NAVAL
OPERATIONS
ANALYSIS

NAVAL OPERATIONS ANALYSIS

Third Edition

EDITED BY Daniel H. Wagner

W. Charles Mylander

Thomas J. Sanders

Department of Mathematics, U.S. Naval Academy

NAVAL INSTITUTE PRESS

Annapolis, Maryland

NAVAL INSTITUTE PRESS
291 Wood Road
Annapolis, MD 21402

ISBN 978-1-59114-950-7
Library of Congress Cataloging-in-Publication Data
Naval operations analysis / edited by Daniel H. Wagner, W. Charles Mylander, and Thomas J. Sanders. — 3rd ed.

p.   cm.

Rev. ed. of: Naval operations analysis / prepared by the Operations Analysis Study Group, United States Naval Academy, Annapolis, Maryland. 2nd ed. c1977.

Includes bibliographical references (p.).
ISBN 1-59114-950-9 (alk. paper)
1. Operations research. 2. Decision making. 3. Naval art and science. I. Wagner,
Daniel H., 1925–   . II. Mylander, W. Charles. III. United States Naval Academy.
Operations Analysis Study Group. Naval operations analysis.
V105.U55 1999   99-29072
359.4'01'1—dc21   ∞
25 24 23 22 21 20   26 25 24 23 22 21 20

To the operations analysts who developed the ideas and techniques presented here. In particular, this book is dedicated to Daniel H. Wagner who was an important contributor to naval operations analysis as an analyst, as a mentor of analysts, and as a leader of analysts. He initiated the project to produce this third edition of *Naval Operations Analysis* and did a large part of the work until his untimely death in March 1997.

CONTENTS

PREFACE
TO THE THIRD EDITION

ONE OF THE FOREMOST RESPONSIBILITIES OF A naval officer is decision making, in operations, in procurement, and in other administration. An important aspect of naval decision making is the use of science, i.e., the treatment of naval operations, etc., as objects of scientific analyses to find bases for decisions, which the decision-maker combines with other aspects of decisions. Such application of science to military decisions was essentially born in the advent of World War II and has since flourished in the military, in government, and in industry. It is called **operations analysis (OA),** and related terms, and as applied to naval problems it is the subject of this book. Chapter 1 below elaborates on this statement of subject matter and history.

The primary purpose of this book is use as a textbook at the U.S. Naval Academy (USNA), Annapolis, Maryland, and at the U.S. Naval Postgraduate School (NPS), Monterey, California. Officer and civilian practitioners of OA, in the fleet, the Center for Naval Analyses (CNA), naval laboratories, and contractor organizations may also find it useful. It is the third edition under the same title, preceded by editions in 1968 and 1977, also published by the U.S. Naval Institute and used for the same purposes.

This edition was prepared at USNA, with substantial external authorship contributions and review, notably from NPS and CNA, during 1989–1996. Quite a bit of the material in the first two editions has been retained, some material has been updated or otherwise revised, and some things, largely obsolete material, have been omitted. Considerable new material has been added.

In one respect this edition takes an introductory viewpoint different from its predecessors, viz., the distinction between the terms **operations analysis (OA) and operations research (OR).** The distinction had been that OA was an activity done by officers and applied in actual operations, while OR was done by researchers, ordinarily civilians, apart from operations. The viewpoint here is that it is appropriate that both officers and civilians participate in OA/OR, applied both in operations and in more detached planning analyses. The term OA is used here for emphasis on applications to actual operations and in that sense it is a subset of OR. Of course OA/OR that is detached from actual operations, notably for planning or procurement decisions, should be based on operational assumptions that are as realistic as possible, which blurs the distinction somewhat. It may be noted that the leading pioneers in USN OR/OA, Philip M. Morse, George E. Kimball, and their colleagues, used the term OR, while the USAF and the previous USAAF, for example, have mainly used the term OA.

The main parts of the second edition that have been omitted, largely because of subsequent obsolescence are as follows, in the chapter/section enumeration of the *second* edition: the discrete-glimpse treatment based on conditional probabilities in 402 and 403 (in favor of the lambda-sigma method); the human factors material in 409–411 (important but difficult to teach in a meaningful quantitative way and unrelated to the rest of the text); the radar and sonar technology discussion in 501, 502, and 901–908 (covered in courses outside OR); the blip-scan and "direct method" radar models in 507 and 508 (out of use with contemporary radars); Chapter 10 on screening against straight-running torpedoes (operationally obsolete); 1103 on disposition of CAP (in favor of newer more general models); 1106 on trade-offs between torpedo and AAW threats (the comparisons becoming disparate in contemporary terms); and most of Chapter 14 on special techniques (generally treated too briefly and/or covered in other courses).

The scientific and editorial leadership of this project was begun by USNA Professors Daniel H. Wagner and W. Charles Mylander. Professor Wagner filled a two-year chair as Visiting Research Professor of Operations Analysis, sponsored by the Assistant Chief of Naval Operations (Naval Warfare) via his Director, Tactical Readiness Division. Professor Mylander is the senior faculty member in OA instruction and also served on the committee that prepared the second edition. Professor Wagner was the committee chairman and served as general editor until completion of his appointment in August, 1991. After that these functions were performed by Professor Mylander and Professor Wagner continued to participate informally. During one year of the project Professor Mylander taught at the Britannia Royal Naval College. He continued to participate, but most of his work was carried on by USNA Professor Thomas J. Sanders. Administrative leadership during the bulk of the work was by CDR David Ehemann and CDR William Kroshl, successively Associate Chairman,

Department of Mathematics, the senior naval position in the Department. Unfortunately, Professor Wagner died before the final editing could be done. Professor Mylander then assumed the role of principal editor and was assisted by Professor Sanders.

This document remains as a small part of the legacy of Daniel H. Wagner. The military analysis community is diminished because of his absence. We are grateful for the hard work and long hours he spent working on this document.

Authorship contributions, by USNA Mathematics faculty except as noted, were as follows ("adapted" means adapted from the second edition): The introductory Chapter 1 was adapted; Professor Wagner added most of sections 102, 108, and 109, and Professor Sanders added parts of 108 and most of the problems, including several adapted from the classic Morse and Kimball text. Chapter 2, "Decision Criteria," was adapted; LCDR Charles R. Frye added section 204, Professor Sanders added the problems for 204, and Professor Wagner added section 205. Chapter 3, "Simulation," was by Professor Sanders. In Chapter 4, "Sonar and Radar Sensors," Part A, "Sonar Detection," was by Prof. Emeritus and CAPT, USN (ret) Frank A. Andrews of Catholic University, who was also responsible for the sonar equation sections of the second edition, and Part B, "Radar Detection," was by Dr. David E. Anderson, retired from the USAF Studies and Analysis Agency. Chapter 5, "Cumulative Detection Probability," was by Professor Wagner. Chapter 6, "Lateral Range Curves and Sweep Width," and Chapter 7, "Search and Patrol," were adapted by Professor Mylander. Chapter 8, "Computer-Assisted Search," was by Professor Wagner. Chapter 9, "Barrier Patrols," was adapted by Professor Mylander; Professor Wagner added 906. Chapter 10, "Mine Warfare," was by Professor Alan R. Washburn, Naval Postgraduate School, with help on history from Fred P. Sutter, Coastal Systems Station. Chapter 11, "Bearings-Only Target Motion Analysis," was by Professor Wagner assisted by LT Mark S. Meltser. Chapter 12, "Target Coverage," was by LCDR Steven C. Rowland, based largely on results of Professor Washburn; the problem solutions were provided by LT Arthur F. Brock. In Chapter 13, "Fleet Air Warfare," Professor Sanders adapted section 1301 and added section 1302, section 1303 was adapted by LCDR Richard Phares, and the history was added by Richard J. Hunt, retired from The Johns Hopkins University Applied Physics Laboratory. Chapter 14, "Reliability," was by Professor James D. Esary, Naval Postgraduate School. Appendix A was adapted by Professor Thomas D. Quint and Professor Sanders. Appendix B on the linear programming formulation of a game was by Professor Quint. Appendix C, "Use of Decibels," was by Professor Andrews and Dr. Anderson.

Comprehensive external reviews by the Naval Postgraduate School and the Center for Naval Analyses were conducted as follows: At NPS were Professor and CAPT USN (ret) Wayne P. Hughes, coordinator, Professor James N. Eagle, Professor Esary, Professor Peter A. W. Lewis, and Professor Washburn. At CNA were Dr. Peter P. Perla, coordinator, Dr. George Akst, Ms. Sabrina Edlow, Dr. Mark Lewellyn, Dr. Bryce Parry, Dr. Matthew Shaffer, Dr. Harvey Spivack, and Dr. David Zvijac. Additional reviews of particular topics were made by LT Brock, CDR June Bishop, LCDR Paul A. Povlock, and CDR James O. Wilson of USNA, Dr. David C. Bossard of DCBossard, Inc., Dr. Edward P. Loane of EPL Analysis, Dr. Henry R. Richardson and Dr. Lawrence D. Stone of Metron, Inc., and Dr. Stanley J. Benkoski, Dr. W. Reynolds Monach, and Dr. Walter R. Stromquist of Daniel H. Wagner, Associates. The immense value of the comments of these reviewers is very gratefully acknowledged.

Graphics were prepared by Professor Sanders.

Needless to say, the present edition owes a great deal to the committees of the 1967 and 1976 eras who prepared the first two editions with great dedication and professional knowledge and skill. The list of those acknowledged as contributors in the Preface to the second edition bears repeating: for the revision resulting in the second edition CDR J. L. Bagby, LCDR R. T. E. Bowler III, Professor T. D. Burnett, LCDR G. M. Marlowe, Professor W. C. Mylander, LCDR J. F. Sigler, and MAJ E. A. Smyth; and for earlier contributions, F. A. Andrews, P. G. Shenk, and P. M. Tullier of USNA and R. N. Forrest and J. K. Hartman of NPS. Going deeper into the historical roots of the three editions of this text, a great deal is owed to the two World War II classics, Operations Evaluation Group Report 54, *Methods of Operations Research,* by Morse and Kimball, and Report 56, *Search and Screening*, by Bernard O. Koopman, for the seminal influence of their work, much of which survives in the present edition.

Gratitude is also expressed for permission to use excerpts from other documents as follows: to John Wiley and Sons for use of an excerpt on OR history from *The Encyclopedia of Statistical Sciences, Volume 6,* Samuel Kotz and Norman L. Johnson, editors; and to the Department of Operations Research, NPS, for use of excerpts on computer-assisted search and on the (λ, σ) model from its publication *Naval Tactical Decision Aids*, by D. H. Wagner.

To better serve the readers and instructors using this book, the editors have established a web page providing an errata sheet, additional problems, and some additional answers to problems. The URL of this page is http://www.nadn.navy.mil/Users/math/tjs/NOA/index.htm. Links are also provided at the USNA Department of Mathematics' home page http://www.usna.edu/MathDept/. Instructors and nonstudents may request copies of *Solutions with Comments for Instructors* from the editors.

Finally the committee immensely appreciates the splendid cooperation of the Naval Institute Press in the preparation of this edition and the Institute's continued publication of this text. The editors believe this text remains as a fundamental vehicle for the instruction of naval operations analysis that in turn continues to be very important to the conduct and planning of naval operations.

1

OPERATIONS ANALYSIS: A SCIENTIFIC BASIS FOR OPERATIONAL DECISIONS

A naval officer is a leader. An officer's primary mission is to conduct successful operations of the Navy both in war and in peace. The primary functions of an officer are to organize, plan, and supervise tasks necessary to accomplish the assigned mission. The single most needed attribute is the ability to make wise decisions that are paramount in determining the success of an operation.

The executive who is effective in all aspects of decision making is in demand in any organization. But what are these aspects, and which of them can be learned? Certainly professional knowledge and experience are essential elements and are perhaps the most important aspects in making a decision. Yet no naval officer or any other executive can be exposed to all the situations in which he or she might have to make a decision. In the procurement of a new weapons system, the decision as to which system is *best* must be made in a situation that is different from any previously encountered. In protecting a task force against enemy submarines, the decision as to the *best* screen placement may have to be based on estimates of the capabilities of a submarine never before encountered. Furthermore, in many cases it is impossible to determine, even after the action has been taken, whether the choice was optimum, or whether a better one might have been made. In such cases, little experience is gained that will help to make a future decision, even if the situation is identical.

The term "best" decisions requires qualification. Decision making is subject to time constraints, which might be a few seconds for anti-air combat actions, or be as long as a few years for major procurement actions. Support to decision making by analysis, computation, and experimentation is limited by the resources available. A recommendation for action that is achieved after the decision deadline or that uses more than the allotted decision support resources is obviously not a best recommendation or even a good one, no matter how brilliant and thorough is the investigation on which it is based. This consideration has given rise to the maxim "Best is the enemy of good enough." The point of it is to discourage a prolongation of decision making by "fine-tuning" the investigation that supports the decision. Apart from time consumption, the precision of the factual knowledge that underlies the supporting investigation rarely justifies fine-tuning. The principle behind this maxim is that a decision-maker seeks the best decision that can be attained within the decision time and data available.

A decision, then, can seldom be made merely by referring to experience alone. The crucial element in making a decision becomes one of how to *apply* experience and knowledge to the present problem in order to optimize the results. This requires sound reasoning, clear thinking, and good logic. It requires an approach that guides one to sound conclusions and prevents overlooking any essential elements. It requires sufficient knowledge about fields related to the problem to enable one to make reasonable assumptions and to separate the unimportant details from the essential elements in the problem.

There have been many methods devised for guiding an executive to a *rational* solution of a problem. In the Navy, for example, the established planning process includes the *Estimate of the Situation,* which guides an officer in making the decision as to how best to carry out a mission. This is an efficient and effective guide, tested and tried as it has developed over the years. The objective is studied, courses of action are developed and weighed in terms of enemy capabilities, and a decision is reached as to which course of action is best. In many cases the combined judgment and experience of a commander and his or her staff are sufficient to predict with reasonable accuracy the outcome for each course of action and to weigh its relative merits. In other situations the factors involved are either so numerous or the relations among them so complicated that systematic methods are required.

Herein lies the need for **operations analysis (OA)** in the Navy. The objective of OA is to be systematic in the analysis of possible actions to provide the decision-maker with a basis for making a rational choice.

The OA approach involves the use of scientific methods to bring objectivity to the results, and to make verification possible. The methods are quantitative, using techniques of mathematics and other sciences to deal with the quantifiable aspects of a problem.

This chapter, while discussing general approaches to OA, emphasizes the difficulty of picking measures of effectiveness for use in an analysis. The issues involved will be brought out by considering examples. Specific methodology areas will be presented in the remaining chapters. Appendices are given on probability and statistics, on a special topic in game theory, and on the decibel concept, which is useful in sensor analysis.

Each chapter has a bibliography and exercise problems. In subsequent chapters, the bibliography is preceded by a discussion of history pertaining to that chapter, including acknowledgments of source documents; literature citations are generally deferred to these historical discussions. In this chapter, history is given in the body, in 102. Defined terms are identified by bold face, in the definition statements and, if earlier, when they are introduced.

101   Operations Analysis

A classical definition of **operations analysis (OA)** is as follows:

Operations analysis is a scientific method of providing executives with a quantitative basis for decisions regarding the operations under their control.

The term originally defined by this statement is **operations research (OR).** The term OA is used to imply emphasis on applications to actual operations. Analyses in support of planning and procurement decisions, although detached from actual operations, should be conducted under realistic operational assumptions. In fact, the terminological distinction between OA and OR does not seem important.

Terms closely related to OA and OR include **operational research** (the U.K. term, which originally identified the profession), **management science** (usually used in business applications), **systems analysis, systems engineering**, and some forms of **industrial engineering**.

The Navy's principal educational activities in OA are the OA curriculum at the Naval Postgraduate School and the OA electives in the Mathematics Department of the U.S. Naval Academy. The first of these is advanced and extensive. The conduct of naval OA is by officers who are graduates of these and other curricula, the Center for Naval Analyses (CNA), naval laboratory activities, and contractors in the private sector. All of these resources are applied to procurement and planning decisions in the shore establishment and to tactical development and operations in the fleet, including the Fleet Marine Force. Among the important fleet users of these OA resources is the Tactical Development and Evaluation Program sponsored by the Tactical Readiness Division in the Office of the Chief of Naval Operations.

CNA is an independent, federally funded research organization. It is the Navy's largest OA activity. It is staffed with a few hundred civilian scientists and several OA-trained officers. CNA provides field representatives to numerous fleet commands on a rotating basis, in the spirit of its World War II origins (see 102).

It is to be emphasized strongly at the outset, and elsewhere in this text, that the function of OA is not to present ready-made decisions to the military commander or civilian executive. Rather, the proper function of OA rests in laying out for the decision-maker the essential factors of the real problem, in proper relationship and expressed in terms of a meaningful common reference, the objective aspects of the problem situation. It remains the prerogative, and responsibility, of the commander to integrate these objective considerations with the qualitative and intangible factors in the problem based on experience and professional judgment in arriving at a final decision. Regarding an analysis of alternative weapon delivery tactics, the tactical commander concerned may judge, on the basis of experience, that the tactic ranked best by the analysis in terms of effectiveness will prove undesirable because of the state of pilot training, and therefore is to be rejected for another maneuver that has lower evaluation but is more operationally feasible. OA has presented a quantitative basis for decision to the commander who knows none the less what compromises the decision will entail. Ideally, the analysis has considered such factors as weather, and includes a breakdown according to the different possible general conditions at the target.

The conclusions of an analysis are meaningful only in the context of the assumptions that underlie them. Identification of the assumptions is a valuable part of an analysis provided to a decision-maker. Symbolically, the relationship of OA and the decision-maker's judgment may be represented in Figure 1.1.

FIGURE 1.1. DOMAINS OF OA AND DECISION-MAKERS

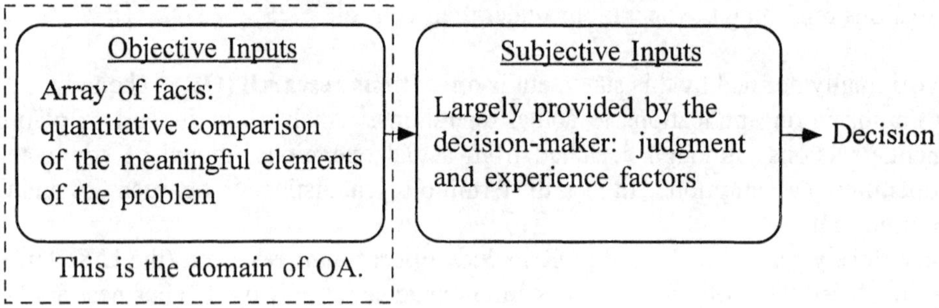

Objective Inputs

Array of facts: quantitative comparison of the meaningful elements of the problem

This is the domain of OA.

Subjective Inputs

Largely provided by the decision-maker: judgment and experience factors

→ Decision

102   Historical Background in the Military

Discussions of the beginnings of OA relate how on the eve of the Second World War the British military turned to civilian scientists for assistance in the resolution of operational problems under the exigencies of war grown more complex than any previously experienced. The American military quickly followed the British lead. The contributions made by these scientists, who came to be called **operations analysts**, were exceptional. Perhaps their greatest and most lasting contribution, however, lay in the *idea* of applying the established methods of science to the resolution of military *operational* problems, problems which at first examination would appear hardly amenable to that kind of treatment. This approach was well established, if not widely known, at the end of World War II.

This resort to civilian assistance, in what had historically been the exclusive province of the military, does not imply that the military officers concerned were incapable of thinking for themselves. In the U.S. Navy, for example, experienced officers were busy organizing a rapidly expanding service and fighting a war in two oceans. They were not afforded the luxury of time to proceed without assistance. Hence they turned to those who already had the scientific competence to cope, in analytical terms, with a burgeoning military technology. The R&D community was producing new weapons and equipment under wartime pressure, at a rate far more rapid than had ever prevailed before.

It may be asked, why, if the scientific method were to prove so effective in analysis of military problems, had it not been applied long before? To a very limited extent, it had. For example, in 1905, Commander (later Rear Admiral) Bradley A. Fiske, USN, published a prize-winning essay [1], which cited little-heralded work by Lieutenant J. V. Chase that anticipated by 10 years analytic ideas more fully developed by Frederick Lanchester [2]. Lanchester's work is a milestone in the mathematical analysis of combat. Lanchester used differential equations and Chase used finite-difference equations to relate force levels during combat to individual "exchange ratios." Thomas

Edison (see [3]) is known to have carried out impressive investigations in antisubmarine warfare during World War I. But these studies were scattered and occasional and *were not done in support of and, in fact, were not known to operational decision-makers.* Certainly in the U.S. Navy between the two world wars there were detailed statistical analyses conducted of naval gun firings, for instance, and of the results of a variety of other competitive evolutions, fleet exercises, and war games. However, none of these statistical studies were true operations analyses. It may be safe to say that scientific methods were not adopted sooner by the military because their power was not recognized.

Speculation will provide several probable reasons why scientists did not venture forth sooner from their laboratories to take part in military problem solving. For one thing, they were not invited. Military operations problems were deemed to be the domain of military experts, not scientists, there was no wartime pressure for their solution, and military thinking produced answers that were presumably adequate unto the time. In fact, before World War II, while naval line officers undoubtedly recognized the importance of technology, there was substantial feeling among them that they need not learn it themselves; they preferred to leave it to non-line billets. Furthermore, weapons and weapons systems changed slowly, and in both the U.S. and the U.K. the military establishment was not popular and budgetary support was meager. Even had such an invitation been tendered, it is doubtful that it would have generated much of a response in the civilian academic community prior to the imminence of war in the late 1930s.

The world today is vastly different from the 1930s. Scientific analysis is a generally accepted feature of problem solving in the military, by professional officers as well as civilians, for reasons which will be elicited. In the ensuing historical account, taken largely from Wagner [4], the term OA is intended to include the term OR.

As an organized body of activity, OA had its origin in the planning, and later the execution, of the air defense of Britain in the late 1930s. Excellent accounts of the early history of OA are given in Trefethen [5], Larnder [6], and Cunningham et al. [7].

Radar developments in the 1930s gave the U.K. radically new capabilities in early warning of air attack. These capabilities raised numerous questions of operational employment, initially in terms of integration with existing warning-response organizations based on visual detections. The earliest study of such questions and accordingly the birth of organized OA is attributed to a group of scientists at Bawdsey Research Station under A. P. Rowe in 1937-39. Radar scientist R. Watson-Watt was an early instigator. This OA work was of enormous importance to the effectiveness of fighter and antiaircraft gun response to air attack during the Battle of Britain. (Now this area is known collectively as command, control, and communications, C^3.) OA spread extensively in all three of the U.K. armed services, notably in antisubmarine warfare, offensive air attack, and civil defense. The most prominent British OA pioneer was P. M. S. Blackett, later a Nobel laureate in physics. He was the first to staff OA work with scientists from diverse fields unrelated to the technology of the equipments employed. Early writings of his reproduced in [8] were influential on OA in the U.S. as well in the U.K.

Literally the first U.S. OA organization was the Operational Research Group established at the Naval Ordnance Laboratory 1 March 1942. This arose from seminar activity led by E. A. Johnson, and it addressed mining operations.

The greatest thrust in U.S. World War II OA began with the recruitment April 1, 1942, of MIT physicist P. M. Morse to lead OA assistance to the antisubmarine command based at Boston. Morse had experience with naval underwater acoustic devices. A month later his group, the Antisubmarine Warfare Operations Research Group (ASWORG), stood at seven scientists and had produced an impressive report on search analysis. A Columbia University chemist, G. E. Kimball, became Morse's deputy. After three months, ASWORG was transferred to the staff of Commander-in-Chief, U.S. Fleet in Washington where it continued to make significant contributions to the antisubmarine thrust of the Battle of the Atlantic. From that position it extended its influence to most aspects of naval warfare. Hence in October 1944, ASWORG was renamed the Operations Research Group (ORG). ORG grew to about 75 scientists by the war's end. It had very direct involvement with fleet operations through rotation of its analysts on field assignment to combat commands.

In fall 1942, OA got under way in the U.S. Army Air Forces under impetus of its commanding generals in England and Washington, again inspired by U.K. experience in OA. Most USAAF major commands came to have OA groups. In contrast to the Navy's ORG, the Washington headquarters function was largely one of staffing the deployed groups.

For accounts of classic OA work and methods in World War II, see Morse and Kimball [9, 10], and Koopman [11, 12] on work for the USN; Blackett [8], Crowther and Whiddington [13], and Waddington [14] on work for the U.K. forces; and Brothers [15] and McArthur [16] on work for the USAAF. A recent and mature reexamination of naval operations analysis in the conduct of the Battle of the Atlantic is found in McCue [17].

After World War II, military OA staffing in the U.S. and the U.K. temporarily declined but acquired permanence in all of the armed services and higher levels of these defense establishments. The principal U.S. leaders were Morse for the Joint Chiefs of Staff, J. Steinhardt for the Navy, L. A. Brothers for the Air Force, and E. A. Johnson for the Army. Subsequently, U.S. military OA involving both government agencies and private industry has become a much larger community than in World War II. This work extends to a wide variety of studies in current tactics, operational requirements for new systems, and strategic planning. A review of the unusually extensive nine fleet field assignments by H. W. Kreiner of OEG/CNA over the years 1952 to 1984 is given in [18].

In the early 1960s, Secretary of Defense Robert McNamara and his Comptroller C. J. Hitch employed systems analysis ([19] is relevant) at the highest levels of U.S. defense planning. This employment appears to have had mixed success amid controversy over the extent of its contravention of professional judgments and its remoteness from measurable experience.

OA also spread extensively to nonmilitary applications, after World War II, in government and private industry.

Academic programs for graduate work in OA began soon after World War II. The first course offering was at MIT in 1948. Case Institute of Technology and the U.S. Naval Postgraduate School began the first degree programs in 1951. Subsequently many leading universities have offered doctorates in OA.

In its sixth decade, the OA profession still has identification problems among the potential users of its work and problems in quality control of this work. Nevertheless, through a lengthy and extensive record of accomplishments, OA has a firmly established position as a means for science to expand its influence on the improvement of world affairs. With the increased complexity of these affairs and advances in computation tools, unbounded challenges and a wealth of interesting problems await the operations analysts of the future.

103   Operations Analysis and the Naval Officer

Knowledge of basic approaches of OA and competence in the application of fundamental methods are important to the naval officer, for reasons including the following:

a. They engender objective, analytic thought processes, sound reasoning and a logical approach to problems.
b. Greater insight is afforded into the essential features of naval operations.
c. They prepare an officer for a later subspecialty in the field.
d. They contribute to an understanding of technical studies being done for and in the Navy.

Objective, quantitative thought processes are always important to the naval officer. Navigation, for example, is an operational task steeped in scientific quantitative methods. History records the glories of the military leaders who, down through the centuries, have thrown caution to the winds and elected to follow their intuition rather than reason and met with great success. Their contemporaries who followed the same decision criteria and failed tend to be forgotten in ignominy, although one suspects that there were at least as many of the latter as the former and that they were quite as competent. They were simply not as lucky. It is the business of OA to put luck on our side. Opinion, preconceived notions, personal bias, whatever the term chosen to employ for the subjective predilections with which one approaches a decision, are insidious and pervasive. It is a rare human being who can avoid their pitfalls without having made a conscious effort to train the mind. An important benefit to be gained from the OA approach to problem solving is an ability to think through, in a logical and ordered manner, the everyday dilemmas of a junior naval officer. Analytic techniques may or may not be applicable, but logical thinking in the vein of the OA method brings good solutions much faster than trial and error.

Insight into the fundamentals of an operational situation – an appreciation of the fundamental processes operating behind the black box, the tabulated search and attack plans, the operations order – is a quality not always gained with experience. Experience alone is a slow and expensive teaching device, and one which may destroy the student before he or she finishes the course. The naval officer who comes by this insight naturally is gifted indeed. OA, with its attention to the essential features of operational problems, and its consideration of the probabilistic nature of the events that can take place, is of particular value in the development of this insight.

OA is of considerable interest to the junior naval officers as a possible subspecialty. It is a stated goal of the Navy that at least 50 percent of regular officers shall have had significant postgraduate education in a subspecialty area. The nature of the OA subspecialty has already been stated. For the unrestricted line officers, in particular, OA bears as directly upon the essence of the naval profession as any other field of study in the military sciences. OA-educated officers are very much in demand.

Many officers who do not engage in the conduct of OA, nevertheless will often have access to studies that analyze naval problems of interest to them. The ability to understand or to evaluate these studies is greatly enhanced by some insight into the approach and methods of OA.

104   The OA Method

It has been asserted above that OA is essentially the application of scientific methods to the resolution of operational problems. Without digressing for a discussion of what constitutes scientific methods, it is reasonable to state that examination of successful applications of OA reveals a consistent pattern, a general form. That general approach is termed the **OA method**. It is by no means a problem-solving algorithm, but most if not all of its features are to be found in varying degrees of development in all cases of creative problem solving through OA. An outline of the OA method is as follows:

A. Formulation of the problem.
  1. Identification of the objectives of the operation's decision-maker (may or may not be quantitative).
  2. Identification of the reasonable alternative courses of action.
  3. Identification of the variables that impact the courses of action.
  4. Definition of a measure of effectiveness (MOE), i.e., a quantitative yardstick providing an ordering of the alternative courses of action that is consistent within the objective.

B. Analysis of the problem.
  1. Construct a model of the operation by analytic formulas and/or Monte Carlo simulation (see Chapter 3) that is faithful to reality and amenable to analysis.
  2. Evaluate, in terms of the MOE, outcomes of the alternative courses of action by exercising the model and by theoretical analysis.
  3. Conduct operational trials or observation of "real world" operations to obtain data needed in (1) and (2).

C. Communication of the results, orally and in writing.

D. Analyst assistance to implementation of the decision.

The remaining sections of this chapter will discuss each of these topics in turn.

105   The Objective of the Operation

Finding the *real* problem is often one of the most difficult features of operational problems, as exemplified in the following case taken from Morse and Kimball [9, 10]. Early in World War II a great number of British merchant vessels were being sunk or seriously damaged by Axis aircraft attack in the Mediterranean. The obvious answer was to equip these ships with antiaircraft guns and gun crews. This was done at great expense of men and equipment badly needed elsewhere. Questions concerning the soundness of this allocation of scarce resources were raised when reports showed that the gun crews were shooting down only about 4 percent of all attacking aircraft. This was a poor showing and seemed to indicate that the AA guns and crews were not worth the cost of installation. On more careful consideration, it was realized that the guns were not there primarily to shoot German or Italian aircraft, but their objective was to protect the merchant vessels. And, in fact, as figures were accumulated, it became apparent that the AA guns and crews were doing the job rather well; of the ships attacked, 25 percent of those without protection had been sunk, while only 10 percent of the ships with protection were lost in the same period.

The objective being considered here is that of the person who has the ultimate responsibility for making the decision. A commanding officer's objective may often be determined by studying the mission assigned by his or her superior. A business executive's objective is largely determined by, or is at least consistent with, the purpose and goals of his or her organization.

In a typical problem involving a major decision, the analysis would be conducted by the decision-maker's staff or by an external research organization. In either case the analyst must determine exactly what the objective is. It may be very vague and elusive at first, but the analysis cannot proceed far until it is clearly defined. Even then, as the analysis proceeds, it may be determined that the objective as stated is not specific enough and further clarification is necessary. Suppose, in a problem involving excess shipping losses, the stated objective is *to minimize the number of merchant vessels sunk*. One way of accomplishing it would be to keep all merchant vessels in port. In a wartime shipping situation, this would hardly be a reasonable solution; hence, the objective as stated must not be the real one.

The objective is sometimes confused with the action taken to accomplish it. The person considering the purchase of life insurance may state the objective as *to determine how much and what kind of life insurance to buy*. The purchase of life insurance, however, is an action taken to accomplish some real objective such as providing security for one's dependents.

The aim of the analyst should be to provide the decision-maker with a sound and unbiased basis for decision. The objective under consideration is that of the decision-maker in conducting the operation. This objective always exists, however difficult it may be to define or express. The first step in the OA method is to find and clearly state it.

106   The Alternative Courses of Action

While the objective is usually determined first, the steps in formulating a problem do not always follow in any definite sequence. Rather, the analyst must consider each step in terms of the others, going from one to another and back again (see Quade [20], pp.155-160 for amplification). The first questions raised when trying to list reasonable alternatives are the following: *How limited are my choices of course of action, and may I consider alternatives that involve an increase in personnel, material, or equipment; or am I limited to tactics and methods of operation which use the resources at hand?*

Such questions become easier to answer after some consideration of the variables that will be discussed in 107. Very often the immediacy of the problem will not only limit the alternatives to those that can be put into use quickly, but also limit the time that can be spent on the analysis itself. Most of the problems treated by OA during World War II were undertaken under circumstances that required doing *the best you can with what you've got*. In most organizations, moral and social considerations rule out alternatives that involve dishonest or unlawful practices, or that violate accepted standards or customs.

One approach would be to list every conceivable course of action that can reasonably be expected to accomplish the objective, reserving further judgment until later. This approach would tend to decrease the possibility of overlooking the best alternative merely because it didn't occur to the analyst. Sometimes an individual closely associated with an operation finds it difficult to think of any alternatives except those tried previously, where some other individual with identical knowledge and experience, but viewing the situation from a distance, would see other possible courses of action. There is no set procedure for discovering good alternatives, although the ingenuity, experience, and vantage point of the individual surely contribute.

An obvious difficulty arises when the number of alternatives is so large that listing them becomes tedious or impossible. It may be that each can be put in one of several categories. For example, in protecting a task force from aircraft attack with combat air patrol (CAP), an infinite number of alternatives would be included in the category of stationing *x aircraft at altitude h_1 spaced equidistantly on a circle of radius r_1 from formation center, and y aircraft at altitude h_2 spaced equidistantly at radius r_2.*

One test for a valid alternative is that it must, by itself, provide a complete means of accomplishing the objective. If the alternative provides only part of the means then it is not complete. For example, if the objective is to protect the task force against submarines, an alternative that provides only a means for detection is not complete in itself, and hence not valid.

107   Identification and Classification of Variables

For the purpose of this discussion, the term **variable** will mean a quantity whose value is not known and is an element or component of the decision problem, i.e., of the decision-maker's operation affected by the decision. Thus an evaluation of the consequences of the decision will be affected by a choice of the value used for the variable.

A listing of variables that affect the outcomes of courses of action in a decision problem can accomplish several purposes:

a. It should serve as a guide to the data that must be gathered before the problem can be solved.
b. It can indicate the complexity of the problem and help to determine the methods to be used in the analysis.
c. It can help to prevent any important elements in the problem from being overlooked.
d. It can provide a guide to listing alternatives.
e. It should include those quantities that will be useful in computing the measure of effectiveness.

Variables may be classified by category. Some variables can be **controllable** or at least influenced to some degree by the decision-maker. For example, the number of destroyers assigned to an ASW screen is a variable controlled by the Officer in Tactical Command (OTC) at least to the extent of the destroyers available. Other variables that influence the outcome of an operation may be completely **uncontrollable**. Some of these have values that are **known** or can be determined. Others are **estimable** in that their values are not known but can be estimated or assumed. Still other variables are **unknown** as to value. Actions by the enemy at various times fall into all three categories.

As examples, the number of destroyers assigned to a task force is known but cannot generally be controlled by the OTC; hence, it establishes some restrictions on the alternatives at the OTC's disposal. The isothermal surface layer depth is a variable that influences the possibility of detecting a submarine with sonar, is uncontrollable yet measurable. The number of enemy submarines operating in a given area cannot be controlled by the OTC nor can it usually be determined by measurement, but may be estimated from intelligence reports, etc. A list and classification of such variables will provide a guide to needed data.

Further, there are those uncontrollable variables whose values cannot be determined because of their random nature. The time that a radar installation will operate before failure, and the range at which a target will be detected, are variables whose values vary widely even for a given situation because of the numerous unknown factors upon which they depend. Such quantities are called **random variables**, and the uncertain events associated with them can be treated effectively only by using methods of probability and statistics. In distinction to random variables are **deterministic** variables, those that are governed by causal relations that are known with considerable precision. An example is the distance to the visual horizon from a given altitude above the sea surface.

It is important that the variables affecting an operational decision be defined explicitly. Some of them may then be eliminated from further consideration if it can be seen that they have little significant effect on the outcome. In that way the problem can be reduced to its essentials.

In solving a problem, a **sensitivity analysis** should be made in order to determine the variables to which the outcome is most sensitive. Clearly the values assigned to these variables are to be determined or estimated as accurately as possible.

An **alternative course of action** may be thought of as a specific assignment of values to the controllable variables. Accordingly, identification of these controllable variables is a necessary first step to gain insight into the various alternatives that are available.

Another category of variables arises in formulating a model of an operation, discussed in 109. Model formulation often produces a *family* of models, containing a few unknown constants which remain to be estimated. Estimation of these constants, by experimentation or other means, results in a specific model from within the family. These unknown constants are variables that are often called **parameters**.

All of the variables discussed so far have been those whose values could be described by numbers. There are certainly other variables whose nature makes it difficult if not impossible to describe their values in such a quantitative way. Such variables as morale, training, political climate, health, ability, and education are difficult to treat quantitatively. Yet, scales have been devised that quantitatively describe the values of some of these. Other scales and methods are sure to be devised so that more and more of these factors can be treated quantitatively in the future. Since OA is to provide a decision-maker with a quantitative basis for decision, it must leave those factors which are not so treated to the judgment and experience of the decision-maker.

108   Measures of Effectiveness

A basis for decision consists essentially of predicting and describing the expected results of each of the alternative courses of action under consideration. One needs to answer the question: Given two courses of action A and B, is A *better* than B? In fact one usually desires to ask further: *How much* better is A than B? To make these questions meaningful and to attempt to answer them, an operations analyst must assign a numerical value to each course of action. Moreover, these assignments must be consonant with the decision-maker's objective that gave rise to the decision problem. Such an assignment of values to courses of action is called a **measure of effectiveness (MOE)**.

While the decision-maker's objective need not be stated quantitatively, and usually is not, it is essential that an MOE assign numerical values. Much of the role of an MOE is as a quantitative proxy or surrogate for the objective. An MOE, then, must be closely related to the objectives of the operation. For example a decision-maker's objective might be stated as "to find submarines using given assets in a given region in time T." The courses of action would be various search plans. The MOE might be the expected value of the number of submarines found by a given plan.

It is important that the operations analyst seek the counsel and concurrence of the decision-maker in choosing an MOE. Such consultation may forestall misunderstanding of objective or approach.

The properties required of an MOE may be described in summary as follows:

a. It must be quantitative.
b. It must be measurable or estimable from data and other information available to the analyst.
c. A significant increase {decrease} in MOE value must correspond to a significant improvement {worsening} in achieving the decision-maker's objective.
d. It must reflect both the benefits and the penalties of a given course of action.

With respect to (d), the analyst should ask "Am I willing to recommend one course of action over another based on valuation by the MOE *alone?"* (This valuation might mean a neutral recommendation if the MOE values are close.) If the answer is no, then possibly an important component is missing from the formulation of the problem and the MOE. Note that this test does *not* apply in the same way to the *decision-maker*, who ordinarily will look beyond the MOE, notably to non-quantifiable considerations, in making a decision.

Often there is an initial impulse to choose as an MOE the probability that something "good" happens (i.e., furtherance of the objective). Sometimes that is a satisfactory choice, but often this probability will not be realistically estimable and hence will violate (b). Sometimes pursuit of the "good" event incurs a penalty or risk of a penalty, that must be included in the evaluation of the MOE, hence (d) is appropriate.

It is hard to overstate the importance of choosing an appropriate MOE. It is often the most difficult part of the problem, at least in military applications, partly because it does not usually have well-defined unique solutions. There are no explicit procedures to follow in making this choice. Some guidance will be offered by examples.

For decisions by a business executive, the MOE is often controllable revenues minus controllable expenses, which are considered to be a contribution to profit. The benefits and penalties are measured in the same (monetary) units, so they are reasonably combined by addition and subtraction.

In military decisions, the benefits and penalties are usually described in different units, so they are typically combined by division and multiplication. Certainly, adding or subtracting quantities measured in different units does not make sense. Thus the analyst often thinks of amount of benefit per unit penalty or cost (usually not in monetary terms), associated with a course of action.

For example, in choosing among alternative naval vehicles to search out a square region, one might first consider the width, call it "sweep width," w, of the swath in the region that a vehicle can effectively search as it moves along. Then w is indicative of benefit. Time consumed in search is a penalty. Should one consider w per unit time as an MOE? That isn't satisfactory, because as search time progresses it isn't really more width that is being generated; rather it is more *area* that is effectively searched. A little further reflection suggests that wv, where v is search speed, is a good MOE for this problem. It has the dimensions of area per unit time and is usually called "sweep rate" or "search rate." On the other hand if the search unit were a stationary sensor protecting a front, then sweep width would be a good MOE. Sweep width and sweep rate are in fact very important MOEs in search planning and will be examined further in Chapters 6 and 7.

It frequently proves useful for the MOE to be factorable so that the "weak link" can be readily established, as in the example which follows.

An MOE used to evaluate the performance of an attack submarine (SSN) stationed in a barrier to oppose enemy submarines is the probability P_K that an enemy transitor passing through (penetrating) the barrier is killed by the SSN. This MOE can be factored into the following conditional probabilities:

$$P_K = P_D \times P_C \times P_A \times P_{AA} \times P_H \, ,$$

where

$$P_K = \Pr\{\text{kill}\},$$

$$P_D = \Pr\{\text{SSN detects transitor} \mid \text{transitor enters barrier}\},$$

$$P_C = \Pr\{\text{SSN correctly classifies transitor} \mid \text{detection}\},$$

$$P_A = \Pr\{\text{SSN attacks} \mid \text{correct classification}\},$$

$$P_{AA} = \Pr\{\text{attack is accurate} \mid \text{SSN attacks}\},$$

$$P_H = \Pr\{\text{weapon hits} \mid \text{accurate attack is made}\}.$$

The MOE P_K is useful because

a. it is quantifiable, i.e., $0 < P_K < 1$;
b. it is estimable, i.e., P_K can be measured by conducting at-sea exercises and taking data such as

$$P_D = \frac{\text{\# transitors detected}}{\text{\# transitors going through}},$$

$$P_C = \frac{\text{\# transitors correctly classified}}{\text{\# transitors detected}}, \text{ etc.}$$

Some of the variables which must be considered in the above are as follows:

1. SSN class/performance (known),
2. enemy transitor characteristics (unknown but can be estimated),
3. sea state and other environmental conditions (can be measured or predicted),
4. transitor path (track) through barrier (can be considered random).

The MOE P_K, also called WSE for weapon system effectiveness, was originated by Submarine Development Group Two in the evaluation of the SSN 594 class during the 1960s. Its use by that command and its successor, Submarine Development Squadron Twelve, has been influential at the DoD level in SSN procurement decisions.

The following example from World War II illustrates the importance of using an appropriate MOE.

Early in the U-boat war in the Atlantic an attempt was made to save merchant vessels by equipping them with antitorpedo nets which were swung out by booms. These nets were capable of stopping some 85 percent of the German electric torpedoes (G7E) but only 20 percent of the German air-propelled torpedoes (G7A). Taking the armament of U-boats as about 60 percent G7E and 40 percent G7A gave an average protection against these torpedoes of 59 percent. Since the nets covered only about 75 percent of the ship, the resulting probability of a net stopping a torpedo was 44 percent:

$$(.6 \times .85 + .4 \times .2) \times .75 = .44.$$

This appears to be a strong argument in favor of equipping all merchant vessels with nets. But the cost was extremely high and the nets slowed down the ships, making an additional cost for fuel, time lost, and added exposure to attack. Against some opposition, about 600 ships were fitted with nets before enough operational experience had been obtained to make a reappraisal possible. This reappraisal was quite broad in scope, as it involved (1) cost in dollars as against the cost of ships saved by the net, (2) cost in time and in cargo space, and (3) cost in manpower to build and maintain the nets. The research on the cost in dollars found that the net program did not pay for itself. The operational data on the 25 ships which were torpedoed and which were fitted with nets are shown here:

	Sunk	Damaged	Undamaged
12 ships, nets not in use at time of attack	9	3	0
10 ships, nets in use	4	3	3
3 ships, use of nets unknown	3	0	0
Totals	16	6	3

If the 10 ships with nets streamed had not had their nets in use, one should expect $7\frac{1}{2} = (9/12) \times 10$ to have been sunk and $2\frac{1}{2}$ damaged. The nets had thus saved the equivalent of $3\frac{1}{2}$ ships and cargoes. But a total of almost 600 ships had been fitted with nets at an initial cost equal to about twice that of $3\frac{1}{2}$ ships and cargo, not to mention costs of maintenance, etc. Thus the program had not paid for itself, and the report of the findings recommended that no further ships be equipped with nets.

A decision problem in the Air Warfare Division in OPNAV in the 1950s was to choose among competing designs for fighter-borne machine guns. The MOE adopted was

$$\frac{\text{rate of fire} \times \left\{ \left[\begin{matrix} \text{kinematic energy} \\ \text{of a round} \\ \text{leaving barrel} \end{matrix} \right] + \left[\begin{matrix} \text{chemical energy} \\ \text{of a round} \\ \text{exploding on impact} \end{matrix} \right] \right\}}{\text{cost of procuring required number of guns}}.$$

This MOE afforded a relatively quick but meaningful comparison that favored a particular Gatling design and agreed with an independent recommendation based on an engineering analysis by the cognizant technical bureau. The Navy adopted the recommended design.

The significance of dimension in factors of an MOE is illustrated in another example, which also illustrates relevance and irrelevance of various parameters. Suppose a procurement manager is choosing between two types of submarine-laid mines, A and B. The purpose of the mines is area denial against hostile ships. The following information has been gathered:

a. Radius of horizontal effectiveness is 12 feet for A and 18 feet for B.
b. Mine length is 30 inches for A and 60 inches for B.
c. Mine storage competes for space with storage of torpedoes, which are also needed for the submarine's ASW/ASUW missions.
d. Both A and B fit in 21-inch torpedo tubes. They have the same vertical effectiveness and have similar life cycle costs.

The significance of (d) is that the factors noted there may probably be ignored in choosing the MOE. Fixed costs incurred by all alternatives *might* be relevant to the MOE -- see the next example. The significance of (c) is that storage space may not be ignored. Thus space is regarded as a penalty and may be considered proportional to mine length. This and the *area* clearance mission suggest the MOE

$$\frac{[\text{radius of effectiveness}]^2}{\text{mine length}}.$$

By this MOE, B is preferred to A. If the numerator were not squared, the comparison would be reversed. On the other hand, the numerator should not be squared if the mission were to lay a *linear* barrier against transitors using a given transit course. Examine Figure 1.2.

In general an analyst should consider the possibilities and implications of increasing or decreasing the importance of a given factor in an MOE by raising that factor to a power, which is possibly fractional.

As another construction, consider

$$\frac{x}{y + a},$$

where x is a benefit, y is a penalty, and a is a constant, a fixed penalty incurred by all alternatives. By adjusting a, the relative importance of y compared to x is adjusted. In particular, if the MOE were x/y, then it would grow indefinitely large as y approached zero, and that may not be at all what was intended. This point is one of the lessons of the next example, from Quade [20], which illustrates two alternative ways of using benefit/cost ratios to solve a problem. The MOE that an analyst would use in an actual study depends on the situation, the decision-maker, and the analyst's individual judgment.

FIGURE 1.2. MINE EFFECTIVENESS AGAINST TARGETS OF KNOWN AND UNKNOWN COURSES

Note: In (a), target course is known, so effectiveness is length of frontal coverage.
In (b), target course is equally likely in all directions, so effectiveness is an area.

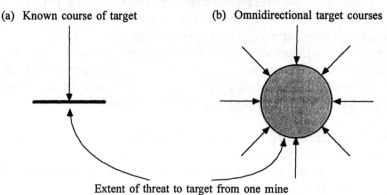

(a) Known course of target   (b) Omnidirectional target courses

Extent of threat to target from one mine

Suppose the procurement of a new electronic countermeasures (ECM) system for installation on an existing aircraft is being studied. The replacement cost of an aircraft is $50,000,000. Two ECM systems are under consideration, A and B, which have anti-jamming and threat warning capabilities. The probability of mission survival with the present system is .8. The estimated parameters for the new systems are as follows:

System	No ECM	A	B
Unit cost ($)	0	1,000,000	5,000,000
Pr{mission survival}	.80	.90	.95

There are three alternative courses of action available. First, no ECM system is added to the aircraft. Second, system A is installed on an aircraft. Third, system B is installed on an aircraft.

The first MOE to be considered might be "number of missions survived per million dollars." To evaluate this MOE, the analyst must first determine the expected number of missions that an aircraft will fly under each of the three options. The probability that an aircraft will be shot down on the nth mission is given by a geometric distribution,

$$\Pr\{E_n\} = p(1-p)^{n-1},$$

where E_n is the event the plane is shot down on its nth mission and $p = \Pr\{\text{not survive a mission}\}$. The expected number of the mission when an aircraft is shot down is then $1/p$. For the three alternatives, the values of $1/p$ are 5, 10, and 20, respectively. Thus the expected numbers of missions survived by an aircraft under the three alternatives are 4, 9, and 19, respectively.

Note that aircraft cost plus ECM system costs must be included in total cost, since the option of not adding an ECM system incurs no cost and would yield an infinite value of the first MOE.

There is also a case for including values for the crew, training costs, etc., but it is difficult to attach dollar amounts to these factors and they will not be considered in this example for simplicity. Thus the following is obtained, where MOE = expected number of survived missions per $10,000,000 cost:

Option	E[# missions]	Cost ($)	MOE value
No ECM	4	50,000,000	0.80
A	9	51,000,000	1.76
B	19	55,000,000	3.45

Notice that the numerator of the MOE, E[# survived missions], is to be maximized, while the denominator, cost, is to be minimized. Thus the largest value of the MOE is the optimal one. Then system B is expected to give the largest number of successful missions for each dollar spent, providing all the existing aircraft are fitted with this system.

Now suppose that discussions with the client have disclosed that there are only five aircraft that are to be equipped with the ECM systems and the amount that has been budgeted is $5,000,000. This changes the available options to the following:

a. Equip one of the planes with system B and leave the other four without ECM gear.
b. Equip each of the five planes with system A.

The MOE that will be used is the numerator of the previous MOE, E[# survived missions], because the denominator remains constant for each. For the first option, the expected number of missions for the plane with system B is 19, while the remaining four are expected to complete four missions each for a total of 16 missions. Thus the total number of missions for option (a) is expected to be $19 + 16 = 35$. Since option (b) has $5 \times 9 = 45$ successful missions expected, it is the optimal choice.

Notice that the new information affected the available options, the MOE chosen, and the final recommendation. This illustrates that it is of utmost importance for the analyst and the client to communicate well and often. The complete definition of the problem and the objective must not be ambiguous or in question, or the analyst may select an incorrect MOE and reach a conclusion that is not in harmony with the client's objectives.

The concept of expected value, employed in the preceding example, is very useful in devising MOEs. It reduces an array of possible outcomes of a course of action, expressed as a distribution of payoffs, to a single number, the mean or average payoff. This particular choice of a single number is not always appropriate, however. For instance it might be better to evaluate the payoffs in terms of "utility," to be discussed in Chapter 2. Also, a better MOE might be the probability of obtaining *at least* some critical value, such as the range from a protected body at which an attacker is stopped. As a related point in the context of defense plans, if plans A and B are predicted to stop 90 and 95 of 100 attackers respectively, does one say that B is 5.6 percent better than A? Considering the purpose of defense, it would be more appropriate to regard B as twice as effective as A since it has half as many predicted leakers.

Decision making is not always a matter of maximizing an MOE. For one thing, an MOE may reflect penalty or cost rather than benefit and therefore is to be *minimized*. Moreover, Chapter 2 discusses various criteria for decision making, all of which center on MOEs. In particular, Chapter 2 treats the division of benefit and penalty considerations into separate MOEs, with a view to basing a decision on maximizing benefit subject to a ceiling constraint on penalty or on minimizing penalty subject to a floor constraint on benefit. This is often called a **cost-effectiveness** criterion. The ECM example above could be approached from that viewpoint.

Two MOEs are said to be **decision-equivalent** if they rank all alternative courses of action in the same order. As a trivial example, suppose the above MOE for mines were revised to make the numerator the *exact* area of horizontal effectiveness; that requires multiplying the numerator by π, which would not affect the comparisons. Decision-equivalent MOEs are not necessarily equally desirable. For example, if x is an MOE, then x^4 is an MOE which is decision-equivalent to x, and so is $x^{1/4}$, but these three MOEs differ greatly in portraying *how much* better one course of action is than another, and that might be important to a decision-maker.

The foregoing provides guidance in the very important problem of choosing an MOE. As additional sources on MOEs, Morse and Kimball [9, 10] and Rockower [21] should be particularly helpful. The best way for a student to acquire competence in this area is by practice. The exercises below are a start. Better practice is confrontation with real decision problems.

109   Models

Analysis of a decision problem almost inevitably involves a **model** of the operation which is to be improved by the chosen course of action. Simply stated, a model is a *quantitative* description of the operation. It typically embodies the operation's dynamics: its cause-and-effect relationships. The primary qualities needed in a model are that it be reasonably *faithful to reality* and *amenable to analysis*. These two qualities unfortunately tend to conflict with each other: The more structure and details included for the sake of fidelity, generally the more difficult it is to understand the cause-and-effect relationships between parameters and to use the model in analysis. Note also that increased detail does not necessarily improve the fidelity of a model, because it may require estimation of too many parameters from the available data.

The ability to strike a good compromise between fidelity and amenability to analysis in model building is possibly the most valuable trait an operations analyst can possess. Usually model building requires a majority of the effort in an OA investigation.

The main thrust of this text is to provide the reader with tools for devising models of various facets of naval operations.

Of course, use of models is by no means peculiar to OA. It is prevalent in all scientific fields. The formula $y = xz$ is simply an abstract equation relating the quantities x, y, and z. It cannot be called a model since it represents no particular physical phenomena. However, if this formula is written as $F = ma$, it is recognized as a model in mechanics that represents the relationship among mass, acceleration, and the resultant force on a physical body. It may be safely stated that until this model was formulated and verified, these concepts could not be well understood. Similarly in a decision problem, if a model can be discovered which expresses the relationships among the variables involved, then predictions can be made about the outcomes of the courses of action and the problem itself can be better understood.

A model need not consist solely of analytic formulas. Simulation by "Monte Carlo" methods is a powerful tool for model building, which has become increasingly important as the power, size, and cost of computers have dramatically improved. This modeling method will be discussed in Chapter 3.

It is usual in OA for at least some of the phenomena being modeled to be probabilistic in nature, whether the model is analytic or Monte Carlo simulation. That is because chance affects the results of most decision choices, and probability theory is a tool to deal with uncertainty in a controlled manner.

Construction of a model enhances an analyst's understanding of the problem. It also may raise issues which cause reexamination of the choice of MOE and problem definition. As with these related phases, model building should be done in consultation with the decision-maker. It is emphasized that this must be done in terminology that the decision-maker understands.

Examples of analytic models are the sonar equation, instantaneous detection models in Chapter 4, the detection rate and (λ, σ) models of Chapter 5 used to represent cumulative detection processes, and the random search and inverse cube models of Chapter 7. These models are probabilistic, and most of them contain parameters that must be measured or estimated. Examples of deterministic, i.e., non-probabilistic, analytic models are the radar equation in Chapter 4 and models of stationing combat air patrol (CAP) in Chapter 13. Various parameters in these models are probabilistic in reality, but they are modeled deterministically because the causal relationships are deemed to be more important than the uncertainties.

An example of modeling by Monte Carlo simulation is the target motion model used in the discussion of computer-assisted search in Chapter 8. Various target tracks are postulated and a probability is assigned to each. Each track amounts to a Monte Carlo "repetition," and this collection of tracks with associated probabilities gives a description of the target motion which is very useful to the search planning process. Also, Monte Carlo modeling is prominent in the methodology for mine warfare analysis discussed in Chapter 10.

One way to change a probabilistic model into a deterministic one is to replace each random variable by its mean, which is treated deterministically. That characterizes an **expected value model**. This method is generally more useful in an analytic than in a Monte Carlo approach. It can provide substantial computational saving or it can be a substitute for data that are in inadequate supply. In any event an analyst using an expected value model must realize that unless the operations on the random variables are linear, approximations, possibly rather poor ones, are being employed, even if one is content with mean values as ultimate outputs. In effect, the approximations are of the form

$$E[g(X)] \approx g(E[X]), \qquad (1\text{-}1)$$

where g is some function representing a (deterministic) operation in the model and X and hence $g(X)$ are random variables. If g is linear, then (1-1) is an equality, but generally not otherwise. For example, suppose X is uniformly distributed over [0, 1] and $g(x) = x^2$ for x in [0, 1]. Then $E[X] = 1/2$, $g(E[X]) = 1/4$, and

$$E[g(X)] = \int_0^1 \frac{g(x)}{1-0} \, dx = \int_0^1 x^2 dx = \frac{1}{3} \neq \frac{1}{4}.$$

The approximation (1-1) may or may not be satisfactory in a given application. A case where it is entertained is in 1004 of the mine warfare discussion in Chapter 10.

Model validation alone is a very important topic. All models should be checked to ensure the level of fidelity to the real world is sufficient. Statistical inference from relevant operational data should be employed but such data may be very difficult or expensive or even impossible to obtain. In naval OA the best source of these data is fleet exercises designed for the purpose of data collection and model validation.

As with MOEs, the best way to learn model building is by doing. The examples and tools in the ensuing chapters should help toward this end.

110   Problem Analysis

After one or more MOEs have been chosen and a model of the operation has been constructed, the model is used to winnow and evaluate the options for the decision-maker. In some models, such as simulation models, each course of action being considered leads to a set of inputs to the model and the model outputs are then used to evaluate the MOEs. Other models, such as linear programming and other optimization models, identify an optimal course of action from the set of actions in the domain of the model as well as the optimal value of the MOE used. It is customary to have a base case and then a number of excursions are done off the base case using different assumed values for parameters. In the majority of cases, it is not possible to determine absolutely correct values for MOEs, but it is possible to compare alternatives as to which yields better values of the MOEs for the model used. As a result of this "exercising the model," the analyst may identity several different courses of action for consideration by the decision-maker. These options are ranked using the MOEs and any non-quantifiable factors used in the ranking process are made explicit. Since the values selected for many of the model's parameters are either estimated from data or simple guesses, it is incumbent on the analyst to provide information to the decision-maker on the impact of poor choices of these parameters. One approach is to explore the sensitivity of the model to parameters believed to be critical. A common method for doing this is *value ranging*.

Value Ranging for a parameter x is done by determining the range of values for x for which the form of the solution remains valid. To do this, the analyst often determines *critical values* where the form of the solution changes. The *allowable range of values* for x consists of the intervals over which the form of the solution is the same as the form for the value of x used in the study.

Example: Consider the ECM procurement example given in 108. The analysis is based on two types of parameters: cost and probability of a successful mission. The table of values is given below. Let us do the value ranging for p_B, the probability of a successful mission when system B has been installed on an aircraft, using the first model having MOE the expected number of missions per $10 million cost.

System	No ECM	A	B
Unit cost ($million)	0	1	5
Pr{successful mission}	.80	.90	.95

The probability p of a successful mission was used to determine the expected number of successful missions by the formula $E[X] = 1/(1-p) - 1 = p/(1-p)$, which was derived from the geometric distribution. Calculations for the respective options gave the results in the following table.

Option	E[X]	Cost ($million)	MOE
No ECM	4	50	.80
A	9	51	1.76
B	19	55	3.45

The largest value of the MOE is 3.45 for option B, and so the recommendation is to equip all aircraft with system B, if there are no budget caps. What we wish to determine is the range of values of p_B (current value of .95) for which system B remains the best choice. The critical value $p*$ for p_B would satisfy the equation $\dfrac{p*/(1-p*)}{5.5} = 1.76$, since this is where the transition from recommending system B to recommending system A would occur (if all the other parameters remain fixed). Solving gives the critical value $p* = \dfrac{(5.5)(1.76)}{1+(5.5)(1.76)} = 0.906$. That is, as long as $p_B > 0.91$, system B would have the largest value of the MOE.

One way to present the sensitivity of the model to a parameter's value is to give the *percent allowable variation* for the parameter. This would be found by taking the difference of the current value and the closest critical value, dividing by the current value, and multiplying by 100. In the example, the percent allowable variation for p_B would be $\dfrac{|.95-.906|}{.95} \times 100 = 4.6\%$. Since this is small, the model is sensitive to the value of this parameter, and it is very important that the decision maker is made aware of this. The value of the percent allowable variation at which a model becomes "sensitive" to the parameter is not well defined. A "rule of thumb" used by some analysts is that values less than 10 percent indicate that the model is sensitive to the parameter and values larger than 25 percent indicate that the model is not sensitive to the parameter.

111   Communication of Results

An OA investigation is not complete until the results have been communicated to the decision-maker, necessarily in writing and ideally orally as well. The assumptions, the data and their sources, the MOE, the model, the reasoning in employing the model, and the conclusions and recommendations must all be clearly elucidated. They must be summarized in terminology understandable by the decision-maker. More detail than the decision-maker needs should be included, ordinarily in appendices and ideally enough to permit the study results to be reproduced by others, for review by the decision-maker's staff and potentially by external technical experts.

The reporting process helps to sharpen the investigation itself. As in any scientific investigation, it is not until the investigator reviews the final written report that he or she can be confident that the assumptions, data, and reasoning hang together and the conclusions make sense. Moreover, documentation of the data and the reasoning and methodology may be as valuable to the decision-maker as the recommendations.

Objectivity is an essential ingredient of OA. OA is by definition an application of *science*, and science is a disciplined search for truth. It is essential that an operations analyst "see it and tell it as it is." Indeed an important role of OA is often one of overcoming preconceived notions. Objectivity is stressed in this discussion of reporting, because that is where it comes under the greatest strain.

The decision-maker is senior to the analyst, though not necessarily via chain of command, and it is necessary at times to report conclusions and recommendations which come as unpleasant news. Such issues also arise in staff work other than OA, but the role of science places especially strong demands for objectivity.

Maintaining objectivity goes to the basic integrity that is expected of naval officers and to the mutual respect that must exist between juniors and seniors. Mutual respect in the context of OA is built on quality of performance by the operations analyst and soundness of decisions by the decision-maker, whether or not they depart from OA recommendations.

112   Implementation

If and when the decision-maker decides on a course of action, based at least in part on the OA investigation, it is desirable to test the recommendations by operational trials before, say, an important change is made in conduct of the operation. Limitations on calendar time and resources may preclude this.

Whether or not testing is done, the operations analyst should stay with the problem during implementation of the decision. Primarily this is to minimize possible misunderstanding, particularly with respect to the assumptions which underlay the action as recommended and decided. Furthermore the implementation may center on a computerized decision aid, notably as a tactical decision aid on a desk-top computer, and for this an operations analyst's talents and knowledge may play an important role.

113   Concluding Remarks

This completes the discussion of the interrelated phases of conduct of an OA investigation. The process may seem discouragingly formidable. On the other hand, some reviewers of OA results may perceive the methods to be deceptively easy. Neither excessive pessimism nor excessive optimism is justified in approaching this subject. Opportunities for real improvements of important magnitude, via the approaches discussed in this chapter and methods given in the rest of this text, abound in large complex operations such as naval operations. Achieving these potentialities is realizable and requires considerable talent, training, and hard work in the investigations themselves.

This text with its exercises can help with the training. It is much to be desired that it be supplemented by confrontation with real decision problems in assistance to real decision-makers.

114   Other Literature and History

Several references have already been cited on the history and methodologies of military OA. Students are particularly encouraged to see Morse & Kimball [9, 10] and Koopman [11, 12], all of which contain and expand upon considerable material used in this text. References [22] through [30] are sources on the general subjects of operations research and management science, generally aimed at non-military rather than military audiences, while Jaiswal [31] is an OR text aimed at a military audience. An excellent case-study book for the budding military operations analyst is Shephard et al. [32].

[1] Fiske, Bradley A. "American Naval Policy." *Naval Institute Proceedings* (March, 1905): 1-79.

[2] Lanchester, Frederick W. *Aircraft Warfare, The Dawn of the Fourth Arm*. London: Constable, 1916.

[3] Whitmore, William F. "Edison and Operations Research." *Journal of the Operations Research Society of America* 1 (February, 1953): 83-85.

[4] Wagner, Daniel H. "Operations Research." *Encyclopedia for Mathematical Statistics* 5, S. Kotz and N. Johnson, eds. New York: Wiley, 1985.

[5] Trefethen, Florence N. "A History of Operations Research." *Operations Research for Management*, Joseph F. McCloskey and Florence N. Trefethen, eds. Baltimore, MD: Johns Hopkins University Press, 1954.

[6] Larnder, Harold. "The Origin of Operational Research." *Operations Research* 32 (March-April, 1984): 465-475.

[7] Cunningham, W. Peyton; Denys Freeman; and Joseph F. McCloskey. "Of Radar and Operations Research: An Appreciation of A. P. Rowe." *Operations Research* 32 (September-October, 1984): 958-967.

[8] Blackett, P. M. S. "Operational Research." *Studies of War. Part II*. New York: Hill and Wang, 1962.

[9] Morse, Philip M., and George E. Kimball. *Methods of Operations Research*. Operations Evaluation Group Report 54. Washington, DC: Office of the Chief of Naval Operations, 1946.

[10] Morse, Philip M., and George E. Kimball. *Methods of Operations Research*. Cambridge, MA: MIT Press, 1951.

[11] Koopman, Bernard O. *Search and Screening*. Operations Evaluation Group Report 56. Washington, DC: Office of the Chief of Naval Operations, 1946.

[12] Koopman, Bernard O. *Search and Screening*. New York: Pergamon, 1980.

[13] Crowther, J. G., and R. Whiddington. *Science at War*. New York: The Philosophical Library, 1948.

[14] Waddington, G. C. *O.R. in World War 2, Operational Research Against the U-Boat*. London: Elek Science, 1973.

[15] Brothers, Leroy A. "Operations Analysis in the United States Air Force." *Journal of the Operations Research Society of America* 2 (February, 1954): 1-6.

[16] McArthur, Charles W. *Operations Analysis in the U.S. Army Eighth Air Force*. Vol. 4 of *History of Mathematics*. Providence, RI: American Mathematical Society and London Mathematical Society, 1990.

[17] McCue, Brian. *U-Boats in the Bay of Biscay: An Essay in Operations Analysis*. Washington, DC: National Defense University Press, 1990.

[18] Kreiner, Howard W. *Fields of Operations Research*. Baltimore, MD: Operations Research Society of America, 1992.

[19] Hitch, Charles J., and Roland N. McKean. *The Economics of Defense in the Nuclear Age*. Cambridge, MA: Harvard University Press, 1960.

[20] Quade, Edward S., ed. *Analysis for Military Decisions*. Santa Monica, CA: The Rand Corporation, 1951.

[21] Rockower, Edward. *Measures of Effectiveness*. Monterey, CA: Naval Postgraduate School, 1985.

[22] Gass, Saul I., ed. *Operations Research Mathematics and Models*, *Proceedings of Symposia in Applied Mathematics* 25. Providence, RI: American Mathematical Society, 1981.

[23] Churchman, C. West; Roy L. Ackoff; and E. L. Arnoff. *Introduction to Operations Research*. New York: Wiley, 1957.

[24] Hillier, F. S., and Gerald J. Lieberman. *Introduction to Operations Research*. 5th Edition. New York: McGraw-Hill, 1967.

[25] Starr, M. K. *Systems Management of Operations*. Englewood Cliffs, NJ: Prentice-Hall, 1971.

[26] Wagner, Harvey M. *Principles in Operations Research*. Englewood Cliffs, NJ: Prentice-Hall, 1975.

[27] Wagner, Daniel H. "Mathematicians in Operations Research Consulting." *American Mathematical Monthly* 82 (April, 1975): 895-905.

[28] Raisbeck, Gordon. "Mathematicians in the Practice of Operations Research." *American Mathematical Monthly* 83 (November, 1976): 681-701.

[29] Eppen, G. D., and F. J. Gould. *Quantitative Concepts for Management*. Englewood Cliffs, NJ: Prentice-Hall, 1979.

[30] Miser, Hugh J. "Operations Research and Systems Analysis." *Science* 209 (July, 1980): 139-146.

[31] Jaiswal, N. W., *Military Operations Research*. Norwell, MA: Kluwer Academic Press, 1997.

[32] Shephard, R. W., et al. *Applied Operations Research: Examples from Defense Assessment*. New York & London: Plenum Press, 1988.

Problems

Problems 7, 8, 9, and 15 are based on information and data taken from Morse & Kimball [9].

1. Answer the following:

a. In what combat problem area was the identifiable origin of OA (i.e., OR)?
b. Who was the leading U.S. pioneer in OA in World War II?
c. In what theater and type of combat did the OA work in (b) originate?
d. What were the first two academic institutions to initiate degree programs in operations research?

2. Assume you are the decision-maker concerned with each of these problems. State what your real objective would be in each case:

a. A midshipman first class about to graduate considering the best automobile to buy
b. A commanding officer considering the best action to take concerning Seaman Jones' return from liberty two hours late
c. The decision-maker faced with excess shipping losses referred to in 105
d. A married Lieutenant junior grade with one child considering the buying of life insurance

3. In 106, how many ways are there of assigning CAP as described by the example if the following conditions exist:

a. $x \geq 1, y \geq 1, x + y \leq 6$, x and y integer valued?
b. $h_1 < h_2$, where h_1 and h_2 have as possible values 5,000, 10,000, ... , 30,000 feet?
c. r_1 and r_2 have as possible values 10, 20, ... , 50 nm?

4. For one of the situations in Problem 2, list several reasonable alternative courses of action.

5. A decision-maker is considering the problem of detecting a target. Consider each of the following variables,

(1) the amount of money available for procuring new detection equipment
(2) the size of the enemy target
(3) the target aspect angle during the search
(4) the search time necessary for detection
(5) the speed of the search unit
(6) the speed of the target
(7) the radar operator's current state of training
(8) the distance between adjacent search units.

Determine which of the following categories best describes each of the above variables.

    a. controllable,
    b. uncontrollable, but one whose value is known or can be measured,
    c. random,
    d. one whose value must be estimated or assumed.

6. For the situation you used in Problem 2, do the following:

a. List as many variables as you can that will significantly influence the outcome.
b. For each of your variables indicate which of the categories listed in Problem 5 applies.
c. Of these variables, indicate which have values that can be represented quantitatively.
d. Determine whether any of your nonquantitative variables can be changed or rephrased to make them quantitative.

7. The following data were collected on the sighting of merchant vessels by submarines on patrol during World War II. Since the average number of ships present in a region is estimated, the other numbers are rounded to one or two significant figures.

Region	A	B	C
Area of region (sq. nm.), a	80,000	250,000	400,000
Patrol time in region (days), t	800	250	700
Number of sightings, c	400	140	200
Avg. No. ships in region, n	20	20	25

The objective is to compare the effectiveness of the search and patrol efforts of the submarines in each region and to determine how well it is being done.

a. Discuss the usefulness of the following MOEs for use in the analysis of this problem:
   i. The number of sightings in an area, c.
   ii. The number of sightings per unit area, c/a.
   iii. The number of sightings per unit search time, c/t.
   iv. The number of sightings per unit search time divided by the density of targets,
$$\frac{c/t}{n/a} = \frac{c \times a}{t \times n}.$$

b. Using an appropriate MOE, discuss the relative effectiveness of the search and patrol efforts in each of the three areas.

c. Suppose the effective lateral range of detection of a merchant vessel by a submarine, r, is between 15 and 20 nm, and the speed of a patrolling submarine in each of these regions during WWII allowed for a search of length $l = 200$ nm per day. If the (normalized) density of merchant vessels in a region is assumed to be one vessel per sq nm, a theoretical estimate of the maximum possible effectiveness of the patrol could be $q_{th} = 2rl$. How do the search efforts in each of the regions compare to this theoretical maximum value?

d. Discuss the sensivity of your model to the assumed value for the average number of ships in the region, n.

8. In an attempt to help protect merchant vessels from aircraft attack during WWII, it was suggested that the vessels be equipped with antiaircraft (AA) guns and crews. This was done for some ships and data were collected from engagements involving these ships and low-level attacks by aircraft. Suppose that these data, as well as data from similar engagements involving ships not having AA, are as given in the following table:

	AA fired	AA not fired
Attacks	331	155
Ships attacked	155	71
Bombs dropped	632	304
Bombs which hit	50	39
Ships sunk	16	18
Planes shot down	13	---

a. Give a concise statement of the objectives of the study.
b. State the alternative courses of action available.
c. Identify any MOEs that could be used in the analysis of this problem. State whether each is a principal MOE, a secondary MOE, or not acceptable as an MOE in this case. Be sure to explain your reasoning in each case.
d. Analyze the problem using the appropriate MOEs from c. If possible give a mathematical

statement of the model used for the analysis.

e. Decide which parameters are critical and discuss the sensitivity of your model to these parameters.

f. Write a paragraph on your conclusions and recommendations. Discuss how reasonable they are and provide arguments for the reasonableness of your conclusions.

9. The use of early-warning (EW) radar on submarines by the U.S. in WWII provided the submarine with an improved chance of detecting a patrol aircraft and diving before being spotted. The average range of detection of a Japanese plane by a U.S. submarine using an EW radar was only about 1.4 times the average range of visual detection for these planes. When radar detectors were subsequently developed, there was concern that the Japanese might have developed a similar instrument. If radar detectors were being used on Japanese planes, then the use of EW radar by U.S. submarines could have been helping the Japanese locate U.S. submarines. Operational data were collected to help decide whether or not the Japanese were using radar detectors in this fashion. Suppose that the data set collected is given as:

Region	A	B
Area (sq nm)	250,000	400,000
Patrol time in region (days)	250	700
Contacts, EW radar used	86	67
Contacts, EW radar not used	61	51

No information is available concerning the actual number of Japanese planes in the regions during the patrol periods. Provide analysis of this problem by answering questions a to f given in Problem 8.

10. Suppose the Navy has been ordered to consolidate all fleet units on the East Coast at a single port. The candidates are ports A, B, C, and D. Estimates of the cost of relocation at each of the candidate ports are given below. The probability of war over the next several years is considered small, but the Navy may have to respond quickly to several crises at locations W, X, Y, or Z. Assume there will be three future crises. The distance between the candidate ports and the possible crisis locations and the probability of a crisis at each location are given below. Political pressure to relocate at each port is roughly equal. A variety of other external factors have been considered and do not favor any particular port.

Port	Consolidation cost ($ billion)	Location	Location probability
A	2.7	W	.4
B	3.5	X	.2
C	3.8	Y	.3
D	3.0	Z	.1

Distance in 100s of nm

	W	X	Y	Z
A	38	32	24	25
B	32	27	20	28
C	27	22	23	26
D	28	24	22	30

Provide analysis of this problem by answering questions a to e given in Problem 8.

11. Suppose that after further investigation into the situation described in Problem 10, the following additional assumptions were made:

i. In responding to a crisis, a carrier battle group (CVBG) should average 25 knots.
ii. When steaming at 25 knots, a CVBG can transit without replenishment for between 8 and 10 days, depending on sea state, weather, type of ships, initial stores on board, maneuvering during transit, and possibly other factors.
iii. Only about 10 percent of the crises will occur during the winter months, about 20 percent will occur in each of the spring and fall months, and about 50 percent will occur in the summer months.
iv. During the past 10 years, there have been on the average one crisis every two years.
v. The time interval to be considered in the planning of the port consolidation is the next five years.
vi. Delay in responding to a crisis usually results in an escalation of the problem which increases the cost associated with that crisis. The table below gives estimates of the cost (in $100 million) associated with a crisis at each of the locations and for the indicated response times. A response time of zero would mean that the CVBG is at the site when the crisis begins:

Estimated Cost ($100 million)

Location	Number of days to respond to crisis								
	0	1	2	3	4	5	6	7	>7
W	2.5	3.7	4.9	6.5	8.3	10.0	11.8	13.3	14.9
X	3.2	4.8	6.1	7.3	8.7	10.0	11.5	12.6	13.8
Y	3.0	4.5	5.9	7.3	8.5	9.7	10.9	12.2	13.5
Z	2.7	3.8	5.0	6.3	7.7	9.2	10.7	11.9	13.1

a. Provide analysis of this problem by using total cost (relocation cost plus expected cost of crises) as the principal MOE.
b. As a beginning of a sensitivity analysis of your model for this problem, determine the range of values of expected number of crises per year for which your solution remains optimal.

12. A large corporation has 10 computer lines that it rents to 40 smaller companies. All customers have access to all lines, but only one customer at a time can use a line. The corporation wishes to extend this service to encompass 80 companies. Executives of the corporation feel that since the number of customers would double, if the number of computer lines were also doubled, then the current customers would not experience a reduction in their level of satisfaction with the service. Since computer lines are expensive, it is hoped that fewer than 20 lines would be sufficient.

a. Give a concise statement of the objectives of the study.
b. State the alternative courses of action available.
c. In this problem, one must first decide what is meant by maintaining the current customer's level of satisfaction. Three candidates are as follows:

S_1 – the probability of getting a busy signal when trying to use a line,
S_2 – the expected number of customers using a line at any time, and
S_3 – the expected time that a customer has to wait to obtain a free computer line.

Discuss these three measures of customer satisfaction for possible use in this study. In particular, what would be required in order to estimate each for the current system and can they be used to obtain an MOE?
d. Suppose that each customer is expected to use a computer line about three hours each (24-hour) day, and that the line use is spread uniformly about the day. Analyze the problem using an appropriate MOE. Since no measure is given for current customer satisfaction, your analysis should include solutions for representative samples of reasonable levels of customer satisfaction.
e. Write a paragraph on your conclusions and recommendations. Discuss how reasonable they are and provide arguments for the reasonableness of your conclusions.

13. Suppose that you are part of an analysis team that has been given the task of making a recommendation on the procurement of an electronic countermeasures (ECM) package for a type of cruise missile. The budget calls for an expenditure of at most $50 million for this type of cruise missile during the coming year. The cost of a missile without an ECM package is estimated to be $1 million. Two ECM packages are being considered. Package A is estimated to cost an additional $10,000 per missile and Package B is estimated to cost an additional $50,000 per missile.

An ECM package functions to defeat jamming radars aboard a target vessel. They contain a "home on jamming" (HOJ) option that should increase the probability that the missile's seeker will acquire a target whenever the target is actively trying to jam the seeker. Estimates are that 40 percent of the weapons will be used in an environment where the ECM package would be of benefit.

Tests were done on cruise missiles without ECM and on cruise missiles with each of the ECM packages. The results are given in the following table:

Option	No. fired	No. hits	Target type
Current	5	4	Hulk without jammer
Current	7	5	Hulk with jammer
Pkg. A	5	4	Hulk with jammer
Pkg. B	8	7	Hulk with jammer

Provide analysis of this problem by answering questions a to f given in Problem 8.

14. A farmer wishes to purchase a combine for use in harvesting his crops. Assume that he wishes to use it the next five years. He has narrowed his choice to two brands, JD and IH. Each combine can be operated by one person and requires one truck and driver to haul the harvested crops from the field to storage facilities, so the labor cost is proportional to the time required to do the harvesting. The two combines have the following characteristics:

Combine	Cutting speed (ft/min)	Cutting width (ft)	5-year cost ($) (purchase + maintenance)
JD	50	10	120,000
IH	60	12	150,000

a. Give several (at least three) MOEs that could be used in the analysis that could be done to help the farmer make his decision as to which combine to purchase. Indicate circumstances under which each would be appropriate to use.

b. If no additional information is necessary, do the analysis and determine which combine the farmer should purchase. If additional information is needed, indicate what is needed and explain (in detail) how the analysis would be done. Give all relevant formulas that would be needed.

15. A significant problem faced by the U.S. Navy toward the end of WWII was Japanese suicide planes (Kamikazes). As soon as it was clear that a plane was in a dive heading for a particular ship, the ship could attempt to avoid being hit by violent maneuvers in addition to continuing to fire at the plane with its AA guns. It was important to find out whether radical ship maneuvers would spoil the aim of the incoming Kamikaze more than they would spoil the aim of the defensive AA fire. The results of 365 Kamikaze attacks are summarized in the table below. The data have been divided into two categories, those against larger units, including CV and BB fleet units, and smaller units, including DD and LST fleet units.

	Larger units	Smaller units
Maneuvering		
No. attacks	36	144
No. ships hit	8	52
No. planes hit	28	85
Nonmaneuvering		
No. attacks	61	124
No. ships hit	30	32
No. planes hit	45	82

Provide analysis of this problem by answering questions a to f given in Problem 8.

16. Cooperative Engagement. Consider the scenario of a naval battle group defending itself against air attacks. The battle group is equipped with SAMs, search radars, and target illumination radars. The search radars track incoming targets (aircraft, high flying missiles, and surface skimming missiles), and provide in-flight guidance for the SAMs. Each target must be illuminated during the last few seconds of the SAM trajectory for it to "home-in" on its target. The number of illuminators in a battle group is small compared with the number of SAMs and potential targets. In scheduling the illuminators to focus on targets there may be times an illuminator is unavailable due to prior assignments. Start by considering the following example.

The time a target has to be illuminated is five seconds. The battle group has three illuminators. Eight targets have be picked up and must be assigned to illuminators. Targets 5 through 8 can not be assigned to illuminator 3 because its view of them is blocked by other ships. Information about the targets including the time windows for homing in on it is given in the following table. Targets with the highest priority are most dangerous. Note that the target illumination windows' start and ending times are multiples of five seconds.

Target information		Window times	
Id No.	Priority	Open time	Close time
1	10	15	25
2	10	20	30
3	10	35	45
4	10	25	35
5	15	25	30
6	20	25	35
7	35	45	50
8	40	50	60

Prior engagements restrict the illuminator availability as follows:

Illuminator	Time available
1	20-35, 45-60
2	0-30, 50-60
3	0-20, 30-60

Provide analysis of this problem by answering questions a to f given in Problem 8. In doing this keep in mind the fact the "real" problem is much larger, many more targets.

Answers to Problems

1. a. Use of radar in U.K. air defense. b. P. M. Morse. c. ASW in the North Atlantic.
d. U.S. Naval Postgraduate School and Case Institute of Technology.

3. a. 15 combinations of x and y. b. 15 combinations of h_1 and h_2. c. 25 combinations of r_1 and r_2 (therefore, there are $15 \times 15 \times 25 = 5,625$ ways).

5. (1) b. (2) d. (3) c. (4) c. (5) a. (6) d. (7) b. (8) a.

7. a. i. Takes no account of A, T, or N. ii. Same objections as i. plus desire to maximize if A is constant and to minimize if C is constant. iii. Better, but doesn't account for A or N. iv. Good MOE, takes all information into account consistently.
b. MOE value (sq nm/day) is 2000 in A, 7000 in B, and 4500 in C, thus search best in B.
c. $6000 \le Q_{th} \le 8000$, so effort in B is in range of Q_{th}, effort in C is 25 percent outside, which may not be significant, and effort in A is definitely outside.

8. a. Protect merchant vessels from air attack. b. Equip ships with AA or not.

9. a. Give surfaced submarines early warning against air attack. b. Do air search by radar or visually.

10. a. Maintain timely response to likely threats while keeping down relocation costs.
b. Relocate to any of $A, B, C,$ or D.

2
DECISION CRITERIA

Chapter 1 placed considerable emphasis on devising an MOE to be maximized. The obvious variant of devising an MOE with the intent that it be *minimized*, i.e., the MOE indicates penalty to be made small, does not need separate discussion. In either case, the decision making procedure may not be simple maximization or minimization, because the consequences of an action may not be predictable, due to chance events or the actions of an opponent. Other decision criteria may be relevant when unpredictability plagues a decision problem. Some options for assessing an array of actions in the face of unpredictability are discussed in this chapter. Underlying the choice among these various decision criteria is the decision-maker's attitude toward *risk*.

This chapter will begin, in 201, with the concept of a **payoff matrix**. This is an orderly way to list available actions and their consequences. Given a payoff matrix, 202-203 will present several different decision criteria to accommodate risk attitudes and uncertainty, with and without estimates of probabilities of chance events. In section 204 an alternative approach will be studied called **utility theory**. This considers the possibility that the same size change in the payoff for different payoff levels results in different degrees of change in the *satisfaction* with the payoffs. A common example, which arises in personal decision making, is purchase of insurance. If one transforms MOE values into utility values via this theory, which requires interaction with the decision-maker, then the decision problem can be dealt with using one of the decision criteria in 202-203.

Chapter 1 cites single-valuedness as an essential attribute of an MOE, and that is retained in

201-204. Section 205 gives a method of dealing with multiple MOEs via maximization of one MOE subject to constraints on one or more other MOEs. This is in contrast to the examples of 108 which combined multiple evaluative quantities into a single MOE by forming products, quotients, etc. The situation presented in 205 involves the most frequent occurrence of multiple MOEs, a "cost" MOE and an "effectiveness" MOE, and the decision criterion is accordingly labeled **cost-effectiveness.**

The longest section of the chapter, 206, studies decision making when the payoff is influenced by the action of another decision-maker with opposing interests. This is called **game theory**. It is approached in terms of each of two opponents simultaneously analyzing the strategies for both adversaries.

Among the decision criteria presented, by far the most used by naval commanders and other decision-makers are the two most elementary ones: maximizing an MOE or maximizing the expected value of an MOE. The cost-effectiveness approach has been frequently used in procurement decisions. Utility theory is seldom used explicitly, probably because it requires the decision-maker to answer difficult questions to implement it. Game theory is seldom used, because the conditions which underlie the well-developed theory are rarely realized in practice. However, it is important for an OA student to study and to understand these little-used theories, because the *ideas* of utility theory and of game theory often influence successful decision making, even without formal use of their theories.

201   Payoff Matrix

A fundamental concept in describing decision criteria is that of the **payoff matrix.** This is a simple powerful aid to *organizing* decision making. The rows of a payoff matrix are associated with the various courses of action, the choice of which constitutes the decision problem. Each column represents either a possible event, which may be a chance event, or a willful choice of action by an opponent. A matrix entry is the payoff, i.e., the MOE value, that results from the choice of a row and the occurrence of a column. Recall that the payoffs, being MOE values, could be probabilities, expected values, or ratios of such quantities, among other possibilities.

As an example, consider a decision problem consisting of a choice among four search plans, S_1, S_2, S_3, and S_4, with detection probability as the MOE. Suppose the detection probability resulting from each plan is affected by sea state, which is a chance event. Three states of nature, N_1, N_2, and N_3, are identified, each being a range of sea states. Further it is supposed that for each search plan and each state of nature the detection probability can be estimated. The payoff matrix, which neatly embodies this information, is shown as Figure 2.1(a). This example will be used to illustrate decision criteria in the next two sections. Figure 2.1(b) illustrates another payoff matrix. Here each column heading corresponds to a choice by the enemy, rather than the outcome of a chance event. Decision making with this type of payoff matrix will be the subject of 206.

The difference between these two cases is that in Figure 2.1(b), the choice of enemy tactic is a source of uncertainty based on a *willful* act with malevolent intent toward our side, whereas in Figure 2.1(a) the source of uncertainty is chance rather than will or malevolence.

Both of these sources of uncertainty could be presented in a single matrix. In Figure 2.1, that would be a matrix of six columns, one for each pair of nature's state and enemy tactic. Theory for such a combined approach will not be given in this text, however

FIGURE 2.1. ILLUSTRATIVE PAYOFF MATRICES

a. Uncertain states of nature

Alternatives	N_1 Sea state 0 or 1	N_2 Sea state 2 or 3	N_3 Sea state 4 or more
S_1: Search plan one	.9	.4	.1
S_2: Search plan two	.7	.5	.4
S_3: Search plan three	.8	.7	.2
S_4: Search plan four	.5	.5	.5

b. Uncertain enemy tactics

Alternatives	Enemy tactic one	Enemy tactic two
S_1: Search plan one	.9	.5
S_2: Search plan two	.7	.6
S_3: Search plan three	.8	.3
S_4: Search plan four	.5	.4

202   State Probabilities Known or Estimable

This section describes fundamental decision criteria used when the probabilities of relevant states of nature are known or can be estimated. These are the most basic and frequently used decision criteria.

The simplest of these, maximizing the MOE, arises when the payoff matrix is simply a single column. This means there is no uncertainty beyond those in calculation of the MOE values, i. e., the payoff values in the column. Then the course of action is chosen to maximize the payoff. For example, in Figure 2.1(b) if it were known that the state of nature N_1 would occur, then the payoff matrix (transposed) would reduce as follows:

	S_1	S_2	S_3	S_4
N_1	.9	.7	.8	.5

The first strategy clearly yields the highest payoff and is the indicated choice. This is the decision criterion implicit in Chapter 1.

The criterion of maximizing expected value arises when it is not known which state of nature will occur, but the *probability* that each will occur is known (or can be reasonably estimated). Suppose the occurrence probabilities of the states of nature, N_1, N_2, and N_3, in Figure 2.1(a), are .4, .5, and .1, respectively. If the first strategy were chosen, the payoff would be .9 with probability .4, .4 with probability .5, and .1 with probability .1. The *expected payoff* would then be the weighted average: $.9 \times .4 + .4 \times .5 + .1 \times .1 = .57$. If expected payoffs for each course of action are similarly computed, the results can be tabulated as in Figure 2.2. The optimal choice is the strategy which *maximizes the expected value* of the MOE. For the given payoff matrix it can be seen that the strategy S_3 maximizes the expected payoff. By regarding the expected values as forming a single-column payoff matrix, this of course reduces to the previous decision criterion.

FIGURE 2.2. EXPECTED PAYOFF

	N_1	N_2	N_3	
	.4	.5	.1	Expected payoff
S_1	.9	.4	.1	$.9 \times .4 + .4 \times .5 + .1 \times .1 = .57$
S_2	.7	.5	.4	$.7 \times .4 + .5 \times .5 + .4 \times .1 = .57$
S_3	.8	.7	.2	$.8 \times .4 + .7 \times .5 + .2 \times .1 = .69$
S_4	.5	.5	.5	$.5 \times .4 + .5 \times .5 + .5 \times .1 = .50$

203   State Probabilities Unknown

Suppose a decision-maker is faced with the earlier payoff matrix as follows, but has *no* knowledge concerning the probable state of nature:

	N_1	N_2	N_3
S_1	.9	.4	.1
S_2	.7	.5	.4
S_3	.8	.7	.2
S_4	.5	.5	.5

How can one determine *which course of action is best?* It will be seen presently that the word *best* takes on meaning only when considered in conjunction with a *particular* criterion. In this matrix, S_1 is best if the state of nature is N_1, likewise S_3 is best for N_2 and S_4 is best for N_3. Also, S_1 offers the highest possible payoff, S_3 the highest average payoff, and S_4 the highest guaranteed payoff. In addition, it will be shown that S_2 is the strategy which will guarantee a decision-maker the "least regret." As the following four different decision making criteria are discussed, it should be kept in mind that the question of *which criterion is best* cannot be answered in general. Only for a particular decision-maker facing a particular problem does a best criterion exist.

A conservative approach would be to look for the course of action which offers the *best guaranteed payoff*. The decision-maker can easily determine the guaranteed payoffs by asking, for each course of action: *What is the worst that can happen if I use this strategy?* The resulting guarantees for the previous matrix would be as in Figure 2.3. The course of action which yields the highest guaranteed payoff is S_4. The decision-maker who chooses this course of action can do so knowing the payoff will be *at least .5 no matter what state of nature occurs*. This pessimistic criterion minimizes the risk in picking an action. It is referred to as the **maximin** criterion since the minimum payoff for each course of action is first found and then the action is chosen which yields the maximum value of these minimum guaranteed payoffs. If the payoffs were such that the decision-maker wants them small rather than large, the minimization and maximization would be interchanged and the criterion would be termed **minimax**.

The second criterion, while similar to the first, rejects the idea of being pessimistic. In the previous matrix, a complete optimist would be tempted, by the prospect of getting a payoff of .9, to pick the first course of action despite the possibility of getting its less desirable payoffs. This **maximax** choice is equivalent to assuming that nature is benevolent and thus will cause that state of nature to occur which is best for the decision-maker no matter which decision is made. A more rational use for maximax thinking is its identification of the best payoff possible for each decision available. It also may be thought of as a state of mind in which, for this example, .9 is a satisfactory payoff and anything less in the matrix is unsatisfactory. Hence the only choice that has a satisfactory prospect is S_1. This may be thought of as a "go-for-broke" or "desperation" criterion.

FIGURE 2.3. GUARANTEED PAYOFF

	N_1	N_2	N_3	Guaranteed payoff
S_1	.9	.4	.1	.1
S_2	.7	.5	.4	.4
S_3	.8	.7	.2	.2
S_4	.5	.5	.5	.5

The third criterion is based on the tendency of some decision-makers to look back on their decision after the action is completed to see how much better they could have done by predicting the correct state of nature. This gives rise to the possibility of **minimizing regret** as a criterion for decision making. Suppose the decision-maker computes the regret he or she could experience and constructs a **regret matrix** from the payoff matrix as in Figure 2.4.

Here the decision-maker would have no regret if the first course of action were chosen and the state of nature N_1 occurred, since a better result could not have been obtained. If N_2 were to occur, however, the regret would be .3 (i.e., .7 - .4) since one could have done that much better by using strategy S_3. This suggests what is known as the **least regret** criterion: Applying the minimax criterion to the regret matrix will determine the strategy which has the least of the highest regrets. The first strategy guarantees a regret of not more than .4, the second a regret of not more than .2, etc., as in Figure 2.5. The second strategy thus yields the least of the maximum regrets, called "least regret" for short.

FIGURE 2.4. PAYOFF AND REGRET MATRICES

	Payoff Matrix			Regret Matrix		
	N_1	N_2	N_3	N_1	N_2	N_3
S_1	.9	.4	.1	.9 - .9	.7 - .4	.5 - .1
S_2	.7	.5	.4	.9 - .7	.7 - .5	.5 - .4
S_3	.8	.7	.2	.9 - .8	.7 - .7	.5 - .2
S_4	.5	.5	.5	.9 - .5	.7 - .5	.5 - .5

FIGURE 2.5. REGRET MATRIX

	N_1	N_2	N_3	Maximum regret
S_1	0	.3	.4	.4
S_2	.2	.2	.1	.2
S_3	.1	0	.3	.3
S_4	.4	.2	0	.4

The fourth criterion to be presented, when state probabilities are unknown, takes the viewpoint that complete uncertainty about the probable state of nature is equivalent to assuming each state of nature equally probable. That is, if any state is assumed more likely than another, it is because more information is known and the decision-maker is not faced with complete uncertainty. The validity and implications of this argument have long been debated and remain debatable. However, to use this criterion, the expected payoff for each course of action can be computed as in maximizing expected payoff where each state of nature is now weighted equally, as shown in Figure 2.6. The third course of action then is best under this criterion.

In discussing these four criteria for decision making under uncertainty, it was shown that for the payoff matrix used, four different courses of action resulted as best. This is not generally the case, but it is by no means unique and points to the importance the decision criterion plays in choosing the best course of action.

204   Utility Theory

The preceding section described some decision criteria which reflect conservative or venture-some attitudes, i.e., pessimism or optimism, by the decision-maker. This section addresses a different approach to this end in the form of **utility theory**.

FIGURE 2.6. EQUAL PROBABILITIES

	N_1	N_2	N_3	
	⅓	⅓	⅓	Expected Payoff
S_1	.9	.4	.1	.467
S_2	.7	.5	.4	.533
S_3	.8	.7	.2	.567
S_4	.5	.5	.5	.500

The purpose of utility theory is illustrated by a decision to purchase home fire insurance. A decision-maker owns a home valued at $200,000 and there is one chance in 1,000 (probability .001), that the house will burn down this year. The *expected* loss is .001×$200,000 = $200. The insurance premium for the home costs $250. If the decision-maker's objective is to maximize expected assets the insurance should not be purchased. However, since the loss of the home would be such a financial setback, most likely that objective will be disregarded, and the insurance will be bought at a disadvantage in expected value of $50. Utility theory helps to explain why a rational decision-maker will not always choose the course of action that maximizes expected value, even if expected value is computable.

Every decision-maker has a personal level of acceptable risk associated with the relative value placed on possible outcomes and their probabilities of occurrence. Utility theory enables a decision-maker to rescale an MOE consistent with his or her subjective judgments and personal views of risk.

Utility theory uses the concept of a lottery to describe a situation in which a person will receive, for $i = 1, 2, \dots , n$, a reward r_i with probability p_i denoted as $(p_1, r_1; p_2, r_2; \dots ; p_n, r_n)$. For example, suppose one were asked to choose between the certain lottery of receiving $30,000 or playing a lottery with a 50 percent chance to win $100,000 and a 50 percent chance to receive $0. The lotteries (1.0, $30,000) called L_1 and (.5, $100,000; .5, $0) called L_2 are depicted as follows:

$$L_1 ---[1.0 : \$30,000$$

$$L_2 --- \left[\begin{array}{l} .5 : \$100,000 \\ .5 : \$0 \end{array} \right.$$

The lottery L_1 has an expected value of $30,000, and L_2 has an expected value of $50,000, that is, .5×$100,000 + .5×$0. Although L_2 has a larger expected value than L_1, most people would prefer L_1 to L_2, because L_2 offers the certainty of an attractive reward while L_2 has a .5 probability of $0 reward.

One method that enables a decision-maker to choose consistently among different lotteries is the construction and application of a **utility function** which gives the evaluations of possible outcomes in light of the decision-maker's views on risk. The construction of a utility function involves assigning a utility value to each reward r_i, written $u(r_i)$. The procedure begins by giving the least favorable reward a value of 0 and the most favorable reward a utility of 1. Then one determines the utility of intermediate outcomes by finding the decision-maker's level of indifference between the certain lottery of an intermediate reward and a lottery based on known utility values. The utility value of each reward determines a point on the utility function. In the previous example, the most favorable reward was $100,000 and the least favorable was $0, hence $u(\$100,000) = 1$ and $u(\$0) = 0$. Suppose the decision-maker states indifference between receiving the certain reward of $10,000 and receiving $100,000 with probability .2 and receiving $0 with probability .8, i.e., between the following lotteries:

$$---[1.0: \$10,000 \quad \text{and} \quad ---\begin{bmatrix} .2: \$100,000 \\ .8: \$0 \end{bmatrix}$$

Since the decision-maker is indifferent between the two lotteries, they must have the same expected utility. Therefore

$$\begin{aligned} u(\$10,000) &= .2u(\$100,000) + .8u(\$0) \\ &= .2 \times 1 + .8 \times 0 \\ &= .2. \end{aligned}$$

This procedure yields a utility value of .2 for $10,000. Similarly, suppose the decision-maker states indifference between the following lotteries:

$$---[1.0: \$50,000 \quad \text{and} \quad ---\begin{bmatrix} .75: \$100,000 \\ .25: \$10,000 \end{bmatrix}$$

Using the equivalence of expected utility,

$$\begin{aligned} u(\$50,000) &= .75u(\$100,000) + .25u(\$10,000) \\ &= .75 \times 1 + .25 \times .2 \\ &= .8. \end{aligned}$$

Suppose furthermore that the decision-maker states indifference between

$$---[1.0: \$85,000 \quad \text{and} \quad ---\begin{bmatrix} .7: \$100,000 \\ .3: \$50,000, \end{bmatrix}$$

yielding $u(\$85,000) = .94$. Now the utility function can be approximated by drawing a piece-wise linear curve joining the points (0, 0), (10,000, .2), (50,000, .8), (85,000, .94), and (100,000, 1), shown in Figure 2.7.

The shape of the utility function contains information about the decision-maker's attitude toward risk. In Figure 2.7, the graph of the utility function is concave down (see 205 below for a definition of concavity), indicating a risk avoidance attitude. This explains why the decision-maker chose to keep the certain $30,000 instead of playing the lottery which gave a 50 percent chance to win $100,000 and had an expected value of $50,000. Utility functions that are concave up demonstrate risk-preferring behavior. A straight line indicates risk indifference.

The next example is a combat situation where the relative values of the rewards are more difficult to assess. A Marine Corps infantry Lieutenant is leading a platoon of 20 men and has been ordered to hold a position to which there are 12 possible approaches. As long as he has 12 men he can guard each of the approaches, but if he suffers more than 8 casualties, he must abandon the position. He must judge the relative importance (value or utility) of two goals:

(a) maximize the number of survivors under his command;

(b) maximize the probability that he will be able to hold his position.

It seems reasonable that 2 casualties are approximately twice as bad as 1 casualty. Perhaps 8 casualties are about 8 times as bad as only 1 casualty, but clearly 9 casualties (and having to abandon the position) are far worse than 9 times as bad as 1 casualty. In fact, looking at it in terms of survivors, there is a step increase in utility for having 12 survivors as compared with having only 11 survivors. How does one compare different plans for carrying out the mission?

FIGURE 2.7. UTILITY FUNCTION

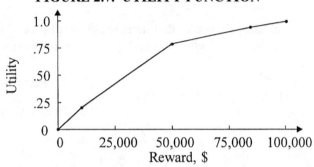

Suppose that the Lieutenant has two plans for carrying out this mission. Plan 1 has a .5 probability of 10 casualties and a .5 chance of 0 casualties. Plan 2 has a .8 probability of incurring 8 casualties and a .2 probability of incurring 0 casualties. The two plans can be shown in terms of lotteries as follows:

$$\text{Plan 1} ---\begin{bmatrix} .5: 10 \text{ survivors} \\ .5: 20 \text{ survivors} \end{bmatrix} \quad \text{and} \quad \text{Plan 2} ---\begin{bmatrix} .8: 12 \text{ survivors} \\ .2: 20 \text{ survivors} \end{bmatrix}$$

The expected number of casualties and the probability of a successful mission are as follows:

Plan	E[# survive]	Pr{successful mission}
1	15.0	0.5
2	13.6	1.0

If the Lieutenant is willing to suffer 1.4 additional expected casualties by using plan 2, he will be assured of holding the position. The decision as to which plan to use depends on the Lieutenant's perception on how critical (in terms of troop losses) it is to hold this position.

In order to assist the Lieutenant in making rational, consistent choices between alternative courses of action, a utility function can be constructed using techniques shown in the first example. The most favorable reward of 20 survivors is assigned a utility of 1, and the reward of 0 survivors is assigned a utility of 0. The assumption that 2 casualties are approximately twice as bad as 1 casualty implies that the utility function is (approximately) composed of straight lines, except at the discontinuity of 12 survivors. In order to find the slopes of the two line segments, the Lieutenant says that he is indifferent between a certain reward of 17 survivors and the scenario (lottery) where there are 20 survivors with probability of .98 and 0 survivors with probability of .02. The two lotteries are as follows:

$$---[1.0 : 17 \text{ survivors} \quad \text{and} \quad ---\begin{bmatrix} .98 : 20 \text{ survivors} \\ .02 : 0 \text{ survivors} \end{bmatrix}$$

Since he is indifferent between the two scenarios they must have the same expected utility:

$$\begin{aligned} u(17) &= .98u(20) + .02u(0) \\ &= .98 \times 1 + .02 \times 0 \\ &= .98. \end{aligned}$$

Similarly, suppose the Lieutenant indicates that he is indifferent between a certain reward of 10 survivors and one having 20 survivors with probability .2 and 0 survivors with probability .8, i.e., between the following:

$$---[1.0 : 10 \text{ survivors} \quad \text{and} \quad ---\begin{bmatrix} .2 : 20 \text{ survivors} \\ .8 : 0 \text{ survivors} \end{bmatrix}$$

The utility of 10 survivors is found by

$$\begin{aligned} u(10) &= .2\,u(20) + .8\,u(0) \\ &= .2 \times 1 + .8 \times 0 \\ &= .2. \end{aligned}$$

Four points, (# survivors, u(# survivors)), on the Lieutenant's utility function have been established: (0, 0), (10, .2), (17, .98), and (20, 1.0). The graph of the utility function is given in Figure 2.8. Notice that the utility assigned to the certain outcome of 12 survivors is around .95. This

FIGURE 2.8. UTILITY FUNCTION FOR INFANTRY EXAMPLE

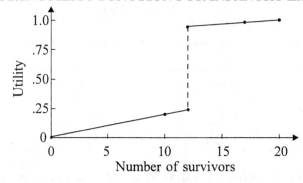

value is chosen over the lower point (about .24) since a reward of having 12 survivors results in a successful mission. The *expected* utility of each of the two battle plans can now be calculated, and they can be ranked as to which one the Lieutenant would prefer:

$$\begin{aligned} \text{expected utility of plan 1} &= .5\,u(10) + .5\,u(20) \\ &= .5 \times .2 + .5 \times 1 \\ &= .6, \end{aligned}$$

$$\text{expected utility of plan 2} = .8\,u(12) + .2\,u(20)$$
$$= .8 \times .95 + .2 \times 1$$
$$= .96.$$

Thus, if the Lieutenant bases his decision on the above utility values using expected utility, he should choose plan 2 for his defense of the position.

The limiting factor in applying utility theory is the difficulty in eliciting from the decision-maker equivalences between lotteries according to his or her attitudes. Nevertheless, the theory is a rational approach to reflection of risk attitudes in decision making.

205   Cost-Effectiveness -- Multiple MOEs

Attention now turns to decision making when more than one MOE, which amounts to an MOE with values having dimension greater than one, is deemed needed for a quantitative characterization of payoff. This arises most naturally when benefit and penalty are treated as *separate* MOEs, to be considered simultaneously. The discussion which follows will consider just two MOEs, called "effectiveness" and "cost." "Cost" may be any form of penalty, not necessarily financial. Also, the ideas below are readily extended to the case of more than two MOEs.

One desires that effectiveness be high and cost be low. These desiderata usually conflict.

Suppose courses of action $S_1, \ldots, S_k$ are available, and action S_i has effectiveness e_i and cost c_i for $i = 1, \ldots, k$. Then S_i is said to **dominate** S_j if S_i is at least as effective as S_j and has less cost than S_j or S_i is more effective and has no more cost, i.e.,

$$(e_i \geq e_j \text{ and } c_i < c_j) \quad \text{or} \quad (e_i > e_j \text{ and } c_i \leq c_j).$$

If for some i, S_i dominates S_j for all $j \neq i$, then S_i is an obvious choice, but that wouldn't be much of a decision problem, and things seldom happen that way.

A sensible approach is to seek an S_i (expecting that there will be more than one) which is not dominated by any S_j, $j \neq i$,

$$e_j < e_i \quad \text{or} \quad c_j > c_i$$

Such an S_i is said to be **cost-effective**.

An easy geometric description of cost-effectiveness is obtained by plotting the (c_i, e_i) pairs for $i = 1, \ldots, k$ as shown in Figure 2.9 (where k = 6). Then for each plotted point, which represents an action, draw or visualize the upper left quadrant whose vertex is that action; the action is cost-effective if the quadrant contains no other actions. In Figure 2.9(a) this is illustrated for action S_2. All of the points that are not cost-effective are dominated by some cost-effective point and are obviously eliminated from the decision choices. In Figure 2.9, S_4 is dominated by S_3, while S_1, S_2, S_3, S_5, and S_6 are all cost-effective.

It is further useful to plot a graph of the most effectiveness that can be obtained for a given cost. This graph consists of a step function with steps parallel to the cost axis, each of whose left end-point is a cost-effective action and whose right end-point is not on the graph. This is illustrated in Figure 2.9(a). The actions that are not cost-effective lie strictly below the graph (S_4 in the figure). If a cost budget (illustratively 1.5 in the figure) is given as a constraint, then the available effectiveness is the ordinate on the graph above that cost (0.5 in the figure) and is attained by the action (S_1 in the figure) at the left end-point of the step for that cost.

Similar reasoning and symmetric graphing, illustrated in Figure 2.9(b), lead to the least cost that must be incurred (3 in the figure) to meet a given effectiveness requirement (1.5 in the figure).

Within the cost-effective actions, there is a preferred set known as **efficient** actions. These are the action points that lie on the **concave envelope**, which in this context is called the **efficiency frontier**, of the cost-effective action points. The graph of a function is **concave** if the chord between any two points on the graph lies on or below the graph (equivalently, the slope of the graph is non-increasing as the horizontal coordinate increases). The **concave envelope** of a set of plotted points is the lowest concave function graph which lies on or above the set.

The reason the efficient actions are preferred is that if one moves from such an action (e.g., S_3 in the figure) to a cost-effective action which has higher cost and is *not* efficient (S_5 in the figure), then the increase in effectiveness per increase in cost $((2.5 - 2)/(5 - 3) = \frac{1}{4})$ is not as much as could be obtained by moving to another efficient point (S_6 in the figure, for which the ratio is $(3 - 2)/(6 - 3) = \frac{1}{3}$). If the cost budget in the figure were 2.5 instead of 1.5, it would oblige one to use an action (S_2 in the figure) which is not efficient. This could also be a guide to choosing an efficient budget, e.g., in the latter example, one might argue for a budget of 3, since it would permit the efficient action S_3.

The foregoing discussion is in terms of a *finite*, i.e., discrete, set of alternative actions. The concepts readily extend to a continuum of alternative actions, e.g., see problem 8.

As an example of the kind of decision to which the cost-effectiveness approach might be applied, suppose the problem were to choose a type of system to be procured. Available are k system types, and procurement cost and operational effectiveness have been evaluated for each. Then one could plot as in Figure 2.9, and use cost-effectiveness as a decision criterion, possibly refined in terms of efficiency as defined above.

As a tactical application, consider a variation on the platoon leader example of 204. Suppose that instead of having a critical number of approaches to protect, there are various degrees of strength, evaluated as effectiveness, of holding the platoon's position, and it is very important to maintain as much effectiveness as possible. It is also important to minimize the expected number of casualties, which is the measure of cost. Various plans to defend the position are considered, and cost and effectiveness are estimated for each. Then the cost-effectiveness pairs may be plotted and a cost-effectiveness approach to a decision may be made. An advantage of this approach is that it avoids combining human casualties with the effectiveness objective, which is always difficult, until relatively late in the decision process. Thus the decision-maker may weigh the increase in casualties against an increase in effectiveness, in comparing plans, which might be a less difficult rationale than forming a single MOE which embodies both.

Thus cost-effectiveness is yet another simply-described decision criterion which can contribute greatly to orderliness in decision making.

206   Game Theory

Military decisions are usually made in *conflict situations*. That is, one side has goals and desires opposed to those of the other side. These conflicts exist in politics, business, parlor games, and many other activities. This section presents a mathematical framework known as **game theory** for justifying simultaneous choices by two adversaries in a conflict situation.

FIGURE 2.9. COST-EFFECTIVENESS

Index, i	Action, S_i	Cost, c_i	Effectiveness, e_i
1	S_1	1	0.5
2	S_2	2	1.0
3	S_3	3	2.0
4	S_4	4	1.5
5	S_5	5	2.5
6	S_6	6	3.0

(a)

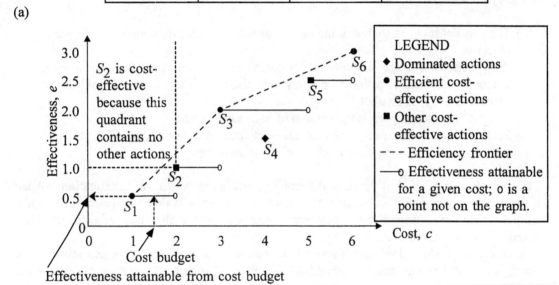

Effectiveness attainable from cost budget

(b)

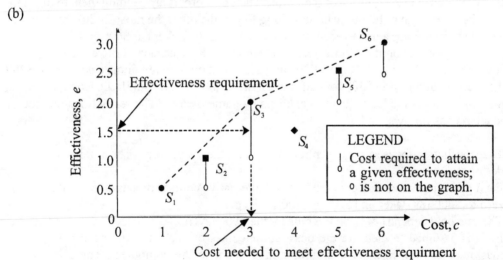

Cost needed to meet effectiveness requirment

Preliminary discussion. Application of the theory has been made in tactical situations, weapons system analysis, logistics, and economics. More important to the military planner, the implications of the theory can be brought to bear on situations more complicated and less precise than those to which it was originally applied. However, many of these applications are tentative and limited in scope. A naval operations analyst should, however, have a knowledge of the way in which game theory can assist in decision making. It is the purpose of this section to give a simplified explanation of what game theory is, how it can be applied in its pure form to various conflict situations, and how the reasoning employed in game theory may aid in arriving at sound military decisions.

There are several restrictions on the types of conflicts which are amenable to analysis by the game theory presented in this text:

(a) The conflict must be such that the participants have opposing interests in the same objective.
(b) Participants must make simultaneous or concurrent decisions as to which of a set of alternative courses of action to employ, and these decisions cannot be subject to revision during the conflict.
(c) The outcome depends upon the choices of *both* participants.
(d) Each of the participants must measure the worth of all possible outcomes on the same scale and must have the same estimate of these outcomes.

In general, restriction (d) is the most difficult to meet in real world conflict situations. Apart from the problem of outcome estimation, two adversaries usually evaluate outcomes differently, particularly in military engagements. They tend to have different intelligence and different utility functions, whether or not the latter are explicitly estimated.

As an example which does meet these restrictions, consider the conflict which arises in the following situation: Ensigns James Baker and William Rogers have equal investments in a computer they jointly purchased at the beginning of their tour. Their new orders are sending them to different stations, and they decide that the one who is willing to pay the other the most for his interest will become the sole owner. They agree the computer is worth $1,000. Baker has $600 and Rogers $400 in cash, and they agree to submit bids in whole $100 amounts. For instance, if Baker bids $300 and Rogers bids $200, then Baker pays Rogers $300 and gets the computer, obtaining a net gain of $200 (because he is essentially paying $300 for half interest in a $1,000 asset). Similarly, Rogers is losing $200. This conflict situation lends itself to analysis by game theory. The restrictions previously mentioned are met as follows:

(a) The conflict is focused on a central issue, i.e., the computer. The interests are definitely opposed.
(b) Each participant must select one of several alternative courses of action, i.e., bids of zero to $600 for Baker and zero to $400 for Rogers.
(c) The outcome depends only on the bids by the two players.
(d) Each is assumed to measure the possible outcomes on the same (monetary) scale inasmuch as they each have a similar investment in the computer. There is no difficulty in estimation of outcome -- it is clearly known to both!

Game theory provides a basis for each participant to decide what bid to make.

Before making such a choice, the decision-maker must choose a criterion, several of which have already been discussed. In what follows, it is assumed that each player tries to gain as much as possible, *safely*, in the face of a skillful opponent whose objective is diametrically opposed. This is the maximin criterion (see 203), applied simultaneously to adversaries, while reversing to minimax for one who wants the payoff small. In a game situation, the maximin-minimax criterion will lead each player to a strategy which insures his or her best "worst case" result.

There are certain terms which must be defined at this point. It will be helpful if the reader recognizes these terms as technical words with special meanings for game theory:

(a) A **player** is one of the opposing interests or persons.

(b) A **strategy** is an available action for either player.

(c) A **payoff** is a quantity "paid" by one player, the **minimizing** player, to the other, the **maximizing** player, depending on the choice of strategy made by each.

(d) A **two-person game,** or **game** for brevity, is a pair of players together with a set of strategies for each and resultant payoffs for each strategy pair. Note that this implies that there is a set of rules which define what can and cannot be done, the size of bets or penalties, and payoff methods. The rules must be complete, must not change during the game, and must be known to the participants.

(e) A **zero-sum** game is one in which the payoffs for the two players under any strategy pair sum to zero; that is what one player wins, the other loses.

(f) The **payoff matrix** of a game is the matrix wherein each row corresponds to a strategy of the maximizing player, each column corresponds to a strategy of the minimizing player, and the matrix entry is the payoff resulting from the strategy choices of that row and column.

(g) A **play** of the game is the choosing of a strategy by each player, i.e., a row and column of the payoff matrix, along with the awarding of the payoff which results.

(h) An **optimal** strategy for either player of a two person zero-sum game is one which provides the best guarantee available to that player, i.e., a maximin strategy for the maximizing player or a minimax strategy for the minimizing player.

(i) The **value** of a game is the guaranteed payoff for each player, providing it is the same for each and providing each uses an optimal strategy.

(j) The **solution** of a two-person zero-sum game is an optimal strategy for each player and the numerical value of the game.

Here only two-person zero-sum games, each characterized by a payoff matrix, are considered. In the following discussion on saddle-points and dominance, attention is confined to cases where each player's choice is a *single* strategy (row or column) among those available. Such a choice is called a **pure** strategy. Later, consideration is given to choosing a mix of pure strategies, each with a probability. This is called a **mixed** strategy for a player. The terms "optimal strategy," "value of the game," and "solution" will readily extend to the mixed strategy concept.

In the examples below, the names "Blue" and "Red" will often conventionally be given to the maximizing and minimizing players, respectively.

Once a conflict situation has been formulated as a game, the next objective is to solve the game.

Saddle-point games. Consider again the computer problem. First, it is clear that whatever Baker gains, Rogers loses, and vice versa, so this is a two-person zero-sum game. If Baker bids $300 and Rogers bids $200, Baker gets the computer and pays Rogers $300 for a net gain of $200 on his investment. On the other hand if Baker's $300 is met by a $400 bid from Rogers, then Rogers gets the computer in exchange for $400 and Baker suffers a net loss of $100. Suppose, however, that the bids are equal. In such a case, Baker and Rogers agree to flip a coin to see which of them gets the computer in exchange for his bid. If both bid $300, for example, Baker's net gain is $200 if he gets the computer and -$200 if he receives instead the $300. Either outcome is equally probable and his net expected gain is then zero. In this way, the payoff matrix in Figure 2.10, with payoffs in $100s, is generated.

FIGURE 2.10. SADDLE-POINT GAME

		Red (Rogers)				
		R_1	R_2	R_3	R_4	R_5
		Bid 0	Bid1	Bid 2	Bid 3	Bid 4
	B_1: Bid 0	0	-4	-3	-2	-1
	B_2: Bid 1	4	0	-3	-2	-1
	B_3: Bid 2	3	3	0	-2	-1
Blue	B_4: Bid 3	2	2	2	0	-1
(Baker)	B_5: Bid 4	1	1	1	1	0
	B_6: Bid 5	0	0	0	0	0
	B_7: Bid 6	-1	-1	-1	-1	-1

Baker, when faced with this payoff matrix, can immediately see that a bid of zero may result in as much as a $400 loss while other bids seem to offer less risk. Using the maximin criterion he asks himself what is the worst he can do for each of his alternatives. His findings are shown in the matrix in Figure 2.11, and the zero is starred to represent the highest guarantee he has available–in this case by bidding either $400 or $500.

But Rogers can also exert some influence on the results by the proper choice of his strategies. Being also rational he asks himself the corresponding question for each of his alternatives: *What is the worst possible outcome* (realizing that Baker's gains are his losses)? If he bids $100, for example, Baker's payoff may be as high as $300, whereas by a proper choice he can insure that Baker does not do better than break even. The starred result in the matrix given in Figure 2.12 indicates his best guarantee.

FIGURE 2.11. MAXIMIN

		R_1	R_2	R_3	R_4	R_5	Red (Rogers) guarantee (minimum in each row)
		Bid 0	Bid 1	Bid 2	Bid 3	Bid 4	
	B_1: Bid 0	0	-4	-3	-2	-1	-4
	B_2: Bid 1	4	0	-3	-2	-1	-3
	B_3: Bid 2	3	3	0	-2	-1	-2
Blue (Baker)	B_4: Bid 3	2	2	2	0	-1	-1
	B_5: Bid 4	1	1	1	1	0	0* ← maximum of row
	B_6: Bid 5	0	0	0	0	0	0* ← minima, i.e., maximin
	B_7: Bid 6	-1	-1	-1	-1	-1	-1

FIGURE 2.12. MINIMAX

		R_1	R_2	R_3	R_4	R_5	Red (Rogers)
		Bid 0	Bid 1	Bid 2	Bid 3	Bid 4	
	B_1: Bid 0	0	-4	-3	-2	-1	
	B_2: Bid 1	4	0	-3	-2	-1	
	B_3: Bid 2	3	3	0	-2	-1	
Blue (Baker)	B_4: Bid 3	2	2	2	0	-1	
	B_5: Bid 4	1	1	1	1	0	
	B_6: Bid 5	0	0	0	0	[0]	← saddle-point
	B_7: Bid 6	-1	-1	-1	-1	-1	
Red's guarantee:		4	3	2	1	0*	

(maximum in each column)   ↑ minimum of column maxima, i.e., minimax

In all (two-person zero-sum) games, the *minimax* is greater than or equal to the *maximin*. In this particular game, something of a coincidence appears; the two are *equal* and Blue's best guarantee is equal to Red's best guarantee. When this is the case, a **saddle-point** is said to exist and the optimal strategies for both players are those which yield the saddle-point payoff, which is then the value of the game. In this example, two saddle-points exist as Baker may bid either $400 or $500 while Rogers should bid $400 dollars. The reader may verify that a saddle-point must be both the minimum payoff in its row and the maximum payoff in its column. If either player varies from the saddle-point strategies, he loses his guarantee. The value of this game is zero, the payoff when both players use their optimal strategies. Actually, Baker may prefer to bid $400 rather than $500 since then he would gain more if Rogers bids unwisely.

When considering a game matrix, the first step in finding the solution is always to check for a saddle-point. If one does exist, the solution is immediate because the optimal strategies for the Blue and Red are evident and the value of the game is the saddle-point payoff. If a saddle-point is not found, a more general method is needed.

Dominance. Large payoff matrices can often be reduced in size by inspecting the payoff matrix to discover strategies which a player should never use. A strategy is said to be **dominated**, and therefore may be eliminated from consideration in solving a game, if there is another strategy which is *as good or better* no matter what strategy the opponent may use. Such strategies are evident in the game between Baker and Rogers. For example, compare Baker's first two strategies which are as follows:

		Red				
		R_1	R_2	R_3	R_4	R_5
Blue	B_1:	0	-4	-3	-2	-1
	B_2:	4	0	-3	-2	-1

Here Baker's strategy B_2 is as good or better than B_1 no matter what Rogers does, i.e., 4 is better than 0, 0 is better than -4, -3 is as good as -3, -2 is as good as -2, and -1 is as good as -1. Hence, the strategy B_1 may be eliminated in searching for a solution to the game. In like manner, Baker's sixth and seventh strategies may be eliminated by dominance. The reduced matrix is then as in Figure 2.13.

FIGURE 2.13. REDUCED MATRIX

		Red (Rogers)				
		R_1	R_2	R_3	R_4	R_5
	B_2	4	0	-3	-2	-1
Blue	B_3	3	3	0	-2	-1
(Baker)	B_4	2	2	2	0	-1
	B_5	1	1	1	1	0

It can be reduced even further because Rogers also has dominated strategies. His strategy R_2 is as good or better than strategy R_1 no matter which of the four strategies Baker may now use (remember that large payoffs are good for Baker, poor for Rogers). Hence R_1 can be eliminated. Also, R_2 is worse for Rogers than any of his remaining strategies and the game can now be reduced to the following:

		Red (Rogers)		
		R_3	R_4	R_5
	B_2	-3	-2	-1
Blue	B_3	0	-2	-1
(Baker)	B_4	2	0	-1
	B_5	1	1	0

Further dominance can be found by alternating between Blue and Red strategies. This matrix would finally be reduced to the single strategies B_5 and R_5 with payoff (value) 0, a previously found solution to the game.

Not all games with saddle-points can be so reduced by dominance, however, as the matrix in Figure 2.14 shows. Here a saddle-point is found at the intersection of Blue's first and Red's first strategies. Hence, the solution is (B_1, R_1) and the game value is 2. If, however, dominance is considered, only B_4 and R_4 can be eliminated.

FIGURE 2.14. SADDLE-POINT

		Red				
		R_1	R_2	R_3	R_4	
	B_1	2	3	3	4	2*
Blue	B_2	1	0	4	3	0
	B_3	1	4	0	2	0
	B_4	1	2	3	1	1
		2*	4	4	4	

Whether or not a saddle-point exists, the matrix should be reduced as far as possible, discarding poor strategies by dominance. Dominance could in fact have been applied to the choices of strategies in the decision problems considered in 202 and 203, although the computational effort involved might not have been worthwhile. However, *those* decision cases are made against *future states of nature*, so dominance there would be applied *only to the rows* and *not to the columns*. A future, indifferent state of nature will not rationalize dominance, as will a logical opponent who controls the column choices with deliberate objectives.

Mixed strategies. Next consider a matrix without a saddle-point in which each player has only two pure strategies, i.e., the payoff matrix is 2×2. This matrix may appear after reducing a larger game by dominance or it may be originally a 2×2 game. As an example consider the following operational problem.

Suppose a submarine transitor (Red) has a choice of running in or below the isothermal layer below the surface. These two strategies for Red will be called "run shallow" (R_1) and "run deep" (R_2). Suppose also that a patroller (Blue, which might be an aircraft, surface ship, or submarine) attempting to detect the transitor, has a choice of placing its sensors in or below the layer, but not both -- Blue's strategies will be called "search shallow" (B_1) and "search deep" (B_2). Let the payoff to Blue (the patroller) be the probability that it detects Red (the transitor). The payoff is enhanced if the choices are both deep or both shallow. It is significantly lessened, but not to zero, if the choices are not the same. Specifically, assume that the payoff matrix is as follows:

		Red	
		R_1	R_2
		Run shallow	Run deep
Blue	B_1: Search shallow	.6	.3
	B_2: Search deep	.4	.7

In checking for a saddle-point, guarantees are found for Blue and Red as before:

		Red		Blue's guarantees
		R_1	R_2	
Blue	B_1	.6	.3	.3
	B_2	.4	.7	.4*
Red's guarantes:		.6*	.7	

Blue can assure a payoff of at least .4, his maximin, by choosing strategy B_2. Red's best guarantee, his minimax, is .6, using R_1. There is significant difference between the maximin and the minimax in this matrix. In such a case either player could benefit greatly by knowing what strategy the other player is using. Hence each player must take care that the opponent does not discover his strategy ahead of time.

Without knowledge of Red's strategy, a reasonable choice for Blue is the maximin strategy, i.e., to place the sensors deep and guarantee a payoff of at least .4. Is there any way for Blue to increase this guarantee without undue risk? Suppose that instead of making a single choice, Blue decides to search deep *with a certain probability*, in hopes of increasing the *expected value* of his payoff. Blue might, for example, use the **mixed strategy** of searching deep in 8/10 of the patrols and searching shallow in 2/10 of the patrols. If only one play of the game occurs, Blue might equivalently choose to search deep if and only if a draw from cards numbered 1 to 10 is 8 or less. What would be the expected outcome (computed before the draw of the card) using this mixed strategy?

If Red were certain to run shallow, Blue's payoff would be .4 on 8/10 of the plays and .6 on

$2/10$ of the plays for an expected (average) payoff of $.4 \times (8/10) + .6 \times (2/10) = .44$. If, however, Red were certain to run deep, Blue's expected payoff would be $.7 \times (8/10) + .3 \times (2/10) = .62$. Then by using this mixed strategy, Blue would have an expected payoff of at least .44 no matter what Red does. This minimum expected payoff of .44 is higher than the payoff of .4 that Blue can guarantee by *always* playing B_2:

		Red	
		R_1	R_2
Blue	B_1 (2/10):	.6	.3
	B_2 (8/10):	.4	.7

Blue's expected payoff: .44*   .62

Notice that if Red knew what Blue's mixed strategy was (without knowing whether Blue is searching shallow or deep on a particular play), Red would prefer to run shallow (R_1) and make Blue's expectation only .44 rather than .62.

Blue may now try mixing the strategies B_1 and B_2 in the ratio $4/10$ to $6/10$. Against R_1, this mixed strategy would yield $.6 \times (4/10) + .4 \times (6/10) = .48$, and against R_2 Blue's expected payoff would be $.3 \times (4/10) + .7 \times (6/10) = .54$. The minimum expected payoff would now be .48 which is better than what was obtained from the previous mixed strategy:

		Red	
		R_1	R_2
Blue	B_1 (4/10):	.6	.3
	B_2 (6/10):	.4	.7

Blue's expected payoff: .48*   .54

Note that as Blue's strategy mix changes from $(0, 1.0)$ to $(.2, .8)$ and then to $(.4, .6)$, not only does Blue's guaranteed expected payoff improve from .4 to .44 and then to .48, but also the separate expected payoffs corresponding to Red's two pure strategies come closer together: from .4 and .7 to .44 and .62 and then to .48 and .54. It is a reasonable conjecture at this point that Blue's highest (optimal) expected payoff is achieved by a mixed strategy which has the same expected payoff for each of Red's two pure strategies. A solution will be found by following that conjecture for both players, and the result will be shown to be indeed an optimal mixed strategy for each.

Let x and $1 - x$ be the respective fractions of patrols in which Blue uses B_1 and B_2. Then $.6x + .4(1 - x)$ is the expected payoff against Red's R_1 and $.3x + .7(1 - x)$ is the expected payoff against R_2. Pursuant to the conjecture, set these two expected payoffs equal:

$$.6x + .4(1 - x) = .3x + .7(1 - x),$$

so $x = 1/2$. Also, the common value of the two expected payoffs is $.6 \times 1/2 + .4 \times 1/2 = .5$. Now apply the same reasoning to Red's point of view. Let y and $1 - y$ be the respective fractions of transits on which Red uses R_1 and R_2. Proceeding as before,

$$.6y + .3(1-y) = .4y + .7(1-y),$$

so $y = 2/3$. Again the common expected payoff is .5. Thus according to the conjecture, the solution of the game is that $(1/2, 1/2)$ is an optimal mixed strategy for Blue, $(2/3, 1/3)$ is an optimal mixed strategy for Red, and the value of the game is .5. To see that these mixed strategies are in fact optimal, observe that if Blue plays his conjectured optimal strategy, his expected payoff is .5 regardless of what Red does, and a reciprocal remark applies to Red. Hence Blue's strategy is maximin and Red's is minimax. Since the maximin expected payoff equals the minimax expected payoff, each side can achieve no better guarantee, which proves the conjecture for this example.

The formal definition of a **mixed strategy** for a player is that it is a probability distribution over the set of pure strategies available to the player. To review, a pure strategy for Blue is optimal if it is maximin among Blue's pure strategies against Red's pure strategies. A Blue mixed strategy is optimal if it is maximin among Blue's mixed strategies against Red's mixed strategies. Optimality is defined for Red similarly using minimax instead of maximin. A strategy for Blue and a strategy for Red (pure or mixed) are optimal *as a pair* if Blue's maximin expected value equals Red's minimax expected value. An optimal pair of pure strategies exists if and only if the payoff matrix has a saddle-point. Otherwise an optimal pair of *mixed* strategies always exists, although so far this has been indicated only by example. For a general proof of this, see Appendix B.

When an optimal mixed strategy is used, an opponent cannot benefit from knowing what that strategy is, provided the opponent does not know what particular course of action will be used on a specific play. In using a mixed strategy, then, a player must insure secrecy by using some random device immediately before each play to select the particular course of action for that play. For example, Red could use the mixed strategy $(2/3, 1/3)$ by marking a spinner into three equal sectors, two marked R_1 and one marked R_2. Red could even allow Blue to see the completed spinner without affecting success. But before each play Red must spin the spinner and take the resulting course of action without Blue finding it out.

Note that in the above 2×2 matrix, the differences within a row are the same for the two rows, i.e., $.6 - .3 = .3 = .7 - .4$, and the two fractions in Blue's optimal mixed strategy are also the same. Also, the differences within a column for the two columns, i.e., $.6 - .4 = .2$ and $.7 - .3 = .4$, are in the same ratio as the two fractions in Reds optimal mixed strategy taken *in reverse order*. These are not coincidences (in a 2×2 game) — see problem 18.

Graphic solution of a $2 \times n$ game. A method will now be provided for solving $2 \times n$ or $n \times 2$ games graphically. As an illustration modify the above searcher-transitor game by adding a third column to the payoff matrix:

		Red		
		R_1	R_2	R_3
Blue	B_1	.6	.3	.4
	B_2	.4	.7	.5

As before, Blue is trying to maximize the payoff and Red is trying to minimize. Blue uses a mixed strategy choosing pure strategy B_1 the fraction x of plays of the game and B_2 the remainder, i.e., the fraction $1 - x$.

To solve this game graphically, define p_i to be the expected payoff to Blue if Red plays R_i, for $i = 1, 2, 3$. Each p_i is related linearly to x as follows:

$$p_1 = .6x + .4(1 - x) = .4 + .2x,$$
$$p_2 = .3x + .7(1 - x) = .7 - .4x,$$
$$p_3 = .4x + .5(1 - x) = .5 - .1x.$$

These three equations are representations of lines, which are shown in Figure 2.15 for x in the interval $[0, 1]$, the interval of interest. The expected payoff to Blue if Red plays R_i is the vertical coordinate, i.e., p_i, in each of the three lines. The bold-line graph in this figure is the minimum p_i (over the three Red strategies) for a given x. An optimal solution for Blue is an x which maximizes this minimum payoff, i.e., a maximin point.

One of the three intersections of pairs of the three lines is necessarily at a maximin point. In the Figure 2.15, these intersections are lettered a, b, c. However b does not lie on the bold-line graph, so it is eliminated. In general, it is possible for two or more pairwise intersections to lie on the heavy graph and to have the same vertical coordinate at the maximum of the vertical coordinates of the bold-line graph. Then both or all of these intersections would be maximin points, and so would all points in between.

FIGURE 2.15. GRAPHICAL SOLUTION OF 2×3 GAME

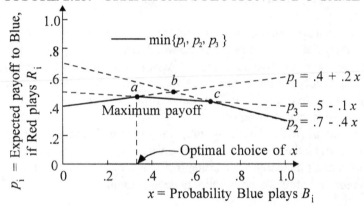

However, in this example there is only one optimal x, the horizontal coordinate of point a. This is found by equating p_1 to p_3 and solving for x:

$$.4 + .2x = .5 - .1x,$$
$$x = \frac{1}{3}.$$

Thus the optimal mixed strategy for Blue is $(x, 1 - x) = (1/3, 2/3)$. The value of the game must be $.2(1/3) + .4 = 7/15$.

To find an optimal mixed strategy for Red an additional useful fact maybe obtained from the graph in Figure 2.5: Red should never use R_2, because if Blue uses his optimal strategy ($x = 1/3$), then Red can do better (lower expected payoff to Blue) by playing R_1 or R_3, compared to playing R_2. Let y be the probability (fraction of times) Red plays R_1 under an optimal strategy; then he plays R_2 with probability 0 and R_3 with probability $1 - y$. Moreover, following the methodology of the transitor-patroller game, the payoff must be 7/15 if Red chooses y optimally, regardless of what Blue does, so

$$.6y + .4(1 - y) = \frac{7}{15},$$

hence $y = 1/3$. This completes the graphical solution of this game. Note that the method easily extends to more than 3 pure strategies by either player, so long as the opponent has only 2, but if both players have 3 or more pure strategies, a graphical representation for this purpose is not practical.

Games of higher dimension. The general solution of games of dimension higher than $2 \times n$ and $n \times 2$ is beyond the scope of this text. To tie this theory to something more recognizable, it is observed that a two-person zero-sum game can be solved by linear programming (LP). This connection is described in Appendix B for the student who has studied LP but not its connections to game theory.

Military decisions and game theory. As implied earlier, when it comes to applying two-person zero-sum game theory to military decisions, there are serious difficulties. In the first place, military adversaries seldom have the same intelligence and estimates about each other as to the tactical choices that are available to each or as to outcomes that would ensue from particular tactical choices by each. Moreover, the adversaries usually judge by different scales of values the outcomes that they can foresee as possibilities.

One comment is that approaches exist without the zero-sum limitation which help to overcome these obstacles, notably that of a bi-matrix game which deals with a pair of matrices each giving payoffs as viewed by one of the two adversaries. Another comment is that despite its limitations, the principles of game theory as presented above are worth study by a student operations analyst who is a prospective scientific adviser to a decision-maker, military or otherwise. For one thing, it is very desirable to present to a decision-maker a payoff matrix with columns representing relevant decisions by the opponent (with or without being combined with states of nature). Such a payoff matrix probably will not be the same as would be constructed by the opponent, but using one's best estimates of the opponent's plausible actions and their consequences in orderly payoff matrix form, and variations thereon, is surely an aid to rational decision making. Haywood [1] puts it strongly as follows:

"If the commander is not prepared to make a matrix of the opposing strategies for the situation, he is not prepared to make a decision."

Given a payoff matrix, the decision might be simplified by eliminating dominated strategies. Next, it is worthwhile finding the maximin pure strategy choice and payoff for the maximizer and the minimax choice and payoff for the minimizer, as having relevance to either or both sides for whom conservatism may be deemed desirable. The matrix further portrays the value of obtaining intelligence on the opponent's decisions and of protecting the security of one's own decisions. The difference between minimax and maximin is some indication of the value of intelligence, but even if this difference is zero (a saddle-point exists), one should examine the possibility of either side taking advantage of a mistake by the other. If a saddle-point does exist, it should be regarded that this represents a pair of choices to which each side should be attracted. All this should be done with the caution that the opponent may take quite a different view of the situation and of the matrix.

Consideration of mixed strategies presents more profound issues. A military commander does not need to be convinced that it is important to make it difficult for the opponent to predict his decisions and actions. Just as a football quarterback mixes between passing and running plays and variations thereon to keep the defense guessing, in a *sequence* of encounters with the same adversary, a commander will tend to vary his tactics for the sake of unpredictability. This is the essence of employment of a mixed strategy. Guidance for choosing the mix might be found from analysis of a payoff matrix, via minimax, maximin, etc., again with the caution that the opponent may in effect consider the matrix to be different.

An important instance of use of a chance device to implement a mixed strategy was by the Soviet army against the Germans in World War II. In early stages, the Germans found the timing and range of the Soviet artillery barrages quite predictable, and directed their ground force movements accordingly. When the Soviets became aware of this, they started mixing their timing and range, according to a chance device, with great effect. Use of the chance device also had the advantage of better security for their planning, which in other respects was vulnerable to espionage.

In 906 in Chapter 9 an example will be given of game theory applied to SSN ASW. This example, not drawn from actual operations, plausibly comes close to meeting the requirements for two-person zero-sum game theory to be applicable, as does, perhaps, the deep-shallow ASW game described above.

How do the ideas and methods of game theory change if a commander has a *one-time* very important encounter with a particular adversary? In such a situation one is not contemplating "playing for the long-run averages." Even in a situation which is one-shot, and subject to chance, *expected value* retains its relevance. Expected value has its limitations in decision criteria, as stressed earlier in the chapter. However, given that allowance has been made for risk-averse or venturesome attitudes, use of expected value in a one-shot situation is simply a matter of "putting luck on our side," as stressed in Chapter 1 as an objective of OA. After one has done one's best to predict states of nature (e.g., the weather at D-Day for the Normandy invasion), enemy capabilities and intentions, and probabilities of these and ensuing outcomes, and to account for risk aversion, etc., what better rationale remains than expected value, even in the absence of opportunity to verify through repeated trials? In particular, it makes perfectly good sense that after going through all that is outlined in the preceding sentence, a commander uses a chance device to make a one-time crucially important choice among tactical options for the purpose of unpredictability, in light of corresponding unpredictability by his opponent.

Williams [2] puts it this way:

"Consider a non-repeatable game which is terribly important to you, and in which your opponent has excellent human intelligence of all kinds. Also assume that it will be murderous if your opponent knows which strategy you will adopt. Your only hope is to select a strategy by a chance device which the enemy's intelligence cannot master -- he may be lucky of course and anticipate your choice anyway but you have to accept some risk. Game theory simply tells you the characteristics your chance device should have.

You may also adopt the viewpoint that you will play many one-shot games between the cradle and the grave, not all of them being lethal games, and that the use of mixed strategies will improve your batting average over this set of games."

The reference to a lifetime of decisions helps to make the point, but would not of itself convince a combat commander confronted with what looms as the most important decision of his career. For the latter, reference is made to the relevance of expected value as discussed above.

The algorithms to compute *optimal* mixed strategies are both the most mathematically interesting parts of the chapter and the least likely to be used in OA practice. It is advisable to learn these algorithms, by study and exercises, because this should help to illuminate the ideas involved in game theory. As just discussed these ideas can be very useful to military decision making, despite the departures in practice from the idealizations of the theory.

207   Other Literature and History

The material in sections 201, 202, and 203 consists of basics in the elementary aspects of what is known as **statistical decision theory**. A general treatment of this theory is given in Luce [3]. The basics appear in many, perhaps most, texts in operations research, such as those cited at the end of Chapter 1, often using alternative terminology in addition to some terms used here. For example, the maximin and least regrets criteria were originally proposed by the eminent mathematical statisticians Abraham Wald and Leonard Savage, respectively, and are often referred to by their names.

The criteria in these sections are also sometimes categorized by the terms "certainty," "risk," and "uncertainty." Thus when the relevant state of nature is known, so the payoff matrix is a single column, the decision making is "under certainty." When probabilities of the states of nature are estimable, the decision making is "under risk." When there is no basis for estimating probabilities of states of nature one decides "under uncertainty." Within this category, the view that all the states of nature (with unknown probability) should be treated as equally likely is sometimes called the "criterion of rationality." The latter concept and term originated with the French mathematician Laplace, a pioneer in probability theory, at the beginning of the 19th century.

Among these alternative terminologies, that used in sections 202 and 203 is chosen to be as descriptive and concise as feasible.

The origin of utility theory is attributed to the 18th century Swiss mathematician Daniel Bernoulli. He proposed the natural logarithm function as a useful tool to model a risk-averse viewpoint. The platoon leader utility example in 204 is taken from Rockower [4]. Utility theory was more well developed and formally axiomatized by John von Neumann and Oskar Morgenstern in reference [5]. Von Neumann is considered the greatest mathematician of the 1930s and 1940s and Morgenstern was a prominent mathematical economist. A good axiomatic treatment of utility theory may be found in the chapter on decision making under uncertainty in Winston [6].

Cost-effectiveness as described in section 205 was originated in the late 19th century by the Italian economist Vilfredo Pareto and is often called "Pareto optimality." It came to particular prominence in the operations research/systems analysis profession during the tenure of Robert McNamara as Secretary of Defense, through its use under the DoD Comptroller Charles Hitch [7] in high level procurement decisions. This usage became highly controversial among senior uniformed personnel, who felt that their professional experience and judgments were not being adequately reflected. Whatever the merits of those controversies may have been, it is the case that when a decision-maker is confronted with multiple MOEs, cost-effectiveness, i.e., Pareto optimality, is a reasonable criterion to be considered.

As a method to find the efficient points in a cost-effectiveness plot, see the "generalized Lagrange multiplier" treatment of Everett [8]. In [9], Wagner relates this approach to the constrained optimization method of mathematical statistics known as the Neyman-Pearson lemma. In a complicated logistics problem, for example, the efficient points might be quite numerous, in contrast to the simple examples given here. What is usually much more difficult, and often needed to apply a budget optimally, is to find cost-effective actions, among a discrete set, which are *not* efficient, i.e., which have costs intermediate to the efficient cost budgets. A method of doing this, which extends the Lagrange multiplier approach, is given by Loane [10]; more generally, one uses methods of integer programming (not necessarily linear).

The French mathematician Emile Borel pioneered important elements of game theory in the early 20th century. It was von Neumann who first proved, in a 1929 paper, existence of an optimal solution by mixed strategies and developed much of the further theory. Reference [5] was the first general treatment of the subject. Considerable research literature on game theory is in reports of the Rand corporation and in proceedings of a sequence of symposia at Princeton University throughout the 1950s into the 1960s. Washburn's monograph [14] is an excellent place to go beyond this chapter's presentation on matrix games. It comes complete with military examples and PC programs to solve matrix games. McKinsey [11] and Dresher [12] are recommended as more general texts on the theory of games. Linear programming, which is associated with game theory, was pioneered by the Soviet mathematician Kantorovich in the late 1930s and the American mathematician and operations analyst George Dantzig in the 1940s (see his book [13] for the history and theory of the connections between game theory and linear programming). Also see the Appendix showing the relationship between linear programming and 2-person zero-sum games.

[1] Haywood, O. G., Jr. *Military Decision and the Mathematical Theory of Games*. Maxwell AFB, AL: Air University Press, Rev. 4, 1950.

[2] Williams, J. D. *The Compleat Strategist*. New York: McGraw-Hill, 1954.

[3] Luce, R. Duncan, and Howard Raiffa. *Games and Decisions, Introduction and Critical Survey*. New York: Wiley, 1957.

[4] Rockower, Edward. *Measures of Effectiveness*. Monterey, CA: Naval Postgraduate School, 1985.

[5] von Neumann, John, and Oskar Morgenstern. *Theory of Games and Economic Behavior*. Princeton, NJ: Princeton University Press, 1944.

[6] Winston, Wayne L. *Operations Research: Applications and Algorithms*. Boston, MA: PWS-Kent, 1987.

[7] Hitch, Charles J., and Roland N. McKean. *The Economics of Defense in the Nuclear Age*. Santa Monica, CA: The Rand Corporation, 1963.

[8] Everett, Hugh. "Generalized Lagrange Multiplier Method for Solving Problems of Optimum Allocation of Resources." *Operations Research* 11 (1963): 399-417.

[9] Wagner, Daniel H. "Nonlinear Functional Versions of the Neyman-Pearson Lemma." *SIAM*

Review 11 (January, 1969): 52-65.

[10] Loane, Edward P. "An Algorithm to Solve Finite Separable Constrained Optimization Problems." *Operations Research* 19 (October 1971):1477-1493.

[11] McKinsey, J. C. C. *Introduction to the Theory of Games*. New York: McGraw-Hill, 1952.

[12] Dresher, Melvin. *Games of Strategy: Theory and Applications*. Santa Monica, CA: The RAND Corporation, 1961.

[13] Dantzig, G. B. *Linear Programming and Extensions*. Princeton, NJ: Princeton University Press, 1963.

[14] Washburn, Alan R. *Two - Person Zero - Sum Games*. Baltimore, MD: Operations Research Society of America, 1991.

Problems

1. Immediately after takeoff on an important mission a fighter pilot notices his oil pressure low and fluctuating. Should he continue the mission or not? It may be only the gauge; on the other hand it could be loss of oil, which could lead to disaster. His primary consideration is the completion of the mission, yet the safety of himself and the aircraft are also important. Suppose he had anticipated such a situation at a more leisurely time and set up the following payoff matrix:

	N_1: Gauge bad	N_2: Loss of oil
S_1: Continue	10	-20
S_2: Turn back	-5	0

a. What is the maximin choice?
b. Which choice guarantees the least regret?

2. During an automobile trip, Ensign Brown notices that her gas gauge reads zero and doesn't know whether she can make it to her destination before running out of fuel. She judges her chances of making it to be about 80 percent. She could use the extra gallon of gas in the trunk but a heavy rain is falling and she'd rather not get wet. If she runs out and then puts the extra gas in the tank, her car (with a weak battery) may not start again. All things considered, she finds the following payoffs reasonable in estimating the various outcomes.

	N_1: Enough gas to make it	N_2: Will run out
S_1: Put in gas now	-5	-5
S_2: Take a chance	0	-15

What should her decision criterion and decision be?

3. Consider for the following payoff matrix:

	N_1	N_2	N_3	N_4
S_1	5	1	5	2
S_2	3	2	3	3
S_3	4	6	0	5

Which is the best strategy:

a. using the maximin criterion?
b. using the criterion of least regret?
c. maximizing expected payoff if all states of nature are equally likely?

4. Assume that you have been retained as a consultant to an investment firm that wants you to advise them on the decision on how to invest $18,000 in a certain enterprise; there are two investment opportunities. According to the best information available, the possible outcomes and their likelihoods are as given in the following table:

Outcome	Investment 1		Investment 2	
	Profit ($1000)	Prob.	Profit ($ 1000)	Prob.
1	0	.10	0	.20
2	20	.90	11	.25
3			21	.25
4			34	.20
5			90	.10

The CEO of the firm has responded to your queries and indicated the following concerning potential investment opportunities for the firm. All these investments are over a time horizon similar to the investment being considered.

i. The CEO is indifferent between an investment in an enterprise that has a 50 percent chance of a profit of $100,000 and a 50 percent chance of a profit of $0 (the money invested is recovered but no profit is earned), and an investment that assures a profit of $30,000.
ii. He is indifferent between an investment that has a 50 percent chance of a profit of $100,000 and a 50 percent chance of a profit of $30,000, and one that assures a profit of $55,000.

a. What courses of action are available?
b. What is the most appropriate MOE?
c. Determine an appropriate utility function. Both graph it and define it analytically.
d. Analyze the data based on the utility function proposed in (c) and make a recommendation. Provide a justification for your recommendation.

5. Suppose that the Navy is considering the purchase of a new remote sensor. When this sensor erroneously indicates a target contact a loss of resources occurs and additionally if false alarms occur frequently there will be a loss of sensor credibility. A questionnaire was sent to 100 operational users of this type of sensor asking them to rank, on a scale of -10 to 10, the four possible combinations of sensor indication and target presence. The results are tabulated below:

Sensor indication	Target present	Average ranking
no contact	no	.48
no contact	yes	-9.57
contact	no	-5.31
contact	yes	9.83

A target is present only 1 percent of the time.
    There are two versions of the sensor that are under consideration. Laboratory testing was done by an independent contractor on each of the candidates. The results are as follows:

(1) Sensor 1 has an 88 percent chance of showing no contact when no target is present. It has a 70 percent chance of showing a contact when a target is present.
(2) Sensor 2 has a 90 percent chance of showing no contact when no target is present. It has a 67 percent chance of showing a contact when a target is present.

Rank the two candidate sensors based on this information.

6. Suppose that a crisis has occurred and a SAG has been ordered to respond. If the SAG steams at maximum speed, it can arrive at the crisis area in 10 days. It is important that it arrive as soon as possible, but if it arrives within 13 days of the start of the crisis then the effects will be lessened. If the response time is more than 18 days, the mission will be a failure. A complicating factor is that higher speeds tend to cause equipment failure. Equipment failures may be classified either as minor, which results in an average delay of 2 days, or major, which results in termination of the mission. Current data are summarized in the following table:

Speed (percent of maximum)	Response time (days)	Probability of equipment failure	
		Minor	Major
100	10	.35	.15
90	12	.25	.10
80	14	.15	.05
70	16	.10	.01
60	18	.05	.005

Assume the following:

(1) The value of arriving in 13 days instead of 14 is five times the value of arriving in 14 days instead of 15.
(2) The value of arriving in 10 days instead of 19 days is 20 times more important than arriving in 17 days instead of 18 days.

What percentage of its maximum speed should the SAG use in responding to this crisis?

7. Suppose Patty is trying to determine which of two courses to take. She would like to take both, but her schedule will allow only one and so she has decided to base her decision on the anticipated grade she thinks she will receive in the course she takes. If she takes the operations research course, she believes that she has a 10 percent chance of receiving an A, a 40 percent chance for a B, and a 50 percent chance for a C. If she takes the advanced statistics course, she believes she has a 70 percent chance for a B, a 25 percent chance for a C, and a 5 percent chance for a D.

Patty has decided that she is indifferent between a course in which she will receive a certain C and a course in which she has a 25 percent chance for an A and a 75 percent chance for a D. She is also indifferent between a course with a certain B and one with a 70 percent chance for an A and a 30 percent chance for a D.

Which course should Patty take to maximize the expected utility of her final grade?

8. Suppose actions are available as follows, with cost and effectiveness as shown:

Action:	S_1	S_2	S_3	S_4	S_5
Cost:	2	3	5	6	8
Effectiveness:	1	3	5	7	6

a. Which actions are dominated?

b. Which actions are cost-effective?
c. How much effectiveness can be obtained from cost 4 and by what action?
d. What is the smallest cost budget giving at least 4 units of effectiveness and is an efficient action?

9. Analyze Problem 10 of Chapter 1 using a cost-effectiveness graph.

10. Suppose a decision-maker's course of action is to choose a time t such that $0 \le t \le 2$, with cost $c(t)$ and effectiveness $e(t)$. Suppose

$$c(t) = t,$$

$$e(t) = (t-1)^3 - t + 1, \quad \text{for } 0 \le t \le 2.$$

a. Graph the effectiveness that can be obtained from a given cost.
b. Which actions are dominated?
c. Which actions are cost-effective?
d. Which actions are efficient?

11. Blue holds two military positions which are subject to attack. He values installation A at one unit and installation B at three units. He is capable of successfully defending either installation, but not both. His opponent, Red, is capable of attacking either unit, but not both. Blue desires to analyze the situation from the viewpoint of game theory.

a. Set up the game matrix representing this situation.
b. State the measure of effectiveness you used.
c. What strategy guarantees Blue at least the maximin payoff?

12. Consider this game: Player A has three possible strategies, X, Y, and Z. Player B has two possible strategies, W and V. Agreed payments to be made according to the choice of strategies are as follows:

$$X, W: A \text{ pays } B \text{ \$7.}$$
$$X, V: A \text{ pays } B \text{ \$2.}$$
$$Y, W: A \text{ pays } B \text{ \$1.}$$
$$Y, V: B \text{ pays } A \text{ \$1.}$$
$$Z, W: B \text{ pays } A \text{ \$3.}$$
$$Z, V: B \text{ pays } A \text{ \$6.}$$

Find:

a. an optimal pure strategy for A;
b. an optimal pure strategy for B;
c. the value of the game.

13. Solve the following games by finding the optimal strategy for each player and the value of the game:

a.

3	0	3
-3	-2	2
2	-2	-1

b.

0	-4	-5
-2	-3	-2
-5	-4	0
-1	-4	-1

c.

2	5	3	0	1
5	0	1	1	2
3	4	5	3	4
4	1	2	0	3
0	2	0	2	1

14. Solve the following games by finding the optimal mixed strategy for each player and the value of the game:

a.

4	2
2	3

b.

0	7	7
10	4	5

c.

6	3	1	2	6	5
5	3	2	2	7	5
6	5	6	5	4	4
4	6	5	7	5	4
5	7	6	7	4	4

d.

4	-5
-3	5

e.

-1/3	1/4
1/2	0

15. Answer the following in problem 10:

a. What is Blue's optimal pure strategy?
b. What is Blue's optimal mixed strategy?
c. How would Blue execute this optimal mixed strategy?

16. Colonel Blotto (Blue) is defending two positions with three battalions. The enemy (Red), with two battalions, is expected to attack one or both positions. Blotto is trying to decide the optimum allocation of battalions between the two positions. He makes the following judgments about the situation:

   (1) Each battalion has a value of 1.
   (2) Position A is equal in worth to 1 battalion, if captured.
   (3) Position B is equal in worth to 2 battalions, if captured.
   (4) The capture of any enemy battalion is worth the value of 1.
   (5) The side whose force is superior retains or captures the position, and also captures the opposing battalions.
   (6) Where forces are equal, nothing is gained or lost.

a. Set up a matrix whose numbers represent Colonel Blotto's net gain (or loss).
b. With Blotto's optimal pure strategy, what payoff can he guarantee?
c. With Red's optimal pure strategy, what can he guarantee?
d. What do you know about the value of the game?

17. For the Blotto game described in problem 15, do the following:

a. Guess at a good mixed strategy for Blotto and compute the expected payoff against each of Red's possible courses of action. What would Blotto's guarantee be using this mixed strategy? (The value of this game must be no less than this guarantee.)
b. Guess at a good mixed strategy for Red and compute the expected payoff against each of Blotto's possible courses of action. What would Red's guarantee be using this mixed strategy? (The value of the game must be no greater than this guarantee.)
c. What do you know now about the value of the game?
d. Formulate as a linear programming problem the problem of finding the optimal mixed strategy for the Blue player. Solve it. Extract from the solution Red's optimal strategy.

18. Suppose the game whose payoff matrix is

$$
\begin{bmatrix}
a & b \\
c & d
\end{bmatrix}
$$

does not have a saddle-point. Find formulas for the game solution.

19. Show whether or not the strategies Blue (3/8, 0, 5/8) and Red (1/4, 0, 3/4) are optimal in the following game and find the value of the game:

	Red		
	3	12	8
Blue	6	6	5
	9	4	6

20. The transitor/patroller example used in this chapter dealt with only one transit. Suppose two independent transits occur and the ASW forces can not change the depth of their sensor between transits.

a. How many courses of action are available to Red?
b. Compute the payoffs for the resulting matrix.

21. Consider the following with subjective descriptions of the payoffs:

		Red		
		R_1	R_2	R_3
	B_1	Fail	Succeed	Succeed
Blue	B_2	Draw	Succeed	Draw
	B_3	Succeed	Fail	Fail

a. Does the matrix have a saddle-point?

b. Can it be reduced by dominance?

c. If the players were satisfied to assign values to the payoffs as fail = -10, draw = 0, succeed = 5, would the following strategies be optimal: Blue uses (½, 0, ½) and Red uses (½, 0, ½)?

22.   Prove that the proposed strategies for Red and Blue in the following games are (or are not) optimal:

a.

Blue	Red				
	R_1 (½)	R_2 (0)	R_3 (0)	R_4 (0)	R_5 (½)
B_1: (3/10)	4	3	2	1	0
B_2: (1/10)	3	4	3	2	1
B_3: (2/10)	2	3	4	3	2
B_4: (1/10)	1	2	3	4	3
B_5: (3/10)	0	1	2	3	4

b.

Blue	Red				
	R_1 (½)	R_2 (0)	R_3 (0)	R_4 (0)	R_5 (½)
B_1: (3/10)	4	3	2	1	0
B_2: (1/10)	3	4	3	2	1
B_3: (2/10)	2	3	0	3	2
B_4: (1/10)	1	2	3	4	3
B_5: (3/10)	0	1	2	3	4

23. In the following game, suppose Blue intends to use his optimal pure strategy for the next play unless he can get reliable intelligence as to Red's intentions:

		Red	
		R_1	R_2
Blue	B_1	0.6	0.9
	B_2	1.0	0.3

How much would this intelligence increase his (expected) payoff above his payoff with no intelligence, if

a. Red intends to use R_1?
b. Red intends to use R_2 (his best pure strategy)?
c. Red is using his optimal mixed strategy?
d. With correct intelligence, what is Blue's guaranteed payoff no matter what Red does?

24. How could a payoff matrix be set up, without payoff numbers, to depict the results if both sea state and enemy tactics were critical in the text example in 201?

Answers to Problems

1. a. S_2.   b. S_2.

3. a. S_2 is the maximin strategy.
b. S_2 is the minimum regret strategy.
c. S_2 is the maximum expected value strategy when all states are equally likely.

4. d. $u(I_1) = 0.30$, $u(I_2) = 0.33$, thus recommend investment option 2.

6. Use maximum speed, the expected utility of this option is over 30 percent higher than the next best option.

7. Expected utility of the advanced statistics course is 0.5525.

8. a. S_6.
b. S_1, S_2, S_3, S_4, and S_5.
c. 3, S_2.
d. 5, S_3.

10. b. $t > (3 - \sqrt{3})/3$ (c) $t \le (3 - \sqrt{3})/3$ (d) $t \le (3 - \sqrt{3})/3$

14. b. Optimal mixed strategies are: for the row player (6/13, 7/13), and for the column player

(3/13, 10/13, 0) for a game value of 70/13.

d. Optimal mixed strategies are: for the row player (8/17, 9/17), and for the column player (10/17, 7/17) for a game value of 5/17.

18. Let x and y be the probabilities that Blue plays B_1 and Red plays R_1 respectively. Then

$$x \quad \frac{d-c}{a-b+d-c}, \qquad y = \frac{d-b}{a-b+d-c}.$$

The value of the game is $(ad - bc)/(a - b + d - c)$.

3

SIMULATION

Many problems addressed by current analysts have such a broad scope or are so complicated that they resist a purely analytical model and solution. One technique for analyzing these situations is simulation. *Simulation is a technique to perform an experiment on an imitation of a real world system in order to obtain data that can be used to make predictions about the system.* The range of applications of simulation is wide and includes the use of physical models in a wind tunnel as well as the use of statistical models. A statistical model is one that takes random samples from some probability distribution that describes the operation of some aspect of a system, or the total system. Simulations that involve random sampling are usually referred to as **Monte Carlo** simulations. Monte Carlo simulation is the only type of simulation that will be addressed in this chapter, and the term simulation will refer only to this type.

Naval and other operations, are often modeled for OA purposes using Monte Carlo simulation as discussed in 109. If the size of the sample is small and the model is simple, simulation may be done by hand. More commonly it involves the use of a digital computer. In either case, it usually involves the repetitive generation of artificial histories of several time periods during which the system is operating, doing a statistical analysis of the data collected, and drawing inferences about the real world system. Further classifications of (Monte Carlo) simulation often involve how time, when it is a factor, is treated in the simulation. If the treatment of time uses discrete steps, the simulation is called a **discrete-event** simulation. Whenever something of significance (an **event**) happens in a discrete-event simulation, the program determines the time in the "future" that the next event occurs and then advances the clock to that time. If the treatment of time is as a continuous variable, then the simulation is called a **continuous-time** simulation. The clock advance in a continuous-time simulation may be in pre-defined jumps of a uniform size, or they may be determined by the (usually numerical) solution of a differential equation. Sometimes time is handled in discrete steps for some aspects of the simulation and in a continuous fashion for others. In this case, the simulation is said to be a **mixed** simulation. This chapter will be limited to concepts that are associated with the implementation of discrete-event simulations.

The chapter begins with an example to illustrate how a simulation might be done by hand. Section 302 contains a discussion of random numbers. Section 303 addresses some simple statistical techniques that may be used to measure the accuracy of an estimate obtained via simulation, and that provide an estimate of the number of replications needed of the simulation in order to achieve a desired degree of accuracy. Techniques for obtaining simulated values of a random variable are discussed in sections 304 and 305.

301   An Example

As an example of discrete-event simulation from queuing theory, consider a bank that has a single drive-in window. Suppose that data were collected on the operation of the window and a statistical analysis of the data indicated that the distribution of the time between customer arrivals and the distribution of the time to serve a customer are as follows:

Time between arrivals (min)	1	2	3	4	5
Probability	.1	.1	.3	.3	.2

Service time (min)	2	3	4	5
Probability	.4	.3	.2	.1

A simulation to investigate the time the first three customers spend at the bank (waiting in line and being served) is desired.

In order to simulate the operation of the drive-in window, one needs the time of arrival of each customer and how long the service of each customer takes. If there are no customers at the beginning of the simulation, the arrival of the first customer can usually be assumed to occur at a time (after the beginning of the simulation) that has the same distribution as the time between arrivals. Sometimes the simulation begins with the arrival of the first customer, and sometimes a separate distribution is needed for the arrival of the first customer. In this example, the time to arrival, from time zero, of the first customer will be assumed to have the same distribution as the time between arrivals.

In order to sample from a distribution, some method of generating a random number is usually used. A **random number** is an observed value of a random variable that has a uniform distribution on the interval from 0 to 1 (unif(0, 1)). Random numbers may be obtained from a mechanical device, from a table of random digits, or from a random number generator on a calculator or a computer.

For the generation of the arrival times of the customers at the drive-in window, suppose that 10 cards are available that are numbered 1 through 10. The cards are shuffled, and one is drawn at random. The number of the card drawn would be used to determine the simulated time between arrivals of customers at the bank. For example, if the card is a 9 or 10, then the time between arrivals is taken to be 5 minutes. Since drawing 2 of the 10 cards results in a time of 5 minutes, this should give a probability of .2 for an inter-arrival time of 5 minutes. The card number and the associated simulated time between arrivals are as follows:

Card number	1	2	3, 4, 5	6, 7, 8	9, 10
Time between arrivals (min)	1	2	3	4	5

Suppose that the first card drawn is numbered 10. Then the arrival of the first simulated customer would occur at time equal to 5 minutes. That card is then replaced in the deck, the deck is shuffled, and a second card is drawn at random. Suppose the second card drawn is numbered 8. This would then give 4 minutes as the time between the arrivals of the first and second customer. The time that the second customer arrives is then $5 + 4 = 9$ minutes. The time between the arrivals of customers two and three is found by shuffling the 10 cards and selecting a third one at random. Suppose that the third card drawn is a 5, giving a time between arrivals of 3 minutes. Adding this to the time of arrival of the second customer yields the time of arrival of the third customer at 12 minutes.

A similar procedure can be used to generate the service times of each of the three customers. Using the same deck of cards, suppose that three random draws of cards yielded cards numbered 1, 9, and 2. Using the following table, which was constructed from the original probability distribution of service times, the service times of the three customers are simulated as 2, 4, and 2 minutes:

Card number	1, 2, 3, 4	5, 6, 7	8, 9	10
Service time (min)	2	3	4	5

In order to find the total time each customer spends at the bank, one needs to determine the time the customer arrives, the time the customer begins service, and the time the customer ends service. The total time is then the difference between the customer's arrival time and the time service ends. The first customer arrives and begins service at time 5 minutes. The service time for the first customer is 2 minutes, and departure occurs at time 7 minutes. The total time the first customer spends at the bank is 2 minutes. The second customer arrives at time 9 minutes and, since the first customer has already departed, service begins immediately. This service takes 4 minutes, and departure is at time 13 minutes. The time the second customer spends at the bank is then 4 minutes. The third customer arrives at time 12 minutes and begins service at time 13 minutes, when the second customer departs. Service for the third customer takes 2 minutes and departure occurs at time 15 minutes. The total time the third customer spends at the bank is then 15 - 12 = 3 minutes.

An aid in handling simulations done by hand is the use of a table to organize the operation. For the bank's drive-in window, the table might be as follows:

	Card no.	Between arrivals (min)	Arrival (min)	Begin service (min)	Card no.	Service time (min)	Departure time (min)	Total time (min)
1	10	5	5	5	1	2	7	2
2	8	4	9	9	9	4	13	4
3	5	3	12	13	2	2	15	3

There are several concerns involving the use of simulation that will not be addressed in this text, but are important to an analyst who uses simulation. One of these, the generation of random numbers, has already been mentioned. Others include the handling of the initial state of the system, how long to run the simulation (clearly three customers is too small a sample to use for most purposes), validation of the model, and other questions that can be addressed only in a more detailed study of simulation. Any analyst who uses simulation must address these concerns in order to avoid obtaining misleading results from simulation. Topics that will be addressed include the use of the distribution of the sample mean to estimate the size of the error involved in the use of the data, and the generation of values of random variables having some common distributions.

302   Random Numbers

Both computers and calculators make use of algorithms that produce sequences of numbers that pass statistical tests of both randomness and independence. Since they are deterministic and only simulate randomness, they are often called **pseudo-random numbers**. The sequences generated are always the same unless steps are taken to introduce a "random" starting point in the sequence. The careful control and generation of pseudo-random numbers is an important aspect of simulation, but will not be discussed in this text. Analysts that use simulation extensively should be well versed in this important topic, discussions of which can be found in any text on discrete-event simulation.

A table of random digits is given in Figure 3.1 for use in generating pseudo-random numbers. It may be used to generate random numbers by first arbitrarily selecting a starting point in the table, then using each group of five digits as a decimal number between 0 and 1. For example, the first group of five numbers in the table would yield the random number .94737. Subsequent random numbers are then generated by continuing down the column. When the bottom of a column is reached, the next group of five numbers used would be at the top of the next column (or the first column, when the end of the last column is reached).

In order to generate arrival times for the customers at the bank's drive-in window using the table of random digits, the cumulative distribution function is needed. This is given in the table following and, in graphical form, in Figure 3.2:

Time between arrivals (min)	1	2	3	4	5
Cumulative Probability	.1	.2	.5	.8	1.0
Decision Interval	[0, .1]	(.1, .2]	(.2, .5]	(.5, .8]	(.8, 1]

The decision intervals are the intervals determined by the step values of the function. Thus if the random number generated is between 0 and .1, the time between arrivals would be 1 minute. If the random number generated is between .1 and .2 (for example .12), then the time between arrivals would be 2 minutes (as illustrated in Figure 3.2). The endpoints of an interval may be chosen to lie in either the interval to the right, or the interval to the left (as long as the choice is done consistently), since the probability of obtaining exactly that value is small (theoretically zero). The generated random numbers should be carried to an accuracy sufficient to avoid generating the endpoints. This method is called the **inverse (discrete) probability integral method**.

FIGURE 3.1. TABLE OF RANDOM DIGITS

94737	08225	79906	88326	40766	95838	79861	82702
67259	85982	37804	25564	95556	44577	72145	18189
33856	14016	73641	05156	44619	77460	82594	24321
40243	30415	01919	39883	85416	77103	37989	48680
85077	34711	38950	68861	07681	60194	24368	46095
61876	34501	12741	92655	81911	38907	63376	22041
55245	05654	06842	55307	13397	74672	34095	61899
37497	87132	91609	51135	91962	95325	15636	54516
14566	20866	08318	39789	73686	10829	53728	16076
09528	91079	84934	16789	98747	43479	34963	70493
11708	63529	41161	45204	50617	27249	06230	78837
54676	34518	14761	45229	53742	17846	30810	51356
19580	47551	43899	87454	31846	80835	04474	59338
17357	69696	12091	11375	21928	41029	28691	86434
04361	45163	45423	77931	41477	84749	93705	13138
42289	86195	74405	00688	86036	54539	17410	76259
32399	49978	47333	16679	84961	20160	20078	09765
20628	78559	19901	87663	57953	44189	23713	64220
27573	46682	35359	19949	93640	05060	32549	68718
89795	24462	57780	22562	20270	33864	33084	35514
39287	10981	72633	79213	01731	16378	47280	10090
61299	62462	07784	73042	30341	92652	81504	88056
07100	87565	45651	06390	98757	44659	82485	10678
34805	50703	37929	41188	48539	67477	34741	42710
38806	50845	55743	67980	97541	92641	80154	19301

The random digits beginning at the upper left of Figure 3.1 will be used to illustrate the simulation of times between arrivals of the customers at the drive-in window. This is done to aid the reader in following the generation of the arrival times; one would ordinarily select an arbitrary starting point. Thus the first random number to be used is .94737. This then gives the first simulated time between arrivals as 5 minutes. Thus the simulated arrival of the first customer would occur at time equal to 5 minutes. To find the time of arrival of the second customer, select the next set of random digits and generate .67259 as the second random number. This would then give 4 minutes as the time between arrivals of the first and second customers. The time that the second customer arrives is then at $5 + 4 = 9$ minutes. The time between the arrivals of customers two and three is found by using the random number .33856 to obtain a time between arrivals of 3 minutes. Adding this to the time of arrival of the second customer yields the time of arrival of the third customer at 12 minutes.

FIGURE 3.2. SIMULATED RANDOM VARIABLE

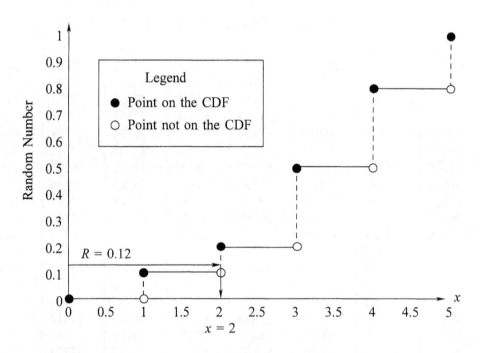

A similar procedure can be used to generate the service times of each of the three customers. Using the second column of random digits in the table, the random numbers are .08225, .85982, and .14016. The cumulative distribution function for the service times is as follows:

Service time (min)	2	3	4	5
Cumulative Probability	.4	.7	.9	1.0
Decision Interval	[0, .4]	(.4,.7]	(.7, .9]	(.9, 1]

The service times thus simulated for the first 3 customers would be 2, 4, and 2 minutes, respectively.

303   Standard Error

A common performance measure used in studies involving simulation is the expected value (or mean) of a random variable that occurs in the system. In the example above of the drive-in window at a bank, the expected time a customer spends at the bank might be desired. Another common measure in such a system is the expected number of customers at the bank at any time. Since the bank has a natural starting and ending time (one day) and a natural starting state (no customers in the bank when it opens), one approach to estimating the expected time a customer spends in the bank would be to replicate n simulations of one day's operation of the bank, to average the times spent in the bank by each customer during a day's simulation (obtaining *one* estimate), then to use the n estimates thus obtained to find both a **point estimate** (the average of the n estimates) and an **interval estimate** (explained below) of the expected time a customer spends in the bank. Note that the time an individual customer spends in the bank on a given day will be correlated to the times spent in the bank by the preceding customers. For this reason, only one estimate (the average) is obtained from each day's simulation. If different random numbers are used in each day's simulation, the n estimates of the average time a customer spends in the bank should be independent and identically distributed. In that case, the following discussion applies.

Suppose that the mean, $E[X]$, of a certain random variable is to be estimated using simulation. In the bank example, the random variable X would be the average time a customer spends in the bank during a day's operation. If the simulation is performed n times and n estimates, $x_1, x_2, \ldots, x_n$, are obtained, then a point estimate of $E[X]$ is the **sample mean**,

$$\bar{x} = \frac{1}{n} \sum_{i=1}^{n} x_i.$$

Each of the sample values, x_i, is a random variable having the same (usually unknown) distribution with mean $E[X]$ and variance σ^2. The sample mean, $\bar{x}$, is a random variable with mean $E[X]$, since

$$E[\bar{x}] = \frac{1}{n} \sum_{i=1}^{n} E[x_i] = \frac{1}{n} \sum_{i=1}^{n} E[X] = \frac{1}{n} n E[X] = E[X].$$

Similarly, assuming that the x_i are statistically independent, the variance of $\bar{x}$ is

$$\mathrm{Var}[\bar{x}] = \left(\frac{1}{n} \right)^2 \sum_{i=1}^{n} \mathrm{Var}[x_i] = \frac{\sigma^2}{n}.$$

The assumption of independence is usually valid whenever the estimates are taken from different replications of the model, the random number streams used are nonoverlapping, and the initial conditions are independently chosen. It would not ordinarily be valid if, for example, the estimates were a sequence of output observations from a single replication of the model. Thus in the simulation of the bank's drive-in window, using the average of the times spent at the window by all customers during a day's simulation would be acceptable, while using an individual time spent at the window by a customer would not.

An unbiased estimate of σ^2 is the **sample variance**

$$s^2 = \frac{1}{n-1} \sum_{i=1}^{n} (x_i - \bar{x})^2.$$

The corresponding estimate of $\text{Var}[\bar{x}]$ can then be found. The resulting estimate of the standard deviation of the sample mean, $\bar{x}$, called the **standard error** and denoted s.e.$(\bar{x})$, can then be found by dividing the sample standard deviation by the square root of the sample size,

$$s.e.(\bar{x}) = \frac{s}{\sqrt{n}}.$$

The standard error is a measure of the accuracy of the estimation of $E[X]$. Note that the sample size must be multiplied by 100 in order to reduce the standard error to one tenth its earlier value.

If $\bar{x}$ is approximately normally distributed, then the standard error may be used to obtain an interval estimate (called a **confidence interval**) for $E[X]$. For $0 \leq \alpha \leq 1$, an α confidence interval for $E[X]$ is given by

$$(\bar{x} - \bar{z} \times s.e.(\bar{x}), \ \bar{x} + \bar{z} \times s.e.(\bar{x})),$$

where $\bar{z}$ is the value for a standardized normal variable Z satisfying the condition:

$$\Pr\{ -\bar{z} \leq Z \leq \bar{z} \} = \alpha.$$

The sample mean $\bar{x}$ is normally distributed if x is normally distributed or by the Central Limit Theorem it is approximately normally distributed when the sample size n is large; in practice n larger than 30 is adequate. For smaller values of n a statistics book must be consulted for ways to obtain a confidence internal for $E[X]$. The α **confidence interval** is the interval centered at the (point) estimate $\bar{x}$ that would be expected to contain the actual mean in α of the cases when the sample experiment (i.e., n replications of the simulation) is repeated many times. Of course, only one sample experiment is ordinarily taken, and there is no way to know whether or not the actual value of the parameter being estimated is really in the confidence interval.

The standard error and resulting confidence interval may be useful in deciding how many estimates must be obtained in order to achieve a desired accuracy. The simulation is usually first done a few times in order to obtain an estimate of the size of sample variance. This estimate is then used to solve for the value of n that should give values close to a desired level of accuracy. For example suppose that an estimate of $E[X]$ was desired to within 0.1 at a confidence level of 95 percent. With $\alpha = .95$ the value for $\bar{z}$ is 1.96. An initial sample of 10 replications was made of the model to compute a sample variance for the purpose to determine the number of replications required to estimate $E[X]$ to the desired accuracy. Suppose the sample variance was found to be 3.2, then

$$\frac{(1.96)\sqrt{3.2}}{\sqrt{n}} = 0.1$$

can be solved for n as $(1.96 \times 1.79/0.1)^2 = 1229.3$. Since the number of replications must be an integer, the estimate for the number of replications needed would be 1230, to estimate to within 0.1 of the actual value of $E[X]$ 95 percent of the time. Of course the actual number of replications needed may vary from this estimate, since the variance may be substantially different than the estimate used.

304   Continuous Random Variate Generation

In order to do a Monte Carlo simulation either by hand or using a computer, techniques must be developed for generating values of random variables having known distributions. These values are often called **random variates**. As was the case in the drive-in window example above, the starting place for random variate generation is usually the generation of random numbers, which are random variates that are uniformly distributed on the interval from 0 to 1 (unif(0, 1)).

If the inverse of the cumulative distribution function for the random variate to be generated can be found in closed form or can be given in a table, the **inverse function technique** used in the drive-in window example may be used. This technique is based on the observation that if the cumulative distribution function for X is F, if F is continuous and one-to-one, and if R is a random variable that has a unif(0, 1) distribution, then $F^{-1}(R)$ has the same distribution as X. A slight variation of this technique has already been used for the discrete case in 302. Figure 3.3 illustrates the technique, which is also called the **inverse transform method**.

FIGURE 3.3. INVERSE TRANSFORM METHOD

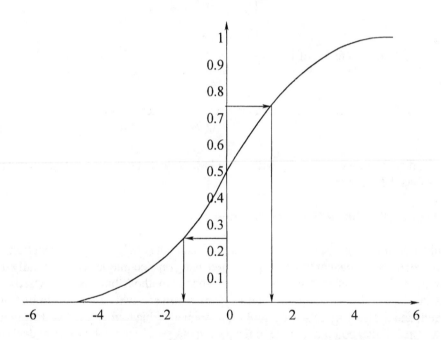

Suppose it is desired to generate random variates having a unif(a, b) distribution. The linear function h given by $h(r) = a + (b - a)r$ would map the interval (0, 1) onto the interval (a, b). A possible way to generate a value for X would be to generate a random number R then to use $h(R) = a + (b - a)R$ as the value. The inverse function technique, illustrated below, will give the same generator.

The probability density function (pdf), f, and the cumulative distribution function (cdf), F, for the unif(a, b) random variable, X, are given by

$$f(x) = \begin{cases} \dfrac{1}{b-a}, & \text{if } a \le x \le b, \\ 0, & \text{otherwise,} \end{cases} \quad \text{and} \quad F(x) = \begin{cases} 0, & \text{if } x < a, \\ \dfrac{x-a}{b-a}, & \text{if } a \le x \le b, \\ 1, & \text{if } x > b. \end{cases}$$

Solving $y = (x - a)/(b - a)$ for x in terms of y yields

$$x = a + (b - a)y.$$

Thus the generator given by the inverse function technique would be

$$X = a + (b - a)R,$$

where R is a random number, and is the same as was obtained above using a linear mapping of the interval $(0, 1)$ onto the interval (a, b).

Another useful random variable generator that can be obtained using the inverse transform method is the one for exponentially distributed random variables. One is needed whenever a simulation of a Poisson process (see Appendix A) is to be done. Let X be a random variable that has an exponential distribution with mean $1/\alpha$. Then the cdf of X is given by

$$F(x) = \begin{cases} 1 - e^{-\alpha x}, & \text{if } x \ge 0, \\ 0, & \text{otherwise.} \end{cases}$$

Solving $y = 1 - e^{-\alpha x}$ for x in terms of y yields

$$x = -\frac{\ln(1-y)}{\alpha}.$$

Since $1 - R$ is unif$(0, 1)$ whenever R is, a random variable generator for X is

$$X = -\frac{\ln(R)}{\alpha},$$

whenever X is distributed exponentially with mean $1/\alpha$. Note that since $R < 1$, $\ln(R) < 0$. Thus $-\ln(R) > 0$, and $X > 0$ as they should be.

305   Normally Distributed Random Variates

Not all random variates may easily be generated using the analytic inverse function technique. One that is often used that cannot be easily generated using this technique is the normally distributed random variable. Since it is used so often, several special methods have been devised to generate it. One method is a "**table look-up**" technique. It may be used whenever the simulation is being done by hand, and is also used in some simulation languages due to the speed with which it can be implemented on a digital computer. One of its disadvantages is that it takes a great deal of effort to implement on a computer, and thus is seldom used whenever the simulation is written in a high level language such as C or FORTRAN. The procedure is basically the inverse function technique with the cumulative distribution function F given in a table rather than a formula. A random number, R, is generated and then the (inverse) value of X that would give R as the value of $F(X)$ is determined. Depending on the desired accuracy, linear interpolation may be used. Thus a table of the standard normal cumulative distribution function may be used to generate values of a standard normal (mean 0, standard deviation 1) random variate. Values of a normally distributed random variate, X, having mean μ and standard deviation σ may be found using the usual transformation

$$Z = \frac{x - \mu}{\sigma} \quad (\text{i.e., } X = \mu + \sigma \cdot Z),$$

where Z has a standard normal distribution.

As an example of this technique, suppose it is desired to generate values of a normally distributed random variable having mean 2 and standard deviation 0.75 using a table of random digits and a table for the standard normal distribution. If the first pseudo-random number generated by the table is .67477, this number is found to lie between the numbers .6736 and .6772 in the (four decimal places) standard normal table. Since the ratio of the difference between .6748 (rounded to four decimal places) and the lower number, .6736, to the difference between the higher number, .6772, and the lower number is 1/3, the ratio of the difference between the desired value of the standard normal random variable, Z, and the value of Z for the lower number, 0.45, to the difference between the values of Z for the upper, 0.46, and lower numbers should also be (approximately) 1/3. Thus $Z = 0.45 + 0.003 = 0.453$. The desired value of the normally distributed random variable having mean 2 and standard deviation 0.75 would be $X = 2 + (0.453)(0.75) = 2.34$ (rounded to two decimals).

A second technique, known as the **6-point method**, that may be used to generate standard normally distributed random variates is based on the Central Limit Theorem. If R_i, $i = 1, 2, \ldots, 6$, are (independent) random numbers, then the sum $\Sigma(R_i - 1/2)$ is approximately normally distributed with mean 0 and, since each R_i has variance 1/12, the sum has variance ½. Thus

$$X = \sqrt{2} \sum_{i=1}^{6} \left(R_i - \frac{1}{2} \right)$$

has an approximately standard normal distribution whenever each R_i has a unif(0, 1) distribution. This generator is easily implemented on a digital computer. Its main disadvantage is the large number of random numbers that must be generated. It is also an approximation and thus some analysts prefer other techniques.

A third technique that may be used to generate standard normally distributed random variates is called the **direct transform method**. It is based on a theorem that says that if R_1 and R_2 are independent random numbers, then

$$Z_1 = \sqrt{-2\ln(R_1)} \cos(2\pi R_2) \quad \text{and} \quad Z_2 = \sqrt{-2\ln(R_1)} \sin(2\pi R_2)$$

are independent standard normal random variates. This technique is also easily implemented on a digital computer. Its main disadvantage is the three function calls (square root, logarithm, and sine or cosine) that are required for each of the (independent) random variates generated.

306   Other Literature and History

Using Monte Carlo techniques to generate artificial histories of systems for study traces its roots to work done modeling nuclear radiation by John von Neumann and Stanislaus Ulam in the late 1940s. Their work was classified, done at Los Alamos, and given the code name "Monte Carlo." With the availability of digital computers, the uses of the techniques have grown in recent years at an extremely rapid pace. The following references should provide a good starting point for further study into simulation and the statistics that support it.

[1] Banks, Jerry; John S. Carson, II; and Barry L. Nelson. *Discrete-Event System Simulation*. 2d ed. Upper Saddle River, NJ: Prentice-Hall, 1996.

[2] Lewis, Peter A., and E. J. Orav. *Simulation Methodology for Statisticians, Operations Analysts, and Engineers*. Vol. 1. Pacific Grove, CA: Wadsworth, 1989.

[3] Lapin, Lawrence L. *Probability and Statistics for Modern Engineering*. Monterey, CA: Brooks/Cole, 1983.

Problems

1. This problem builds on the example used in 301. Suppose in simulating the fourth customer card 2 is drawn for the time between arrivals and card 8 is drawn for the service time. Complete the row of the last table in 301 for the fourth customer. What is the average amount of time the first four customers spend at the bank?

2. This problem also builds on the example used in 301. Use the random numbers shown in figure 3.1 to simulate the arrival and service of the fourth and fifth customers at the drive-in window. Start with the random number at the top of column 2 and work down the column using each group of five digits to give a uniformly distributed random number between 0 and 1. Complete the row of the last table in 301 for the fourth and fifth customers (Drop the two columns recording the Card no.). What is the average amount of time the first five customers spend waiting in line before getting served at the drive-in window?

3. A simulation of a certain system was performed sixteen times with the following results:

Run	Result	Run	Result	Run	Result	Run	Result
1	.808	5	.742	9	.842	13	.850
2	.875	6	.767	10	.817	14	.850
3	.708	7	.792	11	.717	15	.767
4	.842	8	.950	12	.833	16	.817

a. Find an estimate of the mean of the underlying distribution and find the standard error.

b. Based on the results of part a, approximate the number of results that would be needed for a standard error at most 0.005.

c. Estimate the number of times the simulation should be performed in order to obtain an estimate of the mean of the underlying distribution to an accuracy of 0.005 at least 95 percent of the time.

4. A baker is trying to determine how many dozens of doughnuts to bake each day. The probability distribution of the number of doughnut customers is as follows:

Number of customers per day	5	10	15	20
Probability	.15	.40	.35	.10

Customers order 1, 2, 3, or 4 dozen doughnuts according to the following probability distribution:

Number of dozen ordered per customer	1	2	3	4
Probability	.3	.4	.2	.1 .

Doughnuts sell for $3.50 per dozen. They cost $2.00 per dozen to make. All doughnuts not sold at the end of the day are sold at half-price to a local stale baked goods distributor. Mixing size constraints require doughnuts to be made in batches of 10 dozen.

a. Based on 5 days simulation, how many batches (of 10 dozen doughnuts) should the baker make each day? Be sure to clearly identify the MOE you used and how its values were obtained.
b. Instead of simulation, use expected values of the distributions to solve part a.
c. Discuss the relative merits of the solution techniques used in parts a and b.

5. A squadron of 16 H-53 Super Stallion helicopters leave Marine Corps Air Station, New River, NC, en route to Homestead Air Force Base, Miami, where they will conduct hurricane evacuation operations in the Florida Keys. A refueling stop is scheduled at Naval Air Station, Cecil Field, FL. The flight time of each of the two legs (from New River to Cecil, and from Cecil to Homestead) is distributed normally with mean 3 hours and standard deviation 15 minutes. Refueling at Cecil is done at 4 "hot" refueling pits. Each pit handles only 1 helo at a time. Refueling time for 1 helo is constant at 10 minutes. Thirty percent of the helos will experience mechanical difficulties that will further delay their ground time by an amount that is distributed uniformly between ½ and 2 hours. Use simulation to obtain an estimate of the average time that the last helo will reach Homestead.

6. A squadron of bombers is attempting to destroy an ammunition depot which has a rectangular shape and is 1000 meters by 500 meters. The bombing run will proceed down the long center axis of the depot. If a bomb lands anywhere on the depot, a hit is scored. Otherwise, the bomb is a miss. There are ten bombers in each squadron. The aim point is the center of the depot. The point of impact is assumed to have a bivariate normal distribution (see Appendix A) around the aim point with a standard deviation of 600 meters in the down-range direction and 200 meters in the cross-range direction. Simulate 100 bombing runs and obtain an estimate of the probability of a hit. How many bombing runs must be simulated to insure the probability of hit is accurate to two figures?

7. Use a spreadsheet or a computer program to generate 100 values of an exponentially distributed random variate having mean 0.5. Count the number of values of the random variate in each subinterval of length 0.25 and obtain a histogram of the results.

8. Develop a random variate generator for a random variable X with the pdf

$$f(x) = \begin{cases} e^{2x}, & \text{for } x \le 0, \\ e^{-2x}, & \text{otherwise.} \end{cases}$$

9. Consider a random variable X which has pdf

$$f(x) = \begin{cases} x, & \text{for } 0 \leq x \leq 1, \\ 2 - x, & \text{for } 1 < x \leq 2, \\ 0, & \text{otherwise.} \end{cases}$$

This distribution is called a **triangular distribution** with endpoints 0 and 2 and mode at 1. Develop a random variate generator for this random variable.

10.   Consider a detection process where, at time t, the db signal excess, $S(t)$, is the sum of a mean signal strength, $m(t)$, and a deviation $d(t)$, where d is modeled as a (λ, σ) process (Chapter 5) and is such that detection occurs whenever

$$S(t) = m(t) + d(t) > 0.$$

Use the table of random digits to simulate such a detection process where $m(t) = -7 - 4(t - 1.0)^2$, $\lambda = 4$ jumps per hour, and $\sigma = 7$ db. Here it suffices to follow the steps below without knowing the definition of a (λ, σ) process.

a. Simulate the process for 2 hours using the following procedure:
    (1) For $t_0 = 0$, generate an exponentially distributed random variate with mean $1/\lambda$ for the time to the next jump, Δt_1, and let

    $$t_1 = t_0 + \Delta t_1.$$

    (2) Generate a normally distributed random variate with mean 0 and standard deviation σ for the value of $d(t)$ for $0 \leq t \leq t_1$, and determine $S(t)$ for $0 \leq t \leq t_1$.
    (3) Find any sub-intervals of $[0, t_1]$ where detection can occur.
    (4) Continue the above steps until $t_n = t_{n-1} + \Delta t_n$ exceeds 2 hours.
b. If the sensor only glimpses every 0.1 hours, determine the number of glimpses where detection would occur in your simulation in part a.

11.   Below is a spreadsheet model simulating the operation of the bank's drive-in window, the same bank used in the illustrative example of 301. The arrival of 100 customers is simulated and represents one day of operation of the drive-in window. Modify this simulation to model a situation where the inter-arrival time distribution of customers is exponential with the same theoretic mean inter-arrival time, and the service time distribution is normal with same mean as for the discrete distribution used below and with a variance of 0.81. Simulate the operation of the drive-in window for 10 days; a day can be simulated by hitting the recalculate key. Turn in a report summarizing your analysis. It must state for each day simulated, the average inter-arrival time, the average service time, and the average amount of time customers spend both waiting for service and receiving it. Also a print-out of your simulation model similar to the one show below must be included in your report.

\	A	B	C	D	E	F	G	H	I
1		Inter-					Total		
2		arrival	Arrival	Begin	Serve	Depart	time in	Arrival time	
3	n	time	time	service	time	time	system	distribution	
4	0		0			0		0	1
5	1	3	3	3	2	5	2	.1	2
6	2	4	7	7	2	9	2	.2	3
7	3	4	11	11	5	16	5	.5	4
8	4	4	15	16	5	21	6	.8	5
9	5	3	18	21	4	25	7	1	1000
10	6	4	22	25	2	27	5	Service time	
11	7	4	26	27	3	30	4	distribution	
12	8	4	30	30	2	32	2	0	2
13	9	1	31	32	2	34	3	.4	3
14	10	5	36	36	5	41	5	.7	4
15	11	4	40	41	3	44	4	.9	5
16	12	3	43	44	5	49	6	1	1000
17	13	1	44	49	3	52	8		
18	14	4	48	52	3	55	7		
.									
.									
.									
98	94	4	330	331	3	334	4		
99	95	3	333	334	2	336	3		
100	96	3	336	336	2	338	2		
101	97	4	340	340	4	344	4		
102	98	2	342	344	2	346	4		
103	99	5	347	347	3	350	3		
104	100	5	352	352	3	355	3		
105	avg =	3.52		avg =	3.13	avg =	5.28		

B1: [W7] 'inter
B2: [W7] 'arrival
C2: 'arrival
D2: 'begin
E2: [W7] 'Service
F2: 'Departure
G2: [W7] 'total
H2: 'Arrival time
A3: [W4] "n
B3: [W7] 'time
C3: ' time
D3: 'service
E3: [W7] 'time
F3: 'time
G3: [W7] 'time
H3: 'distribution
A4: [W4] 0
C4: 0

A5: [W4] 1
B5: [W7] @VLOOKUP(@RAND,H4..I9,1)
C5: +$C4+$B5
D5: @MAX($F4,$C5)
E5: [W7] @VLOOKUP(@RAND,H12..I16,1)
F5: +$D5+$E5
G5: [W7] +$F5-$C5
H5: 0.1
I5: 2
A6: [W4] 2
B6: [W7] @VLOOKUP(@RAND,H4..I9,1)
C6: +$C5+$B6
D6: @MAX($F5,$C6)
E6: [W7] @VLOOKUP(@RAND,H12..I16,1)
F6: +$D6+$E6
G6: [W7] +$F6-$C6
H6: 0.2
I6: 3

12.   The manager of the bank whose drive-in window operation was simulated in problem 11 realizes the long waiting times incurred by drive-in customers is irritating them and will cause a slowing of the growth of the bank's customer base. Traffic projections made show that in the absence of customer dissatisfaction the demand for drive-in service will grow to result in an average inter-arrival time of 2.3 minutes in the next year or two. The manager has identified two options to handle this situation: (1) build a second drive-in lane equipped identically to the first, and (2) replace the equipment used to handle customers with new, high-tech gear. Thus in option (1) the service time distribution for all customers remains as given in problem 11. In option (2) the service time distribution is normal with mean 1.8 minutes and variance 0.64. The cost of both options is about equal on per year basis. Simulate the operation of both options for 10 days and based on the results recommend the best option. Assume in option (1) cars waiting form a single line feeding into both lanes. Provide printouts of key sections of the spreadsheets used to do the simulations and printouts of typical formulae used in the simulations. Be sure to explain the MOE used to evaluate the options.

Answers to Problems

1.

	Card no.	Between arrivals (min)	Arrival (min)	Begin service (min)	Card no.	Service time (min)	Departure time (min)	Total time (min)
1	10	5	5	5	1	2	7	2
2	8	4	9	9	9	4	13	4
3	5	3	12	13	2	2	15	3
4	2	2	14	15	8	4	19	5

The average is 3.5 minutes.

2.

	Between arrivals (min)	Arrival (min)	Begin service (min)	Service time (min)	Departure time (min)	Total time (min)
1	5	5	5	2	7	2
2	4	9	9	4	13	4
3	3	12	13	2	15	3
4	1	13	15	4	19	6
5	2	15	19	2	21	6

The average time waiting to be served is $(0 + 0 + 1 + 2 + 4)/5 = 1.4$ minutes.

3. a. Mean 0.811, standard error 0.015. b. 154. c. 588.

4. b. Make 30 doz. for an expected profit of $36.60 per day.
c. Solution technique in b is quicker, easier, exact, and wrong.

8. $(1/2)\ln(2R)$ for $0 \le R \le 1/2$, $-(1/2)\ln[2(1 - R)]$ for $1/2 \le R \le 1$.

9. $\sqrt{2R}$ for $0 \le R \le 1/2$, $2 - \sqrt{2(1 - R)}$ for $1/2 \le R \le 1$.

4
SONAR AND RADAR SENSORS

Search and detection play a central role in the next five chapters. Fundamental to search and detection is performance of the sensors that are employed. Sensor performance is the subject of this chapter.

Attention is confined to the two categories of sensor systems that are most important in naval warfare. These are sonar for underwater targets and radar for surface and air targets. Infrared and laser sensors are increasing in importance; visual search is still significant. These sensors, however, are not considered here.

A significant objective of sensor analysis as applied to OA is to find the probability that a given sensor will detect a given target at a given instant under given environmental conditions. Such a probability is called **instantaneous** or **single-glimpse detection probability**. Although a detection is considered instantaneous, the information contributing to the detection might be "integrated" over a finite preceding time interval. This latter interval is usually short, lasting at most a few seconds for radar and anywhere from 20 seconds or less to perhaps 20 minutes for sonar.

This chapter will address the single-glimpse case. The next chapter, Chapter 5, will address the problem of measuring the effectiveness of a *sequence* of single glimpses over a time interval of detection opportunities by combining the separate single-glimpse probabilities, each of which might have its own integration time interval.

PART A: Sonar Detection

Sea water is almost 100 percent opaque to light and radar transmission. Acoustic energy on the other hand will travel for many thousands of yards under water with little absorption. Hence, sonar systems both active and passive, have become the principal sensors in underwater warfare starting at the beginning of WWI in 1914.

Sonar is used in many operational actions. These include searching out and killing submarines; mine field location, penetration, and clearing; target acquisition by torpedoes and mines; ocean bathymetry; ocean floor target location and navigation of remotely operated deep search vehicles; under-ice transit; swimmer navigation and object detection; and underwater communications between surface ships and underwater vehicles. Within these missions the tasks carried out include detection, classification, target or object localization, measurement of depth (by fathometer), and code or voice communications.

OA studies that involve sonar are usually concerned first with detection since one can hardly execute the other tasks unless one knows that a proper target has been detected. The detection process answers the question: is a target present or not? Other questions follow from detection. Classification asks: what kind of target? Localization asks: what is the approximate position of the target? Tracking asks further: what are the target's course, speed, and depth?

The sonar portion of this chapter covers detection in antisubmarine warfare (ASW) scenarios. The primary models for analyzing sonar detection performance are the sonar equations. As explained at the start of 403, there are a passive equation and two active equations.

Sonar equations are baseline models that support all levels of ASW modeling. In Figure 4.1 the triangle's base identifies models associated with a single sonar on a single platform. Other levels identify one-on-one engagement models, multi-platform engagement against one or more targets, and finally models associated with major campaigns of a month or more such as the Battle of the Atlantic in WWII.

FIGURE 4.1. HIERARCHY OF ANTISUBMARINE WARFARE MODELS

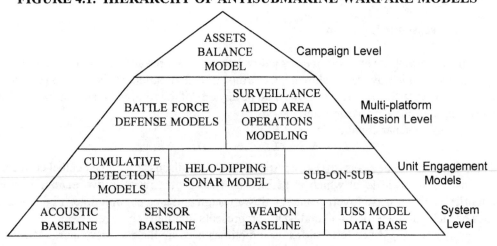

In the discussion below, occasional reference is made to types of acoustic propagation paths. Although the physics of propagation is not described in any depth, the reader should be aware of the three principal types of path: In **direct path (DP)** propagation, the path is fairly close to a straight line, perhaps moderately bent by refraction, but with no reflection off the ocean bottom or surface. In **bottom bounce (BB)** propagation, the path is reflected off the bottom; the segments before and after reflection are fairly linear, perhaps moderately refracted. In **convergence zone (CZ)** propagation, the path is significantly refracted downward into a fairly horizontal "deep sound channel" and is then refracted upward, reaching roughly 30 nm in the first of possibly multiple cycles of these effects. Which type of path prevails depends on local depth and oceanographic conditions. The foregoing describes "one-way" propagation, from a target source to a detecting receiver or from a searcher's transmission point to a target's reflecting surface; in the latter case, the "return trip" would follow a similar path.

Reference is also made below to acoustic frequency, measured in hertz (Hz), equivalently cycles per second. The effects of frequency on detection is a subject beyond the present scope. It is noted here merely that acoustic energy is propagated from a source at various frequencies which have different propagation paths and that, generally speaking, a decrease in frequency increases the range at which acoustic energy is detectable.

Section 401 presents the passive sonar equation. In 402 the concept of figure of merit is introduced as a yardstick for comparing the performance of sonar sets as well as for estimating the detection range of a single sonar under specified environmental conditions. Sections 403 and 404 parallel 401 and 402 but pertain to active sonar where performance is noise-limited. Sections 405 and 406 treat in a similar fashion the reverberation-limited case of active sonar.

The terms in the sonar equation are random variables. In 407 each of the terms is assumed to be a normally distributed (see Appendix A) random variable with variance and mean that are either known or that can be estimated. When the geographic operating region of a sonar is specified, one can estimate the instantaneous probability of detection at a fixed range and also establish a range interval in which detection is likely to occur. Section 408 describes Navy programs to collect and disseminate data for use in sonar equations.

401   Passive Sonar Equation

Sonar equations are an audit of energy flow between a source and a sonar receiver. For passive sonar the path is one way from a ship or submarine target that radiates noise to a sonar receiver that is mounted on a platform. The platform could be any one of the following: submarine, surface ship, air dropped sonobuoy, or ocean floor.

The passive sonar equation is

$$L_S - N_W - (L_N - A_G) - DT = SE. \qquad (4\text{-}1)$$

All parameters are in decibels (dB). (See Appendix C for a discussion of the decibel concept.) Each represents an acoustic level which is defined as 10 log of a ratio of two **acoustic or electric intensities**, each defined as average energy flow through unit area per unit time. Figure 4.2 lists the names of each parameter in (4-1) and what it represents qualitatively.

The symbol N_{DI}, **directivity index,** is sometimes used in place of array gain. The directivity index is a special case of array gain (A_G). Both account for the ability of a sonar array to screen out the effect of omni-directional noise. A value for N_{DI} can be calculated from the geometry of the array, but this makes the assumption of an isotropic noise field. Array gain makes more realistic assumptions about the interfering noise field and is therefore a more accurate term. In this chapter A_G is used in the various sonar equations.

FIGURE 4.2. TERMS IN THE PASSIVE SONAR EQUATION

L_S	**Source level** radiated by the target and measured at the target.
N_W	**Propagation loss** en route to the receiver.
L_N	Omni-directional sonar **self-noise** measured at the sonar receiver.
A_G	**Array gain**, how much omni-directional noise the sonar array cuts out.
DT	**Detection threshold**, the **signal-to-noise ratio**, SNR, required for detection.
SE	**Signal excess**, the difference between provided SNR and SNR required for detection.

The first two terms ($L_S - N_W$) give the level of signal received by the platform receiver. The next two terms ($L_N - A_G$) give the level of interfering **noise** after processing by the array. The four terms taken together give the signal-to-noise ratio (SNR) *provided* to the sonar receiver for processing and subsequent decision by a human operator.

The possible sources of sonar self-noise are (1) ocean noise including that due to wind, waves, bubbles, and distant shipping; (2) flow noise over the receiving sonar dome; and (3) own ship's noise which arrives at own ship's sonar via hull structure paths or through the water.

The parameter DT is the signal-to-noise ratio *required* for detection with a detection probability of 50 percent and a false alarm probability that must be specified by the operator or in some cases the system designer. Signal excess, SE, is the difference between provided and required SNR. For a single sonar glimpse on a given bearing at a given center frequency, detection will take place if $SE \geq 0$.

The terms in a sonar equation are all random variables. If one assumes that each term in the equation is the *mean* of the random variable, then the equation is in deterministic form. In 407 the fact that the terms in a sonar equation are random variables will be used to compute the instantaneous probability of detection. Analysis to determine the cumulative probability of detection resulting from a *sequence* of glimpses is treated in Chapter 5.

If SE is set equal to zero and N_W placed on the left side of (4-1), the resulting quantity is called **figure of merit** (FOM). Thus

$$N_W = FOM = L_S - (L_N - A_G) - DT. \tag{4-2}$$

Propagation loss, N_W, is range dependent; FOM and the terms on the right of (4-2) are not. Thus FOM is a good measure of a sonar's capability against a particular target independent of geographical operating region.

402 A Passive Sonar Problem

Figure 4.3 gives examples of the calculation of *FOM*, using (4-2), for passive sonars. Detection range can be estimated using data such as those given in Figure 4.4. The examples illustrate two points: (1) two or more sonars can be compared without selecting an operating region, and (2) one can find an anticipated detection range by use of *FOM* with propagation loss curves for a specific operating region.

FIGURE 4.3. CASE PROBLEMS FOR PASSIVE SONAR
All entries except range are in dB.

Parameter	Case 1	Case 2	Case 3	Case 4
L_S	120	120	132	115
L_N	58	58	60	65
A_G	10	15	15	15
DT	-6	-15	-7	-7
FOM	78	92	94	72
Range	NA	NA	See Fig. 4.4 & 4.5	See Fig. 4.4 & 4.5

In Cases 1 and 2, an *FOM* is calculated for two different sonars operating against the same target. "Same target and noise conditions" means same values for L_S and L_N. "Different sonars" means different values for A_G and *DT*. The Case 2 sonar is considerably more capable at detecting in that its *FOM* is 14 dB better than that of the Case 1 sonar. That is because the former has a larger array (higher A_G) and an improved receiver (lower *DT*). Both A_G and *DT* are controlled by sonar designers. The value -6 dB for *DT* is typical for aural processing of broad band signals while -15 dB for *DT* is typical for a time bearing readout (DIMUS display). Both of the latter detection technologies are used by modern submarine and surface ship platforms.

In Cases 3 and 4, we have the same sonar operating against different targets and under different sonar self-noise conditions. The sonar might be a towed array listening for tonal signals using a "waterfall display." The values chosen for *DT* and A_G are typical for this type of sonar system.

A set of propagation curves for areas of operational interest is needed to determine the detection range. Figures 4.4 and 4.5 are such curves, obtained from actual at-sea measurements. For Case 3, *FOM* and therefore N_W are 94 dB when *SE* = 0. Using Figure 4.4 (Norwegian Sea) the anticipated detection ranges are by direct path 7,500 yards, by bottom bounce 20,000 yards, and by first convergence zone 60,000 yards. For Case 4, the *FOM* is smaller and the anticipated detection range is far less (direct path only, at 3,200 yards).

Using Figure 4.5 (Iceland operating region), the Case 4 platform performs about the same as for the Norwegian Sea area with an expectation of detecting by direct path only at 3,400 yards. Detection in the Icelandic operating region is far better for the Case 3 sonar and target with detection ranges as follows: direct path 20,000 yards, bottom bounce 50,000 yards, and convergence zone 80,000 yards.

FIGURE 4.4. PROPAGATION LOSS VS RANGE, NORWEGIAN SEA

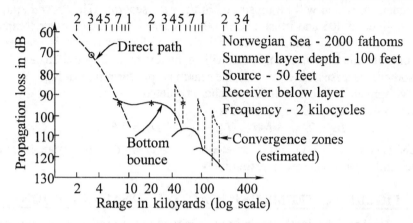

FIGURE 4.5. PROPAGATION LOSS VS RANGE, ICELAND

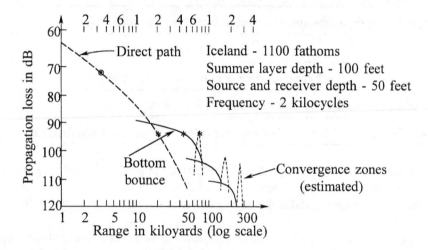

403   Active Sonar Equation (Noise-Limited)

Analysis of active sonar detection involves two sources of interference at the sonar receiver: noise, which arises as in the passive case, and **reverberation**, which is peculiar to the active case. A sonar equation can be given pertaining to each of these two interference types. In practice it is usual for both of these types of interference to be present. They can be combined into a composite interference, but this is not done by combining decibels. Instead one converts the dB amounts back to the power amounts that the dB amounts represent. The power amounts may then be combined by addition and the sum may be converted back to dB, following Appendix C. This is called **power**

summation and will not be treated here. It is simply noted that if the two dB amounts differ by more than 3 dB, then it is usually not a bad approximation to take their power sum to be the larger of the two amounts.

Proceeding without this complication, this section presents the "noise-limited" version of the active sonar equation, which will be illustrated in the next section. The "reverberation-limited" version will be given in 405 and illustrated in 406. When, in practice, power summation is not employed, one would solve for detection range using each of these two equations and use the shorter of the ranges thus obtained. In most cases that will be the reverberation-limited case, but the noise-limited case sometimes arises, notably when the searching platform runs at high speed, depending also on the environment and how well the searcher is quieted.

The **noise-limited** active sonar equation is

$$L_S - 2N_W + Nts - (L_N - A_G) - DT = SE. \qquad (4\text{-}3)$$

As for the passive equation, (4-1), all parameters in (4-3) are in dB. In Figure 4.6 is the name of each parameter and what it represents qualitatively.

FIGURE 4.6. TERMS IN THE ACTIVE SONAR EQUATION

L_S	**Source level** radiated by the ensonifying sonar and measured at the ensonifying sonar.
N_W	One-way **propagation loss** en route to the receiver or return.
Nts	**Target strength**, a measure of sound reflected by a target .
L_N	Omni-directional sonar **self-noise** measured at the sonar receiver.
A_G	**Array gain**, how much omni-directional noise the array cuts out.
DT	**Detection threshold**, the *SNR* required for detection.
SE	**Signal excess**, the difference between provided *SNR* and *SNR* required for detection.

The first three terms of (4-3), (L_S - $2N_W$ + Nts), give the level of signal received back at the ensonifying sonar platform. A signal level is radiated, it loses intensity en route to the target, a portion is reflected by the target, and its intensity is diminished on the return trip to the ensonifying sonar.

The next two terms, (L_N - A_G), give the level of interfering **noise** inboard at the receiver. The five terms taken together give the signal-to-noise ratio (*SNR*) that is *provided* to the sonar receiver for processing and subsequent decision by a human operator.

As in the passive case, the parameter *DT* is the signal-to-noise ratio *required* for detection with a detection probability of 50 percent and a false alarm probability that must be specified by the operator or in some cases the system designer. Signal excess (*SE*) is the difference between *provided and required SNR*. For a single sonar glimpse on a given bearing at a given center frequency, detection will take place if $SE \geq 0$.

Active figure of merit (*FOM*) is found by setting *SE* equal to zero in (4-3) and moving N_W to the left side of the equation:

$$N_W = FOM = \frac{1}{2}\{L_S + Nts - (L_N - A_G) - DT\}. \qquad (4\text{-}4)$$

404   An Active Sonar Problem (Noise-Limited)

Figure 4.7 tabulates calculations of noise-limited active *FOM*s, using (4-4) and reasonable values for the sonar variables. The resulting *FOM*s can be used to determine the corresponding 50 percent probability detection ranges for the four cases.

FIGURE 4.7. CASE PROBLEMS ACTIVE SONAR
All entries except range are in dB.

Parameter	Case 1	Case 2	Case 3	Case 4
L_S	196	184	197	197
Nts	15	15	25	12
L_N	58	58	60	65
A_G	15	13	15	15
DT	20	14	19	19
FOM	74	70	79	70
Range	NA	NA	Fig. 4.4 & 4.5	Fig. 4.4 & 4.5

In Cases 1 and 2, *FOM* is calculated for two different sonars operating against the same target under the same noise conditions. "Same target and noise conditions" means the same values for *Nts* and L_N. "Different sonars" means different values for L_S, A_G, and *DT*. The Case 2 sonar is less capable at detecting in that its *FOM* is 4 dB poorer than that of the Case 1 sonar. Why? Because the Case 2 sonar has a smaller array (lower A_G), and lower source level (L_S). Its poorer performance is offset partially by an improved receiver (*DT* is 14 dB versus 20 dB).

For active sonars, *DT* is given as $10 \log (S/N_0)$, where S is the signal intensity in the band of the receiver and N_0 is noise in the receiver band per Hz. Typical values for the *DT* of active sonars are +14 dB to +24 dB, rather than the -6 dB to -15 dB values that one sees for passive sonars. For the latter, *DT* is defined as $10 \log (S/N)$ where S is the same as for active sonar, but N is the total acoustic intensity in the receiver band.

In Cases 3 and 4, the same sonar operates against different targets and under different sonar self-noise conditions. The sonar could be a cylindrical array sonar mounted in a streamlined dome on the bow of an ASW frigate. The values chosen for *DT* and A_G are typical for this type sonar.

An anticipated detection range is obtained using *FOM* and propagation loss curves as was done in the passive sonar problem.

The Case 3 sonar has an *FOM* of 79 dB and can anticipate detection on its designated target (*Nts* = 25 dB) at 4,200 yards in the Norwegian Sea and 5,400 yards in the Icelandic operating region.

The Case 4 sonar has a *FOM* of 70 dB and can expect to detect its designated target (*Nts* = 12 dB) at 3,000 yards in the Norwegian Sea and at 2,500 yards in the Icelandic region.

In Case 3, the sonar faces a submarine target that is probably presenting a beam aspect (high *Nts*); and in a lower sea state or at a lower own ship's speed (L_N = 60 dB). In Case 4, the submarine target is one that is presenting a bow or stern aspect (*Nts* = 12 dB), and sonar self- noise is higher.

As was true for passive sonar, *FOM* is a good way to compare two different active sonars, *when noise-limited*, versus the same target independent of the operating region in which they might operate. Additionally one can identify the sources of difference (i.e., L_S, *DT*, A_G, or even L_N for the same ships' speeds). Also *FOM* gives a method for translating dB into anticipated detection ranges given a defined operating region with known propagation loss curves. In the presence of reverberation as in the next two sections, however, these remarks are modified by the need to take account of the dependence of reverberation on range and operating region.

The curve of N_W versus range, *R*, is non-linear. Moreover, it is not given by an analytic formula. Where the curve also has a shallow slope, small changes in *FOM* can often lead to large changes in *R*. For example using data in Figure 4.4 (Norwegian Sea), an *FOM* of 80 dB gives the anticipated detection range as 5,000 yards by direct path. If however the *FOM* increases to 86 dB, anticipated range is now 42,000 yards by convergence zone propagation.

405   Active Sonar Equation (Reverberation-Limited)

The reverberation-limited equation is

$$(L_S - 2N_W + Nts) - [L_S - 2N_W + Nrs + 10\log(V \text{ or } A)] - DTR = SE. \qquad (4\text{-}5)$$

The terms sonar source level (L_S), target strength (*Nts*), and propagation loss (N_W) are the same as in (4-3). *DTR* is used instead of *DT*, to signify 10 log (signal intensity in the frequency band of the receiver divided by reverberation intensity in the receiver band). A typical value for *DTR* is −6 dB.

The source of interfering noise is reverberation, i.e., echoes received from scatterers in the three-dimensional region V^* surrounding the target and having volume *V*, or in the planar region A^* nearby the target and having area *A*; both are at the same approximate range, *R*, as the target.

See Figure 4.8(a) for volumetric reverberations and Figure 4.9(a) for surface reverberations. In the graphics assume the target to be located at the center of the space V^* or nearby the region A^*. Within V^* are minute scatterers such as particulate matter, thermal microinhomogeneities, or minute biologic life. Each scatterer returns echoes which in sum contribute to the total return echo. Surface roughness of the bottom or sea surface make up the scattering ensemble for surface reverberation originating in A^*.

To obtain a value for the volume *V* or the area *A*, one must calculate the length in the direction of the sonar transmitted beam from which overlapping echoes are returned.

In Figure 4.8(a), the graphic shows an example of V^*, centered about a target at range *R* yards. The target is not shown. Reverberation echoes from within this region will be superposed onto the echo return from the target and hence will be interfering noise.

The area of the front face of V^* is equal to $(R\psi_1)(R\psi_2)$ with ψ_1 and ψ_2 being the horizontal and vertical sonar beam widths in radians. The length of the V^* is Δx, as shown in Figure 4.8(b). As indicated, $\Delta x = c\tau/2$ yards (see below), where *c* represents sound velocity in water in yards per second and τ is the time duration of the transmitted echo in seconds. Echoes E_1 have been returned from the front face of V^*. Echoes E_2 are acoustic energy that has penetrated into V^* and has been reflected by scattering centers on the rear face.

FIGURE 4.8. VOLUMETRIC REVERBERATIONS

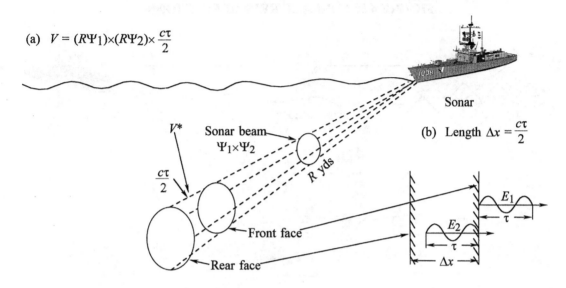

(a) $V = (R\Psi_1) \times (R\Psi_2) \times \dfrac{c\tau}{2}$

(b) Length $\Delta x = \dfrac{c\tau}{2}$

The distance Δx must be such that echoes E_2 will just barely overlap echoes E_1 when all return to the sonar. The length of a pulse in water is $c\tau$. Thus twice Δx must equal the distance that echoes E_1 can be delayed and still barely overlap echoes E_2. Hence Δx equals $c\tau/2$. If τ equals 200 milliseconds, and c is 1,650 yards per second then Δx will be 165 yards.

Assume $\psi_1 = \psi_2 = 30° = 30\pi/180$ radians. Assume target range is 2,000 yards. The term $10 \times \log(V)$ would be $10 \log(165 [2000 (30\pi/180)]^2)$ dB = 83 dB.

The parameter Nrs is reverberation scattering strength per unit volume V, or per unit area A. The term $10 \log V$ or $10 \log A$ (written in (4-5) as $10 \log (V \text{ or } A)$) converts scattering strength per unit volume or per unit area value into total scattering strength.

If Nrs is -70 dB per cubic yard, then total volume reverberation strength in the above calculation will be $-70 + 83 = 13$ dB.

Figure 4.9(a) and (b) show how surface area A is calculated for surface reverberation. The platform in 4.9(a) transmits a signal via a bottom bounce beam that has an effective beam width of ϕ and is depressed at angle θ. The slant range to the target and hence to the region A^* of interfering reverberations is R. The width w of the region A^* will be ϕR.

In 4.9(b), the ray (containing reverberation) that returns to the sonar from point #1, will arrive first. The ray from point #2 returns last. In order for the echoes to overlap, the slant distance indicated in the graphic must be $c\tau/2$. Thus if R equals 12,000 yards, ϕ equals 20°, τ equals 250 milliseconds, and θ equals 30°, then w will be $(12,000)(20\pi/180) = 4,188$ yards; and l will be $(1,650$ yards/sec $\times 0.25/2)/\cos 30° = 238$ yards. The term $10 \log A$ will be 60 dB. And if Nrs is -50 dB per square yard, then total scattering strength for surface reverberations will be $+10$ dB.

By eliminating like terms in (4-5) a simplified equation is

$$Nts - (Nrs + 10 \log (V \text{ or } A)) - DTR = SE. \qquad (4\text{-}6)$$

The term A_G is missing from the reverberation-limited equation. Array directionality (as beam width) is introduced in the calculation of the volume V or area A.

FIGURE 4.9. SURFACE REVERBERATIONS

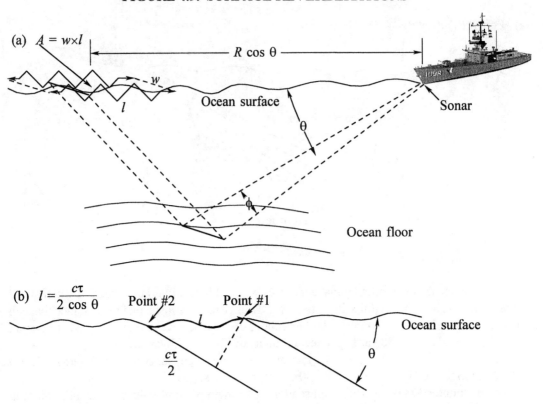

A figure of merit (*FOM*) calculation would not have the same usefulness in the active sonar reverberation-limited as in the passive or noise-limited active cases. Again that is because reverberation depends on range and operating region. If compute value of *SE* happens to be zero in a reverberation-limited active sonar problem, then the range used in calculating V or A will be the 50 percent detection probability range.

406   An Active Sonar Problem (Reverberation-Limited)

The following problem assumes an active sonar that is reverberation-limited, as a result of low search speed and typical environmental conditions to produce reverberation that dominates noise at ranges of interest.

The problem is to calculate the predicted signal excess (*SE*) in the active detection of a submarine by bottom bounce propagation mode.

Picture a submarine target directly under the center of the planar region A^* of Figure 4.9(a) at perhaps 150 feet depth. The target echo and the surface reverberation echoes received from $A*$ will overlap at the surface ship sonar receiver.

Assumed data are R (slant detection range) = 12,000 yards, $\theta = 30°$, Nts = 10 dB, Nrs = -50 dB per yards^2, DTR = -6 dB, 10 log A = 60 dB.

The pertinent equation is the area version of (4-6) as follows: the value for A in yards^2 is that from 405:

$$Nts - (Nrs + 10 \log A) - DTR = SE,$$

$$10 - (-50 + 60) - (-6) = 6.$$

If the assumed detection range to the target is increased, the value A increases and hence SE decreases. Note that this analysis does not involve an FOM calculation. Note also that range enters the problem through the area A.

407   Glimpse Probability of Detection

Previously in this chapter all values in the sonar equations have been treated as if they were deterministic. If the sonar equation is to be used to predict a future detection outcome in terms of a detection probability and a detection range, the sonar terms may be considered to be random variables, each normally distributed (in dB), and independent. The distribution of each term is characterized by its mean and standard deviation (σ). Examples follow.

The passive case. Equation (4-1) for passive sonar is written as a sum of mean values totaling a mean value for SE. A second equation for the variance of the signal excess σ_{SE}^2 is

$$\sigma_{LS}^2 + \sigma_{NW}^2 + \sigma_{LN}^2 + \sigma_{AG}^2 + \sigma_{DT}^2 = \sigma_{SE}^2,$$

$$3^2 + 4^2 + 2^2 + 1^2 + 1^2 = 5.6^2,$$

(4-7)

where σ_{LS} is the standard deviation of L_S, etc. Typical variance values are listed beneath each term in (4-7). For any random variables the sum of the means equals the mean of the sum, and if they are independent, the sum of the variances equals the variance of the sum. Note negative signs in (4-1) but not in (4-7). The standard deviation of SE in the example is 5.6 dB.

Consider the graph of the density function of SE (in dB); it is that of a normally distributed random variable with its mean obtained from (4-1) and a 6 dB standard deviation obtained using (4-7). The normal curve represents a probability density distribution of all possible SE values that one might encounter in a future target and sonar interaction. For any given single outcome, detection will take place any time instantaneous SE is equal to or greater than zero. Why? Because for that glimpse the "provided SNR" is equal to or greater than the "required SNR."

If the mean value of SE happens to be 0, then the percentage of all instances for which detection occurs will be 50 percent. (Recall that for the normal distribution the mean equals the median.) The probability of detection is given by the area under the normal culrve to the right of the zero mean. See Figure 4.10(a). That is why when SE was set to 0 in (4-2), the solution range is the 50 percent detection probability range.

If mean SE = 6 dB and σ = 6 dB, the probability of detection, p, will be 84 percent, which is the area to the right of the one standard deviation point under the standardized normal density function as shown Figure 4.10(b). Likewise if mean SE = -6 dB, p will be 16 percent, as shown in Figure 4.10(c).

FIGURE 4.10. SIGNAL EXCESS PROBABILITY DENSITY CURVES FOR THREE VALUES OF THE MEAN

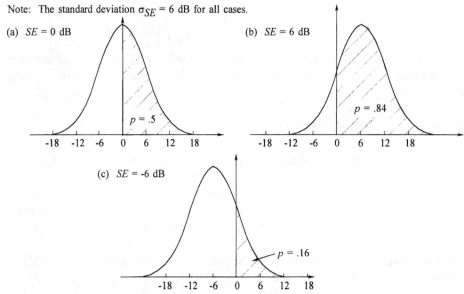

Note: The standard deviation σ_{SE} = 6 dB for all cases.

(a) SE = 0 dB

p = .5

(b) SE = 6 dB

p = .84

(c) SE = -6 dB

p = .16

One still solves for N_W in the mean value equation, (4-1), setting mean SE to values as indicated in Figure 4.11. A propagation loss curve is used to translate the N_W value into detection range assigning it a probability of detection p appropriate for the value of mean SE.

Five passive cases treating the terms of the sonar equation as random variables are worked out in Figure 4.11 below. All cases, except 3B, are for a same range of 6,000 yards with the value for N_W taken from Figure 4.4 (the Norwegian Sea region). The detection probabilities vary because of a variation in target, self-noise, or sonar parameters. Still one could possibly detect all targets at the same range. The predicted probability of doing so will vary from 16 percent to 84 percent. Case 3B is a take off of Case 3A, in which the detection range has been increased at the cost of a lower value for p. For Case 3B, median detection range is 40,000 to 45,000 yards by BB or CZ modes.

A more usual situation is to ask for the median, i.e., 50 percent probability detection range along with the spread about this range–all for the same target, environment, and sonar. The results of doing this are displayed in the next table, Figure 4.12, assuming σ_{SE} = 6 dB as before.

The transformation between N_W and log range is near linear for direct path (DP) propagation, but highly non-linear for bottom bounce (BB) and convergence zone (CZ). The result is that the probability 16 percent and probability 84 percent predicted ranges can vary widely from the median (probability 50 percent) detection range. Indeed this is the story of sonar detection both passive and active. There will always be wide variation in actual sonar performance because of the great uncertainty in predicted sonar system values. Improved *in situ* data will help, but one requires good on-board measurements plus quick and accurate calculation models that use the collected data.

**FIGURE 4.11. CALCULATION OF PROBABILITY OF DETECTION
FOR PASSIVE SONAR**

All entries except for p and range are expected values in dB.

Parameter	Case 1	Case 2	Case 3A	Case 3B	Case 4
L_S	126	120	134	134	115
N_W	90	90	90	96	90
L_N	58	60	60	60	50
A_G	10	15	15	15	15
$D\dot{T}$	-6	-15	-7	-7	-7
SE	-6	0	6	0	-3
p	.16	.50	.84	.50	.30
Detection range	6,000 yd DP	6,000 yd DP	6,000 yd DP	See text	6,000 yd DP

The calculation of the probability of detection, p, is based on a single glimpse of the target. For readouts like the broad band Bearing Time Recorder or narrow band waterfall display, a single glimpse can be 5 to 15 minutes long. The actual integration time before a single mark is made on the readout is much shorter. However, the readout will present a series of sequential marks before the operator decides to call "Target."

For aural detection the single glimpse time might be even longer for a very weak target. Alternately if the target has some pronounced salient feature like a particular tonal frequency or pinging or cavitation, the glimpse time could be very short.

The subject of combining the results of sequential observations of single glimpses will be covered in Chapter 5, Cumulative Detection Probability.

The active case. The basis for calculating the glimpse probability of detection for active sonar, both noise and reverberation-limited, is the same as that for passive sonar.

There will be an uncertainty in the selected values of the active sonar equation parameters. Each parameter is treated as an independent, normally distributed random variable and the mean and standard deviation of the signal excess (SE) is calculated as in the passive case.

In the problem below, the glimpse probability of detection, p, is calculated for the reverberation-limited interaction worked out in 406. The mean value equation with illustrative values is again the area version of (4-6):

$$Nts - (Nrs + 10 \log A) - DTR = SE,$$

$$10 - (-50 + 60) - (-6) = 6.$$

Assume the value for σ_{SE} to be 10 dB. From figure 4.13(a) the area to the right of $SE = 0$, is .73.

Hence $p = .73$ for this condition, where $\sigma_{SE} = 10$ dB and mean SE = 6 dB.

FIGURE 4.12. ILLUSTRATIVE DETECTION PROBABILITIES AND THE SPREAD OF RANGES ABOUT THE MEDIAN VALUE

All entries except range are expected values in dB.

Parameter	Case 1	Case 2	Case 3
L_S	128	128	128
L_N	60	60	60
A_G	10	10	10
DT	-10	-10	-10
N_W	94	88	82
SE	-6	0	6
p Detection probability	.16	.50	.84
Range (yd) Icelandic Area	20,000 DP	12,000 DP	8,000 DP
	45,000 BB	No BB	No BB
	70,000 CZ	No CZ	No CZ
Range (yd) Norwegian Sea	7,500 DP	6,000 DP	5,000 DP
	20,000 BB	No BB	No BB
	90,000 CZ	40,000 CZ	No CZ

If sea state were to roughen such that *Nrs* became -46 dB, then *SE* would equal +2 dB and, as indicated in Figure 4.13(b), *p* would be .58. For a given range, changes in environmental conditions show up as changes in the probability of detection.

The procedure above is for a single ping. Active sonar systems are often designed to transmit three or more sequential pings. The operator's detection probability would increase with the observation of multiple pings. Also some prior knowledge of the target's presence before pinging could mean the operator might detect at a lower value of *DT* or *DTR* than was assumed. This prior alert could come from a passive detection by airborne sonar buoys launched from a LAMPS helicopter or from a towed array. Both the above conditions and many others mean that the operation analyst must be most precise in defining the details of an interaction.

FIGURE 4.13. DETECTION PROBABILITY FOR TWO VALUES OF MEAN SE

Note: The standard deviation σ_{SE} = 10 dB for all cases.

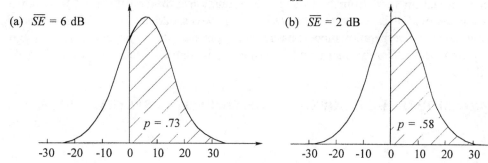

(a) $\overline{SE}$ = 6 dB

$p = .73$

-30 -20 -10 0 10 20 30

(b) $\overline{SE}$ = 2 dB

$p = .58$

-30 -20 -10 0 10 20 30

408   Data and Data Sources

For the operational analyst, two concerns occur in using sonar equations. First is understanding and using the correct definition of specific terms. This will include signal and noise frequencies and precise spatial location of where parameters are defined. The second is obtaining valid numerical data.

Figures 4.2 and 4.6 are descriptive definitions only for terms in the sonar equations. For precise physical definitions, the more comprehensive texts on sonar should be consulted. See for example Burdic [1] or Urick [2].

Textbooks have only limited value in providing valid data to use in the sonar equations. These books will certainly give the reader some idea of the order of magnitude of values as do the examples in this chapter. However, for acceptable numbers for real world ASW situations, one must go to official U.S. Navy publications. Locating these sources is often not easy and many are classified.

Sonar equation terms can be divided into three categories:

a. target terms: L_S (radiated noise) and Nts (target strength);
b. system terms: L_S (active sonar transmission level), A_G (array gain), N_{DI} (directivity index), DT or DTR (detection threshold), array beam angles needed for calculating A and V associated with back scattering, and L_N (the portions of self-noise from own ship mechanical and hydrodynamic sources);
c. environmental terms: N_W (propagation loss), L_N (the portion of self-noise from ocean sources and from distant shipping), Nrs (reverberation strength per unit volume or area).

Figure 4.14, taken from Etter [3], illustrates the support of sonar performance models by sub-models of terms in Category (c). In the figure, the sub-models are called "basic acoustic models" and "environmental models."

Sonar performance models are mostly the sonar equations, but could also be acoustic ray tracing programs showing the best depth to locate a sonobuoy or towed array or one's own submarine. Signal processing includes models to calculate spectral and spatial characteristics of ocean noise, for both active and passive sonars, on which DT and A_G are dependent. The top of Figure 4.14 feeds into the bottom of Figure 4.1. The latter then shows the sonar equations as the sub-models for higher order battle models.

Basic acoustic models in Figure 4.14 include: (1) the many ways to calculate propagation loss in deep as well as in shallow water from the acoustic wave equation or from ray theory; (2) self-noise models and sea noise models based on the physics of ocean waves, and empirical distributions of distant shipping; and (3) reverberation models based on the physical theory of scattering by rough surfaces or by particles randomly distributed in volumes, including calculation or coding of coefficients of back-scatter.

FIGURE 4.14. MODELS DEVELOPED TO SUPPORT SONAR SYSTEMS MODELS

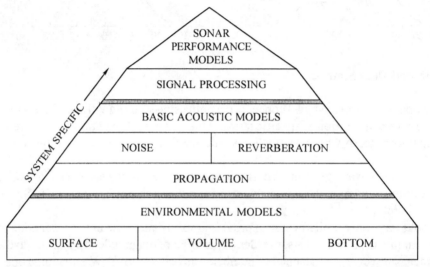

Most models are validated by sea measurement which is the job of Navy laboratories particularly those responding to the Naval Oceanographic Command. The Oceanographer of the Navy takes a big interest in and assumes accountability for these models. See the reference text Etter [3] for an excellent survey of ocean acoustic models.

Environmental models are mostly large data bases that store in an organized and user-friendly fashion, worldwide information on the physical properties of ocean bottoms, including roughness and structural characteristics; volumes, including salinity and distribution of particulate matter; and surfaces including roughness.

Data for terms in categories (a) and (b) are more difficult to obtain because of security. Official and authoritative sources that are readily obtainable by naval activities with appropriate security clearance are Naval Warfare Publications (NWPs). This series originates in various fleet centers (such as Submarine Development Squadron 12) and is printed by the Naval Tactical Support Activity in Washington, DC. A staff group within the office of the Chief of Naval Operations is responsible for overall coordination of the NWP series and for the authenticity of data.

Topics covered in the NWP series include: ASW by Surface, Air, and Submarine units; guidance to warfare commanders; passive classification guide; surface sonar; mine countermeasures; and many more. Many of the publications are now available on CD-ROM discs for use aboard ship with desktop computers.

Other sources of data are also available from naval laboratory reports. For example the Naval

Ships Research and Development Center at Carderock, Maryland, publishes a Detection and Detectability Report on all U.S. Submarines and Surface Ships. This report is an authoritative listing of L_S values for individual and first-of-class ships. The Naval Technical Intelligence Center also publishes available data on foreign naval ships and submarines.

Some terms in category (b) (system) can be calculated with a considerable degree of confidence. The values so calculated might be degraded by operator or system degradation. However, the results are often surprisingly close to values achieved in fleet use of a system. Examples are DT and N_{DI}. For active sonar L_S can actually be measured alongside a pier.

Finding valid numbers for use in sonar equations is not easy. Data from standard textbooks will be useful only as an indicator of the possible range of values. The best sources are actual measurements at sea where possible or are official U.S. Navy publications.

409   Summary

Sonar is the principal sensor used by the U.S. Navy for underwater operations. Radar does not work below the sea surface. The three sonar equations are the prime models for analyzing sonar performance. For passive and noise-limited sonar detection, a figure of merit (FOM) can be defined that is not range dependent. Thus two such sonars can be compared without having to assume an operating area. The FOM can be translated into a median detection range by use of propagation loss curves which are region specific. Active detection under reverberation is more complicated. The use of sonar equations pertains to a single glimpse to obtain the detection. A variety of glimpse probabilities versus range can be obtained. The median detection range (50 percent probability of detection) is but one. Finding valid data for use in the sonar equations is a big problem. Using the equations is usually not.

410   Other Literature and History

References [1] through [4] will help readers to expand their understanding of the concepts presented in this part of the chapter. The level of presentation in each text is that for a third or fourth year undergraduate or a first year graduate student.

An excellent history of sonar *equipment development* is given in Burdic [1]. What follows is a history of methodology in sonar *performance prediction*.

Performance prediction at the end of World War II.   At the end of World War II detection ranges for *active* sonar were determined by comparing a plot of echo level versus range with a second plot of minimum detectable signal level versus range. Both plots were based on either computed or historically-measured values of components of the sonar equation. The range at which the two plots intersected was taken to be the range at which the target echo would be detected with a 50 percent probability of detection. The detection ranges were determined for both reverberation-limited and noise-limited conditions, with the lesser range selected as the best estimate of detection range from a combined background of noise and reverberation. For *passive* sonar both propagation loss and allowable loss were plotted as a function of range and frequency; the intersection was the predicted range corresponding to a 50 percent probability of detection. (See [5].)

Figure of merit. Referring to the allowable loss as "figure of merit" became popular during the immediate post-WWII years (see Horton [6], Chapters 7 and 8). For a passive sonar the figure of merit was equal to the target source level minus the minimum detectable signal level capability of the sonar. For an active sonar the figure of merit was initially defined as the sonar source level minus the sonar minimum detectable signal level. The sonar range was solved by determining the range at which the active figure of merit was equal to the propagation loss minus the target strength. The parallel in the passive situation was not complete because the figure of merit thus defined was no longer equal to the allowable propagation loss, unless the target reflectivity was considered to be a part of the propagation loss. To preserve the more conventional definition of propagation loss and equate figure of merit to allowable propagation loss, another definition of **active figure of merit** was coined which included the target strength as a part of the figure of merit. Both definitions have been widely used over the years and have been a source of confusion concerning what a stated active figure of merit value really means.

Another complication in the active sonar figure of merit concept concerned its dependence upon reverberation interference. Since reverberation depends on both range and environmental condition, the active figure of merit lost the attractive feature of the passive figure of merit of being a quantity that is independent of both range and the propagation characteristics of the environment. The active figure of merit, no matter how defined, was dependent on both. Although in the early 1950s there was an attempt to have the shipboard operators measure active figure of merit versus range in the environment of interest (Schulkin et. al. [7]), this was later found to be impractical. The figure of merit measurement concept was later supplanted by a shipboard measurement of *in situ* reverberation which was then used to provide the same type of information that was dependent on range and environment, in solving the sonar equation. As a result of the foregoing problems the active sonar figure of merit concept today has fallen into disuse in both shipboard detection range prediction or in sonar system design. Instead the individual components of active sonar equations (source level, recognition differential, interference background, and possibly target strength) are each considered separately in arriving at a performance prediction.

Expansion of underwater acoustic knowledge. Propagation loss, reverberation, and minimum-detectable-level measurement programs started to expand rapidly in the 1950s, which enormously increased the understanding of the impact of the environment on items in the sonar equation affecting performance (Urich [8] and Marsh and Morris [9]). *Average* values of inputs to the sonar equation for any particular type of environment, as well as the *statistical variability* about the average, as discussed in this chapter, were estimated. This permitted much more accurate predictions of detection range in terms of environmental conditions by the use of semi-empirical formulas. The formulas were first embedded in charts and tables for shipboard use ([10] and Bell [11]), and later programmed in digital computers.

Signal excess and detection probability. Information on the statistical variability of propagation loss and operator minimum detectable level performance permitted the introduction in the early 1950s of the ability to compute detection ranges corresponding to probabilities other than the standard 50 percent value. This was accomplished by the formulation in 1951 by Morris Schulkin [12] of the "signal excess" form of the sonar equation. Instead of determining only the range corresponding to a 50 percent probability as the range at which the allowable loss equaled the actual propagation loss, the average excess of signal over that required for 50 percent detection was determined as a function of range. From the average signal excess and the knowledge of the variability of the average of all components of the sonar equation for a given environmental condition, the detection probability versus range was determined in that environment. The variability in signal excess about its computed average was found to be Gaussian distributed with typical standard deviations of 9 dB for passive sonar and 12 dB for active sonar. These values have been inferred both from experimental detection results from sea and from observations of the variability of the components of the sonar equation (Marsh [9], pp. 57-64, DelSanto and Bell [13], and Bell [14]). The signal excess *variability* is not greatly affected by environmental conditions.

With the introduction of the signal excess concept the methodology of separately solving for reverberation and noise-limited conditions became generally inadequate for determining the operational signal excess versus range, although it can have the benefit of providing visibility on the relative contributions of reverberation and noise to the detection probability result. Beginning in the 1960s these two sources of interference were usually combined by power summation along the lines mentioned at the start of 403.

Single-glimpse probability interpretation. The probability obtained from signal excess is said to be a "single-glimpse" probability, based on an effective observation interval usually of the order of 5 minutes, the exact value depending on the display presentation history. The standard deviation of instantaneous signal excess as determined from the sum of the variances of each term in the sonar equation is based on a long-term variability, determined from sampling individual values over a long period of time with an average time between samples of many days. Thus one has to be careful not to assume that probabilities can accumulate with time over a short period of time. Thus two 50 percent probability glimpses made over a period of 10 minutes, where each glimpse is based on a 5-minute observation time, will not lead to a 75 percent probability of detection. The conditions over 10 minutes are highly correlated as compared to the sampling times of the components of the sonar equation. In reality the detection probability over 10 minutes will be only slightly higher than it would over the basic 5-minute display history period. The appropriate computation of cumulative probabilities is discussed in detail in Chapter 5.

[1]   Burdic, William S. *Underwater Acoustic Systems Analysis*. Englewood Cliffs, NJ: Prentice-Hall, 1984.

[2]   Urick, Robert J. *Principles of Underwater Sound*. 3d ed. New York: McGraw-Hill, 1983.

[3]   Etter, Paul C. *Underwater Acoustic Modeling*. New York: Elsevier Applied Science, 1991.

[4]   Clay, Clarence S., and Herman Medwin *Acoustical Oceanography*. New York: Wiley, 1977.

[5]   National Research Council. *Principles of Underwater Sound*. Washington, DC: Originally issued as Division 6, Volume 7, NDRC Summary Technical Reports; reprinted and distributed by the Research Analysis Group, Committee on Undersea Warfare, 1946.

[6]   Horton, J. Warren. *Fundamentals of Sonar*. Annapolis, MD: United States Naval Institute, 1957.

[7]   Schulkin, Morris; Frank S. White, Jr.; and Raymond A. Spong. *QHBa Figure of Merit Tests*. New London, CT: Navy Underwater Sound Laboratory Report No. 187, 3, 1953.

[8]   Urick, Robert J. *Sound Propagation in the Sea*. Los Altos, CA: Peninsula Publishing, 1982.

[9]   Marsh, H. Wysor, Jr., and Morris Schulkin. *Report on the Status of Project AMOS*. New

London, CT: Navy Underwater Sound Laboratory Research Report No. 255, 1955.

[10] Naval Ship Systems Command. *Manual for Estimating Echo Range*. NAVSHIPS 900,196, 1959.

[11] Bell, Thaddeus G. *Sonar Detection and Detectability Ranges for Submarines*. New London, CT: Navy Underwater Sound Laboratory Report No. 491, 1960.

[12] Schulkin, Morris. *History, Development, and Present Status of Project AMOS (Acoustic, Meteorological, and Oceanographic Survey)*. New London, CT: Navy Underwater Sound Laboratory Report No. 132, 1951.

[13] DelSanto, Ralph F., and Thaddeus G. Bell. *Comparison of Predicted Vs Actual Submarine Sonar Detection Ranges*. New London, CT: Navy Underwater Sound Laboratory Report No. 544, 1962.

[14] Bell, Thaddeus G. *Comparisons of Target Detection Results with Expectations Based on USL Range-Prediction Methods*. New London, CT: Navy Underwater Sound Laboratory Report No. 576, 1963.

PART B: Radar Detection

A **radar** (for **RA**dio **D**etection **A**nd **R**anging) is any device that emits electromagnetic radiation signals and detects their echo. All radars operate in only a small portion of the total spectrum of electromagnetic radiation. The total spectrum stretches from very long waves on the order of the size of the earth to very short waves on the order of the size of an atom, and includes everything from extremely low frequency (**ELF**) waves, to ordinary radio waves (ordinary radar waves), infrared, visible light, ultraviolet, X-rays, up to gamma rays at the very top. The portion used by radar stretches from a few **megahertz** (millions of cycles per second) to about 300 **gigahertz** (300 billion cycles per second), plus some laser radars (**ladars**) that operate near the frequency of visible light. All electromagnetic waves move at the same speed, the speed of light, and all obey the same fundamental physical laws. The operation of most radars relies on very accurate measurement of the time for emitted pulses to travel to and be reflected back from an object to be detected or ranged. *Electromagnetic detectors* that detect light waves exist in nature–they are called eyes.

Radar serves as the indispensable eyes of surface naval and aircraft fleets. Radar offers unmatched advantages of early warning, detection, and tracking. With ten or more times the distance of human daylight vision, at night, in fog, in bad weather, and at all altitudes, and with accurate and rapid ranging, radar's contributions are unequaled by other sensors. Many military analysts view *stealth* design in aircraft, ships, and missiles as the greatest advance in military technology in the last quarter of the twentieth century – primarily because it offers a chance to hide from radar.

This section on radar starts with a treatment of how to compute the distance to the **radar horizon** from any height above the earth's surface. It then moves on to the problem of predicting the range capability of a radar and the impact of the radar antenna's on performance. It gives a heuristic description of countermeasures used in air vehicle design and tactics to counteract radar operation.

Figure 4.15 depicts a **radar beam** emanating from an antenna with the **sidelobes** indicated as annular rings or lobes around the **mainlobe** or **main beam**. Radar radiation and light are both examples of electromagnetic radiation and behave in similar ways. Radar sidelobes are analogous to the diffraction patterns observed when light passes through a pinhole. In the case of the sidelobes of the radar, they become of progressively decreasing intensity, and spread farther and farther to the side until there is a weak signal out the back end of the antenna, opposite to the main beam.

FIGURE 4.15. ANTENNA PATTERN WITH MAINLOBE AND SIDELOBES

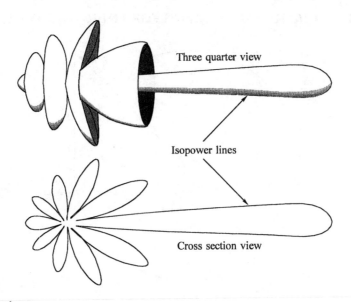

Three quarter view

Isopower lines

Cross section view

411   Radar Horizon

The earth's atmosphere has a density that decreases exponentially with altitude. Because of this density gradient, light is refracted as it passes through the atmosphere so that at the latitude of Washington, D.C., on the days of the solar equinoxes, the sun appears to come up some four minutes before it would if there were no refraction. Radar waves are also refracted so that targets can be tracked even beyond the visual horizon. This effect is more pronounced at the lower frequencies than at the higher frequencies. To correct for refraction at conventional radar frequencies, an analytical approximation is commonly used called the **four-thirds earth approximation**. This approach assumes that the earth is four-thirds the size of its actual radius and that radar waves travel in a straight line. Figure 4.16 shows how this physical relationship may be approximated for search radar frequencies.

As can be seen from Figure 4.16,

$$r^2 + d^2 = (r + h)^2.$$

Solving for d yields

$$d^2 = 2rh + h^2.$$

Since h^2 is small compared to $2rh$, the approximate value for d (the distance to the horizon) can be approximated closely by

$$d \approx \sqrt{2rh}, \quad [r \gg h].$$

This assumes that h and d are expressed in the same units as r. A nautical mile is 6,076 feet, the radius of the earth at the equator is 3,354 nautical miles (nm), and the 4/3 radius r is 4,473 nm. Setting r equal to 4,473 nm and using h in feet, the equation for d in nautical miles becomes

$$d \approx \sqrt{2rh/6076}, \quad [r \gg h],$$

or

$$d \approx 1.21\sqrt{h}, \quad [r \gg h]. \tag{4-8}$$

FIGURE 4.16. RADAR HORIZON FOR FOUR-THIRDS EARTH

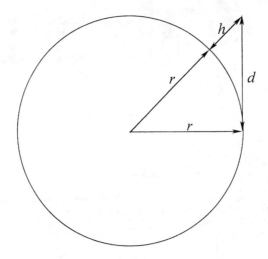

As an example, an aircraft flying at 10,000 feet will be able to see, or be seen, out to a horizon at distance $d = 1.21 (10,000)^{1/2}$ or 121 nautical miles. This approximation is valid for radars that operate in the lower frequency bands. For higher frequencies, the refraction effect becomes less pronounced until at the frequencies of visible light the effect may be approximated by making a seven-sixths earth's radius assumption. This can be important for laser radars, or **ladars**, which operate at, or near, visible light frequencies.

Light travels at 161,830 nm per second in air. Thus, it takes light, or a radar signal, 6.18 microseconds (μsec) to travel one nautical mile. If a target is one mile away, it will take 12.36 μsec for a signal to go out one mile and come back. This echo time, 12.36 μsec, is called a **radar mile**. In statute miles, the number is 10.74 μsec, which is also an often used baseline by radar specialists.

412   Radar Scattering

When a radar wave strikes a target, it causes an excitation of the electrons in the target's surface. This excitation in turn causes a reradiation of the signal by the target. This process is referred to as **scattering** by radar experts. Loosely, both radar experts and non-experts refer to this as **reflection** of the energy – just as we refer to reflection of light from a mirror. However, both light reflection from a mirror and radar wave reflection from a surface are really *reradiation* phenomena.

When a radar beam encounters a target, it usually exhibits a mirror reflection in which the angle of incidence equals the angle of reflection, provided the wavelength is long compared to the surface roughness of the target (Figure 4.17(a)). With most radars, the wavelength is measured in centimeters and most target exterior surfaces are smooth by comparison so that mirror-like, or **specular**, "reflection" occurs. However, if the wavelength is short compared to the surface roughness as in Figure 4.17(b), then diffuse, or **spectral**, "reflection" will occur.

FIGURE 4.17. RADAR REFLECTION

(a) Specular (mirror) reflection.   (b) Spectral (diffuse) reflection.

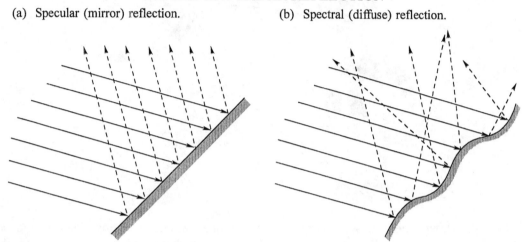

If one looks at an early stealth aircraft such as the F-117 (see Figure 4.18), one can think of the specularly reflected radar signals as bouncing off its faceted surfaces much as bullets might ricochet off an armored plate or light would reflect from mirror surfaces. Antenna theory says that the larger the antenna of a radar in terms of wavelength, the more focused the beam. Similarly, the larger the facets on the surface of an aircraft such as the F-117, the more focused the deflected radar wave energy will be. This can be thought of as the bullets reflecting off within a narrow angle as opposed to splaying off in diverse directions. In addition to this shaping effect, radar absorbing material (RAM) and radar absorbing structure (RAS) may be used on any surfaces not expected to offer a "glancing blow" to the impinging radar waves.

413   Radar Range Equation

Much of the theory of radar is based on the law of conservation of energy. The radar range equation is based on fundamental physical principles including the inverse square law of dissipation of radiation.

A basic form of the radar range equation is derived by taking the **transmitted power** (P_T) that is radiated from the antenna estimating the ability of the antenna to focus this power (called **gain** or G or the antenna), computing the power density that reaches the target as a result of the inverse square law of spatial attenuation, determining what part is intercepted by the target and reflected or reradiated by the target back toward the radar (measured as the **radar cross section** or σ), computing the power density level achieved back at the radar as a result of spatial attenuation again, and computing what part of that energy is captured by the receiver antenna (A_e).

FIGURE 4.18. F-117 AND RADAR REFLECTION

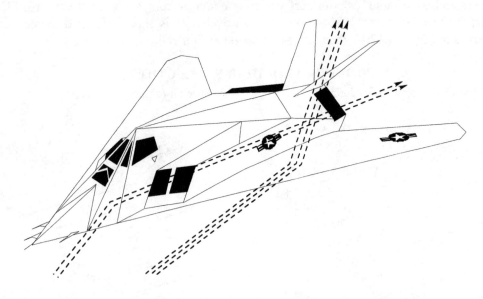

Consider a transmitter of power P_T sending out electromagnetic energy **isotropically** (i.e., equal in all directions) as shown in Figure 4.19(a). At a distance r to the target, the power density over the surface of the sphere of radius r will have dissipated by the inverse square law of radiation, or by $1/(4\pi r^2)$. This energy may be focused by an antenna, as shown in Figure 4.19(b) where the power density only is spread over a region of the sphere of area approximately $\theta^2 r^2$.

FIGURE 4.19. SIGNAL TRANSMISSION TYPES

(a) Isotropic signal.   (b) Focused signal.

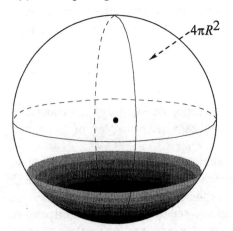
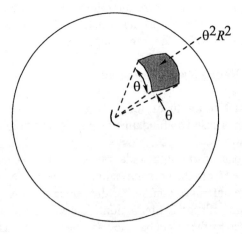

The power radiated per unit area on a sphere of radius r with the radar at the center defines the **power density** of the signal at that range. The ratio of the power density in the direction toward which the antenna is focused compared to the power density of an **isotropic** (equal in all directions) radiator is called the **gain** of the antenna. Using only this term and other basic concepts, one can derive the radar range equation in its simplest form by following the sequence of events in the propagation of the radar signal as shown in Figure 4.20.

One can set the **power received**, P_R, equal to the **minimum detectible signal**, S, and then gather terms in the above relationship, to obtain the basic form of the radar equation as

$$S = P_R = P_T G \sigma A_e / (4\pi r^2)^2 \tag{4-9}$$

or

$$r = \{P_T G \sigma A_e / [(4\pi)^2 S]\}^{1/4}. \tag{4-10}$$

Equation (4-10) is the basic radar range equation. It does not take into account a number of things that affect range performance such as the degree to which the target is off-center in the beam, weather, atmospheric effects including electrical disturbances, system losses, and dynamic variability in the various factors including σ, G, and S. Thus, it is important to remember in an analysis that the strength of a radar return is a random variable and not a deterministic value.

As a result of these highly variable terms, the radar range predicted by the equation may be off by a factor of 2, which means that the terms inside the parentheses may be off by a factor of 16. Nevertheless, the equation is useful since taking the fourth root dampens the variability, even though the terms inside the brackets may vary over a large range. Also, as with almost all analysis, the important thing is to be able to *compare* two systems, and the theoretical performance of radar A relative to radar B may be very pertinent for comparison purposes even though both theoretical performance estimates are higher than real-world values.

FIGURE 4.20. RADAR POWER RETURN SIGNAL

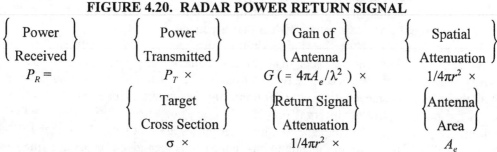

Antenna theory provides the following relationship between G, A_e, and wavelength λ:

$$G = 4\pi A_e / \lambda^2.$$

Thus range r becomes

$$r = \{P_T G^2 \sigma \lambda / [(4\pi)^3 S]\}^{1/4}. \tag{4-11}$$

A useful abbreviated form of the radar range equation is to collapse all the terms for a given case except σ into a constant to show the effects of changes in radar range based on changes in cross section alone, so that

$$r_1/r_2 = (\sigma_1/\sigma_2)^{1/4}. \tag{4-12}$$

In any form of the radar equations, units must be consistent. One consistent set is to use watts and meters. Thus, P_T becomes the transmitted power in watts, G the antenna gain (a dimensionless quantity relative to an isotropic radiator with a gain of one), σ the radar cross section of the target in square meters, λ the wavelength in meters, and S the minimum detectable signal in watts. If, as may happen, range is desired in nautical miles and minimum detectable signal is expressed in milliwatts, then appropriate adjustments must be made in the units of the terms in the equations.

Many calculations with radar rely on calculations based on **decibels** (dB), in which a quantity or a ratio in decibels is computed by

$$x \text{ in dB} = 10 \log_{10} x.$$

All of the terms in (4-11) can be expressed in decibels, in which case they are ratios relative to some base value. By convention, dBW expresses power relative to one **watt**, and a transmitted power, P_T, of 30 dBW would be 1000 watts. A minimum detectable signal, S, may be expressed relative to a **milli**watt so that 30 dBw, for example, would be 1000 milliwatts, or one watt. The radar cross section and wavelength, σ and λ, would be expressed relative to one **square meter** (dBSM) and one **meter** (dBM), respectively.

Radar cross section in dBSM is a much used way of referring to the radar cross section of vehicles, and especially low-observable vehicles. In this framework, 10 dBSM would be 10 square meters, and -20 dBSM would be 0.01 square meters.

With (4-12), one can easily calculate how effective radar cross section will be in reducing range. To take an example, if the target cross section were reduced by a factor of 4000, the range would only be reduced by a factor of $4000^{1/4}$, or only a factor of 7.95. To illustrate, consider a radar with a range capability of 200 miles against a 10-square-meter target. The range for stealthier targets is easily derived as shown in Figure 4.21.

In Figure 4.21, the σ values are changed by 12 dB (a factor of approximately 16) in each step so that the range is approximately halved ($16^{1/4} = 2$) in each step as shown in the second line. The more precise range calculations (line 4), based on the true value of 12 dB and its effect on $\sigma^{1/4}$ values (line 3), differ from the approximations by less than 1 percent.

The range equation (4-11) defines the maximum range in terms of sensitivity as where only one pulse was sent out and its echo detected. In practice, sending out later pulses imposes an ambiguity problem on the designer. When a pulse returns from a target just before a second pulse is to be emitted, the radar has achieved its **maximum unambiguous range**. This is calculated from *PRI*, which is the **pulse repetition interval** (or time between pulses), or *PRF*, which is the **pulse repetition frequency** (or the frequency with which pulses are emitted). Note that PRF is the reciprocal of PRI. The maximum unambiguous range (r_u) is then given by using c (the speed of light, 161,830 nm per sec. in air) and either of these ratios in which

$$r_u = PRI\,(c/2) = c/(2\,PRF).$$

FIGURE 4.21. EFFECT OF RCS REDUCTION ON RADAR RANGE

σ (dBSM)	10	-2	-14	-26	-38
r (nm)	200	100	50	25	12.5
σ (SM)	10	.63	.04	.0025	.00016
R (nm)	200	100.2	50.2	25.2	12.6

Any pulse arriving later, as from a more distant target, will appear to the radar as if it were much closer somewhere within the maximum unambiguous range. Radar designers use *PRF* staggering techniques to resolve such ambiguities.

There is also a radar **dead zone** due to the finite width (duration) of the radar pulse. Pulse radars operate in either transmit or receive mode, but not both at the same time. That is, the radar operates in transmit mode for a few microseconds or milliseconds, and then switches over to receive mode to pick up the returned echo. Until the transmitter is turned off, the receiver is disconnected from the antenna to protect it from being burned out by the transmitter's enormously greater power. This is necessary, because the transmitted pulse may be 10^{15} (150 dB) or more times greater than the received signal and would burn out the amplifier stages if it were to go directly into the receiver. This ultra-rapid switching between transmit mode and receive mode is accomplished by an electronic switching device, called a **duplexer**.

If there is a target so near that the pulse will go out to the target and come back while the receiver is turned off by the duplexer, the target will not be detected. This period of no reception is called the radar's dead zone, and is dictated by the width of the transmitted pulse in microseconds. If the pulse width is defined as τ, then the dead zone range is defined as

$$r_d = \tau \, c/2.$$

In addition, radars often have cone-shaped **dead zones** overhead due to angular motion limitations on the antenna. These factors impinging on range are portrayed in Figure 4.22.

FIGURE 4.22. RANGE LIMITATIONS

(a) Side view.   (b) Top view.

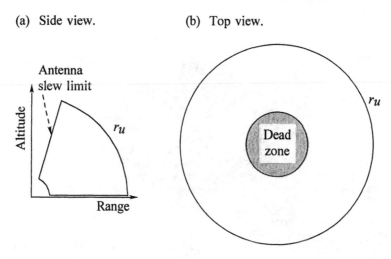

414   Radar Reflection and Radar Cross Section

By convention, the **radar cross section** (*RCS* or σ) of a target is defined as the cross-sectional area of an isotropic reflector that would reradiate the same amount of energy back to the radar receiver antenna. Loosely, *RCS* is also sometimes defined as the cross-sectional area of a sphere that would radiate the same amount of energy back to the radar, but that is true only in cases where the circumference of the sphere would be more than ten times the radar wavelength (λ). For small

RCS targets, even those physically large but of small radar target size such as a stealth bomber, the definition by analogy with a sphere is no longer applicable. Also, the analogy with light is not directly applicable here as those targets that are physically large and large in the visible light regime may be very small in the region of radar waves.

RCS is critically dependent on the aspect angle from which the radar views the target, the shape of the target, the materials used in fabrication, and the radar's frequency. *RCS* always has a strong probabilistic aspect shown in the wild fluctuations in the signal strength reflected back toward the receiver, even at nearly the same aspect angles. Figure 4.23 indicates how this variability manifests itself in the case of a pioneer jet fighter aircraft, the Messerschmitt 262. Note that the figure uses the a dB scale to relate the cross section to a one-square-meter cross section isotropic scatterer. This spiked appearance is typical of all radar targets, although for analytical purposes such plots, called **waterline plots**, are sometimes given as smoothed lines or even as a nominal numerical value for analytic purposes. Many computer programs are set up to use such smoothed values or even a single number for defining the radar cross section. However, it should always be kept in mind that the basic picture is highly irregular despite appearances, and lesser representations are mere analytic conveniences such as were in fact used in Figure 4.21. Also, even the plot in Figure 4.23 is only good for one operating frequency and a family of plots is needed to define the cross section at various frequencies.

FIGURE 4.23. THE RADAR WATERLINE CROSS SECTION OF THE MESSERSCHMITT ME-262 (COURTESY OF THE BOEING COMPANY)

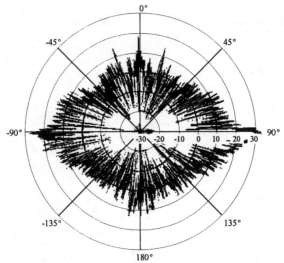

The equations so far have assumed that the same antenna is used for transmission and reception, and that is usually the case, as most radars are **monostatic**, (i.e., they use only one antenna). Where one antenna is used, antenna area and gain are interrelated at a given frequency/wavelength. In some radars, however, there are separate antennas for transmission and reception. In such cases two G terms must be carried for G_t and G_r and the radar range equation is otherwise unchanged. Where the two antennas are separated, it is called a **bistatic** radar, and in fact the first steps in 1925 toward an operating radar to measure the height of the ionosphere had the two antennas separated by eight miles. Also, the experimental Over-the-Horizon-Backscatter radar built in the 1970s to detect aircraft and ships out to a range of 1800 nm by reflecting a radar signal off the ionosphere had the transmitter in Moscow, Maine, and the receiver in Bar Harbor, Maine, 95 nm away.

415   Antennas

Antennas focus the energy radiated by a radar set and collect the reflected energy reradiated by a target. The radar equation underscores the big impact antenna design has on the range of the radar. The ability of a radar to specify the location of a target depends on the shape of the beam it radiates. This ability must be traded off against the volume of space a radar can illuminate in one instant of time. There are two classes of antenna: reflectors and phased-array antennas. Both types are used to focus the energy of the radar set into beams. Reflectors reradiate energy off the reflector of the antenna to send it in a desired direction. **Phased-array antennas** are made up of many individual antenna elements that are controlled electronically so the phase-effect causes the energy emitted to be shaped into a desired beam pattern.

A pencil beam, which can be formed by a parabolic reflector, is used to accurately determine a target's height and azimuth. A fan beam, typically used in search radars, has a narrow width in azimuth, but a wide beam in elevation. These characteristics allow it to give precise direction information, but do not give the elevation of a detected target.

Because the radiation of energy from the antenna must conserve (not create) energy, the integral of the gain about the waterline of an antenna is equal to one (referred to as zero dB, since $10^0 = 1$). Thus, the energy that an antenna focuses in one direction, is at the expense of energy radiated in other directions. As a rule of thumb, approximately 90 percent of the energy lies in the main beam, with the remainder spilling into the sidelobes.

In reflector antennas the beam is moved using a mechanically steerable dish. Phased-array antennas achieve beam steering by means of controlling the phase of the signals out of individual antenna-elements buried in the face of the array. Radars with such antennas are also called **agile beam radars**. Figure 4.24 depicts how this is done by emitting signals from each element in the face in sequence so as to establish a phase front that can be electronically steered in any direction within about $\pm60°$ of the axis of the antenna. The technique can be used with tracking radars as well as search radars. It can even be combined in a **track-while-scan** mode as on some interceptor aircraft radars, which can search the sky in front of the aircraft while tracking specific targets to keep track of their location. The radar in Army's Patriot air-defense system and the Navy's Aegis system for ship air-defense use electronically steered phased-array antennas.

416   Signal to Noise/Interference and Probability of Detection and False Alarm

It is important to keep in mind that the signal must be pulled out of an underlying blanket of noise as shown in Figure 4.25(a). Some of the thermal noise power created in the receiver will be amplified along with the incoming signal and may be the dominant form of noise to contend with where other interference such as clutter or active jamming is not an issue

From Figure 4.25(a), it can be seen that one can increase the probability of detection by lowering the threshold for the minimum detectable signal. However, lowering the threshold increases the chances of a noise spike being large enough to mislead the radar to indicate that a target has been detected, when in fact it was only noise in the receiver. Because of these factors, detection is based on probability functions called the probability of detection (P_d) and the probability of false alarm or (P_{fa}), which are dependent on each other and the signal to noise (S/N). Assuming that the target signal is a sine wave to be extracted from a noise background, these probabilities can be described as in Figure 4.26. This is a matter of balancing what statisticians call type-one and type-two errors. Since P_d and P_{fa} are always mutually interdependent, it is always necessary to specify them together in order to give complete meaning to either. Frequently, radar professionals will accommodate to this need by showing how P_d changes at a **constant false alarm rate** (called CFAR). In Figure 4.26, the steeply upward sloping graphs are a family of CFAR curves

FIGURE 4.24. ANGLED WAVEFRONT FORMED BY A PHASED-ARRAY ANTENNA

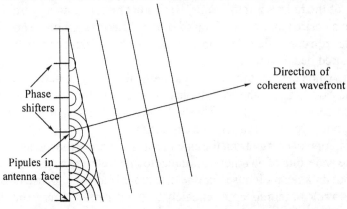

FIGURE 4.25. RADAR SIGNAL THRESHOLD

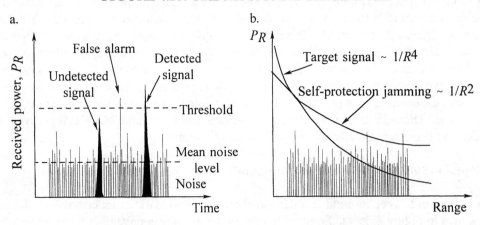

From Figure 4.26, it can be seen that a signal-to-noise ratio of 13 dB will give a good probability of detection while at the same time suppressing the false alarm probability to an acceptably low rate. (A ratio of 13 dB is widely considered adequate for early warning and detection. For tracking, a higher ratio of up to 22 dB may be used to suppress the chances of falsely identifying non-target signals as targets.)

Thermal noise in the receiver is generated by the thermal energy there. The noise power due to temperature alone is given by Boltzmann's law as

$$N = kTB_R.$$

In this equation, k is Botzmann's constant, which is 1.38×10^{-23} Joules per degree Kelvin, T is the temperature in degrees Kelvin, and B_R is the bandwidth of the receiver amplifier. One watt equals one Joule per second, and bandwidth has the units of frequency (i.e., one over time). Hence, at room temperature (75°F or 297°K), the factor kT equates to $1.38 \times 10^{-23} \times 297 = 4.1 \times 10^{-21}$ Watts/Hz of receiver bandwidth.

Given the desired signal-to-noise ratio and the value for the noise figure, one can derive a term for the S as follows:

$$S = S/N \times kTB_R.$$

This can be substituted into (4-11) to give

$$r = \{P_T G \sigma A_e^2 / [(4\pi)^2 S/N \times kTB_R]\}^{1/4}. \tag{4-13}$$

FIGURE 4.26. PROBABILITY OF DETECTION AND FALSE ALARM

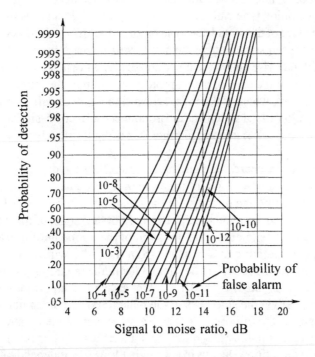

Radars operating against their own internal noise power, are said to be operating in the **blue-sky** mode – that is, against a benign background, so that their primary limitation is their own internal noise generated in the receiver that competes with the signal return. It is in these blue-sky situations where (4-13) is most applicable.

417   Electronic Warfare

Not all radars operate in the blue-sky or noise-limited mode, and many must cope with interference introduced by the environment as well as by opposing forces trying to deny detection of a target. Air vehicle designers and opposing radar designers are in a continuing battle to foil one another. Military combat aircraft often resort to various forms of electronic warfare that can be broadly classified as active or passive.

Active electronic warfare (also called **jamming** or **electronic-countermeasures**), is further broken down into self-protection or support jamming. **Self-protection jamming** is when a combat aircraft is equipped with its own electronic jammers to foil radar. A **support jammer** may be another aircraft or a drone that acts against radar in support of an aircraft or missile that carries home the attack. Passive counters to radar includes such measures as stealth or low-observables designs for potential radar targets. **Stealth** sometimes denotes a vehicle of very low cross section and usually is one built to be stealthy from its initial inception. A **low-observable** vehicle is often defined as one with some radar cross section reduction, but not so stealthy as a true stealth vehicle.

The most basic active countermeasures to radar detection are noise jammers that generate noise in the bandwidth of the radar receiver to increase the denominator of the range equation and thus decrease range. In that case, interference and not receiver noise becomes the basis for computing the signal-to-interference ratio. One can then enter the P_d versus P_{fa} curves by using the signal-to-interference ratio in the place of the signal-to-noise ratio. Noise may indeed deny detection at longer ranges, but if range is reduced sufficiently, the signal will increase with $1/r^4$, and a point may be reached where the signal may rise above the noise and detection will occur – this is called the **burn-through range**. Note that in the case of a self-protection jammer, the jamming signal power will increase in proportion to $1/r^2$, whereas the radar return signal power will increase in proportion to $1/r^4$, so that range reduction has a much more pronounced effect on signal than it does on the interference signal. If a stand-off or support jammer is causing the interference, the jamming signal may not increase at all.

Also, if the jammer is on-board the penetrating aircraft, the radar may be able to detect the direction of the signal even though range information may be denied. By increasing the required signal-to-noise ratio sufficiently, the direction of the jamming may be defined by a **strobe**, or line that appears on the radar screen showing the direction, if not the range, of the target. It may then be possible to fly an intercept missile out in the direction of the strobe until it is able to intercept the target. A support jammer operating at a distance from the radar will try to inject noise into the radar's receiver. Since this aircraft may not be a target itself, the radar may not be pointing at it, and it will not then be in the mainlobe of the radar. In that case, the support jammer tries to inject its signal into the radar receiver via the sidelobes of the radar to poison the mainlobe detection signal.

Another option open to the offense is to use decoys, which make no attempt to hide or deny detection but instead try to mimic the radar return characteristics of a target vehicle so as to mislead the radar into indicating a detection. Decoys may be either towed or independent flying vehicles that fly at some distance from the aircraft. They also may be either passive or may actively emit a signal to emulate important target radar cross-section characteristics.

An air vehicle may also detect the radar's signal and emit a return signal that is bounced off the ground toward the radar as in Figure 4.27. This **terrain bounce** signal may be 20 dB (100 times) or so stronger than the echo signal from the vehicle. In this case the radar has no difficulty following the target, but a missile launched toward the target may be decoyed off course to attack the return from the ground and will thus be lured into flying into the ground. Since this technique is employed during the final attack, it is called an **end game** or **spear-catcher** technique to distinguish it from electronic countermeasures that try to foil detection or tracking before an attack missile is launched.

FIGURE 4.27. TERRAIN BOUNCE SIGNAL COUNTERMEASURES

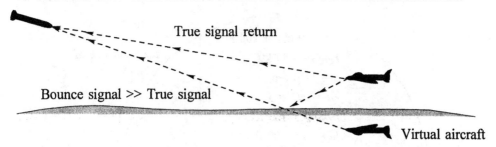

In World War II, the British initiated the use of chaff (they called it window) to fill the air with small dipoles that would resonate at the frequency of the radar. **Chaff**, which consists of fine metal filaments long enough to make half-wavelength metal dipoles, may be dispensed into the air in quantities of thousands or even millions to simply swamp, or clutter, the radar's return signal with unwanted echoes. However, such filaments drifting through the air will not have similar velocity characteristics to an aircraft, and many radars are designed to see only moving targets by **filtering out** (or eliminating) all targets having a radial component of velocity toward the radar of less than 80 to 100 miles per hour or so. **Moving target intercept (MTI)** radars and **pulse Doppler** radars have this capability.

Both MTI and pulse Doppler radars rely on the **Doppler effect** in which a target moving toward or away from the radar imparts a frequency change to the signal that allows determination of its radial velocity component. Besides chaff drifting through the air, this allows the radar to eliminate signal returns from most ground vehicles such as cars and trucks that move at velocities relatively slower than most aircraft. Unfortunately, it will make the radar ignore even fast-moving air vehicles that are moving perpendicular to, or nearly perpendicular to, the radar line of sight so that the target's radial velocity is less than the target cutoff value. Because of this feature, the radar detection footprint will display a Doppler notch characteristic that gives a butterfly-like appearance as shown in Figure 4.28. Since Doppler effect indicates only the rate of change of range (called R-dot, $\dot{r}$), it is the component of velocity in the direction of the radar that determines whether or not the target's motion is greater than the cutoff velocity.

The Doppler effect for the increase in the frequency of the radar's return signal when looking at a fast approaching target, may be easily visualized. Consider a stationary radar of frequency f that is illuminating a stationary target, where f is the underlying or **carrier frequency** of the radar as distinguished from the pulse frequency or PRF. For this case, the target will then have f waves sweeping over it each second. Another way of looking at this is that (since $f = c/\lambda$) the target will have c/λ waves washing over it each second, where c is the velocity of light and λ is the wavelength.

Now suppose the target is moving toward the radar at velocity v so that it travels a distance v in one second. The wavelength (λ) of the radar will indicate that v/λ *additional* waves will be intercepted by the target and the *apparent* frequency of the radar *as detected by the target* will be $f + v/\lambda$. But, the target will then reradiate the radar signal back toward the radar *at this new frequency* while again adding the effect of its own motion, so that the returning frequency detected by radar will be $f + 2v/\lambda$. This second term, $2v/\lambda$, is called the **Doppler frequency** (f_d).

FIGURE 4.28. GROUND DETECTION FOOTPRINT FOR A SAM RADAR

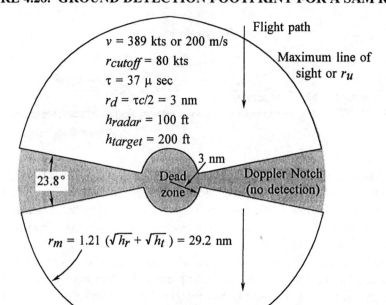

$$v = 389 \text{ kts or } 200 \text{ m/s}$$

Flight path

Maximum line of sight or r_u

$$r_{cutoff} = 80 \text{ kts}$$
$$\tau = 37 \ \mu \text{ sec}$$
$$r_d = \tau c/2 = 3 \text{ nm}$$
$$h_{radar} = 100 \text{ ft}$$
$$h_{target} = 200 \text{ ft}$$

23.8°

3 nm

Dead zone

Doppler Notch (no detection)

$$r_m = 1.21 \ (\sqrt{h_r} + \sqrt{h_t} \ ) = 29.2 \text{ nm}$$

For example, a radar with three gigahertz (GHz) carrier frequency will have a wavelength (λ) or 10 centimeters. A target moving toward such a radar with a radial velocity of 300 meters per second will increase the frequency of the return signal seen by the radar by an amount, $f_d = 2\times (300/0.1)$ or 6000 Hz. If the carrier frequency had been 9 GHz, the Doppler shift would have been 18,000 Hz. As a target flies past a radar site, the radial component of its velocity is easily computed and there will be a radial line along which the component of velocity toward the target will be equal to the **Doppler cutoff velocity** and a **Doppler notch** in the detection and tracking map will appear. When the target goes far enough past the target that the radial velocity component again becomes greater than the cutoff velocity, the target will reappear on the screen. The angular region between where the approaching target is lost and the retreating target is gained is referred to as the Doppler notch. The added Doppler frequency will be positive for an approaching target, and negative for a receding target.

Some radars do not measure range. A police radar, for example, need only measure velocity of a vehicle moving toward or away from it, so it needs only determine f_d. Such a radar does not require pulse operation at all, but can simply emit a continuous sine wave signal or tone and measure the change as above.

When combined with the radar dead zone and the range limitation due to radar antenna height, a SAM radar footprint pattern such as the one shown in Figure 4.28 may be obtained assuming the earth is a smooth sphere. The spherical earth assumption is a valid representation for most ocean environments, but for land-based missile acquisition radars, masking of the radar angle occurs where topography, vegetation, or the artifacts of man block a view of the horizon that a bald spherical earth would reveal. Where the radar looks over a sharp ridge, sharp-edged beam diffraction can occur so that detection may occur far beyond what would normally be called the line of sight. A smooth spherical earth may also cause diffraction, and computer codes have been written to compute effect of **spherical diffraction**.

When combined with the radar **dead zone** and the range limitation due to radar antenna height, a SAM radar **footprint pattern** such as the one shown in Figure 4.28 may be obtained assuming the earth is a smooth sphere. The spherical earth assumption is a valid representation for most ocean environments. For land-based missile acquisition radars, masking of the radar angle occurs where topography, vegetation, or man-made artifacts block a view of the horizon that a bald spherical earth would reveal. Where the radar looks over a sharp ridge, **sharp-edged beam diffraction** can occur so that detection may occur far beyond what would normally be called the line of sight. A smooth spherical earth may also cause diffraction, and computer codes have been written to compute effect of **spherical diffraction**.

In the naval environment particularly, humid air near the sea may create a zone of lower density (called an **inversion layer**) so that a radar signal will follow the curvature of the earth (see Figure 4.29). This phenomenon, called a **tunneling effect**, can also extend detection of low flying targets well beyond the horizon. However, the tunneling effect can complicate the detection of targets flying just above the inversion layer, since the radar energy pulled into the inversion layer will not be available at the higher altitude where it would normally have gone.

FIGURE 4.29. TUNNELING EFFECT AT SEA

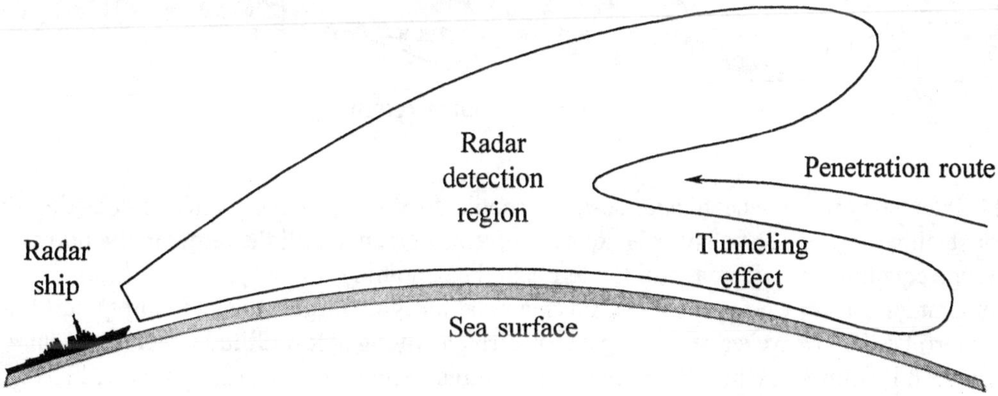

418   **Clutter**

Whether or not support jamming is available, a target may be able to hide in radar signal returns from the ground, from atmospheric interference, or the returns from chaff. All of theses unwanted signals are broadly termed **clutter**. When a target flies in at low altitude against a surface-to-air missile (SAM) site, the SAM radar may receive **interference** or clutter from the ground between it and the target. This arises because the radar sidelobes impinge on the ground in front of the site as shown in Figure 4.30. The radar operator might think of turning up the power in this situation so as to see a low-observable target more clearly. But this can be self defeating, as turning up the power in the main beam turns up the power in the sidelobes commensurately, the clutter then increases commensurately, and no net advantage may be gained. In this way, attack aircraft can hide in the ground clutter return as they approach target defenses. Ground clutter that is closer to the radar than the target may simply be **range-gated** out (eliminated from consideration) by instructing the radar software to ignore targets too close to be of concern. This can be so arranged that the software can make the range gate move with the target as the tactical situation develops.

419   Passive Countermeasures and Stealth

The most basic **passive countermeasure** that air vehicle designers can use to deny radar detection is to reduced the radar cross section of the vehicle. One may build a low-observable aircraft by shrinking the σ waterline pattern as in Figure 4.23 at least in some major aspects, angles near the direction of flight. One may suppress the return from regions that are within ±30° off the heading of the aircraft. This may be done by shaping the vehicle so as to deflect the radar signals harmlessly into directions away from the radar, by coating the vehicle with **radar absorbing material** (or RAM), and by using a **radar absorbing structure** (or RAS)

FIGURE 4.30. GROUND CLUTTER RETURN TO THE RADAR

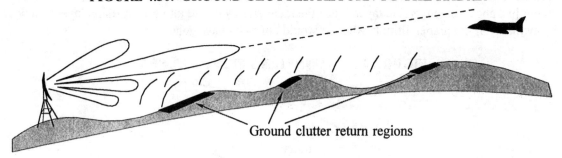

Ground clutter return regions

It is interesting to ask what a radar designer should do to increase the chance of detecting very small or stealthy targets. The answer is not so simple as to increase all the terms in the numerator of the range equation or to decrease all the terms in the denominator.

For example, a surface-to-air (SAM) missile radar designer might consider simply building a more powerful radar. However, if the target is an airplane flying at low altitude, then the radar will have to search low upon the horizon to pick up potential targets. For the radar, this will have the unfortunate effect of causing the sidelobes of the radar to illuminate the large area of the ground between it and the target with more power, which will increase the signal back to the radar (**clutter return**) from the ground reflection. As the radar turns up the power (P_T in the equation), the clutter return simply goes up commensurately with the mainlobe return from the target. Since in this type of situation the ground clutter return tends to dominate over the thermal noise in the receiver, little or nothing may be gained in terms of signal to interference ratio. Where clutter is not a problem as where the radar is operating in a blue-sky environment, then turning up the power will have the desired effect, and detection of stealthy targets will be improved.

Suppose the designer simply increases antenna gain, say by doubling the diameter of the antenna, then the radar will concentrate all of its mainlobe energy into an area one-fourth the original size. This will mean that the antenna will be able to pour four times the amount of energy into one-fourth as much area for one-fourth as long. Thus if the radar is a search or early warning radar, it will still take the same time to search a given area so that nothing will be gained on transmission.

On reception, however, the four times larger capture area of the antenna will indeed be effective and the radar will quadruple its sensitivity. (Another way of saying this is that the antenna will achieve 6 dB of improvement since $10 \times \log(4) \approx 6$.)

One can demonstrate a more general result mathematically from 4-9

$$S_{min} = P_R = P_T G \sigma A_e / (4\pi r^2)^2.$$

Since $N = kTB_R$, the signal to noise required for minimum signal, S_{min}, becomes

$$S_{min} = S/N \, kTB_R = P_R = P_T G \sigma A_e / (4\pi r^2)^2. \tag{4-14}$$

Considering that the gain, G, of the antenna concentrates the energy that would have covered 4π steradians (if radiated isotropically) into a solid angle approximated by θ^2, if the beam half angles are equal, one can compute G as

$$G = 4\pi/\theta^2,$$

or

$$\theta^2 = 4\pi/G.$$

In radar parlance, squaring the antenna beam's included angle gives a solid angle, θ^2, that is called an **angle bin**, and from Figure 4.31 one can see that the solid angle covered per pulse (or pulse train) is somewhat less than θ^2 since some degree of overlap will be required between successive pulses. Nevertheless, θ^2 is a good measure of the solid angle illuminated per pulse and it captures the essential relationship. Thus, if the radar is to scan some solid angle, Φ, in scan time, t_s, then n angle bins will be required to fill the area, where n is given by (4-15).

$$n = \Phi/\theta^2 = \Phi G/(4\pi), \tag{4-15}$$

and

$$n/t_s = \Phi G/(4\pi t_s).$$

Solving (4-14) for the transmitted power, P_T, gives

$$P_T = (S/N)[(4\pi r^2)^2 \, kTB_R/[G \sigma A_e]],$$

or

$$(n/t_s)P_T = (\Phi G/(4\pi t_s))(S/N)[(4\pi r^2)^2 \, kTB_R/[G \sigma A_e]].$$

This is the total pulse power in n angle bins (or pulse trains) taking t_s seconds of scan time to scan the solid angle, Φ. Note that the antenna gain term, G, will now cancel out and does not contribute to the scan performance. However, the antenna capture area, A_e, remains and will contribute to performance. The other terms can all be treated as a constant for a given case to show the signal-to-noise as

$$(S/N)_{scan} = constant \, [(n/t_s)P_T]A_e.$$

On balance then, the designer gains in the blue-sky case directly in proportion to the power of the radar signal and the increased antenna capture area. This is called the **power-aperture** of the radar system. Power-aperture is the term radar experts use to describe the target detection capability of a radar. It should be noted that it is the power in the transmitted signal, and the aperture to capture the weak return signal coming back that defines the radar's performance. It is not, as is sometimes thought, the aperture in the sense that increased aperture increases the antenna gain, which cancels out and has no direct effect as shown above.

FIGURE 4.31. ANGLE BINS AND SCAN REGION

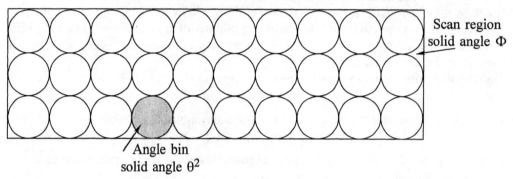

Scan region solid angle Φ

Angle bin solid angle θ^2

One sees also that the analogy with light applies yet again. Recall that astronomers use the capture area of a telescope to define that instrument's ability to see very faint objects (given that the instrument is operating at the diffraction limit of the lens). Thus for a given brightness of a star (i.e., the power of the signal), it is the aperture of the telescope that is important, or overall the power-aperture of the relationship, that the astronomer is concerned with.

Finally, the SAM radar designer can raise his antenna off the ground on a tall mast, thus reducing the impingement of the sidelobes on the ground, and making them impinge at a greater range. The greater antenna height will also move the radar horizon out to greater distances according to the formula in (4-8). This will increase the area illuminated by the sidelobes in proportion to the square of the distance. However, clutter return is often approximated as decreasing with the eighth power of the distance along the ground from the site, and the net effect of a weaker return from a larger area will be to decrease the clutter. For these reasons surface-to-air missile (SAM) radars are often mounted on tall masts or high on the superstructure of a ship.

420   Other Literature

[1] Stimson, George W. *Introduction to Airborne Radar*. El Segundo, CA: Hughes Aircraft Company, 1983.

[2] Page, Robert Morris. *The Origins of Radar*. Westport, CT: Greenwood Press, 1962.

[3] Barton, David K. *Radar System Analysis*. Norwood, MA: Artech House, 1976.

[4] Skolnix, Merrill I. *Introduction to Radar Systems*. New York, NY: McGraw-Hill, 1962.

[5] Considine, Douglas M., ed. *Van Nostrand's Scientific Encyclopedia*. 7th Edition. New York, NY: Van Nostrand and Reinhold, 1989.

[6] Gilbert, Stephen M. *Tactical Radar Systems Course*. Huntsville, AL: Dynetics, Inc., 1986.

[7] Heilenday, Frank. *Principles of Air Defense and Air Vehicle Penetration*. Rockville, MD: Mercury Press, 1988.

[8] Toomay, John C. *Radar Principles for the Non-Specialist*. Belmont, CA: Lifetime Learning

Publications, 1982.

[9] Olenick, Richard P.; Tom M. Apostol; and David L. Goodstein. *Beyond the Mechanical Universe: From Electricity to Modern Physics*. London, U.K.: Cambridge University Press, 1986.

Sonar Problems

1. Write the passive sonar equation as a product of terms. Use the definition as follows: I_0 is a constant (1 micro-pascal), and I (with a subscript) is a variable equal to acoustic intensity at a given spatial point.

Definition of Terms in the Passive Sonar Equation

L_S	Radiated Signal Level	10 log of I_S @ 1 yard from source / I_0
N_W	Propagation Loss	10 log (I @ 1 yd / I @ R yds from source)
L_N	Omni-Directional Noise	10 log of I_N @ own sonar / I_0
A_G	Array Gain	10 log (*SNR* in array / *SNR* in omni-phone)
N_{DI}	Directivity Index	10 log (I_N in array / I_N in omni-phone)
DT	Detection Threshold	10 log (*SNR* required to detect)
SE	Signal Excess	Provided *SNR* (dB) minus required *SNR* (dB)

2. What is the probability of a passive sonar set detecting a submarine in an interaction where the expected $SE = 2$ dB and $\sigma_{SE} = 6$ dB?

3. Construct a matrix of terms from the sonar equations (rows) and the three different equation types – passive, active-noise limited, active-reverbs limited – as three columns. Fill in typical dB values for sonar terms versus type of sonar interaction.

4. Solve the active reverberation equation limited sonar equation given that R (slant range) is doubled in the sample problem in Section 406. What is the mean SE? What is the probability of detection if $\sigma_{SE} = 10$ dB?

5. Verify the ranges in Figure 4.12. Write new predicted ranges for the spread of $P\{\text{Detection}\}$ values, for the case when $\sigma_{SE} = 10$ dB instead of the value of 6 dB.

6. Do the case 2 problem in Figure 4.3, but substitute aural detection ($DT = -6$ dB) for bearing time recorder (BTR) detection ($DT = -15$ dB). Compare the new sonar setup to the old cases 1 and 2.

7. Do the case 4 problem Figure 4.7, but assume a less powerful active sonar ($L_S = 190$ dB) and a beam aspect submarine ($Nts = 22$ dB). What is the *FOM* and the 50 percent probability detection range?

8. What is the volume V for the problem on three-dimensional reverberations in section 406, assuming $\tau = 250$ milliseconds and $R = 4000$ yards? Calculate V and $Nrs + 10 \log V$ assuming $Nrs = -90$ dB/yards^3.

9. The reverberation level at the receiving sonar is given as
$$L_S - 2N_W + N_{rs} + 10 \log (V) = L_r$$
How does L_r vary with range to target? Choices are R, R^2, R^3, R^{-1}, R^{-2}, R^{-3}, and R^{-4}. Hint: Assume that $2N_W$ increases as R^4.

10. Same question as number 9, but for
$$L_r = L_S - 2N_W + Nrs + 10 \log (A).$$

11. Consider the case of seeking a target by passive means in the Norwegian Sea when the propagation loss curve is as shown in Figure 4.4. The values of the terms in the sonar equation are: $L_S = 130$, $L_N = 60$, $A_G = 10$, $DT = -10$, and $\sigma_{SE} = 7$ dB. What is the probability of detecting the target at a range

a. of 6,000 yards?
b. of 15,000 yards?

12. The situation is a Red sub is closing with a Blue sub in the Norwegian area during the summer. The Blue sub expects to gain initial detection using passive sonar. You must provide detection probabilities and range information assuming the glimpse theory of detection applies. To do this task fill in the values missing in the following table. The value for σ_{SE} in all cases is 8 dB.

Parameter		Case 1	Case 2	Case 3
L_S		128	128	128
L_N		63	63	63
A_G		15	15	15
DT		-10	-10	-10
N_W		___	___	___
$\overline{SE}$		___	0	___
$\Pr\{\text{Det.}\} = \Pr\{SE \geq 0\}$		.2	___	.8
Range (yds)	DB	___	___	___
Norwegian Area	BB	___	___	___
	CZ	___	___	___

Radar Problems

13. Do you agree that radar was the most important technological innovation of World War II? State your reasons for thinking so. How would you rate it with Asdic (sonar) for example and the submarine threat to England's survival during the war? Do you think the assertion that the war could have been won without the atomic bomb but not without radar is the correct way to put the question?

14. If a radar echo returns in 618 μsec, what is the target range?

15. If a radar has a maximum range of 100 nm, what is the maximum PRF (pulse repetition frequency)?

16. Derive the radar range equation in terms of power received at the receiver assuming the same antenna is used for transmitting and receiving. (Hint: You may group the various terms in order of (a) power at a distance r, (b) radar cross section*, (c) power density back at the receiver based on attenuation on the return path, and (d) antenna collection area.)

17. How would you design (what features would you emphasize) a radar to detect a low-observable target (i.e., a weak return signal)?

18. How does a radar determine range? What is the major limitations on radar range for detection against a blue-sky background? What factors are most important in the case of normal sized targets coming over the horizon? What factors are most important in the case of low-observable targets coming over the horizon?

19. Derive an approximate equation for the distance to the radar horizon for a light-frequency radar (ladar) assuming a seven-sixths earth to account for atmospheric refraction of the beam.

20. How must one describe the radar cross section (more properly radar backscatter cross section) of an airborne target?

21. Computer programs may call for the radar line of sight based on an airplane's altitude in meters. How would Equation 4-8 be changed to use the height in meters and still give the range d in nautical miles? Show how your result would work in the case of an aircraft at 10,000 feet.

22. If by clever design and by adding radar absorbing material, it were to be possible to reduce the radar cross section of an air vehicle by a factor of 100, what would be the effect on the maximum range of radar detection? What if the cross section were reduced by a factor of 10,000, what would be the effect on radar range?

23. If radar absorbing material were added to a design that gave a reduction in radar cross section by a factor of 30 dB, what would be a reasonable range reduction to expect in terms of percentage?

24. The radar range equation can be in error by as much as a factor of two in predicting radar range. What factor would that equate to in terms of the power required for a given range? (Express the

answer both in terms of an integer and in terms of decibels.)

25. A SAM radar is mounted on a 120 foot mast so as to extend the radar horizon. The radar has a pulse width (τ) of 25 μsec, and a frequency of 10 GHz. If a prospective target has a true velocity of 500 knots, and the designer designs circuitry to eliminate targets with a radial velocity of less than 100 knots, what will the radar footprint pattern look like? That is, what will be the radius of the radar's dead zone? What will be the range to the radar horizon against a target flying at 300 feet? What will be the angle of the Doppler notch?

Answers to Problems

2. .63

5.

Parameter	Case 1	Case 2	Case 3
N_W	98	88	78
SE	-10	0	10
p Detection probability	.16	.50	.84
	23,000 DP	12,000 DP	5,800 DP
Range (yd)	55,000 BB	No BB	No BB
Icelandic Area	80,000 CZ	No CZ	No CZ
	8,000 DP	6,000 DP	4,500 DP
Range (yd)	41,000 BB	No BB	No BB
Norwegian Sea	130,000 CZ	40,000 CZ	No CZ

11. a. $N_w = 88$, b. $P[SE > 0] = .24$

12.

Parameter	Case 1	Case 2	Case 3
N_W	97	90	83
$\overline{SE}$	-7	0	7
Pr{Det.} = Pr{*SE* ≥ 0}	.2	.5	.8
Range (yds) DP	7,000	6,000	5,000
Norwegian BB	40,000	NA	NA
Area CZ	120,000	50,000	NA

5
CUMULATIVE DETECTION PROBABILITY

Chapter 4 addressed capabilities of a sensor to detect a target *at a fixed point in time* under particular target and environmental conditions. This chapter considers an *aggregate* of such instantaneous detection possibilities and evaluates capabilities over the aggregate by *cumulative* detection probability defined below. Chapters 6, 7, 8, and 9 will be using both instantaneous and cumulative detection probabilities, but primarily the latter.

To be more specific, consider the question: If a sensor searches for a target over a time interval [0, *T*], what is the probability that detection occurs *at least* once? This is called **cumulative detection probability (cdp)**. It is assumed that at each instant between 0 and *T*, detection capability is known. To this must be added knowledge of interdependence of the separate glimpses in order to obtain cdp. To a tactical decision-maker, and consequently to a tactical analyst, cdp is generally of *much* greater importance than instantaneous detection probability. This is also true of analysis for decision making in planning and system procurement which evaluates outcomes in operational situations.

Why is cdp important? Typically a decision-maker for whom a detection effort is made contemplates certain action, possibly offensive, defensive, or intelligence acquisition, once detection occurs. Usually the success of such actions depends on the range to target at detection, and the longer the detection range the better. However, it is usually *crucial* to the decision-maker's objective that this range be *at least* some critical value. For example, in carrier task group air defense, this would be the detection range required in order to intercept a hostile attacker prior to the attacker reaching weapon launch point; then success of the detection system/tactic is measured by the probability of detection at or beyond this critical range, which is a cdp.

This illustration envisions an *absolute* evaluation of cdp, which is needed if it is to be part of a larger analysis that goes beyond the detection phase. However, cdp is also preferable to instantaneous evaluations in *relative* comparisons. It is possible, although not usual, that system/tactic *A* has a higher cdp than system/tactic *B*, whereas *B* has a higher *instantaneous* detection probability than *A* at particular instants or ranges.

It must also be noted that cdp is generally much more difficult to evaluate or estimate than is instantaneous detection probability.

Distinction is made between two sensor types: those which use **discrete glimpses** and those which use **continuous looking**. These terms and **instantaneous detection probability** deserve clarification. In this paragraph, a "detection" is not necessarily an *initial* detection. It is a sensor/-operator indication that a target is present at a particular time instant. In discrete-glimpse search, these or contrary indications occur only at isolated time instants, called **glimpse times**. Examples are active, i.e., pinging, sonar and radar with a rotating antenna. In continuous-looking search they occur at each instant in a substantial time interval. Examples are passive reception of acoustic or electromagnetic signals emitted by a target. In either case, instantaneous detection probability refers to the probability that a target-present indication is correctly made at a particular instant, given the conditions that prevail at that instant and without regard to indications at other instants. There are two caveats: First, in a continuous-looking search, the time interval in question might be divided into relatively short nonoverlapping sub-intervals, ordinarily of uniform length, with the probability of detection during a sub-interval treated as a single-glimpse probability. This sub-interval probability is really a cdp, but because it is relatively short, it might be treated more simply than the general cdp problem. In this approach, the continuous-looking analysis is approximated by a discrete-glimpse analysis. Second, the indication of detection at a given discrete glimpse or instant in continuous looking might be based on "integration" of information received by the sensor in the recent past, as noted in both the sonar and radar parts of Chapter 4. Such integration refers to coherence analysis in the realm of signal processing; it is not to be confused with the cdp problem, which refers to probability of at least one success during several opportunities. The sensor output at a given instant, even when based on integration, is one such opportunity.

After some definitions in 501, discussion of methods of finding cdp begins in 502 in an easy case, where the glimpses are discrete and statistically independent. Unfortunately, inter-glimpse independence is not realistic in most detection situations. A method is needed to avoid the usually spurious assumption of independence. A model given in 503 for this purpose is the (λ, σ), "lambda-sigma," model, to which most of the chapter is devoted. Incorporating interdependence among glimpses necessitates some mathematical complication, but the (λ, σ) method appears to be the best available compromise, within present empirical knowledge, between simplicity and reality. The principal tools for computing cdp under a (λ, σ) model, other than by recursion or simulation, are the "unimodal" formulas. These are given for discrete glimpses in 504 and for continuous looking in 505. Here unimodality refers to detection capability being nondecreasing up to some time point and thereafter being nonincreasing.

A recursive method of computing cdp under (λ, σ), without assuming unimodality, is given in 506. An alternative approach by simulation is also noted.

In 507 an extension of the notion of independent glimpses (502) to independent continuous looking is achieved by the **detection rate** model. Despite the unrealism of independence, this model can be quite useful. For one thing it leads to the very important **random search formula**. Another application of detection rate is the **inverse cube law** of detection , which applies to search from aloft for a planar object on the ocean surface. (This must be distinguished from the inverse cube formula introduced in Chapter 7. That formula is derived from the inverse cube law.)

Some additional cdp methods are outlined in 508. Illustrative numerical examples are given in 509. These examples also afford some comparisons among alternative cdp methods. Some empirical results are reviewed in the literature and history discussion at the end.

501   Basic Definitions

It is assumed that a search is proceeding in time. The search starts at time 0 and might consist of a sequence of discrete glimpses or it might be continuous looking. In continuous looking, the search is conducted throughout the time interval $[0, T]$ and a time instant in that interval is typically denoted by t. In discrete-glimpse search, $n + 1$ glimpses will be assumed to occur at uniform time intervals of length Δ; thus $n\Delta = T$. The uniform separation is merely for notational simplicity; there would be no difficulty in generalizing to nonuniformly spaced glimpses. Thus discrete glimpses will be indexed by $i = 0, \dots , n$, so glimpse i occurs at time $i\Delta$ and is the $(i + 1)$st to occur.

For $0 \le t \le T$, **cumulative detection probability** (cdp) at time t, denoted $F_d(t)$, is defined to be the probability that detection occurs *at least* once during $[0, T]$, i.e.,

$$F_d(t) = \text{Pr}\{\text{at least one detection occurs no later than time } t\}$$
$$= \text{Pr}\{\text{time-to-initial-detection} \le t\}.$$

Under discrete glimpses, the cdp when glimpse i is made is $F_d(i\Delta)$, which will be abbreviated as F_{di}. Thus F_d is the cumulative distribution function (cdf) for the random variable time-to-detection, *providing* F_d approaches 1 as time grows indefinitely; otherwise F_d is a "defective" cdf. Whether or not F_d is defective, the convention is adopted that, as in a cdf, F_d is right continuous, i.e., for any $u > 0$, $F_d(t)$ approaches $F_d(u)$ as t approaches u through values greater than u. This makes the definition of F_d unambiguous at any jump discontinuity — it takes the upper value of the jump.

For $0 \le t \le T$ in continuous-looking search, $p(t)$ will denote the instantaneous probability that the target is detected at time t, not necessarily initially. The sensor might include information acquired before time t as well as information at time t as its basis for indicating at time t that a target is present. E.g., as noted above, the prior information might be used in a coherence analysis typical of signal processing, but the detection indication pertains to the t instant. In discrete-glimpse search, the instantaneous detection probability on glimpse i, $p(i\Delta)$, is abbreviated p_i.

502   Independent Discrete Glimpses

In a discrete-glimpse search suppose that the glimpses are statistically independent of one another. Then the probability of *no* detection by any of these n glimpses, $1 - F_{dn}$, is the probability that *all* glimpses *fail* to detect, i.e.,

$$1 - F_{dn} = \prod_{i=0}^{n}(1 - p_i),$$

so

$$F_{dn} = 1 - \prod_{i=0}^{n}(1 - p_i). \tag{5-1}$$

Unfortunately, more often than not in practice this independence is not realized, unless only widely separated glimpses are considered, in which case much intermediate information may be wasted. If glimpses are close together, then the physical characteristics of the transmission path, sensor, and target vary relatively little from glimpse to glimpse, and one expects the independence assumption to be a poor one.

To illustrate the unrealism of (5-1), consider the following example of a sequence of glimpses, e.g., active sonar pings, taken at short intervals:

i	0	1	2	3	4	5	6	7
p_i:	.15	.18	.23	.28	.33	.38	.39	.40

i	8	9	10	11	12	13	14	
p_i:	.39	.38	.33	.28	.23	.18	.15	

Note that the single-glimpse probabilities rise to a maximum and then decrease as is typical of a target whose range decreases until closest approach is reached (at $i = 7$) and then increases. By applying (5-1) to the first five glimpses, one obtains

$$\begin{aligned}
F_{d4} &= 1 - (1 - .15)(1 - .18)(1 - .23)(1 - .28)(1 - .33) \\
&= 1 - .85 \times .82 \times .77 \times .72 \times .67 \\
&= 1 - .26 \\
&= .74.
\end{aligned}$$

Thus the five single-glimpse probabilities ranging from .15 to .33 combine into a probability of .74 that at least one of the glimpses will succeed. Although it is true that the cdp for the five glimpses is greater than any of the individual p_i's, in reality the increase for sonars, or other sensors, is usually not nearly as great as in this example. To carry this further, if this calculation is made for all 15 glimpses, the result is $F_{d14} = .994$, which seems quite unrealistic. Thus a way must be found to account for inter-glimpse dependence.

503   A Model that Incorporates Sequential Dependence

In order to incorporate sequential dependence, more structure is needed in the model of the detection process. Initially this will be done in terms of $n + 1$ discrete glimpses as before and then the model will be generalized to continuous looking.

The methodology below was developed for sonar detection; it might be adaptable to radar and other types of sensors, although there is much less experience in it outside sonar applications.

Define a "signal excess" process $(S_0, S_1, \ldots, S_n)$. Ordinarily, the units of this process and its additive components are decibels (dB). Each S_i is a random variable. Assume that the sensor "sees" the target on glimpse i if and only if $S_i > 0$. Express S_i as the sum of a deterministic component m_i and a random component D_i:

$$S_i = m_i + D_i, \text{ for } i = 0, \ldots, n.$$

Here m_i is the signal excess on glimpse i resulting from the known causal relationships that bear on the sensor's ability to see the target, e.g., range from sensor to target, target "visibility," sensor operator efficiency, etc. These quantities, which are inputs to the causal estimation of S_i, are in general random, and m_i is the mean of this estimation. The random deviations of S_i from its mean m_i are given by D_i, which is a 0-mean random variable.

To illustrate, suppose each glimpse is an active sonar ping. Then m_i is the value of signal excess on ping i predicted from the values of the terms of the active sonar equation (Chapter 4), each term being predicted separately from known conditions and relations.

It is in a model for the sequence of random variables, i.e., stochastic process, $(D_0, D_1, \ldots, D_n)$ that sequential dependence is incorporated. Specifically, a useful model of this sequence is formed as follows: Suppose events occur in a Poisson process at rate λ per unit time. See Appendix A for details on the Poisson process, but its most important characteristic for this discussion is that the time intervals between events are given by independent draws from an exponential distribution with mean $1/\lambda$ time units. Each time an event occurs, draw a sample value from a fixed normal distribution which has mean zero and standard deviation σ. Let this sample value be the value of the D process until the time of the next event in the Poisson process. Upon that next event a sample value is drawn from the (fixed) normal distribution, independent of previous values. This is the new value of the D process. This model of the D process is called a **(λ, σ)**, i.e., **lambda-sigma**, process; it is characterized, of course, by the two parameters λ and σ.

If t_i is the time of glimpse i, then D_i denotes the value of the D process, modeled as a (λ, σ) process, at time t_i. A particular sampling of the D process, called a "sample path" in stochastic process terminology, is a "step function," illustrated in Figure 5.1. The deviation values could be taken from this sample path at discrete times as shown or they could be taken continuously.

FIGURE 5.1. ILLUSTRATIVE SAMPLE PATH FROM (λ, σ) PROCESS

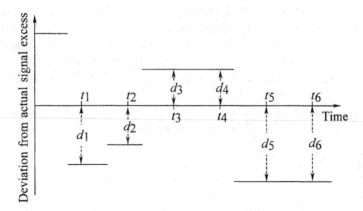

Figure 5.2 illustrates how the (λ, σ) example in Figure 5.1 would apply to detection. Mean signal excess is shown as a continuous curve. The result of adding the step function sample path to the continuous curve is also shown; this represents actual signal excess and must exceed the zero threshold (shown) for detection to occur. Although the actual signal excess does not behave in this fashion, by averaging the effects of the population of such discontinuous curves, it is plausible to obtain realistic cdp's.

FIGURE 5.2. ILLUSTRATIVE MEAN AND ACTUAL SIGNAL EXCESS

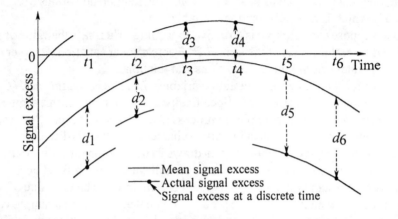

If it were known that, as for t_1 and t_2 in Figure 5.1, t_i and t_j are separated by one or more jump times, then D_i and D_j would be independent of each other. However, absent that knowledge there is a dependence between D_i and D_j which derives from the uncertainty that a jump occurs between them. From the properties of Poisson processes it is known that the probability of no jump event between t_i and t_j is

$$\exp(-\lambda|t_j - t_i|),$$

and it is not hard to show that the correlation coefficient (see Appendix A) between the random variables D_i and D_j is that same quantity. Note that if t_i and t_j are close to each other, then this correlation is close to 1, i.e., D_i and D_j are highly correlated with each other. Also if t_i and t_j become increasingly farther apart, then this correlation decreases toward zero, i.e., toward independence. These observations agree with one's intuition as to appropriate correlation behavior. Note further that $\lambda = \infty$ corresponds to zero correlation, i.e., sequential independence, and $\lambda = 0$ corresponds to complete correlation among the glimpses, i.e., the deviation in one glimpse would be repeated in all of them. The same correlation remarks apply to signal excess.

To extend the foregoing discrete-glimpse discussion to continuous looking, the following definitions are made at time t, $0 \le t \le T$: $S(t)$ is signal excess, $m(t)$ is the mean of $S(t)$, and $D(t)$ is $S(t) - m(t)$, so

$$F_d(T) = \Pr\{S(t) > 0 \text{ for some } t, 0 \le t \le T\}$$
$$= 1 - \Pr\{S(t) \le 0 \text{ for all } t, 0 \le t \le T\}$$
$$1 - \Pr\{D(t) \le -m(t) \text{ for all } t, 0 \le t \le T\},$$
$$p(t) = \Pr\{D(t) > -m(t)\} \text{ for } 0 \le t \le T.$$

The discrete-glimpse discussion then carries over in obvious ways. Note that $p(t)$ is *not* a probability density or a detection rate as defined below in 507; it is a probability.

It is important not to confuse the D process (modeled as a (λ, σ) process) with noise. In effect, prediction of noise is included in the prediction of signal excess, i.e., in m_i. What D_i represents is the deviation between predicted signal excess (noise included) and actual signal excess (noise included). Next the above modeling is applied to computing cdp.

504   Unimodal Formula for cdp (Discrete Glimpses)

A formula will now be given for cdp under the above modeling and discrete-glimpse search, for a case which has rather wide applicability in tactical analysis. In 505 this will carry over to continuous looking. Both these results are given in closed form, in contrast to recursions given in 506 for a broader case.

Recall that the criterion for the sensor being able to detect the target on glimpse i, not necessarily initially, is that

$$m_i + D_i = S_i > 0, \quad \text{equivalently} \quad D_i > -m_i.$$

Thus for detection to occur, the random deviation D_i, modeled as a (λ, σ) process, must exceed a threshold $-m_i$ which is deterministic. Recall that the probability of this event is denoted by p_i, i.e.,

$$p_i = \Pr\{D_i > -m_i\} \quad \text{for} \quad i = 0, \dots, n.$$

Suppose $0 \le i \le j \le n$. A sequence $(x_i, \dots, x_j)$ is called **monotone nondecreasing** if

$$x_i \le x_{i+1} \le \cdots \le x_j.$$

Similarly, $(x_i, \dots, x_j)$ is said to be **monotone nonincreasing** if

$$x_i \ge x_{i+1} \ge \cdots \ge x_j.$$

If there is an index h such that $(x_0, \dots, x_h)$ is monotone nondecreasing and $(x_h, \dots, x_n)$ is monotone nonincreasing, then $(x_0, \dots, x_n)$ is said to be **unimodal.** Note that h need not be unique; any h such that p_h is a maximum of $\{p_0, \dots, p_n\}$ will do. The illustration in Figure 5.2 is an example where $(m_0, \dots, m_n)$ is unimodal, hence so is $(p_0, \dots, p_n)$.

If instantaneous detection probability is non-increasing as range increases (not true of sonar search using convergence zones), this unimodality condition is realized in cases of passing targets, i.e., when a target is on constant course passing a fixed sensor, a moving sensor on constant course is passing a fixed target, or, simply when relative velocity is constant with moving sensor and target. These cases occur frequently in tactical analyses.

Equation (5-3) in Theorem 5.1 given next constitutes the very useful discrete-glimpse unimodal formula for cdp under a (λ, σ) model.

Theorem 5.1. Suppose the search is by discrete glimpses, $(p_0, \dots, p_n)$ is unimodal (equivalently, $(m_0, \dots, m_n)$ is unimodal), $0 \le h \le n, p_h$ is the maximum over $\{p_0, \dots, p_n\}$, and the deviation process $(D_0, D_1, \dots, D_n)$ is modeled as a (λ, σ) process. Then

$$F_{dn} = 1 - \frac{1 - p_h}{1 - a p_h} \prod_{i=0}^{n} (1 - a p_i), \tag{5-2}$$

where $a = 1 - \exp(-\lambda \Delta)$ and Δ is the time between glimpses.

Proof: For $0 \leq j \leq h \leq k \leq n$, let

$$Q_{jk} = \Pr\{\text{no detection occurs on glimpses } j, \ldots, k\}.$$

Obviously the theorem is true if there is only one glimpse, so that $n = h = 0$, i.e., $Q_{hh} = 1 - p_h$. Suppose that $0 \leq j \leq h \leq k \leq n$ and that it has been shown that

$$Q_{jk} = \left[\prod_{i=j}^{h-1} (1 - ap_i) \right] [1 - p_h] \left[\prod_{i=h+1}^{k} (1 - ap_i) \right]. \tag{5-3}$$

The proof will be by induction on k and j. Next it is to be shown that (5-3) still holds if $k < n$ and k is replaced by $k + 1$. It is the case that

$$Q_{j(k+1)} = Q_{jk} \Pr\{D_{k+1} \leq -m_{k+1} \mid D_i \leq -m_i \text{ for } i = j, \ldots, k\}. \tag{5-4}$$

The condition in (5-4) says in particular that $D_k \leq -m_k$. There are two disjoint events: between glimpses k and $k + 1$ at least one jump occurs or no jump occurs. If no jump occurs, and the probability of this event is $1 - a$, then $D_{k+1} = D_k \leq -m_k \leq -m_{k+1}$, by the unimodality assumption, so non-detection on glimpse $k + 1$ is certain. If a jump occurs, and the probability of this is a, the probability of no detection on glimpse $k + 1$ is $1 - p_{k+1}$. Thus

$$Q_{j(k+1)} = Q_{jk}[1 - a + a(1 - p_{k+1})]$$

$$= Q_{jk}(1 - ap_{k+1}).$$

Similar reasoning is used for glimpses prior to h, moving backwards in time, i.e., away from h, *except* that the reasoning might break down where a jump time coincides with a glimpse time. The event that some jump time coincides with some glimpse time has probability 0 and may be ignored. That said, it follows that if $0 < j$, then

$$Q_{(j-1)k} = (1 - ap_{j-1})Q_{jk}.$$

The completion of the proof now follows by induction.

Note that in the foregoing proof, the assumption of normality of the after-jump distribution in the D process is not needed. Any fixed distribution will do, but normality is a natural assumption when the S process has decibel values.

The discrete-glimpse unimodal formula, (5-3), will now be illustrated by some computed examples. For this purpose, illustrative instantaneous detection probabilities in Figure 5.3 are developed first.

In this example suppose that the target is an SSN whose motion relative to the sensor is at 30 knots on a constant relative track, with 20 nm range at the closest point of approach (CPA). Glimpses occur every .1 hour and begin when the target is 21 nm from CPA (29.0 nm from the sensor). Note that mean signal excess is negative throughout, so that if there is no deviation from the mean, the target would never be detected. However, the example assumes $\sigma = 6$ dB.

Single-glimpse detection probabilities are given in the last column and are obtained by using the standardized, cumulative normal distribution evaluated at the value given in the next to last column shown in Figure 5.3. The last column has already been used to illustrate (5-1) for independent glimpses. This yielded the presumably unrealistic values of $F_{d4} = .74$ and $F_{d14} = .994$.

Now suppose deviations from mean signal excess are modeled as a (λ, σ) process with $\lambda = 1$ per hour. Note that $(m_0, \ldots, m_{14})$ is unimodal, so apply the discrete unimodal formula, (5-3). Since $\Delta = .1$ hour,

$$a = 1 - e^{-\lambda\Delta} = 1 - e^{-.1} = .095.$$

Hence the cdp for the first five glimpses is, by (5-2),

$$F_{d4} = 1 - (1 - .33)(1 - .095 \times .15)(1 - .095 \times .18)(1 - .095 \times .23)(1 - .095 \times .28)$$
$$= 1 - .67 \times .986 \times .983 \times .978 \times .973$$
$$= 1 - .62 = .38.$$

Note that the p_h in (5-2) is .33. A similar computation for all 15 glimpses (where $p_h = .4$) yields $F_{d14} = .59$.

FIGURE 5.3. EXAMPLE SINGLE-GLIMPSE DETECTION PROBABILITIES

Target speed relative to sensor = 30 kts.   Range at closest point of approach (CPA) = 20 nm.
Glimpses are every .1 hr, i.e., every 6 min. $\sigma = 6$ dB.

Time (hours)	Glimpse i	Distance to CPA (nm)	Range (nm)	Mean Signal Excess, m_i (dB)	(m_i/σ)	$\Pr\{S_i > 0\}$
0	0	21	29.0	-6.3	-1.05	.15
.1	1	18	26.9	-5.4	-0.90	.18
.2	2	15	25.0	-4.4	-0.73	.23
.3	3	12	23.3	-3.5	-0.58	.28
.4	4	9	21.9	-2.7	-0.45	.33
.5	5	6	20.4	-1.8	-0.30	.38
.6	6	3	20.2	-1.6	-0.27	.39
.7	7	0	20.0	-1.5	-0.25	.40
.8	8	3	20.2	-1.6	-0.27	.39
.9	9	6	20.4	-1.8	-0.30	.38
1.0	10	9	21.9	-2.7	-0.45	.33
1.1	11	12	23.3	-3.5	-0.58	.28
1.2	12	15	25.0	-4.4	-0.73	.23
1.3	13	18	26.9	-5.4	-0.90	.18
1.4	14	21	29.0	-6.3	-1.05	.15

Note that in the formula for F_{d4}, glimpse 4 (maximum p_i) dominates the computation. The influence of the other factors is reduced through the .095 factor. This does not mean that these other glimpses, *taken individually*, have abnormally reduced effectiveness. It merely means that when all five glimpses are considered *in aggregate*, glimpse 4 has the main influence and the other glimpses augment glimpse 4, but the interdependence makes this augmentation substantially less than it would be if the glimpses were independent of each other.

If one repeats the above computations with $\lambda = 2$ per hour, then $a = 1 - \exp(-.2) = .18$, and one obtains $F_{d4} = .43$ and $F_{d14} = .71$ versus .38 and .59 respectively when $\lambda = 1$ per hour.

505   Unimodal Formula for cdp (Continuous Looking)

In this section the main result of the preceding section is extended to continuous looking. The definitions of monotonicity and unimodality carry over to continuous looking in obvious ways.

Equation (5-5) in the following theorem is the cdp formula under unimodal p, continuous looking, and D modeled as a (λ, σ) process.

Theorem 5.2.   Suppose p (equivalently m) is unimodal on $[0, T]$, $0 \le h \le T$, $p(h)$ is the maximum value of p over $[0, T]$, and D is a (λ, σ) process. Then

$$F_d(T) = 1 - (1 - p(h))\exp(-\lambda \int_0^T p(t)dt). \tag{5-5}$$

Outline of a Proof: The idea of this proof is to approximate the continuous-looking search by a sequence of discrete searches. Let the first search have glimpses at times 0, $T/2$, and T. Let the successor to each search be formed by adding glimpses at inter-glimpse mid-points. Let P_k be the cdp of the kth search. Clearly $P_1 \le P_2 \le ... \le F_d(T)$, so the P_k's approach a limit, P_∞, such that $P_\infty \le F_d(T)$. It remains to show that $P_\infty \ge F_d(T)$ and P_∞ is the right side of (5-5). To this end, (5-2) is applied to express $\ln(1 - P_k)$ as the sum of logarithms of the factors of $1 - P_k$. One uses Taylor series approximations and several convergence details to complete the proof.

An alternative (complete) Proof: For a given step function sample path of D, certain jump times will be **counted**. At a given jump time t, the step function has steps on both sides of t. If the step farther from h has value exceeding $-m(t)$, consider t a counted jump time; otherwise, don't count t. (The possibility that a jump occurs at h has probability 0 and will be ignored.) See Figure 5.4.

Let N be the number of counted jumps in $[0, T]$, a random variable. Then no detections occur in $[0, T]$ if and only if (a) there is no detection at time h and (b) $N = 0$. To see this note that if for some t, $D(t) \le -m(t)$, then this inequality remains true as t moves away from h until a jump is encountered, because m is unimodal.

To evaluate $\Pr\{N = 0\}$, note that the occurrence of counted jumps in D is a non-homogeneous, i.e., variable-parameter, Poisson process (see A22 in Appendix A) whose parameter at time t is $\lambda p(t)$ for t in $[0, T]$. Hence

$$E[N] = \int_0^T \lambda p(t)dt,$$

so

$$\Pr\{N = 0\} = \exp(-\int_0^T \lambda p(t)dt).$$

Also, the events (a) and (b) above are independent, hence the product of $1 - p_h$ and the last expression is the probability of no detections in $[0, T]$, which proves the theorem.

FIGURE 5.4. ILLUSTRATION OF COUNTED JUMPS

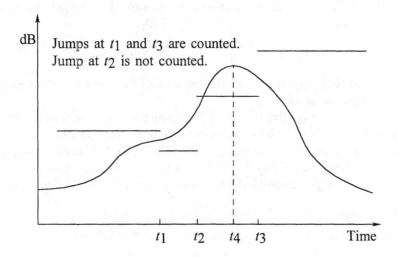

506   A General cdp Algorithm Under (λ, σ)

In this section, a recursive algorithm, Theorem 5.3, is given to compute cdp when the deviation process, D, is modeled as a (λ, σ) process as before. However, here there is no restriction on the instantaneous detection probabilities. Simulation is noted as an additional method of achieving this objective.

Theorem 5.3. Suppose the deviation process D is modeled as a (λ, σ) process. Define
$$H_{ik} = \min\{1 - p_j : i \le j \le k\} \quad \text{for} \quad 0 \le i \le k \le n,$$
for discrete-glimpse search, and for continuous-looking search define
$$H(t, u) = \min\{1 - p(s) : t \le s \le u\} \quad \text{for} \quad 0 \le t \le u \le T.$$
Then for discrete-glimpse search, with $a = 1 - e^{-\lambda\Delta}$,
$$F_{dk} = 1 - (1-a)^k H_{0k} - a\sum_{q=1}^{k} [1 - F_{d(q-1)}]H_{qk}(1-a)^{k-q}, \quad \text{for} \quad 0 \le k \le n, \tag{5-6}$$
and for continuous looking, assuming m is continuous,
$$F_d(t) = 1 - e^{-\lambda t}H(0, t) - \lambda\int_0^t [1 - F_d(s)]H(s, t)e^{-\lambda(t-s)}ds, \quad \text{for} \quad 0 \le t \le T. \tag{5-7}$$

Proof: In (5-6) each term in the summation on q is conditioned on a jump occurring between glimpses $q - 1$ and q, and no jump occurring thereafter, while the first term is conditioned on no jumps anywhere. These terms each contain factors of a and of powers of $1 - a$ that constitute the probabilities of the conditioning events. Also these conditioning events are mutually exclusive, term by term, and exhaust all possibilities of jump time sequences during glimpses 0 to k inclusive. In each term, the remaining factors constitute the probability of non-detection through relevant glimpse intervals given the conditioning on jumps. In each jump-free interval between glimpses q and k inclusive, the probability of non-detection is the lowest single-glimpse probability of non-detection,

H_{qk}; this multiplies the probability of non-detection on the interval between glimpses 0 and $q - 1$ inclusive, because a jump between these two intervals makes them independent.

To prove (5-7), for $i = 1, 2, ...$, approximate the continuous-looking search by a discrete-glimpse search with glimpses at times $0, t/i, 2t/i, ... , it/i = t$. By (5-6),

$$F_d(t) \approx 1 - (1 - \lambda\frac{t}{i})^i H(0, t) - \lambda\frac{t}{i} \sum_{q=1}^{i} [1 - F_d((q-1)\frac{t}{i})]H(q\frac{t}{i}, t)(1 - \lambda\frac{t}{i})^{i-q}. \qquad (5-8)$$

As $i \to \infty$, the right side of (5-8) approaches the right side of (5-7) (various convergence details are omitted). This completes the proof.

For computation of (5-6), note that the only F_d terms on the right side have argument less than k, so one can compute the desired F_{dn} by a straightforward one-dimensional recursion.

An example to illustrate application of (5-6) is given in Figure 5.5. In this example p does *not* satisfy the unimodality condition of 504 and 505 — it falls, then rises. This could occur if, for example, the target opens range from own ship and then closes after the third glimpse.

FIGURE 5.5. EXAMPLE OF cdp UNDER (λ, σ)

This search has five glimpses with single-glimpse probabilities as follows:

	0	1	2	3	4
i:	0	1	2	3	4
p_i:	.3	.2	.1	.4	.6
$1 - p_i$:	.7	.8	.9	.6	.4

The probability of at least one jump during inter-glimpse time Δ is $a = 1 - e^{-\lambda\Delta}$ and is assumed to be .2, so $1 - a = .8$. To apply (5-8), it helps to make a table of H_{ik}, for $0 \le i \le k \le 4$:

Table of H_{ik}

$i = $	$k = $ 0	1	2	3	4
0	.7	.7	.7	.6	.4
1		.8	.8	.6	.4
2			.9	.6	.4
3				.6	.4
4					.4

One may now apply (5-8) to find cdp after each of the five glimpses:

$$F_{d0} = 1 - (1 - a)^0 H_{00}$$
$$= 1 - .7 = .3,$$

$$F_{d1} = 1 - (1 - a)^1 H_{01} - a\{[1 - F_{d0}]H_{11}(1 - a)^0\}$$
$$= 1 - .8 \times .7 - .2 \times .7 \times .8 = 1 - .672 = .328,$$

$$F_{d3} = 1 - (1 - a)^3 H_{03} - a\{[1 - F_{d0}]H_{13}(1 - a)^2 + [1 - F_{d1}]H_{23}(1 - a)^1 + [1 - F_{d2}]H_{33}(1 - a)^0\}$$
$$= 1 - .8^3 \times .6 - .2\{.7 \times .6 \times .8^2 + .672 \times .6 \times .8 + .659 \times .6\} = 1 - .505 = .495,$$

$$F_{d2} = 1 - (1-a)^2 H_{02} - a\{[1 - F_{d0}]H_{12}(1-a)^1 + [1 - F_{d1}]H_{22}(1-a)^0\}$$
$$= 1 - .8^2 \times .7 - .2\{.7 \times .8 \times .8 + .672 \times .9\} = 1 - .659 = .341,$$
$$F_{d4} = 1 - (1-a)^4 H_{04} - a\{[1 - F_{d0}]H_{14}(1-a)^3 + [1 - F_{d1}]H_{24}(1-a)^2$$
$$+ [1 - F_{d2}]H_{34}(1-a)^1 + [1 - F_{d3}]H_{44}(1-a)^0\}$$
$$= 1 - .8^4 \times .4 - .2\{.7 \times .4 \times 8^3 + .672 \times .4 \times .8^2 + .659 \times .4 \times .8 + .505 \times .4\} = 1 - .309 = .691.$$

In the five-glimpse search of Figure 5.5, (5-6) is easily manageable by hand computation. However, notice that to compute F_{dn}, as n increases by 1, so do both the number of terms in the sum on q *and* the number of factors in each term. This has the effect that the length of computation is of the order of n^2, so that computation can become cumbersome. There are algorithms for this problem whose computation length is of order n (see the discussion at the end of the chapter). However, (5-6) itself is easy to program and somewhat easier to understand than the more efficient algorithms. In some important applications, such as computer-assisted search as discussed in Chapter 8, many cdp's must be computed. However, with contemporary microcomputers, computing time will usually not be a difficulty with any of these algorithms.

An additional powerful approach in the absence of unimodality is to *simulate* a (λ, σ) process, especially when cdp computation is part of a larger simulation model. Using methods of Chapter 3 it is easy to simulate the exponential distribution of time between jumps and the normal distribution of the after-jump values. By draws from these distributions, one easily obtains step-functions which are "sample paths" of a (λ, σ) process. By comparing each such step function with the causal m function, one determines whether detection occurs in a given interval of opportunity. By averaging such outcomes over the set of sample paths for the opportunity interval, cdp's are obtained. This approach will work for arbitrary sensor-target capabilities and tracks and propagation behaviors, without assuming unimodality.

507   Independent Continuous Looking – Detection Rate Models

To extend the notion of independent glimpses to continuous looking, it is necessary to give meaning to independence in this situation. This is achieved by the notion of **detection rate**. Suppose that in a continuous-looking search, detections, not necessarily initial detections, occur as a Poisson process that has a variable rate parameter, i.e., is nonhomogeneous; see A22 in Appendix A. Denote the rate parameter at time t by $\gamma(t)$. Then the search is said to have the (variable) **detection rate** $\gamma(t)$ at time t. This implies the following:

(1) For any time t, for small h > 0,
$$\Pr\{\text{at least one detection occurs in } [t, t+h]\} \approx h\gamma(t),$$
and
$$\Pr\{\text{more than one detection occurs in } [t, t+h]\}$$
is negligible compared to $h\gamma(t)$.

(2) Occurrences of detections in nonoverlapping time intervals are independent.
Property (1) is made more precise in A22.

Detection rate cdp formula. A formula for cdp can be derived from these two properties. The probability of *no* detection in $[0, t + h]$ is the product of the probabilities of no detection in $[0, t)$ and in $[t, t + h]$, i.e.,

$$1 - F_d(t + h) \approx [1 - F_d(t)][1 - \gamma(t)h],$$

so

$$\frac{- F_d(t + h) + F_d(t)}{h} \approx - [1 - F_d(t)]\gamma(t).$$

Letting $h \to 0$ (the limit exists because on the right the only dependency on h is via the error terms not shown, which go to zero) and dividing by $1 - F_d(t)$,

$$\frac{- F_d'(t)}{1 - F_d(t)} = - \gamma(t).$$

The prime denotes *right* derivative, in consonance with the convention in 501 that F_d is right continuous. This variables-separable differential equation, with boundary condition $F_d(0) = 0$, has the solution

$$F_d(t) = 1 - \exp(- \int_0^t \gamma(u)du). \tag{5-9}$$

This derivation is given because such differential equation methods have frequent application when modeling by continuous-parameter Markov processes, such as F_d is here. A shorter derivation can be given using, from A22 of Appendix A, facts on a Poisson distribution associated with a variable-rate, i.e., non-homogeneous, Poisson process. One of these facts is of independent interest: The expected number of detections in $[0, t]$, is

$$E[\text{number of detections in } [0, t]] = \int_0^t \gamma(u)du.$$

The difficulties with applying (5-9) are in finding an expression for γ and, as in 502, in the issue of how valid is the independence assumption (2) above. Some special cases of γ are of interest and will be studied in chapter 7. An attempt to determine the probability of detecting an evading target is studied in 705 and results in a model with a detection rate function that varies over time.

Constant detection rate. In this simplest case, $\gamma(t)$ is a constant, γ^*, for t in $[0, T]$, i.e., detection is equally likely to occur at all times t in $[0, T]$ at this same rate. In this case, time-to-initial-detection is an exponentially-distributed random variable and

$$F_d(t) = 1 - e^{-\gamma^* t} \quad \text{for} \quad 0 \le t \le T.$$

Also, as one would expect, if γ^* persists over all future time ($T \to \infty$), then the mean time-to-initial-detection is $1/\gamma^*$, since

$$E[\text{time - to - initial - detection}] = \int_0^\infty t F_d'(t)dt = \int_0^\infty t\gamma^* e^{-\gamma^* t}dt = \frac{1}{\gamma^*}.$$

Random search formula. An application of constant detection rate, which is a convenient and useful approximation encountered in later chapters, is as follows. Suppose one is searching for a target in a region of area A that contains the target, using a sensor which detects the target if and only if the target is within range r of the sensor. Suppose further that (1) the behavior of the searcher is sufficiently random that at each instant, all points in the search region are equally likely to be the point of placement of the sensor and (2) in a short time interval of length Δt the sensor covers an incremental region of area $2rv\Delta t$, so the probability of detection in that interval, given no earlier detection, is $2rv\Delta t/A$. This is an idealization (no sensor behaves that way), but again it leads to a useful approximation to cdp, when sensor movement has speed v and is unsystematic. Then $2rv/A$ may be reasonably said to be a constant detection rate for this situation.

The resulting cdp formula is

$$F_d(t) = 1 - e^{-2rvt/A}, \quad \text{for } t \geq 0. \tag{5-10}$$

Equation (5-10) is the **random search formula**, applications of which will be prominent in Chapters 6, 7, and 8. In the present formulation, no assumption is made on the distribution of target position, whereas most formulations assume that it is uniform.

Inverse cube law of sighting. Another useful example of detection rate occurs when an observer aloft searches visually for a rectangular wake (or other rectangular object) on the ocean surface. The following assumptions are made:

(a) The observer is at height h above the ocean, on which the target is cruising.
(b) The observer detects the target by seeing its wake. (For an airborne visual observer the wake of a moving target is usually more readily sighted than the target itself.)
(c) The instantaneous detection rate, $\gamma(t)$, at time t is proportional area of the wake projected into the plane perpendicular to the line of sight (what may be called the "cross section" of the wake) or equivalently it is proportional to the solid angle subtended at the point of observation of the wake.

The solid angle, shown in Figure 5.6, can be calculated as subtended by a rectangle on the surface with length a toward the observer and width b perpendicular to the direction of observation (perpendicular to the page in Figure 5.6(a)). The small solid angle is the product of the angle α subtended by a, and the angle β subtended by b. The radian measure of α is c/s, where s is slant range. By approximately similar triangles, $c/a \approx h/s$ and hence $\alpha \approx ah/s^2$ and the radian measure of β is b/s. Hence the solid angle, $\alpha\beta$ is abh/s^3, the area of the rectangle times h/s^3. The actual target's wake is not rectangular, but can be regarded as being made up of large numbers of rectangles as in Figure 5.6(b), the solid angle being the sum of the corresponding solid angles. Hence when the dimensions of the rectangle are small in comparison with h, $r(t)$, and s, letting $r(t)$ be the horizontal range at time t to the viewed part of the ocean and w be the area of the wake,

$$\alpha\beta = \frac{wh}{s^3} = \frac{wh}{(h^2 + r(t)^2)^{3/2}} \quad \text{for } t \geq 0.$$

Since $\gamma(t)$ is assumed proportional to the solid angle,

$$\gamma(t) = \frac{kh}{s^3} = \frac{kh}{(h^2 + r(t)^2)^{3/2}}, \quad \text{for } t \geq 0, \tag{5-11}$$

where the constant k depends on all factors that are regarded as fixed and not introduced explicitly, such as contrast of the wake with the ocean, number of lookouts and their facilities, meteorological conditions, etc., and of course k contains w as a factor. Dimensionally, k is in area per unit time. In the majority of cases $r(t)$ is much larger than h and (5-11) can be replaced by the satisfactory approximation

$$\gamma(t) \approx \frac{kh}{r(t)^3}, \quad \text{for } t \geq 0, \quad r(t) >> h. \tag{5-12}$$

The property of detection expressed by (5-11) or (5-12) is called the **inverse cube law of sighting**.

FIGURE 5.6. SOLID ANGLE SUBTENDED BY WAKE

(a) Two dimensional side view

(b) Three dimensional view

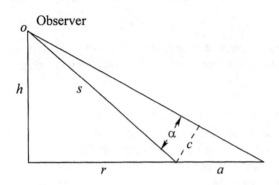

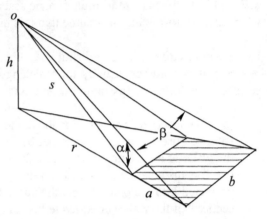

It should be noted that this development results in a law that gives detection rate, which is a *time* rate, in terms of range. Hence, it is useful only when range is known as a function of time. Moreover, the effect on detection capability in a short time increment, which underlies the definition of detection rate and (5-12), can change if a change is made in the function which relates range to time. This impairs the consistency of some applications of the above inverse cube law of sighting and of the detection rate approach in general. The approach can still be useful, but one must at least avoid expressing detection rate as purely dependent on range, when time variation of range is involved.

The following example illustrates this and indicates how cdp may be found when detection rate depends on range under an inverse cube law.

Suppose that at time $t = 0$, a radar site reports an enemy missile 500 nm away and closing on an anti-missile site at a speed of 10,000 knots. In order to counter the attack, acquisition must be accomplished by the site's fire control radar before the range closes to 200 nm. If the detection rate for the fire control radar follows the inverse cube law of sighting with $kh = 10^9$ nm³ and $r(t)$ in nm, then the detection rate at time t is

$$\gamma(t) = \frac{10^9}{r(t)^3} \text{ hr}^{-1}.$$

What is the probability of acquiring the missile in time to counter the attack?

Range can be given by $r(t) = 500 - 10,000t$ nm, where t is in hours, and the detection rate is given by

$$\gamma(t) = \frac{10^9}{(500 - 10,000t)^3} \text{ hr}^{-1},$$

so the probability of acquisition by range 200 nm is equivalent to the probability of acquisition by time .03 hours. This probability can be calculated from (5-9) as follows:

$$F_d(.03) = 1 - \exp\left(-\int_0^{.03} \frac{10^9}{(500 - 10,000\,t)^3}\,dt\right)$$

$$= 1 - e^{-1.05}$$

$$= .65 .$$

508   Some Alternative cdp Methods

Some alternative methods for finding cdp will now be considered, with some comparisons by numerical examples.

One approach to cdp is to introduce an adjustment factor A, $0 < A < 1$, into the independence formula, (5-1):

$$F_{dn} = 1 - \prod_{i=0}^{n} (1 - A\,p_i). \tag{5-13}$$

The factor A reduces cdp below the value obtained under independence and is intended to adjust for sequential correlation. In the absence of an established name for this method it is referred to here as the "adjustment factor" method. Estimation of A might be done by fitting data in one or more combinations of sensor, target, and environment, in hopes that the estimated A will be appropriate for other combinations. Formula (5-13), which does not require unimodality, bears striking resemblance in form to (5-2). The distinction is that (5-13) contains a factor $(1 - A\,p_h)$ in place of $(1 - p_h)$. However, the distinction in substance is much greater than the apparent difference in form as seen in the discussion of the example following Theorem 5.1.

Another cdp method in use is to apply the independence formula, but confine attention to glimpses that are so widely separated that they are deemed to be approximately independent. This time separation is usually called "relaxation time." This has been a fairly frequently used cdp method, at least in ASW modeling. However, it begs the question as to what glimpse separation achieves independence, and it ignores intermediate glimpses. Incidentally the term "relaxation time" is sometimes used for $1/\lambda$ in a (λ,σ) process. That is an unfortunate confusion of terms, since at separation $1/\lambda$ the inter-glimpse correlation is $\exp(-1) = .36$, and that is usually too high for approximate independence to be considered present.

Still another cdp method is to compute cdp separately under assumptions of independence, i.e., formula (5-1), and complete dependence, i.e., $F_{dn} = \max\{p_0, ..., p_n\}$, and use a weighted average of these two as an estimate of cdp. This approximation appears to be too crude to inspire confidence. Its main use has been to estimate the probability that at least one out of k sonobuoys detects (a spatial rather than a temporal cdp), with weight .45 on independence and .55 on dependence, and in that context this approach apparently has done not badly. This is often called the "45-55 rule." The numbers 45 and 55 come from experimentation with sonobuoy data, pertaining to *spatial* cdp. It is emphasized that this approach is not recommended for temporal cdp.

Some numerical comparisons of the (λ, σ), independence, adjustment factor, and relaxation time methods are shown in Figure 5.7. Note that the adjustment factor method with $A = .39$ matches the

$F_{d4} = .38$ obtained by the (λ, σ) method for $\lambda = 1$ per hour; however the resulting comparison of F_{d14}'s is a bad mismatch, .83 versus .59. Similarly with $A = .45$, F_{d4} matches that of (λ, σ) for $\lambda = 2$ per hour, i.e., .43; however this again produces a mismatch in F_{d14}, .87 versus .71.

FIGURE 5.7. ILLUSTRATIVE COMPARISON OF ALTERNATIVE CDP METHODS
Data of Figure 5.3 apply.

cdp Method	F_{d4}	F_{d14}
(λ, σ) method, $\lambda = 1$ / hr	.38	.59
(λ, σ) method, $\lambda = 2$ / hr	.43	.71
Independence method	.74	.94
Adjustment factor method, A = .39	.38	.83
Adjustment factor method, A = .45	.43	.87
Relaxation time method, relaxation time = .6 hrs		.60
Relaxation time method, relaxation time = .4 hrs		.69

A relaxation time of 0.6 hours can be used to obtain $F_{d14} = .60$, approximately that of (λ, σ) with $\lambda = 1$ per hour; the rule here is to apply (5-1) to the best glimpse, glimpse 8, and those removed from it by integral multiples of 0.6 hours, glimpses 2 and 14. One can similarly approximate the $F_{d14} = .71$ using $\lambda = 2$ per hour by a relaxation time of 0.4 hours, using glimpses 8, 4, and 12, to obtain $F_{d14} = .69$. However, this choice of relaxation time suggests that one should extrapolate to include times -.1 and 1.5 (which would be glimpses 0 and 16). That calculation would say that relaxation time 0.4 hours is too short to achieve the approximation. However a longer relaxation time would lead one to extrapolate uncomfortably far into time regions where no search is being conducted. This illustrates some difficulties in using the relaxation time method.

Consider the method of combining the independence estimate, $F_{d(ind)}$, and complete dependence estimate, $F_{d(dep)}$, as a weighted sum:

$$kF_{d(dep)} + (1 - k)F_{d(ind)} \approx F_d.$$

Now $F_{d(dep)}$ is just the maximum single-glimpse probability among those considered, and $F_{d(ind)}$ is given by (5-1). To approximate the results of $\lambda = 1$ per hour, one would need $k = .15$ for F_{d4} and $k = .35$ for F_{d14}; for the result of $\lambda = 2$ per hour, one would need $k = .29$ for F_{d4} and $k = .63$ for F_{d14}.

The above comparisons of alternative methods appear to assume implicitly that the (λ, σ) method is "ground truth," given knowledge of the values of λ and σ. That has by no means been proved. What has been shown is that a choice among these alternative methods does make a material difference in cdp estimation, apart from the problem of estimating the key parameters, i.e., a single choice of A, relaxation time, or k will not produce a consistent approximation to the (λ, σ) results for a given λ.

Because there is an empirical basis, albeit a modest one (see below), for the (λ, σ) model and because of its basic plausibility, it is recommended as the soundest approach to cdp that has yet been found for general tactical analysis, at least in sonar search. It has been frequently used, e.g., in models employed in OPNAV studies and games and Fleet tactical decision aids. It has reasonable motivation insofar as aberrations from causal predictions in environmental impacts, humans, and equipments behave in toto as being fairly constant between random fades and surges. Of course such effects are never precisely step functions.

509   Other Literature and History

It is important to provide one's cdp model with empirical links to reality. Strong empirical bases are not at hand, but more has been done with (λ, σ) methods than with other methods, at least in ASW applications. Some history of cdp methods, both empirical and theoretical contributions, will now be reviewed.

The detection rate method and its by-products, the random search and inverse cube law formulas, all were developed by ORG (see Chapter 1) in World War II and were worked into a coherent theory by B. O. Koopman [1]. Also, the "blip-scan" formula for scanning radar cdp given in [1] is an example of the "adjustment factor " method for cdp noted in 508. The factor p_o in [1], referred to as probability that the radar operator would see a blip if it appeared on a scope, was actually found in practice as a parameter to fit empirical cdp data.

The (λ, σ) process was first used as a tool to find cdp in ASW by J. D. Kettelle [2] in 1960. Kettelle was motivated by reviewing data on propagation loss versus time, at convergence zone range, as found by E. A. Anderson of what is now the Naval Command and Control Ocean Systems Center. Kettelle found fairly constant levels between random fades and surges.

In 1962, R. F. DelSanto and T. G. Bell of what is now the Naval Undersea Warfare Center (NUWC) reported in [3] a good basis for assuming that deviations of actual signal excess from predicted signal excess have a normal distribution and for estimating its mean to be zero and its standard deviation to be 9 dB. They did not address temporal behavior. They examined substantial exercise data on detection of submarines by passive submarine sonars. For each detection, they predicted detection ranges from data known in advance and they estimated the dB adjustment needed to make predicted range agree with actual range. A histogram of these deviations was approximately normal with mean zero and standard deviation 9 dB. Their method is worthy of application to contemporary sonars and exercises.

The 9 dB standard deviation was further supported in the 1960s era by NUWC estimates synthesized from estimates of variability of the separate terms in the sonar equation.

The theory of cdp was investigated extensively in the 1960s, under sponsorship of NUWC and what later became the Naval Air Warfare Center (NAWC) Warminster, reported primarily in Loane et al. [4], Curtis et al. [5], and Arnold et al. [6]. This work was largely on (λ, σ) themes and variations thereon. Chapter 1 of [4] reviews some earlier approaches to cdp by OEG and others, notably a Markov chain approach by Koopman, also explored in Chapter 2 of [4].

The unimodal formula for cdp under (λ, σ) for the case of monotone p with continuous looking was first found by Kettelle [2] in 1960 and proved using a differential equation approach. The unimodal cases, both discrete-glimpse and continuous-looking, as stated in Theorems 5.1 and 5.2, were first found and proved by E. P. Loane [4] in 1964. The evolution of the proof of Theorem 5.1 given in 504 has been influenced mainly by J. D. Kettelle, E. P. Loane, H. R. Richardson, R. B. Parry, and D. H. Wagner. Loane's original proof of Theorem 5.2 used a sequence of discrete-glimpse searches, which approach the continuous-looking search, with application of Theorem 5.1. The alternative and shorter proof given in 505 is due to L. F. Takács (informal communication soon after Loane's proof – see [7]) and to A. R. Washburn (see [8]).

Excellent recursive algorithms for computing cdp under (λ, σ) and discrete glimpses without unimodality were obtained by Loane in 1966 in Appendix A of [5]. His 1966 development began with (5-8), which has computation length of order of n^2, where n is the number of glimpses. He then refined (5-8) to an algorithm of order n, also in [5]. This was improved in 1970 by L. K. Arnold and Loane [9]. A computational improvement was introduced in 1984 by M. E. Grunert and S. J. Benkoski [10]. A simpler statement of the algorithm in [9] is given by Loane in [11]. The first treatment of the non-unimodal problem under continuous looking was by Belkin [7]. He gave a recursive algorithm for cdp when m is a step-function and showed how to approximate cdp for general m through step functions above and below m. The first version of (5-7), i.e., the continuous-looking version of (5-6), is in [7].

Reference [12] is a theoretical investigation by B. J. McCabe and B. Belkin. They explored use of a mixture of a (λ, σ) process and a Gauss-Markov process as a model for D, including each process separately. Analytic computation of cdp under Gauss-Markov can be done only in special cases.

The most extensive empirical investigation ever made of cdp and of (λ, σ) methods in particular, was undertaken in 1969-70 by Commander Submarine Development Two (CSDG-2, now Submarine Development Squadron Twelve), CAPT C. E. Woods, and his Director, Tactical Analysis Group, CDR L. M. Stoehr. This was supported by J. Pulos and G. Elmer of what is now the David Taylor Naval Ship Research and Development Center (DTNSRDC), D. C. Bossard and B. J. McCabe of Daniel H. Wagner, Associates, M. M. Fox of Analysis and Technology, and C. E. Gasteyer of General Dynamics – see [13] and the Elmer article in Volume 2 of [14]. This investigation analyzed data from numerous CSDG-2 submarine ASW exercises in an effort to validate (λ, σ) methods and to estimate λ and σ. The estimation of λ and σ was done jointly with estimation of an additive dB adjustment to figure of merit, which improved the fit but weakened the conclusions. The estimates were made in varied environments; the values which were most generally consistent with the data were $\lambda = 2$ per hour and $\sigma = 9$ dB (the latter as in [3]). Experienced analysts advise that for contemporary passive sonars, lower values of λ and σ are more appropriate. This investigation appeared to confirm the adequacy of (λ, σ) cdp methods for the environments considered, but it cannot be considered a general validation, which indeed would be difficult to achieve.

Various articles relevant to cdp are in [14], which reports a 1975 workshop on the subject at DTNSRDC.

The use of a weighted sum of cdp's under independence and complete dependence assumptions has been primarily to combine single-buoy detection probabilities (each being a temporal cdp) into a field cdp, accounting for spatial buoy-to-buoy dependence. This method originated in [15], where the weights were taken to be equal. G. Marin [16], CNA representative to Commander Patrol Wings Pacific (CPWP), supported the weights .45 and .55 based on analysis of exercise results in [15]. This was for use in the SPAM model for evaluation of sonobuoy fields. In 1977, McCabe [17] investigated for CPWP a more elaborate model, CSPAM, for spatial correlation. He found that the CSPAM results were well approximated by the simpler SPAM, so he recommended continued use of the latter. For more discussion of spatial cdp see [18].

W. Hurley has given a review [19] of various cdp methods.

A workshop [20] at the Surface Warfare Development Group in Little Creek, 19 January 1989, sponsored by the surface ASW desk in OPNAV, was devoted almost half to cdp methods (with emphasis on (λ, σ)).

Radar cdp is a somewhat open question. Reference [21] supports use of what amounts to a relaxation time method applied to single pulses. The methods discussed in this chapter have largely been used in sonar applications. By and large they are plausible for radar applications, but there seems to be a lack of experience to support that. The blip-scan method of radar cdp is no longer in use.

Much of the material in this chapter has been taken from Appendix C of Wagner [22].

[1] Koopman, Bernard O. *Search and Screening*. Operations Evaluation Group Report 56. Washington, DC: Office of the Chief of Naval Operations, 1946.

[2] Kettelle, John D., and Daniel H. Wagner. *Influence of Noise on SSK Effectiveness*. Kettelle & Wagner Report to David Taylor Model Basin, DTIC AD C959083, 31 December 1960.

[3] DelSanto, Ralph F., and Thaddeus G. Bell. *Comparison of Predicted Versus Actual Submarine Sonar Detection Ranges*. New London, CT: Naval Underwater Sound Laboratory Report 544, 1962.

[4] Loane, Edward P.; Henry R. Richardson; and Edward S. Boylan. *Theory of Cumulative Detection Probability*. Paoli, PA: Daniel H. Wagner, Associates Report to Naval Underwater Sound Laboratory, DTIC AD 615497, 10 November 1964.

[5] Curtis, E. Count; Henry R. Richardson; and Edward P. Loane. *Cumulative Detection Probability for Continuous-Parameter Stochastic Processes*. Paoli, PA: Daniel H. Wagner, Associates Report to Naval Air Development Center, DTIC AD 803585, 30 July 1966.

[6] Arnold, Leslie K., and Henry R. Richardson. *Cumulative Detection Probability for Passive Sonobuoy Fields*. Paoli, PA: Daniel H. Wagner, Associates Report to Naval Air Development Center, DTIC AD 829337L, 14 December 1967.

[7] Belkin, Barry. "First Passage to a General Threshold for a Process Corresponding to Sampling at Poisson Times." *Journal of Applied Probability* 8 (1971): 573-578.

[8] Washburn, Alan R. *Search and Detection*. Baltimore, MD: Operations Research Society of America, 1980.

[9] Arnold, Leslie K., and Edward P. Loane. *Cumulative Detection Probability (cdp) for a Step Process*. Paoli, PA: Daniel H. Wagner, Associates Memorandum to Commander Submarine Development Squadron Two, 8 January 1970.

[10] Grunert, Margaret E., and Stanley J. Benkoski. *Modified Version of the cdp Algorithm for a Step Process*. Paoli, PA: Daniel H. Wagner, Associates Memorandum to Commander Patrol Wings, Pacific Fleet, 7 March 1984.

[11] Loane, Edward P. "General cdp Methods Under Lambda-Sigma." Article 2.5, Search, Detection and Tracking Area, *MORS Analysts' Handbook*. Alexandria, VA: Military Operations Research Society, to be published.

[12] McCabe, Bernard J., and Barry Belkin. *A Comparison of Detection Models Used in ASW Operations Analysis*. Paoli, PA: Daniel H. Wagner, Associates Report to the Office of Naval Research, DTIC AD 531985, 31 October 1973.

[13] Stoehr, Leonard M.; Maurice M. Fox, Jr.; Charles E. Gasteyer; David C. Bossard; and Glenn

A. Elmer. "*COMSUBDEVGRU TWO Presentation on cdp Project.*" Proceedings 25th Military Operations Research Symposium, Alexandria, VA: Military Operations Research Society, June 1970.

[14] Naval Ship Research and Development Center. *Proceedings, First Workshop on OR Models of Fluctuations Affecting Passive Sonar Detection.* 19-21 March 1975. Washington, DC: NSRDC Report 76-0063.

[15] COMASWFORPAC. *VASSEL XIII Report.* ser 7/00170, May 1967. (DTIC AD391953L.)

[16] Marin, Gerald. *Modeling Passive Detections by ASW Aircraft.* Arlington, VA: Center for Naval Analyses, CRC 430, 1980.

[17] McCabe, Bernard J. *Comparison of SPAM and CSPAM.* Paoli, PA: Daniel H. Wagner, Associates Memorandum Report to COMPATWINGSPAC, DTIC AD A956319, 30 August 1977.

[18] McCabe, Bernard J. "Spatial-dependence cdp Methods." Article 2.7, Search, Detection and Tracking Area, *MORS Analysts' Handbook.* Alexandria, VA: Military Operations Research Society, to be published.

[19] Hurley, W. J. *An Introduction to the Modeling of Cumulative Probability of Detection in Underwater Acoustics.* Arlington, VA: Center for Naval Analyses Report CRC 395, July 1986.

[20] Commander Surface Warfare Development Group. *Conference on ASW Measures of Effectiveness, Reconstruction and Analysis, and Data Collection.* 18 January 1989 (Presentation slides).

[21] Schlerer, D. Curtis. *Introduction to Electronic Warfare.* Norwood, MA: Artech House, 1960.

[22] Wagner, Daniel H. *Naval Tactical Decision Aids.* Military Operations Research Lecture Notes, NPSOR-01, Monterey, CA: Naval Postgraduate School, 1989.

Problems

1. What is the important difference between cdp and instantaneous detection probability?

2. Suppose a sensor has constant single-glimpse probability .1.

a. What is its cdp for 10 independent glimpses?
b. How many independent glimpses are needed to attain cdp = .99?

3. Show that if a sensor has constant single-glimpse probability p and makes independent glimpses, then the mean number of glimpses to detection is $1/p$.   (Hint: recall that

$$\sum_{n=0}^{\infty} (1-p)^n = \frac{1}{p}, \quad \frac{d}{dp}(1-p)^n = -n(1-p)^{n-1}.)$$

4. What is the purpose of including a (λ, σ) process in a method to compute cdp?

5. What part of a detection process is modeled by a (λ, σ) process?

6. In the example of Figure 5.3, suppose the sonar is effective only on glimpses 5, 6, 7, 8, and 9. What is the cdp for these glimpses under the following assumptions?

a. The (λ, σ) assumptions of Figure 5.3.
b. Independence among glimpses.

7. Suppose a (λ, σ) model is being used for a sonar's detection of a target by discrete glimpses.

a. If $\sigma = 5$ dB, complete the last column of the following table with single-glimpse detection probabilities:

Time (hours)	Glimpse i	mean signal excess, m_i (dB)	Pr{signal excess > 0 on glimpse i}
.1	0	-10.8	
.2	1	-5.4	
.3	2	-3.2	
.4	3	-2.5	
.5	4	-2.8	

b. If $\lambda = 1.5$ jumps per hour, find the probability that the sonar detects the target on at least 1 of the 5 glimpses.

8. A submarine moves at 15 knots directly towards a sonar hydrophone fixed on the ocean floor. The sonar glimpses the submarine once per half-hour. The sonar's capability to detect the submarine is modeled by (1) a time process representing mean signal, (2) a (λ, σ) process representing deviation from the mean signal, and (3) a level that the total signal must exceed for detection to occur. Suppose $\lambda = 2$ jumps per hour, and from other model parameters it has been determined that single-glimpse detection probabilities at various ranges are as follows:

Range (1,000s of yards):	20	35	50	65	80	95
Single-glimpse detection probability:	.90	.80	.65	.45	.15	0

a. What is the probability that the submarine will be detected at or beyond 50 kyds?
b. What would this probability be if the glimpses were independent?

9. In a 4-glimpse search, where D is a (λ, σ) process and $a = .25$, suppose $p_0 = .2$, $p_1 = .3$, $p_2 = .1$, and $p_3 = .3$.

a. Apply Theorem 5.3 to find cdp after each glimpse.

b. Apply Theorem 5.1 to find cdp after the third glimpse and compare to a.
c. Show that for arbitrary a and for $p_0 \le p_1$ and $p_1 \ge p_2$ but otherwise arbitrary, the cdp's for the three glimpses computed by Theorems 5.1 and 5.3 are the same.

10. Suppose a ship is searching visually for a life raft and that at time t, range is $r(t)$ and detection rate is

$$\gamma(t) = \frac{40}{r(t)^3} \; hr^{-1},$$

with t in hours, and $r(t)$ in nm. The ship starts the search at an initial range of 2 nm and approaches the life raft on a direct course at a speed of 10 knots. Answer the following:

a. What are $r(t)$ and $\gamma(t)$?
b. What is the probability that detection will occur before the range decreases to 1 nm?

11. In a continuous-looking problem the maximum range of detection is 200 nm and the target will approach directly at 400 knots. At time t in hours let range be $r(t)$ in nm and detection rate be $\gamma(t)$ = $1000/r(t)$ hr^{-1}.

a. Determine $r(t)$ measured in nm at time t measured in hours.
b. Determine the function γ.
c. Find the probability that detection occurs by the time the range closes to 100 nm.
d. Find the probability density function of time-to-detection and state the times for which it holds.
e. Write an expression which will give mean time-to-detection and evaluate it.
f. Write an expression which (if evaluated) will give the variance of time-to-detection.

12. Two detectors are being considered for installation on a destroyer in order to provide early warning against enemy air targets. The CO desires the device which will detect most targets before they close to 300 nm. The targets are expected to be flying directly towards the destroyer at a speed of 800 knots.

　　Device I is a continuous-looking type, having a maximum range of 400 nm and a detection rate of $(400 - r)/6.25$ detections per hour at range r.

　　Device II is an independent-glimpsing type, having a maximum range of 400 nm, glimpse rate of two glimpses per minute, and a single-glimpse detection probability .2.
Compare the effectiveness of the two detectors and recommend one.

13. If p is a constant, can (5-5) be reformulated in detection rate terms, and why?

Answers to Problems

2. a. .65 b. 44

6. a. .48

7. a. Glimpse probabilities are in order .015, .14, .26, .31, .29. b. .38

8. a. .77 b. .84

9. a. $F_{d0} = .2$, $F_{d1} = .335$, $F_{d2} = .352$, $F_{d3} = .425$. b. Both are .352.

10. a. With t in hrs, $r(t) = 2 - 10t$ nm, $\gamma(t) = 40/(2 - 10t)^3$ hr^{-1}. b. .78

11. a. $r(t) = 200 - 400t$ nm, for $0 \le t \le .5$ hr
b. $\gamma(t) = 1000/(200 - 400t)$ hr^{-1}, for $0 \le t \le .5$ hr
c. .82
d. $f(t) = 5(1 - 2t)^{1.5}/hr$ for $0 \le t \le .5$ hr
e. Letting T = time-to-detection, $E[T] = \int_0^{.5} 5t(1 - 2t)^{1.5} dt = 1/7$ hr
f. Variance of T is $\int_0^{.5}(t - 1/7)^2 5(1 - 2t)^{1.5} dt$ hr^2

12. For device I, $F_d(400$ nm$)$ is .63 and for device II it is .96.

13. Not unless $p(t) = 0$ for all t.

6
LATERAL RANGE CURVES AND SWEEP WIDTH

In searching for targets with any kind of detection device, it will almost always be the case that either the target or the searcher, or both, will be in motion. Detection becomes possible because the relative motion between target and searcher brings them sufficiently close together for detection to occur. If the path of the target relative to the sensor is known and has a model of the detection process, then the cumulative detection probability can be determined. Chapter 4 presented detection models for common sensors, and Chapter 5 presented techniques for converting instantaneous detection probabilities produced by some detection models into an estimate of cumulative probability of detection. In planning and analyzing search operations it is desirable to characterize the capability of the sensors being used in a manner not dependent on knowledge of the relative path of the target.

In this chapter the performance of a sensor will be summarized first by a function called the **lateral range curve**, and its use in analyzing certain phases of a search operation will be presented. A lateral range curve for a sensor-target combination is built on the capability to determine the cumulative detection probability along straight line paths of the target relative to the sensor. The concept of a lateral range curve leads naturally into the concept of **sweep width**. The sweep width of a searcher is a number that gauges its effectiveness under specified environmental conditions against a given class of targets. This measure of effectiveness for a sensor is an important parameter used in planning and analyzing search operations. In Chapter 8, sweep width is seen to be the key parameter characterizing the capability of a sensor when determining the allocation of search effort among different parts of a region being searched.

Lateral range is defined in 601. In 602, a lateral range curve is defined in terms of the cumulative detection probability of a passing target versus the lateral range. Examples illustrate methods for obtaining a lateral range curve by analytic and statistical means. Section 603 addresses the use of a sensor's lateral range curve in determining the probability of detecting a target when the sensor is placed in a channel or choke point. The concept of sweep width is introduced in 604 and then used to simplify the analysis of some of the barrier examples of 603.

601   Lateral Range

Rarely will a target's relative motion bring it directly towards the sensor. Generally, the target moves along a path of relative motion into and through the zone of possible detection. Assume that the target's path of relative motion is a straight line. The distance to the target at its *closest point of approach* (CPA) to the sensor is called **lateral range**. The convention will be followed that lateral ranges on one side of the sensor will have positive values and lateral ranges on the other side will have negative values. In analyzing target detection opportunities lateral range is a random variable and it will be represented by the symbol X. When lateral range takes on a sample value in a specific situation it will typically be denoted by x.

In this chapter the zone of possible detection is assumed to be the region enclosed by a circle centered on the detection device having a radius equal to the maximum possible detection range, r_m. A geographic presentation of the movement situation is shown in Figure 6.1.

FIGURE 6.1. PASSING TARGET'S RELATIVE TRACK

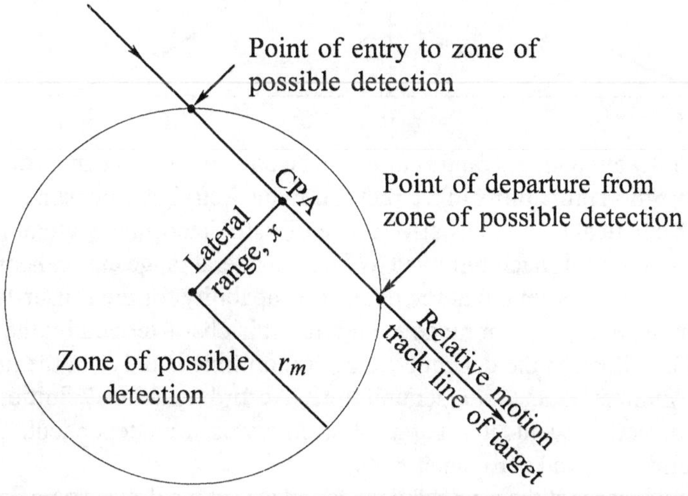

602   Lateral Range Curve

Suppose a target is moving along a line which will cause it to pass at some lateral range x within the detection zone of a particular detection device. The cumulative chance of detecting the target increases from the time the target enters the detection zone until the moment it reaches the point of departure from this zone as illustrated in Figure 6.1. When the target departs the zone of detection all chance (probability) of detecting the target has passed. The cumulative detection probability along a straight line path for which the lateral range is x is denoted by $p_\ell(x)$ and p_ℓ is called the **lateral range function**. The graphical representation of $p_\ell(x)$ for all values of x is known as the **lateral range curve**. Hereafter, the terms "lateral range curve" and "lateral range function" will be used interchangeably. The proper interpretation of the quantity $p_\ell(x)$ is that it is a conditional cumulative detection probability, conditioned on the target's range at CPA being x. A typical lateral range curve is shown in Figure 6.2. For each sensor, set of environmental conditions, and target there exists one lateral range curve. If the detectability of the target changes, for example with changes in the environmental conditions, with the physical aging of a submarine resulting in its becoming noisier, or with the target's speed, then the lateral range function is changed.

FIGURE 6.2. LATERAL RANGE CURVE

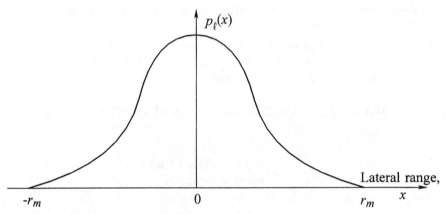

There are several ways a lateral range curve can be constructed. It can be derived theoretically if the cumulative detection probability of a target following a straight line path relative to the sensor can be computed. Statistical techniques also can be used to determine a lateral range curve.

To give an idea of the approach followed to derive a lateral range curve theoretically, a simple situation will be explored. Assume that the detection capability for the sensor-target combination under consideration depends only on range r, and that it is characterized by the detection rate (as defined in 507) $\delta(r)$. Although the dependence of $\delta(r)$ on time is only via the dependence of r on time, its units are in number of detection per unit time. According to the definition of detection rate, the occurrences of detection events in separate short intervals are independent. Also the detection rate is positive when $r \le r_m$, and zero when $r \ge r_m$.

Suppose the sensor is at the origin and the target is moving down a path parallel to the y-axis in the xy-plane at a rate of v distance units per unit time. Let (x, y_0) be the location of the target when it enters the zone of possible detection. It moves with the x value constant and y decreasing, hence

$$r_m = \sqrt{x^2 + y_0^2}.$$

See Figure 6.3. Start the clock when the target enters the zone of detection at the point (x, y_0). The location of the target at time t is $(x, y(t)) = (x, y_0 - vt)$. In this case the detection rate at time t is

$$\gamma(t) = \delta(\sqrt{x^2 + (y_0 - vt)^2}).$$

Then as shown in (5-9) the probability that the target is detected before it reaches the point $(x, y(t))$ is

$$\text{Pr\{detection by time } t\} = F_d(t) = 1 - \exp(-\int_0^t \gamma(u)du).$$

Note that the target reaches its CPA at time $t = y_0/v$ and moves out of the zone of detection at time $t = 2y_0/v$. Thus $p_\ell(x) = F_d(2y_0/v)$.

FIGURE 6.3. TARGET PASSING AT FIXED LATERAL RANGE

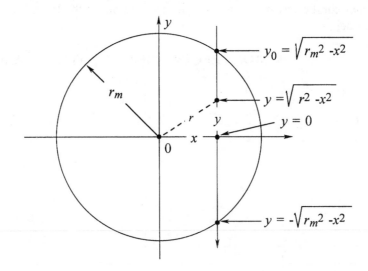

To make the example more concrete, consider the case where the detection rate in the zone of detection is a constant 0.6 detections per unit time and 0 outside the zone of detection. Thus $\delta(r)$ = 0.6 detections per unit time when $r \leq r_m$, hence $\gamma(t) = 0.6$ per unit time for $0 \leq t \leq 2y_0/k$ and

$$p_\ell(x) = F_d\left(\frac{2y_0}{v}\right) = 1 - \exp(-\int_0^{2y_0/v} .6\,dt) = 1 - \exp\left(-\frac{1.2y_0}{v}\right).$$

Since $y_0^2 = r_m^2 - x^2$, substituting in the above expression for $p_\ell(x)$ gives

$$p_\ell(x) = \begin{cases} 1 - \exp(-1.2(\sqrt{(r_m^2 - x^2)}/v), & \text{when } |x| \leq r_m, \\ 0, & \text{otherwise.} \end{cases}$$

Of course, the assumption that the probabilities of detection from one glimpse to the next are independent in determining the cumulative detection probability is unrealistic. A more realistic, but more complex, construction of a lateral range curve can be done, at least for sonar detection, using a signal excess model to predict a sensor's performance, as in Chapter 4, Part A, and the (λ, σ) model as developed in Chapter 5.

Statistical estimates for the lateral range curve may be made if data from trials or exercises are available or can be collected. For example, to approximate the lateral range curve of a sonobuoy for one set of environmental conditions against one class of submarines, trials could be conducted with the submarine making numerous runs past the sonobuoy in various CPA (lateral range) bands on a test range. The number of runs and the number of detections made in each range band are recorded. From these data an unbiased estimate of the probability of detection in each range band is the ratio of the number of detections to the number of runs in the range band. A typical example of this approach is shown in Figure 6.4. These detection probabilities can be graphed as shown in Figure 6.5. If the sonobuoy has a symmetric region of detection about an axis parallel to the runs, then the data can be extended to a symmetric lateral range histogram. A continuous curve may be faired through the lateral range histogram. The resulting graph is an estimate of the lateral range curve. (See Figure 6.6.) This curve depicts the probability that the sonobuoy will detect a submarine of the same class under similar environmental conditions in terms of the lateral range (or CPA) of the relative target track.

FIGURE 6.4. DETECTION FREQUENCIES IN LATERAL RANGE BANDS

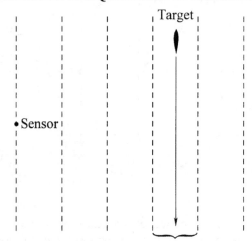

Range band Δr in width

Range band Δr = 5 kyds	# Runs of Target thru Δr	# Det. in band Δr	P_D
0-5	15	15	1.00
5-10	10	8	.80
10-15	12	6	.50
15-20	16	4	.25

Since a lateral range curve represents the cumulative detection probability for a *particular target*, under a *particular set of environmental circumstances*, with a *particular detection device*, a detection device is associated with a family of lateral range curves. This family contains one function for each combination of target type and set of environmental conditions that may be encountered. The dilemma of developing and maintaining a large number of lateral range curves for the large number of detection devices in the fleet (including the eyeball for visual search) against many different targets in a multitude of situations can be partially overcome by grouping targets into basic types (such as small, medium, and large), tactics (shallow or deep), and environmental conditions into categories (such as smooth sea, moderate seas, and high seas), with one lateral range curve representing the average conditions existing within each grouping. Even with such grouping, estimation of such a family of curves requires considerable effort. It will be seen in the following section that it is possible in many situations to replace the problem of working with lateral range curves by carefully choosing a single parameter to represent an entire lateral range curve.

FIGURE 6.5. HISTOGRAM OF DETECTION FREQUENCIES

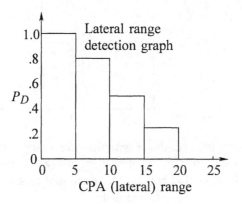

FIGURE 6.6. THE FAIRED LATERAL RANGE CURVE

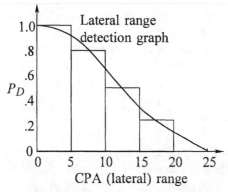

The lateral range curve usually is a symmetric curve about the detection device, from maximum range on one side to maximum range on the other, as in Figure 6.2. One may think of a sensor platform as moving through a region containing potential targets. In this sense, the platform is *sweeping* through the region. This concept may be applied to stationary sensors, such as sonobuoys, where the targets move past it, or where both target and search platform are moving, as is generally the case in naval operations.

It must be re-emphasized that the lateral range function is *neither* a probability density function *nor* a cumulative distribution function. It is a *conditional* cumulative probability function. Using a lateral range function, one may pick any lateral range x and find the probability that a target will be detected at some time if it passes at CPA $= x$ from the sensor. (See Figure 6.7.)

FIGURE 6.7. THE FULL LATERAL RANGE CURVE

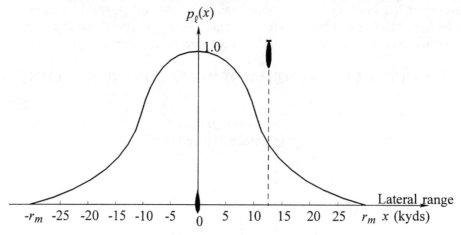

For example, if a searcher is using a sensor with the lateral range curve depicted in Figure 6.7 and a target passes the searcher at a lateral range of 13 kiloyards (kyds), the probability that the target will be detected is $p_\ell(13) = .4$. Note that beyond the maximum range r_m, in this example $r_m = 30$ kyds, the probability that a target will be detected is 0.

603   Detection of Randomly Distributed Targets

Consider the case where either the target or the searcher or both are moving at constant velocity. Further assume all lateral ranges between $-r_m$ and r_m are equally likely. Mathematically, this means that the random variable, X, defined above as the lateral range to this target, has a *uniform probability distribution* over the range of values from $-r_m$ and $+r_m$. It follows (from basic probability theory) that the *probability density function f* of the random variable X is

$$f(x) = \begin{cases} 1/(2r_m), & \text{for } |x| < r_m, \\ 0, & \text{elsewhere.} \end{cases}$$

Recall that $p_\ell(x)$ is the probability of detecting a target which transits *at some specific lateral range x*. If f is the probability density function of X, then the probability of detection is given by

$$\text{Pr\{detection\}} = \int_{-\infty}^{\infty} p_\ell(x) f(x)\, dx.$$

In the above case, where $p_\ell(x) = 0$ if $|x| > r_m$ and between $-r_m$ and $+r_m$, X is uniformly distributed, the probability of detection becomes

$$\text{Pr\{detection\}} = \frac{1}{2r_m} \int_{-r_m}^{r_m} p_\ell(x)\, dx,$$

because $f(x) = 1/(2r_m)$ for $|x| < r_m$. This gives, then, the probability of detection of a target which randomly transits the zone of possible detection, given the path of relative motion is a straight line.

Suppose an SSN conducts a stationary patrol in the center of a barrier of length b, and it is not known what track (lateral range or CPA) a target will have in passing through the barrier. (See Figure 6.8.) It is reasonable to assume that a target is equally likely to come through the barrier at any point along it, thus the target's lateral range or CPA from the SSN will be assumed to be uniformly distributed between $-b/2$ and $b/2$, and f, the probability density function of the target's lateral range, is given by

$$f(x) = \begin{cases} \dfrac{1}{b}, & \text{for } |x| \leq \dfrac{b}{2}, \\ 0, & \text{elsewhere.} \end{cases}$$

FIGURE 6.8. BARRIER LENGTH EXCEEDS TWICE MAX RANGE

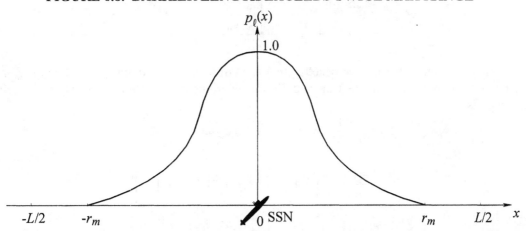

Furthermore, it is assumed the target follows a straight line path, perpendicular to the barrier. One can now compute the probability of detecting the target, henceforth to be denoted by P_d, assuming that the target is equally likely to transit through the barrier starting at any point along the barrier front of length b:

$$P_d = \Pr\{\text{detection}\} = \int_{-\infty}^{\infty} p_\ell(x) f(x) \, dx.$$

Now if $b/2 \geq r_m$, then

$$P_d = \frac{1}{b} \int_{-r_m}^{r_m} p_\ell(x) \, dx.$$

The integrand is zero over the intervals $-\infty$ to $-r_m$ and r_m to ∞. This also is intuitive to the situation, as regions beyond the maximum detection range of the sensor cannot contribute to the probability of detection.

For the specific example, assume that an SSN has a passive sonar with a lateral range function given below and whose graph is shown in Figure 6.9:

$$p_\ell(x) = \begin{cases} 1 - |x|/25, & \text{for } |x| \leq 25, \\ 0, & \text{elsewhere.} \end{cases}$$

FIGURE 6.9. TRIANGULAR LATERAL RANGE CURVE

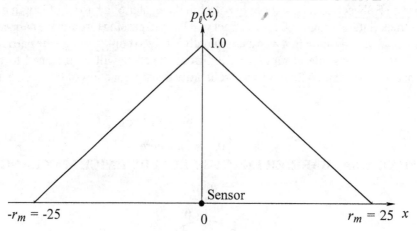

Assume a target takes a track penetrating a front of length $b = 60$ nm centered on the SSN's sonar and the point of crossing the front is uniformly distributed. Then the probability of detecting this target is

$$P_d = \int_{-\infty}^{\infty} \frac{1}{b} p_\ell(x)\, dx = \frac{1}{b} \int_{-r_m}^{r_m} p_\ell(x)\, dx$$

$$= \frac{1}{60} \left[\int_{-25}^{0} \left(1 + \frac{x}{25} \right) dx + \int_{0}^{25} \left(1 - \frac{x}{25} \right) dx \right]$$

$$= \frac{1}{60} \left[x + \frac{x^2}{50} \Big|_{-25}^{0} + \left| x + \frac{x^2}{50} \right|_{0}^{25} \right]$$

$$= \frac{1}{60} [25 - 12.5 + 25 - 12.5] = \frac{25}{60} = .42.$$

Symmetry can often be used to reduce the computational workload of these problems.

Observe the situation of Figure 6.10. Here, several searchers are conducting a search at a distance apart, called the **track spacing**, denoted by s, such that there is no overlap of detection zones, i.e., $s > 2r_m$. If the target is randomly located in the region being searched, what is the probability of detecting a given target as it passes through the line of searchers? In this case let X be the lateral range of the target from the nearest searcher. Then the value of X is uniformly distributed between $-s/2$ and $+s/2$ and over this interval f has the value $1/s$. The probability of detection by one of the searchers would then be

$$P_d = \int_{-s/2}^{s/2} \frac{1}{s} p_\ell(x)\, dx = \frac{1}{s} \int_{-r_m}^{r_m} p_\ell(x)\, dx, \qquad (6\text{-}1)$$

since for all values of x outside of the range of detection $p_\ell(x) = 0$.

Finally, consider the situation where one sensor is being used and the length of the barrier b is less than $2r_m$ so all of the possible target tracks fall *within* the interval $-r_m$ to r_m. Here the expected probability of detection is

$$P_d = \frac{1}{b} \int_{-b/2}^{b/2} p_\ell(x)\, dx.$$

This expression reflects the fact that the detection capabilities of the lateral range curve p_ℓ at points where the target is not going to pass do not make contributions to the probability of detection.

FIGURE 6.10. PARALLEL SEARCHERS

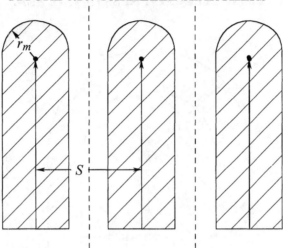

The foregoing methodology easily extends to cases where some lateral ranges are more likely than others, that is, cases were the function f is not the probability density function of a uniformly distributed random lateral range. Problem 6 explores such a case.

604   Sweep Width

It is desirable, where possible, to characterize the complex capability of each detection device (radar, sonar, eyeball, and so on) by a single number that is operationally meaningful. One such quantity might be the maximum detection range. Another might be the range for 50 percent probability of detection. Still another could be that range beyond which as many targets are detected as are missed at lesser ranges. Such a quantity would be useful, for instance, in deciding how far apart searchers may be stationed and still effectively conduct a search. Whatever the quantity used, it must be clearly defined and understood by those who use it.

The most widely used concept to summarize a sensor's capability in search planning is **sweep width**. This concept assumes that as a detection device searches for targets randomly distributed over a region, it *effectively* sweeps out a path of a certain width. For example, in the case resulting in (6-1) the problem is to detect targets which pass within a distance $s/2$ on either side of the sensor. In Figure 6.11 only one of the several searchers is shown, since the situation is the same for each of the others. If all targets within the sweep width were detected and none detected outside, then the probability of detection of a single target would be just the fraction of all targets within the sweep width, which for this case is

$$P_d = \frac{\text{sweep width}}{s}.$$

Using (6-1) it is seen that this probability of detection is

$$P_d = \frac{1}{s}\int_{-r_m}^{r_m} p_\ell(x)\,dx.$$

FIGURE 6.11. EFFECTIVENESS OF ONE SEARCHER

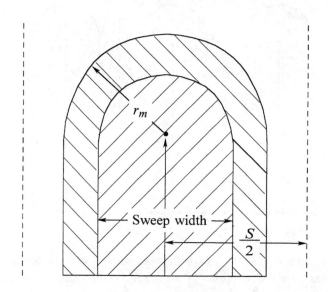

Notice that in this example if merely *the area under the lateral range curve* were known, the probability of detection could be determined without reference to the lateral range curve itself. Search for targets which can be considered to have random locations is a common operational situation and a mathematical fortuity, since it allows one to work with a single quantity, the *area* under the lateral range curve. This quantity, denoted by w, is

$$w = \int_{-r_m}^{r_m} p_\ell(x)\,dx.$$

From (6-1) it can be seen that in a search for a target whose lateral range is uniformly distributed over an interval completely containing the maximum range interval of the search sensor, the probability of detection is directly proportional to the number, w, the area under the lateral range curve. *Hence w is as good a measure of detection capability as the lateral range curve itself.* Therefore, the **sweep width** *is defined to be* equal to the area, w, under the lateral range curve. In essence, this defines an equivalent "cookie cutter" lateral range curve with a base of width w and height 1.0. The symbol w then physically represents the *effective* width of the sensor's detection zone. An alternative interpretation of sweep width is that $w/2$ is the *lateral range beyond which as many targets are detected as are missed at lesser ranges*. This is seen in Figure 6.12. The area of the hatch region is the probability a target passing at a lateral range less than $w/2$ is missed and the area of the shaded region is the probability a target passing at a lateral range greater than $w/2$ is detected. The area of these two regions is the same. (The equivalence between this interpretation of sweep width and the definition given is derived in problem 8 at the end of this chapter.) Although sweep width is defined as an area under a curve it has dimension of distance. The cookie-cutter interpretation implies that the probability of detecting a target with a uniformly distributed lateral range from $-s/2$ to $s/2$ is

$$P_d = \frac{w}{s}.$$

As discussed in Chapter 4, the range usually quoted for a sonar set in an operational situation against a specified target is the range at which there is a 50 percent chance of detection. At this "quoted range" a sonar set has an instantaneous detection probability of 50 percent. Consider the use of the lambda-sigma model (presented in Chapter 5) to determine the cumulative detection probability (cdp) of a target passing by the sonar set. If the lateral range to the target is equal to the 50 percent probability of detection range and the parameter lambda has the value zero, then as many targets will be missed at shorter lateral ranges as are detected at longer lateral ranges. By the equivalent characterization of sweep width given above, the sweep width of a sonar set is equal to twice the 50 percent detection range. Even if the lambda-sigma model is an appropriate way to compute the cdp, it is unlikely that lambda equals zero, but it is likely its value is small. Thus it can be concluded that twice the 50 percent sonar detection range is a useful estimate, but one on the low side, for a sonar set's sweep width.

FIGURE 6.12. STEP-FUNCTION APPROXIMATION TO LATERAL RANGE CURVE

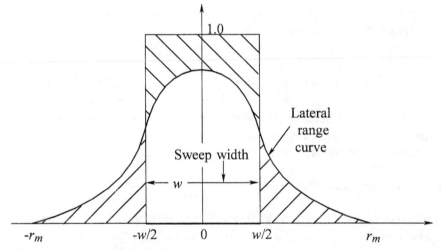

When the mission is to search a *region* for one or more targets, in contrast to a barrier patrol, an appropriate MOE is the product of the sweep width times the search speed. This value (vw, where v is the relative search speed) is called **sweep rate** and it has dimension area per unit of time. Many sensors mounted on a moving platform have their detection effectiveness degraded when the speed of the platform is increased, that is the sweep width is a decreasing function of speed. In such cases sweep rate is a useful measure for analyzing the tradeoff of the impact of increasing the search platform's speed. For instance it has been determined that the most effective speed for a patrol plane conducting a visual search for a small target on the surface of the ocean is below 200 knots.

In the earlier example of an SSN patrolling a barrier of width b where target transits are uniformly distributed along the barrier using sweep width w, the probability of detecting a target becomes simply

$$P_d = \frac{w}{b}, \quad \text{provided that } \frac{b}{2} \geq r_m.$$

It can easily be shown that using sweep width w in the above fashion yields the same answer as when the complete functional form of the lateral range curve is used; that is

$$P_d = \int_{-\infty}^{\infty} f(x) p_\ell(x)\, dx = \frac{1}{b} \int_{-r_m}^{r_m} p_\ell(x)\, dx = \frac{w}{b},$$

provided, of course, that $b \geq 2r_m$.

The SSN stationary barrier example given earlier will be reconsidered from the point of view of sweep width. Recall that the lateral range function defined in that example is

$$p_\ell(x) = \begin{cases} 1 - |x|/25, & \text{for } |x| \leq 25, \\ 0, & \text{elsewhere.} \end{cases}$$

Thus the sweep width is

$$w = \int_{-r_m}^{r_m} p_\ell(x)\, dx = \left[\int_{-25}^{0} \left(1 + \frac{x}{25}\right) dx + \int_{0}^{25} \left(1 - \frac{x}{25}\right) dx \right]$$

$$= (25 - 12.5 + 25 - 12.5) = 25 \text{ nm.}$$

In this example the barrier front is 60 nm wide ($b = 60$) with the SSN more than 25 nm from either edge. So the probability of detecting the target is

$$P_d = \frac{w}{d} = \frac{25}{60} = .42.$$

In actual practice, sweep width w for acoustic detectors usually is determined based on forecasts of sonar range made by a computer, that is fed environmental observations and information about the target. It should be noted that so far only searches in which there is no overlap of detection zones have been discussed. Situations in which searchers are placed more closely together so there are overlapping zones of detection are presented in the next chapter.

605   Other Literature and History

The material in this chapter is largely drawn from B. O. Koopman's World War II classic [1]. Reference [2] is a revised edition of [1]. The book by McCue [3] includes an interesting exposition on the concepts of lateral range curves and sweep width and their use in ASW operations during the campaign against U-boats in World War II. Also he uses sweep rate, sweep width times the speed of the search platform, in his historical analysis of the U-boat campaign.

[1] Koopman, Bernard O. *Search and Screening*. Operations Evaluation Group Report 56, Washington, DC: Office of the Chief of Naval Operations, 1946.
[2] Koopman, Bernard O. *Search and Screening*. New York: Pergamon Press, 1980.

[3] McCue, Brian. *U-Boats in the Bay of Biscay – An Essay in Operations Analysis.*
       Washington, DC: National Defense University Press, 1990.

Problems

1. A target is 20 nm bearing 000 degrees true from the searcher. Target course and speed are 090 degrees true, at 10 knots. The searcher's course and speed are 000 degrees true, at 10 knots.

a. What is the relative speed of the target at times $t = 0$, $t = 3/4$ hours, and $t = 2$ hours?
b. What is the target's direction of relative movement?
c. If the maximum detection range is 20 nm, then how long will the target be in the zone of detection and what is the lateral range?
d. When will the target be at CPA?

2.   The lateral range curve, p_ℓ, for a certain radar is represented by

$$p_\ell(x) = .9\left[1 - \left(\frac{x}{50}\right)^2\right], \quad |x| < 50.$$

a. If targets pass the radar at lateral ranges uniformly distributed between -50 and 50, what is the probability of detecting a given target?
b. If targets pass the radar at lateral ranges uniformly distributed between -100 and 100, what is the probability of detecting a given target?
c. If targets pass the radar at lateral ranges uniformly distributed between -25 and 25, what is the probability of detecting a given target?
d. What is the sweep width of this radar?

3. Answer the questions posed in problem 2 for the following lateral range curve:

$$p_\ell(x) = .8\left(1 - \frac{|x|}{75}\right), \quad |x| < 75.$$

(Note: if the curve is sketched, integration will be unnecessary.)

4. The lateral range curve of a particular radar can be represented by the following figure:

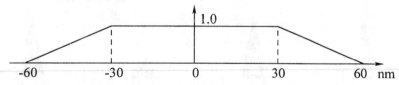

a. What is the maximum range, r_m, of the radar?
b. What is the probability that the radar will detect a target passing at a lateral range of 45 nm?
c. What is the sweep width of the radar?
d. What is the probability of detecting a target that passes in a random manner within 60 nm of the

radar?

e. What is the probability of detecting a target that passes in a random manner between 30 nm and 60 nm of the radar?

f. What is the probability of detecting a target that passes in a random manner within 45 nm of the radar?

5. A radar which is located at the center of a 100 nm wide channel has the following lateral range curve:

$$p_\ell(x) = \begin{cases} .8(1 - |x|/60) & \text{for } |x| \le 60, \\ 0, & \text{elsewhere.} \end{cases}$$

a. What is the probability of detecting a target which passes down the channel at a distance of 10 nm from the edge of the channel?

b. What is the probability of detecting a target which is as likely to transit the channel at one point as any other?

c. If the target has a greater probability of transiting near the center of the channel than near the edges, would you expect the probability of detecting the target to be higher, lower, or the same as in part b?

6. Suppose a target is more likely to transit near the center of the channel than near the edge as indicated by the following probability density function:

$$f(x) = \begin{cases} \dfrac{1}{40} - \dfrac{|x|}{1600}, & \text{for } |x| < 40, \\ 0, & \text{elsewhere.} \end{cases}$$

Using the lateral range curve from problem 5, what is the probability of detecting such a target?

7. A division of destroyers using visual means, is searching in a line abreast for a small life raft. Course is 000 degrees true. The life raft passes between the two easternmost destroyers as shown in the next figure. From the lateral range curve for visual detection of this target under existing conditions, it is determined that destroyers A and B each have a probability of detection of .6, destroyer C has a probability of detection of .1, and destroyer D has a probability of detection of 0. The probability of detection by each destroyer is independent of the others

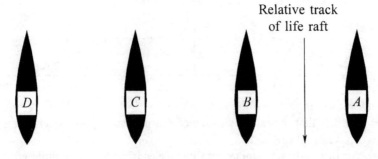

Relative track
of life raft

D   C   B   A

a. What is the probability that the life raft is *not* detected?
b. Compute the probability of detection of the life raft by the division of destroyers.
c. What is the probability that destroyers A, B, and C each detect the life raft?
d. What is the probability that both destroyers A and B, but no others, detect the life raft?

8.   The sweep width, w, can be defined as the quantity such that as many targets are missed at lateral ranges less than $w/2$ as are detected at lateral ranges greater than $w/2$. One hundred targets pass the searcher at lateral ranges uniformly distributed between $-r_m$ and r_m.

a.   Compute the number of targets *missed* which pass at lateral ranges between $-r_0$ and r_0, where r_0 is some range between 0 and r_m.
b.   Compute the number of targets *detected* which pass at lateral ranges between $-r_m$ and $-r_0$ or between r_0 and r_m.
c.   Show that if the answers to (a) and (b) are equal, then

$$r_0 = w/2 = \frac{1}{2} \int_{-r_m}^{r_m} p_\ell(x)\,dx.$$

d.   Show that the definition of w given in this problem is equivalent to that given in the text.

9.   Derive the lateral range curve based on the assumption the inverse cube law of sighting holds when the target is at a range less than the maximum possible range of detection r_m. That is, assume the detection rate model is

$$\gamma(t) = \frac{kh}{[h^2 + r^2(t)]^{3/2}},$$

when the target is in range and the detection rate is 0 otherwise. In developing the lateral range function let x be the lateral range and let the point where the target enters the zone of detection be (x, y_0) and the point at which it leaves the zone of detection be $(x, -y_0)$. The parameters in the detection rate function are
    $k = $ a proportionality constant, $h = $ height, $v = $ relative speed of the target.
After deriving the lateral range function plot it using the following values for the parameters:
    $r_m = 10$ nm, $k = 40$ sq nm, $h = 1$ nm, $v = 10$ kts.
Make a second plot for the case when $h = 0.4$ nm.

10. Use a computer plotting package and plot the lateral range curve derived in 602. That is, plot the function

$$p_\ell(x) = \begin{cases} 1 - \exp(-1.2(\sqrt{(r_m^2 - x^2)}/v)), & \text{when } |x| \le r_m, \\ 0, & \text{otherwise.} \end{cases}$$

a. Do this when $v = 10$ knots and $r_m = 10$ nm and the detection rate is as given in 602.
b. Plot the function with $v = 10$ knots and $r_m = 10$ nm and the detection rate that is (1) half the rate given in 602, and (2) twice the rate given in 602.

Answers to Problems

1. a. 14.14 knots at all times. b. 135°. c. 2 hours. d. 1 hour.

2. a. .6. b. .3. c. .825. d. 60 nm.

3. a. .532. b. .3. c. .67. d. 60 nm.

4. a. 60 nm. b. 0.5. c. $w = 90$ nm. d. $P_d = 3/4$. e. $P_d = 15/30 = .5$. f. $P_d = 82.5/90 = .92$.

5. a. $.8/3 = .27$. b. $(46\ 2/3)/100 = .47$. c. higher.

6. $P_d = .622$.

7. a. .144. b. .856. c. .036. d. .324.

8. Define the events: A = the event the target passes in the interval $(-r_0, r_0)$,
   B = the event the target passes in the intervals $(-r_m, -r_0)$, or (r_0, r_m),
   D = the event that a particular target is detected.

   a. $N(A \cap \text{not } D) = \dfrac{100 r_0}{r_m} - \dfrac{100}{r_m} \int_0^{r_0} p_\ell(x)\, dx.$

   b. $N(B \cap \text{not } D) = \dfrac{100}{r_m} \int_{r_0}^{r_m} p_\ell(x)\, dx.$

7
SEARCH AND PATROL

This chapter develops methods to evaluate search by a patrolling vehicle, which uses its motion to broaden the extent to which its sensor covers the search region. The principal input to these methods is sweep width as developed in the preceding chapter. Also the very important **random search formula** derived in Chapter 5 is applied to evaluating search plans. Chapter 8 continues the analysis of search plans; it addresses the issue of the allocation of search effort over a large region. An important category of search patrols, called **barrier patrols**, will be developed in Chapter 9.

The random search formula is reviewed in 701. It is a generally conservative evaluation of a search patrol, because searchers attempt to be systematic. Random search in strips of the search region is discussed in 702. Section 703 presents a related topic of searching in parallel sweeps. In 704 the **inverse cube law of detection** is presented as a powerful method for estimating the effectiveness of using a string of sensors in detecting a target passing between two of the sensors. The estimate of the probability of detection provided by the inverse cube law of detection is bracketed by using coverage factor as a probability of detection and the value given by the random search formula. For this reason the inverse cube law of detection sometimes is used to give an estimate of the probability of detection in the search of a region that is between the conservative random search formula estimate and the optimistic coverage factor estimate.

Section 705 discusses random search of an expanding region of uncertainty. Emphasis is on the case where the search region is a circular disc of increasing radius.

701   Random Search

Suppose it is known that a target is somewhere in a given region of total area A. For lack of information to the contrary, its position may be assumed throughout the search to be uniformly randomly distributed in A, i.e., as likely to be found in one part of the region as in any other.

Suppose also that the observer searches at speed v through the region and that a systematic search path relative to the target is **not** used. In this random search, what is the probability that detection will occur by time t? As in Chapter 5, call this probability $F_d(t)$. For the case where the sensor detects if and only if the target comes within range r (definite range law), this question is answered by (5-10), which is repeated here:

$$F_d(t) = 1 - e^{-2rvt/A}. \tag{7-1}$$

Now assume, instead of a definite range law, that the sensor's lateral range curve is general. As an analytic device it can be replaced by one that is a step-function whose height is one and whose width is w, its sweep width as presented in Chapter 6. Thus (7-1) becomes

$$F_d(t) = 1 - e^{-wvt/A}. \tag{7-2}$$

In (7-2), the time dependency may be replaced by dependency on track length vt, by denoting the latter by L; also denote the probability by P_d to drop the time dependency. Then

$$\Pr\{\text{detection}\} = P_d = 1 - e^{-wL/A}. \tag{7-3}$$

Formulas (7-1), (7-2), and (7-3) are different forms of the random search formula, of which (7-3) is perhaps the most frequently used form.

It is reiterated for emphasis that this development is based on the following assumptions:

(a) The target's position is (and remains until found) uniformly distributed in A.
(b) The search is conducted in a random manner.

The significance of this model is not that it represents a particular type of operational search, but that it represents a theoretical search in which the least information is known about a target and no systematic search plan is used. Hence, *in the case where more is known about a target and a systematic means of searching is used, an equal amount of search effort should yield a higher probability of detection.* On the other hand, it need not be true that the random search evaluation is the worst the searcher can achieve in a given patrol. For one thing, the derivation in Chapter 5 assumes that search efforts in successive small increments of time are independent of each other, which is optimistic to compute cdp. For another thing, one could do worse by unintelligently incurring unnecessary overlap in the search track. The best comparative statement about the random search evaluation is that it is a *conservative* estimate of success probability, even though that is a somewhat loose statement.

The quantity wL/A in the exponent is called the **coverage factor**. It is the ratio of area swept, i.e., the area which lies within the sweep width, to the total area. This coverage factor then measures the amount of effort spent searching. It may take on values greater than one in a search when multiple coverage of the region is incurred.

Figure 7.1 shows the way in which the probability of detection in a random search increases with the coverage factor. Note that always $wL/A \geq 1 - \exp(-wL/A)$ and for small wL/A, $wL/A \approx 1 -$

exp($-wL/A$) (both statements are seen from $e^x = 1 + x + x^2/2! + ...$). Thus when the coverage factor is small, the probability of detection is approximately equal to the coverage factor itself. When the coverage factor is larger, this probability approaches unity, exhibiting a *saturation* or *diminishing returns* effect, due in part to an increase in overlapping of swept areas. Thus an optimistic appraisal of the probability of detection is provided by the formula

$$P_d = \min\left(\frac{wL}{A}, 1\right).$$

This formula provides an upper bound for the probability of detection, while the random search evaluation is generally conservative and often considered to be a lower bound on the probability of detection for a well conducted search.

FIGURE 7.1. COVERAGE FACTOR AND RANDOM SEARCH ESTIMATES OF DETECTION PROBABILITY

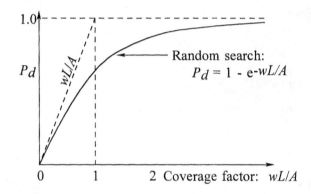

702   Random Search in Strips

It is useful to consider another case of random search in order to see a different aspect of coverage factor. Suppose a rectangular search region is divided into n parallel strips of width s and length b, so that $A = nsb$ (Figure 7.2). Suppose the searcher attempts to cover the region somewhat more uniformly by conducting part of the random search in each strip. An equivalent coverage of the area could be obtained by using n searchers to search the region, every searcher following a path near the center of its strip. In such a search, to be considered in the next section, each observer would patrol a distance b and the total search path length in the region would be nb.

In order that the total search efforts be comparable, let the total search path length for this random search in strips be nb. If the observer spent equal time in each strip, the search path length in each strip would be b, but the path would be random as in Figure 7.2. Now $L = nb$ and $A = nsb$ so that the coverage factor becomes

$$\frac{wL}{A} = \frac{w(nb)}{nsb} = \frac{w}{s},$$

and (7-3) for a random search in strips becomes

$$P_d = 1 - e^{-w/s}. \tag{7-4}$$

As is true for (7-3), this is a generally conservative evaluation of the probability of detecting a target. Random search in strips may cause less overlap in execution, thereby causing the real probability of detection to be greater.

FIGURE 7.2. RANDOM SEARCH IN SEVERAL REGIONS

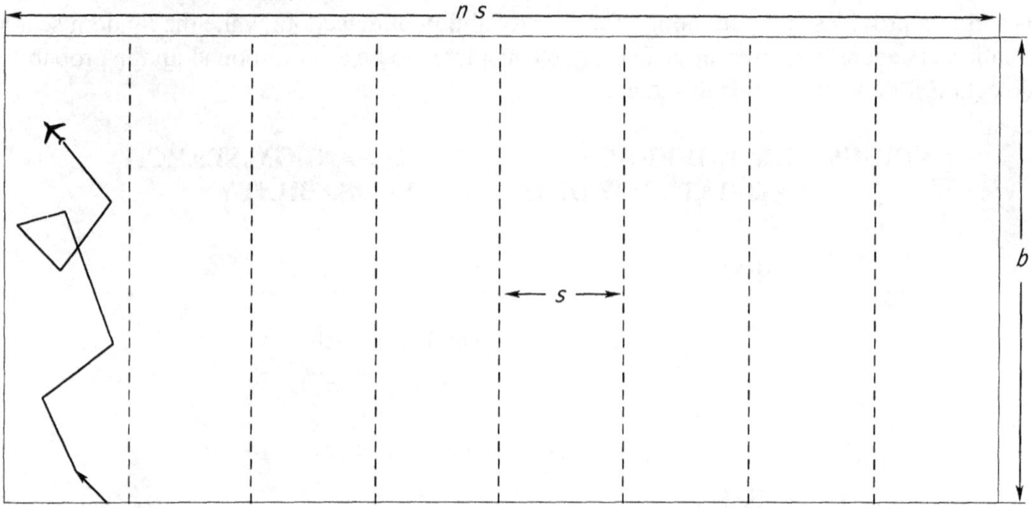

703   Parallel Sweeps

Suppose again a target is known to be located in some particular region of the ocean and is as likely to be in one part as in any other part of that region. A common method of search employed in such a case, in order to cover the region systematically, is known as **parallel sweeps**. Such a search is conducted by several observers searching on parallel tracks through the region, their common distance apart, or track spacing, being s nm.

The objective of this section is to provide a method of arriving at the probability of detection when the lateral range curve of each sensor is known. Below, it is assumed that the separate sensors all have the same lateral range curve (which is easily generalized to a case of different curves) and that they are independent.

Assume the lateral range curve, p_ℓ, for each observer is as given by Figure 7.3, and that several observers are used simultaneously to search the region in Figure 7.2. Each observer covers its strip by patrolling along its center line. The probability of detection when the lateral range curves of adjacent observers do not overlap is given by (6-1).

If the track spacing is less than $2r_m$, then more than one of the sensors may detect the target. Consider the detection potential against targets which come between an adjacent pair of sensors. The probability of detecting a target which passes between the pair is the probability the line of sensors detects the target. Assume, for the moment that a target coming between an adjacent pair of identical sensors is detectable only by that pair, as illustrated in Figure 7.4, i.e, $r_m \leq s \leq 2r_m$. To evaluate the probability of a detection, consider the adjacent pair of sensors to be a composite sensor, and find the composite lateral range curve, p_ℓ^*. In doing this, measure lateral range from the sensor on the left, as shown in Figure 7.4. Then

$$p_\ell^*(x) = 1 - (1 - p_\ell(x))(1 - p_\ell(x - s)), \quad \text{for } 0 \le x \le s$$

provided that the detection probabilities of the two sensors are independent.

FIGURE 7.3. SINGLE SEARCHER LATERAL RANGE CURVE

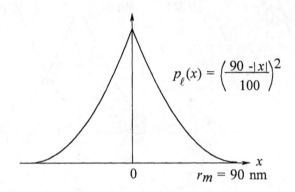

$$p_\ell(x) = \left(\frac{90 - |x|}{100}\right)^2$$

$$0 \qquad r_m = 90 \text{ nm}$$

Let X be the random variable lateral range, measured relative to the sensor on the left, and let f be the probability density function of X. Then detection probability for the pair of sensors, and therefore of the entire sweep, is

$$P_d = \int_0^s p_\ell^*(x) f(x) \, dx. \tag{7-5}$$

FIGURE 7.4. OVERLAPPING ADJACENT SEARCHERS

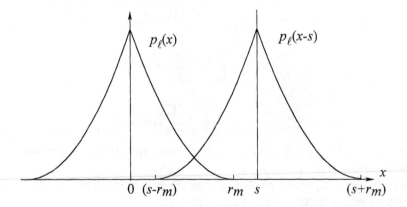

$$p_\ell(x) \qquad p_\ell(x-s)$$

$$0 \ (s-r_m) \qquad r_m \quad s \qquad (s+r_m)$$

For the case where the track spacing, s, is less than r_m, the target could be detected by more than two observers. Let s, for example, be 60 nm so that the overlapping lateral range curves would be as shown in Figure 7.5. Here the tracks for different observers are numbered arbitrarily, and track

1 is used as the reference. Notice that although observers are positioned 60 nm apart, the pattern mirrors itself every 30 nm, and a target 20 nm to the right of track 1 has the same probability of detection as a target 20 nm to the left of track 1, and so on. Every target then will pass within 30 nm of the nearest observer.

FIGURE 7.5. FIVE PARALLEL SEARCHERS

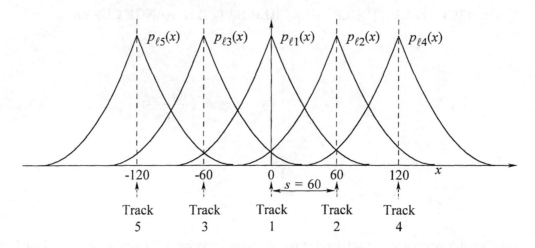

It is easy to extend the case of Figure 7.4 to this situation. For example, if three sensors have overlapping coverage as in Figure 7.5, then the composite lateral range curve is given by

$$p_\ell^*(x) = \begin{cases} 1 - (1 - p_\ell(x))(1 - p_\ell(x-s))(1 - p_\ell(x+s)) & \text{for } 0 \le x \le s/2 = 30 \text{ nm,} \\ 1 - (1 - p_\ell(x))(1 - p_\ell(x-s))(1 - p_\ell(x-2s)) & \text{for } s/2 \le x \le s = 60 \text{ nm.} \end{cases} \quad (7\text{-}6)$$

Now one uses (7-5) as before. Following through on the numerical example with p_ℓ as shown in Figure 7.3 and $s = 60$ nm, by computing (7-5),

$$P_d = \int_{\text{all } x} p_\ell^*(x) f(x) \, dx$$

$$= \int_0^{60} \frac{p_\ell^*(x)}{60} \, dx,$$

$$= 2 \int_0^{30} \frac{p_\ell^*(x)}{60} \, dx,$$

since $f(x) = 1/60$ (X is uniformly distributed between zero and 60) and then by symmetry. Inserting (7-6), the result is $P_d = .68$.

This result may be compared with the previously discussed random search model by computing the single-sensor sweep width:

$$w = \int_{-90}^{90} \left(\frac{90 - |x|}{100} \right)^2 dx = 2 \int_0^{90} \left(\frac{90 - x}{100} \right)^2 dx = 48.6 \text{ nm.}$$

The coverage factor w/s would then be

$$\frac{w}{s} = \frac{48.6}{60} = .81,$$

and so an equivalent search effort as a random search in strips yields a lower, conservative estimate of the probability of detection which is

$$1 - e^{-w/s} = 1 - e^{-.81} = .56,$$

compared with .68 for the systematic coverage given by parallel overlapping sweeps.

The parallel sweep method was developed assuming there are enough observers in a line abreast to cover the area by sweeping through it once. It is assumed the target's location is uniformly distributed over the line between the two sensors it passes between. For a moving target this implies either it is unaware of the searching sensors or it can not maneuver quickly enough to position itself in such a way as to invalidate this assumption. If the target is stationary, then a *single* observer can make successive parallel sweeps through the area at a distance s apart and the same result is obtained. Another equivalent situation occurs when several stationary observers were placed across a channel at a distance s apart to detect transiting targets. Many other types of searches and patrols are nothing more than parallel sweep coverage adapted to a particular situation.

The model developed in this section has led to the computation of the probability of detecting a target passing through a line of sensors at a random point. While this model provides a useful measure of effectiveness in many situations, it is not appropriate in all situations. If, for example, a target has the capability to track the searchers, then it will try to maneuver to avoid detection, and a better measure of effectiveness for the search is the minimum probability of detection. The point to try to cross the line of sensors usually, but not always, is located halfway between adjacent searchers. The best point is the one yielding the minimum value of $p_\ell^*(x)$ in an equation like (7-6).

704   Inverse Cube Law

In the previous section a method for finding the probability of detection with parallel sweeps was demonstrated. In the example, using a particular lateral range curve, the probability of detection, P_d, was found to be .68 for a track spacing, s, of 60 nm. The reader can see that for other lateral range curves and different track spacings the method would be applicable, although graphical approximations or the use of a computer might be necessary to carry through the calculations.

The question arises as to whether the shape of the lateral range curve significantly affects the result. For example, when making parallel sweeps as analyzed in 703 and using a sensor having a lateral range curve with a different shape, but the same sweep width, will P_d still be .68? The answer, for reasonable lateral range curves, is that the result does not differ significantly. It turns out that it is possible to obtain a fair estimate of the probability of detection, using the coverage factor, without knowing the shape of the lateral range curve from which the sweep width was computed. The method of estimating the probability of detection of a target passing between two sensors in a line of identical sensors when only their sweep width is known is called the **inverse cube law** (of detection). It will be given here, but not developed. The probability of detection computed using the inverse cube law is

$$P_d = 2\int_0^z \varphi(t)\,dt, \tag{7-7}$$

where φ is the standardized, normal probability density function with mean zero and variance one, and

$$z = \sqrt{\frac{\pi}{2}\frac{w}{s}} \cong 1.253\frac{w}{s}.$$

(7-8)

Thus this law requires the use of normal probability tables.

To illustrate the use of the inverse cube law recall the example of the previous section, where $w = 48.6$ nm and $s = 60$ nm. Thus

$$z = 1.253\frac{w}{s} = 1.015,$$

and

$$P_d = 2\int_0^{1.015}\varphi(t)\,dt$$

$$= 2(.3449) = .69,$$

which agrees closely with the previously computed value of .68.

Figure 7.6 displays the probability of detection versus coverage factor for the three models presented above in this chapter. In conducting a search of a region the coverage factor itself gives a good estimate of the probability of detection when its value is small or when there is no overlapping of the detection zones of different legs of the search. It is an upper bound on detection probability. The random search model is a generally conservative estimate and is often viewed as a lower bound on the detection probability in a well conducted search of a region. The inverse cube law is a method which is appropriate when multiple search platforms are being used and the target will be forced between two of the search sensors. It also has the attraction of giving an intermediate estimate between the first two estimates. For this reason it often is used to give an estimate of the probability of detection in a search of a region. The coverage factor of the search, wL/A, is used in place of w/s in 7-8.

FIGURE 7.6. COMPARISON OF DETECTION LAWS

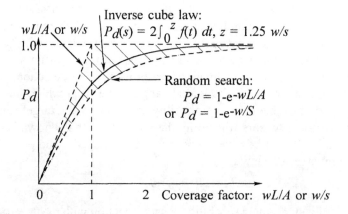

705   Random Search of an Expanding Region (Evading Target)

One form of random search formula gives the probability that the target is detected at least once by time t when the location of the target is uniformly distributed at all time during the search within a *fixed* region of area A. Recall that form

$$F_d(t) = 1 - e^{-wvt/A},$$

and as before, v is the search speed, w is sweep width, and t is the search time. Hence wvt/A is the coverage factor and wv/A is the detection rate which is a constant.

The above formula can be generalized for the case where area of the region changes over time. In this case the probability that the target is detected at least once by time t is

$$F_d(t) = 1 - \exp\left(-\int_0^t \frac{wv}{A(\tau)} d\tau\right), \tag{7-9}$$

where $A(\tau)$ is the area of the region at time τ. This formula is an example of the model given in 507 for a Poisson detection process with the detection rate varying as a function of time. See equation 5-9.

A case which is of particular interest is the case where the region of uncertainty *expands circularly* and target position remains uniformly distributed within the expanding region. If the target's position is assumed *initially* to be uniformly distributed within a circular disc of radius r, and thereafter the target could be *evading* in any direction at a maximum speed u, or could be moving about in some other way, then a reasonable assumption to make about the area of the region containing the target is

$$A(\tau) = \pi(r + u\tau)^2,$$

and

$$\int_0^t \frac{1}{A(\tau)} d\tau = \int_0^t \frac{1}{\pi(r + u\tau)^2} d\tau = \frac{t}{\pi r(r + ut)}.$$

The cumulative detection probability at time t can then be written

$$F_d(t) = 1 - e^{-\gamma(t)}, \tag{7-10}$$

where

$$\gamma(t) = \frac{wvt}{\pi r(r + ut)}. \tag{7-10a}$$

In *prolonged search*, that is as t approaches infinity, the term r inside the parentheses becomes insignificant compared to the term ut, so that:

$$\lim_{t \to \infty} \gamma(t) = \frac{wv}{\pi ru}. \tag{7-10b}$$

Suppose a submarine periscope is sighted and a VP aircraft is sent to datum to conduct a random search. Assume that the submarine can be evading datum at a maximum speed of 10 knots and that the VP aircraft arrives at datum 30 minutes after the submarine was sighted. The VP aircraft conducts a random search about the datum at a speed of 250 knots, and its sweep width is estimated to be 2,000 yards (1 nm).

In this problem, upon commencing search, the target is assumed to be initially uniformly distributed within a circle whose radius is $r = ut_o$, where t_o is the "time late" at datum of the searching aircraft. Therefore, $r = (10 \text{ knots})(.5 \text{ hour}) = 5$ nm. In prolonged search about datum, i.e., no matter how long the VP aircraft conducts a random search about the increasingly expanding region of uncertainty, the probability that the evading submarine will be detected can be computed as (see Figure 7.7)

$$\lim_{t \to \infty} F_d(t) = 1 - e^{-wv/(\pi r u)}$$
$$= 1 - e^{-(1)(250)/(\pi(5)(10))}$$
$$= 1 - e^{-1.59}$$
$$= .80.$$

FIGURE 7.7. DIMINISHING RETURNS

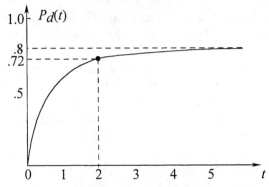

The probability that the aircraft will detect the target within the initial two hours of search time after arrival at the datum region can be computed as:

$$F_d(2) = 1 - e^{-(1)(250)(2)/[\pi 5(5 + (10)(2))]}$$
$$= 1 - e^{-1.27}$$
$$= .72.$$

As can be seen, if the target continues to open (evade) datum as described, the region of uncertainty rapidly becomes very large and, if the target is not detected early, say within the initial two hours after search commences, the chance of detecting the target with continued search effort becomes marginal. By decreasing the variable t_o and calculating the corresponding value of $r = ut_o$, one can readily perceive the importance that time late at datum has in target detection capability.

706   Other Literature and History

The material in this chapter is entirely adapted from B. O. Koopman's World War II classic [1]. It is also found in [2], a later version of [1], somewhat revised. Washburn's book [3] is a outgrowth of his course in Search Theory at the Naval Postgraduate School. It includes coverage of the material presented in this chapter and includes many interesting extensions. Of particular interest are results Washburn reports on man-machine computer games that support the use of the random search formula in naval search operations.

The inverse cube law (of detection) gets its name from the fact that its derivation is based on the inverse cube detection rate model discussed in 507. The derivation, which is lengthy and beyond the scope of this text, may be found in references [1], [2], or [3] with the one in [3] more comprehendible to the reader. It has an excellent development explaining the physical and geometric relationships. (See [3], pp. 2-11 to 2-15.) Many advanced developments in search theory, such as the aggregate effect of sensors search from the same platform and the logic of "forestalling" (counter detection and evasion) are derived under the assumption that the inverse cube law is true or at least "good enough."

[1] Koopman, Bernard O. *Search and Screening*. Operations Evaluation Group Report 56, Washington, DC: Office of the Chief of Naval Operations, 1946.
[2] Koopman, Bernard O. *Search and Screening*. New York, NY: Pergamon Press, 1980.
[3] Washburn, Alan R. *Search and Detection: Second Edition*. Arlington, VA: ORSA Books, 1989.

Problems

1. An aircraft is conducting a completely random visual search over a region of area 20,000 square nm. Assume that the search, which covers a total distance of 800 nm, consists of a total of 20 random legs of equal length. For the prevailing conditions, the visual sweep width of the searching unit is 15 nm.

a. What is the probability of detecting the target on one leg of the search treating each leg as a single glimpse?
b. What is the probability that the target is detected on any of the 20 legs assuming the probability of detection on each leg is independent of the other legs?
c. What is the probability that the target is detected if the random search formula is used?

2. Three aircraft operating independently are assigned to conduct random search sorties in a region 600 nm by 300 nm. The search speed of the aircraft is 180 knots. For the prevailing conditions, the sweep width of the aircraft radar is determined to be 60 nm. Fuel considerations limit the on-station time for each aircraft to 3 hours.

a. What is the probability that the first aircraft detects the target during a single sortie?\
b. If each aircraft flies a single sortie, what is the probability that the target is detected?
c. How many aircraft are required, each flying a single sortie in a completely independent manner, in order to achieve a probability of detection of .9?

3. A parallel-sweep search is to be flown to cover a rectangular region 300 nm by 600 nm. Track spacing, s, for the search will be 60 nm. For the prevailing conditions the sweep width, w, of the aircraft radar is determined to be 60 nm.

a. What total distance is patrolled in the region?

b. Estimate the probability of detection using the random search model.
c. Does the random search model provide an estimate which is too high or too low?
d. What is the coverage factor?

4. An S3 aircraft is assigned to conduct a radar search for a large life raft located somewhere in a region 500 nm by 200 nm in size. Search speed, v, of the aircraft is 150 knots. Under the prevailing conditions and considering the characteristics of the target as well as search altitude, the sweep width of the radar is determined to be 50 nm. Fuel considerations limit the aircraft time on station (in the region) to 4 hours.

a. Using the random search model, compute the probability that the aircraft will detect the life raft in a single sortie.
b. How many aircraft-hours in the area would be required to achieve a probability of detection of .95?
c. What is the expected value of the random variable T which is number of aircraft-hours required in the area to detect the life raft? (Note that $\Pr\{T \le \tau\} = F_d(\tau) = 1 - e^{-wv\tau/A}$.)

5. Suppose six radars are placed across a channel, as shown, to detect targets which are as likely to transit the channel at one point as any other. This situation is similar to a parallel sweep search in which the targets are stationary and each radar moves up the channel.

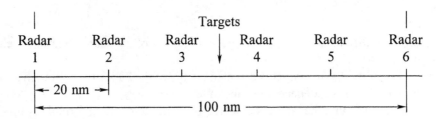

Each radar has the following lateral range curve, p_ℓ, and detects independently of any other radar:

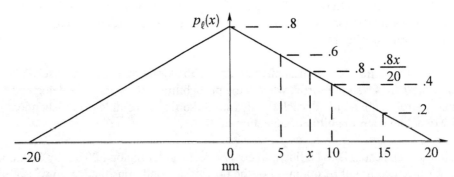

a. What is the probability that a target which transits the channel will be detected:
    (1) at the left edge zero nm from radar number one?
    (2) 5 nm to the right of radar number one?

(3) 10 nm to the right of radar number one?
(4) 15 nm to the right of radar number one?
(5) 20 nm to the right of radar number one?
(6) x nm to the right of radar number one (find the answer in terms of x, where $0 \le x \le 20$)?

b. Could you now easily extend this for a target passing at some other point in the channel?
c. What is the average probability of detecting a target which may pass at any point between zero and 20 nm to the right of radar number one? Would the answer to this question change if radars number two, three, four, or five were substituted for radar number one?
d. What would be the coverage factor?
e. Using the inverse cube law, compute the probability of detection and compare the answer to that for (c).

6. A square region 200 nm by 200 nm is completely searched one time by means of parallel sweeps using a track spacing of 40 nm. Sweep width for this particular search is determined to be 30 nm.

a. Estimate the probability of detecting a randomly located target using the random search model.
b. Using the inverse cube law, compute the probability of detecting the target.
c. What track spacing would be required to produce a probability of detection of .95 (using the inverse cube law)?

7. A Navy oiler supporting an aircraft carrier task force is torpedoed 100 nm offshore from a hostile power. This small belligerent nation purchased several Romeo diesel submarines from the former USSR. The radioman on the oiler reported the crew could see a periscope close by when he made his last distress call. An S3 happens to be 15 minutes away from the sinking oiler. The TACCO considers two options for his attempt to gain detection on the submarine. He could immediately begin a MAD search about the oil slick or he could lay a ring of passive sonobuoys about the slick and drop an active buoy in the slick to drive the submarine through the ring. He estimates that the sub is very unlikely to exceed 12 knots for the first 10 minutes and 8 knots thereafter because it will attempt to return to coastal waters under battery power.

a. What is the probability the MAD search will detect the submarine in an hour of search? The S3 flies at 170 knots during a MAD search. The sweep width of MAD is 200 yards. (Assume one nm = 2000 yards.)
b. What is the probability the submarine will be detected when it penetrates the ring of sonobuoys? The ring will have a radius of 5 nm and 12 buoys will form the ring. The sweep width of the passive buoys is 1 nm.
c. The random search formula for an expanding circle gives a conservative, and hence likely low, estimate of the probability of detection in part a. Can an optimistic or an intermediate case estimate (like the one expected in part b) be found?

Answers to Problems

1. a. .03. b. .46. c. .45.

2. a. .16. b. .42 (assuming each aircraft proceeds independently). c. 13.

3. a. 3,000 nm. b. .63. c. too low. d. one.

4. a. .26. b. 40 hours. c. 13.3 hours.

5. a. (1) .8. (2) .68. (3) .64. (4) .68. (5) .8. (6) $.0016x^2 - .032x + .8$.
   b. yes. c. .693, no. d. .8. e. .683.

6. a. .528. b. .653. c. 19 nm.

7. a. .17. b. .37.

8
COMPUTER-ASSISTED SEARCH

The preceding four chapters addressed successive stages of the search and detection process: Chapter 4, evaluation of naval sensors, given target detectability and position and environmental factors; Chapter 5, cumulative evaluation as sensors are applied over time; Chapter 6, the tactically useful MOE sweep width; and Chapter 7, evaluation of some types of search plans. This chapter discusses methods usable on a desktop computer to present to a search planner a probability map of target position at a user-chosen time. These implementations of search methodology are an important category of tactical decision aids known as **computer-assisted search (CAS)**. CAS programs have been applied with much success in exercises and operations in ASW and in Coast Guard search and rescue.

CAS usually employs methods from all of the preceding four chapters. The principal new methods in this chapter are (a) modeling target motion as a simply-described probabilistic, i.e., **"stochastic" process** (defined below), (b) application of Bayes' theorem from probability theory to account for unsuccessful search, i.e., **"negative information"** (defined below), and optimal allocation of search effort. Both (a) and (b) are important to preparation of a current or future probability map of target position. While the emphasis is on moving targets, the discussion begins with the much easier stationary-target case.

Usually CAS systems are also updated for "positive" information, i.e., information provided by target contacts with uncertain position and credibility, and present a recommended search plan in addition to the descriptive probability maps. Positive information updating is beyond the scope of the present treatment.

The target motion model employed in 803 is sometimes called a **track bundle** approach. This is a Monte Carlo method and has been a much-used approach to motion modeling in CAS systems. Analytic motion models have also been used in CAS, notably Markov chains. Markov chains as such are easily described, but they typically use a very large number of states to model target motion realistically. This poses a computation challenge that can be overcome in a significant class of cases by recursion under Bayesian filtering (not treated here).

To convey some of the basic concepts, section 801 gives an elementary example of search for a *stationary* target. Construction of a prior distribution of target position, Bayesian updating for negative information, and optimal allocation of search effort, based on the Bayesian updating method, are illustrated.

The main elements of a CAS system for a *moving* target are outlined in 802. These are a **prior probability map** of target position; a model of target motion; updates of the probability map for target motion, for negative information (which requires a model of cumulative detection probability), and for positive information; and search plan recommendations.

The usual Monte Carlo approach to CAS is illustrated in 803 by an idealized elementary example in which probabilistic target motion is represented by a bundle of only 16 tracks. The probability of occurrence of each track is derived from simple assumed distributions. The probabilistic behavior is quite visible. Motion updating is done by moving the target along each track according to the effect of that track, without changing track probabilities. Updating for negative information is done by changing track probabilities rather than geographic cell probabilities as in the stationary target case. These are important features of this Monte Carlo approach to CAS.

An algorithm for optimal allocation of search effort in space and time against a moving target is given in 804. It is illustrated by an example, which also shows that it need not be optimal to allocate myopically at each instant, without considering later instants. However, myopic search is usually fairly close to optimal.

801   Stationary Target

This section treats an elementary example of search for a stationary target, to illustrate some basic CAS concepts that are used in planning a search for either moving or stationary targets. The topics illustrated are map discretization, multi-scenario construction of a prior distribution (prior probability map) of target position, Bayesian updating for negative information, and optimal allocation of search effort.

Map discretization. In CAS applications, geographic positions in a search region are always shown by dividing the region into a rectangular array of discrete cells. A simple example of a 3 × 3 array of such cells is shown in Figure 8.1. Here the cells are indexed 1, 2, 3 in latitude and the same in longitude. They could just as well be indexed by mid-latitudes and mid-longitudes of the cells. A CAS program usually chooses cell size, but it is desirable and usual to let the user change this choice. The main factors influencing this choice are accuracies in placement of search effort and in estimation of positional probabilities. It is usually desirable to **smooth** the displayed probabilities in a map that has a realistic number of cells. This might be done by averaging each interior cell with its (pre-smoothing) neighbors, using suitable weights.

Multi-scenario construction of a prior. In Figure 8.1 (a) and (b), two scenarios, I and II, are assumed. Each **scenario** is a postulation as to what caused the target to be wherever it is. Associated with each scenario is a distribution of target position that has been derived from that scenario. Preferably this derivation is based on the information of the scenario as to *causes* of the target position; that is called a **causal** derivation. The distribution is given by assigning a number between 0 and 1 to each cell, with these numbers adding to 1. Each assigned number is the probability, before the search begins, that the target is in that cell, providing that scenario is valid. Also associated with each scenario is a number between 0 and 1 called the **scenario weight**. The scenario weights (here two) also add to 1. Each weight is an estimate of the probability that that scenario is valid. It is usually arrived at by consulting opinions of experts and may be regarded as a "subjective probability."

FIGURE 8.1. MULTI-SCENARIO CONSTRUCTION OF PRIOR DISTRIBUTION OF TARGET POSITION (STATIONARY TARGET)

(a) Scenario I
       Weight = .7

		Longitude Index		
		1	2	3
	1	.1	.3	.0
Latitude Index	2	.3	.3	.0
	3	.0	.0	.0

(b) Scenario II
        Weight = .3

		Longitude Index		
		1	2	3
	1	.00	.00	.00
Latitude Index	2	.00	.25	.25
	3	.00	.25	.25

(c) Composite Scenario

		Longitude Index		
		1	2	3
	1	.070	.210	.000
Latitude Index	2	.210	.285	.075
	3	.000	.075	.075

The composite distribution in Figure 8.1(c) is obtained by combining the single-scenario cell probabilities according to the scenario weights. E.g., the composite for latitude index 2 and longitude index 2 is

$$.3 \times .7 + .25 \times .3 = .285.$$

The distribution is also called the probability map of target position or probability map for short. In particular, it is the prior probability map, further abbreviated as the prior.

FIGURE 8.2. SCORPION SEARCH PRIOR DISTRIBUTION OF TARGET POSITION

NOTE: Shading indicates magnitude as follows: | x | $0 \leq x \leq 10$ | x | $10 < x \leq 100$

* Indicates location of Scorpion. | x | $100 < x \leq 1000$ | x | $1000 < x \leq 10,000$

Convert numbers to probabilities by dividing by 10,000.

Row		A	B	C	D	E	F	G	H	I	J	K	L	M	N	O	P	Q
														5	7	1		
													3	11	14	24	6	
1												5	26	35	22	26	9	1
2											18	46	74	42	18	10	4	2
3									8	60	140	99	45	20	4	2	1	1
4			2	21	137	16	7	1	20	215	239	105	30	5	3	1	1	1
5			18	40	46	747	30	1250	205	571	277	38	5	2	1	1	1	
6		14	326	3	1	28	31	63	*85	62	1	8	7	10	7	3	4	
7	1	359	175	174	1096	282	245	82	71	65	35	27	9	12	6	5	4	
8		24	25	42	82	297	230	129	115	61	33	14	14	10	6	2	5	1
9		17	25	20	20	20	19	55	99	46	30	14	15	3	5	1	6	
10		2	13	14	25	20	24	45	34	27	19	15	5	7	5	5	1	
11			7	13	12	9	1	3	3	11	14	5	4	3	2	1		
12									1	4	4	10	5	4	1			
											1	3	2					
												3	2					

Figure 8.2 presents a real-life prior, from the 1968 *Scorpion* search. It was constructed as a weighted composite of nine single-scenario priors, as above, and of course is much more complicated than Figure 8.1. Among the scenarios were (I) *Scorpion* struck a sea mount and glided to the bottom, and (II) a torpedo turned active in a tube and *Scorpion* was unsuccessful in her maneuver prescribed for that emergency. For each of these and various other scenarios, a position distribution on the ocean bottom was causally derived, and scenario weights were obtained by expert opinion. Figure 8.2 ensued. The remains were found within a submarine length of the highest-

probability cell, after a five-month search. For planning purposes several probability distributions of time-to-detection, measured in search time on the bottom, were derived from this prior using different assumptions regarding such factors as the quality of navigation.   The mean for each distribution was computed. The actual search time of 43 days turned out to be within the interval defined by the computed means, which was 35 to 45 days.

FIGURE 8.3. APPLICATION OF SEARCH EFFORT (STATIONARY TARGET)

		Longitude Index		
		1	2	3
	1	.0	.3	.0
Latitude Index	2	.0	.4	.0
	3	.0	.0	.0

Negative information update. An update for negative information will now be illustrated. Suppose search effort is applied to the 3×3 array of cells resulting in the probabilities of detection shown in Figure 8.3. The detection probabilities given in Figure 8.3 are conditional probabilites, conditioned on the presents of the target in the cell being searched, and are indicative only of quality and amount of search effort, and tell nothing about target location. The latter remains as in Figure 8.1(c).

Suppose this effort is unsuccessful. What is the new, i.e., **posterior**, probability map? It is known that the target is now less likely to be in the cells searched than it was and consequently it is more likely to be in the other cells. That is valuable information and should not be ignored, but how does one adjust the prior probability map accordingly? The answer is to apply Bayes' theorem (see Appendix A). This may be done in spreadsheet fashion as follows (of course, a CAS program would do this for a user):

[1]	[2]	[3]	[4]	[5]=[4]/S
Cell lat/lng index (i,j)	Pre-search (prior) probability target is in (i,j)	Search *failure* probability *if* target is in (i,j)	[2]×[3]	Posterior probability target is in (i,j)
(1,1)	.070	1.0	.070	.085
(1,2)	.210	.7	.147	.179
(1,3)	.000	1.0	.000	.000
(2,1)	.210	1.0	.210	.255
(2,2)	.285	.6	.171	.208
(2,3)	.075	1.0	.075	.091
(3,1)	.000	1.0	.000	.000
(3,2)	.075	1.0	.075	.091
(3,3)	.075	1.0	.075	.091
	1.000		S = .823	1.000

Column [2] is the prior. Column [3] is usually called the **likelihood** of the observed event given the inferred event. Column [4] is proportional to the **posterior** distribution, which reflects real-world observations. Until this information is output to a user, it may be left in this unnormalized form. That is the reason the term "weights" is used. If probabilities are needed column [4] is normalized. This is done by dividing column [4] by its sum, S, resulting in the posterior, column [5]. The posterior is shown geographically in Figure 8.4.

FIGURE 8.4. PROBABILITY MAP UPDATED FOR NEGATIVE INFORMATION

Probabilities that a given cell contains the target given that the effort in Figure 8.3 did not succeed in detection.

		Longitude Index		
		1	2	3
	1	.085	.179	.000
Latitude Index	2	.255	.208	.091
	3	.000	.091	.091

The foregoing implements Bayes' theorem for this application. For cell (i,j) this result is given by the formula

posterior Pr{target in (i,j) | no detection} $=$

$$\frac{\text{Pr\{no detection} \mid \text{target in } (i,j)\} \times \text{prior Pr\{target in } (i,j)\}}{\text{normalizing factor}}.$$

Here the first probability on the right side is the likelihood factor. The normalizing factor (S in the above table) is the probability that the search fails.

Optimal search against stationary target – example. The probabilities in Figure 8.3, and hence those in Figure 8.4, depend on the amount of search effort applied to the various cells. Usually a search planner can choose among various allocations of effort, cell by cell, and would prefer to do so optimally.

To illustrate this, suppose the search is by an aircraft looking for a life raft assumed to be stationary. Suppose the nature of the search is such that the cumulative detection probability through search time t, $F_d(t)$, is given by the random search formula (7-2):

$$F_d(t) = 1 - e^{-wvt/A},$$

where w is sweep width, v is search speed, and A is the area of the cell searched. Assume $w = 30$ nm, $v = 200$ knots, and $A = 20,000$ sq nm. Then

$$F_d(t) = 1 - e^{-.3t}.$$

(It might be that w, and accordingly the coefficient .3 in $F_d(t)$, change from cell to cell, but assume here that they do not.)

Referring to Figure 8.1(c), it is clear that initial effort should be applied to cell (2, 2), since it has the highest probability of containing the target, .285. The question is how long should the search remain in (2, 2) before putting effort into (1, 2) and (2, 1), which have the second highest prior probability of containing the target, .21? One might apply the Bayesian algorithm to find the value of t which drops the posterior probability in (2, 2) to .21. However, that ignores the fact that as the posterior probability falls in (2, 2), it rises in (1, 2) and (2, 1). The solution, of course, is to find the *t* where these falling and rising posterior probabilities meet. Noting that cumulative *failure* probability is $\exp(-.3t)$ and setting the posterior probabilities of cells (2,2) and (1,2) equal to each other gives

$$\frac{.285e^{-.3t}}{S} = \frac{.21}{S}$$

and solving for *t* gives

$$t = \frac{\ln(.21/.285)}{-.3} = 1.02 \text{ hrs.}$$

Thus after 1.02 hours the effort should be divided equally among (2, 2), (1, 2), and (2, 1), since all three have the same probability (which has not been calculated) at that point.

This procedure can be continued until all cells which initially had non-zero probability of containing the target have equal probability, and accordingly, subsequent search is divided equally among them.

Optimal search against stationary target – general algorithm. The foregoing procedure may be restated as an algorithm in more general form as follows.

Let *C* be a finite set of cells, one of which contains the target. An amount of search effort is available, which the searcher may divide among the cells in *C*. Assume exponential effectiveness of search effort in the sense that there is a $\beta > 0$ such that if *z* is an amount of search effort applied to the cell containing the target, then $1 - \exp(-\beta z)$ is the probability that detection results from *z*. (The dimensions of β and *z* must be such that βz is dimensionless.) The initially available effort is fully applied in a sequence of application steps.

An application step begins with the total then-remaining effort *z* and for *c* in *C*, the probability $p(c)$ at that point that *c* contains the target; it may just as well be assumed that $p(c) > 0$, since if $p(c) = 0$, no search effort should be applied to *c*. If when the step begins, all cells have the same *p* value, then divide *z* equally among them. Otherwise choose c_1 and c_2 in *C* such that $p(c_1)$ and $p(c_2)$ are respectively the highest and second-highest (different) values of *p*. Then to every *c* in *C* whose *p* value is $p(c_1)$ apply

$$-\frac{1}{\beta}\ln\left(\frac{p(c_2)}{p(c_1)}\right)$$

amount of search effort, unless this would exhaust *z*, and none to other cells. If exhaustion would occur, then instead divide *z* equally among the cells with probability $p(c_1)$ and the allocation is complete. Whether or not exhaustion occurs, compute

$$S = \sum_{c \text{ in } C} p(c)e^{-\beta x(c)},$$

where for each *c*, $x(c)$ is the effort applied to *c* in this application step. Then *S* is the non-detection probability for this application step. If the target has not been found and effort remains, then $p(c)\exp(-\beta x(c))/S$ is *c*'s containment probability at the start of the next application step (*S* is the normalizing factor). Repeat the procedure until the effort is exhausted. This results in an optimal allocation. The failure probability for the entire procedure is the product of the *S* factors over all the application steps. If the total-procedure failure probability is not needed, there is no need for normalization – numbers proportional to containment probabilities suffice to produce the allocation.

Note that this algorithm is "myopic," i.e., one always searches in the cell(s) of highest current probability. This optimizes the *currently* available effort without regard to what additional effort may become available thereafter. E.g., suppose a planner were initially allowed 4 units of search effort and planned accordingly by the above method. Then suppose the planner is allowed an additional 3 units of effort. Might it then be wished that the first 4 units had been used differently in light of having a total of 7 units available? The answer is no – myopic search is optimal. This statement depends very much on the target being stationary. As will be seen in 804, if the target is moving, myopic search need not be optimal.

802   Principal Requirements for Moving Target CAS

As a lead-in to CAS for *moving* targets, the requirements for such a system and means by which these requirements can be met are noted succinctly.

Prior map. A CAS analysis begins with a prior map (probability map of the target's position). This may be constructed as a weighted sum of single-scenario maps, each derived causally, preferably. Typically it begins with a single report of a target's approximate location at a particular time. Alternatively, it may be derived from historical analysis of past target habits.

Target motion model. Target motion must be described in probabilistic terms. This inevitably means that it is given as a stochastic process. Motion models are illustrated here in a Monte Carlo framework.

Most CAS systems have used Monte Carlo target motion models consisting of a bundle of (typically 500) target tracks, each labeled with the probability that it is (approximately) the actual track. A method is needed for the CAS user to construct this bundle and the associated probabilities from a menu of building blocks and the user's knowledge or assumptions of target behavior. Alternatively, the bundle of tracks may be constructed from historical analysis, and this may be done simultaneously with construction of the prior map. Whether a structure of building blocks with prior assumptions or historical analysis is used, it is usually most efficient to construct the track bundle by random sampling, as described below, after Figure 8.6.

The track probabilities in a Monte Carlo model are converted at any time to geographic cell probabilities by adding for each cell the probabilities of the tracks with positions in that cell.

Updated maps. The main object of CAS is to produce a probability map of target position *at a user-chosen time* and to do so from time to time. To do this, updates are needed for target motion and negative information. CAS systems also update for positive information, i.e., contact reports of uncertain position and credibility, which is not addressed here. When one utilizes positive and negative information jointly to estimate target state, notably position and velocity, one is engaged in **tracking**.

Target motion is updated in track bundle modeling rather simply: The tracks remain fixed, and in motion updating without new information the track probabilities remain fixed. For each track, the target position is simply moved along the track to the position of the chosen time. In the illustration of 803, the track mechanism is deterministic, but in some systems it is probabilistic.

Track speeds as well as courses may differ from track to track. An update for motion under an analytic model follows the mechanism of the model.

Updating for negative information is done by application of Bayes' theorem. In Monte Carlo modeling this is best done by updating the *track* probabilities, and going from there to geographic cell probabilities.

Negative information updating also requires an estimate of the effectiveness of the (unsuccessful) search effort applied. This in turn requires a model of cumulative detection probability (cdp), a subject discussed in Chapter 5.

Optimal search plans. For a CAS system to compute optimal search plans may be considered highly desirable rather than a necessity. If the user is provided with good probability maps, guidance to search planning is at hand – search in the cells of highest detection probability (myopic search). However, it may not be practical to place the next increment of search effort on just the high probability locations, so an optimal practical plan is desired also. It is also often possible to improve significantly on myopic approaches. Most CAS systems provide methods of doing both of these things. The methods include selectively exhaustive examination of a reasonable set of alternatives, optimal placement of a rectangular application of search effort, and more sophisticated algorithms to compute optimal allocation of effort in time as well as space. For the latter, see 804. The theory of optimal allocation of effort is much better developed than the theory of optimal choice of path by which to deliver that effort.

803   Simplified Illustration of Moving Target Monte Carlo CAS

This section illustrates the principal method used in Monte Carlo CAS against moving targets. It does so by a simplified example of target motion, application of which captures the main principles involved. This approach is an excellent example of tactical decision aid modeling in that the modeling ideas and computer implementation are intimately and effectively intertwined. This point applies in particular to updating track weights rather than cell position probabilities, as described below.

Construction of target motion model. Figure 8.5 gives assumptions from which one can quickly build a model of target motion in a simplified search example.

Suppose there are two scenarios, I and II, representing two principal courses of action by the target. These have respective probabilities of occurrence .6 and .4. For each scenario, assumptions are made of target initial position, course, and speed. For each of these there are four possibilities, but for a given scenario only two positions, two courses, and two speeds have non-zero probability. It is assumed here that course and speed remain fixed once chosen. Realistic implementations provide for course changes and much richer distributions of initial course, speed, and position and of scenarios than the two-point distributions assumed here.

Each choice of scenario, initial position, course, and speed, all four being deemed independent, determines a sample target track. There are 16 such tracks and they are tabulated in Figure 8.5 along with probability of occurrence in the last column. For example, the prior probability that track 5 occurs is

$$.6 \times .3 \times .8 \times .4 = .058,$$

as seen from the four two-point distributions. A geographic plot of these 16 tracks is given in Figure 8.6, which identifies the four possible initial positions *A*, *B*, *C*, and *D*. For each start point and course, there is a track for each of two speeds, and these are plotted close to each other as dashed and solid lines. Each track is labeled with probability of occurrence. The 16 tracks together with their probability labels constitute a "stochastic process." This is one type of definition of the stochastic process concept: a probability distribution over a set of "sample paths." In operational CAS systems the bundle would contain 500 or more tracks, each generally having more complexity than the 16 illustrated here. A CAS user usually does not *see* the bundle of tracks, although some systems provide the user an option to view randomly selected tracks to obtain a view of the flow of the problem.

FIGURE 8.5. INPUTS TO TARGET MOTION ILLUSTRATION

| Scenario | | Position at time 0 | | | | Course | | | | Speed (kts) | | | |
#	Probability	A	B	C	D	060T	075T	090T	105T	8	9	10	11
I	.6	.7	.3	*	*	*	.8	*	.2	.4	*	.6	*
II	.4	*	*	.6	.4	.5	*	.5	*	*	.7	*	.3

Track	Scenario	Position at time 0	Course	Speed (knots)	Initial track weight (probability)
1	I	A	075T	8	0.134
2	I	A	075T	10	0.202
3	I	A	105T	8	0.034
4	I	A	105T	10	0.050
5	I	B	075T	8	0.058
6	I	B	075T	10	0.086
7	I	B	105T	8	0.014
8	I	B	105T	10	0.022
9	II	C	060T	9	0.084
10	II	C	060T	11	0.036
11	II	C	090T	9	0.084
12	II	C	090T	11	0.036
13	II	D	060T	9	0.056
14	II	D	060T	11	0.024
15	II	D	090T	9	0.056
16	II	D	090T	11	0.024
					1.000

The user does see on request a probability map pertaining to a given time, e.g., as in Figures 8.7 and 8.8, pertaining to times 0 and 3 hours. The probabilities might be color coded rather than be presented as numbers. To find the probability that the target is in a given cell of a map, the program determines which tracks have the target position in the chosen cell *at the map time* and simply adds the probabilities of those tracks to obtain the cell probability. In Figure 8.7 the prior distribution of the target position is given, taken directly from the scenario weights and initial position distributions of Figure 8.5. In Figure 8.8 the map is derived from moving the target along each track at the speed of that track for 3 hours.

FIGURE 8.6. ILLUSTRATIVE MONTE CARLO TARGET MOTION MODEL

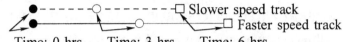

Time: 0 hrs   Time: 3 hrs   Time: 6 hrs

Note: (n, p) means track number n and track probability p.
The tracks from A and B are Scenario I.
The tracks from C and D are Scenario II.
Cells are 10 nm by 10 nm.

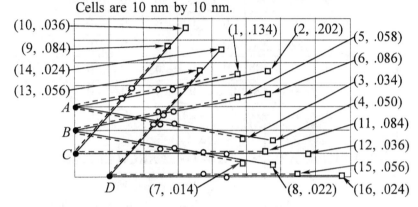

FIGURE 8.7. TARGET POSITION PROBABILITY MAP (TIME = 0)

Convention: A cell boundary point is considered in the cell above or to the right of the boundary. Cells are 10 nm by 10 nm.

	0	0	0	0	0	0	0	0
	0	0	0	0	0	0	0	0
	0	0	0	0	0	0	0	0
A	.42	0	0	0	0	0	0	0
B	.18	0	0	0	0	0	0	0
C	.29	0	0	0	0	0	0	0
D	0	.16	0	0	0	0	0	0

An important remark is to be made about generating a track bundle by sampling. In the 16-track example it is feasible to use *all* the points in the four two-point distributions, in fact with such small sample spaces there is no reasonable alternative. When a more realistic number of choices of course, speed, changes in these, etc., are available, a bundle of tracks (typically 500 or more) is usually constructed by *sampling* each of the distributions of course, speed, etc. This is where the method really becomes Monte Carlo. When the construction is by sampling, the initial weight (probability) is assigned to be the same for all tracks. The probability structure over the track bundle comes from the relative densities of tracks, i.e., there will be relatively numerous tracks with high-probability courses, etc. As the search progresses without success, the track weights will shift, as described below.

FIGURE 8.8. TARGET POSITION PROBABILITY MAP (TIME = 3 HRS)

Convention: A cell boundary point is considered in the cell above or to the right of the boundary. Cells are 10 nm by 10 nm.

0	0	0	0	0	0	0	0
0	0	0	0	0	0	0	0
0	0	0	0	0	0	0	0
0	.120	.336	0	0	0	0	0
0	0	.308	0	0	0	0	0
0	0	.120	.036	0	0	0	0
0	0	0	.056	.024	0	0	0

A is at left of row 4, B at left of row 5, C at left of row 6, D at bottom left.

FIGURE 8.9. APPLICATION OF SEARCH EFFORT

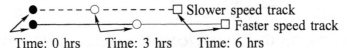

●- - - - - -○- - - - - - - -□ Slower speed track
Faster speed track

Time: 0 hrs   Time: 3 hrs   Time: 6 hrs

Note: (n, p) means track number n and track probability p.
The tracks from A and B are Scenario I.
The tracks from C and D are Scenario II.
Cells are 10 nm by 10 nm.

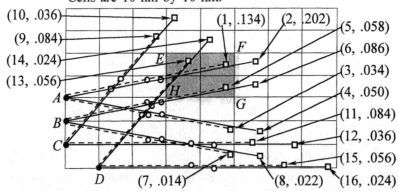

Updates for new information. Now updating for negative information is illustrated. Suppose that from time 3 hours to time 6 hours search effort is applied uniformly over the square shown in Figure 8.9 as $EFGH$. Suppose that as of time 6 hours no detection has been made, and it is desired to update the probability map to reflect this negative information. First one needs an estimate of the

FIGURE 8.10. CUMULATIVE DETECTION PROBABILITY

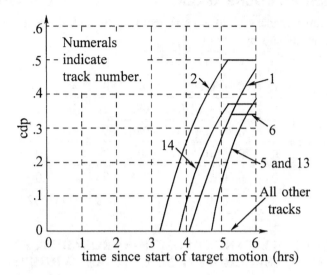

Numerals indicate track number.

cdp

time since start of target motion (hrs)

FIGURE 8.11. UPDATE FOR NEGATIVE INFORMATION

Search effort is applied uniformly over rectangle *EFGH* from time 3 hours to time 6 hours. No detection occurs.
What are the inferred new (posterior) track weights?

[1]	[2]	[3]	[4]	[5]
Track # i	Pre-search (prior) track weight (normalized)	Search failure probability if track i is actual	[2]x[3] = posterior track weight (unnormalized)	Normalized weight [4]/S
1	0.134	0.52	0.070	0.093
2	0.202	0.50	0.101	0.134
3	0.034	1.00	0.034	0.045
4	0.050	1.00	0.050	0.066
5	0.058	0.60	0.035	0.046
6	0.086	0.67	0.058	0.077
7	0.014	1.00	0.014	0.019
8	0.022	1.00	0.022	0.029
9	0.084	1.00	0.084	0.112
10	0.036	1.00	0.036	0.048
11	0.084	1.00	0.084	0.112
12	0.036	1.00	0.036	0.048
13	0.056	0.60	0.034	0.045
14	0.024	0.64	0.015	0.020
15	0.056	1.00	0.056	0.074
16	0.024	1.00	0.024	0.032
	1.000		$S = 0.753$	1.000

FIGURE 8.12. TARGET POSITION PROBABILITY MAP
(TIME = 6 HOURS AFTER NEGATIVE INFORMATION)

Convention: A cell boundary point is considered in the cell above or to the right of the boundary. Cells are 10 nm by 10 nm.

0	0	0	.048	0	0	0	0
0	0	.112	0	.020	0	0	0
0	0	0	.045	.093	.134	0	0
0	0	0	0	.046	.077	0	0
0	0	0	0	0	0	0	0
0	0	0	0	.045	.178	.048	0
0	0	0	0	.019	.029	.074	.032

A •
B •
C •
D •

FIGURE 8.13. TARGET POSITION PROBABILITY MAP
IF NO SEARCH WERE MADE (TIME = 3 HOURS)

Convention: A cell boundary point is considered in the cell above or to the right of the boundary. Cells are 10 nm by 10 nm.

0	0	0	.036	0	0	0	0
0	0	.084	E 0	.024	F 0	0	0
0	0	0	.056	.134	.202	0	0
0	0	0	0	.058	.086	0	0
0	0	0 H	0	0	G 0	0	0
0	0	0	0	.034	.134	.036	0
0	0	0	0	.014	.022	.056	.024

A •
B •
C •
D •

effectiveness of the search effort cell by cell, and one must combine that with the assumptions of target motion track by track. As to search effectiveness, one must find a curve of cumulative detection probability (cdp) *for each track*. This is illustrated in Figure 8.10. In most CAS systems this is done by a (λ, σ) model (Chapter 5). The negative information update is now applied to the track probabilities, as shown in Figure 8.11. This again applies Bayes' theorem in analogy to 801, where the updating is on cell probabilities. Column [2], the prior for the current Bayesian update, is obtained from the track probabilities in Figure 8.5. Column [3], the likelihoods, is obtained by complementing the 6-hour probabilities in Figure 8.10. Column [4] is the product of columns [2] and [3] and is proportional to the posterior track probabilities at time 6 hours. The posterior probabilities, column [5], are obtained by normalizing column 4 and reflect the 3 hours of unsuccessful search as desired. The posterior distribution over the tracks is translated into the posterior distribution over the cells by the method used to produce Figure 8.8. This results in Figure 8.12 which is the probability map for time 6 hours, reflecting the 3 hours of unsuccessful search as well as 6 hours of target motion. Figure 8.13 shows what the distribution of target position would have been at time 6 hours if there had been no search. Note that in the searched rectangle, *EFGH*, the unsuccessful search drove the probabilities lower in Figure 8.12 than in Figure 8.13, but not to 0, except for the cell that was 0 initially. Note also that in the two cells to the east of *EFGH* and in one cell to the north the probabilities also decreased; that is because the tracks with positions in these cells at 6 hours had *passed through EFGH* while it was being (unsuccessfully) searched. To offset these decreases, in all other cells the probability is higher in Figure 8.12 than in Figure 8.13.

This completes the description of updating for negative information in Monte Carlo moving target CAS. As review, the use of Bayes' theorem is analogous to the stationary case, but the updated probabilities pertain to tracks rather than positions. The track probabilities are readily converted to position probabilities at any desired time.

804   Optimal Search for a Moving Target

In this section an algorithm is given to allocate search effort optimally against a moving target. After the algorithm is specified, an example illustrates its mechanism.

The target motion is now assumed to be a Markov chain moving among a finite set C of cells at search times $i = 0, 1, \ldots, n$. (Treatment of other types of motion such as that of 803 is noted at the end of the section.) An optimal plan (allocation of search effort in space and time) maximizes probability of detection by time n. The target occupies one cell at a given time. It is also assumed that search effectiveness is exponential as defined in the stationary search algorithm in 801, final subsection, using β as specified there. One unit of search effort is available at each search time and may be allocated over the cells as the searcher desires. It is easy to generalize what follows to let β and the available effort depend on time. With added complication, β may depend also on cell.

The algorithm is a sequence of iterations indexed $m = 1, 2, \ldots$; iteration m outputs a search plan x^m and the probability Q^m that the search *fails* at every search time and cell during the iteration. Here $x_i^m(c)$ is the amount of search effort that the plan x^m applies to cell c at time i. For each $m > 1$, iteration m is at least as good as its predecessor: $Q^m \le Q^{m-1}$. The sequence of plans $(x^1, x^2, \ldots)$ converges to a limit. The limit plan minimizes the probability that detection fails at every time and cell. For initiation of iteration 1, one may choose an arbitrary plan, x^0; this may be thought of as an output of an artificial iteration 0. For example, one might choose $x_i^0(c) = 0$ for c in C and $i = 0, \ldots, n$. If that choice is made, then iteration 1 will output a myopic plan, i.e., one that does not look ahead in search times.

It is interesting that the plan produced in a given iteration allocates effort optimally, at each search time i, against a *stationary* target, *given* non-detection at all times *before i* using the plan of the *current* iteration and *given* non-detection at all times *after i* using the plan of the *previous* iteration. That is the heart of the algorithm. It reduces the problem of allocating effort in space and time to a time sequence of problems of instantaneous allocation over space against a stationary target (whose position distribution is suitably conditioned as just noted). An algorithm to solve such a stationary-target problem has been given at the end of 801. Recall that algorithm is composed of "application steps." These are within a search time of the present algorithm, and the search times are within an iteration. One must not confuse these three sequences with one another.

Additional inputs are, for c, d in C and $i = 0, \ldots, n$,

$$g(c) \equiv \Pr\{\text{cell } c \text{ contains the target at search time } 0\},$$

$$\tau(c, d) \equiv \Pr\{\text{the target is in cell } d \text{ at a given search time } | \text{ it is in cell } c \text{ at the preceding search time}\}.$$

The containment probabilities will shift between search times because of Bayesian updating for unsuccessful search and because of target motion. It is assumed that containment and search effectiveness probabilities are independent of cell, search time, and each other.

Specification of the algorithm. The algorithm initiates by a choice of x^0 as above. For $m > 0$, iteration m proceeds by computing a backward recursion for search times $i = n$ down to $i = 0$:

$$b_i(c) \equiv \Pr\{\text{a target in cell } c \text{ at time } i \text{ will not be detected by search after time } i\}$$

$$= \begin{cases} 1, & \text{if } i = n, \\ \sum_{d \text{ in } C} \tau(c, d) \exp(-\beta x_{i+1}^{m-1}(d)) b_{i+1}(d), & \text{if } i < n, \end{cases} \tag{8-1}$$

for c in C.

$$f_i(c) \equiv \Pr\{\text{the target is in cell } c \text{ at time } i \text{ and was not detected by search before time } i\}$$

$$= \begin{cases} g(c), & \text{if } i = 0, \\ \sum_{d \text{ in } C} f_{i-1}(d) \exp(-\beta x_{i-1}^m(d)) \tau(d, c), & \text{if } i > 0. \end{cases} \tag{8-2}$$

The iteration next does a forward recursion for search times $i = 0, \dots, n$. Fix i, $0 \le i \le n$. Compute

$$s_i(c) \equiv \Pr\{\text{the target is in cell } c \text{ at search time } i \text{ and is not detected by search at any time other than } i\} \tag{8-3}$$

$$= f_i(c) b_i(c),$$

for c in C. One can now compute, with i still fixed,

$$x^m = \text{optimal search plan for a stationary target with defective distribution } s_i \text{ using one unit of search effort, computed as in 801.} \tag{8-4}$$

In (8-2), "search before time i" refers to plans x_0^m at time 0, x_1^m at time 1, ... , x_{i-1}^m for time $i - 1$. Similar remarks apply to (8-1) on b, referring to plans at *future* times from the *previous* iteration, $m - 1$, and to (8-3) on s.

Unless $i = n$, one replaces i by $i + 1$ and proceeds with the forward recursion. If $i = n$, the forward recursion is complete and so is iteration m. As the iterations progress, the plans $x^1, x^2, \dots$ converge to a single, and optimal, plan. The failure probability, Q^m, under plan x^m, is given by

$$Q^m = \text{probability of non-detection using plan } x^m = \sum_{c \text{ in } C} s_n(c) \exp(-\beta x_n^m(c)). \tag{8-5}$$

The next iteration ensues. The algorithm stops when $Q^{m-1} - Q^m$ becomes less than a pre-assigned threshold.

Example. In this example, C consists of three cells, indexed $c = 1, 2, 3$. There are two search times, 0 and $1 = n$. The target's prior position, i.e., containment, distribution is $g(1) = .6$, $g(2) = .4$, and $g(3) = 0$. If the target is in cell 1 or 2 and if z amount of search effort is applied to that cell, then detection probability is $1 - \exp(-1.5z)$, thus $\beta = 1.5$. When the target is in cell 3, it is undetectable, so cell 3 is excluded from allocations of effort; only 0 effort is applied to cell 3. Also, between successive search times, if the target is in cell 1, it moves to cell 2, if in cell 2, it moves to cell 3, and if in cell 3, it stays there; thus $\tau(1, 2) = \tau(2, 3) = \tau(3, 3) = 1$, while otherwise $\tau(c, d) = 0$. At each search time, 1 unit of search effort is available.

Although it is quite instructive to carry out the lengthy hand computation of the algorithm for this example, in this particular case a much easier solution is available by calculus – see problem 10. Examples with substantially greater numbers of cells and search times are generally not practical to compute by hand, and generally they do not have convenient alternative solution methods.

The computation of the algorithm will be presented as a sequence of numbered statements, followed by explanation or other comments. Attention is particularly directed to statement (14).

Initiation by artificial iteration 0:
  (1)   Set $x_i^0(c) = 0$, for $i = 0, 1$, $c = 1, 2, 3$.
Iteration 1:
  Time 1:
  (2) Set $b_1(1) = b_1(2) = b_1(3) = 1$.
  Applies (8-1), noting that $1 = n$.
  Time 0 (time has moved backward):
  (3) Set $b_0(1) = b_0(2) = b_0(3) = 1$.
  Applies (8-1), (1), and (2). Note that for each c, in the summation in (8-1) there is one term (one d) with $\tau(c, d) = 1$ and the other τ factors are 0.
  (4) Set $f_0(1) = .6$, $f_0(2) = .4$, $f_0(3) = 0$.
  Applies (8-2). This is the prior containment distribution.
  (5) Set $s_0(1) = .6$, $s_0(2) = .4$, $s_0(3) = 0$.
  Applies (8-3), (4), and (3).
  (6) Compute $x_0^1(1) = .635$, $x_0^1(2) = .365$, $x_0^1(3) = 0$.
  Applies (5) and 801, last subsection, to find best allocation of 1 unit of effort over cells 1 and 2 with containment probabilities .6 and .4 respectively. Application step 1 applies $(1/1.5)\ln(.6/.4) = .270$ to the higher probability cell, cell 1, since that does not exhaust 1, and 0 effort to cell 2.

For application step 2, necessarily the containment probabilities for cells 1 and 2 are equal, even without computing $S = .4 + .4 = .8$, so that step divides the remaining effort between the two cells: $.635 = .270 + (1 - .270)/2$, and $.365 = 1 - .635$.

  Time 1 (time has moved forward):
  (7) Compute $f_1(1) = 0$, $f_1(2) = .6e^{-1.5 \times .635} = .231$, $f_1(3) = .4e^{-1.5 \times .365} = .231$.
  Applies (8-2), (4), and (6). For any cell d, $\tau(d, 1) = 0$. For $c = 2$ or 3, a remark on τ similar to (3) applies here also.
  (8) Set $s_1(1) = 0 \times 1 = 0$, $s_1(2) = .231 \times 1 = .231$, $s_1(3) = .231 \times 1 = .231$.
  Applies (8-3), (7), and (2).

(9) Set $x_1^1(1) = 0$, $x_1^1(2) = 1$, $x_1^1(3) = 0$.

Applies (8-4) and (8). This does not need 801 because $s_1(1) = 0$ and the target is undetectable in cell 3, so all effort must be applied to cell 2.

(10) Compute $Q^1 = 0 + .231e^{-1.5\times1} + .231\times1 = .283$.

Applies (8-5), (8), and (9). Thus .283 is the failure probability for myopic search over the two search times.

Iteration 2:

Time 1:

(11) Set $b_1(1) = b_1(2) = b_1(3) = 1$.

Same as (2).

Time 0:

(12) Compute $b_0(1) = e^{-1.5\times1} = .223$, $b_0(2) = b_0(3) = 1$.

Applies (8-1) and, for $c = 1$, (9), otherwise same as (3).

(13) Set $f_0(1) = .6$, $f_0(2) = .4$, $f_0(3) = 0$.

Same as (4).

(14) Compute $s_0(1) = .6\times.223 = .134$, $s_0(2) = .4\times1 = .4$, $s_0(3) = 0$.

Applies (8-3), (13), and (12). *Important note*: At this point the conditioned containment probabilities *at time* 0 shift so the majority is in cell 2 rather than cell 1. That is how the computed plan improves over the myopic plan. It results from the time 0 backward recursion in this iteration, i.e., (12).

(15) Compute $x_0^2(1) = .135$, $x_0^2(2) = .865$, $x_0^2(3) = 0$.

Similar to (6), applies (8-4), 801, and (14).

Time 1:

(16) Compute $f_1(1) = 0$, $f_1(2) = .6e^{-1.5\times.135} = .490$, $f_2(3) = .4e^{-1.5x.865} = .109$.

Similar to (7), applies (8-2), (13), and (15).

(17) Set $s_1(1) = 0$, $s_1(2) = .490$, $s_1(3) = .109$.

Applies (8-3), (16), and (11).

(18) Set $x_1^2(1) = 0$, $x_1^2(2) = 1$, $x_1^2(3) = 0$.

Same as (9).

(19) Compute $Q^2 = 0 + .490e^{-1.5} + .109 = .219$.

Similar to (10).

It is easily confirmed that if iteration 3 is undertaken, it repeats iteration 2. Therefore the algorithm stops at this point. For this example, it provides the optimal allocation of unit effort over the two search times: At search time 0, apply .135 amount of effort to cell 1, .865 to cell 2, and none to cell 3, and at time 1 apply the entire unit of effort to cell 2. The myopic plan is the same for time 1, but at time 0 applies .635 to cell 1 and .365 to cell 2. The failure probability is $Q^1 = .283$ for the myopic plan and is $Q^2 = .219$ for the optimal plan, a 23 percent improvement. In many, perhaps most, realistic moving target search allocation problems a myopic plan is much closer to optimality than in this example. As one can see from this relatively simple example, the algorithm is rather lengthy to compute by hand, but it is not difficult to program for a computer.

Suppose that target motion is given as a track bundle, call it B, as illustrated in 803, instead of assuming that it is a Markov chain. The above algorithm might be adapted to such motion. To illustrate, suppose the problem is to plan placement of a sonobuoy field (a timed collection of patterns) during each of a sequence of VP ASW patrol sorties. Regard each sortie as a time step. Let the assignment of effort on sortie i be determined by choice of a timed point, call it x_i, at which to anchor the buoy field for that sortie. For any track T in B, let $g(T)$ be the pre-search probability that T is the correct track; let $u_i(x_i, T)$ be the probability that if T is the correct track, and x_i is chosen to anchor the field on sortie i, then detection will not occur on that sortie. Because the field has a lifetime, to evaluate u_i, a cdp model, e.g., Figure 8.10, is needed. As before, iterations will be computed, indexed by m.

Now define b_i, f_i, and s_i as before, but using tracks in place of cells, somewhat in analogy to the cell definitions: For each track T in B, and for $i = n$ down to 0, let

$$b_i(T) = \text{Pr\{if } T \text{ is the correct track then no}$$
$$\text{detection occurs after sortie } i\}$$

$$= \begin{cases} 1 & \text{if } i = n, \\ b_{i+1}(T)u_{i+1}(x_{i+1}^{m-1}, T), & \text{otherwise.} \end{cases}$$

Next, for $i = 0, \dots , n$ and T in B, let (as before iterations are indexed by m)

$$f_i(T) = \text{Pr\{} T \text{ is the correct track and no detection occurs before sortie } i \}$$

$$= \begin{cases} g(T) & \text{if } i = 0, \\ f_{i-1}(T)u_{i-1}(x_{i-1}^{m}, T) & \text{otherwise,} \end{cases}$$

$$s_i(T) = \text{Pr\{} T \text{ is correct and no detection on other than sortie } i\}$$
$$= b_i(T)f_i(T),$$

$$x^m = \text{optimal anchor point for buoy field on sortie } i$$
$$\text{given that the defective track distribution is } s_i.$$

The plans $x^1, x^2, \dots$ converge to a limit plan, which is approximately optimal. This leaves unanswered the question of how to compute an optimal anchor point for single sortie and a given distribution of tracks, but it does reduce the multiple-sortie problem to a sequence of single-sortie problems. The single-sortie problems may be generalized to choice of optimal *configuration* of the buoy field, in addition to optimization of its placement.

805   Other Literature and History

Figure 8.2, was taken from H. R. Richardson and L. D. Stone [1]. The algorithm described at the end of 801 for optimal allocation of search against a stationary target is given more formally in 2.2.8 of Stone [2, 3], where it is credited to A. Charnes and W. W. Cooper [4]. Monte Carlo CAS, illustrated in 803, was originated by Richardson; the illustration is taken from Wagner [5].

The exposition of the optimal moving target search algorithm given in 804 follows S. S. Brown [6] with different notation. The three-cell example in 804 illustrating that algorithm and the two-cell example in Problem 11a were inspired by A. R. Washburn's example in 6.2 of [7], which illustrates dramatically that myopic search need not be optimal. In the example of [7], at a given time instant all of the effort must be placed in a single cell.

The first operational CAS system was the U.S. Coast Guard search and rescue program, Computer-Assisted Search Planning, developed 1970-72 under Richardson [8]. LCDR J. H. Discenza, USCG, was instrumental in implementation of CASP (see [9]). The multi-scenario method of constructing a prior was originated by J. P. Craven in the 1966 H-bomb search off Palomares, Spain. Perhaps the first application of Bayes' theorem to update for negative information in actual search planning was by Richardson on scene in that operation (without electronic computation). A multi-scenario prior was again applied in the *Scorpion* search in 1968, as noted in 801; this time electronic computation was used (remotely). Bayesian updating of the prior was done by hand on the search scene.

Richardson and his colleagues extended these methods to develop and to apply successfully various ASW CAS systems in the 1970s. The first desktop-calculator and seagoing CAS system was developed by T. L. Corwin at COMSUBPAC in 1975. It used analytic rather than Monte Carlo methods.

The progress of the 1970s culminated in development of VPCAS under COMPATWINGSPAC and COMPATWINGSLANT, led by S. J. Benkoski and R. P. Buemi. VPCAS was a Monte Carlo program to assist mission planning in VP ASW and was introduced to ASW Operations Centers (ASWOCs) in late 1983. Successor extensions, developed primarily by W. R. Monach, were the search and tracking systems PACSEARCH, under COMOCEANSYSPAC, and the OCAS module [10] in the ONR system OPTAMAS. These programs included algorithms for optimal multi-sortie sonobuoy search along the lines of that given at the end of 804. The 1987 prototype SALT was developed primarily by Stone, D. A. Trader, and Corwin and evolved into Nodestar [11]; these systems used Markov-chain target-motion modeling and recursive Bayesian filtering methods [12], which make combined inference from positive and negative information. OCAS and Nodestar are much more sophisticated than the CAS systems of the early 1970s, and their hardware hosts are much more powerful.

The algorithm for optimal search for moving targets presented in 804 was given in 1977 by Brown [13]; see also Brown [14] and Stone, et al., [15]. Assuming that the amount of effort allocable to a given cell is arbitrary and effectiveness is exponential, both as assumed here, he showed that for a plan to be optimal it is necessary and sufficient that all instantaneous allocations, conditioned on non-detection in the future and past, be optimal. He proved that under arbitrary discrete target motion, the algorithm converges to a limit plan and that the limit plan satisfies this instantaneity condition.

Although the algorithm in 804, sometimes called "Brown's algorithm" and sometimes the "FAB algorithm" (for forward and backward), is extremely interesting and sometimes useful, in most practical applications a myopic plan is quite close to optimality. In [16], Washburn showed that even if at a given instant all effort must be allotted to a single cell, then the above instantaneity condition is still necessary (true for any restriction on the amounts allocable to a single cell), and showed by example that sufficiency may fail. In [17] Washburn gave a bound which enables one to tell when a solution comes within a given ϵ of optimal detection probability. In [18] he extended the algorithms of [15] and [16] to payoffs other than probability of detection in specified time. For further results and history on optimal moving target search see Appendix C of [3].

Richardson and Corwin in reference [19] is an article on the principal methods used in Monte Carlo CAS. An excellent tutorial on CAS, with very modest mathematical prerequisites, is given in [20]. It contains an eight-track example similar to the above sixteen-track example, but shows only what the user would see and not the tracks themselves. References Koopman [21, 22], Stone [2, 3], and Washburn [7] are general texts on methods in search analysis. Reference [2] was awarded the Lanchester Prize of the Operations Research Society of America as the best 1975 publication in English on operations research. Stone it reference [23] describes the search planning processes. Richardson et al., [24] is a manual for analysis of deep ocean search; among other things it gives guidance for choosing cell size. More detailed history and some elaboration on VPCAS, PACSEARCH, and SALT are given in Wagner [5]. Extensive bibliographies of search literature are given in Benkoski [25] and Stone [2, 3].

Koopman's pioneering role in search theory and its applications is noted in Chapter 6. Craven was Technical Director of the 1966 H-bomb search and the 1968 *Scorpion* search, while he was Chief Scientist at Special Projects, the developers of Polaris missiles and submarines. Richardson, Stone, Corwin, Benkoski, Buemi, and Monach, were with Daniel H. Wagner, Associates, during their cited contributions, except for the work on SALT through Nodestar by Stone, Trader, and Corwin, which was at Metron, Inc. Discenza's work on CASP was at the USCG Rescue Coordination Center, Governor's Island, N.Y. Washburn's various contributions were as an operations research professor at the Naval Postgraduate School. Andrews commanded the *Thresher* search in 1963-64 as CAPT, USN, and consulted on scene to the H-bomb and *Scorpion* searches. Stone [26] details the search planning done for the search for the SS Central America, a side-wheel steamer that sunk in 1857 with over 3 tons of gold. The use of the multi-scenario approach for obtaining the initial probability map is laid out in detail.

[1] Richardson, Henry R., and Lawrence D. Stone. "Operations Analysis During the Underwater Search for Scorpion." *Naval Logistics Research Quarterly* 18 (June, 1971):141-157.

[2] Stone, Lawrence D. *Theory of Optimal Search*. New York: Academic Press, 1975.

[3] Stone, Lawrence D. *Theory of Optimal Search*. 2nd edition. Baltimore: Operations Research Society of America, 1989.

[4] Charnes, A., and W. W. Cooper. "The Theory of Search: Optimum Distribution of Search Effort," *Management Science* 5 (1958): 44-50.

[5] Wagner, Daniel H. *Naval Tactical Decision Aids*. Military Operations Research Lecture Notes, NPSOR-1. Monterey CA: Naval Postgraduate School, 1989.

[6] Brown, Scott S. "Optimal Search: Markov Chain Motion, Exponential Effectiveness Function." *Search, Detection, and Tracking*. Vol. II, Area 2, *Military OR Analyst's Handbook*. Alexandria, VA: Military Operations Research Society (to be published).

[7] Washburn, Alan R. *Search and Detection*. Baltimore, MD: Operations Research Society of America, 1981.

[8] Richardson, Henry R. *Final Report on Computer-Assisted Search Planning System (CASP)*. Paoli, PA: Daniel H. Wagner, Associates Memorandum to Commandant, U. S. Coast Guard Headquarters, July 17, 1975.

[9] Richardson, Henry R., and Joseph H. Discenza. "The United States Coast Guard Computer-Assisted Search Planning System (CASP)." *Naval Research Logistics Quarterly* 27 (December, 1980): 659-680.

[10] Director ASW Environmental Acoustics Support Program. *OPTAMAS Version 2.0 System Description*. AEAS Report 900-001. Office of Naval Research, March, 1990.

[11] Stone, Lawrence D.; Thomas L. Corwin; and James B. Hoffman. *Technical Documentation of*

Nodestar. Reston, VA: Metron, Inc. Report to the Naval Research Laboratory, December 11, 1995 (DTIC No. AD-A302 458/XAG).

[12] Corwin, Thomas L., and Lawrence D. Stone. "Bayesian Filtering." *Search, Detection, and Tracking*. Vol. II, Area 2, *Military OR Analyst's Handbook*. Alexandria, VA: Military Operations Research Society (to be published).

[13] Brown, Scott S. *Optimal and Near Optimal Search for a Target with Multiple Scenario Markovian, Constrained Markovian, or Geometric Memory Motion in Discrete Time and Space*. Paoli, Pa: Daniel H. Wagner, Associates Memorandum Report to the Office of Naval Research, June 14, 1977.

[14] Brown, Scott. S. "Optimal Search for a Moving Target in Discrete Time and Space." *Operations Research* 28 (November-December, 1980):1275-1289.

[15] Stone, Lawrence. D.; Scott S. Brown; Robert. P. Buemi; and Carol R. Hopkins. *Numerical Optimization of Search for a Moving Target*. Daniel H. Wagner, Associates Report to the Office of Naval Research, 1978 (DTIC No. AD-A058 470/XAG).

[16] Washburn, Alan R. "On Search for a Moving Target." *Naval Research Logistics Quarterly* 27 (June, 1980): 315-322.

[17] Washburn, Alan R. "An Upper Bound Useful in Optimizing Search for a Moving Target." *Operations Research* 29 (November-December, 1981): 1227-1230.

[18] Washburn, Alan R. "Search for a Moving Target: the Fab Algorithm." *Operations Research* 31 (July-August, 1983): 739-751.

[19] Richardson, Henry R., and Thomas L. Corwin. "An Overview of Computer-Assisted Search." Haley, K. Brian, and Stone, Lawrence D., eds., *Search Theory and Applications*. New York: Plenum, 1980.

[20] Benkoski, Stanley J. *Introduction to ASW and Computer-Assisted Search*. Commander Patrol Wings, Pacific Fleet Tactical Study sz033-z-83, 26 September, 1983.

[21] Koopman, Bernard O. *Search and Screening*. Operations Evaluation Group Report 56. Washington DC: Office of the Chief of Naval Operations, 1946.

[22] Koopman, Bernard O. *Search and Screening: General Principles with Historical Applications*. New York: Pergamon Press, 1980.

[23] Stone, Lawrence D. "The Process of Search Planning: Current Approaches and Continuing Problems." *Operations Research* 31 (March-April, 1983): 207-233.

[24] Richardson, Henry R.; Lawrence D. Stone; and Frank A. Andrews. *Manual for Operations Analysis of Deep Ocean Search*. Supervisor of Salvage, Naval Ships Systems Command Publication 0994-010-7010, 1971.

[25] Benkoski, Stanley J.; Michael G. Monticino; and James R. Weisinger. "A Survey of Search Theory Literature." *Naval Research Logistics*. 38 (August 1991): 469-494.

[26] Stone, Lawrence D. "Search for the SS Central America: Mathematical Treasure Hunting." *Interfaces* 22 (January-February 1992): 32-54.

Problems

1.   A stationary object has been lost in cell 1, 2, or 3. Scenarios I and II have been postulated for the loss. A priori under I, it is twice as probable that the object is in cell 2 as in cell 1 and three times as probable that it is in cell 3 as in cell 1. Under II, all three cells are equally likely to contain the

target. Scenario II is deemed twice as likely as I.

a. Under the composite of I and II, which cell has the highest probability of containing the target?
b. What is that probability?
c. Why is no calculation needed to answer a.?

2. A stationary object is lost at a point on a line with a coordinate scale and origin. There are two equally likely scenarios for the loss, I and II. The distribution of the position is normal for both. For I and II respectively, the means are 0 and 2 and the variances are 4 and 9. Under the composite of these scenarios, what is the probability that the object is at a negative coordinate?

3. For the optimization example in 801, answer the following:

a. After the 1.02 hours of search effort have been applied to (2, 2), how much additional search time should be applied to (2, 2), (1, 2), and (2, 1) before effort should begin in (3, 3), (2, 3), and (3, 2)?
b. What is the distribution of position at that point?
c. What computation saving in CAS programs is suggested by this exercise?

4. Why are the track probabilities the same in Figures 8.6 and 8.9, while the cell probabilities in Figures 8.7 and 8.8, at the corresponding times, are different?

5. In the prior distribution of tracks in Figure 8.5, find the distributions of

a. target course and
b. target speed.

6. As of the update in Figure 8.11, compute the posterior distributions of

a. target speed,
b. target course, and
c. target scenarios.
d. How has inference from unsuccessful search changed one's view of the scenarios compared to the pre-search situation?

7. Using Figures 8.10 and 8.11, given unsuccessful search through time 4 hours, what is the probability that the actual track is number 1?

8. A target moves among the following nine boxes:

1	2	3
4	5	6
7	8	9

There are four tracks the target can take, given as follows, with the stated probabilities:

Track Number	Box number at time 0	Box number at time 1	Box number at time 2	Prior probability that the track occurs
1	1	2	3	.1
2	1	5	3	.3
3	7	5	9	.2
4	7	8	9	.4

At time 1, box 5 is searched with detection probability .4, given that the target is in box 5 at time 1. The search does not succeed. What is the probability that the target is in box 9 at time 2?

9. A momentary contact on an enemy submarine occurred in cell (3, 1), shown below. Note that cell (i, j) is row i, column j. It is postulated that the submarine is en route to one of two harbors to sow a minefield. A bottom chart of the area is examined in detail resulting in the postulation of two possible tracks to each of the two harbors, totaling four tracks. Their a priori probabilities are also shown in the figure below. The postulated tracks are converted to positions for each of three times t following the initial contact.

Track:		T_1	T_2	T_3	T_4
A priori probability		.4	.2	.1	.3

a. It is now time 1 and searches are conducted in cells (2, 1) and (4, 1) in such a manner that the probability of detection is .7, given the target was in the cell searched. There were no detections. Update the *track* probabilities.
b. Construct a probability map of target location for time 2 using the track probabilities from a.
c. The weather turns bad and further search is impossible. What is the probability that Harbor B is the submarine's destination?

10. In the example of 804, observe that the choice of the amount of effort applied to cell 1 at time $0, x_0(1)$, determines the amount applied to cell 2 at time 0, since no effort is applied to cell 3. Also, at time 1, all available effort is applied to cell 2, since there is 0 probability that the target is in cell 1. Thus $x_0(1)$ determines the entire search plan. Use this fact and calculus to show that the optimal plan is in fact as found by the algorithm in 804.

11. Suppose at time 0, a target is in cell 1 with probability .3 and in cell 2 with probability .7. After 1 unit of search effort is applied at time 0, divided equally between the two cells, the target moves to cell 1 if it was in cell 2 and to cell 2 if in cell 1. Then at time 1, another unit of effort is applied. When effort z is applied to a cell containing the target, detection probability is 1 - exp(-2z), except that at time 1, if the target is in cell 2 it is undetectable.

a. For this problem apply the algorithm of 804 to find the myopic search plan and the probability that this plan finds the target in one of the two search times, 0 and 1.
b. Continue the algorithm to find the optimal plan and its success probability.
c. Use a method similar to that of problem 10 to verify independently (and more easily) that the solution found in b is correct.

Answers to Problems

1.   a. Cell 3. b. 7/18. c. Because cell 3 is not bettered under either I or II.

2.   .38.

3.   a. 3.43 hrs. b. Distribution:

	1	2	3
1	.135	.144	.000
2	.144	.144	.144
3	.000	.144	.144

c. Postpone calculation of normalizing factors in Bayesian analysis until needed. Much useful information can be gained without them.

4.   Motion has occurred to change the cell probabilities, but no search has occurred to change the track probabilities.

5. Distributions:

a.		b.	
Course	Probability	Speed	Probability
060T	.200	8 kts	.240
075	.480	9	.280
090	.200	10	.360
105	.120	11	.120

6. Distributions:

a.		b.		c.	
Speed	Probability	Course	Probability	Scenario	Probability
8	.203	060T	.225	I	.509
9	.343	075	.350	II	.491
10	.306	090	.266		
11	.148	105	.159		
	1.000		1.000		1.000

7. .141.

8. .65.

9. a. The track probability updates are .235, .392, .196, and .176 for tracks 1, 2, 3, and 4, respectively.

    b. The probabilities of being in cells (1, 2), (2, 2), (4, 2), and (5, 2) are respectively .235, .392, .196, and .176; all other cells have probability 0.

    c. .373.

10. Additional hint: Apply the methods of 801 for optimal search for a stationary target at each time.

11. a. At time 0, put .788 amount of effort in cell 2 and .212 in cell 1. At time 1, put the entire 1 unit of effort in cell 1. Success probability is .876.

    b. At time 0, the myopic plan puts .288 amount of effort in cell 1 and .712 in cell 2; at time 1, all effort is in cell 1. Success probability is .808, compared to .876 for the optimal plan.

9
BARRIER PATROLS

The preceding chapter addressed search for a target whose motion is modeled as a stochastic process of a rather general nature. It is assumed in this chapter that the target's intention is to traverse a fairly straight channel (which may be a wide portion of the ocean). The target's velocity vectors at all points are parallel and equal. The time that the target's transit initiates is unknown and is assumed to be equally likely throughout the time interval under consideration. The opposing search is called a **barrier patrol**. It is also assumed that detectability of the target does not change during the search or patrol. In particular, in the case of sonar detection of submarines, the target is regarded as constantly submerged on nuclear power. This avoids the complication of the snorkel cycle of diesel submarines.

For convenience of wording, in the first three sections the target will be referred to as a "ship" and the searcher as an "aircraft." While this corresponds to a prominent situation, the same mathematical ideas apply to other vehicles.

Crossover barriers are analyzed in 901. Section 902 treats in more detail the case of a symmetric barrier. This leads to a discussion of parameter selection issues in 903. Section 904 compares a symmetric barrier with a linear back-and-forth barrier. Kinematic enhancement of a barrier is treated in 905. This is applied in 906 to a game analysis of choice of speeds by a submarine transitor and a submarine patroller, involving the tradeoff between kinematic enhancement and acoustic degradation arising from increased speed.

901   Crossover Barrier Patrol

Under a wide variety of circumstances, the problem of detecting a target in transit through a channel by means of a searcher whose speed, v, considerably exceeds the target speed, u, for example, an airborne searcher and ship target, can be simplified to the following mathematical statement. Given a channel bounded by two parallel lines d miles apart (the vertical lines of Figure 9.1) and a target moving through this channel and parallel to it at a fixed speed, u (downward in Figure 9.1(b)), how shall the searcher fly from one side of the channel to the other and back, etc., in order to be most effective in detecting the target?

FIGURE 9.1. FLIGHT PATH RELATIVE TO TARGET

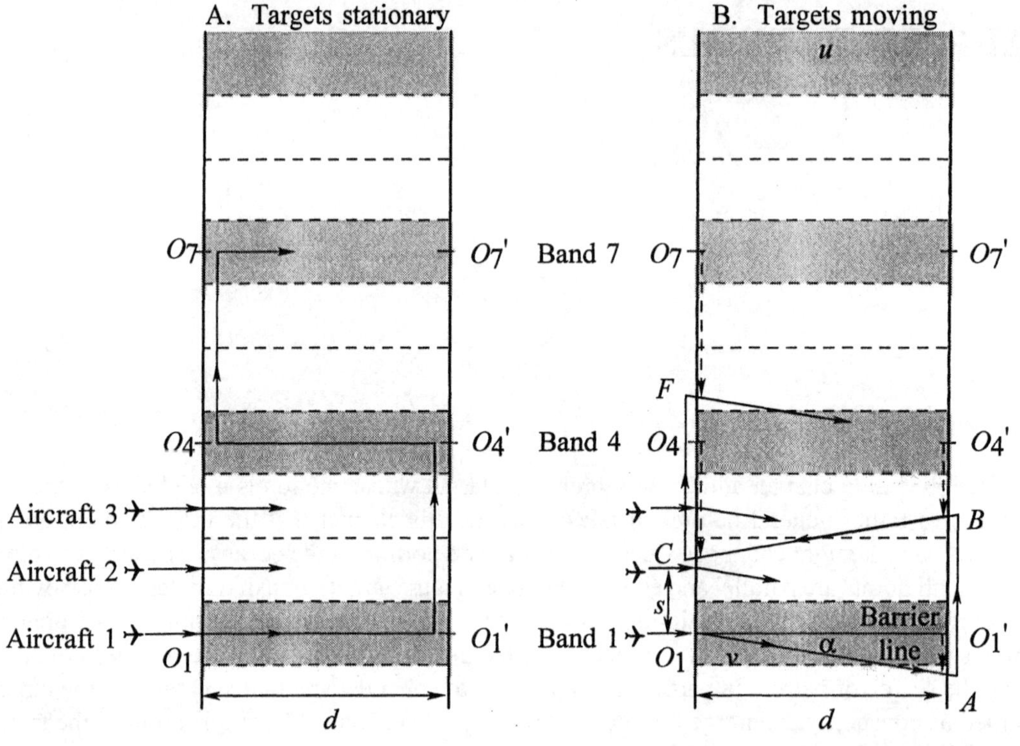

It is necessary to orient the flights relative to a fixed reference point, O_1, from which they start or take their direction. Thus O_1 may be a convenient geographic point at or near the narrowest part of the actual channel. The line, O_1O_1' (in Figure 9.1) is drawn across the perpendicular to the channel as a purely mathematical reference line called the **barrier line.**

Suppose three aircraft are available to prevent targets from transiting the channel undetected. Let s be the track spacing used between aircraft and consider this problem as a special case of parallel sweeps. In Figure 9.1, the channel is divided into several bands of width s. If targets are stationary, as in Figure 9.1(a), the three aircraft could search the first three bands while crossing the channel, then move up the opposite side of the channel and search bands four, five, and six on the return trip, etc., with the first aircraft taking each third (shaded) band. However, with targets moving down the channel, as in Figure 9.1(b), such a search would let some targets transit with an unnecessarily low probability of detection. With slight modification, the parallel sweep method can be made more effective.

Let the first aircraft fly the pattern O_1ABCF, as indicated by Figure 9.1(b), where the angle α is computed such that a target originally at O_1' will be at A when the aircraft reaches A. The location of point A then depends on u, v, and d. In effect, the first aircraft has searched for targets originally located in band 1 and moves next to search for targets that originally were located in band 4. It must fly up the channel to intercept at B, any target originally at O_4. Denote the distance between two arbitrary points H and K by $|HK|$. After flying the **upsweep**, $y = |AB|$, it returns across the channel at the necessary lead angle to keep it over the collection of possible targets that originally were in band 4. Then it flies an upsweep leg up the channel from C to F where it intercepts the position of a target originally at O_7, thus completing one basic element of the search. At point F, it begins another cycle identical to the first, covering targets originally in band 7.

At the same time, the second and third aircraft, flying parallel to the first, cover bands 2 and 3 on the first leg, 5 and 6 on the return. Before computing the times and distances involved, it should be pointed out that there are three possibilities:

(a) The barrier may progress further up the channel with each basic element flown. This is called an **advancing barrier**.
(b) The barrier may retire down the channel with each succeeding element. This is referred to as a **retiring barrier**.
(c) The barrier may remain stationary. This is called a **symmetric barrier**.

Which of these three types occurs depends on target speed (u), search speed (v), channel width (d), track spacing (s) of the search aircraft, and the number of aircraft (n).

To proceed further, it is necessary to develop certain relationships that follow from the preceding description. The angle α is dependent solely on the two speeds, v and u, of the aircraft and target respectively. From the requirement that the aircraft reaches point A when a target originally at O_1' also reaches point A, it can be seen in Figure 9.1(b) that $\sin \alpha = |O_1'A|/|O_1A|$, $|O_1'A| = ut_1$, and $|O_1A| = vt_1$, where t_1 is the time required for the aircraft to reach point A. Thus

$$\alpha = \arcsin\left(\frac{u}{v}\right). \tag{9-1}$$

To find the time, t_0, for an aircraft to complete one basic element requires some intermediate computations:

$$d = \sqrt{(vt_1)^2 - (ut_1)^2} = t_1\sqrt{v^2 - u^2};$$

so

$$t_1 = \frac{d}{\sqrt{v^2 - u^2}}.$$

When the first of n aircraft, and also a target originally at O_1', are at point A, the aircraft proceeds next to intercept a target originally located n bandwidths, distance ns, above point O_1'. This target must now be a distance ns above point A and traveling down the channel with speed u. Let t_2 be the time it takes for the aircraft to proceed up the channel to intercept such a target. Then

$$t_2 = \frac{ns}{u + v},$$

and the total time, t_B, for the first aircraft to reach B is $t_1 + t_2$:

$$t_B = \frac{d}{\sqrt{v^2 - u^2}} + \frac{ns}{u + v}.$$

The length of the upsweep, $y = |AB|$, is the distance traveled by the aircraft in the time t_2 so that $y = vt_2$, i.e.,

$$y = \frac{vns}{u + v}. \tag{9-2}$$

This completes half of one basic element and the remaining half is seen to be identical. Therefore, the time for one complete basic element, t_0, is given by $2t_B$, i.e.,

$$t_0 = \frac{2d}{\sqrt{v^2 - u^2}} + \frac{2ns}{u + v}.$$

902   Symmetric Crossover Patrol

The question arises as to whether the resulting barrier with n aircraft flying parallel is advancing, retiring, or symmetric. It would be symmetric only if the starting point for the second element were the same as the first, i.e., if F and O_1 coincided. Note carefully that the time for a target originally at O_7 in Figure 9.1(b) to reach point F is equal to t_0, the same time as that required for the aircraft to reach F. If F were located at O_1, the target originally at O_7 would have to travel six bandwidths to reach point F. If n aircraft were used, the number of bands swept during one basic element is $2n$ and the first unswept band is the one originally located a distance $2ns$ above the barrier line. When will this band, or rather a target in this band, reach the barrier line? Let t^* be this time. Thus

$$t^* = \frac{2ns}{u}.$$

For an advancing barrier, as in Figure 9.2(a), F is above O_1; therefore

$$t^* > t_0.$$

For a retiring barrier, as in Figure 9.2(b), F is below O_1; therefore

$$t^* < t_0.$$

For a symmetric barrier, as in Figure 9.2(c), F and O_1 coincide; therefore

$$t^* = t_0.$$

From these relationships, it is possible to determine the number of aircraft required or the track spacing necessary for a symmetric barrier to be maintained. Since $t^* = t_0$ in this case,

$$\frac{2ns}{u} = \frac{2d}{\sqrt{v^2 - u^2}} + \frac{2ns}{v + u}.$$

Solving for n and letting

$$K = \sqrt{\frac{v + u}{v - u}}$$

gives

$$n = K\frac{d\,u}{s\,v}, \qquad (9\text{-}3)$$

and solving for s gives

$$s = \frac{Kdu}{nv}.$$

FIGURE 9.2. ADVANCING, RETIRING, AND SYMMETRIC CROSSOVER BARRIERS

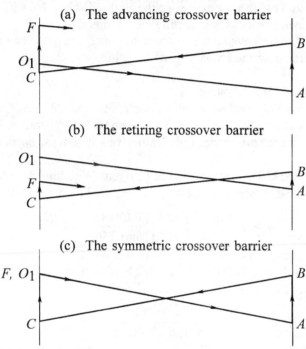

(a) The advancing crossover barrier

(b) The retiring crossover barrier

(c) The symmetric crossover barrier

903   Barrier Patrol Selection Considerations

For a crossover barrier patrol, the probability of detection is computed in exactly the same manner as for parallel sweeps with the same track spacing, s. That is the inverse cube law of detection presented in 704 is used to determine the barrier's probability of detection. However, the accuracy of the computed probability of detection depends on two additional variables, the estimated target course and estimated target speed.

If the target's speed, u, has been overestimated, some portions of each band will be searched more than once and the true probability of detection will be higher than computed. The true probability of detection will not, however, be as high as it would be if the search were planned (and s reduced) for the correct value of u. Underestimating the target speed produces the opposite effect, and the probability of detection will be less than predicted.

If the target is moving obliquely down the channel instead of exactly parallel to the banks as has been assumed, the effective value of the target speed as far as the tightness of the barrier is concerned is the downward component of the speed. This reduces the effective speed and produces the same result as when the target speed is overestimated.

In designing a symmetric barrier the analyst can adjust the values of n and s used within limits:

(a) Given a required effectiveness, i.e, probability of detection, $p(s)$, design a barrier to provide or exceed this requirement. Use the inverse cubed law of detection to compute the required detection probability. Then using (9-3) to compute n, round n up to an integer value and use (9-4) to determine s. The values of n and s thus obtained will result in a symmetric barrier having a probability of detection equaling or exceeding the required value. No smaller number of planes, n, can be used in a symmetric barrier meeting the requirement.
(b) Given the number of aircraft available s can be determined using (9-6) and the inverse cube law will provide an estimate for the probability of detection, $p(s)$.

The following example is illustrative.

It is desired to close a 300 nm channel with a barrier having an 87 percent chance of detection. The speeds are $v = 150$ knots and $u = 14$ knots. The sweep width is 20 nm, and the inverse cube law is assumed. How many aircraft are needed in order to have a symmetric barrier, and how should the flights be conducted?

Using the inverse cube law, s is required to be 16.6 nm. With this value for s the number, n, of aircraft must be the smallest integer, not less than that required for a symmetric barrier in (9-5), i.e.,

$$n \geq K\frac{d}{s}\frac{u}{v} = \sqrt{\frac{164}{136}\frac{(300)(14)}{(16.6)(150)}} = 1.85.$$

In other words, two aircraft are necessary. But with two aircraft, an advancing barrier will result because t^* will be greater than t_0. To have a symmetric barrier, the two aircraft must fly more closely together, and their track spacing, s, is determined using (9-4) to be

$$s = \frac{Kdu}{nv} = \sqrt{\frac{164}{136}\frac{(300)(14)}{(2)(150)}} = 15.4 \text{ nm.}$$

With this reduced track spacing, the barrier gains in tightness. In fact the probability found from the inverse cube law now becomes 90 percent, which is all to the good. The length of upsweep given by (9-2) is $y = 28.2$ nm. Finally, the lead angle given by (9-1) is $\alpha = 5° 21'$.

904   Barrier When Target Speed Is Close to Searcher's Speed

So far it has been assumed that v considerably exceeds u. When $v \leq u$, the crossover type of barrier is impossible. Even when u is nearly as great as v, the angle α is so large that a crossover barrier is inefficient. This does not arise when the searcher is airborne and the target is a ship, but when both searcher and target are units of the same type (both ships or both aircraft), the situation excluded heretofore becomes important. Although many barrier plans for a channel can be devised for this situation, attention will be confined here to several simple patrols. First to be examined is the patrol in which the searcher moves back and forth across the channel on a straight path perpendicular to its (parallel) edges. Such a barrier, called a **linear patrol**, is always possible as its design does not involve the speed ratio, u/v.

This linear patrol is then compared with the symmetrical crossover patrol (when $u < v$). Since only a rough comparison is sought here, the definite range law will be assumed, i.e., those and only those targets coming within range $w/2$, will be detected. A more sophisticated detection law is not likely to alter the comparison appreciably.

The diagrams in Figure 9.3 show the geographic as well as the relative tracks for the two types of patrol. In both cases the searcher moves only to a distance $w/2$ from the channel boundary, so that for the crossover patrol some coverage is obtained on each upsweep. Only one searcher is used in each case, and for the crossover patrol there is an implicit track spacing for the relative track.

FIGURE 9.3. COMPARISON OF CROSSOVER AND LINEAR PATROLS

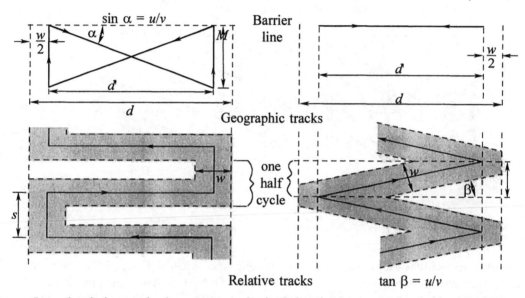

In each relative track, the swept area is shaded and a representative half cycle shown. In deriving (9-5) and (9-6) below, for simplicity the detection circle has been "squared off" so these equations slightly overstate performance. It is assumed that barrier penetrations are uniformly distributed across the front. The probability of detection for each case is taken as the ratio of the shaded area to the total area in the channel between the two dashed lines marking off the half cycle.

Let d be the channel width, as before, and let $d' = d - w$. It is convenient to introduce two new variables to describe the probability of detection, $\rho = v/u$ and $\lambda = d'/w$. For the case of the crossover patrol, the probability of detection, $P_{\bowtie}$, is given by (recall that u must be $\leq v$)

$$P_{\bowtie} = \min\left\{1, \left(1 + \frac{\rho\sqrt{\rho^2 - 1}}{\rho + 1}\right)\frac{1}{\lambda + 1}\right\}. \tag{9-5}$$

For the linear patrol, the probability of detection, P_{-}, is given by

$$P_{..} = \begin{cases} \left[1 - \left(\lambda - \dfrac{\sqrt{\rho^2 + 1} - 1}{2}\right)^2 \dfrac{1}{\lambda(\lambda+1)}, & \text{if } \rho \le 2\sqrt{\lambda(\lambda+1)}, \\ 1, & \text{otherwise.} \end{cases} \qquad (9\text{-}6)$$

In Figure 9.4, the values of $P_{\bowtie}$ and $P_{..}$ from (9-5) and (9-6) are plotted versus ρ with λ kept fixed for a given curve. In comparing crossover patrols with linear patrols, curves having the same value of λ should be compared. The solid curve passes through the points of intersection of the curves being compared and marks the boundary between the regions where linear is preferable and where crossover is preferable.

FIGURE 9.4. THE COMPARATIVE EFFECTIVENESS OF LINEAR AND CROSSOVER PLANS

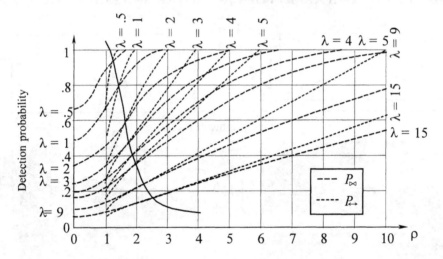

In order to facilitate the selection of the preferable type of patrol, Figure 9.5 is included. This curve shows the relation between λ and ρ for the points of intersection of curves in Figure 9.4. An example will illustrate the use of the curves. Suppose a ship making 12 knots is trying to prevent undetected penetration of a barrier by a submerged submarine traveling at 6 knots. Assume further that the channel being guarded is 8 nm wide and that the sonar sweep width, w, is 2 nm. Then $d' = 8 - 2 = 6$ nm, $\lambda = 6/2 = 3$, and $\rho = 12/6 = 2$. Entering Figure 9.5 with these values for λ and ρ, one discovers that a crossover patrol is preferred.

905   Kinematic Enhancement of Linear Patrols

This section considers enhancement of sweep width that arises from motion when the tactic is to patrol back and forth to protect a front of length d against transitors. Specifically it is again assumed as before that transit tracks are perpendicular to the front and that their penetrations are uniformly distributed across the front, as illustrated in Figure 9.6.

Let w be the patroller's sweep width against the transitors. As an approximation, it is assumed that detection capability is cookie cutter to distance $w/2$ from the patroller. That is,

$$p_\ell(x) = \begin{cases} 1, & \text{if } 0 \leq x \leq w/2, \\ 0, & \text{otherwise.} \end{cases}$$

FIGURE 9.5. REGIONS OF EFFECTIVENESS OF LINEAR AND CROSSOVER PLANS

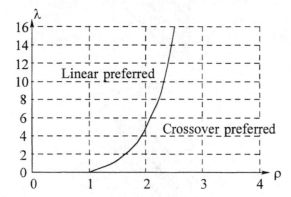

Figure 9.6 shows two cases, where the patroller's turnaround points are at boundaries of the transit channel (the end points of the front) and where the turnaround points are short of the boundaries. Consider the case of turning around at the channel boundary.

FIGURE 9.6. TWO TURNAROUND ASSUMPTIONS

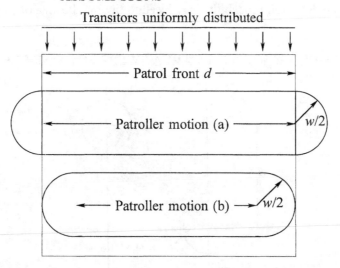

The method of gauging kinematic effects is to consider the transitor position fixed and to analyze the motion of the patroller and its detection circle relative to the transitor. The region swept in three legs of relative motion is shown in Figure 9.7. The angle θ is given by arctan u/v.

FIGURE 9.7. RELATIVE AREA SWEPT WITH PATROLLER REVERSING COURSE AT BOUNDARIES

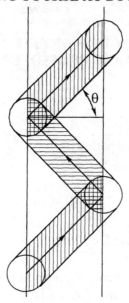

Figure 9.8 shows a single leg. It is evident that the detection probability on that leg is the ratio of the area of the shaded region to the area of the rectangle of length d and height $d\tan\theta$, i.e., du/v, and, from Figure 9.7, this same ratio is the detection probability over multiple complete legs. Thus the problem of finding detection probability is reduced to finding the area of the shaded region in Figure 9.8.

FIGURE 9.8. RELATIVE AREA SWEPT FOR ONE LEG

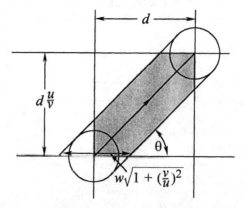

Consider now the parallelogram formed by adding to the shaded region the right triangle shown at each end. It is seen from either of those triangles that half the base of the parallelogram is

$$\frac{w/2}{\sin \theta}.$$

Since $\tan \theta = u/v$ it follows that $\sin \theta = u/(u^2+v^2)^{1/2}$, so the area of the parallelogram is

$$wd\frac{u}{v}\sqrt{1 + \frac{v^2}{u^2}}.$$

Now make the important assumptions that d/w is sufficiently large and v/u is sufficiently close to 1 so that the area of the parallelogram is a good approximation to the area of the shaded region. Then the triangles mentioned above have small area compared to the parallelogram and by dividing by d^2u/v, which is the area of the rectangle, the probability p of detecting a given transitor is

$$p = \frac{w}{d}\sqrt{1 + \frac{v^2}{u^2}}. \tag{9-7}$$

Since w/d is the detection probability if the patroller were motionless, the factor

$$\sqrt{1 + \frac{v^2}{u^2}} \tag{9-8}$$

represents the multiplicative enhancement to the patroller's detection probability that arises from motion of the two ships, providing the barrier length is large compared to sweep width; (9-8) is called the **kinematic enhancement factor**. Note that the term (9-8) also appears (as $(\rho^2 + 1)^{1/2}$) in (9-6), the formula for probability of detection by a linear patrol.

When the area of triangles by which the parallelogram differs from the shaded area is removed, it is not hard to show that the patroller's detection probability is

$$p - \frac{1}{4}p^2,$$

where p is as in (9-7). If p is .2 or smaller, the error due to neglecting the end-effect triangles is $(.2)^2/4 = .01$ or less, thus the error in using (9-7) is at most 5 percent of the correct value.

Tactic (b) in Figure 9.6, was the case analyzed in 904 and the probability of detection is given by (9-6). In this case it can be shown that if d/w is large, (9-7) is a good approximation to detection probability, so (9-8) again approximates kinematic enhancement. In fact, in many cases the error caused by using (9-7) for tactic (b) is less than the error resulting from its use for tactic (a).

Note that if the two speeds are equal, the kinematic enhancement factor is 1.41 so patrol motion improves search effectiveness by 41 percent over standing still. If v/u is 3/2, then patrol motion improves search effectiveness by 80 percent.

The discussion in this section assumes that w does not change with speed of patroller or transitor. The next section explores what happens when this is not the case.

906   Kinematic Enhancement Versus Acoustic Degradation

Now assume that the patroller and transitor are submarines and that they are nuclear-powered. (The diesel-snorkel cycles of diesel submarines would greatly complicate what follows.)

Most of the things a submarine CO wants to do can be done better at high speed than at low speed, from a *kinematic* standpoint. However, an increase in a submarine's speed is generally accompanied by an increase in noise, in fact two types of noise: self-noise, which interferes with her listening ability, and radiated noise, which discloses her presence to hostile units. These are denoted L_N and L_S respectively in Chapter 4. They are measured in dB and are reflected additively in sonar figure of merit (*FOM*) as L_S - L_N. Thus an increase in speed incurs acoustic degradation as well as kinematic enhancement. Tradeoffs thereby arising in the tactical situation of a submarine patrolling a back-and-forth barrier versus a submarine transitor trying to penetrate the barrier undetected will now be examined.

For modeling purposes, first consider the forms of the relationships of self-noise versus speed and radiated noise versus speed.

At speeds below some "breakpoint" speed, self-noise is independent of speed. In this speed regime, self-noise is governed by the ambient, by electronic self-noise, and by the speed-independent non-propulsion machinery necessary for the submarine's "hotel" functions. At speeds above this breakpoint, self-noise is governed mainly by flow noise, from water passing the hull. It is assumed that noise versus speed is linear in this regime. Thus the relation between self-noise and speed is determined by three parameters: the breakpoint speed, the constant self-noise below that speed, and the slope (in dB/knot) of the linear graph of self-noise versus speed above that speed. For the patroller call these v_s, n_{sp}, and m_{sp}, respectively, and for the transitor call them u_s, n_{st}, and m_{bt}. These parameters vary from submarine to submarine.

Similarly, at speeds below some possibly different breakpoint speed, radiated noise is independent of speed, being dominated by that arising from the hotel machinery. Linearity of radiated noise versus speed above the breakpoint speed is assumed. For the patroller, the breakpoint speed, the constant radiated noise at speeds below that speed, and the slope of radiated noise versus speed above that speed are denoted v_r, n_{rp}, and m_{rp}, respectively, and for the transitor denote them u_r, n_{rt}, and m_{rt}.

Illustrations of these four noise-speed relations are given in Figure 9.9. Their formulas are as follows (z^+ is defined as max $\{z, 0\}$ for any z):

$$\text{transitor self-noise} = n_{st} + m_{st}(u - u_s)^+,$$
$$\text{transitor radiated noise} = n_{rt} + m_{rt}(u - u_r)^+,$$
$$\text{patroller self-noise} = n_{sp} + m_{sp}(v - v_s)^+,$$
$$\text{patroller radiated noise} = n_{rp} + m_{rp}(v - v_r)^+.$$

It is further needed to model propagation loss, N_W, in terms of range, r. This is taken to be a "spreading law":

$$N_W = k\log_{10}r,$$

where k is the "spreading factor." Hence

$$r = 10^{N_W/k}.$$

For detection to occur, $N_W \le FOM$ (see Chapter 4).

The foregoing will now be combined to measure the patroller's detection capability against the transitor, ignoring for the moment the transitor's capability to counterdetect the patroller. Assume a cookie-cutter detection model where the sweep width of the patroller is twice the detection range r. Assume also that the patroller's speed, v, and the transitor's speed, u, remain at or above v_s and u_r, respectively (in the ensuing analysis, there is no point in using lower speeds). For detection, $N_W =$

FOM, so

$$r = 10^{FOM/k}.$$

Following (4-2), let

$$FOM = n_{rt} + m_{rt}(u - u_r) - n_{sp} - m_{sp}(v - v_s) + L$$

$$= J + Z,$$

where

$$J = m_{rt}u - m_{sp}v,$$

and *L* and hence *Z* do not depend on *v* or *u*. Thus the kinematically-enhanced sweep width may be expressed as

$$Q10^{J/k}\sqrt{1 + \frac{v^2}{u^2}} \equiv Qf(u, v), \tag{9-9}$$

where Q embodies the effects of all components of *FOM* that do not depend on the speed of either unit. Note that while Q need not be computed, for purposes of derivation it is $2 \times 10^{Z/k}/d$.

FIGURE. 9.9. ILLUSTRATIVE NOISE-SPEED CURVES

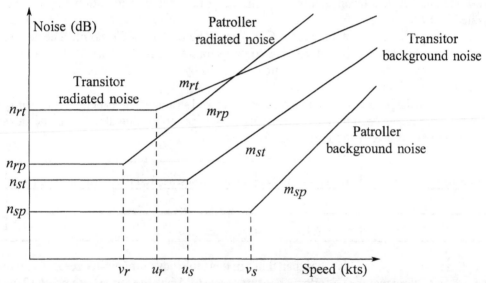

Thus *f* defined by (9-9) embodies both the kinematic and acoustic effects on sweep width that arise from the choices of speed by both the patroller and the transitor. Hence *f* may be used as the payoff function in a game theory analysis (Chapter 2) of these speed choices.

As examples, fix the spreading factor *k* at 20 ("spherical" spreading) and the breakpoint speeds v_s and u_r both at 6 knots. Each pure strategy for the two players is a choice of speed, *u* for the transitor and *v* for the patroller. For a pair of such choices, the payoff to the patroller is *f(u, v)*.

Again, there is no point in either player using a speed lower than the breakpoint speed, under the assumptions. Assume that speeds greater than 20 knots will not be entertained and that the speed choices for each player will be restricted to 6, 8, 10, ... , 20 knots.

Payoff matrices for this situation for each of four pairs of noise-speed slopes are shown in Figure 9.10. Again, these are values of f and are (dimensionless) numbers proportional to the patroller's sweep width.

Consider first part (a) of Figure 9.10, where m_{sp}, the patroller's self-noise slope, and m_{rt}, the transitor's radiated noise slope, are both 0.1 dB/knot. These are the lowest noise-speed slopes considered in these examples. The payoff matrix has a saddle-point (payoff is highest in its column and lowest in its row – see Chapter 2) at $u = v = 20$ knots. Thus both players are advised to run at the highest speed under consideration. That is not surprising since the low noise-speed slopes mean that there is only slight acoustic degradation from high speed and one can take full advantage accordingly of kinematic enhancement.

On the other hand, in part (b), where $m_{sp} = m_{rt} = 0.8$ dB/knot, the highest noise-speed slope of these examples, there is a saddle-point at $u = v = 6$ knots, the lowest speed considered. Thus both are advised to use minimum speed because of the high acoustic penalties from high speed.

In part (c), $m_{sp} = 0.5$ dB/knot and $m_{rt} = 0.7$ dB/knot. Here there are saddle-points at $u = 8$ knots, $v = 10, 12,$ or 14 knots. This is an example of saddle-point solutions that are interior to the extreme speeds of 6 and 20 knots among those considered. Among the patroller's three speeds which are optimal with respect to the payoff function f, probably the highest, 14 knots, is preferred, since it provides better ability to outrun a torpedo. (Indeed the latter consideration might better be incorporated into f.)

In part (d), $m_{sp} = 0.5$ dB/knot and $m_{rt} = 0.6$ dB/knot. There is no saddle-point. The next step is to eliminate dominated rows and columns. The columns for $u = 12, 14, 16, 18,$ and 20 are dominated by $u = 10$. The rows for $v = 16, 18,$ and 20 are dominated by $v = 14$. These eliminations result in the payoff matrix in Figure 9.11.

By formulating the problem of finding an optimal mixed strategy to two-person zero-sum game as a linear program (see Appendix B) and applying a linear programming algorithm, one can show that the optimal pair of mixed strategies is as follows:

Patroller use speed v	with probability	Transitor uses speed u	with probability
6	.08	8	.75
12	.92	10	.25

In these optimal strategies, speeds other than those in this table have probability zero. The value of the game is 1.567. Note that the patroller can insure at least 1.56 by the pure strategy $v = 12$ and the transitor can insure no more than 1.57 by the pure strategy $u = 8$; thus this pair of speeds is an approximate saddle-point. The advantage to either player of the optimal mixed strategy over the approximate saddle-point pure strategies is slight. That is fairly typical of the payoff function f as defined by (9-9). There is often an approximate saddle-point in the neighborhood of which payoff is insensitive to speed choices. In such a situation, computation of optimal mixed strategies is probably not worth the effort. However, in the tactical situation giving rise to this analysis, it certainly is important to pay attention to breakpoint speeds and noise-speed slopes, and a saddle-point analysis, albeit in approximate terms, can be a useful assist to decision making.

FIGURE 9.10. ILLUSTRATIVE SPEED-CHOICE PAYOFF MATRICES

(a) Spreading factor = 20.0, Patroller self-noise slope = .1 dB/kt, Transitor radiated noise slope = .1 dB/kt

$v\backslash u$	6	8	10	12	14	16	18	20
6	1.41	1.28	1.22	1.20	1.19	1.20	1.21	1.23
8	1.63	1.41	1.31	1.26	1.23	1.23	1.23	1.24
10	1.86	1.56	1.41	1.33	1.29	1.26	1.25	1.25
12	2.03	1.72	1.53	1.41	1.35	1.31	1.29	1.28
14	2.32	1.88	1.64	1.50	1.41	1.36	1.33	1.31
16	2.54	2.04	1.76	1.59	1.48	1.41	1.37	1.34
18	2.75	2.19	1.88	1.68	1.56	1.47	1.41	1.38
20	2.96	2.35	1.99	1.77	1.63	1.53	1.46	1.41

(b) Spreading factor = 20.0, Patroller self-noise slope = .8 dB/kt, Transitor radiated noise slope = .8 dB/kt

$v\backslash u$	6	8	10	12	14	16	18	20
6	1.41	1.50	1.69	1.94	2.27	2.68	3.18	3.79
8	1.39	1.41	1.54	1.74	2.00	2.34	2.75	3.25
10	1.34	1.33	1.41	1.56	1.78	2.05	2.39	2.81
12	1.29	1.25	1.30	1.41	1.58	1.81	2.09	2.44
14	1.22	1.16	1.19	1.28	1.41	1.60	1.83	2.12
16	1.13	1.07	1.09	1.15	1.26	1.41	1.61	1.85
18	1.05	0.98	0.99	1.04	1.13	1.25	1.41	1.62
20	0.96	0.89	0.89	0.93	1.00	1.11	1.24	1.41

(c) Spreading factor = 20.0, Patroller self-noise slope = .5 dB/kt, Transitor radiated noise slope = .7 dB/kt

$v\backslash u$	6	8	10	12	14	16	18	20
6	1.62	1.69	1.85	2.08	2.38	2.75	3.18	3.70
8	1.71	1.70	1.81	1.99	2.25	2.56	2.95	3.41
10	1.77	1.72	1.78	1.93	2.14	2.41	2.74	3.15
12	1.82	1.72	1.75	1.86	2.04	2.27	2.57	2.93
14	1.84	1.72	1.72	1.81	1.95	2.16	2.41	2.73
16	1.84	1.70	1.68	1.75	1.87	2.04	2.27	2.56
18	1.82	1.66	1.64	1.68	1.79	1.94	2.14	2.39
20	1.78	1.62	1.58	1.62	1.70	1.84	2.02	2.24

(d) Spreading factor = 20.0, Patroller self-noise slope = .5 dB/kt, Transitor radiated noise slope = .6 dB/kt

$v\backslash u$	6	8	10	12	14	16	18	20
6	1.52	1.54	1.65	1.81	2.03	2.28	2.59	2.94
8	1.59	1.55	1.61	1.74	1.91	2.13	2.39	2.71
10	1.65	1.56	1.59	1.68	1.82	2.00	2.23	2.50
12	1.70	1.57	1.56	1.62	1.74	1.89	2.09	2.33
14	1.72	1.56	1.53	1.57	1.66	1.79	1.96	2.17
16	1.72	1.55	1.50	1.52	1.59	1.70	1.85	2.03
18	1.70	1.52	1.46	1.47	1.52	1.61	1.74	1.90
20	1.67	1.48	1.41	1.41	1.45	1.53	1.64	1.78

FIGURE 9.11. REDUCED PAYOFF MATRIX

Spreading factor = 20
Patroller self-noise slope = 0.5 dB/kt
Transitor radiated noise slope = 0.6 dB/kt

$v\backslash u$	6	8	10
6	1.52	1.54	1.65
8	1.59	1.55	1.61
10	1.65	1.56	1.59
12	1.70	1.57	1.56
14	1.72	1.56	1.53
16	1.72	1.55	1.50

This approach can be extended to take account of counterdetection by the transitor as well as detection by the patroller. One method would be to replace J in (9-9) by

$$[n_{st} + m_{st}(u - u_s)^+ + n_{rt} + m_{rt}(u - u_r)^+]$$
$$- [n_{sp} + m_{sp}(v - v_s)^+ + n_{rp} + m_{rp}(v - v_r)^+].$$

A better method of bringing counterdetection into this analysis is to compute sweep width as the area under a redefined patroller's lateral range curve: let the ordinate at a given lateral range be cumulative probability that the patroller detects without being *previously* counterdetected by the transitor. The area under this curve is an MOE that has been called **secure sweep width**. That term is not to be interpreted as implying that the patroller is secure against counterdetection out to a stated width, but it is a measure of the patroller's ability to detect without prior counterdetection. (It is also complicated to compute.)

907   Other Literature and History

Most of the material in 901 through 905 is taken from the World War II classic, Koopman [1]. The kinematic enhancement factor is at least implicit in that work. Its role in submarine ASW barrier patrols and tradeoffs with acoustic effects of speed were emphasized in Loane and Wagner [2] and in later work on submarine ASW search manuals. Washburn [3] supports the accuracy of the simplifying approximation given by the kinematic enhancement factor by showing that (9-7) is an upper bound on detection probability and that one can come close to this bound by feasible patrol plans. The game analysis of choice of speeds by transitor and patroller originated in Kettelle and Wagner [4], a precursor to [2], and was developed analytically for a continuum of speed choices by Langford [5]. The concept of secure sweep width mentioned at the end of the chapter is developed in [4] and [2].

[1] Koopman, Bernard O. *Search and Screening*. Operations Evaluation Group Report 56.

Washington, DC: Office of the Chief of Naval Operations, 1946.

[2] Loane, Edward P., and Daniel H. Wagner. *Submarine-versus-Submarine Secure Sweep Width Manual*. Paoli, Pa: Daniel H. Wagner, Associates Report to Bureau of Ships, Commander Submarine Group Two, and David Taylor Model Basin, 17 December, 1964.

[3] Washburn, Alan R. "On Patrolling a Channel." *Naval Research Logistics Quarterly* 29 (December, 1982): 609-615.

[4] Kettelle, John D., and Daniel H. Wagner. *Acoustic Effectiveness of Specific Nuclear Submarines*. Kettelle & Wagner Report to David Taylor Model Basin, March 31, 1963.

[5] Langford, Eric S. "A Continuous Submarine Versus Submarine Game." *Naval Research Logistics Quarterly* 20 (September, 1973): 405-417.

Problems

1. A single patrol aircraft is assigned to fly a crossover barrier across a channel 150 nm wide to detect surface vessels transiting parallel to the channel boundaries on course 225° true. The following parameters prevail:

Visual sweep width:	15 nm
Track spacing:	25 nm
Maximum expected target speed:	20 knots
Aircraft cruising speed:	120 knots

a. What is the initial true heading of the aircraft on the first leg if the barrier starts on the northwest side of the channel?
b. What is the time (in hours) required to fly one upsweep along the channel boundary?
c. What is the time (in hours) required to fly one complete basic element?
d. What type of crossover barrier results?
e. What courses of action are open to the patrol squadron commander that would result in an advancing barrier?

2. Preliminary calculations by a task group staff operations officer indicate that utilizing one aircraft under the conditions given, a retiring crossover barrier with the following parameters would result:

Time for target to move two track spacings:	2.50 hours
Time for aircraft to complete one basic element:	2.65 hours
Channel width:	175 nm
Track spacing:	25 nm
Target speed:	20 knots
Aircraft speed:	150 knots

a. What is the minimum number of aircraft that will change the retiring barrier into either a symmetric or an advancing crossover barrier?
b. With the number of aircraft determined in part a, what track spacing results in a symmetric crossover barrier?

3. A merchant ship, with an estimated speed of 20 knots on a westerly course, is expected to pass through an approach zone to a harbor. A patrol squadron, utilizing aircraft with a cruising speed of 160 knots, has been assigned the task of flying a barrier across this approach zone and taking photographs of all merchant vessels for intelligence purposes.

Assuming the squadron can maintain one aircraft on station for 6 hours at a time, and using a track spacing of not more than 16 nm, answer the following:

a. How long will it take the aircraft to fly one complete basic element of its patrol if the approach zone is 100 nm wide?
b. What type of crossover barrier results if the track spacing is 16 nm?
c. What track spacing results in a symmetric barrier?
d. How many complete basic elements can an aircraft fly within its 6-hour patrol period?

4. The coverage of a 500 nm wide channel is required using a barrier with a 95 percent chance of detection. Aircraft search speed will be 190 knots. The best estimate of enemy transiting speed is 18 knots. For existing conditions, the sweep width is 25 nm. The inverse cube law for detection is assumed.
a. What is the maximum track spacing that can be used?
b. How many aircraft are needed in order to have a symmetric barrier?
c. Using the minimum number of aircraft required, what must be the values of s, y, and α?
d. What is the probability of detection?

5. You have been assigned to provide a 90 percent chance of detecting and photographing any ship that transits a certain channel for the next two-week period. You must decide how to use your squadron of ten patrol planes most effectively to accomplish the objective. The inverse cube law applies and the following data are known or assumed:

Channel width:	100 nm
Maximum search speed:	200 knots
Maximum expected target speed:	30 knots
Predicted sweep width:	30 nm
Aircraft endurance (takeoff to landing):	12 hours
Distance from base to channel:	80 nm
Maximum number of aircraft airborne at one time:	4

a.   State the objective of the operation.
b.   What measure of effectiveness can be used?
c.   What is the maximum allowable track spacing?
d.   What is the maximum number of basic elements that will be flown each day?
e.   What is the minimum number of aircraft that must be on station?

6.   The United States as part of a naval blockade wishes to detect ships moving through a choke point. The choke point is 1000 nm wide and intended targets move through the choke point at a maximum speed of 20 knots. The means of detection is a radar set mounted on planes having a cruising speed of 250 knots. The sweep width of the radar is 40 nm.

a.   Using a flight of only 2 planes flying the barrier at a time, what track spacing should be used to give a symmetric crossover barrier. What is the estimated probability of detection?
b.   To insure a probability of detection that equals or exceeds .90, how many planes are needed to fly in parallel to establish a symmetric crossover barrier? What track spacing should be used? What is the estimated probability of detection?

7.   A destroyer can conduct a sonar search at 15 knots. It is to prevent the undetected penetration of a barrier across a channel of width 10 nm by enemy submarines. Assume the maximum speed of a submarine in this channel is 12 knots. The sweep width of the destroyer's sonar is 2 nm.

a.   What patrol type (crossover or linear) is preferred?
b.   What is the probability of detection using the preferred patrol type?
c.   Compute the probability of detection for the non-preferred patrol type when the destroyer can conduct a sonar search at 22 knots.
d.   How much of a speed change would have to be made by the destroyer in order for the two patrol types to give about the same probability of detection?
e.   What is the probability of detection when the destroyer's speed is 15 knots and it conducts a linear patrol from channel boundary to channel boundary?
f.   What is the value of the kinematic enhancement factor in this case?

8.   Compute the probabilities of detection when (i) doing a linear patrol and turning around at the distance $w/2$ from the channel boundaries, (ii) doing a crossover patrol and turning around at the distance $w/2$ from the channel boundaries, (iii) doing a linear patrol and turning around on the channel boundaries and using the "approximation" formula, and (iv) doing a linear patrol and turning around on the channel boundaries and using the "exact" formula for the following cases. Before doing the calculations state for which cases you believe the approximation formula will give a good approximation to the value produced by the exact formula and for which cases it will give a poor approximation. Here v and u are in knots and w and d are in nm:

a. $v = 15, u = 10, w = 2,$ and $d = 12,$
b. $v = 12, u = 6, w = 2,$ and $d = 8,$
c. $v = 12, u = 6, w = 2,$ and $d = 20,$
d. $v = 12, u = 10, w = 2,$ and $d = 20.$

9.   An ASW helicopter is assigned to protect an area with patrol front length d by dipping its active sonar for time t_{dp} at intervals $2r$ between dips, while traveling parallel to the front at speed v back and forth between the boundaries. Transiting submarines enter the region at speed u uniformly distributed across the front on a course perpendicular to the front. Any transitor which closes the helo to within range r from the sonar is detected.

a.   Assuming $d \gg r$, derive an expression to estimate the probability that a transitor will be detected.
b.   Use this model to compute the probability of detection, where $u = 10$ knots, $r = 3$ nm, $v = 60$ knots, $d = 60$ nm, $t_{dp} = .1$ hour.

10. Suppose that in (9-9), the admissible speeds are $u = 6, 10, 14$ kts and $v = 6, 10, 14$ kts, the spreading factor is 20, patroller's self-noise speed slope is 0.5 dB/knot, and transitor's radiated noise speed slope is 0.3 dB/knot.

a.   Compute the payoff matrix for f (hint: use spreadsheet format).
b.   What is the solution of this game?

Answers to Problems

1.   a. $144° 36'$. b. 0.18 hour. c. 2.89 hours. d. retiring. e. (1) increase number of aircraft, sweep d' instead of d, increase aircraft speed.
2.   a. 2 aircraft. b. 13.3 nm.

3.   a. 1.44 hours. b. advancing.

4.   a. 16 nm. b. 4. c. $s = 13$ nm, $y = 47.5$ nm, $a = 5° 26'$. d. .984.

5.   a. Detect and photograph shipping(with assigned probability of 90 percent).
b.   Number of aircraft hours flown for a two-week period.
c.   22.85 nm. d. 14. e. 2.

7.   a. linear patrol. b. .32. c. .40. d. An increase of 7 knots. e. .29 ("exact"), .32 ("approximate").
f. a 60 percent increase.

8.   a. .29, .27, .30, .28. b. .53, .54, .56, .48. c. .22, .22, .22, .21.

9.   a.

$$\frac{2rut_{dp} + \pi r^2}{du\left[2\dfrac{r}{v} + t_{dp}\right]}.$$

b. .28.

10. a.

$v\backslash u$	6	10	14
6	1.23	1.17	1.25
10	1.34	1.12	1.12
14	1.40	1.09	1.02

b.   There is a saddle-point at $v = 6$ kts, $u = 10$ kts. The value is 1.17.

10
MINE WARFARE

In October 1950, an amphibious task force of 250 ships with some 50,000 troops embarked steamed back and forth outside the approaches to Wonsan harbor in Korea. D-day for the landing at Wonsan had been set for 20 October, but a week after D-day the task force still marched and countermarched offshore while food supplies ran low. The landing was delayed because the approaches to Wonsan were mined. The situation was reported to the Chief of Naval Operations by Rear Admiral Allan Smith in a message which began:

> *"The U. S. Navy has lost control of the sea to a nation without a navy, using pre-World War I weapons laid by vessels that were utilized at the time of the birth of Christ."*

Admiral Forrest Sherman, who was then CNO, later explained:

> *"When you can't go where you want to, when you want to, then you haven't got command of the sea."*

The minefield shown in Figure 10.1 had a similar effect in Desert Storm, except the landing never occurred. Mines are a menace to naval operations.

It wasn't always that way. At one time mines were generally rejected for naval use because they were considered too clandestine for a chivalrous nation to use. That stopped being true at about the time of the Civil War. It was actually a minefield that Admiral Farragut so heartily *damned* at Mobile Bay (the terms *mine* and *torpedo* were used interchangeably during that period). The Civil War taught that, whether or not mines are regarded as "distasteful," navies must be prepared to defend against them and to use them whenever they can be employed productively. Mines have shown themselves to be effective naval weapons in every major conflict since the Civil War. Two-thirds of the ship casualties in the Russo-Japanese War of 1904 were due to mines. In WWI, thousands of mines were used by both sides in the North Sea, and the mining of the Dardanelles by the Turks was the event that precipitated the disastrous British invasion. In June 1942, the German submarine U-701 planted 15 mines off the Chesapeake Capes. Five of those mines sank or damaged ships, while also bottling up shipping in Hampton Roads and Newport News for two days. The WWII mine campaign against Japan sank or damaged over 2 million tons of enemy shipping , and was a crucial factor in ending the war. Literature describing this history is cited in the final section of the chapter.

FIGURE 10.1. DESERT STORM MINEFIELDS

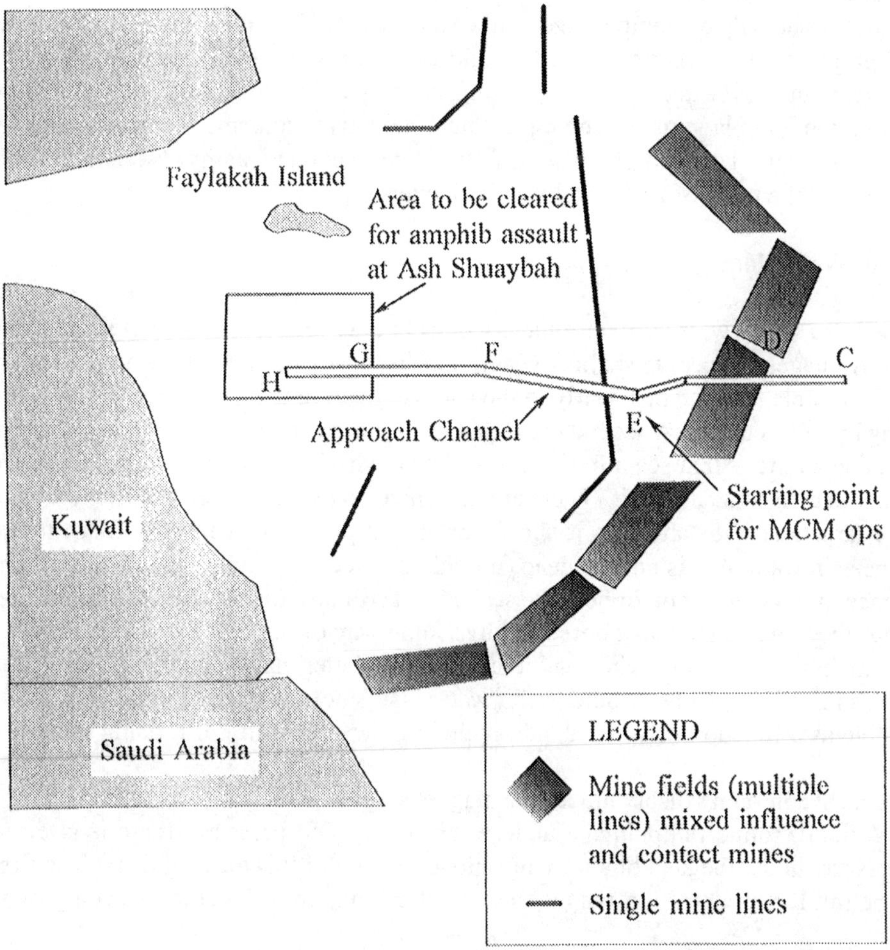

Mines will continue to be an important part of naval warfare. The availability of cheap micro-processors with low power requirements has given mines a technological advantage, and even mines designed decades ago have shown themselves to be effective in modern combat.

This chapter develops mine warfare models. The motivation includes the possibility that they might be used to study broader issues than just mine warfare, as is brought out in 1002, after some technology background in 1001. Section 1003 on minefield planning introduces several functions, e.g., actuator functions, used in minefield planning that are mathematically similar to the lateral range function, which was introduced in Chapter 6 and is key to the concept of sweep width.

Analytic mine warfare models are often compelled to reduce multiple actuation curves to a single actuation curve by an averaging process. The pros and cons of this **pre-averaging** are the subject of 1004. In 1005 a simulation model is outlined as an alternative to the analytic model of 1003. Section 1006 is a brief reexamination of mine warfare from the point of view of the side encountering a minefield. The problem of estimating the number of active mines left in a field that has been swept is addressed. Mine warfare is a situation with two sides having opposing interests making tactical decisions. Applications of two-person zero-sum game theory to explore decision options are discussed in 1007.

The Navy relies heavily on computerized mine warfare models, which are gradually replacing formulas and graphs as a means of developing and assessing the effectiveness of tactics. This movement began in the 1970s and is still continuing, encompassing dozens of computer programs designed to aid minefield planning, sweeping and hunting, navigation, and record keeping. Some of these models will be used as examples below, and the final section contains a brief history of mine warfare analysis and the models mentioned in this chapter.

1001   A Little Technology

The earliest sea mines were **contact** mines. Contact mines are still in use, but they have some important disadvantages. Except in shallow water, one disadvantage is that they must be anchored to the seabed by a cable that extends nearly to the surface, making them vulnerable to mechanical **minesweeping** by cable cutters. A second disadvantage is that the radius of action is limited by the target's width, and a third is that sea mines are most lethal when they detonate significantly below the target, rather than in contact with it. There are thus three powerful reasons for employing mines that can sense targets at a distance, so it should not be surprising that most modern mines are **influence** mines. In water that is not too deep (roughly 200 feet, depending on charge weight and target), influence mines can rest on or near the seabed and still be a threat to targets on the surface. In deeper water they must either be moored or have some way of moving toward the target. The former choice makes the mooring cables vulnerable and the latter makes the mines expensive, so, given a choice, a minefield planner would prefer water that is not too deep. Figure 10.2 shows the options available as a function of water depth, including the possibility of a rising mine in deep water.

The three most common sensory modes are magnetism (the passage of a steel ship changes the local magnetic field), sound (ships make underwater noise), and pressure (there is a temporary decrease in pressure under the keel of a moving ship, especially if it is moving fast). The first two sensor types permit longer detection ranges than the third, but are subject to sweeping by minesweepers or helicopters that artificially create the magnetic/acoustic signatures characteristic of target ships. The advantage of the pressure sensor is that there seems to be no way to create the pressure effect except by having a large "guinea pig" ship pass over the mine, an awkward sweeping technique. A pressure sensor, however, is subject to false alarms due to waves, so it is usually used in combination with other sensors. Using a combination of sensors also tends to frustrate mine-sweeping, as does the employment of other counter-countermeasures such as delay timers or ship-counters that actuate the mine only after the required influence has been sensed a certain number of times.

Mines can also be countered by **hunting,** by which is meant locating a mine by some mechanism (eyeball, sonar, laser, ...) independent of the mine's sensors. Detected "mine-like-objects" are typically examined more closely and, if judged to be mines, either avoided or destroyed. Hunting has an advantage over sweeping in that most counter-countermeasures are without effect, but hunting suffers from false alarms and a relatively low sweep width, particularly against bottom mines that are partially buried. The proper division of effort between sweeping and hunting is one of the reasons for developing mine warfare models.

A third countermeasure is to cover a given area with such intense lethal effects that all mines contained in it are necessarily destroyed. This "destruction" alternative has the advantages that it can't be outwitted (as sweeping can) and that false alarms are not an issue, and the disadvantages that it is very expensive and (of course) destructive. It is generally implemented either by line charges or intense air strikes, and used only when minefields are both dense and unavoidable.

Water is denser and less compressible than air, so sea mines tend to have a much larger radius of action than land mines, particularly against targets subject to damage by shock waves. Sea mines are also harder to sweep and hunt than land mines, so mine warfare is an essentially different topic in the Navy, where mines are a potential show stopper, than in the Army, where mines tend to be viewed as a nuisance, albeit one that has to be planned for. An exception to this is the availability of artillery in conjunction with minefields on land. Artillery does well against concentrated targets, and since one countermeasure to minefields is concentration, the two measures can be particularly effective if used together. Naval minefields typically do not have the counterpart of artillery to support them

One general consideration which must be noted in mine warfare is that mines, once planted, do not distinguish between friend and foe. They will destroy one's own or neutral forces as indiscriminately as those of an enemy. It is therefore essential that the presence of minefields be carefully published to all friendly forces who may traverse the mined area. It is required by international law (The Hague Convention, 1907) that the presence of minefields which threaten neutral shipping be published to the neutrals concerned. Consideration must also be given to sterilization of the mine-field once hostilities cease. Historically, mines have caused more damage to noncombatants than they have to combatants.

1002   Modeling Mine Warfare in Theater Level Models

In spite of its importance, mine warfare is often a peripheral consideration in operational studies. For example one might be concerned with whether a planned logistic system for a battle fleet is sufficient to sustain it in combat, and might begin the study by using a wargame within which mine warfare is not even represented. But on second thought minefields are relevant to sustainability, so how can they be included in the study without imposing a big computational or conceptual burden? The answer will be a very simple kind of minefield model, one that omits most of the minefield detail while still capturing the essence of the matter. Such models are the subject of this section.

FIGURE 10.2. MINING OPTIONS DEPEND ON WATER DEPTH

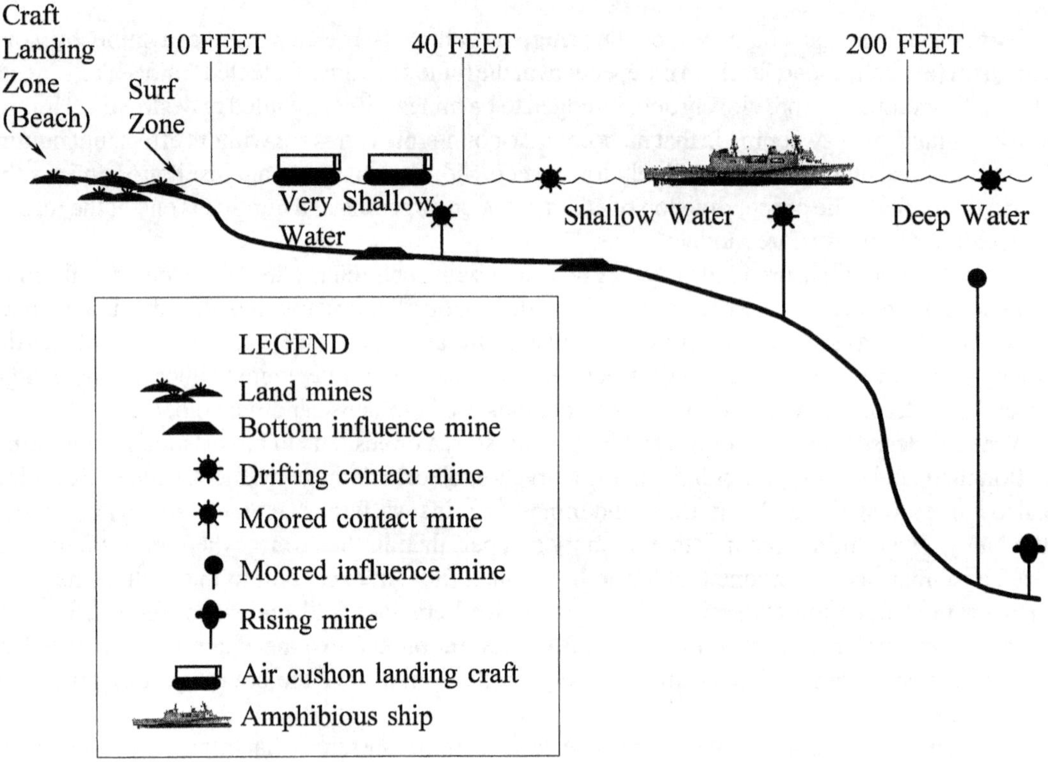

In a wargame, a "minefield" might be as simple as a prohibited region with an associated story line. The designers might announce, "Supply ships are not allowed to transit XYZ Strait because of the presence of minefields in the region." The implied model of mine warfare is that countermeasures are impossible, reconnaissance is perfect, and logistic problems in placing the minefield at XYZ are not relevant to the question being studied. None of those statements are really true, but even so the model might be satisfactory. XYZ Strait might be a shallow, easily mined region that, in the judgment of the designers, would simply be avoided in favor of other alternatives in the event of a conflict.

Wargame players might also be allowed to create their own minefields if the game included realistic rules and constraints. A possible set of rules in a Red versus Blue wargame might be as follows:

a. Red may construct only 10 square miles of minefield during the game, and each minefield requires the presence of a Red unit somewhere within it when the minefield is created.

b. Except for minesweepers, any Blue ship entering a Red minefield is sunk immediately, and the outlines of the minefield are then immediately revealed to the Blue commander. Red units are unaffected by Red minefields.

c. Entry of any Blue minesweeper into a minefield will immediately reveal the minefield's outlines to the Blue commander, and furthermore the minefield will disappear 48 hours later.

There would be similar rules for minefields created by Blue. These rules are probably overly simple, since they permit a single unit to create or counter a minefield, but still they are easily understood, easily implemented, and adequate for some purposes. They permit mine warfare to be "played" in a way that is impossible if minefields are simply announced by the game designers. A rough replication of what happened at Wonsan, for example, might happen within these rules.

The above sketches might be called "permission" models, since the central idea is a region that every unit either has permission to enter or not. While such models are useful for some purposes, an important idea is missing – the idea that a ship might enter a minefield without permission, but still not be damaged. The fact is that *most* ships that enter real minefields emerge undamaged, either by luck or design, so there is a danger of overstating the effectiveness of minefields if the possibility is ignored. To include it in a quantitative way will require the introduction of probability theory, a characteristic of all of the models that follow.

The Enhanced Naval Wargaming System (ENWGS) incorporates a minefield model that is basically a permission model with another level of detail – the number of mines m in the minefield and a sweep width w associated with each mine. The idea is that every ship that comes within $w/2$ of a mine will be damaged (or sunk, not distinguished here) by it and in the process decrease m by one. ENWGS does not actually keep track of mine locations. To decide whether a ship is damaged over a given time interval, ENWGS first computes the ship's incremental length of track l within the minefield, and then an actuation probability wl/A, providing $wl \ll A$, where A is the minefield's area. The implied assumption is that each mine is uniformly distributed over the minefield. In its Monte Carlo mode, ENWGS selects a uniform random number U and compares U to wl/A. If $U < wl/A$, the mine actuates and damages the ship; otherwise the next mine is tested using a new independent random number until finally all m mines have been considered. Since the number of mines decreases with every actuation, the minefield gradually becomes less effective with time; this is an important feature of mine warfare that cannot be included in a simple permission model.

In using an independent random number to make each of its comparisons, ENWGS is implicitly assuming that the mines are located independently as well as uniformly at random within the minefield. There is an odd dissonance here: Platforms responsible for laying mines usually practice laying them accurately, especially relative to each other, whereas ENWGS and practically every other minefield model begin by assuming that mines are simply strewn about at random. The reasons for this curious situation are worth a digression.

Seemingly a minefield planner would want to arrange mines in such a manner as to leave no gaps in coverage, which would typically have them being evenly spaced on a single line perpendicular to the direction of ship traffic, rather than spaced randomly throughout the minefield. Laying mines in lines is also tactically convenient, so one would expect to encounter lines of mines in practice, rather than random fields of them. In fact one *does* encounter mine lines in practice. Figure 10.1 shows the locations of the mine lines/fields laid by Iraq before Desert Storm. Even the regions shown as fields actually consisted of multiple lines. Incidentally (to digress a bit within this digression), Figure 10.1 also makes it clear that the original U.S. sweeping plan was in a region where there were no mines. The hits on the *Tripoli* (moored mine) and *Princeton* (bottom mine) were the first indications that the minefields were actually located as shown – the exact locations were not known until after the war. The *Tripoli* and *Princeton* paid for the lack of surveillance of minelaying operations.

Even though Desert Storm mines were laid in lines, they were not laid in a *single* line. There are two advantages to the miner for not using a single line. One is the avoidance of fratricide among the mines or minelayers. The other is complication of the mine countermeasures job, since mines in a single line would be easy to sweep or avoid if the orientation of the line were discovered. At the end of World War II, Japanese Navy Captain Tamura was interviewed about the effectiveness of the massive B-29 drops of mines in Japanese waters. He said that the drops were on the whole very effective, but he had the following caveat:

> "The mine laying planes always laid their mines in a simple row which made it easy for our lookout activities to analyze the plan and determine where the mines were and adopt effective countermeasures. It is necessary to vary the plan of laying occasionally."

And so, partly because a minefield planner is already thinking of counter-countermeasures, a given "approach channel" like the one in Figure 10.1 is likely to include parts of several mine lines. Straighten out the approach channel into a long, narrow rectangle, and speculate about the cross-channel coordinates of the enclosed mines. They are unlikely to be evenly spaced for two reasons. First, the *effective* mines on a given line will not be evenly spaced because some mines are duds, some are deliberately configured differently from their neighbors, and because of navigation or timing errors in minelaying. Second, the mine positions on the various lines can reasonably be assumed independent – how could they be coordinated when the minefield planner doesn't know exactly where the channel will be or whether it will be slightly crooked, such as the one in Figure 10.1? The net result of superimposing the cross-channel coordinates of the mines on different lines, each with a different spacing, will be much closer to the cross-channel coordinates of a random minefield than to a minefield with regular spacing. In other words the random minefield assumption is robust to the kinds of deviations from the ideal of regularity that actually occur in practice. It may not be true that mines are *deliberately* placed at random, but the effect is much the same.

This long digression has had the purpose of justifying the assumption of independence used by ENWGS. The independence assumption is not always so easily justified, and has caused considerable mischief when employed in the wrong circumstances. The assumption usually leads to simple, transparent computations, so it is often tempting to make it "as an approximation" to avoid some analytical complexity or database deficiency. If the assumption is substantially wrong, garbage in will lead to garbage out. The probability that the first ship to enter a minefield is damaged is known as **Simple Initial Threat** (*SIT*). In ENWGS, since all m mines are treated independently,

$$SIT = 1 - (1 - wl/A)^m.$$

The threat to the second ship should not be as high. To some extent this is handled in ENWGS by decrementing the number of remaining mines whenever a mine actuates, but there is an implied assumption about reality in proceeding with that method. The assumption is that the remaining mines have locations that are independent of the locations of the original mines, as if the passage of the first ship caused all of the mines to activate a little motor and move to a new position. The assumption is incorrect, since the remaining mines are a subset of the original mines and *mines don't move*. The falsity of the assumption might not be important if the second ship chose a track far away from that of the first ship, but in fact the second ship is likely to take great pains to follow the first ship's track as closely as possible, especially if the first ship makes it through the minefield. That being the case, this second independence assumption is disastrous to the verity of the model for anybody wishing to explore the benefits of channelization, a basic mine countermeasure. If the first ship actuates no mine, then the following ship's chances should be improved by the knowledge, but the ENWGS model gives the same chance to both. A naive user might conclude from experience with the model that channelization is actually ineffective, which is not true.

It does not follow from the above comments that the ENWGS minefield model is useless, but only that it should not be used to explore the benefits of channelization. ENWGS comes closer to reality than a simple permission model, and it does so without being excessively complicated, an important property in a wargame where more important things than minefields must be represented accurately. This kind of situation is typical in studying mine warfare – models are neither good nor bad in any absolute sense, but only for specific purposes.

1003   Minefield Planning

A minefield model useful for minefield planning will have to be different from the one used by ENWGS. This is partly because of the channelization issue discussed above, but there is also the question of sensor sensitivity. A minefield planner must consider the possibility of **wasted fires** – mines that detonate without damaging anything. Wasted fires are possible because a mine actually has two radii of effectiveness, one for the sensor's range and one for the warhead's range. Neither one is predictable exactly, so one can have wasted fires as well as wasted opportunities where a mine does not detonate when damage is possible. Using the sensor's sensitivity to balance these two types of error is one of the functions of a minefield planner, so the cookie-cutter model where actuation and damage both happen at range $w/2$ must be abandoned in favor of something that reflects uncertainties about these phenomena.

Probabilistic actuation and damage models can be based on actuation and damage curves a and d, both dependent on the distance between mine and target at the closest point of approach; call the distance x. By definition $a(x)$ is the probability of actuation; it depends on the target as well as the mine's sensitivity. The quantity $d(x)$ is by definition the probability of damage *given* actuation; it has nothing to do with the mine's sensors and can be measured independently of them. Now consider a situation where n ships attempt to transit a minefield by following each other through it, an extreme form of channelization. More precisely, consider a minefield consisting of a single mine whose distance from this track is x. The probability that none of the n ships actuates this mine is $(1 - a(x))^n$. Each of the ship tracks has the same distance x from the mine, so the required independence assumption here is that actuations are independent given a fixed geometry – the mine remains at the same distance x for all n ships, in contrast to the ENWGS model. The probability that one of the ships is damaged is therefore

$$r_n(x) \equiv d(x)(1 - (1 - a(x))^n). \tag{10-1}$$

If the minefield has width b in the direction perpendicular to the ship track, if the mine is equally likely to be anywhere in this interval, and if the ship track is in the center of the interval, then the average value of this quantity is

$$r_n{}^* \equiv \frac{1}{b} \int_{-b/2}^{b/2} r_n(x)dx, \tag{10-2}$$

and $r_n{}^*$ is the probability that one mine damages one out of n ships. The only other possibility is that no ships are damaged, since one mine cannot damage multiple ships. The assumption that the ship track is in the center of the interval is not essential as long as it is not too near an edge. It turns out that the numbers $r_n{}^*$ can be used to analyze a minefield consisting of multiple mines, even though only a single mine has been considered so far, but first it is necessary to consider possible quantitative goals for the minefield planner.

It is not obvious what measure of effectiveness (MOE) to use in planning a minefield. Simple Initial Threat is one option, but *SIT* gives no clue to the threat to following ships, which can be much smaller than the threat to the first (imagine a minefield with one *big* mine). Other options might be the average number of wasted fires, the average number of wasted opportunities, the average number of ships damaged, the probability that two or more ships are damaged, the probability that the second ship to enter the minefield is damaged, etc. There are clearly many statistics that might be of interest. Among all these consider first the "catastrophe probability," the probability that no ships at all are damaged. Let $CAT(m, n)$ be the probability that n ships suffer no hits in a minefield of m mines. Then, since each mine must fail to damage all n ships, and since mine locations are all independent of each other,

$$CAT(m, n) = (1 - r_n{}^*)^m.$$

The assumption that all mine locations are independent also simplifies other computations. For example the probability that exactly 1 ship out of 2 is damaged in a transit of a minefield of 2 mines is $r_2{}^*(1 - r_1{}^*) + (1 - r_2{}^*)r_2{}^*$. Think of the group of surviving ships as encountering the mines in sequence, with the number of ships possibly diminishing with each encounter. The first term corresponds to the two mines hitting and missing, in that order, and the second term to a miss by the first and a hit by the second. As long as the mines are located independently of each other, the numbers $r_n{}^*$ suffice to calculate most MOE's of interest.

The Navy has used a minefield planning tool called the Uncountered Minefield Planning Model (UMPM), a computer program that makes calculations essentially as outlined above. The principal difference is that UMPM includes the possibility of navigation errors when the ships attempt to follow the channel centerline. The MOE's computed by UMPM are as follows:

a.   **Sustained threat:** The probability that the ith ship activates a mine, $i = 1, \dots, n$. For $i = 1$ this is *SIT*.

b.   **Casualty distribution**: The probability that k out of n ships actuate a mine, $k = 0, \dots, n$. For $k = 0$ this is the catastrophe probability.

c.   **Stopped penetrator distribution:** For an additional user input, "number of damaged ships after which no further transits will be attempted," UMPM outputs the probability that i ships will penetrate. That is, UMPM outputs the probability that k out of n ships will neither turn back nor be damaged, $k = 0, ..., n$. This MOE is in response to the idea that a minefield may be successful by forcing the enemy to avoid it, even if it doesn't damage anything.

If the minefield planner desires to increase the sustained threat to ships that enter the minefield late in the sequence, possibly because low numbered "ships" are actually expected to be mine-sweepers, then the planner may wish to make the mines insensitive or employ some other counter-countermeasure such as a probability actuator. Doing so will decrease *SIT*, but may increase the threat to high numbered ships. Probability actuators are easy for UMPM to handle because the only effect is to multiply the actuation curve by whatever probability is built into the probability actuator. Other generalizations are more difficult. For example mine counters and delay arms cannot be evaluated. Neither can UMPM be used to analyze mixed minefields or minefields with mixed targets, since only a single actuation curve is input, unless several such curves are "pre-averaged" as in the next section. Like ENWGS, UMPM is good for some things and not for others.

1004   The Pre-averaging Problem

As mentioned in 1003, UMPM assumes that actuations are independent when the locations of mines and ships are given. Whether this is a good assumption depends on the unpredictable quantity that causes actuations to be uncertain. The best case for the assumption would be where actuations are driven mainly by a probability actuator or some other phenomenon that fluctuates independently every time a ship passes by a mine. If the uncertainty is mainly about target or mine physical properties, however, then the assumption may be incorrect because those properties are constant from encounter to encounter.

For example, suppose that half of all ships have actuation curve a_1, while the other half have actuation curve a_2. Let $a(x) = .5a_1(x) + .5a_2(x)$, so that $a(x)$ represents the probability that a ship actuates a mine when the range at closest point of approach is x. There would be nothing wrong with using actuation curve a in UMPM if every ship somehow mutated between mines so that its type was independently selected for the next mine. Unfortunately, a given ship's type remains fixed from encounter to encounter. Displacement, magnetic moment, speed, and noisiness are all important determinants of the actuation curve for which there is no reason to expect any significant fluctuation during a transit. The independence assumption that UMPM requires is not true in these cases. Suppose $a_1(x) = 1$ and $a_2(x) = 0$ for all x, possibly because the mines are magnetic and type 2 ships are made of wood. The planner's object is to make $SIT = .9$. Using $d(x) = 1$ and $a(x) = .5$ in UMPM would lead to the conclusion that 4 mines are required. In actuality SIT cannot be made larger than .5 no matter how many mines are used, and only one mine is required to do so. This is an extreme example, but the effect can be significant even in non-extreme situations.

The act of replacing $a_1(x)$ and $a_2(x)$ with $a(x)$ in the above paragraph is an example of what is called "pre-averaging." Ideally one would analyze all possible combinations of two ship types and then average the outputs, but it is much easier to pre-average the actuation curves and then use UMPM as if there were only a single ship type. The two methods give different answers. A similar problem occurs if the unpredictable quantity is a mine characteristic, rather than a ship characteristic. The curve a_1 might be for a mine with high sensitivity while a_2 is for a mine with low sensitivity (problem 9). The UMPM calculations assume implicitly that sensitivity is independently determined for each interaction with a ship, which isn't true if a mine's sensitivity never changes. If mines differ from each other, it may not be possible to define an "average mine" that produces the same results as a truly mixed minefield. Here are some reasons why mines might differ significantly from each other:

a. Magnetic mines that lie on the bottom typically measure only one component of the magnetic field. Therefore the actuation curve depends on the orientation of the mine when it hits the bottom. The orientation is random, but does not change with time.
b. The mines might be of different types (mixed minefield).
c. Tactical parameters such as sensitivity or actuation probability might be deliberately varied by the minefield planner. Indeed, it was the presence of some very sensitive mines at Wonsan that made clearance especially difficult.

To summarize, while UMPM correctly handles the fact that the *location* of a mine does not change between transits (this is the main difference between UMPM and the ENWGS model), all other uncertainties about mine and ship characteristics are necessarily pre-averaged into the actuation curve. Mines have many properties other than location that, while random, are not *independently* random for each mine-ship interaction. The resulting deviations from reality, for UMPM or any other model that employs actuation curves, are potentially significant.

In spite of all these reservations, pre-averaging is common enough to have earned a name for itself. The reason for this is that the choice is often between a model with pre-averaging or no usable model at all. To consider all scenarios involving at most 10 ships of a single type in 1003, it was necessary to first compute $r_1, \dots, r_{10}$, a total of 10 integrals that could easily be computed numerically. If the 10 ships could be of two types, then the order in which the ships follow each other would be important – results can depend strongly on whether big ships follow small ones or vice versa. There are 2^{10} sequences where each of 10 ships can be one of two types, and each sequence requires 10 integrals because any one of the 10 ships might be damaged. So the need to compute 10 integrals is replaced by the need to compute 10,240 integrals to merely accommodate the possibility of two ship types. With three ship types there would be 590,490 integrals, and consideration is yet to be given to the logic required to analyze minefields consisting of more than a single mine! This is a combinatorial explosion, the bane of analytic models. It is the specter of just such an explosion that prevents the development of a multi-ship counterpart to UMPM. A multi-mine extension also leads to a combinatorial explosion.

Outside the context of mine warfare, pre-averaging is more likely to be called "expected-value analysis," as discussed in 109 in Chapter 1. The general situation is that one has a function $f(X)$, of the random variable X, and a desire to know $E[f(X)]$. Often the function f is a computer program, with X being the inputs. Correctly evaluating $E[f(X)]$ involves running the program for all values of X and then weighting the results by the probability mass function of X before summing. It is tempting to shortcut all this effort by first computing $\mu = E[X]$, which is often relatively easy, and then using the computer program once to determine $f(\mu)$. Doing so would be expected-value analysis; essentially the idea is to replace things that are random by their expected values before proceeding further. Unfortunately $E[f(X)]$ is not in general equal to $f(E[X])$, unless f is linear, so the shortcut will probably produce a wrong answer. Whether the error is *significant* depends on the circumstances. The important thing is to recognize that expected-value analysis is a method for saving computational effort at the cost of introducing an error in the answer. That is exactly what happens when UMPM is employed with pre-averaged actuation curves.

1005   Monte Carlo Simulation Versus Analytic Methods

It is often the case that probability questions can be answered either by Monte Carlo simulation, the subject of Chapter 3, or analytic methods. Analytic models are often difficult to formulate, even for skilled analysts, and may require questionable assumptions to the effect that various things are independent of each other. Once set up, however, analytic models are efficient and precise. Monte Carlo models are easier to formulate, but can be time consuming to implement, be difficult to verify, and suffer from sampling errors that can be reduced only by large numbers of replications. Sampling errors can be particularly annoying in optimization problems where neighboring decisions may differ from each other by so little that the difference gets lost in the noise. The choice of model type is something that requires careful consideration at an early stage of a study. This section considers an alternative Monte Carlo model for the UMPM scenario described in 1003.

Figure 10.3 is a flow diagram of a Monte Carlo simulation that measures the casualty distribution c, $c(k)$ being the probability that k out of n ships will be damaged in attempting a transit of a minefield containing m mines. The number of casualties, CAS, is accumulated in the appropriate cell of c at the end of each replication. "Ship properties" would include at least a track for each ship through the minefield, and "mine properties" would include at least a location for each mine. To parallel the calculations of 1003, each ship would transit the same straight line through the center of the minefield. The actuation question would be answered by first finding the closest distance x between mine j and ship i, and then testing a uniform random number against $a(x)$. The damage question would test another (independent) uniform random number against $d(x)$. If $REP = 10,000$, then $c(k) \pm .01$ is at least a 95 percent confidence interval on the true probability of k casualties, sufficiently accurate for most minefield planning. Modern (1999 vintage) computers are fast enough to do 10,000 iterations of Figure 10.3's logic in a few seconds.

However, there is no point in estimating c with a Monte Carlo simulation when c can be calculated exactly in milliseconds by UMPM. The real value of the simulation is that it can measure c even in circumstances where no analytic model is available.

To illustrate the adaptability of the simulation, consider ship navigation errors. So far it has been assumed that the ships all follow exactly the same track through the middle of the minefield, but in reality the tracks will be slightly different. To be definite, suppose that the minefield is rectangular, paralleling the ship tracks, so that only the cross-channel location of mines and ships is important, and that the distribution of the ship's location X is known. Consider the following two methods of carrying out the simulation:

a. Assign ship i a location x_i as a ship property, and mine j a location y_j as a mine property. The actuation and damage tests then use $|x_i - y_j|$ as the distance between ship and mine.

b. Do the same as (1) except that the ship location is independently set at each actuation test, rather than as a ship property.

FIGURE 10.3. MONTE CARLO SIMULATION OF CASUALTY DISTRIBUTION

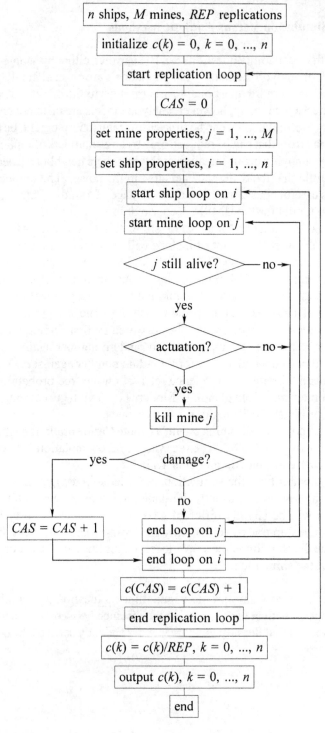

Methods a and b correspond to different assumptions about reality, call them Cases 1 and 2. In Case 1 ships move in parallel straight lines, so that a ship has the same location for every mine. In Case 2 a ship can be thought of as trying to follow a channel centerline, but wobbling enough in the channel to make the ship's location independent for every mine. In either case the simulation will still determine $c(k)$ to within .01 in a few seconds. The analytic computations described in 1003 can be adapted to handle Case 2, and in fact UMPM does so, but no useful analytic technique for handling Case 1 is known. Analytic techniques thrive on independence assumptions; the difficulty in Case 1 is that the location of a ship relative to mine 1 is not independent of its location relative to mine 2. While the choice of case is crucial for UMPM and its analytic generalizations, it is almost immaterial for simulation; in fact Case 1 is slightly easier for simulation because fewer random numbers are required.

Simulation could also be used to provide a way to deal with the pre-averaging problems described in 1004. The actuation curve could depend on ship properties such as magnetic moment or on mine properties such as orientation, each property set once per replication. The damage curve might depend on ship displacement or some better measure of a ship's ability to withstand underwater explosions. However, each of these changes would require either a more extensive data base or a good physical understanding of the processes involved. To make the actuation curve "depend on" the mine's orientation requires either an expansion in the amount of data that have to be measured and stored (8 orientations would require 8 times as much data, etc.), or an ability to determine whether actuation criteria are met when ship and mine properties are given. The attractiveness of simulation as a technique will depend on whether actuation and damage tests can be made accurately and quickly, with quickness being important because the problem with simulations tends to be long run times.

Monte Carlo simulation and analytic techniques can be expected to continue to compete with and complement each other, in mine warfare as in other areas. Each method is an important part of the OA toolkit.

1006   Mine Countermeasures (MCM)

In the rest of this chapter the ships that are the target of the minefield will be referred to as "transitors." The MCM ships (or helicopters) that employ countermeasures will be called "minesweepers" or simply "sweepers," a term that is meant to include hunting as well as sweeping.

MCM planning has some features that make it more difficult than minefield planning. Minefields are usually laid in secrecy, so the location and even existence of the minefield may be initially unknown to MCM forces. If at least the identity of the miner is known, it may be possible to make some inferences about the type of mines to be expected, but even in that case the mines will still have unknown sensitivity, unknown mine count, and unknown delay arming adjustments. Mines can be threatening even to minesweepers, as at Wonsan. In the face of all this uncertainty, MCM forces must make clearance plans and eventually decide when to say "all clear."

The simplest clearance model would be based on the idea of exhaustive search: Establish a distance z such that all mines that come within z of a sweeper will be swept, patrol in such a manner that all points of a region come within z of some sweeper, and then announce that the region is clear of mines. Unfortunately, the uncertainties of the previous paragraph usually make it impossible to establish z. Minehunting would be a better case for exhaustive search than minesweeping, but even in that case mines may be moored or not, buried or not, etc. For these reasons mine clearance models are almost never based on the idea of exhaustive search, but rather on the idea of sweeping mines to a certain "level." Sweeping a minefield to level p simply means that, with probability p, each mine is detected and either marked or removed.

Putting ship counters and arming delays aside, there isn't much conceptual difference between the level-of-clearance problem and the minefield planning problem. Figure 10.3 could be made into a mine clearance simulation by simply changing the ship properties and collecting statistics about killed mines, rather than damaged ships. If the sweepers were helicopters, or if the risk to minesweepers were negligible for other reasons, the "damage?" question in that figure could simply be omitted. Omitting the damage question would also make the clearance level independent of the number of mines m, a parameter that is usually unknown.

Depending on the contents of the ship and mine properties boxes in Figure 10.3, the level of clearance can be assessed analytically as well as by simulation. The Navy's analytic model NUCEVL (Non Uniform Coverage EVaLuator) accomplishes this when ship and mine properties are restricted to cross-channel locations and sweepers cannot be damaged; the user inputs a set of sweeper tracks that constitute the sweeping plan, and NUCEVL outputs the level of clearance as a function of the cross-channel location of a hypothetical mine. NUCEVL also has a companion model UCPLN (Uniform Coverage PLaNner) that outputs a sweeping plan that will accomplish a given clearance level. NUCEVL and UCPLN accept only "squared-off" actuation curves of height B and width A, a restriction that can be thought of as one of the prices that must be paid for relying on an analytic model, rather than a simulation. The benefit is that each provides its answer instantly and without sampling error.

NUCEVL's output includes the probability of clearing a mine at least k times for some $k > 0$, if the user inputs a maximum ship count k. In this sense NUCEVL could be said to deal with ship counters, since, if the user happened to know that all mines were on ship count 3 or smaller, the user could interpret the probability of sweeping a mine 3 or more times as the probability that the mine will have been eliminated by the end of the sweeping plan. However, NUCEVL does not deal in any sense with delay arming devices that simply turn off the mines' sensors for some time after the mine has been laid. In fact no tactical decision aid for mine warfare does so, in spite of the existence of the mechanism in some mines. The trouble is that any decision about time must take into account so many consequences of the pace of battle, from the viewpoint of both sides, that it becomes very difficult for either side to quantify its importance. So far, the employment of arming delays is an example of an important tactic that has not been the object of very much quantitative analysis.

At the end of minesweeping, a clearance level of .95 may be of scant comfort to a transitor who thinks there may have been 100 mines to begin with. It would be nice to say something about the number of mines that haven't been cleared yet, the difference between the unknown initial number of mines (call it m) and the known number that have been swept (call it s). If the clearance level is p, it is tempting to argue that the number of mines swept is both s and mp, so m must be s/p and the number of mines remaining must be $s/p - s$. This argument can be formalized by employing the Principle of Maximum Likelihood, which says that the best estimate of m is whatever maximizes the probability of sweeping s mines, the observed event. The number of mines swept, S, in a field of m mines is binomially distributed (see Appendix A) with probability

$$\Pr\{S = s\} \equiv B(m, s) = \binom{m}{s} p^{s}(1 - p)^{m-s}. \tag{10-3}$$

The Maximum Likelihood Estimate of m is the value of m that makes $B(m, s)$ as large as possible. This value turns out to be the largest integer not exceeding s/p (problem 11), so the informal argument is correct except that s/p needs to be truncated to an integer. However, the Maximum Likelihood Estimate is not the only estimate that should be considered. If there is prior information about the number of mines, then it is reasonable to use Bayes' theorem to derive the posterior distribution (problem 12). The posterior distribution could then be used as the basis for further action.

1007 A Game Theory View of Mine Warfare

Mine warfare is an area where each side takes pains to conceal its habits and capabilities from the other. The minefield planner conceals the location of the minefield, the number and type(s) of mine, the sensitivity settings, and the use of various counter-countermeasures. Furthermore, all of the miner's choices must be made without knowing the extent to which the minefield will be swept, hunted, destroyed, or avoided once it is laid. Either side might begin by saying, "If he thinks that I think that he thinks ...," in trying to decide what to do. Two-Person Zero-Sum (TPZS) games were invented to deal with such situations; they hold out the hope of basing actions on the enemy's capabilities, rather than his intentions. The purpose of this section is not to be exhaustive, since TPZS formulations quickly become very complicated, but merely to give some mine warfare examples that illustrate the theory of Chapter 2.

Is it better to hunt for mines or to sweep them? Hunting has the advantage of working equally well regardless of the mine sensor type, mine count setting, or delay arming, since it is completely independent of the mine's sensors. On the other hand hunting usually has a comparatively small sweep width. The decision must depend on the options available to the miner, and of course the miner must allow for both sweeping and hunting in designing the minefield in the first place. For a simple example suppose that there are only two mine types (MAG and ACU) and three possible countermeasures (SMAG, SACU, and HUNT). The miner has only one mine, but can choose the type of sensor, and the minesweeper elects to sweep or hunt without knowing the miner's choice. The sweeper is the maximizing player, so his three pure strategies are by convention shown as rows:

	MAG	ACU
SMAG	1.0	0.0
SACU	0.0	0.5
HUNT	0.3	0.3

The mine removal probability depends on the choices of both players, as shown in the matrix. For the first two countermeasures the matrix entry is an actuation probability, since no mine counters or arming delays are assumed. For the HUNT countermeasure the matrix entry is the probability of detecting the mine, which is again equivalent to removal.

The solution of this game is the pair of mixed strategies (1/3, 2/3, 0) for the sweeper and (1/3,

2/3) for the miner. The value of the game is 1/3. Note that MAG mines are used 1/3 of the time in spite of the fact that they are more easily swept than ACU mines, that the sweeper is more likely to do what he is bad at (SACU) than what he is good at (SMAG), and that the HUNT option is never used. If the HUNT detection probability were raised from .3 to .35, the sweeper would switch from exclusive sweeping to exclusive hunting and the value of the game would be .35. Some of these results are mildly surprising, and it is hard to imagine discovering them by any means other than analysis of a TPZS game.

One can also formulate TPZS matrix games where the miner selects a ship count while the sweeper selects the number of sweeps (problem 13), or where other combinations of measure and countermeasure are played against each other. The results of solving these abstract games are often instructive, but even so there are some good reasons why TPZS game analysis has been and will likely remain on the sidelines of minefield theory. The most important of these is the combinatorial explosion in the number of strategies that needs to be considered in "scaling up" to realistic values. Suppose there were m mines in the previous example, each of which could be of t types. A pure strategy for the miner then consists of t nonnegative integers that sum to m, for which there are

$$\binom{m+t-1}{t-1}$$

possibilities. This combinatorial coefficient is only 2 when $m = 1$ and $t = 2$, but it is 910 when $m = 10$ and $t = 5$. If the order in which the mines are encountered by the sweepers were important to assessing the outcome, then there would be t^m possibilities, an even larger number. Similar considerations apply to sweeper strategies; if there were a sequence of 10 sweeps, rather than just one, then the sweeper would have $3^{10} = 59,049$ strategies. TPZS games on that scale are usually not solvable, for computational reasons and also because of the data requirements implied by such a large payoff matrix.

It is common for a decision problem to be easy to solve with only a few alternatives, complicated for combinatorial reasons as the number of alternatives is increased, and then become easy again in the limit as the set of alternatives becomes a continuum. The problem considered above is like this. The number of strategies available to the minesweeper increases fast if the number of sweep/hunt opportunities is increased, or if devoting part of a period to one activity and part to another is permitted, or if there are multiple units available for sweeping/hunting. This rapid increase destroys any hope of a matrix game analysis. But if h_j is the number of unit-hours devoted to activity j, for $j = 1, 2, 3$, and if a total of h unit-hours are available, then $h_1 + h_2 + h_3$ must not exceed h for *any* feasible strategy. If scheduling details and all constraints other than this one are ignored, the game once again becomes subject to analysis, albeit not as a matrix game. While techniques for solving TPZS games with a continuum of strategies are beyond the scope of this book, they exist and are effective. Solutions often have the characteristic of frequently employing relatively ineffective mine clearance strategies, as in the example above; in warfare, the enemy is motivated to test weakness, rather than strength.

1008   Other Literature and History

The 1942 actions by the U-701, noted in the introduction, are described by Lott in [1]. Historical details on WWII against Japan can be found in [2], Hartmann [3], and Melia [4]. Captain

Tamura's quote, given in 1002, is in [2], p. 37. Figures 10.1 and 10.2 are taken from Lyons [5]. The contemporary relevance of mine designs decades old is noted in Wettern [6], p. 36.

Melia [4] claims that Farragut's famous "Damn the torpedoes ..." quote has had the unfortunate consequence of making his actions at Mobile Bay appear reckless, when actually he had a good understanding of the risk and had surveyed, and swept the Confederate minefield before entering it. Farragut's "model" of the minefield no doubt consisted of annotations on a chart, but the increasing sophistication of mines subsequently led to increasingly abstract minefield models, particularly with the advent of digital computers after WWII. The rest of this section reviews a few of these models that have taken the form of tactical decision aids (TDAs). Most have been developed either by or under the supervision of the Navy's laboratories at White Oak, Maryland, and at Panama City, Florida. Many owe a debt to the work of R. K. Reber, who developed analytical foundations such as [7] at the Bureau of Ships (Minesweeping Branch). Sutter and Cushman [8], pp. 10-19 to 10-23, provide a more extensive review.

The first MCM TDA was developed in the 1970s as a desktop calculator computerization of calculations found in tactical publications. This machine language calculator program was subsequently translated to FORTRAN for the Korean Navy, and the FORTRAN program was itself later restructured to be the Mine Warfare Trainer (MWT). The MWT was implemented on a mainframe at the Fleet Mine Warfare Training Center, with a similar system installed at the Mine Warfare Command. The mainframe implementation permitted the inclusion of a database of relevant mine and ship data, plus the routines necessary to convert the data to tactically relevant quantities. While the MWT was not designed as a TDA, some of its models were subsequently included in TDAs as personal computers became more powerful. In addition to UMPM, NUCEVL, and UCPLN, these models included the Analytical Countered Minefield Planning Model (ACMPM, [9]), a minefield planning model for use when minesweeping was to be expected, and the Batch Minefield Evaluation Model (BAMEM).

The inclusion of a database was an important feature of the MWT that was at first omitted from some of the derived personal computer TDAs, but which was subsequently reintroduced as hardware improved. MCM85 was introduced in 1985 with a built-in database, and similarly named updated versions have been released every two years since then.

Throughout the 1970s and 1980s, there was a debate about exactly what quantities were relevant for minefield planning and clearance. The "stopped penetrator distribution" was added to the output of UMPM during this period, as a response to the idea that the tendency of a ship to enter a minefield might depend on the fate of preceding ships. The details of the required calculations, as well as for calculation of the other two MOEs mentioned in 1003, can be found in Odle [10]. Neither NUCEVL nor UCPLN addresses the possibility that minesweeping assets might be lost in the process of clearing a minefield, but the possibility is a real and important one, particularly for clearance by surface minesweepers. A new TDA (COGNIT) was developed to simultaneously manipulate *three* MOEs: the minefield clearance level, the expected minesweeper casualties, and the total time required for minesweeping. The user sets requirements for two of the MOEs, and COGNIT finds the tactic that optimizes the remaining one. The required computations were essentially impossible in the 1970s, but had become routine by the 1980s. Minesweeping TDAs sometimes employ MOEs that are driven more by necessity than by tactical relevance. NUCEVL and UCPLN deal in "clearance level," for example, rather than more relevant MOEs such as the threat to follow-on traffic, partly to avoid asking the user to estimate the number of mines present. Even so, minesweeping TDA users must often squirm when asked for answers to certain questions. "What is the distribution of mine counts?" is one such question, since the number of times a mine must be actuated before detonating is a tactical parameter set by the enemy. It might seem natural to assume that the enemy will set the mine count distribution to be whatever is "optimal" from his standpoint, and to construct a minesweeping plan in the context of a TPZS game. Attempts have been made along this line, but the nature of the resulting minesweeping plan is sensitive to exactly how the game's payoff is measured. So far none of these attempts has resulted in a deployable TDA, so the question about mine counts must still be answered by the user.

The early 1990s saw the development of the Mission Planning System (MPS), an integrated TDA which for the first time does not require the user to transfer intermediate data from one module to another. MPS also integrates data from the Global Positioning System, and includes an improved version of NUCEVL. After Desert Storm, the need for a comprehensive command and control system was evident and the MIW Environmental Decision Aid Library (MEDAL) was designed as a segment of the Joint Military Command Information System (JMCIS). MPS and MEDAL both take advantage of modern computer graphical capabilities, and are in other ways designed to be more user-friendly than earlier systems.

[1]   Lott, Arnold. *Most Dangerous Sea: A History of Mine Warfare and an Account of U. S. Navy Mine Warfare Operations in World War II and Korea*. Annapolis, MD: Naval Institute Press, 1959.

[2]   U.S. Navy. *The Offensive Mine Laying Campaign Against Japan, U. S. Strategic Bombing Survey*. Washington, DC: Department of the Navy, 1946.

[3]   Hartmann, Gregory. *Weapons That Wait*. Annapolis, MD: Naval Institute Press, 1979.

[4]   Melia, Tamara. *Damn the Torpedoes, a Short History of U. S. Naval Mine Counter-measures*. Contributions to Naval History No. 4, Naval Historical Center, Department of the Navy, 1991.

[5]   Lyons, H. Dwight; Eleanor Baker; Sabrina Edlow; and David Perin. *The Mine Threat: Show Stoppers or Speed Bumps?* Alexandria, VA: Center for Naval Analyses, 1993.

[6]   Wettern, Desmond. "Coping with the Hidden Threat." *Sea Power*, March, 1991, p. 36.

[7]   Reber, R. K. *A Theoretical Evaluation of Various Search Salvage Procedures for Use with Narrow Path Locators*. Washington, DC: Bureau of Ships Technical Report 117, 1956.

[8]   Sutter, Fred, and Diane Cushman. "Mine Countermeasures Tactical Models." *Proceedings of the Autonomous Vehicles in Mine Countermeasures Symposium*. Monterey, CA: Naval Postgraduate School, April, 1995.

[9]   Bronowitz, Richard, and Charles Fennemore. *Mathematical Model Report for the Analytical Countered Minefield Planning Model (ACMPM)*. NSWC/DL TR-3359, White Oak, MD: Naval Surface Weapons Center, July, 1975.

[10] Odle, John. *Minefield Analysis for Channelized Traffic*. NSWC/WOL TR77-109, White Oak, MD: Naval Surface Weapons Center, August, 1977.

Problems

1. Consider a minefield laid in secrecy. As soon as the enemy is aware of it he can redirect his shipping. Magnetic mines with an influence diameter of 80 yards and a kill diameter of 60 yards are

to be used. Twenty mines will be laid in two lines across a channel a 9,500 yards wide. The lines will be perpendicular to the flow of traffic. Each mine will be laid at least 100 yards from its nearest neighbor in the line. The mines will be active for two weeks and 4 ships per week will transit the channel. What is the probability this minefield will sink a ship?

2. Consider the ENWGS model of a minefield where 200 mines planted in a 10 square nm region. Each mine has an effective radius of 40 yards. What is the probability a ship passing on a 12 nm track through the region will be damaged by a mine? (Assume 1 nm = 2000 yards).

3. In 1003 the functions $a(x)$ and $d(x)$ are introduced.

a. Where have you seen a similar function earlier in this text?
b. Sketch these two functions as they are implicitly defined in problem 1 and then as they might appear in a more realistic version of problem 1.

4. In 1002, it is described how ENWGS decides on actuation for a given ship by comparing at most m random numbers to wl/A, potentially one comparison for every mine. Describe a test involving a single random number that would have the same effect.

5. Consider the ENWGS model of 1002. Suppose that m mines with action radius $w/2$ remain in a minefield of area A at the beginning of the fixed time interval δ that ENWGS uses to advance time, and consider an arbitrary ship that will travel some length l in the minefield over δ. As explained above, in the stochastic mode ENWGS compares a random number to wl/A to decide whether the ship is damaged by each of the m mines, subtracting one from m if any mine is struck. ENWGS also has a "deterministic" mode in which no random numbers are employed, the idea being to avoid the vagaries associated with randomness and assure reproducibility of results. The simplest deterministic model would be to replace all random numbers by .5, the midpoint of the interval $[0, 1]$. Explain why this won't give satisfactory results, and suggest a better deterministic model. The principle should be that, since δ has no physical meaning and is chosen for reasons having nothing to do with the minefield, results should not depend strongly on what value happens to be chosen for δ.

6. Find a formula analogous to (10-1) for the probability of a wasted fire, and another formula for the probability of a wasted opportunity.

7. Suppose that $m = 8$ mines and that r_5^* as given by (10-2) is .2. If 5 ships transit the minefield, what is the probability that none of them are damaged (i.e., what is catastrophe probability)? Now suppose that, with probability .1, each mine develops a leak that renders it harmless, independently of the others. Now what is the catastrophe probability?

8. Five ships transit a minefield of three mines. In terms of r_1^*, ..., r_5^*, what is the probability that exactly two of the ships will be damaged?

9. Consider the extreme example of 1004, but this time suppose that there are $n = 10$ identical

transitors and a single mine that is equally likely to be type 1 or type 2. What is the actual probability of a single casualty? What would that probability be if each mine somehow selected its type independently for each encounter?

10. In 1005, a claim is made about the size of a confidence interval for $REP = 10,000$ replications. Verify it, and also give the size if $REP = 1000$.

11. Show that $B(m, s)$ (see (10-3)) is maximized when $m = [s/p]$, the greatest integer in s/p. Hint: Consider the ratio $B(m + 1, s)/B(m, s)$; m is too small if the ratio exceeds 1.

12. Suppose that the number of mines m is a priori equally likely to be 10 or 15, and that 7 mines are found in the process of sweeping to level .5. Using Bayes' theorem (see Appendix A), find the probability that the original number of mines was 10, given the observed result.

13. There are two mines, each of which must be assigned a "count" of 0, 1, or 2 by the miner, a total of 9 possible joint assignments. The sweeper can sweep each mine either 0, 1, or 2 times, but the total number of sweeps cannot exceed 2 so there are only six joint possibilities. The sweeper wins if and only if both sides select different numbers for both mines, so the payoff matrix is a 9×6 matrix of 0s and 1s. This TPZS game models a situation where each mine is "ripe" only if its count is reduced to exactly 0 by sweeping, and where the sole transitor will encounter both mines. Show that the value of the resulting 9 by 6 game is 2/3.

14. Suppose that a single mine must be placed at y in the unit interval $[0, 1]$, while a transitor simultaneously selects a point x in the same interval in an attempt to pass safely by the mine. The transitor will be sunk if and only if $y - x \le .2$. Obviously the location of the mine should be uniformly distributed over the interval and the game value is .4, since the mine can cover 40 percent of the interval. But not so fast ...

a. Show that a clever choice of x would result in a sinking probability of only .2 against the uniform strategy.
b. Find a strategy for placing the mine that will always sink the transitor with probability 1/3 or more, regardless of x. Hint: The optimal distribution for y is discrete, not continuous.
c. Find a strategy for transiting (a distribution for x) that will result in being sunk with probability 1/3 or less, regardless of y.

The moral of this story is that end effects are potentially important.

Answers to Problems

1. Pr[Kill|Explosion] = 3/4, Pr[Explosion] = 0.9477, Pr[Kill] = 0.71.
2. $SIT = .62$

4. Test a uniform random number against SIT as given by (10-1).

5. If δ is small, the stochastic version of ENWGS makes many tests, a small fraction of which result in damage. The small fraction would be 0 in the deterministic version, so there would be no damage at all. The two versions cannot be made equivalent, but there are deterministic versions where results do not depend so strongly on the size of the time interval.

6. For a wasted fire, replace $r_n(x)$ by $(1 - d(x))(1 - (1 - a(x))^n)$ in (10-2). For a wasted opportunity, replace $r_n(x)$ by $d(x)(1 - a(x))^n$.

7. .1678, .2040.

8. $r_5*r_4* (3 - r_5* - 2r_4*)$.

9. .5000, .9990.

11. To be precise, the confidence interval extends .0098 each side of the sample proportion when $REP = 10,000$; that is, the length of the interval is .0196. If $REP = 1,000$, the length of the interval is .0620.

12. .3737 = 256/685.

13. Row 00 (both mines immediately "ripe") in the payoff matrix should have a payoff of 1 against all but 1 of the 6 columns. The 9×6 matrix reduces to a 6×6 by dominance. The 6×6 can be further reduced by exploiting symmetry between mines 1 and 2.

14. a. Choose either endpoint.
b. An equally likely choice of .15, .50, .85 will do, but there are other correct answers.
c. An equally likely choice of .00, .50, 1.00 will do, but there are other correct answers .

11
BEARINGS-ONLY TARGET MOTION ANALYSIS

Target motion analysis (TMA) is defined as the estimation of a detected target's range, course, and speed. This chapter addresses TMA in the situation where the data on which the estimation is based are directional, i.e., consist of bearings from own ship to target.

In bearings-only TMA, particular importance is attached to range estimation. This is because knowledge of range is equivalent to knowledge of target position, since bearing is presumed known. Target position is the prime determinant in deciding whether to fire a weapon, to commence evasion, or to continue pursuit. Also, with target range at hand, course and speed may be estimated by finding position at two distinct times.

Bearings-only TMA is very important because bearings may be obtained *passively*, without disclosing one's own presence. The methods described here are usually applied to bearings obtained by underwater acoustics, but in principle they could apply to TMA based on interception of electro-magnetic signals. It may also be noted that if the detection is made by receiving echoes from *active* sonar or radar transmission, then TMA is relatively easy, since these devices provide range as well as bearing to the target, with high accuracy. Active sensors have a major disadvantage, however, in that the transmitted energy discloses own ship's presence. Also, passive sensors usually afford longer detection ranges.

The stealth advantage of passive sensors is particularly important to submarines. Since the early 1950s, antisubmarine warfare (ASW) has been an important mission of U.S. submarines. To maintain the advantages that U.S. submarines have had over potential adversaries, enormous investigative efforts have been devoted to improving ASW sensors as well as the TMA techniques applied to the data from these sensors. These efforts have been primarily in a submarine context, but they have also become important to surface and airborne ASW and to anti-surface warfare (ASUW) by all platforms.

TMA is almost synonymous with the term "tracking" and the objectives are identical. In tracking, updates of the estimate of target position and velocity alternate between a motion update based on prior target motion assumptions and an information update based on new information from observations. Both updates are probabilistic. This is akin to the alternation between updates for motion and negative information (unsuccessful search) described in Chapter 8 in search for moving targets. Tracking, however, involves positive as well as negative information (as does search in more advanced treatments). Tracking algorithms typically process numerous observations via sophisticated forms of statistical regression, notably Kalman filtering, which are beyond the scope of this text.

A vessel's track will be said to be **linear** if its course and speed are constant. *Throughout this chapter* it is assumed that the target is on a linear track. The focus is on how much TMA can be done with two, three, or four bearings.

Some notation is defined in 1101. Section 1102 examines what can be obtained from bearings if own ship is also on a linear track. In that circumstance, a complete TMA solution is not possible no matter how much bearing information is available, but the direction of relative motion can be determined from three or more bearings. The important **Ekelund ranging** method, based on bearing rates before and after a turn by own ship is presented in 1103; these two rates may be approximated by use of four bearings. Section 1104 gives the time correction method for improving the Ekelund range estimate, by finding times at which the range estimation is insensitive to target speed in the line of sight.

Section 1105 develops the techniques of **Spiess** TMA. Given bearings at three times, the locus of target positions at a chosen fourth time is a computable straight line called the **Spiess line** at that time. Also discussed are connections among time correction, Spiess lines, target tracks consistent with three bearings, and the parabolic envelope to the latter two sets of lines.

1101   Notation

The following notation conventions will apply throughout the chapter. As elsewhere, target speed is u and target true course, i.e., relative to 000, is c. Time instants will be denoted $t_0, t_1, \ldots$. At these respective times the bearings from own ship to target will be $b_0, b_1, \ldots$, and the ranges will be $r_0, r_1, \ldots$. The following definitions are made for $i, j = 0, 1, \ldots$ (a double subscript ij refers to a change taking place from time t_i to t_j):

a. $t_{ij} = t_j - t_i$,
b. $b_{ij} = b_j - b_i$,
c. DOA_{ij} = distance own ship moves from t_i to t_j perpendicular to bearing b_i, i.e. *across* the b_i line of sight (if the motion is to the left of b_i, the distance is negative),
d. DOI_{ij} = distance own ship moves from t_i to t_j in the direction b_i, i.e. *in* the b_i line of sight (if the motion opens own ship from the target, the distance is negative),

e. DTA_{ij} and DTI_{ij} are the corresponding distances for *target* motion.

The above definition of b_{ij} must be interpreted in the arithmetic of the nautical compass. Specifically, b_{ij} is the change in bearing from time t_i to time t_j, measured as an angle between -180° and 180°, a clockwise change being positive. E.g., if $b_i = 010$ and $b_j = 355$, then $b_{ij} = -15°$. (See problem 22.)

The **direction of relative motion** (*DRM*) is defined as the direction of the vector of target motion relative to own ship, when own track is linear – see Figure 11.1. This should not be confused with target relative course, which is the angle measured clockwise from own course to target course.

FIGURE 11.1. DERIVATION OF *DRM*

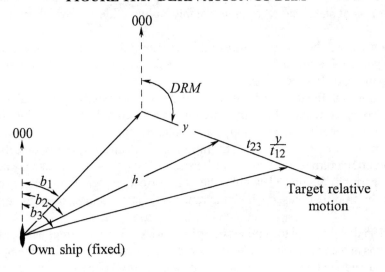

1102   Own Ship on Linear Track

In this section it is assumed that own ship's track is linear, as has already been assumed for the target. The theorems below identify certain features of target motion that can and cannot be determined from bearings only in this case.

Two tracks are said to be on a **collision course** if at some instant of time they are at the same point – this could occur in past or future time.

Theorem 11.1. If the two tracks are on a collision course, then all bearings are equal.

Proof: Consider the track of the target plotted relative to own ship. Bearings are the same in the relative and true plots. If the two true tracks are on a collision course, then the relative track will pass through own ship. Each bearing runs from own ship to target in the relative plot; thus all bearings coincide.

Theorem 11.2. If the bearings at two distinct times are equal, then all bearings will be equal and the two tracks are on a collision course or are parallel.

Proof: In the plot relative to own ship, both bearing lines coincide at own ship (which is fixed), so they coincide entirely. Hence the relative motion lies within the bearing line. If target position relative to own ship is constant, then the two tracks are parallel. Otherwise, the constant relative velocity must take the target through own position, i.e., the two tracks collide, and by Theorem 11.1 all bearings are equal.

Theorem 11.3. If t_1, t_2, and t_3 are distinct times, then
$$t_{23}\cot(DRM - b_1) = t_{13}\cot b_{13} - t_{12}\cot b_{12}. \tag{11-1}$$
In particular, if the times are uniformly spaced, i.e., $t_{23} = t_{12}$, then
$$\cot(DRM - b_1) = 2\cot b_{13} - \cot b_{12}.$$
Also, defining b_0 as the bearing at closest approach of the two tracks,
$$t_{23}\tan b_{01} = t_{13}\cot b_{13} - t_{12}\cot b_{12}. \tag{11-2}$$
Equation (11-1) is solved for DRM, by computing the two values, which differ by 180°, of
$$b_1 + \operatorname{arccot}\left(\frac{t_{13}\cot b_{13} - t_{12}\cot b_{12}}{t_{23}}\right), \tag{11-3}$$
and adding or subtracting an integer multiple of 180° to each value to make both lie between 0 and 360. The DRM is that direction, of these two, which is on the side of b_1 to which the bearings draw. Similarly, one can solve (11-2) for b_0.

Proof: Referring to Figure 11.1, apply the law of sines twice to obtain (recall $\sin(180° - x) = \sin x$)
$$\frac{\sin(DRM - b_1)}{h} = \frac{\sin b_{12}}{y},$$
$$\frac{\sin(DRM - b_3)}{h} = \frac{\sin b_{23}}{yt_{23}/t_{12}}.$$
Hence,
$$\frac{\sin(DRM - b_1)}{\sin(b_2 - b_1)} = \frac{t_{23}\sin[(DRM - b_1) - (b_3 - b_1)]}{t_{12}\sin[(b_3 - b_1) - (b_2 - b_1)]}.$$
By applying the formula for the sine of a sum to the numerator and denominator on the right and manipulating the result, one may obtain equation (11-1). Equation (11-2) follows from the perpendicularity of b_0 to DRM. The remainder of the theorem follows from the fact that arccot x has two reciprocal values between 0° and 360°.

Application of Theorem 11.3, including the high sensitivity of DRM to bearing errors, is illustrated in problems 1, 2, and 3.

Theorem 11.4. One cannot obtain target course, speed, or range from bearings only, no matter how numerous, when own track is linear.

Proof: If the bearings are constant, the target's relative motion is along the bearing line; obviously there is no unique range, speed, or course which produces the observed bearing.

Suppose the bearings are distinct. Let b_0, t_0, and r_0 be bearing, time, and range at closest approach of the two tracks and let w be *relative* speed. Then at any time t_j,

$$\tan b_{0j} = \frac{w}{r_0} t_{0j} \qquad (11\text{-}4)$$

(see Figure 11.2), so

$$b_j = b_0 + \arctan(\frac{w}{r_0} t_{0j}). \qquad (11\text{-}5)$$

Equation (11-5) thus gives a complete bearing history and forecast in terms of b_0, t_0, and w/r_0.

If w and r_0 are multiplied by any non-zero constant, (11-4) and (11-5) are unaffected. Thus, there is an infinite family of target tracks each of which produces the same observed bearing history. For each of these tracks, the *DRM* is perpendicular to b_0, the bearing at closest approach. Hence, in relative motion, these tracks are all parallel (see Figure 11.2). At any instant, the ranges of the positions on these tracks are distinct, since the values of r_0, the range at closest approach, are distinct. Therefore, there is no unique range solution. Also, the values of w are distinct, since if two of these tracks had the same relative speed, being separate and parallel, they could not produce the same bearing history. Given that *DRM* is fixed by Theorem 11.3 and own course and speed are known, neither target course nor speed can be unique, because otherwise one could solve a relative motion diagram for a unique value of w. This completes the proof.

FIGURE 11.2. RELATIVE MOTION PLOT

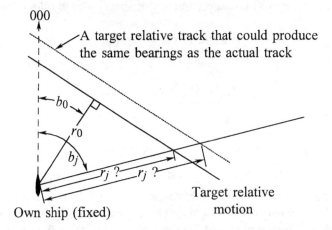

Equation (11-4) can also be used to show that bearings at three distinct times determine all bearings. Given three distinct bearings, equation (11-4) is written for three pairs of values of t_j and b_j, and the equations are solved for t_0, b_0, and w/r_0. The solution is then inserted in (11-5). A better form of this result, however, is given in Theorem 11.7 of 1105.

Some summary remarks are in order on what is learned from bearings when own track as well as target track is linear. Given that constraint, a remarkable result is that the values of own course and speed are not relevant to TMA efforts. After gaining a contact, the first significant TMA information is available after just two bearings (assuming the ideal situation that there is no error in bearings). If the bearings are (approximately) equal, indicating a collision course, this may dictate that own ship commence evasion to avoid collision or coming too close and being counterdetected. For distinct bearings, the important information is whether they draw left or right. This initial bearing drift is the first piece of information from which an approach plan can begin to be formed. The *DRM* can then be determined once three bearings are available. It is important to remember, however, that when both own ship and the target have linear tracks, bearings alone are insufficient to determine target range, course, or speed.

1103   Ekelund Ranging

Once *DRM* is determined and an initial approach plan is developed, the next objective is to get a rough idea of target range. Possibly the best known of all submarine TMA ranging techniques is the Ekelund method of bearings-only ranging. It requires a maneuver by own ship and uses observed bearings before and after a turn by own ship to estimate the target range.

Consider a single leg of own ship's track as in Figure 11.3. The figure shows range and bearing at times t_i and t_j and also distances across the b_i line of sight moved between these times by own ship and target. From the figure one sees that

$$r_j \sin b_{ij} = DTA_{ij} - DOA_{ij}.$$
(11-6)

Equation (11-6) will be applied to each leg of a two-leg maneuver. On the first leg, bearings are observed at times t_1 and t_2, and by (11-6)

$$r_2 \sin b_{12} = DTA_{12} - DOA_{12}.$$
(11-7)

By dividing both sides by t_{12} and letting t_1 approach t_2, $\sin b_{12}$ approaches b_{12} (in radians) and b_{12}/t_{12} approaches *BR*, defined to be the bearing rate at time t_2. Also $(DTA_{12} - DOA_{12})/t_{12}$ approaches $STA - SOA$, where *STA* and *SOA* are defined to be respectively target and own speed across the b_2 line of sight. Thus,

$$r_2 BR = STA - SOA.$$
(11-8)

Now suppose, idealistically, that own ship makes an instantaneous turn at time t_2. At this point, *BR* and *SOA* may be interpreted as one-sided derivatives just before t_2. The corresponding one-sided derivatives just after the turn will be designated *BR′* and *SOA′*. Since it is assumed that the target does not change course or speed, *STA* is the same before and after the turn. Then by the same reasoning that led to (11-8),

$$r_2 BR' = STA - SOA'.$$
(11-9)

One eliminates the unknown *STA* from (11-8) and (11-9) to obtain

$$r_2 = \frac{SOA' - SOA}{BR - BR'}.$$
(11-10)

Formula (11-10) is the Ekelund range formula: the change at the turn in own speed across line of sight divided by the reverse change in bearing rate. Note that its inputs are entirely measurable on own ship. This is a very convenient estimate of range. It applies at the time of own ship's turn in a two-leg maneuver.

Of course (11-10) must be applied with consistent units, e.g., knots, nm, and radians per hour. To compute *SOA*, it can help to note that

$$SOA = (\text{own speed}) \times \sin(\text{own true course} - \text{true bearing to target}).$$

An example of Ekelund ranging follows: Suppose own ship makes 10 knots on course 030 for 5 minutes and then makes an instantaneous turn to 120, same speed. Exact bearings are observed as follows:

Time (min):	0	4	6	10
Bearings (deg):	090	088.9	085.3	070.3

Then $BR \approx [(88.9° - 90°)/(4 \text{ min})](60 \text{ min/hr})(\pi \text{ rad}/180°) = -.29$ rad/hr. Similarly, $BR' = (70.3 - 85.3)(\pi/12)$ rad/hr $= -3.92$ rad/hr. Also, $SOA = 10\sin(30° - 88.9°)$ kts $= -8.56$ kts and $SOA' = 10\sin(120° - 85.3°)$ kts $= 5.69$ kts. Hence

$$\text{range at the turn} \approx \frac{5.69 + 8.56}{-.29 + 3.92} \text{ nm} = 3.93 \text{ nm} = 7966 \text{ yards.}$$

The actual target track from which the above bearings are taken is 10 knots due north bearing due east at 10,000 yards at time 0, and the actual range at the turn is 9158 yards. Thus the Ekelund range estimate is 13.0 percent low. Since the bearings are exact (to within .1°), the range error is mainly attributable to estimation of bearing rates by difference quotients and to these quotients being centered 3 minutes away from the turn time.

FIGURE 11.3. EKELUND RANGING DERIVATION

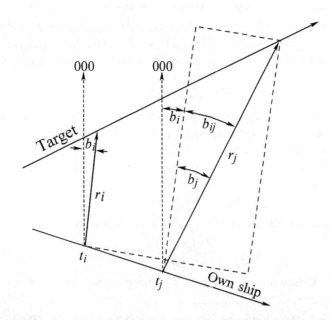

Additional examples of Ekelund ranging, showing effects of bearing observation errors and bearing spacing, are given in problems 4 to 10.

Of course the idealized assumptions of instantaneity of turn and of estimation of bearing rates immediately before and after the turn cannot be realized in practice. Departures from these idealizations introduce errors in the Ekelund estimate, as was just seen. The next section gives a method of sharply reducing these and other errors in bearings-only TMA.

1104   Time Correction

This section describes the powerful and interesting method known as **time correction**, which reduces errors in bearings-only range estimation.   As before, it is assumed that the target track is linear. To help to clarify the development, some simplifying assumptions are made, while the main principles of time correction are preserved. The method is readily extendable to apply without these simplifications.

An outline of this development is as follows: From bearings at four times, a formula, (11-22), will be found for range at one of those times. This formula will be related to the Ekelund range formula but will contain troublesome terms involving target motion in the line of sight. To eliminate these terms, it is observed that by changing the time at which the range estimate applies, the range itself is changed by an increment of own motion in the line of sight, which is calculable, and an increment of target motion in line of sight. The trick is to determine the range time at which the target motion increment cancels the troublesome terms in the range formula thus eliminating the major source of error. An important feature of this procedure is that by suitable choice of own ship maneuvers, the new range time can be caused to occur roughly when a range estimate is most needed.

The four bearing times will be denoted by t_1, t_2, t_3, and t_4. These times may occur in any order and own track may be quite irregular, although one usually considers that own ship is conducting a two-leg ranging maneuver with t_1 and t_2 occurring on the first leg and t_3 and t_4 on the second.

As one simplification, it is assumed that $t_{12} = t_{34}$. No other restrictions are made on time spacing.

As an additional simplification, it is assumed that the four observed bearings, b_1 through b_4, are sufficiently close to each other that the "small angle" approximations may be applied to differences between them, i.e., for $i, j = 1, \ldots, 4$, $\sin b_{ij} \approx b_{ij}$, if b_{ij} is in radians, and $\cos b_{ij} \approx 1$. Small bearing differences tend to arise in range estimation at relatively long range with relatively accurate bearing estimation. Note that if b_{ij} is as much as $15°$, i.e., .2618 radians, then the small angle approximations overestimate $\cos b_{ij}$ by only 3.5 percent, since $\cos 15° = .9659$, and overestimate $\sin b_{ij}$ by only 1.2 percent, since $\sin 15° = .2588$.

The previous notation will be expanded to define STI_i and STA_i to be target speed respectively in and across the b_i line of sight. Thus, e.g., $STI_i = DTI_{ij}/t_{ij}$ for any j.

Recalling that u and c are target speed and course, respectively, it is easily seen that

$$DTA_{ij} = ut_{ij}\sin(c - b_i), \tag{11-11}$$

$$DTI_{ij} = ut_{ij}\cos(c - b_i). \tag{11-12}$$

From (11-6) and further reference to Figure 11.3 (again, b_{ij} is in radians),

$$DTA_{ij} - DOA_{ij} = r_j\sin b_{ij} \approx r_j b_{ij} \tag{11-13}$$

$$DTI_{ij} - DOI_{ij} = r_j\cos b_{ij} - r_i \approx r_j - r_i. \tag{11-14}$$

Applying (11-13) and (11-14),

$$DTA_{12} - DOA_{12} \approx r_2 b_{12}, \tag{11-15}$$

$$DTA_{34} - DOA_{34} \approx r_4 b_{34}, \tag{11-16}$$

$$DTI_{12} - DOI_{12} \approx r_2 - r_1, \tag{11-17}$$

$$DTI_{14} - DOI_{14} \approx r_4 - r_1. \tag{11-18}$$

Note that the subscripting in (11-18) does not follow the pattern of (11-15), (11-16), and (11-17). This will aid in achieving the desire to express target motion relative to a single direction, namely, b_1. Now eliminate r_2 from (11-15) and (11-17) and r_4 from (11-16) and (11-18):

$$r_1 b_{12} \approx DTA_{12} - DOA_{12} - (DTI_{12} - DOI_{12}) b_{12}, \tag{11-19}$$

$$r_1 b_{34} \approx DTA_{34} - DOA_{34} - (DTI_{14} - DOI_{14}) b_{34}. \tag{11-20}$$

The DTA terms can be referred to the direction b_1 as follows, using (11-11), (11-12), and the assumption $t_{12} = t_{34}$:

$$
\begin{aligned}
DTA_{34} - DTA_{12} &= ut_{12}\left[\sin(c - b_1 + b_1 - b_3) - \sin(c - b_1)\right] \\
&\approx ut_{12}\left[\sin(c - b_1) + b_{31}\cos(c - b_1) - \sin(c - b_1)\right] \\
&= \left[ut_{12}\cos(c - b_1)\right](-b_{13}) \\
&= -DTI_{12} b_{13}.
\end{aligned}
\tag{11-21}
$$

Noting that

$$DTI_{14} = DTI_{12}\frac{t_{14}}{t_{12}}$$

and $b_{13} - b_{12} = b_{23}$, subtract (11-19) and (11-21) from (11-20), and solve for r_1:

$$r_1 \approx A - B \cdot STI_1, \tag{11-22}$$

where

$$A = \frac{DOA_{12} - DOA_{34}}{b_{34} - b_{12}} - \frac{DOI_{12} b_{12} - DOI_{14} b_{34}}{b_{34} - b_{12}}, \tag{11-23}$$

$$B = \frac{1}{b_{34} - b_{12}}(b_{23} t_{23} + b_{34} t_{14}). \tag{11-24}$$

The first term of (11-23) is, when its numerator and denominator are divided by t_{12} ($= t_{34}$), a discrete difference version of the Ekelund range estimate in (11-10). The remaining terms in (11-23) amount to errors introduced by departures from the idealizations which underlie the derivation of (11-10). The DOI terms are easily found by own ship so (11-23) may be calculated. Also B, (11-24), is readily calculable. However, the STI_1 term of (11-22) involves target motion in line of sight which is unknown to own ship and is the greatest source of error in Ekelund and other bearings-only ranging techniques. The essence of time correction is to *eliminate* this source of error by judicious choice of the time at which the range estimate is to apply. The method by which this time is determined is explained next.

Let time t^* be an arbitrary time, which will be chosen judiciously, and r^* and b^* be the corresponding range and bearing. Also let DTI_{1*} and DOI_{1*} be the distances target and own ship move in the b_1 line of sight from time t_1 to t^*. Then the equality version of (11-14) may be combined with (11-22) using $t_j = t^*$ and $t_i = t_1$ to extrapolate from r_1 to r^*:

$$r^* \cos(b^* - b_1) \approx r_1 + DTI_{1*} - DOI_{1*}$$

$$= A - B \cdot STI_1 + STI_1(t^* - t_1) - DOI_{1*} \qquad (11\text{-}25)$$

$$= A - \left[B - (t^* - t_1) \right] STI_1 - DOI_{1*}.$$

Now, to make r^* independent of STI_1, t^* is chosen such that the coefficient of STI_1 in (11-25) is equal to zero:

$$B - (t^* - t_1) = 0,$$

$$t^* = t_1 + B = t_1 + \frac{b_{23} t_{23} + b_{34} t_{14}}{b_{34} - b_{12}}. \qquad (11\text{-}26)$$

This value of t^* is known as a **best range time**. By (11-22) through (11-26), r^*, the **time-corrected range** at t^*, is given by

$$r^* = \frac{1}{\cos(b^* - b_1)} \left(\frac{DOA_{12} - DOA_{34} - DOI_{12} b_{12} + DOI_{14} b_{34}}{b_{34} - b_{12}} - DOI_{1*} \right), \qquad (11\text{-}27)$$

provided $\cos(b^* - b_1) \neq 0$.

Formula (11-27) is entirely in terms of the original four bearings, b^*, and distances travelled by own ship. This range estimation, applicable to a particular time t^*, is insensitive to target speed in line of sight. There remains, however, the problem of finding b^*. Sometimes one can conclude that b^* is close enough to b_1 that $\cos(b^* - b_1)$ is approximately equal to one. One may also extrapolate or interpolate bearings linearly or by Theorem 11.6 below or, finally, there remains the possibility of finding b^* by observation, waiting if necessary.

An example of best range time and time-corrected range will now be given, as a continuation of the example of Ekelund ranging given in 1103. The four times and bearings given in 1103 will play the roles here of $t_1, b_1, \dots, t_4, b_4$. From (11-26), the best range time for this time-bearing sequence is

$$t^* = 0 + \frac{(85.3 - 88.9)(6 - 4) + (70.3 - 85.3)(10 - 0)}{(70.3 - 85.3) - (88.9 - 90)} \text{ min} = 11.3 \text{ min}.$$

Since t^* occurs after t_4, and not long after, b^* is found by linear extrapolation:

$$b^* = \left[\frac{70.3 - 85.3}{4} \times 1.3 + 70.3 \right]^\circ = 65.4^\circ.$$

Thus $\cos(b^* - b_1) = \cos(65.4^\circ - 90^\circ) = .909$. Now

$$DOI_{12} = \frac{(10 \text{kts})(4 - 0) \text{min}}{60 \text{min/hr}} \cos(30^\circ - 90^\circ) = .33 \text{ nm},$$

$$DOI_{14} = \frac{(10)(5 - 0)}{60} [\cos(30^\circ - 90^\circ) + \cos(120^\circ - 90^\circ)] \text{nm} = 1.14 \text{ nm},$$

$$DOI_{*1} = \frac{10}{60} [5 \cos 60^\circ + 6.3 \cos(120^\circ - 90^\circ)] \text{nm} = 1.33 \text{ nm}.$$

In (11-27), the first two terms of the four-term quotient are just the Ekelund range found in 1103 to be 8027 yards. Hence, the range at time $t^* = 11.3$ minutes is

$$r^* = \frac{1}{.909}\left[8027 + \frac{-.33(88.9 - 90) + 1.14(70.3 - 85.3)}{-15.0 + 1.1} - 1.33\right] = 8830 \text{ yards.}$$

The actual range at time 11.3 minutes is 8071 yards. Thus time correction overestimates the range (at time 11.3 minutes) by 9.4 percent, in this example, in comparison with Ekelund ranging which underestimates the range at time 5 minutes, the turn time, by 13.0 percent. Again, exact bearings were used in both methods.

Additional examples of time correction, including effects of bearing errors, are given in problems 11, 12, and 13. In these examples, the improvement of time-corrected Ekelund over Ekelund without time correction is sharper than in the above example.

Note that the development of t^* distinguishes t_1 among the four times t_1, t_2, t_3, and t_4. If instead t_2 were distinguished, for example, then the ensuing r^* would be insensitive to target speed in direction b_2, i.e., to STI_2, rather than to STI_1. With the bearings close enough for the small angle approximations to apply, that change in sensitivity should not be important.

Apart from the choice of the distinguished time, by permutating the indices $(1, 2, 3, 4)$, various values of t^* can be obtained from the four given times and associated bearings. Recall, however, that the above simplified derivation assumes $t_{12} = t_{34}$, so unless also $t_{12} = t_{23}$, there are only four permutations that meet this constraint. Among these, there are only, at most, two different values of t^*. Under derivation without the present simplifications, there are 24 possible permutations, but there are at most twelve different values of t^* for a given set of four observation times. Some of the values of t^* will be too far in the future or past to be tactically useful, but others may be opportune times for own ship to make relatively accurate range estimates which will be insensitive to target speed in the line of sight.

Bearings only TMA is generally more accurate when own ship uses lead-lag, e.g., problems 4 to 14, compared to lag-lead, e.g., the above example.

For most purposes, notably weapon launch, a best range time in the future is highly desirable. (The above time-correction example is an improvement over the Ekelund version of the same example, in this respect as well as in accuracy.) Own ship can effect partial control on this by carefully choosing when and how to maneuver. If, for example, own ship points the target on the first leg and maneuvers to lag the line of sight for the second leg, then a best range time will occur after the last time of the input bearings. Of course, the further into the future the best range time is, the more one must be concerned about a possible course change by the target.

Convenient graphical methods are available for computing t^* under the small angle approximations used here and can be useful in a shipboard tactical situation. Exact formulas without the approximations used here are also available and are easily implemented on a desktop computer.

1105   Spiess TMA

Although not as widely used as Ekelund ranging, another source of range estimation is **Spiess TMA**. Spiess TMA is a technique requiring bearings at four times. Theorem 11.5 below states that given three bearings at distinct times, the locus of target positions at a selected fourth time is a computable straight line. This locus, known as a **Spiess line**, is then simply laid down on a plot and the target position is determined by the intersection of the Spiess line with the observed target bearing at t_4, *unless* the two lines coincide, which is termed a **singularity**. The Spiess line and the fourth bearing line will coincide, if, for example, own track is linear throughout. Once again, target range cannot be determined from bearings only if both own ship and target have linear tracks.

The Spiess range technique will require the following additional notation: As earlier, assume that bearing b_i is observed at time t_i, for $i = 1, 2, \ldots$. Specify a rectangular coordinate system (see Figure 11.4) by fixing the origin at own ship position at time t_1, giving the y-axis direction b_1, and the x-axis direction $b_1 + 90°$. Denote target position at time t_i in these coordinates by (x_i, y_i). The previous double subscript convention is extended to position coordinates: $x_{ij} = x_j - x_i$, etc.

FIGURE 11.4. COORDINATE SYSTEM FOR SPIESS LINE DERIVATION

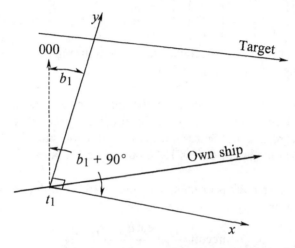

Theorem 11.5. Given bearings b_1, b_2, b_3 at respective times t_1, t_2, t_3, the locus of target positions at a given fourth time, t_4, with all four times distinct, is a straight line comprised of points (x_4, y_4) such that

$$y_4 t_{23} t_{14} = x_4(t_{13} t_{24} \cot b_{13} - t_{12} t_{34} \cot b_{12})$$

$$+ t_{14} t_{24}(DOI_{13} - DOA_{13} \cot b_{13}) \tag{11-28}$$

$$- t_{14} t_{34}(DOI_{12} - DOA_{12} \cot b_{12}).$$

Proof: Note that

$$y_i - DOI_{1i} = (x_i - DOA_{1i}) \cot b_{1i}, \tag{11-29}$$

for $i = 2$ and 3, and for a constant target speed,

$$\frac{x_{12}}{t_{12}} = \frac{x_{13}}{t_{13}} = \frac{x_{14}}{t_{14}} \quad \text{and} \quad \frac{y_{12}}{t_{12}} = \frac{y_{13}}{t_{13}} = \frac{y_{14}}{t_{14}}, \tag{11-30}$$

where $x_1 = 0$ from the coordinate system. These are six linear equations in $x_2, x_3, x_4, y_1, y_2, y_3, y_4$. Using the four equations in (11-30), x_2, x_3, y_2, and y_3 may be eliminated from the two equations in (11-29). The two resulting equations are then solved simultaneously to eliminate y_1 and the result is (11-28). This completes the proof.

The linear locus of points given by (11-28) is called the **Spiess line** at time t_4. It is denoted L_4, or at an arbitrary time t_j playing the role of t_4, it is denoted L_j. As described above, once L_4 has been determined from three bearings using (11-28), the target position is simply the point of intersection of L_4 with the bearing observed at t_4, *unless* these two lines coincide, which is a singularity. If a singularity does occur, range cannot be obtained from this technique with the available data.

One way to obtain target course and speed is to reverse the order of the four time indices and repeat the above procedure to obtain target position at (the original) t_1. It is then a simple computational or graphical manipulation to obtain course and speed. Another possible technique, although more tedious, is to compute the complete solution to the six equations in (11-29) and (11-30) and also (11-29) for $i = 4$. From these solutions, the target speed and course are given by

$$ u = \left[\left(\frac{x_{14}}{t_{14}} \right)^2 + \left(\frac{y_{14}}{t_{14}} \right)^2 \right]^{1/2} \quad \text{and} \quad c = b_1 + \text{arccot} \left(\frac{y_{14}}{x_{14}} \right) . $$

Spiess TMA is greatly simplified if own track is linear through the three bearings. The next two theorems pertain to this.

Theorem 11.6. If own track is linear, then the Spiess line at a chosen time t_j, corresponding to bearing observations at three other times, is the bearing line observed at t_j.

Proof: If the bearing line and Spiess line at time t_j did not coincide, then it would be possible to find the range at that time by the Spiess TMA procedure, violating Theorem 11.4.

Theorem 11.7. If own track is linear and distinct bearings b_1, b_2, b_3 are observed at respective times t_1, t_2, t_3, then the bearing b_4 at a different arbitrary time t_4, past or future, is found by computing

$$ b_4 = b_1 + \text{arccot} \left(\frac{t_{13} t_{24} \cot b_{13} - t_{12} t_{34} \cot b_{12}}{t_{23} t_{14}} \right) , \tag{11-31} $$

and adding, if necessary, an integer multiple of $180°$ to make the sum the value between 000 and 360 which draws in the same direction as b_1 through b_3.

Proof: The Spiess line at t_4 coincides with the bearing line at t_4, by Theorem 11.6. The slope of the Spiess line given by (11-28) is the ratio of the coefficient of y_4 to the coefficient of x_4. This slope may also be determined trigonometrically to be $\cot b_{14}$. Equation (11-31) comes from setting the two expressions for slope equal to each other and solving for b_4. This completes the proof.

Figure 11.5 illustrates Spiess ranging via Theorems 11.6 and 11.7. Own track is linear through three bearings, and a fourth bearing is taken after a port turn. The initial leg is extrapolated to the fourth bearing time, and the bearing at the extrapolated position is calculated by Theorem 11.7. By Theorem 11.6, this extrapolated bearing line is the Spiess line at that time. Theorem 11.6 still applies even though own ship maneuvered, since the maneuver in no way affected the Spiess line, given the bearings and times. Target position at t_4 is the intersection of the actual fourth bearing with the extrapolated fourth bearing (Spiess line).

Figures 11.6 and 11.7 show examples of singularities when own ship's track is not linear. In Figure 11.6, own ship's track is linear through the first three bearings, and a fourth bearing is taken after a maneuver. This time, however, the maneuver is such that the extrapolated bearing and the actual bearing coincide causing no range information to be obtainable. Figure 11.7 is an example of a singularity with two bearings on each of two legs; the Spiess line at any of the four bearing times (with respect to the other three) is necessarily the bearing at that time. In this figure, either of the indicated target tracks would satisfy the bearings, and definitive range information can not be obtained with only the four bearings. Spiess ranging is explored through problems 14 to 21.

FIGURE 11.5. SPIESS RANGE

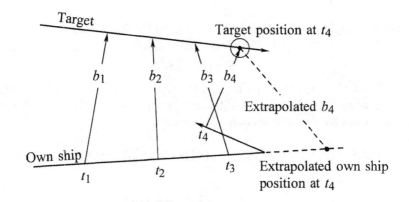

FIGURE 11.6. SINGULARITY IN SPIESS RANGING

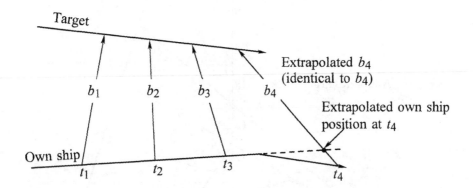

The concept of time correction which was discussed in terms of reducing the error of Ekelund range estimations is equally applicable to Spiess ranging. The same formulas used in 1104 apply and the simplifications that $t_{12} = t_{34}$ and the small angle approximations apply are reinstated. As before, the development could be done without these simplifications. It is further assumed that $t_2 = t_3$, so among t_1, t_2, t_3, t_4 there are only three distinct times and they are uniformly spaced.

Referenced to the coordinate system of Figure 11.7, the target position (x_j, y_j) at an arbitrary time t_j is given by

$$x_j = STA_1 t_{1j} = DTA_{1j}, \qquad (11\text{-}32)$$
$$y_j = r_1 + STI_1 t_{1j} = r_1 + DTI_{1j}. \qquad (11\text{-}33)$$

From (11-19) and (11-22),

$$STA_1 = C - D \cdot STI_1, \tag{11-34}$$

where

$$C = \frac{1}{t_{12}}\left(A \cdot b_{12} + DOA_{12} - DOI_{12}b_{12}\right), \tag{11-35}$$

$$D = \frac{b_{12}}{t_{12}}\left(B - t_{12}\right). \tag{11-36}$$

Combining and simplifying (11-32) through (11-36) and (11-22) yields

$$x_j = \left(C - D \cdot STI_1\right)\left(t_j - t_1\right), \tag{11-37}$$

$$y_j = A - \left(B - t_j + t_1\right)STI_1. \tag{11-38}$$

Note that (11-37) and (11-38) are linear in t_j and are separately linear in STI_1. Now if t_j is fixed as a chosen fourth bearing time, then the set of these (x_j, y_j) points, as STI_1 is varied, is the Spiess line at time t_j. (This proves an alternate version of Theorem 11.5.)

FIGURE 11.7. TWO LEG SPIESS RANGE SINGULARITY

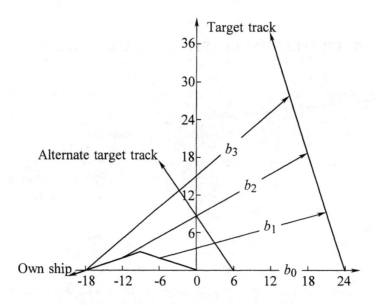

Own ship cannot distinguish between the two constant-velocity targets with bearings only.

Time	0	1	1.5	2	3
Own ship	(0, 0)	(2, -6)	(3, -9)	(2, -12)	(0, 18)
Target track	(0, 24)	(11, 21)	---	(22, 18)	(33, 15)
Alt target track	(0, 6)	(5, 3)	---	(10,0)	(15, -3)

The time quadruple (t_1, t_2, t_3, t_4), with $t_2 = t_3$, and the associated three bearings determine a best range time, t^*. Let L^* be the Spiess line at time t^*. From (11-38) with $t_j = t^* = t_1 + B$, it follows that $y_j = A$ *independent of* STI_1. Hence L^* is *perpendicular* to b_1, the y-axis of the coordinate system. If b^* is not far from b_1, this means that L^* and b^* will have a good cross-cut and Spiess ranging at time t^* will be relatively accurate.

Unfortunately, quite the opposite case is also possible. Suppose own track is linear through t_1, $t_2 = t_3$, t_4, and t^*. Then at t^*, the bearing line b^* and Spiess line L^* coincide by Theorem 11.6. Since L^* is perpendicular to b_1, so is b^*. Hence, the $\cos(b^* - b_1)$ factor of the r^* equation, (11-27), equals zero and r^* cannot be computed. This is consistent with Theorem 11.4 and is an inevitable singularity.

An additional observation arises from the linearity of (11-37) and (11-38) in t_j and in STI_1. For a fixed value of STI_1, the (x_j, y_j) values for various values of t_j given by these equations define a linear track. This linear track is the target track which is consistent with the three observed bearings and the chosen value of STI_1. Note the duality: For a fixed t_j, one gets a locus of position as STI_1 is varied; and for a fixed STI_1, one gets a target track as t_j is varied. It can also be shown from (11-37) and (11-38), that at a chosen t_j there is a value of STI_1 whose resultant track coincides with the Spiess line at t_j, and vice versa. More simply, a given bearing triple defines both a set of Spiess lines and a matching set of target tracks. Finally, if the chosen time is the best range time for the triple of bearings, regarded as a quadruple as before, then the corresponding STI_1 is zero.

Figure 11.8 shows the relation between Spiess TMA and time correction when own track is linear throughout. Bearings are taken at times 0, 10, and 30 minutes and a best range time of 48 minutes is calculated from these bearings, regarding the 10-minute observation as both t_2 and t_3. Spiess lines from the three bearings are shown for $t_4 = 18$, 28, 48($= t^*$), and 68. Note how the direction of the Spiess line swings as t_4 changes. At $t_4 = t^* = 48$, L^* is perpendicular to the bearing at time 0, and both own ship and target are on that line. Also shown are target tracks consistent with two separate values of STI_1, +15 knots and -15 knots. If one assumes that the actual STI_1 is between these limits, then the target position at time 48 is limited to the portion of L^* which lies between the 15 knot and -15 knot tracks. Thus, while a complete TMA solution is not possible from bearings only when own track is linear, the target's position can be narrowed down by reasonable assumptions of STI_1.

Figure 11.9 shows a Spiess plot with an own ship turn to port at time 10. Bearings are taken at 0 and 5 minutes on the first leg and at 15 minutes on the second. Spiess lines are shown for various values of t_4, and the target tracks for STI_1 at 15 and -15 knots are also shown. Note how slowly the Spiess lines change direction between times -20 and 5 and between 15 and 40, while direction changes rapidly between 5 and 15. Time 10 is a best range time, and the Spiess line at that time is narrowly delimited by the bounding tracks. Additionally, L^* is roughly perpendicular to the bearing at time 10.

The potential for an accurate estimation of target position at a best range time is clearly demonstrated by this figure. Even without the bearing at time 10, the target's position can be estimated as the intersection of the two possible target tracks since the range at t^* is independent of STI_1. In shipboard use, multiple estimated target solutions are continuously laid out on the plot in an attempt to narrow in on the actual solution. While Figure 11.9 represents a somewhat idealistic plot since there is no bearing scatter and the target conveniently does not maneuver for greater than an hour, all that is required for a rather accurate estimate of target position at $t = 10$ is to lay down the bearing at $t = 10$ minutes and circle the point of intersection with the Spiess line at 10 minutes.

FIGURE 11.8. SPIESS LINES WITH LINEAR OWN SHIP TRACK

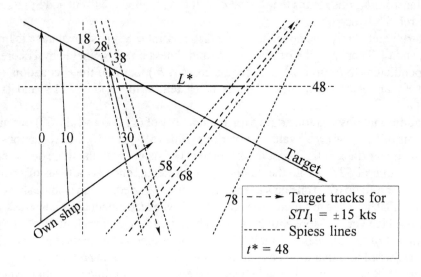

FIGURE 11.9. SPIESS PLOT RELATED TO BEST RANGE TIME

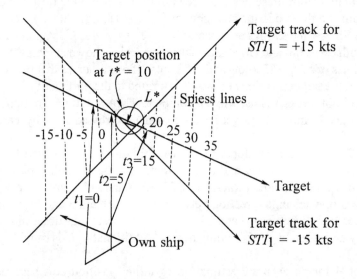

Theorem 11.8, given next without proof, is the "parabola theorem" for bearings-only TMA when own track is linear. From this is derived a generalization to non-linear own track, Corollary 11.9. These results further tie together the above theory.

Theorem 11.8. Suppose own track is linear and distinct bearings at three times are given. A parabola is defined by those bearings and times such that (a) all bearing lines are tangent to the parabola, and (b) so too are the target tracks which are consistent with the bearings for various values of STI_1 as given by (11-37) and (11-38). The axis of this parabola will parallel the DRM.

Corollary 11.9. Without assuming that own track is linear, suppose distinct bearings are observed at three times. A parabola is thereby determined which is tangent to all Spiess lines arising from the three bearings and times and to all target tracks consistent with the three bearings and times.

Proof: A linear track is said to **agree** with a bearing if the track position lies on that bearing at the time of the bearing. A point on one of the three bearing lines but not on the others is selected and a linear track through this point which agrees with the three bearings is found. (From linear equations representing the three bearing lines, deduce three equations for the coefficients of the track's equation and solve; these are solvable because the three bearings are distinct.) Theorem 11.7 gives future and past bearing lines from this linear track. Now consider the Spiess line determined by own track, the three bearings and times, and a chosen fourth time. The slope of this Spiess line is the same as that of the bearing line at that time (compare (11-28) and (11-31)). Since the Spiess line and the bearing line both pass through the target and they have the same slope, they coincide. Theorem 11.8 may be applied to find the parabola determined by the three bearings and the linearity of the chosen track. (Although own ship track is not linear, the calculated track is linear so Theorem 11.8 is applicable to it.) As stated in Theorem 11.8, this parabola will be tangent to all the bearing lines. Since the bearings from the linear track and the Spiess lines from own track coincide, this parabola must also be tangent to the Spiess lines. Finally, since the set of tracks consistent with the three bearings coincides with the set of Spiess lines, the parabola must also be tangent to the target tracks. This proves the corollary.

Theorem 11.8 is illustrated by Figure 11.10. Although the parabolic envelope of Spiess lines and target tracks is not explicitly shown in Figures 11.8 and 11.9, a brief reexamination of those figures will show the same principle applies to those figures as well.

As stated early, particular importance is attached to the estimation of range when performing bearings-only TMA. Therefore, the majority of this chapter has been spent in discussing ways of estimating target range. First, it was shown that a complete target solution is not possible if own ship's track is linear. The most common technique of range estimation, Ekelund ranging, and the errors involved in it were discussed next. Also examined was the time correction method to reduce range errors. Finally, the technique of Spiess ranging was explored. Links between time correction and Spiess theory have been found via the parabolic envelope of bearings between linear units. Ekelund ranging, the concept of time correction, and, to a lesser degree, Spiess ranging are not merely techniques used for mathematical discussion. These techniques, and others, have been proven useful in shipboard fire control evolutions, and the creation of these techniques has primarily evolved from shipboard experience.

1106   Other Literature and History

The first complete TMA solution from bearings only was found in 1953 by F. N. Spiess of the Scripps Oceanographic Institution [1], who had considerable submarine war patrol experience in

World War II, became a distinguished oceanographer, and achieved the rank of Captain in the Naval Reserve. Theorem 11.5 and its proof are from that paper. Also given in [1] is a condition which is necessary for a singularity to occur.

FIGURE 11.10. PARABOLIC ENVELOPE OF BEARINGS AND TARGET TRACKS

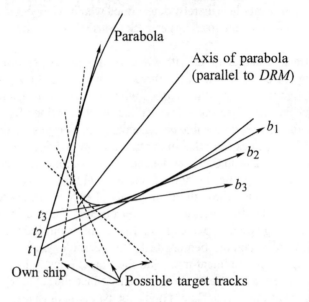

Ekelund ranging was devised in 1958 by LT (later RADM) J. J. Ekelund, while an instructor at Submarine School in Groton, CT. It was disseminated to submariners via [2] and has since become widespread.

Time correction was originated by D. C. Bossard of Daniel H. Wagner, Associates in 1968 while on assignment to COMSUBDEVGRU TWO. It was inspired in part by CAPT J. F. Fagan's analysis [3] of tactics to reduce Ekelund errors. Time correction was a prominent theme in the most extensive passive ranging exercise ever held at sea, LANTSUBASWEX 2-68, and in the ensuing reference [4] written by Bossard. In 1991, Bossard of DCBossard, Incorporated greatly improved the theory of time correction and its relation to Spiess TMA in [5], which is a revision to [4]. The development in 1104 and the time correction part of 1105 follow [5] with simplifying approximations. Figures 11.8 and 11.9 are from [5].

The illustrative singularity in Figure 11.7 is due to W. R. Stromquist of Daniel H. Wagner, Associates. The relevance to TMA of the parabola statement for linear own track, Theorem 11.8, was found independently by J. D. Kettle [6] of Kettle & Wagner and D. J. Bordelon [7] of what is now NUWC/Newport. An abstract mathematical statement of the parabola theorem has long been known in the field of projective geometry – e.g., see Courant and Robbins [8], page 208. E. J. Holder of Wagner Associates found that the axis is the *DRM*. Bossard and W. R. Stromquist contributed to the generalization of Theorem 11.8 to nonlinear own track and Spiess lines stated in Corollary 11.9.

The foregoing gives some historical highlights on bearings-only TMA without use of "filtering" methods. TMA in general has received enormous attention, principally in the submarine community, since the 1950s. Particularly important centers of this activity have been COMSUBDEVGRU TWO (now COMSUBDEVRON TWELVE), notably in 1967-73 under successive commands of CAPTs W. M. Pugh, C. W. Woods, and J. F. Fagan; a group led by E. L. Messere at what is now NUWC/ Newport and its predecessor organizations; prior to the early 1970s, a group led by A. J. Van Woerkom at the Electric Boat Division, General Dynamics Corporation; and prior to the early 1980s, groups at the Naval Ordnance Laboratory, now the Naval Surface Warfare Center, White Oak.

It may also be noted that TMA has attracted considerable investigative attention over the years from naval officers, junior and senior. Among the more successful of these, in addition to Ekelund and Fagan mentioned above, have been LT (later CAPT) F. C. Lynch, who devised the "Lynch plot" shortly before World War II for use in periscope approaches, based on a relation among bearings, bearing rates, and relative motion, and ENS L. A. Anderson who devised a classified TMA method known as FLIT at COMSUBDEVGRU TWO in 1970 (in part independently given by W. C. Queen of General Dynamics in 1969). Also, Kettelle originally found the parabola result as a submarine officer in 1953.

A more extensive history and bibliography are given in Wagner [9].

[1] Spiess, Fred N. *Complete Solution of the Bearings-Only Approach Problem*. San Diego, CA: Scripps Institution of Oceanography, 1953.

[2] Ekelund, John J. "A Means of Passive Range Determination." *Commander Submarine Forces, Atlantic Fleet, Quarterly Information Bulletin*. Summer 1958.

[3] Fagan, John F. "Passive Ranging." *Commander Submarine Forces, Atlantic Fleet, Quarterly Information Bulletin*. Summer 1967.

[4] Bossard, D. C. *Passive Ranging Manual*. Volume 3. Groton, CT: Commander Submarine Development Group Two, 1969.

[5] Bossard, D. C. *Theory of Ranging and Target Motion Analysis*. NWP 71-4, Groton, CT: Commander Submarine Development Squadron Twelve, 1992.

[6] Kettelle, John D. "Parabolic Envelope of Bearings-only Tracks." *Journal of Underwater Acoustics* 11 (October, 1961): 745-747.

[7] Bordelon, Derrill J. *Range-Free Linear Prediction of Target Submarine Location by a Single Attacker*. NAVORD Report 6879. Newport, RI: Naval Underwater Systems Center, 1960.

[8] Courant, Richard, and Herbert Robbins. *What Is Mathematics?* New York, NY: Oxford University Press, 1941.

[9] Wagner, Daniel H. *Naval Tactical Decision Aids*. Military Operations Research Lecture Notes, NPSOR-1. Monterey, CA: Naval Postgraduate School, 1989.

Problems

Note: All courses and bearings are in degrees true. In 1 nautical mile (nm) there are 2027 yards.

In problems 1 through 16, the actual target track is 10 kts on course 180, and at time 0, the target bears 005.3 at 25878 yds from own ship. Own ship makes 10 knots on course 045 from time 0 to time 10 minutes and on course 315 thereafter (assume the turn is instantaneous). Bearing (exact to .1° – this round-off sometimes produces noticeable range errors) and range at various times are as follows:

Time (min):	0	4	6	8	10	12	14	20	45
Bearing:	005.3	003.5	002.5	001.3	000.0	001.4	003.1	009.5	091.3
Range (kyds):	25.9	23.5	22.3	21.6	20.0	18.9	17.7	14.4	8.4

Own ship knows only own motion and bearings observed at certain times, as specified in the problem. Percentage range error is defined as

$$\% \text{ range error} = \frac{\text{estimated range} - \text{actual range}}{\text{actual range}} \times 100 .$$

1. Given bearings observed exactly at times 0, 4, and 8, what is the direction of the target motion relative to own motion on this leg?

2. a. What is the answer to problem 1 if the following bearing errors are *added* to the actual bearings: .4 at time 0, -.1 at time 4, and .2 at time 8?
b. Why do such small bearing errors cause such large *DRM* errors?

3. What is the direction of relative motion on the second leg if exact bearings are observed at times 10, 14, and 20?

4. a. If bearings are observed exactly at times 0, 8, 12, and 20, what is the Ekelund range estimate at turn time? On each leg, approximate the bearing rate at the turn by the difference quotient for the pair of bearing times. Also, since line of sight at the turn is unknown, use line of sight at time 8 on leg 1 and at time 12 on leg 2.
b. What is the percentage range error?

5. Repeat problem 4 for bearings observed exactly at times 6, 8, 12, and 14.

6. Why is the percentage error lower in problem 5 than in problem 4?

7. Repeat problem 4 with errors added to the actual bearings as follows: .4 at time 0, -.3 at time 8, -.3 at time 12, and .2 at time 20.

8. Repeat problem 5 with errors added to the actual bearings as follows: .4 at time 6, -.3 at time 8, -.3 at time 12, and .2 at time 14.

9. Why is the percentage range error lower in problem 7 than in problem 8?

10. What do the answers to problems 6 and 9 suggest about choices of timing of bearings in Ekelund ranging?

11. a.   For the Ekelund range of problem 4, what is the best range time corresponding to the bearings taken in chronological sequence?
b.   What is the time-corrected range at the best range time in a?
c.   What is the percentage range error?
d.   To what should the error in b be attributed?

12. Repeat problem 11 (a through c) for the Ekelund range of problem 7.

13. Comparing the answers to 12c and 7b, what can be said about the accuracy of time-corrected ranging versus Ekelund ranging in these problems?

14. Given exact bearings at times 0, 6, and 10, what is the predicted bearing at time 20 assuming own ship does not turn?

15. a.   Use the answer to problem 14 and the exact bearings at times 0, 6, 10, and 20 to find the Spiess range at time 20.
b.   Find the percentage range error.

16. Repeat problem 15 with errors added to the bearings as follows: .4 at time 0, -.3 at time 6, -.3 at time 10, and .3 at time 20.

17. a.   Using the same three bearings as in problem 14, find the Spiess range at time 45.
b.   If the three given bearings were measured to within .01, they would be 005.30, 002.46, and 000.00. Repeat part a with this change.

18. a.   It is easily seen that the extrapolated own position (without the turn) bears 090 from actual own position at all times after time 10. Find the time at which the target is aligned with the actual and extrapolated own positions.
b.   How does this answer help explain the inaccurate range estimates in problem 17?

19. Suppose own ship turns to 135 at time 10 instead of to 315. At what value of t_4, the fourth bearing time, does a singularity occur in Spiess ranging?

20. Suppose exact bearings are observed at times 0, 8, and 12. Find the Spiess range at time 20.

21. Suppose exact bearings are observed at times 0, 10, and 20.

a.   Regarding these as four times with the second and third coinciding at 10, find the best range time for this chronological sequence.
b.   Given a bearing of 002.8 at this best range time, how does the direction of the Spiess line at this best range time compare to the bearing at time 0? (Spiess line may be found by Theorem 11.5, using the bearings at times 0, 10, and 20.)
c.   Find the Spiess range at this best range time.

22. If for instance $b_i = 010$ and $b_j = 355$, it is relatively easy for a human to recognize that b_{ij}, the bearing change from time t_i to time t_j, is -15, being negative because the change is in the counterclockwise direction. It is not so easy to instruct a computer on this point. A brute force method is to use branched alternatives, instructing the computer case by case. Find a single formula to make this computation, covering all cases, by using the TRUNC function: TRUNC(x) removes the fractional part of a number x, e.g., TRUNC(-1.9) = -1 and TRUNC(1.9) = 1. Hint: In the square set,

$$\{(b_i, b_j): 0 \le b_i \le 360, \quad 0 \le b_j \le 360\},$$

look at the contours of $b_j - b_i$ and the set of points representing left bearing drift.

Answers to Problems

1. 202.6°.

2. a. 162.5°.   b. Since the cotangent of a small bearing difference is large, the difference between two such cotangents is very sensitive to errors in the bearing differences.

3. 156.9°.

4. a. 18.1 kyds. b. -9.5 percent.

5. a. 18.9 kyds. b. -5.5 percent.

6. The derivation of the Ekelund range formula assumes BR and BR' are *at* the turn. In problem 5, the times used for the bearing rates are closer to the turn, and, hence, closer to the assumptions, than in problem 4.

7. a. 16.5 kyds. b. -17.5 percent.

8. a. 13.4 kyds. b. -33 percent.

9. In estimating each bearing rate in problem 8, the bearing times are so close to each other that the difference quotient is very sensitive to errors in its numerator.

10. There is a conflict between two sources of error. If the times are too far apart, the difference quotient is inadequately representative of bearing rate at the turn. If the times are too close together, the difference quotient is too sensitive to bearing errors. Some sort of compromise is usually required.

11. a. 13.4 min. b. 18.7 kyds. c. 3.3 percent. d.   Small angle approximations and slight round-off error.

12. a. 13.0 min. b. 17.1 kyds. c. -6.6 percent.

13. The time-corrected range is less sensitive to bearing errors than the original Ekelund range in these problems.

14. 349.5°.

15. a.   13.7 kyds.   b.   -4.9 percent.

16. a.   16.6 kyds.   b.   15.4 percent.

17. a.   15.8 kyds.   b.   12.5 kyds.

18. a.   44.7 min.   b.   A singularity occurs at time 44.7 and the Spiess range at time 45 would not be expected to be accurate due to the proximity to the singularity.

19. Never.

20. 14.1 kyds (actual range is 14.4 kyds).

21. a.   12.8 min.   b.   They are perpendicular.   c.   18.4 kyds.

22. $b_{ij} = b_j - b_i - 360\ \text{TRUNC}[(b_j - b_i)/180]$ degrees.

12
TARGET COVERAGE

In every type of warfare, a sequence of operations must be completed in order to put ordnance on target successfully. This is true whether one is firing a rifle during a ground battle or engaging sophisticated submarines, aircraft, or surface ships. The ability to achieve the desired level of damage depends on the fire control solution, weapon characteristics such as firing errors and warhead size, and the defensive and counterattack capabilities of the target. The purpose of this chapter is to examine each of those aspects affecting damage.

Section 1201 introduces **damage functions**, **aiming errors,** and **dispersion** of rounds about the point of aim. Damage functions are analogues of lateral range curves as defined in Chapter 6. They lead to **lethal area** and **lethal radius**, which are both analogues of sweep width. **Aiming error** and **dispersion** are modeled collectively as a two-dimensional sum, **firing error**; its bivariate distribution is often assumed to be normal.

In 1203, damage probability for aimed fire is found in terms of lethal radius and standard deviation of firing error. Under circular normality, standard deviation is proportional to the median, called **circular error probable** (*CEP*). Lethal radius and *CEP* may be used to find damage probability for a collection of weapons of differing types. **Shoot-adjust-shoot** and **shoot-look-shoot** firing doctrines are discussed.

The ability to treat multiple weapons leads in 1204 to comparisons of arsenals by an MOE defined as **counter-military potential** (*CMP*) for nuclear weapons and by an equivalent to rate of fire of 8" rounds of gunfire for conventional weapons.

Sections 1205 and 1206 treat layered defenses against both a single attacker and multiple attackers, with defensive weapons that are limited in number or are unlimited. To facilitate treatment of various combinations of events, assumptions of statistical independence are freely made. Some complex tactical situations are noted in 1207, with the suggestion that they be treated by expected-value models (see 109) or be Monte Carlo simulation (see Chapter 3).

1201   Damage Functions and Firing Errors

The primary goal in this section is to compute the probability P_K of inflicting a specified level of damage to a specified target using a specified number of weapons. This must necessarily include a discussion of the lethality of the weapon being used and firing errors (aiming error plus dispersion).

This development of modeling the effects of damage, which will use the MOE's lethal area and lethal radius defined below, will be, as implied above, very analogous to the development in Chapter 6 of lateral range curves, distribution of transits in lateral range, and sweep width. The analogies will be pointed out at each stage, and attention to them should aid reader understanding.

Throughout this section it is assumed that a single round of a weapon is fired at a target whose position is in a horizontal plane. The target may be on land or sea, and the weapon firing platform may be on the surface, airborne, or submerged. If the target is submerged or airborne at an uncertain depth or altitude, the methods could readily be extended to incorporate the depth or altitude uncertainty, but that will not be treated explicitly.

A rectangular coordinate system with origin at the target will be used. The origin is known to the director of the fire only with uncertainty. The position of the impact of the round will be given by the pair of random variables (X, Y). The type of target and a required damage level are assumed fixed; the results of course depend on both.

Damage functions, lethal areas, and lethal radii. Assume that the ability of the fired round to inflict the required damage against the specified target depends only on the distance from the target to the impact point of the round, i.e, the **miss distance**. Specifically, let $D(R)$ be the amount of damage done if the miss distance is R. It will also be useful to define this in terms of impact position: Let $G(X, Y) = D(\sqrt{X^2 + Y^2})$. Then R, $D(R)$, and $G(X, Y)$ are all random variables.

Both D and G are direct analogues of a lateral range curve. Each gives conditional probability of effective action, given the value of a certain parameter. For D, the parameter is the one-dimensional miss distance, and for G it is the two-dimensional impact position of the round; D and G are illustrated in Figures 12.1 and 12.2. Note that D is typically nonincreasing due to the nature of damage effects. As with lateral range curves, it is emphasized that D and G are *not* probability density functions.

It is natural to define the **lethal area** a of the round as the volume under the G surface:

$$a = \int_{-\infty}^{\infty} \int_{-\infty}^{\infty} G(x, y)\,dx\,dy. \tag{12-1}$$

By transforming (12-1) to polar coordinates, a is expressed in terms of D:

$$a = \int_0^{2\pi}\int_0^{\infty} D(r) r\,dr\,d\theta$$

$$= 2\pi \int_0^{\infty} r D(r)\,dr. \tag{12-2}$$

One may approximate D by D^* defined by

$$D^*(r) = \begin{cases} 1, & \text{if } r \le r_d, \\ 0, & \text{if } r > r_d, \end{cases} \tag{12-3}$$

where r_d is $(a/\pi)^{1/2}$ and is called the **lethal radius**. Then D^* leads to the same lethal area as D and may be used to approximate D.

FIGURE 12.1. TYPICAL DAMAGE FUNCTION

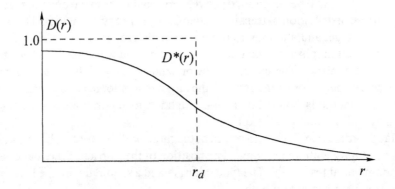

FIGURE 12.2. ILLUSTRATION OF G AND G*

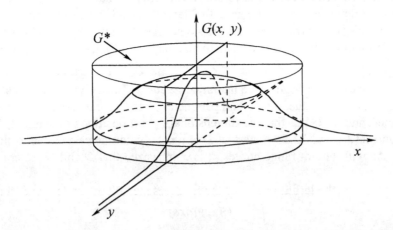

A weapon whose damage function is given by D^* in (12-3) is called a **cookie-cutter** weapon. The lethal area for this type of weapon is $a = \pi r_d^2$ by (12-2). Although most weapons are not strictly cookie-cutter in nature, this assumption enables one to model weapon effectiveness easily.

The lethal area and radius are dependent on the type of round and the target. Sometimes the weapon must actually directly hit the target in order for it to cause the specified level of damage. For example, suppose a five-inch gun is fired at a protected shore battery. The walls of the shore battery may be strong enough to protect the gun and occupants from shells that land outside the walls. If a shell is a direct hit (inside the walls), then both the guns and people are destroyed. The lethal area for such a weapon against that particular target would effectively be the area of the target projected on the plane normal to the trajectory of the incoming rounds.

The lethal area may be very difficult to determine. Past experience has proven that in many cases a single hit may not be sufficient to cause the desired level of damage. A single five-inch round, or even a missile or torpedo, is unlikely to sink a modern warship. In 1987, USS *Stark* absorbed two Exocet missiles in the Persian Gulf without sinking. Sometimes a single round can destroy a target if it hits a "vital spot," such as a magazine, fuel tank, etc., but the area of the vital spot might be very small.

Of course the MOE's lethal area and lethal radius measure only the lethality of a round once it impacts. They reflect nothing about accuracy of fire. That comes next.

Firing errors and damage probabilities. Impact position and therefore miss distance are affected by two random variables. One is the uncertainty about the target's location, which will result in an **aiming error**, and the other is deviation of the round from the point of aim due to a variety of effects that cumulatively are called the **dispersion** of a round. The two effects are often measured separately, but can be totaled as **firing error** to reduce the complexity of the overall model. Let the point (X, Y) be the sum of these two effects, without concern for the separate contributors to (X, Y). Let f be the probability density function of the joint distribution of the pair (X, Y). If one has knowledge of f, and if one scores 1 if the target is damaged to the required degree and 0 otherwise, then P_K, the damage probability, is the expected value of this score and may be expressed in the following ways:

$$P_K = E[G(X, Y)] = \int_{-\infty}^{\infty} \int_{-\infty}^{\infty} G(x, y) f(x, y) \, dx \, dy$$

$$= \int_{-\infty}^{\infty} \int_{-\infty}^{\infty} D(\sqrt{x^2 + y^2}) f(x, y) \, dx \, dy \qquad (12\text{-}4)$$

$$= \int_0^{2\pi} \int_0^{\infty} D(r) f(r\cos\theta, r\sin\theta) r \, dr \, d\theta.$$

Here f is a direct analogue of the function f in 603, where it is the probability density function of the lateral range of a transitor. A uniform distribution over a two-dimensional region could be used to model the present f, but pertaining to impact position as it does, a more realistic model is usually a bivariate normal distribution (see Appendix A). In order to simplify the analysis, assume that the distribution is *circular* normal centered on the target. This assumption means that X and Y have the same standard deviation, σ, and mean, 0, and their correlation coefficient (see Appendix A) is 0. The density function f of (X, Y) is then given by

$$f(x, y) = \frac{1}{2\pi\sigma^2} e^{-(x^2 + y^2)/(2\sigma^2)}, \text{ all } x, y. \qquad (12\text{-}5)$$

Also, if the impact position (X, Y) is circular normal as in (12-5), then the miss distance R has a **Rayleigh** distribution with probability density function f_R given by

$$f_R(r) = \frac{r}{\sigma^2} e^{-r^2/(2\sigma^2)}, \ r \geq 0.$$

1202   Uniform Fire and Area Bombardment

As an alternative to the bivariate normal assumption, (12-5), one might assume that the target position and hence the aiming point are uniformly distributed in a region S having area A and that the dispersion of the weapon is negligible. Then

$$f(x,y) = \begin{cases} 1/A, & \text{if } (x,y) \text{ is in } S, \\ 0, & \text{otherwise.} \end{cases}$$

The probability of damaging the target is found by substituting this f into (12-4):

$$P_K = \frac{1}{A} \iint_{(x,y) \text{ in } S} D(\sqrt{x^2+y^2})\, dx\, dy. \tag{12-6}$$

Suppose also that S is large enough that G vanishes outside S, i.e., any impact outside S will not damage the target. Then the double integral in (12-6) is the lethal area a, so (12-6) reduces to

$$P_K = \frac{a}{A}.$$

If n rounds are fired independently in these conditions, then, in analogy to (5-1) in 502,

$$P_K = 1 - \left(1 - \frac{a}{A}\right)^n.$$

For example, suppose five 16-inch shells are fired at a land target. Assume that each shell falls uniformly in a square with 1000 yards on a side centered on the target, and that each shell is a cookie-cutter weapon with lethal radius 200 yards. The lethal area for one shell is $a = \pi r_d^2 = 125,664$ yards^2. The probability of damaging the target is then found by computing $P_K = 1 - (1 - 125,664\times10^{-6})^5 = .49$.

1203   Aimed Fire

Aimed fire is more difficult to model than uniform fire because the joint density function f is not so easy to work with analytically. Typically one assumes cookie-cutter weapons with firing errors that have a circular normal distribution centered on the target. Thus, the lethal radius, r_d in (12-3), and the standard deviation of miss distance, σ in (12-5), are the only required parameters. The probability of damaging a target can be found by substituting for f from (12-5) and D^* from (12-3) for D in (12-4), and converting to polar coordinates, which results in

$$\begin{aligned} P_K &= 2\pi \int_0^\infty r D(r) \frac{e^{-r^2/(2\sigma^2)}}{2\pi\sigma^2}\, dr \\ &= 2\pi \int_0^{r_d} \frac{e^{-r^2/(2\sigma^2)}}{2\pi\sigma^2} r\, dr \\ &= 1 - e^{-r_d^2/(2\sigma^2)}. \end{aligned} \tag{12-7}$$

Equation (12-7) is sometimes expressed in terms of **circular error probable** (*CEP*), which is defined to be the radius of the circle containing half of the miss distances, i.e., the median of the miss distance distribution. Put another way, if multiple shots were fired at the target, one-half of the rounds would impact within a circle of radius CEP centered on the target. The probability of damaging the target in terms of CEP is

$$P_K = 1 - \left(\frac{1}{2}\right)^{r_d^2/CEP^2}. \tag{12-8}$$

For a circular normal distribution, $CEP = (-2\ln(1/2))^{1/2}\sigma = 1.1774\sigma$. This is an important result because it readily provides a way to estimate the standard deviation σ from the CEP. The CEP could be found by firing a series of rounds and measuring the radius of the circle which contains one-half of the fall of shot. Figure 12.3 illustrates the CEP concept by showing the fall of shot of thirty rounds.

FIGURE 12.3. ILLUSTRATION OF _CEP_

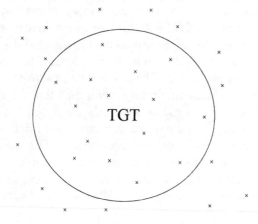

Suppose next that n shots are fired at a target and p_i is the probability that the ith shot damages the target. If each shot is independent of all others, then the overall probability of damaging the target is, again as with (5-1),

$$P_K = 1 - \prod_{i=1}^{n}(1 - p_i). \tag{12-9}$$

If r_{di} and σ_i are the lethal radius and standard deviation respectively of the ith shot, then the probability of damaging the target is

$$P_K = 1 - \prod_{i=1}^{n}\left[1 - \left(1 - \exp\left(-\frac{r_{di}^2}{2\sigma_i^2}\right)\right)\right]$$

$$= 1 - \exp\left(-\frac{1}{2}\sum_{i=1}^{n}\frac{r_{di}^2}{\sigma_i^2}\right). \tag{12-10}$$

Let

$$z = \left(\frac{r_{d1}}{\sigma_1}\right)^2 + \left(\frac{r_{d2}}{\sigma_2}\right)^2 + \ldots + \left(\frac{r_{dn}}{\sigma_n}\right)^2.$$

Then (12-10) can be written more succinctly as

$$P_K = 1 - e^{-z/2}.$$

For targets that are killed by over pressure, lethal radius scales as the cube root of yield; i.e., $r_{di} = ky_i^{1/3}$, where y_i is the energy yield of weapon i and k is target dependent. For such targets,

$$z = k^2 \sum_{i=1}^{n} \frac{y_i^{2/3}}{\sigma_i^2}.$$

The sum depends on properties of weapons but not on targets, a fact that will be exploited in 1204.

Aiming can result in **bias** in impact point, which simply means that the mean aiming error is not zero. Suppose sequential shots are fired at a target for which there is some bias. If the target and fall of shot can be seen well enough to judge the miss coordinates X and Y following each shot, then adjustments to the aim point can be made prior to the next shot. This spotting method is called a **shoot-adjust-shoot** (SAS) firing procedure. The best aim point adjustment following the jth round is accomplished by correcting the azimuth and elevation such that the aim point for the $(j + 1)$st round is the aim point for the previous round, shifted in the X and Y directions by $1/j$ times the amount of observed miss. It can be shown that this procedure minimizes the variance of miss distance, based on observations of previous miss coordinates. The effect of this is to reduce the overall variance and to improve P_K. If n cookie-cutter rounds, each with a lethal radius r_d are fired with circular normal dispersion having standard deviation σ using this SAS doctrine, then the probability of damaging the target with at least one effective round becomes

$$P_K = 1 - \exp\left(-\frac{r_d^2}{2\sigma^2}\left(\frac{1}{2} + \frac{2}{3} + \frac{3}{4} + \ldots + \frac{n-1}{n}\right)\right).$$

Note that $P_K = 0$ when $n = 1$, reflecting the assumption that the aiming bias is large; the first shot provides information, but has no chance of killing the target.

In practice, naval gunfire support often uses a simpler doctrine to get on target. Following the first shot a spotter, either ashore or airborne, radios the number of yards long or short and left or right of the target. The ship's fire control team adjusts the aim point by the full amount of the miss distance in each of two coordinates and fires again. Succeeding shots are "spotted on" in similar fashion until the ship is on target. The ship then fires numerous rounds without further adjustments in what is called "fire for effect."

The naval gunfire support doctrine just described is for *indirect fire*, when the target cannot be seen from the ship, but a similar procedure is followed when the fall of shot can be observed directly. "Spotting on" was first used against enemy warships. An aerial spotter was preferable because his estimate, especially in the direction of fire, was more accurate than estimates from the ship. Because gun errors were large enough to matter, time of flight was significant, and there was a sense of urgency to get on target quickly, it was common practice to fire a full salvo and eyeball the error in both coordinates from the estimated center of the salvo. To further complicate spotting, the target might try to undo the effect of the spot by changing course. Since a clever tactic was to steer out when the salvo was long and in when the salvo was short, the evasive maneuver was called *salvo chasing*. When its salvo "straddled" the target (some shots under and some over), a ship shifted to "rapid continuous fire," but did not cease its attempts to track the motion of the target with its fire control system, which computed the target's future position for the time when shells would impact.

Suppose the magnitude of the miss distances cannot be determined, but an observer can still determine whether a particular shot damaged the target. If the goal is to fire until a damaging hit is made, then the appropriate question becomes: how many shots will be required on average to damage the target? Let N be the number of shots required to damage the target and p_i be the probability of damaging the target with the ith shot. Thus $q_i = 1 - p_i$ is the probability that the target survives the ith shot. Assuming independent shots, the expected value of N using this **shoot-look-shoot** (SLS) doctrine is

$$
\begin{aligned}
E[N] &= \sum_{n=1}^{\infty} n \Pr\{N = n\} \\
&= \sum_{n=1}^{\infty} n p_n \prod_{i=1}^{n-1} q_i \\
&= 1 + q_1 + q_1 q_2 + q_1 q_2 q_3 + \cdots .
\end{aligned}
$$

This type of firing doctrine can be applied to firing surface-to-air missiles (SAMs), providing there is sufficient time between shots to observe damage.

1204   Arsenal Comparisons

In comparing arsenals of weapons, it is necessary to make an assumption about the nature of the targets. If the targets are at known locations and are concentrated in space ("point" targets such as ICBM silos), then delivery accuracy is an important part of the comparison. On the other hand accuracy may be unimportant if the targets are spread out or are loosely located ("area" targets), in which case the object is simply to cover as much area as possible with lethal effects. The problem of comparing arsenals comes up with both nuclear and conventional weapons, although the measurement scales are of course different in the two cases.

For nuclear weapons, it is usual to let the measure of an arsenal for point targets be **counter-military potential** (*CMP*), defined by

$$
CMP = \sum_{i=1}^{n} \frac{y_i^{2/3}}{CEP_i^2},
$$

where y_i and CEP_i are as in 1203. Since CEP_i and σ are related by a scale factor, CMP is the same as z in 1203, except that the target-dependent factor k and the scale factor have been omitted. For purposes of comparing arsenals, it is unimportant whether k is large or small, or even whether k is the same for all point targets in the target set. Against any reasonably diverse set of hard point targets, an arsenal with a big value of CMP is better than an arsenal with a small value.

For area targets, the natural measure of an arsenal is the total area that can be covered with lethal effects. Assuming as before that lethal radius scales with the cube root of yield, and again ignoring the scale factor k, the usual measure of a nuclear arsenal is taken to be

$$EMT = \sum_{i=1}^{n} y_i^{2/3};$$

EMT is "equivalent megatons" if yield is measured in megatons, hence the name.

There was a period of time when the question of whether the United States or the Soviet Union had the more "powerful" nuclear arsenal depended on what one chose to count. The United States, with an arsenal of relatively small but accurate weapons, had more *CMP*, while the Soviet Union had more *EMT*. The power question could not be separated from the question of what the arsenal would be used for.

Similar comparison issues arise for conventional weapons. Which is better, a 3" gun that fires 80 rounds per minute with an explosive weight of 20 pounds per round, or an 8" gun that fires 10 rounds per minute with an explosive weight of 380 pounds per round? One might say that the 8" gun is better because it can apply 3800 pounds per minute to the target area instead of only 1600 pounds per minute. But why should delivering weight be the object? If covering area with lethal effects is the goal, and if lethal radius scales with the cube root of weight, then the 3" gun is actually superior (when in range) because of its high rate of fire. To see this, assume that the weight of a round is proportional to the cube of its diameter, so a 3" round is worth $(3/8)^2 = .14$ of an 8" round in terms of lethal area. The 3" gun can deliver 11.25 equivalent rounds per minute, while the 8" gun can deliver only 10. Generalizing, let

$$E8R = \text{rate of fire} \times \left(\frac{b}{8}\right)^2$$

be the equivalent rate of delivering 8" rounds, where b is bore size. By summing *E8R* over a collection of guns or other delivery systems, the equivalent rate of fire for the collection could be determined and used to compare different collections. This is the conventional analogue of *EMT*, and of course there is also an analog for *CMP*. Note that the conventional comparison is determined by rate of fire, ignoring stockpiles, whereas the nuclear comparison is by stockpiles, ignoring rate of fire. A more sophisticated analysis would acknowledge the importance of both aspects.

One problem with the above gun comparison is that 8" guns have a greater range than 3" guns – outside of the 3" range, the effectiveness of a 3" gun is zero. Range is such an important consideration for most conventional weapon systems that a realistic comparison must include range as a parameter. Figure 12.4 shows total *E8R* versus range for three WWII battleships and two aircraft carriers under the assumption that a 500-pound bomb is equivalent to four 8" rounds. The *New Jersey* is the most effective of the five ships at close range because of her numerous 5" guns. The speed and payload of jet-powered attack aircraft such as the A-6 make a 1977 aircraft carrier completely dominant over a WWII carrier.

Figure 12.5 compares the entire USN fleet in 1947 and in 1977. Including all the CVEs there were 100 aircraft carriers in 1947. The 1977 fleet is similarly effective at long range with far fewer carriers, but much less effective at close range because of having far fewer guns. Of course an *E8R* comparison looks at only one dimension of a complex problem – the "brute force" dimension. The 1977 fleet was superior to the 1947 fleet in many ways having nothing to do with *E8R*, and the modern fleet even more so. A realistic fleet comparison would begin by being specific about the mission. The beauty and also the vulnerability of the comparison in Figure 12.5 is that mission is unspecified.

FIGURE 12.4. EQUIVALENT 8" ROUNDS DELIVERER, FIVE CAPITAL SHIPS

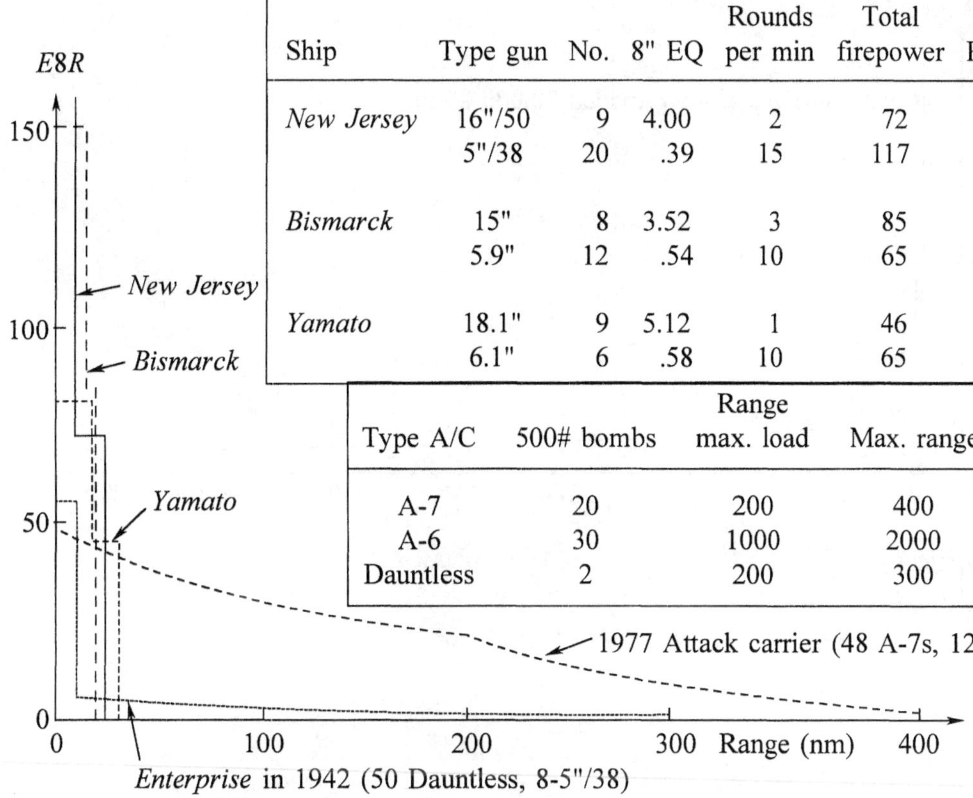

E8R

Ship	Type gun	No.	8" EQ	Rounds per min	Total firepower	Range
New Jersey	16"/50	9	4.00	2	72	24
	5"/38	20	.39	15	117	10
Bismarck	15"	8	3.52	3	85	20
	5.9"	12	.54	10	65	14
Yamato	18.1"	9	5.12	1	46	28
	6.1"	6	.58	10	65	14

Type A/C	500# bombs	Range max. load	Max. range
A-7	20	200	400
A-6	30	1000	2000
Dauntless	2	200	300

1977 Attack carrier (48 A-7s, 12 A-6s)

Enterprise in 1942 (50 Dauntless, 8-5"/38)

Range (nm)

1205   Layered Defense with Unlimited Defensive Weapons

Suppose one or more "attackers" intend to attack a "defender." In general the defender should establish a defense based on mutual support in which the attackers must penetrate as many defensive layers as possible in order to deliver their ordnance to their target. The military term for this concept is **defense in depth**. This section discusses this concept and is general as to permitting diverse types of attackers and defenses which vary from one layer to another. For analytic tractability, the various engagements between attackers and defenders are treated as statistically independent of one another – that assumption especially deserves reexamination when applying these methods to operational problems. Estimation of various one-on-one and many-on-one kill probabilities could use models of the preceding sections.

An attacker could use the models below to estimate the potential losses or the number of platforms required initially in order for some specified number of platforms to penetrate the defenses. A defender could use these models to estimate the effectiveness of the defense and determine the minimum number of defenders required in order to attain some specified probability of survival.

FIGURE 12.5. FIREPOWER OF TOTAL USN FLEET

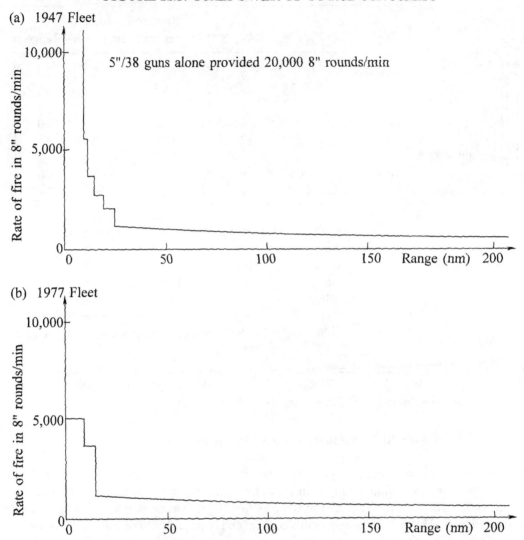

(a) 1947 Fleet

5"/38 guns alone provided 20,000 8" rounds/min

(b) 1977 Fleet

The models are developed with anti-air warfare (and conversely, strike warfare) in mind, where the layered defense consists of combat air patrol (CAP), long and medium range SAMs, and point-defense systems (*short range missiles and guns*). Nonetheless, the models are just as applicable to other warfare areas.

The defenders should establish these defensive layers far enough in the threat direction from the defended units to destroy attackers before they reach their weapons launch range, particularly in the case of missile-firing attackers. How far beyond the minimum distance the stationing should be is a tradeoff between angular sector covered and degree of latitude *of kill* before attacker's launch – such issues are addressed in Chapter 13.

A missile-firing attacker may multiply in that it may launch more than one missile, resulting in an increase in the number of targets for the defenders to engage. Launched weapons are always more difficult to engage than the launch platform due to their smaller size and/or greater speed.

Mathematical models of a layered defense vary widely in complexity, depending on the assumptions made. The most critical assumptions concern the attack size and the defender's weapons limitations in terms of interceptors and the rate of fire. Here "interceptor" refers to any weapon that may be directed at an inbound attacker and includes CAP aircraft, missiles, and guns. The number of interceptors available and rate of fire heavily influence the total number of attackers and the number of attackers arriving per unit time that can be successfully defeated. For example, guided missile-destroyers can engage only a fixed number of targets simultaneously and have relatively small magazines of SAMs.

Throughout the discussion below it is assumed that the number of attackers is fixed and known. In addition, the initial models will be for cases in which the defender's weapon systems are never saturated, that is, the attackers are not so numerous and do not arrive so closely together that the number of defensive weapon systems limits the number of attackers engaged.

The basic goal is to determine, under varying assumptions, the probability of the defender surviving the attack and the average number of attackers surviving all defensive layers. Each attacker is assumed to carry ordnance which has some probability of "damaging" the defender. The ordnance could be one or more bombs or missiles. The "defender" could be a single platform or a group of platforms such as a carrier task group.

Suppose there is only one attacker and the defender has L defensive layers with a probability P_{Ki} of destroying the attacker in the ith layer. The P_{Ki}'s could be determined as in the previous sections. Assuming independence among the L layers, the probability that the attacker survives all L defensive layers is

$$\prod_{i=1}^{L} (1 - P_{Ki}).$$

Let P_{CK} (CK for counter-kill) be the probability that the attacker damages the defender given it survives all defensive layers. Then the probability that the defender survives the attack undamaged is computed by taking the complement of the product of the probabilities that the attacker survives and successfully delivers the ordnance for its kill, to give

$$1 - P_{CK} \prod_{i=1}^{L} (1 - P_{Ki}).$$

If there are n identical, independent attackers, the expected number of attackers surviving to the launch position is

$$n \prod_{i=1}^{L} (1 - P_{Ki}),$$

so the defender's survival probability decreases to

$$\left[1 - P_{CK} \prod_{i=1}^{L} (1 - P_{Ki}) \right]^{n}.$$

Suppose the attacking force is now composed of n platforms that are independent but not necessarily identical. For $j = 1, \ldots, n$, let P_{CKj} be the probability that attacker j damages the defender given it survives all defensive layers. For $i = 1, \ldots, L$, $j = 1, \ldots, n$, let P_{Kij} be the probability that the defender destroys the jth attacker in layer i. Thus the probability of destroying an attacker can vary both by defensive layer and by the type of platform. In addition, attackers may carry weapons with different probabilities of damaging the defender. The probability that the jth attacker survives all defensive layers is

$$\prod_{i=1}^{L} (1 - P_{Kij}).$$

The probability that the defender survives all of the attackers is

$$\prod_{j=1}^{n} [1 - P_{CKj} \prod_{i=1}^{L} (1 - P_{Kij})].$$

1206   Layered Defense with Limited Defensive Weapons

Assume now that there are n identical attackers each with a probability P_{CK} of damaging the defender. Suppose the defender has m weapons, each with a probability P_K of destroying an attacker, available to defend against the attackers. The defender's goal is to maximize the probability of surviving the attack. It can be shown that when the attack size is known it is optimal for the defender to distribute the m defensive weapons over the n attackers as uniformly as possible. Thus m and n are positive integers.

Denote by $[m/n]$, the greatest integer not exceeding m/n and by $(m \bmod n)$ the integer remainder of m/n, so that $m = [m/n]n + (m \bmod n)$. Let $[m/n]$ of the weapons be assigned to each of $n - (m \bmod n)$ attackers and $[m/n] + 1$ weapons to each of the remaining $(m \bmod n)$ attackers. Then the probability that the defender survives the attack is

$$[1 - P_{CK}(1 - P_K)^{[m/n]}]^{n - (m \bmod n)} [1 - P_{CK}(1 - P_K)^{[m/n] + 1}]^{(m \bmod n)}.$$

One may approximate this probability by the following quantity allowing non-integer assignments of interceptors:

$$[1 - P_{CK}(1 - P_K)^{m/n}]^n.$$

The average number of attackers surviving m interceptors is

$$(n - (m \bmod n))(1 - P_K)^{[m/n]} + (m \bmod n)(1 - P_K)^{[m/n] + 1}.$$

These results are essentially for one layer. A multiple-layer defense could be modeled through successive applications of these formulas. The number of attackers surviving a particular layer is then the number of attackers entering the next layer.

1207   Analysis of Complex Tactical Situations

The layered-defense models above result in closed-form solutions under very specific assumptions. They can be very useful for back-of-the envelope calculations and can be successfully used to help to model more complex and realistic scenarios. Two basic approaches may be readily employed, expected-value and Monte Carlo models.

Expected-value multi-layer models. It may be possible to break down a complex scenario into smaller pieces by modeling each layer separately from the others. The output of the model for one layer provides the input for the model for the next layer. The outputs and inputs are generally expected values, for example, the expected number of attackers surviving a particular layer. In this way an approximation to the expected value of the number of attackers surviving to the weapons release point and from that an estimate of the resulting possible damage may be found. This type of approach allows one to model more complex situations such as the case where an attacking aircraft must penetrate some the layers, fire missiles, then turn away. The expected number of surviving aircraft reaching the launch point would first be estimated, then the launched missiles would be the "attackers" for successive layers. The principal disadvantage is that if Z is a random variable and if f is a non-linear function, then $E[f(Z)] \neq f(E[Z])$ – see 109. Thus multi-layer analysis using expected values might yield inaccurate or misleading results.

Monte Carlo analysis. Simulation techniques provide a means to overcome the problem just noted. They are particularly valuable because through repetitions of a Monte Carlo simulation (Chapter 3), it is possible to obtain point estimates and confidence intervals of various MOEs of interest.

1208   Other Literature and History

The intent of this chapter is to provide a survey of plausible target coverage mathematical models that can be understood at the undergraduate level. These types of models were first used extensively during World War II and focused on gunnery, bombardment, depth charge, torpedo, and rocket problems. These models addressed such problems as determining the probability of damaging a target with a given number of rounds, the number of rounds required to achieve a specified level of damage, and the optimal placement of rounds (single or multiple) to achieve the greatest possible level of destruction.

Following World War II additional models were developed as weapon systems became more lethal and complex. Many models were developed to analyze the effects of individual nuclear weapons and to aggregate nuclear arsenals in order to compare the United States' and Soviet Union's capabilities.

Guided munitions have proven to be much more difficult to model. Substantial analysis has been conducted and is ongoing in establishing missile-firing doctrine for various systems currently in use. The basic problem is to determine the number of missiles to allocate to an inbound target, particularly when the number of targets likely to be inbound is unknown. The same type of analysis has been applied to the allocation of aircraft-carried munitions (e.g., infra-red decoys) used to decoy enemy SAMs.

The classic text by Morse and Kimball [1] provides some theory and several World War II examples of the operational use of target coverage models in random and area bombardment, aimed fire, pattern firing without ballistic dispersion (with train bombing and depth charge applications), pattern firing with ballistic dispersion, and sampling (Monte Carlo) methods.

Most of sections 1201-1204 and parts of 1205-1206 were extracted from Washburn [2]. Among the additional concepts in [2] are simultaneous dependent shots, area targets with multiple-error sources, and dynamic programming models, under varying assumptions, for the defense of a target when the attack size is unknown. Reference [2] indicates that Eckler and Burr [4] contains additional references to the literature treating target coverage models. The concept and discussion of weight of a broadside in 1204 was taken from [3], also by Washburn. In [5], Hughes adapts the broadside concept of [3] to construct profiles of firepower versus range with which to make tactical comparisons of a mobile naval task force versus a land-based military complex. The naval force's mission is to strike with bombers and land-attack missiles without being defeated by the land force of bombers carrying air-launched missiles

Section 1201 notes how lethal area might be determined simply in a " vital spot" situation. For an introduction to the more intricate problem of partial damage to a large target, see Esary [6].

[1] Morse, Philip M., and George E. Kimball. *Methods of Operations Research*. Cambridge, MA: MIT Press, 1951.
[2] Washburn, Alan R. *Notes on Firing Theory*. Monterey, CA: Naval Postgraduate School, 1982.
[3] Washburn, Alan R. *Gross Measures of Surface-To-Surface Naval Firepower*. Monterey, CA: Naval Postgraduate School, 1977.
[4] Eckler, A. R., and S. A. Burr. *Mathematical Models of Target Coverage and Missile Allocation*. Alexandria, VA: Military Operations Research Society, 1972.
[5] Hughes, Wayne P., Jr. *Fleet Tactics*: *Theory and Practice*. Annapolis, MD: Naval Institute Press, 1984.
[6] Esary, James D. *Working Papers on Damage Aggregation*. Monterey, CA: Naval Postgraduate School, 1989.

Problems

1. Suppose target location and weapon firing errors are circular normal with the aim point centered on the target and a standard deviation of 170 yds.

a. Graph the distribution of the x coordinate firing errors.
b. If the weapon is cookie-cutter with lethal radius $r_d = 150$ yds, what is the probability of damaging the target?
c. Graph the probability of damage for values of r_d from 0 to 500 yds in 100 yd increments.
d. Find the *CEP* of the weapon based on the information in parts a, b, and c.

2. Use (12-7) to derive (12-8).

3. Conduct a Monte Carlo simulation of a bomber dropping ordnance on a target. Simulate 1000 bombs. Assume the distribution of firing errors is circular normal with the aim point centered on the target. Assume the one-dimensional standard deviation is $\sigma = 170$ yds. Assume each bomb is a cookie-cutter weapon with lethal radius $r_d = 150$ yds. The point of impact of each bomb can be simulated by either the 12-point or "direct transform" method of 305.

a. For each of the bombs generate a point of impact and then the distance from the target. If the miss distance does not exceed 150 yds, the bomb has "hit the target," i.e., caused the required level of damage. Repeat for 1000 independent bomb drops, keeping track of the number of bombs that hit the target. The probability of damaging the target is then the number of hits divided by 1000.

b. Recompute the probability of damaging the target this time assuming that there is a bias error to the aim point. Instead of aiming directly at the target the bomber aims 50 yds to the left and 100 yds long. This can be accomplished by adding -50 to the simulated x coordinate and 100 to the simulated y coordinate or by putting the target at (-50,100) for the purposes of computing the miss distance. Does your result make sense?

c. Compute the CEP. Run your program for a lethal radius equal to the CEP. What should the theoretical value be?

4. Four SAMs are fired at an inbound target with probabilities of kill .3, .4, .5, and .6. Estimate the probability of killing the target.

5. Four different weapons are fired at a target with lethal radii and standard deviations (both in yds) as indicated below. Estimate the probability of damaging the target if one of each is fired at the target.

i	r_{di}	σ_i
1	25	50
2	150	500
3	10	25
4	75	75

6. A destroyer fires ten 5" rounds at a building on the beach. The ship follows an optimal shoot-adjust-shoot firing policy. Each round has a CEP of 20 yds and a lethal radius of 10 yds. Estimate the probability of damaging the building.

7. The destroyer in 6 fires one aiming round then fires continuously at the maximum rate of fire without correcting aim. A spotter is in position ashore to provide damage assessment. What is the expected number of rounds required to damage the target?

8. Type I nuclear warheads have a 10 KT yield and a CEP of 0.25 nm. Type II nuclear warheads have a 20 KT yield and a CEP of 0.50 nm. They cost the same and there are funds to purchase 10.

a. If you have to purchase all of one kind, which would you prefer? What else might you want to know?

b. What would the CEP of the type II weapon have to be in order for the CMPs to be identical?

9. An aircraft shoots a single cruise missile at a destroyer on patrol. The missile has a probability of .6 of damaging the target given it is not shot down. The destroyer has a medium range SAM system and point-defense gun system with probabilities .4 and .3, respectively, of destroying the inbound missile. What is the probability that the destroyer is undamaged?

10. Using the information in 9, what is the probability that the destroyer is damaged if the aircraft

had fired two missiles?

11. Suppose four dissimilar aircraft attack a land installation. The land installation has SAMs and AA guns for defense and each defensive system engages each attacker once before an attack is made. The probability of each defensive system destroying the aircraft is as follows:

Aircraft	1	2	3	4
SAM	.4	.3	.3	.2
Gun	.3	.3	.2	.1

The probability of a surviving aircraft damaging the land installation, P_{CK}, is given for each aircraft as follows:

Aircraft	1	2	3	4
P_{CK}	.6	.5	.4	.3

a. What is the average number of aircraft surviving the defensive systems?
b. What is the probability that the land installation is damaged?

12. A cruiser depleted most of its missile magazine during an engagement in which all but seven of the enemy's aircraft were destroyed. The cruiser has ten SAMs remaining. The seven aircraft return for another attack and the cruiser decides to expend all of its missiles at the seven targets. Each aircraft has a probability of .3 of damaging the cruiser, given it penetrates the defenses. Each SAM has a probability of .6 of destroying an inbound aircraft by the time the aircraft closes to 30 nm.

a. What is the average number of aircraft surviving the defenses?
b. What is the probability that the cruiser survives, if no other defensive systems are available?
c. Suppose the cruiser had a gunnery system with a probability of .3 of destroying an aircraft. Use the result of part a (closest integer) as the input for the second defensive layer and determine the probability of the cruiser surviving with no damage. What assumption does this problem make concerning the weapons release range of the aircraft?

13. Answer problem 12c, assuming the attackers surviving the SAMs each launch two cruise missiles at the ship when they reach 25 nm range. Each of these missiles is engaged by the ship's gunnery system as above. Assume each surviving missile has a probability of .6 of damaging the cruiser.

Answers to Problems

4. .916.

5. .528.

6. .706.

7. 6.3.

8. a. Type I.   b. 80 KT.

9. .748.

10. .44.

11. a. 2.2.   b. .656.

12. a. 4.3.   b. .353.   c. .389.

13. .005.

13
FLEET AIR WARFARE

This chapter is concerned with some of the problems faced by a commander responsible for the air defense of a task group. The objective is to protect the task group from enemy air attack. Each defense option requires many choices, from disposition of ships and aircraft to training of operators and procedures for repair and maintenance of equipment. OA has been used extensively in the analysis of fleet air warfare.

A carrier task group's (CVTG) air defense is often broken into three phases: the inner and the outer air battles, and point defense. Figure 13.1 gives a graphical illustration of a possible composition of a CVTG air defense. For the inner air battle, examples of OA applications include salvo size studies, assignment of SAMs to targets, choices among alternative weapon types, logistic planning factors (to determine the expected materiel needed and potential supply problems for a deployment), trade-offs in the use resources for AW and ASW screening, and measuring the effectiveness of formations and/or compositions of task groups. For the outer air battle, OA studies have included comparisons of defensive postures, the use of aircraft for scouting, and optimal stationing distances for **airborne early warning** (AEW) and **combat air patrol** (CAP) aircraft. Only a few of these issues will be addressed in this chapter.

The outer air battle involves the use of aircraft to detect and intercept potential air threats to the CVTG at ranges beyond the threat's weapons release range. The outer air battle is conducted between the two circles drawn in Figure 13.1 and, in this illustration, uses an AEW radar as well as medium and long range CAP fighter aircraft. The long range CAP is farther from the CVTG (located at reference point *ZZ*) than other elements of the defense, and its mission is to intercept any threats detected by the AEW. The medium range CAP is located closer to *ZZ* in order to help protect the AEW (since it has no weapons to protect itself) and to relieve any of the long range CAP that either intercepts an incoming threat or becomes low on fuel. A tanker may also be stationed in the vicinity of the AEW so fighters that are low on fuel do not have to return to the carrier to refuel.

The inner air battle involves the use of screening ships and surface-to-air missiles (SAMs) to neutralize any "leakers" that survive the outer air battle. It is conducted inside the inner circle drawn in Figure 13.1. Care must be taken to confine the use of SAMs inside this inner boundary so that friendly aircraft are not engaged by the SAMs. If the threat aircraft and/or their weapons survive both the inner and outer air battles, the final point defense is conducted with close range weapons, including rapid-fire guns and shoulder-launched missiles.

FIGURE 13.1. INNER AND OUTER AIR BATTLE

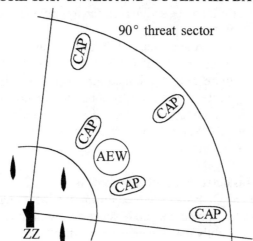

The chapter begins in 1301 with a discussion on some of the insights that OA can provide in the interpretation of the results of fleet exercises. This is followed in 1302 by some of the calculations that may be used when analyzing the outer air battle. In 1303 the chapter concludes with a discussion on the inner air battle.

1301   Exercise Analysis

Fleet AW exercises serve two valuable purposes. First, they provide the pilots, air controllers, commanding officers, and, in fact, all fleet personnel involved with the *training* essential to fleet combat readiness. Second, and equally important, they provide *databases* from which the commander may make realistic appraisals of the capabilities of the CVTG. Shortcomings revealed by close analysis of these data may be corrected, and the readiness of the fleet for future operations thereby improved.

An AW exercise is designed to simulate the defense of a task force against an enemy air attack by using friendly aircraft to simulate the enemy. Some artificialities exist, of necessity, since friendly aircraft cannot actually be destroyed, and any means of countering a given raid must cease prior to the actual firing of weapons. Even so, AW exercises, if properly analyzed, yield much valuable information concerning fleet readiness.

Exercises are expensive; hence they require careful planning, data collecting, and post-exercise analysis in order to derive maximum benefit from the cost and time incurred. In all exercises some sacrifice in realism must be made in order to reduce time and expense. Other means of simulating air defense operations are available in the form of war gaming and computer simulations which are much less expensive, but also less realistic because actual forces are not involved. Such techniques do afford valuable insight and a basis for prediction in areas where exercises are not feasible.

While OA specialists have prominent roles in exercise planning and analysis, experience in these activities as well as the conduct of fleet exercises is part of the professional education of all line officers. Thoughtful analysis is extremely valuable, while, conversely, the consequences of slipshod data recording and analysis can be serious and far-reaching in estimating the readiness and effectiveness of the forces afloat.

In the following example of an AW exercise, 200 "enemy" aircraft attempted to penetrate the force AW defenses which were composed of CAP interceptors and SAMs. In order to gain maximum training and collect more data in a limited time, each raid aircraft continued on to the center of the force whether or not it was successfully countered (intercepted) by CAP forming the outer air battle. For simplicity, the number of raids detected includes only those detected early enough to be opposed by both CAP and SAMs. The data collected were designed to provide information on the following sequence of events in the outer air battle:

a. **Raid detected.** A raid was detected by the task force radar.
b. **CAP assigned.** At least one CAP was vectored toward the incoming detected raid.
c. **Tally-ho.** The CAP visually sighted the raid or locked on with its own fire-control radar.
d. **Intercept.** The CAP successfully maneuvered into position to fire a weapon.

As the raid proceeded inbound to within missile range, another sequence of events was necessary for the raid to be successfully opposed by SAMs forming the inner air battle.

e. **Raid designated.** The raid was assigned to a specific missile system within the ship. This assignment was made by transmitting range, bearing, and altitude of the raid to the weapons system fire-control equipment.
f. **Raid acquired.** The weapons system fire-control radar had begun to track the target, i.e., locked on.
g. **Raid fired on.** The raid was within firing range, the fire-control solution was complete, and a missile was ready for launch.

In Figure 13.2, basic data were collected simply by recording the number of raids for which each successive step was accomplished.

One use for such information is to point out which steps in the inner and outer air battles sequences are weakest. For example, it may be of interest to know the probability of detection resulting from a certain tactical disposition of the air search radar available to the force. It is, of course, impossible to arrive at this number precisely. But when one considers the results obtained from the exercise as a statistical sample, then the data obtained may be used as a best estimate of the true, but unknown, probability of detection. In the discussion which follows, it will be understood that such terms as probability of detection, probability of intercept given tally-ho, and so on, will be the best estimates of these probabilities based upon data obtained from this exercise. If data were available from several exercises, the results might be averaged in order to refine these estimates.

From the data in Figure 13.2, it is seen that of 200 raids, 160 were detected. Thus an estimate of the probability of detection can be obtained by taking the ratio of these two numbers,

$$\text{Pr\{detection\}} = \frac{160}{200} = .80.$$

In a similar manner, conditional probabilities concerning the various phases of the inner and outer air battles can be computed, see Figure 13.3. As a reminder, the notation $\text{Pr\{A|B\}}$ denotes the conditional probability of event A occurring given that event B occurs. Notice that these conditional probabilities are similar to those used in the attack submarine MOE example in 108. With a view to strengthening AW, the above ratios might have provided an argument for improvement in certain factors of the air defense problem.

FIGURE 13.2. TABULATED EXERCISE DATA

Outer Air Battle		Inner Air Battle	
Number of raids	200	Number of raids	200
Number of raids detected	160	Number of raids detected	160
Number of CAP assigned	120	Number of raids designated	155
Number of tally-hos	90	Number of raids acquired	120
Number of intercepts	40	Number of raids fired upon	115

FIGURE 13.3. CONDITIONAL PROBABILITIES

Outer Air Battle	
Pr{CAP assigned | detection}	120/160 = .75
Pr{tally-ho | CAP assigned}	90/120 = .75
Pr{intercept | tally-ho}	40/ 90 = .44
Inner Air Battle	
Pr{designation | detection}	155/160 = .97
Pr{acquisition | designation}	120/155 = .77
Pr{SAM fired | acquisition}	115/120 = .96

A useful measure of effectiveness (MOE) which can be computed from these data is the probability that a raid can penetrate the inner and outer air defenses (i.e., reach the task force without being either intercepted by CAP or fired on with SAMs). This probability is called the **factorized probability** of an unopposed raid (a raid not fired upon), p_{uf}, and can be determined as follows:

p_{uf} = 1 - Pr{intercept or SAM fired}

= 1 - Pr{detection} × Pr{intercept or SAM fired|detection}

= 1 - Pr{detection}[1 - Pr{no intercept and no SAM fired | detection}]

= 1 - Pr{detection}[1 - Pr{no intercept|detection} × Pr {no SAM fired | detection}]

Further substitution gives

$$p_{uf} = 1 - \text{Pr\{detection\}}[1 - [1 - \text{Pr\{intercept | detection\}}][1 - \text{Pr\{SAM fired | detection\}}]]. \quad (13\text{-}1)$$

For this exercise where Pr{detection} = 160/200, Pr{intercept | detection} = 40/160, and Pr{SAM fired | detection} = 115/160, the factorized probability of an unopposed raid is p_{uf} = .37.

Notice that in developing (13-1), independence was assumed in order that

Pr{no intercept and no SAM fired|detect} = Pr{no intercept|detect} × Pr{no SAM fired|detect}.

More precisely this implies that once a raid is detected, the event that the raid is not fired on by SAMs is independent of event of not being intercepted by CAP. For an exercise of the type just described, this assumption seems valid, whereas if not all detected raids were presented to both CAP and SAMs (because some raids were either detected late or destroyed early) the assumption would not be warranted.

If the exercise provided for keeping track of each raid as it approached the task force, some data may be available in addition to the basic information tabulated for the inner and outer air battles. The number of raids for which event A held will be denoted by $n(A)$. The detected raids can thus be further broken down as in Figure 13.4.

FIGURE 13.4. ANALYSIS OF DETECTED RAIDS

Number both intercepted and fired on	n(intercept and SAM fired) = 30
Number intercepted but *not* fired on	n(intercept and no SAM fired) = 40 - 30 = 10
Number *not* intercepted but fired on	n(no intercept and SAM fired) = 115 - 30 = 85
Number *neither* intercepted nor fired on	n(detect and no intercept and no SAM fired) = 35

The probability of an unopposed raid, p_u, can now be found more simply using this additional information:

$$p_u = \frac{n(\text{no detect}) + n(\text{detect and no intercept and no SAM fired})}{\text{number of raids}}. \quad (13\text{-}2)$$

For this example,

$$p_u = \frac{40 + 35}{200} = .375.$$

Considering that opposition to a raid not only could result in killing it before it reached the task force center, but could benefit the task force by other means (such as driving it away sooner or impairing the accuracy of its weapons delivery), the probability of an unopposed raid is a meaningful "inverse" measure of effectiveness. A better measure of effectiveness, however, might be the probability of a raid reaching the task force center without being destroyed, taking into account the kill probabilities for air and surface-fired weapons. If these kill probabilities were known, they could be used with the exercise data to provide the probability of survival. Let S be the event a raid survives and K the event that a raid is killed or destroyed. The probability of raid survival, S, is

$$\Pr\{S\} = 1 - \Pr\{\text{killed}\}$$
$$= 1 - [\Pr\{\text{killed and intercept and no SAM fired}\}$$
$$+ \Pr\{\text{killed and intercept and SAM fired}\}$$
$$+ \Pr\{\text{killed and no intercept and SAM fired}\}]$$
$$= 1 - [\Pr\{\text{killed} \mid \text{intercept and no SAM fired}\} \times \Pr\{\text{intercept and no SAM fired}\}$$
$$+ \Pr\{\text{killed} \mid \text{intercept and SAM fired}\} \times \Pr\{\text{intercept and SAM fired}\}$$
$$+ \Pr\{\text{killed} \mid \text{no intercept and SAM fired}\} \times \Pr\{\text{no intercept and SAM fired}\}]. \quad (13\text{-}3)$$

If the CAP's air-to-air weapon has a .7 single-shot kill probability and a SAM has a .4 single-shot kill probability, and if the exercise data in Figure 13.2 are used, then substituting into (13-3) gives

$$\Pr\{S\} = 1 - \{(.7)(10/200) + [1 - (.3)(.6)](30/200) + (.4)(85/200)\} = .67.$$

If the exercise data in Figure 13.2 are not known, then the probability of survival may be approximated by making the same independence assumption as before — this time to estimate the inputs for (13-3).

It should be noted that time effects are ignored in the analysis. One would not apply these percentages to predict oppositions or kills if the raids were to come in such dense rates as to saturate the capability of some part of the AW system.

Even considering the constraints, artificialities, and assumptions controlling the conduct of this exercise, a probabilistic analysis serves its purpose quite well. It presents the weak areas in the air defense problem that have the most degrading influence on the overall air defense posture, and points out those areas where tactics or equipment need to be investigated. It can also, with careful planning and due consideration of artificialities, give decision-makers better estimates of overall effectiveness, in both absolute and comparative terms, than are otherwise available.

1302   Combat Air Patrol (CAP)

This section is concerned with the kinematics and geometry of the outer air battle. The management of the outer air battle often involves two tactics that are termed **vector logic** and **chainsaw**. Vector logic generally involves setting up a coordinate system, defining a threat sector and potential threat weapon release range (**keep-out range**), and stationing AEW aircraft and/or CAP interceptors in a manner that allows detection and interception of incoming threat aircraft before they close to within the keep-out range. The chainsaw tactic generally uses deck-launched interceptors (DLIs) for scouting and detecting threats (either air or surface) at ranges that exceed other available radar ranges.

Chainsaw Tactic. To initiate chainsaw, a deck-launched interceptor (DLI), call it F_1, is launched and flies away from the carrier along the defined threat axis at a speed v. The DLI's radar is assumed to have a maximum range of distance h, and a maximum azimuth (angle of coverage) of angle 2θ. A second interceptor, F_2, is launched after a time delay of t_S (called the **search interval**) and flies away from the carrier using the same course and speed as F_1. When F_1 has flown out to a range of r_S (called the **search radius**), it turns and flies back to the carrier (see Figure 13.5). The maximum detection range on the threat axis, r_{max}, is then the sum of the search radius and the interceptor's radar range, h:

$$r_{max} = r_S + h.$$

FIGURE 13.5. CHAINSAW DEPLOYMENT OF CAP

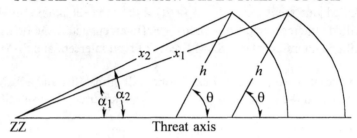

Suppose that when F_1 reaches the turnaround point and turns, a threat aircraft, traveling at a speed u and course directly toward the carrier along the threat axis, is just beyond the detection range of F_1. At this time, F_2 is a distance of vt_S from the turnaround point. Where does F_2 detect the threat aircraft? The distance from the current maximum detection range on axis for F_2 and the threat aircraft, the distance to be closed, is also vt_S. The closing speed is $u + v$, and thus the time elapsed before F_2 detects the incoming threat is

$$t = \frac{vt_s}{u + v}.$$

At the time of detection, F_2 would be at range d from the carrier given by

$$d = r_S - vt_S + vt.$$

The minimum detection range on the threat axis, r_{min}, can then be found as

$$r_{min} = d + h.$$

If interceptors continue to be launched at the same intervals, an on-axis threat approaching at a random time can be detected at a range from the carrier between r_{max} and r_{min}.

For example, if the interceptor's speed is $v = 480$ knots, the threat aircraft speed is $u = 400$ knots, the search interval is $t_S = 30$ minutes $= .5$ hour, the search radius is $r_S = 350$ nm, and the interceptor's radar detection range is $h = 100$ nm, then

$$r_{max} = 350 + 100 = 450 \text{ nm}$$

is the maximum detection range on the threat axis,

$$t = \frac{(480)(.5)}{480 + 400} = .273 \text{ hr}$$

is the time between F_1's turn and detection by F_2, and

$$r_{min} = 350 - (480)(.5) + (480)(.273) + 100 = 341 \text{ nm}$$

is the minimum detection range on the threat axis.

Since the radar on an interceptor can search a sector of azimuth 2θ, threat aircraft that are not on the threat axis may also be detected. One-half of the interceptor's radar azimuth is called the interceptor's *radar coverage angle*, θ (see Figure 13.5). Let x_1 denote the range from the carrier (ZZ) to the point that is at maximum radar coverage angle and distance from F_1 when F_1 reaches the search radius. That is, x_1 is the range from the carrier to a threat aircraft that can just be detected by F_1 (at extreme range and angle) when the DLI reaches its maximum range from the carrier. Let α_1 denote the angle from the threat axis to this point with vertex at the carrier. Let x_2 and α_2 denote the corresponding values from F_2 when it reaches range d. The value of x_1 is called the **maximum detection range at maximum offset angle**, and the value of x_2 is called the **minimum detection range at maximum offset angle**. The law of cosines may be used to determine x_1 and x_2:

$$x_1 = \sqrt{r_s^2 + h^2 - 2r_s h \cos(180° - \theta)},$$

and

$$x_2 = \sqrt{d^2 + h^2 - 2dh \cos(180° - \theta)}.$$

The law of sines can be used to determine α_i for $i = 1, 2$.

$$\frac{\sin \alpha_i}{h} = \frac{\sin(180° - \theta)}{x_i}.$$

For the example begun above, if the interceptor's radar coverage angle is $\theta = 50°$, then calculations using the above formulas give $x_1 = 421.3$ nm, $x_2 = 314.6$ nm, $\alpha_1 = 10.5°$, and $\alpha_2 = 14.1°$.

If DLIs continue to be launched at the same search interval, an on-axis threat approaching at a random time can be detected at a range from the carrier between the minimum and maximum on-axis detection ranges. A similar remark applies to the minimum and maximum detection ranges at maximum offset angle.

AEW Stationing. Suppose that an AEW aircraft has been stationed on the defined threat axis at a range r from the carrier, and has as its mission the detection of any threat aircraft that are incoming at a range that is large enough to allow a DLI to be launched from the carrier in time to intercept the threat aircraft before it reaches the keep-out range k. The assumption of the DLI intercepting, rather than attacking, the threat is made to simplify the problem by ignoring the DLI weapons' ranges. This complication is easily handled, and will be considered later in this section. The AEW's radar is assumed to have a maximum range of h and a full 360 degrees coverage.

If the AEW stationing range, r, is large, then there is more time for a DLI to make the intercept, but the sector, with vertex at the carrier, that the AEW's radar covers is smaller. Thus it is important to find the range at which the AEW aircraft can be stationed and still allow for an intercept to be made outside the keep-out range for the largest possible coverage angle. The optimal AEW stationing range will also depend on the detection range of the AEW's radar, h, the speed of the incoming threat aircraft, u, the delay time to launch the DLI, t_D, and the intercept speed, v, of the DLI.

Let α be the angle (with vertex at the carrier) from the threat axis to the radial on which the incoming threat aircraft is traveling (see Figure 13.6). As a first step toward finding the optimal AEW stationing range, the following problem should be solved: Fix values of r, u, t_D, and v, then determine the largest coverage angle, α, for which intercept can be made on any threat whose path is along a radial that is an angle less than or equal to α from the threat axis. Let θ be the associated angle with vertex at the AEW between the (detected) incoming threat aircraft and the threat axis.

The largest coverage angle, α, will occur when the following are equal:

a. the time t_1 it takes for the threat aircraft to travel from point B (where it is detected) to the point A (where it crosses the keep-out range), and
b. the time t_2 it takes for the AEW to inform the carrier of the detection, for the DLI to be launched (t_D), and for the DLI to travel from ZZ to the point A.

FIGURE 13.6. AEW STATIONING WITH DLI PICKUP

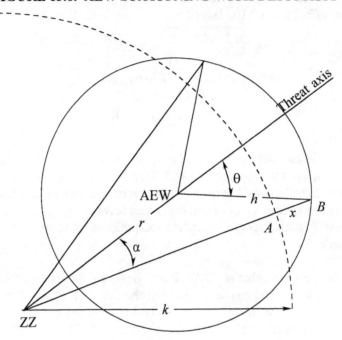

If x is the distance between points B and A, then $t_1 = x/u$, and $t_2 = t_D + k/v$. Thus the largest coverage angle occurs whenever

$$t_D + k/v = x/u \tag{13-4}$$

In order to find the value of α, an expression relating x and α must first be determined. An application of the law of cosines gives

$$h^2 = r^2 + (k + x)^2 - 2r(k + x) \cos \alpha.$$

Solving this equation for x gives

$$x = r \cos \alpha + \sqrt{h^2 - r^2 \sin^2 \alpha} - k. \tag{13-5}$$

Substituting the value of x in (13-5) into (13-4) and solving for α gives

$$\alpha = \arccos\left(\frac{r^2 - h^2 + \left(t_D u + \dfrac{ku}{v} + k\right)^2}{2r\left(t_D u + \dfrac{ku}{v} + k\right)}\right). \tag{13-6}$$

For example, if the AEW stationing range is $r = 100$ nm, the AEW radar maximum detection range is $h = 220$ nm, the threat speed is $u = 400$ knots, the DLI's intercept speed is $v = 480$ knots, the keep-out range is $k = 125$ nm, and the delay time to launch a DLI is $t_D = 7$ minutes $= .117$ hours, then the largest coverage angle is $\alpha = 46.9$ degrees. Notice that if the threat sector is assumed to be 360 degrees, then the minimum number of AEW aircraft on station would be

$$N = \left[\frac{360}{(2)(46.9)}\right] + 1 = 4,$$

where $[\bullet]$ denotes the largest integer function.

Equation (13-6) can be used to determine the largest coverage angle for a particular AEW stationing range, r. The **optimal AEW stationing range** is then the value of r that gives the maximum value of α. It is theoretically possible to use the differential calculus to maximize α, using (13-6) and its derivative. In practice, this is not simple. An easier approach is to determine the value of α for a wide range of values of r and choose the optimal value from the list. Figure 13.7 was generated by changing the values of the AEW stationing range on axis using the input values as in the above example. Since the optimal AEW stationing range is the minimum range having the maximum coverage angle, it would be 150 nm for this example. Notice that the function is "flat" and that varying the AEW stationing range from 120 nautical miles to 220 nautical miles causes a variation of only 2 degrees in the value of α. Since the AEW cannot actually maintain station exactly at the optimal stationing range, this means that the variation of coverage is small as the AEW aircraft changes its position.

FIGURE 13.7. OPTIMAL AEW STATIONING

r (nm)	110	120	130	140	150	160	170	180	190	200	210
α (°)	49	51	52	52	53	53	53	53	53	52	52

CAP Stationing. Perhaps the simplest use of CAP is the stationing of fighters at a predetermined distance from the carrier so that they can detect and intercept incoming threats beyond the keep-out range. Determining the optimal CAP stationing distance is similar to determining the optimal AEW stationing distance, except that both detection and intercept are performed by the same aircraft.

The procedure for determining the optimal CAP stationing distance may be broken into two steps. First, for a fixed CAP stationing range, determine the corresponding coverage angle (see Figure 13.8). The coverage angle is defined to be 2α, where α is the largest angle having vertex at the defended point (ZZ) such that any threat that is incoming on a radial that lies within an angle α of the threat axis (on which the CAP is stationed) can be intercepted outside the keep-out range. Once this problem is solved, it can be repeated as necessary to determine the CAP stationing ranges that have the largest coverage angle (to whatever degree of accuracy is desired). If more than one of the CAP stationing ranges have this largest coverage angle, then the smallest is the optimal CAP stationing range.

FIGURE 13.8. OPTIMAL CAP STATIONING

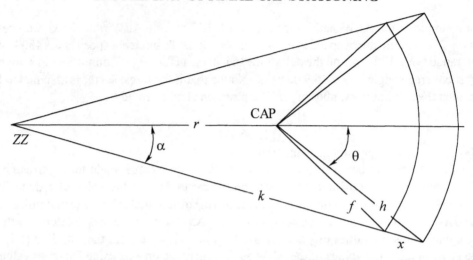

Suppose that the CAP fighter is stationed at a distance r from the defended point, has a radar with range h and radar coverage angle θ_{max} (one-half the azimuth of the radar), and has an intercept speed of v. Let u denote the threat aircraft speed, k the keep-out range, and w the engagement distance between the CAP fighter and the threat when the CAP launches its air-to-air weapon. If θ is the angle with vertex at the CAP between the threat axis and the point where the incoming threat is first detected, then the distance x which the threat aircraft must fly to reach the keep-out range may be found using the law of cosines to be

$$x = -k + \sqrt{r^2 + h^2 - 2rh\cos(180° - \theta)}.$$

A second application of the law of cosines can be solved to find the value of α, the angle with vertex at ZZ between the threat axis and the incoming radial,

$$\alpha = \arccos\left(\frac{r^2 + (x + k)^2 - h^2}{2r(x + k)}\right).$$

The law of cosines may be applied a third time to determine the distance f that the fighter must fly to reach the point where the air-to-air weapons are launched,

$$f = -w + \sqrt{r^2 + k^2 - 2rk\cos\alpha}.$$

For the intercept to be made, the time t_1 that the fighter takes to reach its weapon release point must not exceed the time t_2 that the threat takes to reach the keep-out range. Since $t_1 = f/v$ and $t_2 = x/u$, the intercept is possible if and only if $fu = xv$. By varying the values of θ between 0 and θ_{max}, the maximum coverage angle can be determined for a fixed CAP station range. Figure 13.9 illustrates this procedure using a spreadsheet. Notice that the right most column, $\delta(\alpha)$, has a nonzero value only if a successful intercept is possible, and in this case the value listed is the value for α in degrees. The optimal total coverage angle, $2\alpha^*$, which in this case is 56 degrees, is then found by taking the maximum of this (last) column and multiplying by two.

FIGURE 13.9. CAP STATIONING CALCULATIONS

Fixed CAP Range							
Inputs:		$u =$	480	kts	= Threat a/c speed		
		$v =$	600	kts	= CAP intercept speed		
		$h =$	100	nm	= DLI radar range		
		$\theta_{max} =$	60	deg	= DLI radar cov. angle		
		$r =$	100	nm	= CAP station range		
		$k =$	130	nm	= Keep-out range		
		$w =$	5	nm	= Engagement range		
		step =	1	deg	= Step size for table		
Outputs:		$2\alpha^* =$	56	deg	= Max total coverage angle		
θ (deg)	$x + k$ (nm)	α (radian)	x (nm)	f (nm)	t_1 (hours)	t_2 (hours)	$\delta(\alpha)$ (deg)
60	173.2	.524	43.2	61.2	.102	.090	0
59	174.1	.515	44.1	60.4	.101	.092	0
58	174.9	.506	44.9	59.5	.099	.094	0
57	175.8	.497	45.8	58.6	.098	.095	0
56	176.6	.489	46.6	57.8	.096	.097	28.0
55	177.4	.480	47.4	56.9	.095	.099	27.5
54	178.2	.471	48.2	56.1	.094	.100	27.0
53	179.0	.463	49.0	55.3	.092	.102	26.5
52	179.8	.454	49.8	54.4	.091	.104	26.0

Once the basic spreadsheet calculations are set up, the values of r, the CAP station range, may be varied to obtain a table similar to Figure 13.10, and the optimal CAP station range can then be determined. The optimal CAP stationing is found to be at 105 nautical miles in this example, but the optimum is shallow. Most spreadsheets have an optimization tool that can easily be used to quickly find the optimal CAP stationing once the above spreadsheet is built. The optimization tool in Corel Quattro Pro™ (Tools/Numeric Tools/Optimizer...) gives the optimal CAP station for this example to be 104.8 with a maximum coverage angle of 58.5.

FIGURE 13.10. OPTIMAL CAP STATIONING

r (nm)	100	105	110	115	120
$2\alpha^*$ (°)	56	58	57	55	54

Third Party Detection For CAP Intercept. A CAP intercept may be initiated by detection of an incoming threat by a separate sensor, such as an AEW radar. The separate radar may be more capable or merely positioned for more distant detection. Another possibility is that the CAP radar is intentionally on STANDBY to avoid counterdetection by a threat. The problem is similar to that of the CAP stationing model. It is depicted in Figure 13.11. In the figure, the threat approaches ZZ from the right. An AEW radar is positioned to the north at a station range of r_{AEW}, with a silent CAP to the south at a station range of r_{CAP}. The AEW radar range capability is h. The threat and CAP speeds are u and v, respectively. The threat launch range (keep-out) is k and the CAP engagement distance is w.

The AEW aircraft detects the threat at a distance x from ZZ. A formula for x can be found using trigonometry as

$$x = r_{AEW} \cos\alpha + \sqrt{h^2 - r_{AEW}^2 \sin^2\alpha}.$$

FIGURE 13.11.   AEW DETECTION FOR CAP INTERCEPT

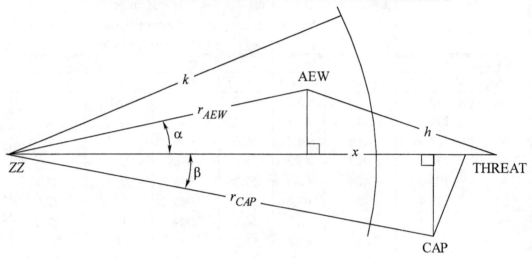

If t_R is the response time to transfer the detection information from the AEW aircraft to the CAP, then the time available for the CAP intercept t_F is given by

$$t_F = \frac{x - k}{u} t_R.$$

The maximum distance r_I from ZZ at which the CAP can intercept the threat, given a speed v and an engagement distance w, can also be found using trigonometry to be

$$r_I = r_{CAP} \cos\beta + \sqrt{(vt_F + w)^2 - r_{CAP}^2 \sin^2\alpha}.$$

If $r_I \geq k$, then intercept can be made prior to anti-surface missile, ASM, launch by the threat.

1303   Inner Air Battle

As stated previously, the inner air battle depends largely on the use of SAMs to neutralize any leakers. As the world situation evolves, the inner air battle may have to deal with more than just leakers from the CAP. A shift towards littoral, rather than open ocean warfare, may shrink the distances from the carrier for the stationing of CAP and SAM ships. Additionally, new technology in the fleet has changed the basic way that SAMs function. It is important to note that the models presented in this section are applicable to most SAM systems, especially those using **proportional navigation** or **intercept** technology. Models presented are for three modes of guidance, command, semi-active homing, and semi-active homing with midcourse guidance.

The first type of guidance discussed is **command guidance.** It uses the fire-control radar to track the aircraft, and the SAM flies toward the point where the target aircraft is currently located. This inevitably leads to a tail chase, with the SAM chasing the target aircraft. The technology involved is called **pursuit** technology. Figure 13.12 illustrates this. At time $t = 0$, the SAM is launched and flies toward the point where the target is at time $t = 0$. As time progresses, the SAM turns and is always flying toward where the tracking radar indicates the target is located. At some time $t > 4$, the SAM reaches a point on the target aircraft's track and begins to overtake the aircraft.

FIGURE 13.12. PURSUIT COURSE GEOMETRY

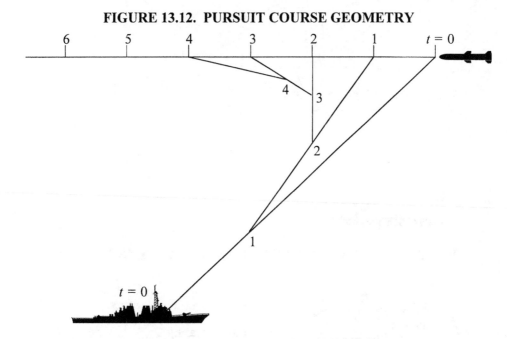

Another type of guidance discussed is **semi-active homing** (SM1). It also involves the use of a fire-control radar to track the target, only this time the missile flies to a computed intercept point, and homes on the target by using the reflected energy from the fire-control radar and a steering technique known as proportional navigation. The technology involved is called **intercept** technology. A possible flight path is illustrated in Figure 13.13. At time $t = 0$, the SAM is launched and flies toward a point where both the target aircraft and the SAM are expected to be located when the SAM reaches the predicted flight path of the target aircraft.

Although systems using semi-active homing guidance were employed in the Vietnam conflict and performed quite well, the major drawback to both command and semi-active homing systems is the fact that the fire-control director has to be "locked on" (tracking) a single target during the entire engagement. This effectively limits surface platforms to a number of simultaneous engagements equal to the number of missile directors present on the ship. For example, on 19 April 1972, USS *Sterett* (DLG-31, now CG-31), was attacked by MiGs in the Gulf of Tonkin while providing AW support to ships engaged in shore bombardment. She shot down two MiGs using Terrier missiles, and also a probable Soviet-made Styx anti-ship missile. What is important is that if all three had arrived at one time (the MiGs arrived first, and the missile some time later), *Sterett* would not have been able to engage all three with her SAMs, since she only had two directors.

FIGURE 13.13. INTERCEPT COURSE GEOMETRY

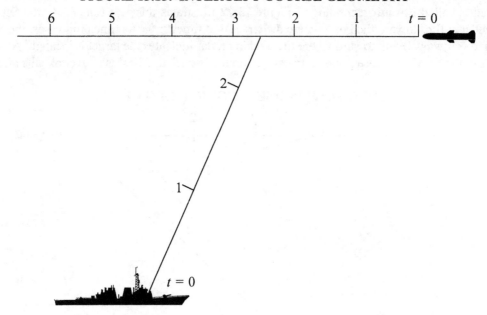

FIGURE 13.14. SEMI-ACTIVE WITH MIDCOURSE GUIDANCE

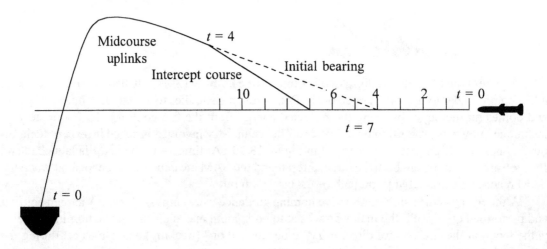

This "lack of firepower" was addressed and partly solved by the introduction of missiles having semi-active homing with midcourse guidance (SM2). These missiles are launched into space towards a midcourse guidance point. Upon arrival at the point, the missile receives updates that direct it towards the target. As the missile approaches the target, the fire-control director provides illumination so that the missile may home on the reflected energy. Note that these updates only occur when required. While this may sound like the previous semi-active homing case, this illumination only occurs during the terminal phase of flight. In other words the director is only used for a fraction of the time required for previous systems, thus a ship can have more missiles in flight towards different targets than it has directors. An illustration of this technology is shown in Figure 13.14. At time $t = 0$, the SAM is launched and flies towards a predetermined point. When the SAM reaches this point, it begins to receive updates from the director that direct it towards the intercept point. At time $t = 4$, the fire-control radar illuminates the target so that the intercept can be made by the SAM.

Missile systems in the fleet are used for both **point-defense** of specific units and **area-defense** of multiple units. Figure 13.15 illustrates these two types of missile use.

FIGURE 13.15. AREA AND POINT DEFENSE

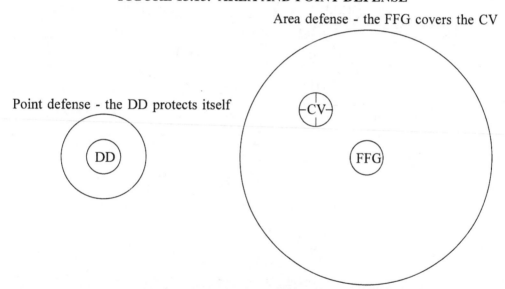

Area defense - the FFG covers the CV

Point defense - the DD protects itself

The basic idea is that an area-defense weapon can protect an area of space which covers the launching ship as well as other units. Point-defense weapons can protect only the firing unit. Many missiles used for point defense (including shoulder-launched missiles) use passive guidance to track their targets (they home on the infra-red signature of the target) while those used for area defense use a longer range guidance system, such as one of those discussed above.

A surface ship's station assignment may result in changes to the effectiveness of missiles used for the area defense of a task group. The assignment problem may be approached as a resource allocation problem. The number of ships assigned to a task group is limited (perhaps 5 or 6 escorts per carrier), and the ships have multiple roles to play. A typical employment starts as was shown previously in Figure 13.1, with the carrier at ZZ, and the escorts generally placed within the inner air battle zone. This does not always have to be the case. A CAP station could conceivably be replaced by a guided-missile cruiser. At least one escort with area-defense weapons may be placed in a "shotgun" position trailing the carrier. An inner screen may be formed by the escorts that carry only point defense, and this screen may be combined with a second area-defense ship. Finally, other area-defense ships may be stationed outside the inner screen along the threat axis, in order to provide a defensive barrier to approaching hostile forces. Figure 13.16 provides an illustration. The FFG represents the "shotgun" position trailing the CV, the DDs represent the point-defense ships forming the inner screen, and the CGs represent the area-defense ships forming a defensive barrier.

FIGURE 13.16. BATTLEGROUP DISPOSITIONS

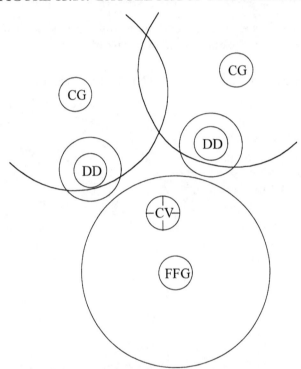

What faces a potential enemy then is a system of layered defenses, starting with the CAP (or a cruiser) in the outer air battle, proceeding through the SAM defenses of the inner air battle, and finally encountering point-defense soft and hard kill weapons. In order to apply different models to the problems often found in the inner air battle, a rather simplistic model of SAM engagements is presented.

Consider a simple engagement model in which a ship fires twenty missiles at approaching targets. If the single-shot kill probability for each SAM is .6, how many SAMs can be expected to hit their target? Treating the problem as a sequence of independent Bernoulli trials (either hit or miss), the binomial distribution may be used. In fact what is needed is the expected value of a binomial (np) where $n = 20$ and $p = .6$. The expected number of targets hit by the 20 SAMs would then be $(20)(.6) = 12$. This model is quite useful for quick answers to questions concerning numbers of weapons to employ in defense, or the number required to overwhelm an enemy's defenses. But a number of important things were not considered. For example, how many targets were there, was a single SAM sent against a single target, when can the ship next shoot at any targets it missed, and under what doctrine was the firing done? One way to begin to address some of these problems is to include time in the model.

Consider an example where an SSN-X missile is to be intercepted by a SM-1 MR missile. Figure 13.17 gives the assumed speeds and effective ranges of the two missiles. Assume further that the SSN-X flies at a very low altitude, and can be detected only just beyond the radar horizon (assume it to be 25 nm). Thus a maximum range intercept can be attempted with the SM-1 MR. The SSN-X is flying at Mach 1.0. Since Mach speeds change with altitude, a good rule of thumb to use is that Mach 1 = 10 nm a minute. Thus the SAM will be flying at 25 nm/minute, or two and a half times as fast as the SSN-X. If the SSN is detected at 25 nm, after one minutes flight it will be 15 nm from the ship. If a SAM is fired at the exact moment of detection, where and when will the intercept occur? The solution is to set up a relationship involving the two speeds, and the initial ranges of the opposing weapons. Using the ship as a reference point, Figure 13.18 shows the geometry of the situation. The closing rate of the two missiles is Mach 3.5 or about 35 nm/minute. The initial distance between the missiles is 25 nm, so the time to intercept is $t_1 = 25/35 = .714$ minute or 42.9 seconds. The distance from the ship where the intercept will take place may be found by multiplying the speed of the SAM by the time to intercept. Thus the first intercept will take place at $d_1 = (25)(.714) = 17.9$ nm from the ship.

FIGURE 13.17. ASSUMED MISSILE PARAMETERS

	SSN-X	SM-1 MR
Speed (Mach)	1.0	2.5
Range (nm)	60	20

FIGURE 13.18. SAM/ASM SPEED AND DISTANCE RELATIONSHIPS

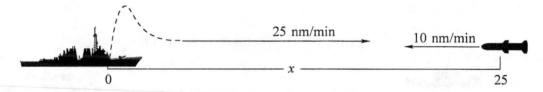

Assuming the SAM missed, the calculation of the next intercept point would use d_1 as the initial distance between the missiles. Thus the next intercept occurs at $t_2 = 17.9/35 = .510$ minutes after the first intercept, or at 1.224 minutes after the incoming missile was first detected. The second intercept will then occur at $d_2 = (25)(.510) = 12.75$ nm from the ship. These calculations can be repeated until the SSN is shot down, the SSN passes inside the minimum range of the SAM system, or the SSN reaches the ship, in which case the SSN either hits or misses the ship. This simple model is based solely on speed and range; several other factors are required to make a more accurate model.

Some of these are as follows:

1. The missiles should fly in 3 dimensional space, not in the linear relationship shown here.
2. Flying in 3 dimensional space also puts physical restrictions on the missiles.
3. These restrictions include the amount of sustained G's the missiles can take.
4. No determination of hit or miss is made.
5. No delay times between detection and acquisition, acquisition and firing, and so forth, are considered.
6. Besides the linear relationship, the model assumes the intended target is the SAM ship; this may or may not be the case.

   This model can be used to track engagements, to find out when the first (or for that matter last) shot can be taken, and to address similar problems involving range and time. With a little modification, this model can be used to find the number of shots available to a particular SAM system.
   To address the problem of determining the number of shots available to a SAM system for a given threat, let r_{max} denote the maximum range of the SAM, r_{min} the minimum firing range of the SAM, x_i the distance of the threat from the ship at the ith intercept which occurs at time t_i, v the speed of the SAM, u the speed of the threat aircraft (which may be a missile), n the number of salvos after the initial intercept, and m_{in} the total number salvos fired at the inbound threat. The following assumptions are made:

1. The raid is directly inbound towards the SAM ship.
2. A shoot-look-shoot model with no time delays is used.
3. The first intercept occurs at the maximum range r_{max} of the SAM.
4. The SAM has a minimum firing range r_{min} inside of which firing is not possible.

   The geometry of this problem is similar to that found in Figure 13.18, and is illustrated in Figure 13.19. The first salvo must be fired so that it will intercept the raid at the maximum range of the SAM. An equation will be derived for the additional number of salvos fired after the threat aircraft has reached r_{max} and one salvo will be added to this number to take into account the intercept which took place exactly at r_{max}.

FIGURE 13.19. INBOUND RAID GEOMETRY

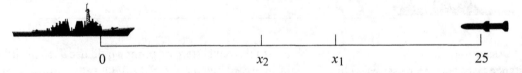

$$0 \qquad\qquad x_2 \qquad x_1 \qquad\qquad 25$$

   With the raid at r_{max} proceeding toward the ship, a salvo is fired. The missile travels a distance x_1, while the raid travels a distance $r_{max} - x_1$, as shown in Figure 13.19. The time of flight for each is the same. Therefore $vt = x_1$ and $ut = r_{max} - x_1$. Solving for time t_1 and equating the two,

$$t_1 = \frac{x_1}{v} = \frac{r_{max} - x_1}{u}. \tag{13-7}$$

Solving (13-7) for x_1 gives

$$x_1 = r_{max} \frac{v}{v + u}. \tag{13-8}$$

Similarly, for the second shot after the raid has passed r_{max},

$$t_2 = \frac{x_2}{v} = \frac{x_1 - x_2}{u},$$

and

$$x_2 = x_1 \frac{v}{v + u}. \tag{13-9}$$

By using the solution for x_1 in (13-8), and substituting into (13-9),

$$x_2 = r_{max} \left(\frac{v}{u + v} \right)^2. \tag{13-10}$$

This can be continued for $x_3, \ldots , x_n$ and, by induction,

$$x_n = r_{max} \left(\frac{v}{u + v} \right)^n. \tag{13-11}$$

Since the minimum missile range is r_{min}, it is practical to shoot only when $x_n \geq r_{min}$. When $x_n < r_{min}$, the missile cannot intercept the raid, so setting x_n equal to r_{min} will determine the maximum number of SAMs that can be fired:

$$r_{min} = r_{max} \left(\frac{v}{v + u} \right)^n. \tag{13-12}$$

Now solving (13-12) for n by using logarithms gives

$$n = \frac{\ln \left(\dfrac{r_{min}}{r_{max}} \right)}{\ln \left(\dfrac{v}{u + v} \right)}. \tag{13-13}$$

Remembering that n is the number of salvos that can be fired after the raid has passed r_{max}, one salvo must be added for the intercept that was made at r_{max}. Also, the value for n in (13-13) may not be an integer. Therefore the maximum number of missiles that can be fired at one incoming threat aircraft is

$$m_{in} = \left[\frac{\ln \left(\dfrac{r_{min}}{r_{max}} \right)}{\ln \left(\dfrac{v}{u + v} \right)} \right] + 1, \tag{13-14}$$

where the square brackets denote the greatest integer contained within (since it would not be possible to fire a fraction of a missile).

Since the SAM ship may be a picket stationed out on the axis of expected threat direction, it is also worth knowing the total number of salvos m_{total} that could be fired at the raid after it has passed overhead the ship and headed outbound. A different equation for the maximum number of missiles m_{out} that could be fired at an outbound threat aircraft can be derived in a manner similar to the incoming derivation, changing only the fact that the velocity of the threat aircraft changes sign. This would give

$$m_{out} = \frac{\left[\ln\left(\dfrac{r_{max}}{r_{min}}\right)\right]}{\left[\ln\left(\dfrac{v}{v-u}\right)\right]} + 1 = \frac{\left[\ln\left(\dfrac{r_{min}}{r_{max}}\right)\right]}{\left[\ln\left(\dfrac{v-u}{v}\right)\right]} + 1. \qquad (13\text{-}15)$$

The total number of salvos $m_{total} = m_{in} + m_{out}$ for a raid that first is inbound, passes overhead, and then is outbound to the firing ship is

$$m_{total} = \frac{\left[\ln\left(\dfrac{r_{min}}{r_{max}}\right)\right]}{\left[\ln\left(\dfrac{v}{v+u}\right)\right]} + \frac{\left[\ln\left(\dfrac{r_{min}}{r_{max}}\right)\right]}{\left[\ln\left(\dfrac{v-u}{v}\right)\right]} + 2 \qquad (13\text{-}16)$$

For the previous example of the SSN-X versus the SM-1 MR, assuming a minimum range of 2 nm for the SAM gives $m_{in} = [8.506] = 8$ SAMs fired at the SSN-X before it passed inside the SM-1 MR's minimum range, and $m_{out} = [5.944] = 5$ SAMs fired at the SSN-X after it passed over the ship. This gives a total of 13 SAMs fired at the SSN-X between the time it was detected and the time it reached the maximum range of the SAM.

Suppose that the threat aircraft arrive in waves, with each wave consisting of several of the aircraft arriving simultaneously. The problem that presents itself to the defending ship is one of how to engage a large number of targets at the same time. As mentioned previously, if either command or semi-active homing guidance is used, each director could engage only one target at a time. If a ship had only two directors, then only two targets could be engaged. The semi-active homing with midcourse guidance system (SM2) avoids this by time-sharing each director, allowing several targets to be engaged by each director. Assume that the SAM ship has SM2, but with the same characteristics as the one used in the earlier examples. It has already been shown that there is only enough time to fire 8 salvos at an incoming SSN-X. What if there were 10 incoming SSN-Xs and the ship can only engage 6 at a time? The possibility exists that not all SSN-Xs would be shot down at the first opportunity, and that in fact some of the SSN-Xs might arrive at the ship without being shot at by the SAM system.

As shown earlier, if six SAMs are shot at the incoming targets, each with a single-shot probability of kill of $p = .6$, it is expected that 3.6 of the SAMs would hit their targets. Assuming that 4 SSNs are hit, that means at the second engagement opportunity, there would be 6 targets left to engage with the SAMs. Another 4 of the targets would be expected to be destroyed by the second launch of SAMs, leaving 2 for the third engagement opportunity. Note that it is actually possible to engage the targets 3 to 8 more times. Figure 13.20 summarizes the fight so far. While it is a reasonable to count the .6 hit as a destroyed target, what about the .2 hit starting at engagement 3? And why were only 2 SAMs used in the third engagement? That depends on the firing doctrine, but since a shoot-look-shoot policy was specified, that typically means shoot a single round, look, and then shoot a second round if the first missed. What if pairs of SAMs were shot at the target (shoot-shoot-look)? Then the kill probability increases, as the target has to be missed by both SAMs in order to survive, so that

$$p = 1 - (1 - .6)^2 = .84,$$

which is a much higher probability of kill than the single salvo. Look at the engagement table once again as shown in Figure 13.21.

FIGURE 13.20. POSSIBLE SHOOT-LOOK-SHOOT RESULTS

Engagement	SSN total	SAMs used	Expected hits
1	10	6	3.6
2	6	6	3.6
3	2	2	1.2
4	1	1	.6
5	0	0	0

The first thing to be noticed is that all of the targets appear to be destroyed by the end of the third engagement. The second thing to be noticed is that the expected number of hits for 12 SAMs seems really low when the probability of kill, p, is .84. However, the number of targets engaged is still only 6, not 10, so $(6)(.84)$ yields 5.04 hits, as the SAMs are fired in pairs at the targets. Finally, notice that 24 SAMs were expended to destroy 10 attackers. This may be over half of the ship's magazine capacity used up in a single raid.

FIGURE 13.21. POSSIBLE SHOOT-SHOOT-LOOK RESULTS

Engagement	SSN total	SAMs used	Expected Hits
1	10	12	5.04
2	5	10	4.20
3	1	2	.84
4	0	0	0

So far the models that have been constructed have depended largely on a target that is directly inbound to the firing ship. Some typical places where SAM ships are located to protect the high value unit (HVU, Figure 13.16 uses a carrier as the HVU) have also been shown. If the carrier is the target, then the incoming raid will be headed towards the carrier, and not necessarily directly towards the SAM ship(s). The next model to be examined determines the number of shots a SAM ship can get off at a given air target as a function of the target's closest point of approach (CPA) to the SAM ship.

The number of shots that the SAM ship can fire during the time the target is within range depends on maximum SAM range r_{max}, target speed u, SAM speed v, and the range to CPA, r_{CPA}. Assume first that the threat aircraft is detected early enough so that the first intercept can be made at the edge of the SAM envelope. As seen from Figure 13.22, the first **target angle**, θ_1, which is the angle between the line of flight of the threat aircraft and the line from the point A where the aircraft enters the SAM envelope and the point Z where the SAM ship is located, can be determined using r_{max} as the length of the hypotenuse and r_{CPA} as the length of a leg of a right triangle. This gives

$$\theta_1 = \arcsin(r_{CPA}/r_{max}). \tag{13-17}$$

The first **lead angle** α_1, which is the angle with vertex at the SAM ship and rays determined by the point A and the point B where the second intercept is made, can be determined by the fact that the time t_1 that it takes for the aircraft to fly from A to B is the same as the time for the SAM to fly from Z to B. Noting that the length of the side opposite θ_1 in the triangle ABZ is vt_1 and the length of the side opposite α_1 in the same triangle is ut_1, and using the law of sines gives

$$\alpha_1 = \arcsin(u \sin\theta_1/v).$$

The range r_1 from the SAM ship where the intercept takes place can also be found using the law of sines as

$$r_1 = \frac{r_{max}\sin(\theta_1)}{\sin(180° - (\alpha_1 + \theta_1))}.$$

Similarly, the distance d_1 that the target has flown into the SAMs envelope is given by

$$d_1 = \frac{r_{max}\sin(\alpha)}{\sin(180° - (\alpha_1 + \theta_1))}.$$

FIGURE 13.22. TARGET TRACK GEOMETRY

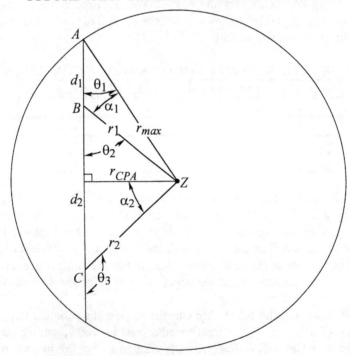

The second target angle θ_2 can be shown to be

$$\theta_2 = \theta_1 + \alpha_1,$$

and the second lead angle α_2 is

$$\alpha_2 = \arcsin(\, u \sin(\theta_2) \,/\, v \,).$$

The range r_2 from the ship to the point where the third intercept takes place may be found using the triangle BZC with known side r_1 found as above:

$$r_2 = r_1 \sin(\theta_2) \,/\, \sin(\alpha_2 + \theta_2).$$

And the distance d_2 that the aircraft flies between the intercepts is given by

$$d_2 = r_1 \sin(\alpha_2) \,/\, \sin(\alpha_2 + \theta_2).$$

The process may be continued, and by induction, as long as the threat aircraft is within the SAMs envelope,

$$\theta_{i+1} = \alpha_i + \theta_i,$$
$$\alpha_{i+1} = \arcsin(u \sin(\theta_{i+1}) \,/\, v),$$
$$r_{i+1} = r_i \sin(\theta_{i+1}) \,/\, \sin(\alpha_{i+1} + \theta_{i+1}), \text{ and}$$
$$d_{i+1} = r_i \sin(\alpha_{i+1}) \,/\, \sin(\alpha_{i+1} + \theta_{i+1}),$$

where $r_0 = r_{max}$ and $\theta_1 = \arcsin(r_{CPA} \,/\, r_{max})$.

The total path length d_{total} of the target aircraft through the SAM envelop can be found by solving the right triangle with side r_{CPA} and hypotenuse r_{max} and doubling the length of the other side:

$$d_{total} = 2\, r_{max} \cos \alpha_1.$$

By keeping a total of the distances between intercepts, or by comparing the range at intercept, r_i, the total number of intercepts possible may be found. Figure 13.23 illustrates how this can be done using a spreadsheet. The example shown is for $r_{CPA} = 2$ nm, $r_{max} = 25$ nm, $v = 25$ nm/minute, and $u = 10$ nm/minute. The column on the extreme right is set to 1 if the intercept can be made, otherwise it is set to 0. Notice that the threat aircraft is within the SAM envelop for 49.84 nm, and no more than 16 intercepts can be made (including the first one at r_{max}). The actual number will likely be smaller than 16, since no delay times for firing SAMs were included in the model.

It is reasonable to assume, and a spreadsheet can be used to verify, that regardless of the values of the other variables discussed above, the number of possible shots will increase as r_{CPA} decreases.

Also notice that as the target changes from an inbound to an outbound presentation, the intercept flight path begins to look more and more like a pursuit (tail-chase) flight path. To see the significance of this, look again at Figure 13.16. In order for the cruisers positioned in the outer screen to have any effect on an attacking force, the attackers need to pass within the missile envelopes of the cruisers. Ideally, the enemy would travel directly towards the defending cruisers, thus presenting the maximum track length for missile engagements. Realistically, the enemy would try to pass between the cruisers, and thus minimize the SAM threat. It is exactly this problem, trying to get an enemy that is much faster than you inside your weapons' envelope, that occupies the majority of a task group staffs' planning considerations. Where do the ships go? What is the optimum stationing for SAM ships? What if your SAM ships are dual purpose (or multi-purpose) –where should they be placed for maximum effectiveness? Some of these questions have been addressed previously, but it is worth reviewing the considerations once again for the placement of AW assets:

1. Try to place the ships near the bearing (or axis) the air threat is expected to come from.
2. Try to place non-AW and HVUs within the missile envelopes of the SAM ships.
3. Try to balance the AW mission area with other comparably important mission areas.

With the changes occurring almost daily in the world military situation, there is no cookbook advice on exactly how to best station both air and surface assets in the AW world. There may or may not be massed bombers striking task groups deep in the ocean; there surely will be small numbers of tactical aircraft trying to penetrate the defenses of a task group operating close to shore. Both threats have to be planned for and dealt with. This chapter has brought out some of the major points and analysis methods to be considered when planning an air defense. With few exceptions (gunboats, submarine-launched torpedoes, and mines), most naval combat evolves into an air battle, whether it be manned aircraft versus ships and aircraft, or air, surface, or submarine-launched cruise missiles versus the same weapons from the adversary. The above text and the problems below are designed to motivate the reader to look at these problems, and perhaps find new solutions.

FIGURE 13.23. NUMBER OF SHOTS

Inputs:	$r_{CAP} = 2$ nm		$v = 25$ nm/min					
	$r_{max} = 25$ nm		$u = 10$ nm/min					
Outputs:	$r_{total} = 49.84$ nm							
	$m = 16 =$ maximum number of intercepts possible							

i	θ		α		r_i	d_i	Σd_i	
	(deg)	(radians)	(deg)	(radians)	(nm)	(nm)	(nm)	
1	4.6	0.08	1.8	0.03	17.9	7.2	7.2	1
2	6.4	0.11	2.6	0.04	12.8	5.1	12.3	1
3	9.0	0.16	3.6	0.06	9.2	3.7	15.9	1
4	12.6	0.22	5.0	0.09	6.6	2.6	18.6	1
5	17.6	0.31	6.9	0.12	4.8	1.9	20.5	1
6	24.5	0.43	9.6	0.17	3.6	1.4	22.0	1
7	34.0	0.59	12.9	0.23	2.7	1.1	23.0	1
8	47.0	0.82	17.0	0.30	2.2	0.9	23.9	1
9	64.0	1.12	21.1	0.37	2.0	0.8	24.8	1
10	85.0	1.48	23.5	0.41	2.1	0.8	25.6	1
11	108.5	1.89	22.3	0.39	2.6	1.1	26.6	1
12	130.8	2.28	17.6	0.31	3.8	1.5	28.2	1
13	148.4	2.59	12.1	0.21	6.0	2.4	30.6	1
14	160.5	2.80	7.7	0.13	9.8	3.9	34.5	1
15	168.2	2.94	4.7	0.08	16.2	6.5	40.9	1
16	172.9	3.02	2.8	0.05	26.8	10.7	51.7	0

1304   Other Literature and History

Instructions for the conduct of exercise analyses are promulgated by the various numbered fleets, fleet commanders in chief, force and type commanders, and the Chief of Naval Operations.

The basic models used in 1302 were taken from Wagner [1] and Handford and Strommen [2]. Alternate current terminologies for combat air patrol (CAP) include carrier defensive air (CDA). The former has been retained here due to the longevity of its usage.

The models presented in 1303 for three modes of guidance (command, semi-active homing, and semi-active homing with midcourse guidance) are from Witte and McDonald [3]. For more on the performance of systems using semi-active homing guidance in the Vietnam conflict consult [4]. The information about the attack on the USS *Sterett* is from [5]. Both [3] and [6] contain additional information about systems having semi-active homing with midcourse guidance.

FIGURE 13.24. EFFECT OF CPA RANGE ON NUMBER OF SHOTS

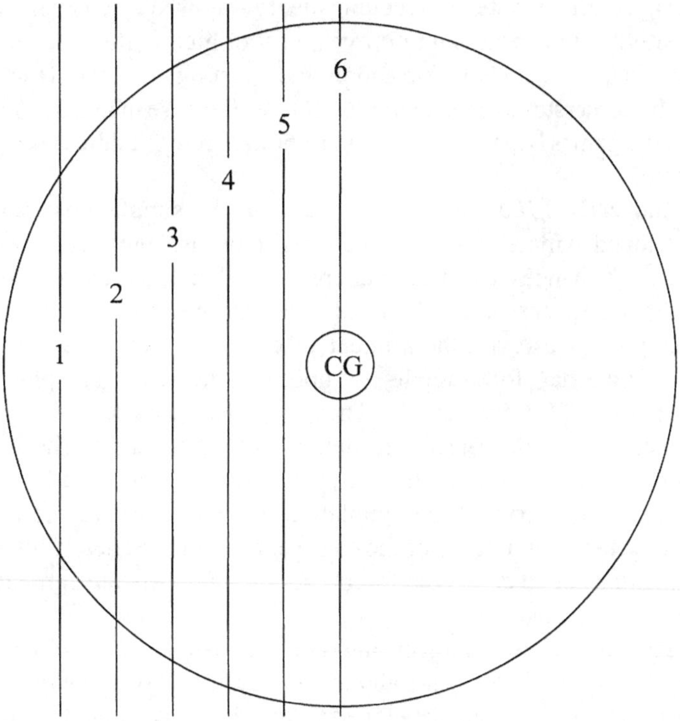

In the problem section that follows, 16 comes from Bond [7]. Problem 18 is based on Farris and Hunt [8]. Problem 19 originally came from Shepard, et. al. [9], and was modified for use in this text. It is ideal for solution by using a computer, or by performing one or two runs by hand. In either case, the goal is to provide the reader with an understanding of the mathematics involved in analyzing a SAM engagement.

Currently, Air Defense analysis methodology is dominated by computer simulations. The complex issues associated with Joint Warfare requirements and operations near land can appropriately be addressed by simulation. For example, protection of amphibious operations or other areas ashore against tactical ballistic missiles requires not only naval forces but Army and Air Force weapon systems. Weapon system requirements, procurement issues, and operational considerations such as employment and doctrine are being addressed by aggregated large scale battle simulations.

Such simulations stand in sharp contrast to the more straightforward mathematical techniques used in the 1950s and 1960s. Most of the analytic derivations in this chapter have their origins in this period. They draw mostly on statistics, probability, queuing, and search theory and for the most part were appropriate to the nature of the problems being addressed in that era. For example, in the 1950s, one of the key issues revolved around single shot kill probability and analytic models of fuzing and guidance accuracy and target lethality models were developed to investigate tradeoffs between various warhead types such as rods, internal and external blast, as well as nuclear. Such models also provided operational insights into salvo firing policies and doctrine for weapon control.

In the 1960s, as the Terrier, Tartar, and Talos missiles began widespread deployment, serious reliability, maintainability, and availability problems surfaced because of the lack of total system integration in the design of these systems. Queuing theory was used extensively to provide the basis for tradeoff and sensitivity studies among improvements for high failure rate components, maintenance practices, logistic factors, and on-line and periodic testing (see, e.g., Hunt [10]). In this era, the F4/sparrow was the cornerstone of the Outer Air Battle. Because manned systems are dominated by human decisions, wargames began to take on an important role to address problems too complex for algorithmic solution.

In the 1950s and early 1960s, manual, tactical, AAW simulations using strip matching techniques were developed to more accurately account for the distribution of fire among raid targets recognizing firing policy changes when targets are not killed. The calculations in (13-14) and (13-15) assume all shots are successful. The manual simulations were intended to better reflect the effects of kill probability. However, the number of cases that could be considered by manual methods was limited. In one day, for example, two good operators, using graphic aids could analyze only about 10 iterations of a 30-target attack. These devices were used in studies on radars, fire-control systems, launchers, missile trajectories, delivery accuracy, and warhead damage. In 1956, the first computer simulation of a missile defense system was programmed for the UNIVAC-1103 computer (32K words of memory!). The simulation was used to compare the Nike and Talos surface-to-air missile systems for defense of the continental United States. This simulation was the first air defense simulation coded and is the forerunner of many existing simulations used in Fleet Air Defense today.

In 1958, the Navy War Games Project, including the Naval War College Naval Electronic Warfare Simulator, the Applied Physics Laboratory, and the Naval Weapons Laboratory, was inaugurated. Computer simulations were developed across all warfare areas including antiair warfare and were especially used to examine the role of the Navy in strategic warfare. The development of these models was particularly valuable in developing much of the underlying technology in simulation. For example, because of computer limitations at that time, all of the warfare area models were deemed feasible because the invention of the "event store" technique (as the means for maintaining sequence control in the air defense simulation program) had provided a new and powerful method for describing the complex interactions of events in Naval tactics.

The original air defense simulation represented a single ship battery or a single CAP station combating a stream of approaching attackers. It was modified to include many batteries and many CAP and an early representation of radar jamming and to permit the study of Threat Evaluation and Weapon Assignment doctrines. The design of the Naval Tactical Data System was influenced by studies using this model. This model went through various evolutions over the decade of the 1960s and was in regular use until 1975.

In the mid-1970s, simulation languages began to be used and models were developed to study Force Mix AAW problems. Later in the 1970s, as a better appreciation developed for the capability of the Soviet Fleet, more sophisticated algorithms were developed to account for enemy countermeasures as well as the effects of clutter from weather, sea-state, and land background.

These early simulations evolved throughout the 1980s and 1990s and continue to provide the cornerstone of much of the operations analyses conducted today.

While the evolution of computer simulations has been of major importance in fleet air defense analysis, analytic and graphical techniques have played a major role in system acquisition decisions and in operations. For example, graphical techniques using range-time plots to calculate firepower coupled with analytic models were the methodology used in technical plans in the 1960s and 1970s for developments and system choices for all Navy air defense systems. In addition, the Advanced Surface Missile System Assessment, which established the technical requirements for the system which eventually became Aegis, used these same techniques. One of the key advantages of analytic and graphical approaches compared to simulation is the ease of comprehension of the underlying results by decision-makers.

A technique that has had considerable input in the 1980s and 1990s is seminar gaming. Many problems faced by decision-makers are too complex for algorithmic solutions. Various techniques have been developed to organize and structure the application of judgment to such problems. Seminar gaming is one such approach. The essence of seminar gaming is an open (all information is known to all participants), two-sided game where snapshots of a scenario are discussed from technical and operational perspectives based on pre-technical analysis. The results provide insight into operational contexts for future systems, provide perspective on boundary conditions, and identify interactions and interrelationships of elements of problems. They are also invaluable as a form to bring together technical, operational, and intelligence personnel particularly at the start of any major study.

One of the significant major analytic thrusts currently being developed is to tie together the high-fidelity simulations of weapons and aggregated effectiveness simulations. Such an approach is being used in the Advanced Surface to Air Missile System program, where high fidelity models of weapon systems provide inputs to an overall effectiveness model. Achieving electronic integration of these models (except for seminar gaming) is a goal and a challenge for future analysts.

In summary, the methodology consistently used by the Navy to predict Fleet Air Defense system effectiveness has been to use a combination of analytic tools, simulation, gaming, and testing. No single simulation, model, or test can by itself provide adequate assessment and prediction. The combined tools of engineering analysis, simulation, component testing, and controlled at-sea operations provide a wide database of performance assessment necessary for predicting system effectiveness.

[1] Wagner, Daniel H. *Naval Tactical Decision Aids*. Monterey, CA: U.S. Naval Postgraduate School, 1989.

[2] Handford, Richard C., and G. A. Strommen, *Engagement Evaluation of Defense Unit Positioning in a Multithreat Environment*. Norfolk, VA: COMSECONDFLT, Final Draft Tacmemo CZ1811-1-89 by Atlantic Analysis Corporation, 1989.

[3] Witte, R. W., and R. L. McDonald. "Standard Missile: Guidance System Development." *The John Hopkins APL Technical Digest*. Laurel, MD, 1982.

[4] "Surface AAW Off Vietnam." *Surface Warfare Magazine*, Mar/April, 1988.

[5] "Action Off Dong Hoi." *Surface Warfare Magazine*, April, 1978.

[6] "Aegis - Forging Ahead." *Surface Warfare Magazine*, March, 1980.

[7] Bond, Larry. *Harpoon–Modern Naval Wargame Rules*. Game Designers Workshop, Blooming-
      ton, IL, 1987.
[8] Farris, R. S., and R. J. Hunt. "Battle Group Air Defense Analysis", *The Johns Hopkins APL
      Technical Digest*. Laurel, MD, 1982
[9] Shephard, R. W.; D. A. Hartley; P. J. Haysman; and M. R. Bathe, *Applied Operations
      Research: Examples from Defense Assessment*. New York, NY: Plenum Press, 1988.
[10] Hunt, R. J. "Availability Model for Shipboard Equipment." *The Johns Hopkins APL Technical
      Digest*, Laurel, MD, 1963.

Problems

1. Given the following data for an AW exercise conducted as described in this chapter:

Outer Air Battle		Inner Air Battle	
Number of raid aircraft	225	Number of raid aircraft	225
Number of detections	210	Number of detections	210
Number of CAP assigned	150	Number of raids designated	200
Number of tally-hos	125	Number of raids acquired	150
Number of intercepts	100	Number of raids fired upon	100
Number intercepted by CAP and fired upon by SAMs			45
Probability of kill for CAP weapons			.75
Probability of kill for SAMs			.75

determine the following.

a. The factorized probability of an unopposed raid, p_{uf}.
b. The simple probability of an unopposed raid, p_u.
c. The probability of survival of a raid, $\Pr\{S\}$.

2. From a different AW exercise, the following data were collected:

Outer Air Battle		Inner Air Battle	
Number of raid aircraft	200	Number of raid aircraft	200
Number of detections	160	Number of detections	160
Number of CAP assigned	130	Number of raids designated	155
Number of tally-hos	115	Number of raids acquired	120
Number of intercepts	88	Number of raids fired upon	115
Probability of kill for CAP weapons			.5
Probability of kill for SAMs			.5

a. Determine the factorized probability of an unopposed raid, p_{uf}.
b. Estimate the probability of survival of a raid, $\Pr\{S\}$.

For Problems 3-12, assume the following unless otherwise indicated:

u	= threat a/c speed	= 480 knots
v	= DLI/fighter speed	= 600 knots
h	= DLI/fighter radar detection range	= 150 nm
θ_{max}	= DLI/fighter radar coverage angle	= 45 degrees
w	= engagement range	= 5 nm.

3. For a chainsaw tactic using a search interval t_S of 20 minutes and a search radius r_S of 400 nm, determine the following:

a. Detection ranges on threat axis, both maximum and minimum.
b. Detection ranges at maximum offset angles (extreme detection azimuth), both maximum and minimum.
c. Maximum offset angles, for both maximum and minimum detection ranges.

4. For a chainsaw tactic, if the minimum range at which an on-axis threat is to be detected is 300 nm, what is the least search radius needed in order that the search interval remain at 20 minutes?

5. For a chainsaw tactic, if the minimum range at which an on-axis threat is to be detected is 300 nm, what is the largest search interval in order that the search radius is 350 nm?

6. Suppose that a chainsaw tactic is to be established using the search interval and radius as given in 3 and so that a detected threat is to be intercepted by a DLI that is launched 5 minutes after the detection occurs. Find the range at intercept from the defended point, ZZ, under the following conditions:

a. The detection occurs at maximum on-axis detection range.
b. The detection occurs at minimum on-axis detection range.
c. The detection occurs at the maximum of the detection ranges at maximum offset angles.
d. The detection occurs at the minimum of the detection ranges at maximum offset angles.

7. Suppose that the USS *Nimitz* has launched fighters along a threat axis using a chainsaw tactic in order to detect an incoming threat that is expected to be flying at 450 knots. A fighter's speed is 500 knots on this mission and the search radius is to be 500 nm. Determine the largest search interval that allows the keep-out range to be 250 nm and the intercept to be made by a DLI that is launched 5 minutes after detection is made and has an intercept speed of 600 knots.

8. Suppose that an AEW having radar detection range h of 300 nm is stationed at a range r of 200 nm from the defended point ZZ. If a threat aircraft is radially inbound on a course that is offset by $\alpha = 30°$ (from the radial containing the AEW), determine the following:

a. The target range r_D from ZZ at detection,
b. The time t_I from detection to intercept , and

c. The maximum intercept range k.

9. Suppose that a CAP has been established with station range (from ZZ) of 180 nm, and keep-out range of 250 nm. Determine the coverage angle.

10. If the keep-out range is to be 250 nm, determine the CAP station range from ZZ that maximizes the coverage angle.

11. Determine the least CAP station range for which an intercept can occur outside a keep-out range of 250 nm for any threat that is detected by the CAP.

12. For the CAP given in problem 9, suppose that a threat aircraft is radially inbound on a course so that the angle off the on-threat-axis measured by the CAP when it detects the threat is $\theta = 30$ degrees. Find each of the following:

a. The range at which the threat will be detected by the CAP fighter.
b. The maximum range at which the CAP fighter can intercept the threat.

13. If an AEW stationed on bearing 065 at range 150 nm detects a radially inbound threat on bearing 075 (from ZZ), can a silent CAP stationed on bearing 090 at range 200 nm make an intercept before the threat closes to 250 nm? Assume that the AEW radar range is 300 nm and that the response time for transfer from the AEW to the CAP is 1 minute.

14. Your ship is under attack by 8 STYX anti-ship cruise missiles. Your main defense consists of a battery of 40 SM-1 MR surface-to-air missiles. Each SAM has a probability of hit of .6.

a. How many SAMs do you expect to expend to destroy the 8 incoming ASMs?
b. If 3 SAMs are fired at one STYX, what is the probability that the third SAM will be the first to hit the target?
c. If the probability of a STYX hitting your ship is .7, what is the probability that more than 6 of the 8 fired will hit your ship?

15. The STYX in problem 14 arrive in range of your SAM system at the rate of 4 per minute.

a. What is the probability that more than 6 STYX arrive in range of your SAMs in 1 minute?
b. What is the probability that the first STYX will arrive in range in the first 10 seconds?

16. A "typical" situation that can occur in restricted waters (like the Persian Gulf) is when a combatant such as a frigate is attacked by missile-armed fast patrol boats. The patrol boats generally have few weapons; a 76 mm gun and 4-8 ASCMs. The frigate typically has more weapons, or weapons that have dual purposes. In this case, the frigate has a CIWS, a 76 mm gun, and a Mk13 launcher that can either launch HARPOONS or SM-1 MRs, but not both. The frigate also has only two directors, so only two targets can be engaged at a time (HARPOONS do not require a director).

The worst case scenario is when the patrol boats attack from within a fairly close range, say, 10 nautical miles. Given the following data, set up an appropriate MOE for the frigate's survival in this worst case scenario:

La Combattante II class PTG (two boats each with)
    76 mm gun (probability of hit = .5), and
    4 HARPOONS (probability of hit = .75).
    It takes 2 HARPOONS or 200 rounds of 76 mm to sink the FFG.
    All 4 HARPOONS can be fired in one time unit; it takes 2 time units to reach the FFG.

Perry class FFG (single ship equipped with):
    76 mm gun (probability of hit = .5),
    4 HARPOONS (probability of hit = .75),
    40 SM-1 MRs (probability of hit = .6), and
    Mk15 CIWS (probability of hit = .9).
    The launcher can fire 3 SM1s or 2 HARPOONS per time unit.
    SM1s can intercept enemy missiles in 1/2 a time unit.
    The frigate can only engage one target at a time with the gun, one with CIWS, and one or two with SM1s (two if the gun engages the same target as the SM1s).

17. Problem 16 above hints at one of the tenets of modern naval warfare–**defense in depth**. Defense in depth basically means that an enemy must pass through several layers of defenses, each of which has some positive probability of destroying the enemy prior to reaching the target of interest. For the frigate in problem 16, the enemy's HARPOONS had to pass first through the SAM system, then if the SAMs missed (and they may get several shots depending on range), then pass through the effective gun envelope and finally get past the CIWS. Using the data given in problem 16, compute the probability that a single HARPOON survives the defenses and impacts on the frigate.

18. This chapter has talked about the use of CAP and SAMs in air defense. Develop a generic model that gives the probability that a target penetrates the defenses, based on the number of weapons that engage the target, and their respective probabilities of kill. Assume that a CAP station, a SAM ship, a non-SAM ship, a SAM ship riding shotgun on the HVU, and the HVU itself are on the target's flight path.

19. Air Defense Naval Engagement. The purpose of this project is to determine, via simulation, the likely outcome of a naval air defense engagement in which a KIDD-class DDG is attacked by a wave of eight (8) SSN-X anti-ship missiles. The ASMs are launched from beyond the KIDD's radar horizon (which is 20 nm) in a single wave with a time lapse of 6 seconds between each missile launch.

    The KIDD is fitted with an SPS-48C three dimensional air search radar, which provides initial target information on the attack. The time delay between an incoming missile crossing the DDG's radar horizon and being detected by the SPS-48C has been found to be 5 seconds. The probability of detection is .8; that is after 5 seconds there is an 80 percent chance that the target will be detected.

If not, then another 5 seconds passes before the detection is checked again.

The KIDD is fitted with two Mk-26 launchers for the SM-1 MR surface-to-air missile. Each launcher has an SPG-51 fire-control radar associated with it. The delay time for an SPG-51 to establish a track, after an incoming missile has been detected by the SPS-48C and the fire-control radar has become free, is 3 seconds. The system of launchers and radars is called the Mk74 fire-control system.

The Mk74 system automatically (for this project) engages any target that enters its engagement envelope, and if more than one target is available, it will select the target that arrives first, except that both SPG-51s will not engage the same target. No battle damage assessment is to be done (that is if a missile hits the ship, note the fact, but do not modify the performance of the ship's weapons or radars).

Using the data listed in the paragraphs above, as well as the information provided below, simulate the attack on the ship. Repeat this simulation 4000 times. Provide the following output:

1. A listing of the program.
2. A listing of the output, containing the following:

a. the number of missiles detected (out of 8 times 4000 or 32,000),
b. the number of missiles shot down,
c. the number of SAMs expended,
d. the number of times the ship was hit,
e. the simulated probabilities of a through d.

Data for the project are as follows:
SSN-X:
    speed = 10 nm/minute,
    probability of hit = .6
SM1:
    min. range = 1.5 nm
    max. range = 20 nm
    speed = 25 nm/minute
    single-shot kill probability = .6

Reaction time between the SPG-51 establishing a track and ready to fire = 2 sec.
Repeat time (between failing to destroy the target and ready to fire next weapon) = 2 sec.
Launcher cycle time = 2 rounds every 8 seconds per launcher (i.e., 4 rounds every 8 seconds).
Firing doctrine = shoot-shoot-look-shoot, that is fire 2 SAMs per target, look to see if one or both or none hit. If none hit, then shoot a third SAM.

For ease of calculations assume that 1 nm = 2000 yards.

Answers to Problems

1. a. .32.   b. .31.   c. .45.

2. a. .30.   b. .49.

3. a. max. 550 nm, min. 461.1 nm.
   b. 517.1 nm and 430.4 nm.
   c. 11.8° and 14.3°.

4. 239 nm.

5. 45 min.

6. a. 277.8 nm. b. 228.4 nm. c. 259.5 nm. d. 211.4 nm.

7. 25 min.

8. a. 456 nm.   b. 29.2 min. c. 292.2 nm.

9. 29°.

10. 38.7° at 196 nm.

11. 196 nm.

12. a. 318.9 nm. b. 255 nm.

13. Yes.

14. a. 13.3. b. .096. c. .2552.

15. a. .0893. b. .342.

14
RELIABILITY

The complex electronic systems that emerged from WWII offered revolutionary capabilities; capabilities compromised by difficulties in keeping the systems operational. The result was a formal emphasis on reliability in their procurement and operation. The same formal concern for reliability, and safety, has been an integral part of the development and employment of complex systems of all descriptions in the postwar era. This chapter is a brief introduction to OA modeling techniques that support the achievement of system reliability and safety.

The premise of OA applied to the reliability of a system is that the potential for effective performance from a system must be complemented by assurance that the system will be *available* when needed, that it will be *reliable* in the execution of its mission when used, and that it can be *maintained* to perpetuate its availability and reliability.

In a technical sense the **availability** of a system is the probability that the system will be found in a satisfactory condition (functioning, operational, "up") at a moment in time when a demand for its services occurs.

In the same sense the **reliability** of a system is the probability that the system will function throughout a period of operation in a service environment or over the course of a specified mission.

The **maintainability** of a system is not a probability, but rather an amalgam of considerations ranging from design for easy fault diagnosis and ready access, to parts needing frequent service or replacement, to a logistics program that assures adequate sparing and provision for field and depot level repairs.

Operational availability and mission reliability are especially critical for tactical military systems. Their achievement is an essential goal in the design, testing, procurement, and operational evaluation of any developing system. Design for maintainability, including planning logistics support, is a vital concurrent activity.

A great deal has and can be said about each of the topics referred to above. The scope of this chapter is much more limited. It introduces some basic mathematical modeling which supports the specification and demonstration of each of these "ilities."

The chapter begins in 1401 with a discussion of life distributions, the no-wear interpretation of exponential distributions, and modeling exposure to service environments with failure rates. In 1402 there is a discussion of mean time to failure and how it relates to the probability of mission survival for exponential distributions, followed in 1403 by an introduction to classes of life distributions that model wearout and how wearout distributions relate to mean time to failure. Modeling survival probabilities over mission profiles with continuous failure rate phases and discrete shock phases is treated in 1404. Series, parallel, and other block diagrammable systems, and their reliability functions, are discussed in 1405, followed in 1406 by a discussion of survival functions, failure rates, and mean times to failure for these systems in a continuous service environment. In 1407 the fault/success tree description of these systems is described. The effect of retrial redundancy is indicated in 1408. In 1409 standby redundancy and sparing are discussed, and the synthesis of block diagrammable systems and standby redundancy is illustrated in 1410.

1401   From Life Distributions to Failure Rates, and the No-Wear Example

The survival of a device exposed to a service environment depends on two factors, one the innate qualities of the device, which may reflect randomness in the processes that created it, and the other the random stresses present in its service environment.

One of the simplest operational scenarios that can be considered is a functioning device operated without interruption in some service environment until it fails. In this scenario the **life**, or equivalently, **time to failure**, T, of the device is a random variable that is nonnegative in the sense that $\Pr\{T \geq 0\} = 1$. The probability that a device survives an exposure (mission) of duration t is described by its **survival function** $\overline{F}$, where $\overline{F} = \Pr\{T > t\}$, $t \geq 0$. The fact that failure times are nonnegative allows the convention that failure probability is confined to the nonnegative real line so that descriptors of **life distributions** such as survival functions need not be specified for negative values of t. The notation $\overline{F}$ for a survival function is used because $\overline{F}$ is the complement $1 - F$ of the customary distribution function F.

One of the simplest operational environments that can be considered is one in which continuous stresses are present, with no scheduled shock events. In this case it is reasonable to suppose that the probability distribution for T can be described by a **failure** (probability). Given a failure density f, the survival function, $\overline{F}$, for the device is related to f by

$$\overline{F}(t) = \Pr\{T > t\} = \int_t^\infty f(s)\, ds, \ t > 0.$$

The probability that the device survives a mission of duration t is the probability that its inevitable failure occurs sometime after t. A survival function $\overline{F}$ generated from a failure density

f starts with $\overline{F}(0) = 1$, and decays continuously to zero as t increases to infinity. The formula for recovering a failure density f from a survival function $\overline{F}$ is

$$f(t) = -\frac{d}{dt} \int_t^\infty f(s) \, ds = -\overline{F}'(t), \; t \geq 0.$$

The most basic life distribution considered in reliability theory and practice is the **exponential** distribution, which has the failure density

$$f(t) = \lambda e^{-\lambda t}, \; t \geq 0$$

and the survival function

$$\overline{F}(t) = \int_t^\infty \lambda e^{-\lambda s} \, ds = e^{-\lambda t}, \; t \geq 0.$$

The parameter λ in the exponential distribution is assumed to be strictly positive. The importance of the family of exponential distributions stems from their memoryless property (see A22 of Appendix A) which says that a device with an exponential life distribution that has survived to any age s has the same probability of surviving an arbitrary additional time t as a new device has of surviving to age t. In the reliability context the memoryless property can be interpreted as a **no-wear** property. Aging in a service environment neither decreases or increases the survival potential of a no-wear device.

The memoryless property is characterized by the equation

$$\overline{F}(x + t) = \Pr\{T > s + t\} = \Pr\{T > s\} \Pr\{T > t\} = \overline{F}(s) \, \overline{F}(t), \; s \geq 0, \, t \geq 0.$$

Arranged in this format the property says that the probability of completing a mission of duration $s + t$ with a memoryless device is the same with or without a preventive maintenance "pit stop" at time s to restore the device or replace it with a new counterpart. When it can be recognized that the exposure of a device is memoryless, it can be shown that its life distribution must be in the exponential class, extended by two special boundary cases $\overline{F}(0) \equiv 0$ and $\overline{F}(\infty) \equiv 0$.

Another way of describing a life distribution is by its **cumulative hazard function** R, defined explicitly and implicitly by

$$R(t) = -\ln \overline{F}(t), \; \overline{F}(t) = e^{-R(t)}, \; t \geq 0.$$

A hazard function R associated with a survival function which is generated from a failure density will start with $R = 0$ and increase continuously to infinity as t increases to infinity. The idea that cumulative hazard is zero for zero exposure, increases as exposure increases, and becomes infinite as exposure becomes infinite is part of what justifies the use of the semantically loaded name given to R, but the real justification is that $R(t) = \lambda t, \; t \geq 0$, for the memoryless exponential distributions. *This reflects the reasonable notion that if a device does not wear, its accumulation of hazard should be proportional to exposure.*

The rate at which hazard accumulates is the primary vehicle for modeling life distributions. The **hazard rate function** r, given by

$$r(t) = R'(t) = \frac{d}{dt}\left(-\ln \overline{F}(t)\right) = -\frac{1}{\overline{F}(t)} \overline{F}'(t) = \frac{f(t)}{\overline{F}(t)}, \; t \geq 0,$$

is the derivative of R. An alternate name for the hazard rate, which tends to be associated with the formula

$$r(t) = \frac{f(t)}{\bar{F}(t)}, \ t \geq 0,$$

is **failure rate**. The ratio at time t of a failure density $f(t)$ to its survival function $\bar{F}(t)$ can be interpreted as the conditional likelihood that failure occurs at time t, given survival to that time, a useful interpretation for modeling purposes.

For a device with a memoryless exponential distribution, the hazard/failure rate

$$r(t) = \frac{f(t)}{\bar{F}(t)} = \frac{\lambda e^{-\lambda t}}{e^{-\lambda t}} = \lambda, \ r(t) = R'(t) = \frac{d}{dt}\lambda t = \lambda,$$

is constant for all values of t, appropriately for a device which does not wear.

Given that a hazard rate has been developed, the process of deriving survival probabilities from it becomes of interest. This process starts with

$$R(t) - R(0) = \int_0^t R'(s)\,ds = \int_0^t r(s)\,ds,$$

and the boundary condition $R(0) = -\ln \bar{F}(0) = -\ln(1) = 0$, so that

$$R(t) = \int_0^t r(s)\,ds$$

and

$$\bar{F}(t) = e^{-R(t)} = \exp\left(-\int_0^t r(s)\,ds\right), \ r \geq 0.$$

Starting with a constant hazard rate $r(t) = \lambda$, $t \geq 0$, and applying the preceding formulas shows that a constant hazard rate leads to a no-wear exponential life distribution. This completes a chain of equivalencies:

memoryless (no-wear) $\Leftrightarrow$ *exponential life distribution* $\Leftrightarrow$ *constant failure rate.*

The process of computing the probability of surviving an exposure (mission) of duration t from an arbitrary failure rate is illustrated in Figure 14.1.

1402 Mean Time to Failure

There is a strong tradition in reliability measurement and specification to focus on the **mean time to failure** (MTTF) of devices. The mean time to failure of a device with a time to failure T is simply the standard expected value of T,

$$E[T] = \int_0^\infty t f(t)\,dt = \int_0^\infty \bar{F}(t)\,dt,$$

where f is the failure density for T, if one exists, and $\bar{F}(t)$ is the survival function. Computing $E[T]$ by integrating the survival function works for nonnegative random variables such as T, and does not depend on the existence of a density or any assumption beyond nonnegativity about the distribution of T. A general proof that *the expected value of a time to failure is the area under its survival function* is beyond the present scope, but a method of proof assuming the existence of a density is indicated in problem 5.

For the exponential distribution,

$$E[T] = \int_0^\infty t f(t)\,dt = \int_0^\infty \lambda t e^{-\lambda t}\,dt = \frac{1}{\lambda}, \ E[T] = \int_0^\infty \bar{F}(t)\,dt = \int_0^\infty e^{-\lambda t}\,dt = \frac{1}{\lambda}.$$

Using $\mu = 1/\lambda$ as a notation for the expected value of an exponential time to failure, its density and survival function can be reparameterized as

$$f(t) = \frac{1}{\mu} e^{-t/\mu}, \quad \bar{F}(t) = e^{-t/\mu}, \quad t \geq 0.$$

FIGURE 14.1. FROM FAILURE RATE TO PROBABILITY OF MISSION SUCCESS

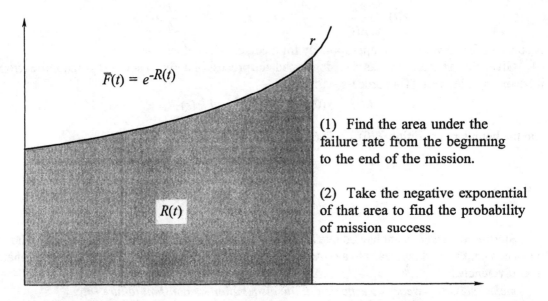

$\bar{F}(t) = e^{-R(t)}$

r

$R(t)$

(1) Find the area under the failure rate from the beginning to the end of the mission.

(2) Take the negative exponential of that area to find the probability of mission success.

Knowledge of the mean time to failure of an exponentially lived device is knowledge of everything there is to know about its reliability. This explains much of the focus on MTTFs in reliability practice.

Notice that the exponential survival function depends only on the ratio t/μ of exposure to MTTF or equivalently on the ratio μ/t of MTTF to exposure. *If the exponential distributions are used to translate mission reliability goals into MTTF specifications*, the necessary ratios of MTTF to mission duration to achieve high probabilities of mission success are illustrated in Figure 14.2.

1403   The Shape of Wearout

There are many uses of the exponential distributions in reliability theory and practice, but because they model no-wear, they are clearly not realistic for the life distributions of mechanical and electronic devices. These devices tend to wear out when exposed to the gravitational, vibrational, thermal, and other stresses present in a service environment.

Given that no-wear is characterized by a constant failure rate, a natural and historically initial way to model wearout is to assume that the hazard rate $r(t)$, $t \geq 0$, of a device is increasing as t increases. **Increasing** as used in this chapter really means nondecreasing, so an increasing hazard rate can run constant over periods of time in which stresses are absent, but cannot actually decrease. This approach leads to the class of **increasing hazard/failure rate** life distributions, often identified by the equivalent acronyms IHR and IFR.

FIGURE 14.2. EXPONENTIALLY SPECIFIED RATIOS OF MTTF TO MISSION DURATION

$\bar{F}(t) = e^{-t/\mu}$	$\dfrac{\mu}{t} = \dfrac{1}{-\ln \bar{F}(t)}$
.999	999.4999
.990	99.4992
.950	19.4957
.900	9.4912

A second way to model wearout is to assume that if a device that is wearing out and a device that is not wearing (in or out) happen to have the same probability of surviving a mission of duration t, then the device that is wearing out must have a larger probability of surviving missions of duration shorter than t and a smaller probability of surviving missions of duration longer than t. Under this approach, if $\bar{F}(s)$, $s \geq 0$, is the survival function of a device that is wearing out, and $\exp(-\lambda s)$, $s \geq 0$, is the survival function of a no-wear device, and if $\bar{F}(t) = \exp(-\lambda t)$, $t \geq 0$, for some t, then it must be that $\bar{F}(s) \geq \exp(-\lambda s)$ for $s \leq t$ and $\bar{F}(s) \leq \exp(-\lambda s)$ for $s \geq t$. The same approach expressed in terms of the cumulative hazard function of the device is that if $R(t) = \lambda t$ for some t, then $R(s) \leq \lambda s$ for $s \leq t$ and $R(s) \geq \lambda s$ for $s \geq t$. This approach leads to the class of **increasing hazard/failure rate average** life distributions, identified by the equivalent acronyms IHRA and IFRA.

The name for the IHRA life distributions is explained by the following derivation. For any $t > 0$ for which $R(t) > 0$, $R(t) = \lambda t$ for some $\lambda > 0$. Then if $s > t$, $R(s) \geq \lambda s$. It follows that

$$\frac{R(t)}{t} = \lambda \leq \frac{R(s)}{s},$$

that is, $R(t)/t$ increases as t increases; it can be observed that

$$\frac{R(t)}{t} = \frac{1}{t} \int_0^t r(s)\,ds$$

is the average of the hazard rate from 0 to t, for $t \geq 0$.

If a hazard rate r is increasing, then its average from 0 to t will be increasing, $t \geq 0$. Thus between the two characterizations of wearout embodied in the IHR and IHRA classes of life distributions, the IHR characterization is the stronger in the sense that an IHR distribution is automatically IHRA. The following comment on MTTFs applies under both approaches to characterizing wearout.

The comparison between an IHRA survival function and any exponential survival function that it happens to intersect is illustrated in Figure 14.3. Recalling that the MTTF of a device is the area under its survival function, *examination of* Figure 14.3 suggests that the necessary ratios of MTTF to mission duration for IHRA devices to achieve high mission reliabilities are not as dramatic as the ratios for no-wear devices shown in Figure 14.2.

FIGURE 14.3. COMPARISON OF IHRA AND EXPONENTIAL SURVIVAL FUNCTIONS

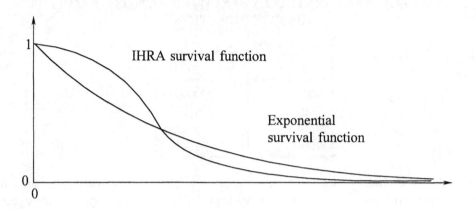

1404   Mission Profiles

A service scenario that frequently occurs in military contexts is a mission of finite duration which can be decomposed into disjoint phases with possibly very different stresses present in each phase. The missions of weapons systems and platforms performing tactical operations tend to have recognizable phase decompositions.

Some mission phases can be periods of time in which continuing stresses (e.g., cruise, approach, patrol), that can be modeled by a failure rate, are present. Other phases can consist of a shock (e.g., launch, firing, takeoff, touch-down) with a discrete probability that the shock is survived. A hypothetical mission profile resulting from decomposing a mission of duration d into a sequence of phases of both kinds is illustrated in Figure 14.4.

FIGURE 14.4. MISSION PROFILE EXAMPLE

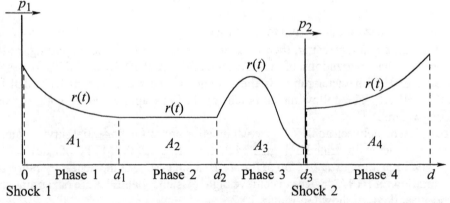

The times d_1, d_2, and d_3 are the boundary points between the continuous phases of the mission. Shock phases have no time duration. The discrete probabilities p_1 and p_2 are the conditional probabilities that shocks 1 and 2 are survived, given that the mission progresses satisfactorily to the point where they occur, and A_1, A_2, A_3, and A_4 are the areas under the failure rate function r for the continuous phases 1, 2, 3, and 4.

The reliability for the mission develops as follows:

Event	Probability
Survive shock 1	p_1
Survive to end of phase 1	$p_1 e^{-A_1}$
Survive to end of phase 2	$p_1 e^{-A_1} e^{-A_2}$
Survive to end of phase 3	$p_1 e^{-A_1} e^{-A_2} e^{-A_3}$
Survive through shock 2	$p_1 e^{-A_1} e^{-A_2} e^{-A_3} p_2$
Survive to end of phase 4	$p_1 e^{-A_1} e^{-A_2} e^{-A_3} p_2 e^{-A_4}$

Variable failure rates within mission phases can be replaced by area-preserving constant failure rates. This would simplify modeling practice in many instances.

1405 Block Diagrammable Systems

Block diagrams are a way of describing the relationship between the performance of the components in a system and the performance of the system. Components and systems are assumed capable of two states of performance, **functioning** and **failed**. Functioning means performing satisfactorily in the mission or service environment. Failure occurs when satisfactory performance stops. The performance of a system is assumed to be determined by the performance of its components. The relationship between the performance of the system and the performance of its components is the **performance logic** of the system.

The simplest examples are the two-component **series** and **parallel** systems. The performance logic for the series system is that the system functions only if both components function. The performance logic for the parallel system is that the system functions if at least one of the two components functions. Block diagrams for the series and parallel systems are shown below:

Series   Parallel

The blocks for components 1 and 2 are abstract representations of switches that are closed if the corresponding components are functioning, and are open if the corresponding components are failed. The system is functioning if there is a closed path between the two ends of the system network.

If components 1 and 2 perform *independently* with probabilities of functioning (reliabilities) p_1 and p_2, then the reliability (probability of functioning) of the series system is

$$p_1 \wedge p_2 = p_1 p_2.$$

and the reliability of the parallel system is

$$p_1 \vee p_2 = 1 - (1 - p_1)(1 - p_2) = p_1 + p_2 - p_1 p_2.$$

The second expression for the reliability of the parallel system is the complement of the probability that both components fail, and the third expression is the result of the inclusion-exclusion formula for the probability of the union of two events. The notation $p_1 \wedge p_2$ is for the **probabilistic "and"** of p_1 and p_2 and the notation $p_1 \vee p_2$ is for the **probabilistic "or"** of p_1 or p_2. The "or" notation is a usefully concise representation of either of its defining expressions, and one which can be readily implemented as a numerical operation. The "and" notation offers no advantage over its defining expression.

In the following examples of three-component systems, components 1, 2, and 3 will be assumed to perform independently with reliabilities p_1, p_2, and p_3, respectively.

The block diagram for the three-component series system is

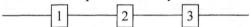

and its reliability is $p_1 p_2 p_3$. This reliability expression is immediately apparent, or formally derivable by considering components 1 and 2 as a series subsystem (module) acting independently in series with component 3.

The reliability of the system

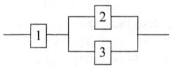

is $p_1(p_2 \vee p_3)$, arrived at by considering the parallel subsystem formed from components 2 and 3 as a module acting independently in series with component 1. The expression $p_1(p_2 \vee p_3)$ can be expanded into a polynomial in p_1, p_2, and p_3 using either of the expressions for $p_2 \vee p_3$, but the efficient way to compute a reliability for the system is to compute the reliability of the parallel module first, and then multiply by the reliability of component 1.

In a similar fashion the reliability of the system

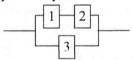

is $(p_1 p_2) \vee p_3$, an expression which corresponds to an efficient reliability computation for this system.

The reliability of the three-component parallel system

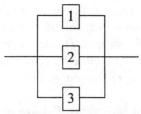

is $p_1 \vee p_2 \vee p_3$, reflecting that the reliability of the system can be found by treating any two components as a parallel module acting independently in parallel with the remaining component. Two very familiar expansions of $p_1 \vee p_2 \vee p_3$ are

$$p_1 \vee p_2 \vee p_3 = 1 - (1 - p_1)(1 - p_2)(1 - p_3)$$
$$= p_1 + p_2 + p_3 - p_1 p_2 - p_1 p_3 - p_2 p_3 + p_1 p_2 p_3.$$

The remaining three-component system to be considered is the "two-out-of-three" system

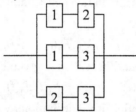

The performance logic for the two-out-of-three system is that the system functions if at least two of its three components are functioning. This performance logic is used in some redundant sensor and control systems which are considered to be functioning so long as two out of three identical components are providing consistent output. In interpreting the block diagram for the system it is necessary to view the two appearances of a component as a ganged switch. Both blocks representing component 1 are open together or closed together, and similarly for the blocks representing components 2 and 3.

The reliability of the two out of three system cannot be found by combining the reliabilities of two-component series modules, as might be suggested by the version of its block diagram shown above, because the appearance of the same components in the potential series modules prevents them from performing independently. The system's reliability can be found, for example, by conditioning on the functioning or failure of component 1. If component 1 is assumed to be functioning, the system block diagram reduces to components 2 and 3 acting in parallel with reliability $p_2 \vee p_3$. If component 1 is assumed to be failed, the system block diagram reduces to components 2 and 3 acting in series, with reliability $p_2 p_3$. The system reliability is then

$$p_1(p_2 \vee p_3) + (1 - p_1)p_2 p_3 = p_1 p_2 + p_1 p_3 + p_2 p_3 - 2 p_1 p_2 p_3.$$

The left side of the preceding identity is computationally simpler than the right-hand side, which is included because it is the commonly published expression.

The expressions for system reliabilities derived above are known as **system reliability functions.** It may seem simplistic to derive system reliabilities in the sometimes termed "one-shot" or "go-no-go" context. However, the one-shot component reliabilities can be component survival probabilities from an elaborate mission profile as considered in 1404, and if the assumption of component independence is reasonable, the component reliabilities can be inserted into the system reliability function to find a system survival probability for the mission.

The failure of any component in a series system causes the failure of the system. Each of the other systems considered in this section is **redundant** in the sense that some of their components can fail without causing the failure of the system. *Designing redundancy into a system is a powerful way to achieve high system reliability from reasonably reliable components, particularly if no single component failure can cause the failure of the system.*

1406   Examples of System Survival Functions, Failure Rates, and MTTFs

The two-component series and parallel systems can illustrate the process of computing survival functions, failure rates, and MTTFs for block diagrammable systems operating in the kind of service environment considered in 1401.

If the components perform independently and have the survival functions $\bar{F}_1$ and $\bar{F}_2$, then by inserting component survival functions into the system reliability functions, the survival function $\bar{F}_S$ for the series system is given by

$$\bar{F}_S(t) = \bar{F}_1(t)\bar{F}_2(t), \ t \geq 0,$$

and the survival function $\bar{F}_P$ for the parallel system is given by

$$\bar{F}_P = \bar{F}_1(t) + \bar{F}_2(t) - \bar{F}_1(t)\bar{F}_2(t), \ t \geq 0.$$

If the components have exponential life distributions with failure rates λ_1 and λ_2, then the survival function for the two-component series system is

$$\bar{F}_S = e^{-\lambda_1}e^{-\lambda_2} = e^{-(\lambda_1 + \lambda_2)t}, \ t \geq 0.$$

From this its cumulative hazard function R_S, found as minus the natural log of the survival function, is

$$R_S = (\lambda_1 + \lambda_2)t, \ t \geq 0,$$

and the derivative of the cumulative hazard function, the system failure rate r_S, is

$$r_S = \lambda_1 + \lambda_2, \ t \geq 0.$$

Two independent no-wear components in series produce a no-wear system whose failure rate is the sum of the two component failure rates.

The formula for r_S is easily understood. Because any component failure in a series system causes a system failure, if the system is functioning, all of its components must be functioning. If also its components are memoryless (do not wear), then the system is as-new and must be memoryless. It follows that the system must have an exponential life distribution. If each component failure *independently* produces a system failure, then the system failure rate will be the sum of the component failure rates.

Under the same assumptions of constant component failure rates and independence the survival function for the two-component parallel system is

$$\bar{F}_P(t) = e^{-\lambda_1 t} + e^{-\lambda_2 t} - e^{-(\lambda_1 + \lambda_2)t}, \ t \geq 0.$$

The failure density for the system, found as minus the derivative of the survival function, is

$$f_P(t) = \lambda_1 e^{-\lambda_1 t} + \lambda_2 e^{-\lambda_2 t} - (\lambda_1 + \lambda_2)e^{-(\lambda_1 + \lambda_2)t}, \ t \geq 0,$$

and its failure rate, found as the ratio of the failure density to the survival function, is

$$r_P(t) = \frac{\lambda_1 e^{-\lambda_1 t} + \lambda_2 e^{-\lambda_2 t} - (\lambda_1 + \lambda_2) e^{-(\lambda_1 + \lambda_2)t}}{e^{-\lambda_1 t} + e^{-\lambda_2 t} - e^{-(\lambda_1 + \lambda_2)t}}, \quad t \geq 0.$$

If the two component failure rates are equal ($\lambda_1 = \lambda_2 = \lambda$), then the system failure rate reduces to

$$r^P(t) = \frac{2\lambda(1 - e^{-\lambda t})}{2 - e^{-\lambda t}} = \frac{2\lambda}{\dfrac{1}{1 - e^{-\lambda t}} + 1}, \quad t \geq 0.$$

In this case it is easy to confirm that $r_P(0) = 0$, that $r_P(t)$ increases as t increases, and that $r_P(t)$ approaches λ as t approaches infinity. In this case the parallel system has an IHR distribution. In the case that the two component failure rates are not equal, it is only slightly more difficult to see that $r_P(0) = 0$ and that $r_P(t)$ approaches the smaller of the two component failure rates as t approaches infinity. In this case $r_P(t)$ increases to a level above the smaller of the two component failure rates and then decreases to its limit. In this case the life distribution of the parallel system is not IHR, but it can be shown to be IHRA.

In redundant systems such as the parallel system, components can fail without causing a system failure. Component attrition without system failure is a system-level form of wearout, and it is not surprising that imposing it on no-wear components results in a wearout system life distribution.

Recalling that the expected value of a time to failure is the area under its survival function from zero to infinity, and assuming independent component performance, the expected value of a two-component series system life T_S is

$$E[T_S] = \int_0^\infty \overline{F}_S(t)\, dt = \int_0^\infty \overline{F}_1(t)\overline{F}_2(t)\, dt.$$

The expected value for a two-component parallel system life T_P is

$$E[T_P] = \int_0^\infty \overline{F}_P(t)\, dt = \int_0^\infty \left(\overline{F}_1(t) + \overline{F}_2(t) - \overline{F}_1(t)\overline{F}_2(t)\right) dt.$$

If in addition the components have exponential life distributions with failure rates λ_1 and λ_2, then

$$E[T_S] = \int_0^\infty e^{-\lambda_1 t} e^{-\lambda_2 t}\, dt = \int_0^\infty e^{-(\lambda_1 + \lambda_2)t}\, dt = \frac{1}{\lambda_1 + \lambda_2},$$

and

$$E[T_P] = \int_0^\infty \left(e^{-\lambda_1 t} + e^{-\lambda_2 t} - e^{-(\lambda_1 + \lambda_2)t}\right) dt = \frac{1}{\lambda_1} + \frac{1}{\lambda_2} - \frac{1}{\lambda_1 + \lambda_2}.$$

Finally if $\mu_S = E[T_S]$ and $\mu_P = E[T_P]$ are the MTTFs of the series and parallel systems, and $\mu_1 = 1/\lambda_1$ and $\mu_2 = 1/\lambda_2$ are the MTTFs of the components, then

$$\mu_S = \frac{1}{\dfrac{1}{\mu_1} + \dfrac{1}{\mu_2}} = \frac{\mu_1 \mu_2}{\mu_1 + \mu_2},$$

and

$$\mu_P = \mu_1 + \mu_2 - \frac{\mu_1 \mu_2}{\mu_1 + \mu_2}.$$

These formulas have an interesting simplification when the components have the same constant failure rate so that $\mu_1 = \mu_2 = \mu$. Then $\mu_S = \mu/2$ and $\mu_p = 3\mu/2$.

It should be emphasized that the relationships between system MTTFs and component MTTFs derived here depend on the assumption that the component life distributions are exponential. There is no relationship between the MTTF of a block diagrammable system and the MTTFs of its components which is comparable to the reliability function relationship between a mission success probability for the system and the mission success probabilities for its components. Specifying MTTFs for the components of a system does not, in itself, result in a specification of an MTTF for the system, and a MTTF specification for a system cannot, without assumptions about component life distributions, be allocated into MTTF specifications for the components.

1407   Fault Trees

Modeling system performance logic by block diagrams started with post-WWII concerns about the reliability of avionics, computers, and other systems whose complexity resulted in reliability problems. The series/parallel switching symbolism employed reflected the contemporary implementation of logical functions by real or electronically emulated switches. Block diagrams relate system success to component successes because of a traditional focus of reliability modeling on success.

An interest in modeling the safety of complex systems arose at a time when the gate symbolism of solid state electronics had replaced the earlier switching symbolism. Safety analysis focuses on combinations of small failures that lead to a major failure. The net result was the **fault tree**, a modeling approach which can be applied in reliability analysis.

A two-component series system fails if at least one of its components fails. The fault tree for the series system processes the failure of components 1 and 2 through an "or" gate to produce a system failure, as follows (the overlines denote component and system failures):

A two-component parallel system fails if both of its components fail. The fault tree for the parallel system processes the failure of components 1 and 2 through an "and" gate to produce a system failure, as follows:

It is possible to represent the performance logic of the three-component systems discussed in 1405 by trees formed using "and" and "or" gates, and to similarly represent the performance logic of larger block diagrammable systems.

System success can be related to component successes using "and" and "or" gates, producing a **success tree.** Both fault and success trees have an interpretive advantage over block diagrams in that the explanatory boxes of flow charting can be inserted into the tree to explain the modeling of the system. A significant advantage of fault-oriented modeling is that it encourages carrying the analysis of the system to a level in which the "components" are the failure modes of the physical components of the system.

1408   Retrial Redundancy

In some mission contexts, for example the launch sequence for a spacecraft, it is possible to monitor each step of the process, repeat the step if necessary, or abort the mission for a total restart if appropriate. This type of **retrial redundancy** can be effective in increasing the probability of mission success in situations where the "parallel" redundancy modeled by block diagrammable systems cannot be employed.

The potential of retrial redundancy can be illustrated by a simple example. Suppose that the first trial of a mission is successful with probability p_1. If the first trial is unsuccessful, suppose that a second trial is successful with probability p_2. If both the first and second trials are unsuccessful, suppose that a third trial is successful with probability p_3. The probability of mission success is then

$$p_1 + (1 - p_1)p_2 + (1 - p_1)(1 - p_2)p_3 = p_1 + p_2 + p_3 - p_1p_2 - p_1p_3 - p_2p_3 + p_1p_2p_3,$$

as if the three trials were three components performing independently in parallel.

1409   Spares and Standby Systems

The simplest example of a system with standby redundancy is an **active** component in service backed up by a **spare** component in **cold standby**. A spare is a component that is intended to replace the active component when it fails, in order to extend the life of the system. Cold standby means that the spare is not subject to failure while it is waiting to take the place of the active component.

If the life of the active component is T_1, and the life of the spare, after activation, is T_2, then the life of the system is $T_1 + T_2$. If T_1 and T_2 are independent, then the survival function $\bar{F}_S$ for T_S is given by

$$\bar{F}_S(t) = \bar{F}_1(t) + \int_0^t \bar{F}_2(t - s)f_1(s)\,ds$$
$$= \bar{F}_2(t) + \int_0^t \bar{F}_1(t - s)f_2(s)\,ds, \ t \geq 0,$$

where $\bar{F}_1$ and f_1 are the survival function and density for T_1, and $\bar{F}_2$ and f_2 are the survival function and density for T_2. In the first equality above, $\bar{F}_1(t)$ is the probability that the active component survives to age t without the need to activate the spare. The integral is the totality of the disjoint events that the active component fails at age s with likelihood $f_1(s)$, and that the spare then replaces the active component and survives the remaining time $t - s$ until system age t. The second equality reflects the fact that $T_2 + T_1$ has the same probability distribution as $T_1 + T_2$, that in this particular scenario the roles of the active component and the spare are interchangeable.

If the active component and the spare have exponential life distributions with the same failure rate λ, the system survival function becomes

$$\bar{F}_S(t) = e^{-\lambda t} + \int_0^t e^{-\lambda(t - s)}\lambda e^{-\lambda s}\,ds$$
$$= (1 + \lambda t)e^{-\lambda t}, \ t \geq 0.$$

The derivation of a system survival function used above is readily modified to deal with some standard variations on the basic standby scenario. If the replacement of the active component by the spare is not certain, but rather occurs with a discrete probability p, the survival function for the system is given by

$$\bar{F}_S(t) = \bar{F}_1(t) + \int_0^t p\bar{F}_2(t - s)f_1(s)\,ds.$$

Now the identification of which component is active and which is the spare is relevant. Again if both components are exponentially distributed with failure rate λ, the system survival function becomes

$$\bar{F}_S(t) = e^{-\lambda t} + \int_0^t p e^{-\lambda(t - s)}\lambda e^{-\lambda s}\,ds$$

$$= (1 - p\lambda t)e^{-\lambda t}, \; t \geq 0.$$

The spare can be in **warm standby**, operating with a reduced load prior to assuming the active role and load. If the active failure rate is a constant λ, and the standby failure rate is a constant η, presumably less than λ, then the survival function for the system is given by

$$\bar{F}_S(t) = e^{-\lambda t} + \int_0^t e^{-\eta s}e^{-\lambda(t - s)}\lambda e^{-\lambda s}\,ds$$

$$= e^{-\lambda t} + e^{-\lambda t}\frac{\lambda}{\eta}(1 - e^{-\eta t}), \; t \geq 0.$$

The term $e^{-\eta s}$ in the integral is the probability that the spare survives to age s at the standby failure rate before assuming the active failure rate and going on to survive to age t with probability $e^{-\lambda(t - s)}$.

It is interesting to note that if the warm standby failure rate η is the same as the active failure rate λ the system survival function reduces to

$$\bar{F}_S(t) = e^{-\lambda t} + e^{-\lambda t} - e^{-2\lambda t}, \; t \geq 0.$$

This is the survival function for two independent exponential λ components operating in parallel, obtained by substituting component exponential survival functions into the reliability function for the two-component parallel system. If the warm standby failure rate η approaches zero, the system survival function approaches $(1 + \lambda t)e^{-\lambda t}$, the result obtained for the cold standby case. It is tempting to think of block diagrams and fault trees as modeling *systems*, and standby sparing as modeling *logistics*, but the preceding example shows how the boundary between the two can be blurred.

1410   Further Examples of Survival Function Modeling

Two examples will suffice to illustrate the modeling of survival functions in mission scenarios where the performance logic of block diagrammable systems is complicated by shifts in component stress levels and the availability of spares. In these examples it is assumed that the failure rates involved are constant, an assumption which may be an acceptable approximation for some reasonably short mission durations.

Suppose that two components operate independently in parallel until the first of the two to fail does so. After the first component failure the surviving component carries on alone. While both components are functioning they share a load and each component experiences the same failure rate λ_1. After the failure of the first component, the surviving component assumes the full load and experiences a presumably larger failure rate λ_2. The survival function for a mission of duration t is given by

$$\overline{F}(t) = e^{-2\lambda_1 t} + \int_0^t e^{-\lambda_2(t-s)} 2\lambda_1 e^{-2\lambda_1 s} ds$$

$$= e^{-2\lambda_1 t} + e^{-\lambda_2 t} \frac{2\lambda_1}{2\lambda_1 - \lambda_2}\left(1 - e^{-(2\lambda_1 - \lambda_2)t}\right), \ t \geq 0.$$

The term $e^{-2\lambda_1 t}$ in the formulation is the (series) probability that both components survive the mission. The factor $2\lambda_1 e^{-2\lambda_1 s}$ in the integral is the likelihood (failure density for the series system) that the first component failure occurs at time s in the course of the mission. The factor $e^{-\lambda_2(t-s)}$ in the integral is the probability that the surviving component completes the balance of the mission. Note that when $\lambda_1 = \lambda_2 = \lambda$ the result reduces to the survival function for two components with constant failure rate λ operating independently in parallel.

Suppose that two components operate independently in series with the same failure rate λ and that there is a single spare available in cold standby to replace the first of the two components to fail. The spare will operate at failure rate λ when it enters active service. The survival function for a mission of duration t is

$$\overline{F}(t) = e^{-2\lambda t} + \int_0^t e^{-2\lambda(t-s)} 2\lambda e^{-2\lambda s} ds$$

$$= (1 + 2\lambda t)e^{-2\lambda t}, \ t \geq 0.$$

The term $e^{-2\lambda t}$ in the formulation is the probability that the original series system survives the mission. The factor $2\lambda e^{-2\lambda s}$ in the integral is the likelihood that the first component failure occurs at time s in the course of the mission. The factor $e^{-2\lambda(t-s)}$ is the probability that the restored series system completes the mission. The result is consistent with the application of the simple cold standby survival function formula found in 1409 for an active component and a spare which both have exponential life distributions with failure rate 2λ.

1411   Other Literature and History

The predominant emphasis in reliability research and development in post-WWII years came from military electronics, primarily airborne. The unreliability of avionics in the early 1950s emerged as a serious threat to defense readiness. Influential documents of that era which pointed up the general problems included Carhart [1] and Mettler [2] for the USAF and Boodman [3] for the USN. Among the major sources of the problem were the predominance of vacuum tubes in electronics, equipment complexity, focus on component rather than system design, inadequate testing, and the lack of quantitative specification of reliability based on mission needs. Reference [2] was particularly strong on the need for incorporation of reliability in the general system analysis of a developmental system, along with other contributors to mission success.

A comprehensive study of the problem was undertaken in 1956-57 by nine DoD and industry task groups sponsored by the Advisory Group on Reliability of Electronic Equipment (AGREE), chartered by the Assistant Secretary of Defense (Research and Engineering). The result was the now famous AGREE report [4]. The first of these task groups addressed the quantitative specification problem and put numerical reliability requirements on various types of non-missile electronics. In the mid-1950s strategic and other missiles posed greatly increased demands on reliability, and since then the need has continued to incorporate reliability into the evolution of electronics, computers, command and control systems, weaponry, and platforms.

A feel for the state of the reliability art in the postwar era can be obtained from the ARINC book on reliability engineering [5] and from the historical remarks in the introductory chapters of Barlow and Proschan [6] and Shooman [7].

The essence of the failure rate concept applied to a population is that it is the instantaneous death rate in the population of survivors of a particular age. The use of failure rates can be traced, at least, back to Gompertz [8], who used the concept deterministically to model human mortality in the early days of life insurance underwriting. Gompertz referred to failure rate as the **force of mortality**. Awareness of the exponential distribution as the model for memoryless waiting times is associated with the earliest work on Poisson processes in traffic and queuing contexts.

The use of MTTFs to specify and demonstrate system and component reliabilities has been strongly embedded in reliability research and practice. While MTTFs have undisputed relevance in some operational scenarios, in other operational scenarios inconsistencies and potential misdirection of effort have resulted from a naive focus on MTTFs.

The IHR class of life distributions was the first class to be studied as a stochastic description of wearout (Barlow and Proschan [6]). The notion that if all the components in a system are wearing out, then the system should wear out, led to the expansion of the IHR class to include the IHRA distributions (Birnbaum, Esary, and Marshall [9]). A variety of related wear-out and wear-in classes have also been studied.

Modeling the dependence of the performance of a system on the performance of its components by a binary performance logic was the norm in post-WWII reliability practice and in early theoretical studies of the benefits of redundancy (von Neumann [10] and Moore and Shannon [11]). The manifestations of Boolean algebra, other than block diagrams and fault trees, that have been used to describe binary performance logics defy enumeration, but truth tables, set theory, and indicator variables are notable examples. The two and three component systems in 1405 are examples of **coherent** systems, roughly systems that can be modeled with block diagrams with series and parallel paths or fault trees using "and" and "or" gates. More precisely a coherent system is one whose performance indicator variable is a monotone increasing function of its component performance indicator variables. An account of the basic theory of coherent systems can be found in the first two chapters of Barlow and Proschan [12], in the reliability chapters of Hillier and Lieberman [13] and Ross [14], and in Henly and Kumamoto [15].

Modeling of standby redundancy can be found in a variety of sources in a variety of styles. The Soviet literature, exemplified by Gnedenko, Belyayev, and Solovyev [16] and Ushakov [17], is strong in this area.

The study of life testing and reliability demonstration, though not discussed here, has developed alongside the probabilistic modeling of systems. References include the early paper of Epstein and Sobel [18] and the books of Mann, Schafer, and Singpurwalla [19], Bain and Engelhardt [20], and Lawless [21].

[1]   Carhart, Richard R. "A Survey of the Current Status of the Reliability Problem." *Research Memorandum* 1131. Santa Monica, CA: The RAND Corporation, August 1953.

[2]   Mettler, Reuben F. "Bombing and Navigation Systems for Manned Strategic Aircraft." *RDB*274/1, February 1955.

[3] Boodman, David M. "The Reliability of Airborne Radar Equipment." *Operations Research* 1 (1953): 39-45.

[4] Advisory Group on the Reliability of Electronic Equipment. *Reliability of Military Electronic Equipment.* Office of the Assistant Secretary of Defense (Research and Engineering), June, 1957.

[5] ARINC Research Corporation. *Reliability Engineering* (Edited by William H. Von Alven). Englewood Cliffs, NJ: Prentice-Hall, 1964.

[6] Barlow, Richard E., and Frank Proschan. *Mathematical Theory of Reliability*. New York, NY: Wiley, 1965.

[7] Shooman, Martin L. *Probabilistic Reliability: An Engineering Approach.* New York, NY: McGraw-Hill, 1968.

[8] Gompertz, Benjamin. "On the Nature of the Function Expressive of the Law of Human Mortality." *Philosophical Transactions of the Royal Society of London* 115 (1825): 513-585.

[9] Birnbaum, Z. W., J.D. Esary, and A.W. Marshall "Stochastic Characterization of Wearout for Components and Systems." *Annals of Mathematical Statistics* 37 (1966): 816-825.

[10] von Neumann, J. "Probabilistic Logics and the Synthesis of Reliable Organisms from Unreliable Components." *Automata Studies*, 43-98, *Annals of Mathematical Studies* 34 (1956).

[11] Moore, Edward F., and Claude E. Shannon, "Reliable Circuits Using Less Reliable Relays." *Journal of the Franklin Institute* 262 (1956): 191-208 and 281-297.

[12] Barlow, Richard E., and Frank Proschan,. *Statistical Theory of Reliability and Life Testing, Probability Models*. New York, NY: Holt, Rinehart, and Winston, 1975.

[13] Hillier, Frederick S., and Gerald J. Lieberman, *Introduction to Operations Research*. 3rd Edition. San Francisco, CA: Holden-Day, 1980.

[14] Ross, Sheldon M. *Introduction to Probability Models*. 5th Edition. San Diego, CA: Academic Press, 1993.

[15] Henly, Ernest J., and Hiromitsu Kumamoto. *Designing for Reliability and Safety Control.* Englewood Cliffs, NJ: Prentice Hall, 1985.

[16] Gnedenko, B. V.; Y. K. Belyayev; and A. D. Solovyev. *Mathematical Methods of Reliability Theory* (Translated by Richard E. Barlow). New York, NY: Academic Press, 1969.

[17] Ushakov, Igor A. *Handbook of Reliability Engineering* (Updated American edition by Igor A. Ushakov and Robert A. Harrison). New York, NY: Wiley, 1994.

[18] Epstein, Benjamin, and Milton Sobel. "Life Testing." *Journal of the American Statistical Association* 48 (1953): 486-502.

[19] Mann, Nancy R.; Ray E. Schafer; and Nozer D. Singpurwalla. *Methods for Statistical Analysis of Reliability and Life Data*. New York, NY: Wiley, 1974.

[20] Bain, Lee J., and Max Engelhardt. *Statistical Analysis of Reliability and Life-Testing Models, Theory and Methods*. 2nd Edition. New York, NY: Wiley, 1982.

[21] Lawless, J. F. *Statistical Models and Methods for Lifetime Data*. New York: Wiley, 1982.

Problems

1. The nominal mission for a reconnaissance sensor is of duration d hours. It is anticipated that 60

percent of the time during the mission the sensor will be passive with the passive failure rate λ_p failures per hour, and that for the remaining 40 percent of the time the sensor will be active with the active failure rate λ_A failures per hour. Find the probability of no sensor failure during a nominal mission. Does it matter if the period of active operation occurs at the beginning of the mission, at the end, or in fragments throughout the mission?

2. The two-parameter Weibull family of life distributions is often assumed in reliability modeling and data analysis. The survival function for a Weibull time to failure is

$$\overline{F}(t) = e^{-(\lambda t)^{\alpha}}, \; t \geq 0,$$

where the parameters λ and α are positive. Find the density, failure rate, and MTTF for a Weibull time to failure. What happens when $\alpha = 1$? Are there values of α for which a Weibull failure rate is increasing? For which a Weibull failure rate is decreasing?

3. Given a time to failure T, the transformation $S = aT$, $a > 0$, is a **change of scale**. It creates a version S of the failure time measured in different units. Given a survival function $\overline{F}_T(t)$, $t \geq 0$, a failure density $f_T(t)$, $t \geq 0$, and a failure rate $r_T(t)$, $t \geq 0$, for T, find corresponding expressions for the survival function $\overline{F}_S(s)$, $s \geq 0$, the failure density $f_S(s)$, $s \geq 0$, and the failure rate $r_S(s)$, $s \geq 0$, for S. What is the effect of a change of scale on a Weibull time to failure T with **shape** parameter α and **scale** parameter λ?

4. The failure rate for a continuously operating device is a constant λ failures per hour. Find the failure rate for the device in failures per minute. The failure rate for another device is a constant λ failures per operating hour. A proportion p of calendar hours are operating hours. Find the failure rate for the device in failures per calendar hour. Still yet another device is installed on a moving platform. If the failure rate for the device is a constant λ failures per hour while the platform is moving, and the velocity of the moving platform is v miles per hour, find the failure rate for the device in failures per mile.

5. Assuming that a time to failure T has a density f, start with the familiar formula for MTTF

$$E[T] = \int_0^{\infty} t f(t) \, dt,$$

make the substitution,

$$t = \int_0^t ds,$$

interchange the order of integration and see what results.

6. Suppose that a time to failure T has the survival function

$$\overline{F}(t) = \frac{1}{1 + \lambda t}, \; t \geq 0,$$

where $\lambda > 0$.

a. Find the density for T.

b. Find the MTTF for T from the formula $E[T] = \int_0^\infty \overline{F}(t)\,dt$.

7. Communications between Facility A and Facility B are routed through Relay Location R. There are two links from A to R, AR1 and AR2. There are also two links from R to B, RB1 and RB2. In configuring R it is possible to connect AR1 to BR1 only and to connect AR2 to BR2 only. It is also possible to connect both AR1 and AR2 to BR1 and to simultaneously connect both AR1 and AR2 to BR2. Treating the links as the components subject to failure decide which configuration option provides the most reliable communication linkage between A and B. Were probability computations necessary to reach your conclusion, or was a choice possible from just the performance logics for the two options?

8. A **path set** of a coherent system is any set of components which by all functioning cause the system to function. A **minimal path set** is a path set which is irreducible in the sense that no component in it can cease to function if the system is to continue to function. A **cut set** of a coherent system is any set of components which by all failing cause the system to fail. A **minimal cut set** is a cut set which is irreducible in the sense that no component in it can resume functioning without causing the system to resume functioning. Find the minimal path sets and minimal cut sets for the three component systems considered in 1405.

9. Assume that each of the components in the three-component systems considered in 1405 fails independently and has reliability .9. Compute the reliability of each system. Observe which system reliabilities are greater than the assumed component reliability .9. What explanatory characteristic do those systems have in common? Now assume that the components fail independently and have reliability .1. Compute the reliability of each system. Observe which system reliabilities are less than the assumed component reliability .1. What explanatory characteristic do those systems have in common?

10. Suppose that a device in continuous service with a constant failure rate λ is backed up by two spares in cold standby. As failures occur the spares will be installed in succession to extend system life. When installed the spares will be subject to the same constant failure rate λ as the original device. Find the survival function for the life of this system. Find the failure density and failure rate for the system. What is the initial (at time zero) value of the system failure rate? What is the terminal (as time approaches infinity) value of the system failure rate? What is the behavior of the system failure rate as time varies from zero to infinity?

11. Suppose that the components in a two-component series system fail independently with constant failure rates λ_1 for component 1 and λ_2 for component 2. Suppose also that each component is backed by a dedicated spare that will replace it from cold standby as soon as it fails, and will then operate at the same component failure rate. Find the survival function for the system, allowing for the effect of the spares.

12. A four-wheeled vehicle is to make a transit over rough, sharp terrain of length d miles. The

vehicle mounts a tire on each wheel, and carries a single spare tire. The spare will be used to replace the first of the four mounted tires to experience a failure. Assume that mounted tires fail independently, each with the same constant failure rate λ, and that the spare is in cold standby until it is deployed, when it also fails at the constant rate λ. Find the probability that the original tires and the spare are sufficient to complete the transit. Are the assumptions realistic that mounted tires fail independently and at the same constant failure rate over the course of the transit?

Answers to Problems

1. $\exp(-(.6\lambda_P + .4\lambda_A)d)$; No.

2. $f(t) = \alpha\lambda^\alpha t^{\alpha - 1}e^{-(\lambda t)^\alpha}$, $t \geq 0$; $r(t) = \alpha\lambda^\alpha t^{\alpha - 1}$, $t \geq 0$; $E[T] = \Gamma\left(\dfrac{1}{\alpha}\right) / \alpha\lambda$; Increasing for $\alpha \geq 1$, decreasing for $\alpha \leq 1$.

3. $\overline{F}_S(s) = \overline{F}_T\left(\dfrac{s}{a}\right)$; $f_S(s) = \dfrac{1}{a}f_T\left(\dfrac{s}{a}\right)$; $r_S(s) = \dfrac{1}{a}r_T\left(\dfrac{s}{a}\right)$; The transformed time S has a Weibull distribution with the same shape parameter α and a new scale parameter λ/a, which explains the names for the parameters.

4. $\lambda/60$; λp; λ/v.

5. $E[T] = \displaystyle\int_0^\infty tf(t)\,dt = \int_0^\infty \int_0^t f(t)\,ds\,dt = \int_0^\infty \int_s^\infty f(t)\,dt\,ds = \int_0^\infty \overline{F}(s)\,ds.$

6. $\dfrac{\lambda}{(1 + \lambda t)^2}$, $t \geq 0$. In both cases the integrals diverge to infinity.

7. That cross-connecting both AR links to both BR links provides greater reliability is clear from block diagrams (or fault trees) for the two options. In the first option AR1 and BR1 are in series, AR2 and BR2 are in series, and these series modules are in parallel. In the second option AR1 and AR2 are in parallel, BR1 and BR2 are in parallel, and these parallel modules are in series. Every path from A to B in the first option is a path from A to B in the second option, and there are additional paths in the second option. This means that the second option will be more reliable for whatever joint probabilities apply to the failure of the links. On the other hand, when all links are functioning, the second option might provide greater capacity.

8. In the order the systems are presented in 1405, the minimal path sets are: {1, 2, 3}, {1, 2} and {1, 3}, (1, 2} and {3}, {1} and {2} and {3}, {1, 2} and {1, 3}and {2, 3}. In the same order the minimal cut sets are: {1} and {2} and {3}, {1} and {2, 3}, {1, 3} and {2, 3}, {1, 2, 3}, {1, 2} and {1, 3} and {2, 3}.

9. In the order the systems are presented in 1405, for component reliability .9 the system reliabilities

are: .729, .891, .981, .999, .972. None of the systems whose reliability is greater than .9 has a cut set with just one component. In the same order, for component reliability .1 the system reliabilities are: .001, .019, .109, .271, .028. None of the systems whose reliability is less than .1 has a path set with just one component.

10. $(1 + \lambda t + \lambda^2 t^2 / 2)e^{-\lambda t}$; 0; λ; System failure rate increases from 0 to λ.

11. $(1 + \lambda_1 t)e^{-\lambda_1 t}(1 + \lambda_2 t)e^{-\lambda_2 t}$, $t \geq 0$.

12. $(1 + 4\lambda d)e^{-4\lambda d}$; Not completely, but the calculation can be useful.

APPENDIX A
PROBABILITY–THE MATHEMATICS
OF UNCERTAINTY

The key phrase appearing in many definitions of OA is *quantitative basis for decision-making*. It is therefore not surprising to find that solving a problem by the OA method usually involves the judicious application of some aspect of mathematics. This is true of both theoretical and empirical models for problem solving, and one finds both classical and modern mathematics being applied extensively in the discipline.

The single most useful field of mathematics in the analysis of naval operational problems is **mathematical probability theory**. In fact, the concepts of probability are indispensable to objective, analytical treatment of those problems. For diverse as is the field of naval operations, there is one factor common throughout. That one factor is *uncertainty*. Not every missile leaves the launcher when the firing key is pressed. Not every attack pilot is able to find and bomb the target. Not every enemy aircraft within theoretical range of the air search radar produces a return on the scope. The list of cases is practically boundless. Whatever the area of naval operations, *uncertainty* is the one quality invariably present. One may deal analytically with these essentially random events thanks to that way of thinking called probability theory.

A closely related field is **mathematical statistics**, which is application of probability theory to making inferences from empirical data.

Accordingly, this appendix is devoted to a coverage of the fundamental concepts of probability theory along with some fundamentals of statistics, with particular emphasis given to those aspects which will prove most useful to naval OA.

A01   Calculation of Simple Probabilities

It is possible to approximate experimentally the probability of a simple event, say the probability of a coin turning up heads, by counting the number of heads which occur in n tosses and dividing by the total number of tosses. As the number of tosses becomes larger and larger, this ratio approaches closer and closer to the precise value of the desired probability. In a similar manner, it would be possible to calculate the probabilities associated with the faces of a die, the probability of a newborn baby being a boy, and so on. Symbolically, the true probability of an event is defined as follows:

$$\Pr\{\text{event}\} = \lim_{n \to \infty} \left(\frac{\text{number of occurrences of the event in } n \text{ trials}}{\text{total number of trials, } n} \right).$$

In the special case where all the **possible outcomes** of a trial are equally likely, the probability of an event may be expressed as

$$\Pr\{\text{event}\} = \frac{\text{number of possible outcomes which constitute the event}}{\text{total number of possible outcomes}}. \qquad \text{(A-1)}$$

The simplification represented by (A-1) applies to all simple chance devices such as fair coins, fair dice, and so forth, and to many of the more common probabilistic situations. For example, consider the probability of a three turning up when a die is tossed:

$$\Pr\{\text{outcome is 3}\} = \frac{\text{number of possible outcomes which constitute a 3}}{\text{total number of possible outcomes}} = \frac{1}{6}.$$

Expression (A-1) is particularly useful in developing the so-called **laws of probability**, which are simply rules for calculating the probabilities of **compound events** in terms of known probabilities of the **simple events** involved. In terms of the die example, one might refer to the rolling of a 3 as a simple event, say event A. Similarly, the rolling of a 4 might be referred to as a simple event, say event B. However, dealing with two dice one would generally refer to the rolling of a seven as a compound event, C, involving two simple events, A and B. It is possible to derive the probabilistic expression for this particular compound event, as well as for other types of compound events, in terms of the simple probabilities, $\Pr\{A\}$ and $\Pr\{B\}$.

The statements made concerning probability have been to a large extent intuitive. It is possible, however, to develop the theory in a completely abstract manner by invoking the mathematics of **set theory**. The set theoretic development was first formulated by the Russian probabilist Kolmogorov in 1933. Because set theory is so useful in probability theory, some fundamentals of set theory are given in the next section in abstraction.

A02   Basic Set Theory

The following definitions embody basics of set theory:

a.   A **set** is a well-defined collection of entities or **elements.**
b.   A set A is a **subset** of a set B, in symbols $A \subseteq B$, if every element of A is also an element of B.

c. A **Venn diagram** is a convenient graphical method for representing various sets and subsets. As an example of its use, consider the simple Venn diagram in Figure A.1, which represents a set S of nine elements, and two overlapping subsets, A and B, each containing two of these elements. This diagram is also useful for illustrating some of the basic types of sets and subsets.

FIGURE A.1. A SIMPLE VENN DIAGRAM

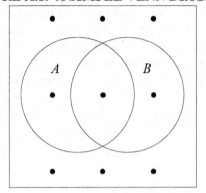

d. The **universal set** is the set containing *all* elements and is denoted by U.
e. The **null set** is the set containing *no* elements at all and is denoted by ϕ.
f. The **intersection** of two sets A and B, in symbols $A \cap B$, is defined as the set of those elements which are common to both A and B. In the example, there is one element in the intersection of A and B. Note that always $A \cap \phi = \phi$ and $A \cap U = A$.
g. The **union** of two sets A and B, in symbols $A \cup B$, is defined as the set of those elements which are in either A or B. In the example, there are three elements in $A \cup B$. Note that always $A \cup U = U$ and $A \cup \phi = A$.
h. The **complement** of a set A, denoted by the symbol $\overline{A}$, is defined as the set of all elements in U *not* in A. In the example there are seven elements in $\overline{A}$. The complement of U is ϕ.
i. Two sets, A and B, are said to be **disjoint** if they have no elements in common, i.e., if $A \cap B = \phi$.

A03   Probability Sample Space

A **sample space** is the collection of all possible outcomes of an experiment. In terms of the above terminology, one thinks of the sample space as a universal set U, and each subset of U is an event. The term **sample point** is used to represent an individual outcome in the sample space. When an event is thought of as a set of possible outcomes in this manner, it then becomes quite easy to express its probability. For example, consider again the probability of a 3 turning up when a die is tossed. The sample space contains six outcomes, each assumed equally likely, i.e., $U = \{1, 2, 3, 4, 5, 6\}$; this expresses a set, but the set may be thought of as an event by inserting the phrase "the outcome is one of the numbers." Let A be the event that a 3 is tossed, i.e., $A = \{3\}$, a subset of U. Let $\Pr\{A\}$ represent the probability that the event A occurs and $n(A)$ represent the number of outcomes in the event A. (As a small point, if $\{3\}$ is substituted for A in "$\Pr\{A\}$," the second pair of "$\{\}$" is omitted.) The possible outcomes can be represented by the Venn diagram in Figure A.2.

The probability of a 3 is then

$$\Pr\{3\} = \Pr\{A\} = \frac{\text{number of outcomes in } A}{\text{total number of outcomes}} = \frac{n(A)}{n(U)} = \frac{1}{6}.$$

FIGURE A.2. VENN DIAGRAM FOR PROBABILITY EXAMPLE

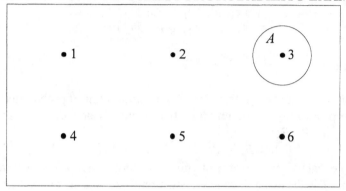

Using the concepts and definitions discussed thus far, the following basic relationships can be derived for any two events A and B:

a.   range of values:

$$0 \le \Pr\{A\} \le 1;$$

b.   complements:

$$\Pr\{\overline{A}\} = 1 - \Pr\{A\},$$
$$\Pr\{A \cap \overline{A}\} = \Pr\{\phi\} = 0,$$
$$\Pr\{A \cup \overline{A}\} = \Pr\{U\} = 1;$$

c.   unions:

$$\Pr\{A \cup B\} = \Pr\{A\} + \Pr\{B\} - \Pr\{A \cap B\},$$
$$\Pr\{A \cup B\} = 1 - \Pr\{\overline{A} \cap \overline{B}\};$$

d.   partitions:

$$\Pr\{A\} = \Pr\{A \cap B\} + \Pr\{A \cap \overline{B}\};$$

e.   subsets:

$$\text{if } A \subseteq B, \text{ then } \Pr\{A \cap B\} = \Pr\{A\} \text{ and } \Pr\{A \cup B\} = \Pr\{B\}.$$

In addition to the relationships previously listed, there are four theorems concerning set operations which will be stated here without proof:

a.   commutative law:

$$\Pr\{A \cap B\} = \Pr\{B \cap A\},$$
$$\Pr\{A \cup B\} = \Pr\{B \cup A\};$$

b.   distributive law:

$$\Pr\{A \cap (B \cup C)\} = \Pr\{(A \cap B) \cup (A \cap C)\},$$

$$\Pr\{A \cup (B \cap C)\} = \Pr\{(A \cup B) \cap (A \cup C)\}.$$

c. associative law:

$$\Pr\{A \cup (B \cup C)\} = \Pr\{(A \cup B) \cup C\},$$
$$\Pr\{A \cap (B \cap C)\} = \Pr\{(A \cap B) \cap C\}.$$

d. de Morgan's laws:

$$\Pr\{\overline{(A \cup B)}\} = \Pr\{\overline{A} \cap \overline{B}\},$$
$$\Pr\{\overline{(A \cap B)}\} = \Pr\{\overline{A} \cup \overline{B}\}.$$

A04   Addition Law

One relationship is commonly referred to as the *addition law* of probability. It provides a rule for calculating the probability of the union of two events, A and B, in terms of the individual probabilities, $\Pr\{A\}$ and $\Pr\{B\}$:

$$\Pr\{A \cup B\} = \Pr\{A\} + \Pr\{B\} - \Pr\{A \cap B\}.$$

Suppose for example that two aircraft are searching for a target. If A is the event that the first aircraft detects the target and B is the event that the second aircraft detects the target, then the event that the target is detected, i.e, by at least one of the aircraft, is represented by $A \cup B$. The addition law provides a method of computing this probability in terms of the simple event probabilities.

In the case where the events A and B cannot occur simultaneously, then $A \cap B = \phi$ and $\Pr\{A \cap B\} = 0$. In this case A and B are said to be **mutually exclusive** events (or that A and B are **disjoint** sets). The addition law then becomes simply

$$\Pr\{A \cup B\} = \Pr\{A\} + \Pr\{B\}.$$

For example let A be the event that an even number is rolled on a die, and B the event that an odd number less than four is rolled. The respective probabilities may be calculated as

$$\Pr\{A\} = \Pr\{2, 4, 6\} = 3/6 \text{ and } \Pr\{B\} = \Pr\{1, 3\} = 2/6.$$

Then $\Pr\{A \cap B\} = \Pr\{\phi\} = 0$, which implies that

$$\Pr\{A \cup B\} = \Pr\{A\} + \Pr\{B\} = 5/6.$$

A05   Conditional Probability and Multiplication Law

An expression was stated in A04 for the probability of the union of two events. In this section an expression will be developed for the probability of the *intersection* of two events (the probability that *both A and B* occur). First, however, the notion of conditional probability will be discussed.

The conditional probability of one event, B, occurring given that another event, A, has occurred is denoted by $\Pr\{B|A\}$. As an aid in visualizing this conditional event consider the Venn diagram in Figure A.3.

In any experiment, only one of the possible outcomes may result. In this diagram depicting nine possible outcomes, it can be seen that if the event A has occurred, the outcome must be one of the two outcomes included in A. Now, given that A has occurred, what is the probability that B occurs? Since A has occurred, one of the two outcomes contained in A must have occurred. One of these lies in B also, so the answer (assuming each outcome is equally likely) is one-half. Mathematically, this used the formula

$$\Pr\{B|A\} \;=\; \frac{n(A \cap B)}{n(A)}, \quad \text{where } n(A) > 0. \tag{A-2}$$

FIGURE A.3. VENN DIAGRAM FOR CONDITIONAL PROBABILITY EXAMPLE

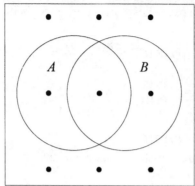

By dividing the numerator and the denominator of the right-hand side of (A-2) by the total number of outcomes in the entire sample space (nine in the example) the conditional probability of B given A becomes

$$\Pr\{B|A\} \;=\; \frac{\dfrac{n(A \cap B)}{n(U)}}{\dfrac{n(A)}{n(U)}} \;=\; \frac{\Pr\{A \cap B\}}{\Pr\{A\}}. \tag{A-3}$$

Equation (A-3) expresses mathematically the conditional probability of B given A, whether or not the outcomes are equally likely. An expression can then be found for the probability of the intersection of two events, A and B, by rearranging (A-3) as follows:

$$\Pr\{A \cap B\} \;=\; \Pr\{A\}\,\Pr\{B|A\}. \tag{A-4}$$

This expression is known as the **multiplication law** of probability.

A06   Statistical Independence

Consider two events, A and B, having non-zero probabilities. The events A and B are **statistically independent** if the conditional probability of event B given event A equals the unconditional probability of event B. In other words, whether or not A is known to occur has no bearing on the probability of B's occurrence. In this case, $\Pr\{B|A\} = \Pr\{B\}$ and the multiplication law simplifies to $\Pr\{A \cap B\} = \Pr\{A\}\Pr\{B\}$.

As an example, consider a simple experiment in which the probability sample space can be represented by the Venn diagram in Figure A.4 depicting three equally likely outcomes. In this case,

$$\Pr\{A|B\} \;=\; \frac{n(A \cap B)}{n(B)} \;=\; \frac{1}{2},$$

$$\Pr\{A\} = \frac{n(A)}{n(U)} = \frac{2}{3},$$

$$\Pr\{A|B\} \neq \Pr\{A\}.$$

Therefore, A and B are not statistically independent. Consider, however, the following slight modification to this probability sample space shown in Figure A.5. With the addition of a point outside both A and B,

$$\Pr\{A|B\} = \frac{n(A \cap B)}{n(B)} = \frac{1}{2},$$

$$\Pr\{A\} = \frac{n(A)}{n(U)} = \frac{2}{4} = \frac{1}{2},$$

$$\Pr\{A|B\} = \Pr\{A\}.$$

Therefore, in this case, A and B are statistically independent.

FIGURE A.4. EVENTS A AND B NOT STATISTICALLY INDEPENDENT

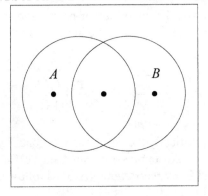

FIGURE A.5. EVENTS A AND B ARE STATISTICALLY INDEPENDENT

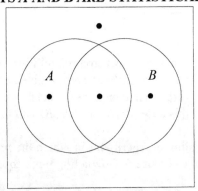

The purpose of these examples is to emphasize the mathematical requirements that must be met before any statements can be made regarding the statistical independence of events. In some practical situations, however, the only information known about the events A and B is their probabilities of occurrence, $\Pr\{A\}$ and $\Pr\{B\}$. With this information only, it is impossible to find $\Pr\{A\cap B\}$ or $\Pr\{A\cup B\}$ unless some assumptions are made. If, for example, it can be reasoned that knowledge of the occurrence of the event A on a particular trial would be of no value in determining whether B did or will occur, then this is equivalent to reasoning that $\Pr\{B|A\}$ is the same as $\Pr\{B\}$ and hence that A and B are *causally* independent.

In practical problems when additional information is lacking, statistical independence is sometimes assumed on the basis of this intuitive (causal) justification, in order to make further computations possible.

A07   Compound Probabilities Involving Three or More Events

Using the simple method of counting sample points in conjunction with a Venn diagram, it is fairly easy to generalize the addition law to three events:

$$\Pr\{A\cup B\cup C\} = \Pr\{A\} + \Pr\{B\} + \Pr\{C\} - \Pr\{A\cap B\} - \Pr\{A\cap C\}$$
$$- \Pr\{B\cap C\} + \Pr\{A\cap B\cap C\}.$$

The expression for the probability of the union of more than three events becomes quite cumbersome in the general case. However, in the special case of *mutually exclusive events*, i.e., $E_i \cap E_j = \phi$ for all $i\neq j$,

$$\Pr\{E_1\cup E_2\cup \ldots \cup E_n\} = \Pr\{E_1\} + \Pr\{E_2\} + \ldots + \Pr\{E_n\}.$$

It is often necessary to find the probability of the *intersection* of several events. To do this, (A-4) can be extended by induction to

$$\Pr\{E_1\cap E_2\cap \ldots \cap E_n\}$$
$$= \Pr\{E_1\}\Pr\{E_2|E_1\}\Pr\{E_3|E_1\cap E_2\} \ldots \Pr\{E_n|E_1\cap E_2\cap \ldots \cap E_{n-1}\}. \qquad \text{(A-5)}$$

If these events are independent, then the multiplication law simplifies to

$$\Pr\{E_1\cap E_2\cap E_n\} = \Pr\{E_1\}\Pr\{E_2\} \ldots \Pr\{E_n\}.$$

Finally, if none of the above conditions hold, there is one more possible approach. The probability of the union of several events E_1, E_2, ... , E_n, represents the probability that *at least one* of these events occurs. The only other possible outcome is for *none* of the events to occur, i.e., each of the events fails to occur. Hence,

$$\Pr\{E_1\cup E_2\cup E_n\} = 1 - \Pr\{\overline{E_1}\cap \overline{E_2}\cap \ldots \cap \overline{E_n}\}. \qquad \text{(A-6)}$$

Equation (A-6) is known as **DeMorgan's Law**, and it relates the probability of the union of events occurring to the probability that the intersection of their complements occur.

A08   Bayes' Theorem

Suppose in some experiment the event B can occur only in conjunction with *one* of several mutually exclusive events A_1, A_2, ... , A_n. Then

$$B \subseteq A_1\cup A_2\cup \ldots \cup A_n,$$

and

$$B = B\cap (A_1\cup A_2\cup \ldots \cup A_n) = (B\cap A_1)\cup (B\cap A_2)\cup \ldots \cup (B\cap A_n),$$

so that

$$Pr\{B\} = Pr\{B \cap A_1\} + Pr\{B \cap A_2\} + ... + Pr\{B \cap A_n\},$$

since these events are mutually exclusive.

If an experiment is conducted and B is observed to occur, what is the probability that the simultaneous event which occurred was A_i? That is, what is $Pr\{A_i|B\}$? From the definition of conditional probability,

$$Pr\{A_i|B\} = \frac{Pr\{B \cap A_i\}}{Pr\{B\}}$$

$$= \frac{Pr\{B \cap A_i\}}{Pr\{B \cap A_1\} + Pr\{B \cap A_2\} + ... + Pr\{B \cap A_n\}},$$

and finally

$$Pr\{A_i|B\} = \frac{Pr\{B|A_i\} Pr\{A_i\}}{Pr\{B|A_1\} Pr\{A_1\} + Pr\{B|A_2\} Pr\{A_2\} + ... + Pr\{B|A_n\} Pr\{A_n\}}.$$

This result is referred to as **Bayes' Theorem**. As an example of its applicability, consider three identical boxes each containing 10 parts as illustrated in Figure A.6. There are 5, 6, and 8 good parts (outside the circle) in boxes 1, 2, and 3, respectively. The remaining parts are defective. First, a box is chosen at random and then a part is drawn from it. If the part drawn is defective, what is the probability that the first box was chosen? To solve, let A_1 denote the event the first box was chosen, A_2 the event the second box was chosen, A_3 the event the third box was chosen, and B the event that a defective part was drawn. Then the desired probability is

$$Pr\{A_1|B\} = \frac{Pr\{B|A_1\} Pr\{A_1\}}{Pr\{B|A_1\} Pr\{A_1\} + Pr\{B|A_2\} Pr\{A_2\} + Pr\{B|A_3\} Pr\{A_3\}}$$

$$= \frac{(5/10)(1/3)}{(5/10)(1/3) + (4/10)(1/3) + (2/10)(1/3)} = \frac{5}{11}.$$

FIGURE A.6. THREE BOXES CONTAINING DEFECTIVE PARTS

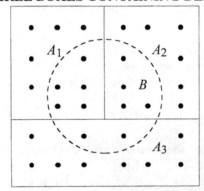

A09   Combinatorial Formulas -- Streamlined Methods of Counting

In the simple case where all possible outcomes of an experiment are equally likely, the probability of an event, A, was given by the following expression:

$$\Pr\{A\} = \frac{\text{number of outcomes corresponding to event } A}{\text{total number of possible outcomes}}.$$

This expression is sometimes referred to as the *classical* definition of probability because it was the original definition adopted in the seventeenth century by mathematicians investigating simple games of chance. In probabilistic situations such as simple games of chance, it is easy to visualize and to list all of the possible outcomes of an experiment as well as those outcomes corresponding to a particular event of interest. For example, it is easy to list the six possible outcomes resulting when a single die is tossed. It is not particularly difficult to list the 36 possible outcomes resulting when two dice are tossed. But it becomes a considerable chore to list the 216 possible outcomes resulting when three dice are tossed, and it becomes a time-consuming task to list the 1,296 possible outcomes resulting when four dice are tossed. Fortunately, in calculating probabilities it is not necessary to list all of the outcomes but simply to be able to *count* all of the outcomes. As will be seen in the next two sections, formulas can be developed without too much difficulty which provide a streamlined method for counting outcomes without having to visualize each individual outcome. These formulas are referred to as **combinatorial** formulas, and they are all based upon one simple, fundamental principle: *If A can be accomplished in n separate and distinct ways and B can be accomplished in m separate and distinct ways, then A and B together can be accomplished in m×n ways.*

A10   Permutations

The first formula to be considered is one for counting the number of **k-object arrangements** which can be made from *n* distinct objects. As an aid in visualizing the development of this formula, consider the simple problem of determining the number of two-letter arrangements which can be made from the letters *a, b, c*. A convenient method of visualizing the situation is to consider filling two boxes with letters drawn from the set *{a, b, c}* by placing the first one drawn in the left box and the second one drawn in the right box as illustrated in Figure A.7.

FIGURE A.7. ARRANGEMENTS OF TWO OBJECTS

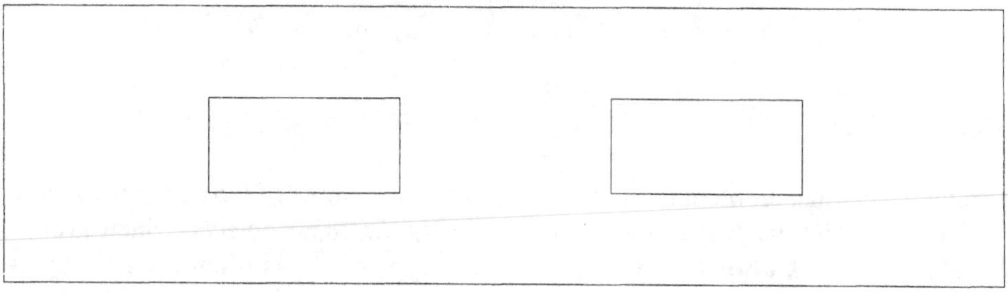

There are three letters to choose from in filling the first box; i.e., there are three ways of filling the first box. With the first box filled, there are now only two letters left to fill the second box.

Therefore, in accordance with the fundamental combinatorial principle, there are a total of 3×2, or six distinct ways of filling the two boxes. In other words, there are six possible two-letter arrangements which can be made up from the letters a, b, c. Specifically, these arrangements are: ab, ba, ac, ca, bc, and cb. The number of arrangements, or **permutations**, of n objects taken k at a time is often represented by the symbol $_nP_k$ ($_3P_2$ in the case of the example). In general, when forming k-object arrangements from n objects, there are n ways of choosing the first object, $(n - 1)$ ways of choosing the second object, etc., until finally there are $(n - k + 1)$ ways of choosing the kth object. Therefore, there are $(n)(n - 1)(n - 2) \cdots (n - k + 1)$ ways of forming k object arrangements. Symbolically,

$$_nP_k = (n)(n - 1)(n - 2) \ldots (n - k + 1).$$

Using the factorial notation, where $n! = (n)(n - 1)(n - 2) \ldots (1)$, this expression can be written in a more compact manner as

$$_nP_k = \frac{n!}{(n - k)!}, \tag{A-7}$$

where it is necessary to define $0!$ to be equal to 1.

Consider, however, the calculation of the number of four-letter arrangements possible from the sequence (a, a, b, b). It is intuitively clear that there would be a smaller number of distinct arrangements possible from a sequence of this kind, where some of the elements are identical. By an extension of the reasoning that led to (A-7), it is fairly easy to develop a formula for determining this number of n-object arrangements possible from n objects, when some of the objects are alike. Without going through the explicit development of the formula, suffice it to say that if there are r distinct types of objects contained in the set of n objects, the total number of n-object arrangements is given by

$$\frac{n!}{(n_1!)(n_2!)(n_3!) \cdots (n_r!)},$$

where n_i is the number of (identical) objects of the ith type.

In the example, the number of four-letter arrangements possible from the a, a, b, b is

$$\frac{4!}{2! \, 2!} = \frac{24}{4} = 6.$$

These 6 possible arrangements are as follows:

a, a, b, b	a, b, a, b	a, b, b, a
b, b, a, a	b, a, b, a	b, a, a, b

A11   Combinations

A similar but distinct problem is that of determining the number of k-object groupings possible from n objects *in which no two groups contain exactly the same objects.* Such groupings are generally referred to as **k-object combinations**. The symbol $_nC_k$ is often used to represent the number of these combinations, but the more commonly used symbol is

$$\binom{n}{k}.$$

The difference between combinations and permutations is that in combinations the order in which the objects are arranged in a particular grouping has no significance. For example, consider the {a, b, c} example. In forming the two-letter *permutations*, ab and ba are considered as two distinct arrangements and would be counted as such. However, since ab and ba contain exactly the same letters with only the order changed, they would not be counted as two distinct two-letter combinations. This point is important enough to be re-emphasized. In permutations *order counts*. In combinations *order does not count*. On the other hand, ab and ac would be counted as two distinct groupings since they contain different letters. It is fairly obvious from this that the number of k-object combinations possible from n objects will always be smaller than the number of k-object permutations for $k > 1$.

To derive an expression for the number of combinations, $_nC_k$, of n objects taken k at a time, consider the set of all $_nP_k$ possible *k-out-of-n permutations*. Consider one of these permutations. How many permutations entail using the *same k* objects, just in a different order? The answer is k!, since using only the k elements, there are k possible choices for the first, $(k - 1)$ choices for the second, and so on. Hence, out of the $_nP_k$ *k-out-of-n permutations*, only one out of every k! of these is a different *combination*. Thus

$$\binom{n}{k} = \frac{_nP_k}{k!} = \frac{n!}{k!\,(n-k)!},$$
(A-8)

which is the desired formula for determining the k object combinations possible from n objects.

As it turns out, the formula for combinations is used much more frequently in probability calculations than is the permutation formula. An example of the use of combinations in calculating probabilities is: *A bridge hand consisting of 13 cards is chosen from an ordinary deck*. What is the probability that such a hand will contain exactly 5 hearts? Since a bridge hand is not affected by the order in which the various cards are obtained, the total number of possible bridge hands is equal to the number of 13-object combinations possible from 52 objects, which is simply $_{52}C_{13}$. This is the total number of sample points in the sample space. The number of hands containing exactly 5 hearts is equal to the number of ways of choosing 5 hearts from the 13 hearts in the deck, i.e., $_{13}C_5$, multiplied by the number of ways of choosing 8 non-hearts from 39 non-hearts, i.e., $_{39}C_8$. Hence, the desired probability is given by

$$\Pr\{5 \text{ hearts}\} = \frac{\binom{13}{5}\binom{39}{8}}{\binom{52}{13}} = \frac{(13!)(39!)(13!)(39!)}{(5!)(8!)(8!)(31!)(52!)} \approx .125.$$

Thus far, only those probabilistic situations having a finite number of possible outcomes have been considered. The next logical step is to consider those situations having an infinite number of outcomes. As an example of such a situation, consider the spinning of a simple pointer. There are an *infinite* number of points between zero and 360 degrees at which the pointer might stop. This continuum of possible outcomes is referred to as a *continuous probability sample space* as opposed to the *discrete probability sample space* associated with a finite or countably infinite number of outcomes.

A12   Random Variable

A definition fundamental to all that follows is that of a **random variable**. *A random variable is a transformation which associates with each point or collection of points in the sample space some real number.* The precise verbal description of the random variable to be used in a particular probabilistic situation will usually be apparent from the nature of the situation itself. For example, in the case of two dice being tossed simultaneously, the outcomes could be represented very conveniently by a random variable, X, where

X = the *sum* of the spots on the dice.

In terms of this random variable, the outcomes would be represented as in Figure A.8. To say that $X = 3$ then, is to say that one of the two outcomes has occurred which results in a sum of 3.

It should be noted that there are other ways of defining the random variable X in this experiment. Instead of the sum of the spots, it might be of interest to define X as the *difference* between the spots on the two dice, the *greater of the two numbers* of spots showing, or the *number of 3s* showing. In each case, the random variable specifies a *number* to be associated with each possible outcome of the experiment. A random variable is said to be *discrete* if it can take on only a finite or countably infinite number of values. Otherwise it is said to be *continuous* and usually takes on as values all the real numbers in some interval.

FIGURE A.8.   SUM OF SPOTS ON TWO DICE

Specific outcomes	Value of the random variable, X
(1, 1)	2
(1, 2), (2, 1)	3
(1, 3), (2, 2), (3, 1)	4
(1, 4), (2, 3), (3, 2), (4, 1)	5
(1, 5), (2, 4), (3, 3), (4, 2), (5, 1)	6
(1, 6), (2, 5), (3, 4), (4, 3), (5, 2), (6, 1)	7
(2, 6), (3, 5), (4, 4), (5, 3), (6, 2)	8
(3, 6), (4, 5), (5, 4), (6, 3)	9
(4, 6), (5, 5), (6, 4)	10
(5, 6), (6, 5)	11
(6, 6)	12

A13   Discrete Probability Functions

When discussing probabilities in terms of random variables, it is convenient to employ the use of certain special functions. In the discrete case the **probability function**, sometimes called **frequency function**, denoted f, is of particular interest. For any real number x, $f(x)$ is the probability that on a particular outcome of the experiment the value of the random variable is x. Symbolically,

$$f(x) = \Pr\{X = x\}.$$

In the previous example where X represents the sum of spots on a throw of two dice, each of the 36 possible outcomes is equally likely. Then

$$f(3) = \Pr\{X = 3\} = \frac{2 \text{ outcomes for which } X = 3}{36 \text{ possible outcomes}} = \frac{1}{18}.$$

The other function of interest for a discrete random variable is the **cumulative distribution function (cdf)**, denoted by F. For any real number x, $F(x)$ is the probability that on a particular outcome of the experiment the value of the random variable is less than or equal to x:

$$F(x) = \Pr\{X \le x\}.$$

In terms of the dice example,

$$\begin{aligned}
F(3) &= \Pr\{X \le 3\} \\
&= \Pr\{\text{sum of spots does not exceed 3}\} \\
&= \Pr\{X = 2\} + \Pr\{X = 3\} \\
&= f(2) + f(3) = 1/36 + 2/36 = 3/36.
\end{aligned}$$

Note that these two functions, f and F, are defined for any real number. The reader should verify that in the dice example, the real numbers, x, in Figure A.9 are the correct values of f and F:

FIGURE A.9. VALUES OF PROBABILITY FUNCTIONS FOR SUM OF TWO DICE

x	$f(x)$	$F(x)$
-3	0	0
0	0	0
2.69	0	1/36
π	0	3/36
11	2/36	35/36
13.2	0	1

For example, $F(\pi)$, from its definition, represents the probability that the sum of the spots is a number not exceeding π (about 3.1416). This event occurs if and only if the sum is a 2 or a 3, hence

$$F(\pi) = \Pr\{X \le \pi\} = f(2) + f(3) = 3/36.$$

In general, if the possible values for the random variable X are denoted by $x_1, x_2, \dots, x_n$, then

$$F(x) = \Pr\{X \le x\} = \sum_{\text{all } x_i \le x} f(x_i),$$

and also

$$\sum_{\text{all } x_i} f(x_i) = 1.$$

As another example of a discrete random variable, consider an experiment in which two coins are tossed. The sample space, S, contains the four outcomes HH, HT, TH, TT (each equally likely). Let the random variable X denote the number of heads appearing. Then X can take on the values 0, 1, and 2. The probability function f could be graphed as in Figure A.10. The formula for f is

$$f(x) = \begin{cases} 1/4, & \text{if } x = 0, \\ 1/2, & \text{if } x = 1, \\ 1/4, & \text{if } x = 2, \\ 0, & \text{if } x \text{ is any other real number.} \end{cases}$$

Likewise the cumulative distribution function would have the graph shown in Figure A.11. The formula for F is

$$F(x) = \begin{cases} 0, & \text{if } x < 0, \\ 1/4, & \text{if } 0 \le x < 1, \\ 3/4, & \text{if } 1 \le x < 2, \\ 1, & \text{if } x \ge 2. \end{cases}$$

FIGURE A.10. GRAPH OF PROBABILITY FUNCTION FOR TOSSING TWO HEADS

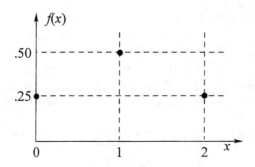

FIGURE A.11. CUMULATIVE DISTRIBUTION FUNCTION FOR TWO HEADS

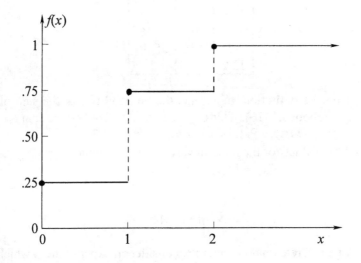

A14   Continuous Probability Functions

Thus far the random variable has been considered to have only a finite or countably infinite number of values. A logical extension of this concept is to let the random variable take on *all* values (-∞ to ∞). The probability associated with a continuous random variable is characterized by a function f called a **probability density function** or simply density function. The area under this function represents probability and hence the total area under this curve is 1. The area $f(x)\Delta x$ gives the approximate probability that the value of the random variable X will occur in an interval of length Δx around x, as shown in Figure A.12. If this interval is considered to be bounded by $x - (\Delta x)/2$ and

$x + (\Delta x)/2$, and $f(x)$ describes the average height of the curve between these two points, then the probability element is

$$f(x)\Delta x \cong \Pr\left\{x - \frac{\Delta x}{2} \le X \le x + \frac{\Delta x}{2}\right\}.$$

FIGURE A.12. PROBABILITY ELEMENT

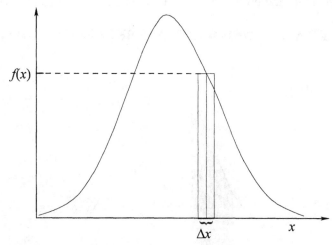

By letting Δx become small and noting that integration is just the limiting form of summation of a large number of small probability elements, the probability that the value of a random variable will fall in an interval $[x_1, x_2]$ is just

$$\Pr\{x_1 \le X \le x_2\} = \int_{x_1}^{x_2} f(x)\,dx.$$

Graphically this is represented in Figure A.13. The probability density function further satisfies

$$f(x) \ge 0, \text{ for all } x,$$

and since

$$\Pr\{-\infty \le X \le \infty\} = 1,$$

it follows that

$$\int_{-\infty}^{\infty} f(x)\,dx = 1,$$

i.e., the total area under the curve must equal 1.

The **cumulative distribution function (cdf)**, F, is defined for a continuous random variable exactly as it was for the discrete case, $F(x) = \Pr\{X \le x\}$. This is equivalent to writing

$$F(x) = \Pr\{-\infty < X \le x\},$$

which can be evaluated using the definition of the probability density function by

$$F(x) = \int_{-\infty}^{x} f(t)\,dt.$$

This is the area to the left of x under the curve defined by the probability density function.

From these definitions, it follows that

$$\lim_{X \to \infty} F(x) = 1, \ \lim_{X \to -\infty} F(x) = 0,$$

and that

$$\Pr\{x_1 \le X \le x_2\} = \int_{x_1}^{x_2} f(x)dx = \int_{-\infty}^{x_2} f(x)dx - \int_{-\infty}^{x_1} f(x)dx$$

$$= F(x_2) - F(x_1).$$

By differentiation of integrals, the probability density function can also be defined as $f = F'$.

FIGURE A.13. PROBABILITY X IS BETWEEN x_1 AND x_2

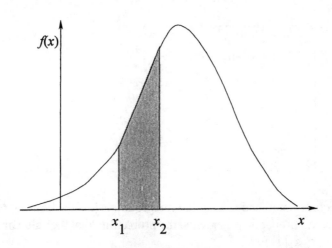

As an example of a continuous random variable consider observing the ship traffic down a channel 1,000 yards wide from a position on one side of the channel. The random variable of interest is the distance (in yards) from the observer to a ship as it passes the observer's position. The probability density function, f, for such a situation might resemble the graph in Figure A.14.

FIGURE A.14. DENSITY FUNCTION FOR RANGE TO SHIP

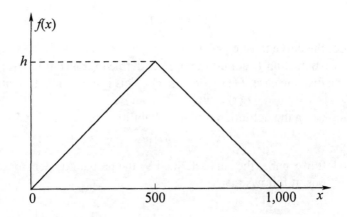

The height h must be chosen so that the area under the curve is 1. In this case, it would require that h be .002. The formula for f is

$$f(x) = \begin{cases} \dfrac{.002}{500}x, & \text{for } 0 \le x \le 500, \\[2mm] .004 - \dfrac{.002}{500}x, & \text{for } 500 \le x \le 1{,}000, \\[2mm] 0, & \text{for all other } x. \end{cases}$$

The probability that a particular ship passes in the middle 500 yards of the channel is then

$$\Pr\{250 \le X \le 750\} = \int_{250}^{750} f(x)dx = \int_{250}^{500} \frac{.002}{500}x\,dx + \int_{500}^{750} (.004 - \frac{.002}{500}x)dx$$

$$= \left[\frac{.002\,x^2}{1000} \right]_{250}^{500} + \left[.004\,x - \frac{.002\,x^2}{1000} \right]_{500}^{750} = .75.$$

Note that this probability could be determined fairly easily from the graph of f.

Suppose one wishes to consider two random variables X and Y arising in the same application. A **discrete joint probability distribution** of X and Y is a discrete function f where $f(x, y) = \Pr\{X = x \text{ and } Y = y\}$. By the laws of probability,

$$f(x, y) \ge 0, \quad \text{for all } x \text{ and } y,$$
$$\sum_x \sum_y f(x, y) = 1,$$

and

$$\Pr\{x_1 \le X \le x_2 \text{ and } y_1 \le Y \le y_2\} = \sum_{x_1 \le x \le x_2} \sum_{y_1 \le y \le y_2} f(x, y).$$

Similarly, a **continuous joint probability distribution** can be defined by a nonnegative density function f satisfying

$$\int_{-\infty}^{\infty} \int_{-\infty}^{\infty} f(x, y)\, dx\, dy = 1,$$

where

$$\Pr\{x_1 \le X \le x_2 \text{ and } y_1 \le Y \le y_2\} = \int_{x_1}^{x_2} \int_{y_1}^{y_2} f(x, y)\, dx\, dy.$$

For instance, let X and Y be the respective fractions of male and female runners who successfully finish a (randomly chosen) marathon race. Suppose their joint density function f is given by:

$$f(x, y) = \begin{cases} 8xy, & \text{if } 0 \le x \le 1,\ 0 \le y \le x, \\ 0, & \text{otherwise.} \end{cases}$$

It is easy to see that f is a true density because $f(x, y) \ge 0$ for all x, y and also

$$\int_{-\infty}^{\infty} \int_{-\infty}^{\infty} f(x, y)\,dx\,dy = \int_0^1 \int_0^x 8xy\,dy\,dx = 1.$$

Finally, the probability that in a random race between 40 percent and 60 percent of all male runners and between 30 percent and 50 percent of all female runners will finish is given by

$$\int_{.4}^{.6} \int_{.3}^{.5} f(x, y)\, dy\, dx = \int_{.4}^{.6} \int_{.3}^{x} 8xy\,dy\,dx = .068.$$

The general term **probability distribution** is used to denote the particular probability functions applicable to a given random variable. In the discrete case, the probability distribution may be specified by stating either the probability function or the cumulative distribution function. The discrete probability distributions encountered most frequently in this text are the **binomial** distribution, the **Poisson** distribution, and the **geometric** distribution, each of which is discussed separately in this appendix.

A continuous probability distribution may be specified by identifying either its probability density function or its cumulative distribution function. Among the most common of these continuous probability distributions are the **uniform**, **normal**, and **exponential** distributions. These and the **bivariate normal** distribution, which is an example of a continuous joint distribution of two variables, are also discussed in this appendix.

Before introducing specific probability distributions, two quantities will be presented which are most important in summarizing the characteristics of all probability distributions. These quantities are the **mean** and the **variance** of a random variable.

A15   Expected Value

As the name implies, the **mean value**, also called **expected value**, of a random variable is a measure of "average value" of the random variable. It is somewhat analogous to the center of gravity used in physics. The symbols commonly used to represent this expected value of a random variable X are $E[X]$ and μ. In the discrete case, the mean is calculated by taking the weighted average of all the possible values of the random variable, i.e., by multiplying each value by its respective probability of occurrence and then summing all of the resulting products:

$$E[X] = \mu = \sum_{\text{all } x_i} x_i f(x_i). \tag{A-9}$$

As an example of the mean value of a discrete probability distribution, consider the probability sample space associated with the rolling of a single die. Let the random variable X be the number of spots showing on the die. The mean value of X is

$$E[X] = \sum_{\text{all } x_i} x_i f(x_i) = (1)\frac{1}{6} + (2)\frac{1}{6} + (3)\frac{1}{6} + (4)\frac{1}{6} + (5)\frac{1}{6} + (6)\frac{1}{6} = 3.50.$$

This agrees with one's intuitive notion as to what an "average die-roll" should be. Note that in this example, where all values of the discrete random variable are equally likely, the calculation of the mean simply consists of taking the arithmetic average of all the values of the random variable. Note also that the mean is not necessarily one of the possible values of the random variable.

Let the random variable X be the sum of spots showing when two dice are rolled. Then the calculation of the mean value of X is done in a similar manner, although in this case the values of the random variable are not equally likely. The result is

$$E[X] = \sum_{\text{all } x_i} x_i f(x_i)$$

$$= (1)(0) + (2)\frac{1}{36} + (3)\frac{2}{36} + (4)\frac{3}{36} + \cdots + (11)\frac{2}{36} + (12)\frac{1}{36} = \frac{252}{36} = 7.$$

The extension of the concept of mean value to the continuous case follows directly in a manner completely analogous to the discrete case. The mean is calculated by taking the limit of the weighted sum of all possible values of the random variable, i.e., by multiplying each value by its associated probability element and then taking the limit of the sum of the resulting products. In this case $f(x)\Delta x$ is the approximate probability that the random variable lies between x and $x + \Delta x$, hence

$$E[X] = \mu = \lim_{\Delta x \to 0} \sum_{i=1}^{n} x_i \, [f(x_i) \, \Delta x] = \int_{-\infty}^{\infty} x f(x) \, dx.$$

As an example of the expected value of a continuous probability distribution, consider the distribution represented by the following function:

$$f(x) = \begin{cases} \dfrac{1}{18} x^2, & -3 \le x \le 3, \\ 0, & \text{elsewhere.} \end{cases}$$

The expected value of a random variable, X, having this distribution is

$$E[X] = \int_{-\infty}^{\infty} x f(x) \, dx$$

$$= \int_{-\infty}^{-3} (0) \, dx + \int_{-3}^{3} x \left(\frac{x^2}{18} \right) dx + \int_{3}^{\infty} (0) \, dx = \left. \frac{x^4}{4(18)} \right|_{-3}^{3} = 0.$$

The mean of this probability distribution occurring at zero is not surprising when one plots the graph of its probability density function as in Figure A.15

FIGURE A.15. DENSITY FUNCTION AND MEAN

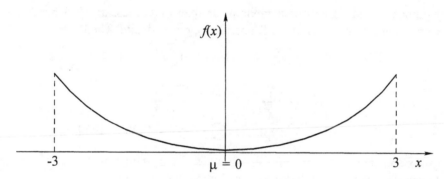

It is possible in a similar manner to compute the expected (or average) value of *any* function g of a random variable X, denoted $g(X)$. For a continuous random variable X,

$$E[g(X)] = \int_{-\infty}^{\infty} g(x) \cdot f(x) \, dx,$$

and for a discrete random variable X,

$$E[g(X)] = \sum_{\text{all } x_i} g(x_i) f(x_i).$$

In computing the expected value of some functions, use can be made of the linear properties of expected value. For example, if $g(X) = aX + b$, where a and b are constants, then when X is continuous,

$$E[aX + b] = \int_{-\infty}^{\infty} (ax + b) f(x) \, dx$$

$$= a \int_{-\infty}^{\infty} x f(x) \, dx + b \int_{-\infty}^{\infty} f(x) \, dx$$

$$= a[E(X)] + b,$$

since $\int_{-\infty}^{\infty} f(x)\, dx = 1$. This property also holds when X is discrete.

If $g(X, Y)$ is a function of the random variables of a discrete joint probability distribution, the expected value of $g(X, Y)$ is defined as follows:
$$E[g(X, Y)] = \sum_{\text{all } x} \sum_{\text{all } y} g(x, y) f(x, y).$$
Similarly, for a continuous joint probability distribution,
$$E[g(X, Y)] = \int_{-\infty}^{\infty} \int_{-\infty}^{\infty} g(x, y) f(x, y)\, dx\, dy.$$
In the marathon example of A14,
$$E[X] = \int_0^1 \int_0^x 8x^2 y\, dy\, dx = 4/5,$$
$$E[Y] = \int_0^1 \int_0^x 8xy^2\, dy\, dx = 8/15,$$
$$E[XY] = \int_0^1 \int_0^x 8x^2 y^2\, dy\, dx = 4/9,$$
$$E[X^2] = \int_0^1 \int_0^x 8x^3 y\, dy\, dx = 2/3, \quad \text{and}$$
$$E[Y^2] = \int_0^1 \int_0^x 8xy^3\, dy\, dx = 1/3.$$

Finally suppose X and Y are discrete random variables, not necessarily independent. Let $f_X, f_Y,$ and f_{XY} be the probability functions for X, Y, and (X, Y), respectively. Then
$$E[X + Y] = \sum_x \sum_y (x + y) f_{XY}(x, y)$$
$$= \sum_x x \sum_y f_{XY}(x, y) + \sum_y y \sum_x f_{XY}(x, y)$$
$$= \sum_x x f_X(x) + \sum_y y f_Y(y) = E[X] + E[Y].$$
This is readily extended to continuous random variables and, by induction, to a sum of finitely many variables. In general, the mean of the sum of random variables is the sum of their means.

A16   Variance, Standard Deviation, and Correlation

As mentioned in the previous section, the mean value might be thought of as the center of gravity of the probability distribution. For many readers, this probably brings to mind the more general notions (which are encountered in the study of mechanics) of the moments of a distribution (of mass) about a particular point. To be specific, the kth **moment of a probability distribution about a point**, a, represented by the symbol μ_a^k, is defined as
$$\mu_a^k = E[(X - a)^k].$$

This can be computed from
$$E[(X - a)^k] = \sum_{\text{all } x_i} (x_i - a)^k f(x_i)$$
for a discrete probability distribution, and from

$$E[(X-a)^k] = \int_{-\infty}^{\infty} (x-a)^k f(x)\,dx$$

for a continuous probability distribution. In terms of this general expression for moments, the **mean** of a probability distribution is simply the *first moment* about the *origin*. Using this notation, the mean should more properly be represented by the symbol, $\mu_0{}'$. However, owing to the fact that the mean is such a commonly used measure, usually the superscript and the subscript are dropped, and it is represented by the symbol μ.

The concept of moments of a distribution serves as a convenient device for the introduction of the second of the two most useful parameters for describing a probability distribution, the **variance**. Whereas the mean is a measure of the *center* of a probability distribution, the variance is a measure of the *dispersion* of the distribution about this central point. In terms of the general expression for moments, the **variance** is defined as the second moment about the mean. The symbol commonly used to represent the variance is σ^2. Thus

$$\sigma^2 = \mu_\mu^2 = E[(X-\mu)^2].$$

The variance of a probability distribution is analogous to the moment of inertia of mechanics.

To illustrate the usefulness of the variance as a measure of dispersion, it is convenient to introduce a unit or measure called the **standard deviation**, σ, which is defined as the square root of the variance. For any probability distribution, the great majority of the distribution falls within the three standard deviation units on either side of the mean, i.e., within the interval $\pm 3\sigma$ from the mean. Therefore, a probability distribution having a small σ^2 and hence a small σ would be concentrated tightly about the mean as shown in Figure A.16. On the other hand, a probability distribution having a large σ^2 would be dispersed more widely about the mean as shown in Figure A.17.

FIGURE A.16. SMALL STANDARD DEVIATION

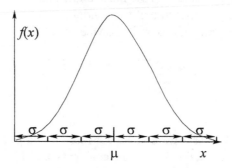

By employing the linearity of the expectation operator E, an alternate expression for the variance can be derived:

$$\sigma^2 = E[(X-\mu)^2] = E[X^2 - 2\mu X + \mu^2] = E[X^2] - 2\mu E[X] + \mu^2$$
$$= E[X^2] - 2\mu^2 + \mu^2 = E[X^2] - \mu^2,$$
$$= E[X^2] - (E[X])^2.$$

It can be shown that if $X_1, \ldots, X_n$ are *independent* random variables,

$$\text{variance}[X_1 + \ldots + X_n] = \text{variance}[X_1] + \ldots + \text{variance}[X_n].$$

FIGURE A.17. LARGER STANDARD DEVIATION

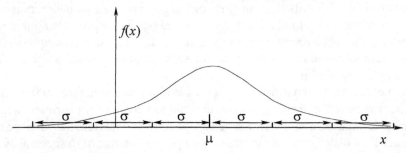

As a numerical example of the computation of the variance in the continuous case, recall the density function given by

$$f(x) = \begin{cases} \dfrac{1}{18} x^2, & -3 \le x \le 3, \\ 0, & \text{elsewhere.} \end{cases}$$

Since the mean for this particular distribution is 0,

$$\sigma^2 = E[X^2] - (E[X])^2 = E[X^2]$$
$$= \int_{-3}^{3} x^2 \left(\frac{1}{18} x^2 \right) dx = \int_{-3}^{3} \frac{x^4}{18} dx = \frac{486}{90}.$$

Higher moments are used (although rarely) to give further information about the probability distribution. For example, the third moment can be used to give a measure of the *skewness* of a non-symmetric probability distribution. The fourth moment is sometimes used as a measure of the *sharpness* or the *peakedness* of the density function. By far the most frequently used descriptive measures are the first and second moments, the mean and variance.

Suppose a joint probability distribution of two random variables X and Y is given. It is desired to measure how dependent the value of X is on Y and vice versa. Define the **correlation coefficient** $\rho(X, Y)$ by

$$\rho(X,Y) = \frac{E[X - E[X]]E[Y - E[Y]]}{\sigma_X \sigma_Y} = \frac{E[XY] - E[X]E[Y]}{\sigma_X \sigma_Y}.$$

It can be shown that

a. $\rho(X, Y) = 1$ if and only if $X = \alpha Y + \beta$ for some constants α and β, α positive;
b. $\rho(X, Y) = -1$ if and only if $X = \alpha Y + \beta$ for some constants α and β, α negative;
c.   if X and Y are independent, then $\rho(X, Y) = 0$;
d.   for any X and Y, $-1 \le \rho(X, Y) \le 1$.

Hence, ρ measures, on a scale from -1 to 1, how "similar" X and Y are likely to be in "random" observations of these variables. In the extreme case where $X = \alpha Y + \beta$ for some $\alpha > 0$, this means that a high value (relatively speaking) of X guarantees a high value of Y and vice versa; we say that X and Y are **perfectly correlated**. At the opposite end of the scale is $X = \alpha Y + \beta$ with $\alpha < 0$, i.e., ρ = -1. Here a high value of X guarantees a low value of Y and vice versa. In the middle, where ρ is close to zero, whether or not X is relatively high has little effect on where the observation of Y will be (hence, independence implies $\rho = 0$). In the marathon example of A15, it can be seen that in general, if X is relatively high (near 1), Y has more of a chance to be high, and vice versa. Also, if X is low, then Y will be low as well. However, these are only general statements, as it is possible to have a high X and low Y for the same race (but not vice versa!). Hence, one would expect $\rho(X, Y)$ to be positive, but definitely less than 1. In fact (see A15), $E[X] = 4/5$, $E[Y] = 8/15$, $E[XY] = 4/9$, $\sigma_X = .163$, and $\sigma_Y = .221$. Hence,

$$\rho = \frac{4/9 - (4/5)(8/15)}{(.163)(.221)} = .492.$$

Up to this point, the primary emphasis has been upon the general mathematical properties of *all* probability distributions. As a consequence, some of the numerical examples used to illustrate the principles have been arbitrary and not necessarily representative of any real-world phenomena. The next step will be to look at those probability distributions which *are* representative of real-world phenomena. Although there are a number of such distributions, each applying to different situations, only six of the most widely applicable will be presented here. These are the binomial, Poisson, geometric, uniform, normal, and exponential distributions. The first three are *discrete* distributions while the others are *continuous* distributions.

A17   The Binomial Distribution

Many situations occur in the real world in the form of a sequence of simple independent trials in which the occurrence or the nonoccurrence of an event is the only item of interest. If, in such a sequence of trials, the individual probability of the event's occurring on any one trial remains constant through the sequence, then these trials are referred to as **Bernoulli** trials. A good example of Bernoulli trials is a sequence of coin tosses for which the probability of a *head* on a single toss is p and the probability of a *tail* is $q = 1 - p$. Another example might be provided by considering defects in a sequence of items being produced on an assembly line in which the probability of an individual item being defective is a constant, p. In situations such as these, it is desirable to know the probability of a specified number of occurrences of the event in a given number of trials. An occurrence of the event is sometimes referred to as a *success*, and a nonoccurrence as a *failure*. The **binomial distribution** provides the means of determining the probability of exactly x occurrences of an event in n independent trials.

The development of the binomial distribution may be visualized by means of the coin-tossing example. Assume that for a particular coin the probability of a head on a single toss is 1/3, and the probability of a tail is 2/3. Let the random variable X be the number of heads occurring in 5 tosses, and find $\Pr\{X = 2\} = f(2)$. A logical approach to such a problem is to consider all of the ways in which 5 heads might occur. Determine probabilities for each of these mutually exclusive occurrences, and then sum the resulting probabilities. One way for the 2 heads to occur in 5 tosses is

$$H\,H\,T\,T\,T$$

and its probability is

$$(p)(p)(q)(q)(q) = p^2 q^3 = (1/3)^2 (2/3)^3.$$

To determine the total number of ways of getting exactly 2 heads in 5 tosses, the total number of possible arrangements must be found. Since order does not matter, this is a matter of counting combinations. From (A-8), the total number of such combinations is

$$\binom{5}{2} = \frac{n!}{n_1!\, n_2!} = \frac{5!}{2!\, 3!} = 10.$$

The 10 combinations that have exactly 2 heads are as follows:

HHTTT   THHTT   TTHHT   HTHTT   THTHT

TTHTH   HTTHT   THTTH   TTTHH   HTTTH

Since the probability associated with each of these combinations is the same, namely $(1/3)^2(2/3)^3$, the overall probability of exactly 2 heads in 5 tosses is given by

$$\Pr\{X = 2\} = f(2) = \frac{5!}{2!\, 3!}\,(1/3)^2\,(2/3)^3 = \binom{5}{2}(1/3)^2\,(2/3)^3 = .31.$$

In general, the probability of exactly x successes in n trials is

$$\Pr\{X = x\} = f(x) = \binom{n}{x} p^x q^{n-x}, \text{ for } x = 0, 1, 2, \ldots, n,$$

which is also the general expression for the probability function of the **binomial distribution with parameters n and p.**

As verification that the previous expression is a probability function, it must be shown that

$$\sum_{\text{all } x_i} f(x) = 1.$$

By its very definition, the particular random variable associated with the binomial distribution can take on all integer values from 0 to n. Therefore,

$$\sum_{\text{all } x_i} f(x_i) = \sum_{x=0}^{n} \frac{n!}{x!\,(n-x)!} p^x q^{n-x}$$

$$= \frac{n!}{0!\, n!} p^0 q^n + \frac{n!}{1!\,(n-1)!} p^1 q^{n-1} + \cdots + \frac{n!}{n!\,(n-n)!} p^n q^0$$

$$= q^n + n q^{n-1} p + \frac{n(n-1)}{2!} q^{n-2} p^2 + \cdots + p^n.$$

A bit of scrutiny of this expression will reveal that it is nothing more than the binomial expansion of $(q + p)^n$. Thus

$$\sum_{\text{all } x_i} f(x_i) = (q + p)^n = 1^n = 1,$$

and the requirement that the probability function sum to 1 is met.

The mean of the binomial distribution is determined to be

$$E[X] = \mu = \sum_{\text{all } x_i} x_i f(x_i) = \sum_{x=0}^{n} x \binom{n}{x} p^x q^{n-x}.$$

Since a 0 value of x does not contribute to the summation, the lower limit of the summation can be changed to $x = 1$:

$$\mu = \sum_{x=1}^{n} x \frac{n!}{x!\,(n-x)!} p^x q^{n-x}.$$

Canceling x gives

$$\mu = \sum_{x=1}^{n} \frac{n!}{(x-1)!\,(n-x)!} p^x q^{n-x},$$

and by factoring out an n and a p, this expression becomes

$$\mu = np \sum_{x=1}^{n} \frac{(n-1)!}{(x-1)!\,(n-x)!} p^{x-1} q^{n-x}.$$

If $x - 1$ is replaced by the dummy variable y, and $n - 1$ is replaced by m, the expression in terms of y and m becomes

$$\mu = np \sum_{y=0}^{m} \frac{m!}{y!\,(m-y)!} p^y q^{m-y}.$$

Since the quantity being summed here is simply the probability of exactly y successes in m trials, and further, since it is summed over all possible values of y, the sum must be 1. Thus

$$\mu = np \cdot 1 = np,$$

which is the expression for the mean of the binomial distribution.

By a similar bit of mathematical manipulation, and by use of the relation $x^2 = x(x - 1) + x$, the variance of the binomial distribution can be found to be

$$\sigma^2 = npq.$$

As an application of the binomial distribution, consider the following hypothetical situation. Merchant vessel losses to enemy submarines are being studied. Statistics on past sinkings indicate that the probability that an individual merchant vessel is sunk on a single crossing is 1/10. What is the probability that exactly two merchant vessels are sunk in a total of 10 attempted crossings? Also, what is the mean number of sinkings in 10 attempted crossings?

Let X = the number of merchant vessel sinkings in 10 attempted crossings. Then

$$n = 10,\ p = 1/10,\ q = 9/10,$$

$$\Pr\{X = 2\} = f(2) = \binom{10}{2}(1/10)^2(9/10)^8 = .19,$$

and

$$\mu = np = (10)(1/10) = 1.$$

Because of the frequent appearance of the binomial distribution in applications of probability theory, standard binomial tables have been compiled in mathematical handbooks giving, for a binomially distributed X, $f(x)$ for various values of x, n, and p.

The binomial distribution is used most frequently in this text to answer the question: *What is the probability that at least one success occurs in* n *trials*? This is computed as follows:

$$\Pr\{\text{at least one success}\} = \Pr\{X \geq 1\}$$
$$= f(1) + f(2) + \ldots + f(n)$$
$$= \sum_{x=1}^{n} \binom{n}{x} p^x q^{n-x}.$$

This may be difficult to evaluate without tables, but may be made much easier by noting that

$$\Pr\{X \geq 1\} = 1 - \Pr\{X = 0\} = 1 - f(0) = 1 - \binom{n}{0} p^0 q^n = 1 - q^n,$$

where one term instead of n terms must be computed. For other required probabilities, the computational effort required can often be reduced by a similar approach.

A18   The Poisson Distribution

Another extremely useful probability distribution is the **Poisson**, which applies in certain situations in which an event occurs repeatedly in a "completely random" or "haphazard" manner. A random variable X which is Poisson distributed will then be the *number* of such occurrences in a certain time interval. The probability function for a Poisson random variable with **parameter** λ is defined by

$$f(x) = \begin{cases} \dfrac{\lambda^x e^{-\lambda}}{x!}, & \text{for } x = 0, 1, 2, \ldots \\ 0, & \text{otherwise.} \end{cases}$$

The fact that $\sum f(x) = 1$ follows directly from the Taylor expansion of e^λ, namely

$$e^\lambda = \sum_{x=0}^{\infty} \frac{\lambda^x}{x!}.$$

Also, it may be shown that $E[X] = \text{variance}[X] = \lambda$.

For an example of the use of the Poisson distribution, suppose that the number of emissions from a radioactive material is a Poisson random variable with parameter $\lambda = 20t$, where t is the time in hours. What is the probability that exactly 5 emissions occur in 1/2 hour? To answer this, let X be the number of emissions in 1/2 hour. Then X is Poisson with parameter $(20)(1/2) = 10$. So, $\Pr\{X = 5\} = f(5) = e^{-10}10^5/5! = .038$.

The Poisson distribution is studied more in the next section, and again in A22 in connection with the Poisson process.

A19   The Poisson Distribution as an Approximation to the Binomial Distribution

In addition to having many applications in its own right, the Poisson distribution can also be used, under certain circumstances, as a good approximation to the binomial distribution. As will be seen, the use of this approximation is most convenient for those situations in which calculations with the binomial formula would be quite tedious.

Recall that the binomial distribution yields the probability of x occurrences of an event in n independent trials when p, the probability of occurrence on one trial, remains constant. In those instances where n is large and p is small, the binomial distribution can be approximated by the Poisson distribution. In making this approximation, substitute the mean of the binomial ($\mu = np$) for the mean appearing in the Poisson density function, i.e.,

$$p(x) \approx \frac{e^{-np}(np)^x}{x!}.$$

In most cases the approximation is quite accurate whenever $n \geq 100$ and $p \leq .05$. In many other cases the approximation is sufficiently accurate for even smaller values of n and larger values of p.

As mentioned earlier, the value of the Poisson approximation lies in the fact that through its use one is able to eliminate much of the tedious arithmetic associated with the combinatorial calculations required for the binomial. Whereas the raising of fractions to large powers can be performed conveniently on a hand calculator, the calculation of combinatorials is usually a long and laborious process (unless the analyst has a calculator that has combinatorial function keys). The following numerical example will illustrate the savings in effort which can be realized by using the Poisson approximation.

Assume that the number X of occurrences of a particular event has a binomial distribution with $p = 1/100$. What is the probability of exactly 6 occurrences of the event in 300 independent trials? The result, using the binomial probability function is

$$f(6) = \binom{300}{6} (1/100)^6 (99/100)^{294}$$

$$= \frac{(300)(299)(298)(297)(296)(295)}{(6)(5)(4)(3)(2)(1)} (10^{-12})(.052) = .0502.$$

The calculation of this expression is quite tedious. However, if the Poisson approximation is used with $\mu = (300)(1/100) = 3$, the result is

$$f(6) \approx \frac{e^{-3}(3)^6}{6!} = \frac{(.05)(729)}{(720)} = .0504.$$

A20   The Geometric Distribution

It has been seen that the binomial distribution applies to situations where the random variable is the number of successes in n independent Bernoulli trials with a constant probability, p, of success on each trial. An associated random variable is the number of independent Bernoulli trials until the first success occurs.

Let N be a random variable defined as the number of the trial on which the first success occurs. For 1 and 2 trials,

$$Pr\{N = 1\} = Pr\{\text{number of trials for first success} = 1\}$$
$$= Pr\{\text{success occurs on the first trial}\} = p,$$
$$Pr\{N = 2\} = Pr\{\text{number of trials for first success} = 2\}$$
$$= Pr\{\text{failure occurs on first trial and success on second trial}\} = (1-p)p,$$

assuming independence. For n trials,

$$Pr\{N = n\} = Pr\{\text{number of trials for first success} = n\}$$
$$= Pr\{\text{failure on first } n-1 \text{ trials and success on } n\text{th trial}\}$$
$$= (1-p)^{n-1}p.$$

By induction,

$$f(n) = \begin{cases} (1-p)^{n-1}p, & \text{for } n = 1, 2, \dots, \\ 0, & \text{for other } n. \end{cases}$$

This is called the **geometric distribution** from its resemblance to a geometric series where the sum of the first n terms is

$$a + ar + ar^2 + \dots + ar^{n-1} = a\frac{(1-r^n)}{1-r}.$$

In this series if $-1 < r < 1$, then the sum as n approaches infinity becomes

$$a + ar + ar^2 + \ldots = \frac{a}{1-r}. \tag{A-10}$$

Use of this fact makes it possible to show that the probability function does in fact sum to 1:

$$\sum_{n=1}^{\infty} f(n) = p \sum_{n=1}^{\infty} (1-p)^{n-1} = p\left(\frac{1}{1-(1-p)}\right) = 1.$$

The mean number of trials required for one success is

$$E[N] = \sum_{\text{all } n} n(1-p)^{n-1} p$$

$$= p + 2p(1-p) + 3p(1-p)^2 + \ldots,$$

which can be evaluated after noting that the derivative with respect to r of both sides of (A-10) is

$$a + 2ar + 3ar^2 + \ldots = \frac{a}{(1-r)^2};$$

using $a = p$ and $r = 1 - p$, this becomes

$$p + 2p(1-p) + 3p(1-p)^2 + \ldots = \frac{p}{p^2} = \frac{1}{p},$$

and the expected value of N then becomes

$$E[N] = \mu = \frac{1}{p}.$$

The variance of N is $(1-p)/p^2$. This can also be computed with slight additional difficulty, using the second derivative of the infinite geometric series and the additional fact that $x^2 = x(x-1) + x$. This computation will be left as an exercise for the interested reader.

A21   The Uniform Distribution

The first continuous probability distribution to be discussed is the **uniform** distribution. It is simply the continuous analogue of the discrete distribution in which each outcome is equally likely. The set of outcomes resulting from the toss of a single die has been used as an example of such a discrete distribution where, if X represents the number of spots showing, then $f(x) = \Pr\{X=x\}$ would be constant for all possible values of x. This constant probability is the distinguishing characteristic of an equally likely distribution. As a continuous analogue to this, consider spinning a pointer which might stop with equal likelihood anywhere between two numbers, say a and b. In complete analogy to the die example, the probability density function associated with the stopping point of the spinner would likewise have a constant value, $f(x) = k$, over the entire range of possible values of the random variable.

The graph of the probability function for the discrete case would have a constant height for each possible outcome as shown in Figure A.18. The graph of the probability density function for the continuous case would be a smooth curve of constant height $f(x) = k$ as in Figure A.19. Because of its characteristic appearance, the uniform distribution is sometimes referred to as the **rectangular** distribution. To find k, recall the fact that the area under the density function must always sum to 1. Since the length of the interval $[a, b]$ is $b - a$,

$$k = \frac{1}{b-a},$$

FIGURE A.18. DISCRETE UNIFORM DISTRIBUTION

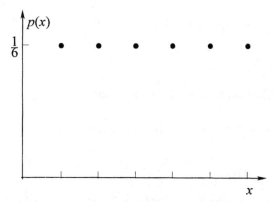

FIGURE A.19. CONTINUOUS UNIFORM DISTRIBUTION

and the probability density function for the uniform distribution is

$$f(x) = \begin{cases} 1/(b-a), & \text{if } a \le x \le b, \\ 0, & \text{otherwise.} \end{cases}$$

The general form of the cumulative distribution function is

$$F(x) = \begin{cases} 0, & x < a, \\ \int_a^x \frac{1}{b-a}\, dt = \frac{x-a}{b-a}, & a \le x \le b, \\ 1, & x > b. \end{cases}$$

Also,

$$\Pr\{x_1 \le X \le x_2\} = \int_{x_1}^{x_2} f(x)\, dx = \frac{x_2 - x_1}{b-a}, \quad a \le x_1 \le x_2 \le b.$$

The mean of the uniform distribution is

$$E[X] = \mu = \int_{-\infty}^{\infty} x f(x)\, dx = \frac{1}{b-a} \int_a^b x\, dx,$$

so

$$\mu = \frac{b+a}{2}.$$

In a similar manner, it can be shown that the variance of the uniform distribution is

$$\sigma^2 = \frac{(b-a)^2}{12}.$$

A22   The Exponential Distribution and the Poisson Process

The **exponential distribution with parameter** λ is defined by its cumulative distribution function:

$$F(t) = \begin{cases} 1 - e^{-\lambda t}, & \text{for } t \geq 0, \\ 0, & \text{otherwise.} \end{cases}$$

Its probability density function is given by $f(t) = F'(t) = \lambda e^{-\lambda t}$ for $t \geq 0$ and $f(t) = 0$, otherwise. If T is the random variable, its mean, $E[T]$, is $1/\lambda$, and its variance is $1/\lambda^2$.

The exponential distribution is also the continuous analog of the geometric distribution in the following sense. In an experiment where the binomial distribution describes the *number of successes in n trials*, the geometric distribution describes the *number of trials necessary for one success*. In an experiment where the Poisson distribution describes the *number of random occurrences of some event in an interval of size* t, of time, distance, area, volume, etc., the exponential distribution describes the *interval required for one such random occurrence.*

An exponential random variable is often used to model the (next) time of occurrence of "random" or "haphazard" events, e.g., the time it takes a "no-wear" part to fail (see Chapter 14), for a radioactive isotope to emit a radiation blast, or a customer to arrive at a bank. This distribution plays a key role in the Poisson process, described next.

A Poisson *process* pertains to events occurring in time and is characterized by a parameter $\lambda > 0$, called the **rate of occurrence of events**. Suppose $t \geq 0$ is arbitrary. Suppose that *independent of* t *and of the number of events in* $[0, t)$, the following hold: For small $h > 0$, the probability that an event occurs during the interval $[t, t + h)$ is approximately λh, specifically

$$\lim_{h \to 0} \left[\Pr\{\text{an event occurs in } [t, t+h)\} - \lambda h \right] = 0; \qquad \text{(A-11)}$$

and for small $h > 0$, the probability of 2 or more events occurring in $[t, t + h)$ is negligible compared to the probability of at least 1 event, specifically

$$\lim_{h \to 0} \left[\frac{1}{\lambda h} \Pr\{\text{at least 2 events occur in } [t, t+h)\} \right] = 0. \qquad \text{(A-12)}$$

Then this event process is said to be a **Poisson process with rate λ (or parameter λ)**. This process (much used in Chapter 5) is closely related to the exponential distribution, which is continuous, and to the Poisson distribution, which is discrete.

To see this, observe the following: For $t \geq 0$, the number of events of the Poisson process with rate λ that occur in $[0, t)$ is a random variable; call it $N(t)$, let $\Pr\{N(t) = n\}$ be denoted $P_n(t)$, for $n = 0, 1, \ldots$, and let T be the time to the first event after time 0. It will be shown, following [1], that (a) $P_n(t) = e^{-\lambda t}/n!$, for $n = 0, 1, \ldots$, i.e., $N(t)$ has a Poisson distribution with mean λt and that therefore (b) T has an exponential distribution with parameter λ.

For $n = 1, 2, \ldots$, $t \geq 0$, and small $h > 0$, the occurrence of exactly n events in $[0, t + h)$ can happen in three mutually exclusive ways: (1) n events in $[0, t)$ and none in $[t, t + h)$, (2) $n - 1$ events in $[0, t)$ and 1 event in $[t, t + h)$, and (3) for some k with $2 \leq k \leq n$, $n - k$ events in $[0, t)$ and k events in $[t, t + h)$. Hence, for some c, $0 \leq c \leq 1$,

$$P_n(t + h) = P_n(t)(1 - \lambda h) + P_{n-1}(t)(\lambda h) +$$
$$c \times \Pr\{\text{at least 2 events in } [t, t + h)\} + \text{error term},$$

so

$$\frac{P_n(t + h) - P_n(t)}{h} = -\lambda P_n(t) + \lambda P_{n-1}(t) +$$
$$\frac{c}{h}\Pr\{\text{at least 2 events in } [t, t + h)\} + \frac{1}{h}(\text{error term});$$

letting $h \to 0$, by (A-11) and (A-12),

$$P_n'(t) = -\lambda P_n(t) + \lambda P_{n-1}(t), \quad \text{for } n = 1, 2, \ldots . \tag{A-13}$$

If $n = 0$, the contingencies (2) and (3) do not arise; in this case, the preceding is replaced by a similar but simpler development leading to $P_0'(t) = -\lambda P_0(t)$. This with the initial condition $P_0(0) = 1$ yields $P_0(t) = e^{-\lambda t}$, for $t \geq 0$, which proves (b) and for $n = 0$ proves (a). From this one proves (a) for $n = 1$ by applying (A-13) with $P_1(0) = 0$. Proceeding similarly by induction one proves (a) for all n.

Other literature sometimes uses the function N, defined above on the time axis, as being *defined* to be a Poisson process. The fact that the distribution of time elapsed from an instant t to the next event of a Poisson process has same exponential distribution for all t, is called the **memoryless property** and is often useful in modeling.

The Poisson process as presented above may be generalized to a **variable-parameter**, also called **non-homogeneous, Poisson process**: Replace the constant parameter λ by a nonnegative *function* λ defined on the time domain. One postulates that at any time t, for small $h > 0$, the probability that an event occurs during $[t, t + h)$ is approximately $\lambda(t)h$, etc. Of course, in contrast to the constant-parameter case, this probability *does* depend on t. Also, the distribution of the number of events in $[t, u)$, for $u \geq t \geq 0$, is again a Poisson distribution, but now with parameter

$$\int_a^b \lambda(t)dt.$$

This value is also the mean number of events in $[t, u)$. Non-homogenous Poisson processes (see Khintchine [2] for theory development) are applied in Chapter 5, in proving Theorem 5.2 and in defining detection rate.

Poisson processes, constant-parameter and variable-parameter, are important examples of **stochastic processes** in time, i.e., probabilistic descriptions of the occurrence of events in time. To specify a stochastic process one must have a means of specifying for any n-tuple of time instants a multivariate random variable corresponding to that n-tuple. Poisson processes have properties that readily afford such means. A stochastic process may alternatively be specified via a set of sample paths and a probability distribution over that set; that is the approach used in 803 of Chapter 8.

A23   The Normal Distribution

The occurrence of many real-world phenomena can be conveniently explained in terms of a well-known continuous probability distribution called the **normal** distribution, also called the **Gaussian** distribution. In general, the normal distribution can be said to apply to many situations involving measurements the frequency of whose values fall within symmetric patterns about a central value, with increasing frequency as one tends toward the central value. In particular, the sum of several random variables tends to have this property, a fact which is formalized in the Central Limit Theorem of mathematical statistics.

For example, consider the values which might be obtained when taking any of the following measurements:

a. the heights of all men, age 21 or older, in a large city;
b. the grades received on the graduate record examination by all college seniors throughout the country;
c. the circumferences of all the full-grown trees in a large forest;
d. the thicknesses of all the metal discs produced by an automatic machine in a 24-hour period.

The measurements in all of these situations would fall into the same general pattern. To emphasize the underlying similarities involved, consider the so-called relative frequency diagrams associated with these measurements. These would be constructed by first grouping the measurements into arbitrary intervals of equal length and then counting the number of measurements falling into each interval and dividing these tallies by the total number of measurements. This gives the **relative frequency** for each interval, which gives estimates for the probability that any one random measurement will fall into any particular interval. Finally, to complete the relative frequency diagram, the results for all of the intervals can be plotted in the form of a bar graph. In many cases, the relative frequency diagrams have the general shape shown in Figure A.20.

FIGURE A.20. RELATIVE FREQUENCY OF MEASUREMENTS

Note that the measurements are grouped in a roughly symmetrical fashion about a central value, and that the relative frequencies drop off as the distance from that central value increases.

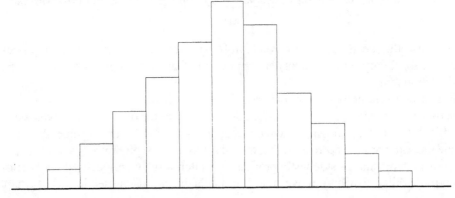

If more and more measurements are tabulated, and if the measuring instruments are sufficiently accurate so as to allow the data to be grouped into finer and finer subintervals, then the bar graph approaches the form of a smooth bell-shaped curve as in Figure A.21. Whereas the bar graph represents a rough approximation of probabilities in the form of a relative frequency diagram, the smooth curve yields a precise representation of probabilities in the form of a smooth probability density curve.

FIGURE A.21. FREQUENCY OF MEASUREMENT APPROACHES NORMAL CURVE

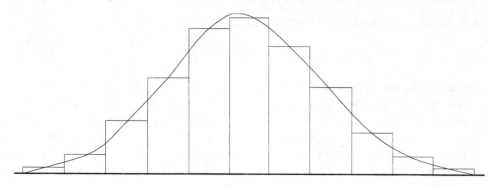

The normal distribution originally received its name because many years ago, it was mistakenly held to be *the one* probability distribution underlying all continuous random variables.

To determine the mathematical expression for the **normal density function**, consider the following function:

$$g(x) = k \exp\left(-\frac{1}{2}\left(\frac{x - \alpha}{\beta} \right)^2 \right), \quad \text{all } x.$$

Note that the function is symmetrical about a central value, α (because of the exponent 2), that for positive values of k, the function is always nonnegative (another requirement of a probability density function), and that as x moves away from α, $g(x)$ decreases. For g to serve as a density function, its integral over all possible values of x must be 1. As in the case for the uniform distribution, this requirement can be met by a suitable choice of k, i.e., the following expression is solved for k:

$$\int_{-\infty}^{\infty} k \exp\left(-\frac{1}{2}\left(\frac{x - \alpha}{\beta} \right)^2 \right) dx = 1.$$

The value of k which satisfies this expression is (by some involved integration)

$$k = \frac{1}{\beta \sqrt{2\pi}}.$$

The probability density function for the normal distribution is in fact given by

$$f(x) = \frac{1}{\beta \sqrt{2\pi}} \exp\left(-\frac{1}{2}\left(\frac{x - \alpha}{\beta} \right)^2 \right), \quad \text{all } x.$$

By a visual inspection of the plot of the normal density function, one can see that the point of symmetry (hence the mean) occurs at the point $x = \alpha$, i.e., $\mu = \alpha$. Also, by some rather complicated integration, it can be shown that the variance for the normal distribution is β^2, i.e., $\sigma^2 = \beta^2$. Hence the expression rewritten in terms of the familiar parameters μ and σ is

$$f(x) = \frac{1}{\sigma\sqrt{2\pi}} \exp\left[-\frac{1}{2}\left(\frac{x-\mu}{\sigma} \right)^2 \right], \quad \text{all } x,$$

from which it follows that the cumulative distribution function is

$$F(x) = \Pr\{X \le x\} = \int_{-\infty}^{x} \frac{1}{\sigma\sqrt{2\pi}} \exp\left[-\frac{1}{2}\left(\frac{t-\mu}{\sigma} \right)^2 \right] dt, \quad \text{all } x.$$

As in any continuous distribution, probability statements are expressed as

$$\Pr\{x_1 \le X \le x_2\} = \int_{x_1}^{x_2} \frac{1}{\sigma\sqrt{2\pi}} \exp\left[-\frac{1}{2}\left(\frac{x-\mu}{\sigma} \right)^2 \right] dx.$$

In the case of the normal distribution, however, the density function cannot be integrated by anti-differentiation in order to find the cumulative distribution function or other desired probabilities. The problem presented by this difficulty is not serious, since the numerical value of a particular integral can be approximated to any desired degree of accuracy and tabulated for use. It is not necessary to tabulate values of $F(x)$ versus x for various values of μ and σ, since any normal distribution can be standardized in order to use tabulated integrals for the special case where $\mu = 0$ and $\sigma = 1$. The standard symbol used to represent the normal distribution with mean μ and standard deviation σ is $N(\mu, \sigma)$. The standardized normal distribution then is denoted by $N(0, 1)$. Let T be a normally distributed random variable having $\mu = 0$ and $\sigma = 1$. Then

$$f(x) = \frac{1}{\sqrt{2\pi}} \exp\left(-\frac{1}{2}x^2 \right), \quad \text{all } x,$$

and

$$F(z) = \int_{-\infty}^{z} \frac{1}{\sqrt{2\pi}} \exp\left(-\frac{1}{2}x^2 \right) dx,$$

where z is a specific value of the random variable X.

This integral is the one tabulated for various values of z, representing the area shaded under the standardized normal density function as shown in Figure A.22. An excerpt from a standardized normal table follows in Figure A.23. In order to use such tables to find probabilities for a given normal random variable X with mean μ and variance σ^2, it is necessary only to standardize this distribution by setting

$$Z = \frac{X-\mu}{\sigma}.$$

Then $dx = \sigma dz$, and as x goes from $-\infty$ to x, z goes from $-\infty$ to $(x - \mu)/\sigma$ so that

$$\Pr\{X \le x\} = \int_{-\infty}^{x} \frac{1}{\sigma\sqrt{2\pi}} \exp\left[-\frac{1}{2}\left(\frac{t-\mu}{\sigma} \right)^2 \right] dt$$

$$= \int_{-\infty}^{(x-\mu)/\sigma} \frac{1}{\sqrt{2\pi}} \exp\left(-\frac{t^2}{2} \right) dt = \Pr\{Z \le \frac{x-\mu}{\sigma}\}.$$

It can be seen that Z measures the distance from X to the mean, μ, in units of standard deviation.

FIGURE A.22. CUMULATIVE STANDARD NORMAL DISTRIBUTION

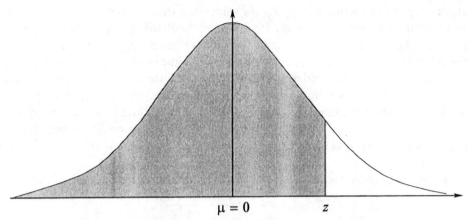

$\mu = 0 \qquad z$

FIGURE A.23. CUMULATIVE STANDARD NORMAL TABLE

z	$F(z)$	z	$F(z)$	z	$F(z)$	z	$F(z)$
0.0	.500	0.8	.788	1.6	.945	2.4	.992
0.1	.540	0.9	.816	1.7	.955	2.5	.994
0.2	.579	1.0	.841	1.8	.964	2.6	.995
0.3	.618	1.1	.864	1.9	.971	2.7	.997
0.4	.655	1.2	.885	2.0	.977	2.8	.997
0.5	.691	1.3	.903	2.1	.982	2.9	.998
0.6	.726	1.4	.919	2.2	.986	3.0	.999
0.7	.758	1.5	.933	2.3	.989		

As an example of normal probability calculations involving the use of the standardized normal tables consider the following: Studies are being conducted concerning the amount of rainfall in Washington, DC. Suppose that Weather Bureau statistics indicate that for the previous five-year period the cumulative rainfall for Spring has been normally distributed with a mean of 10 inches and a variance of 4 inches. Based on these statistics, what is the probability of at least 15 inches of rainfall in Washington, DC during the forthcoming Spring?

Let X be the total amount of rainfall in inches during the Spring; X is distributed N(10, 4). The problem is to find $\Pr\{X \geq 15\}$. Let

$$Z = \frac{X-\mu}{\sigma} = \frac{15-10}{2} = 2.5.$$

Then in terms of the standardized random variable Z, the probability that the amount of rainfall will be at least 2.5 standard deviation units above the mean rainfall is

$$\Pr\{X \geq 15\} = \Pr\{Z \geq 2.5\} = 1 - \Pr\{Z \leq 2.5\} = 1 - \Pr\{-\infty < Z \leq 2.5\}.$$

From the standardized normal table when $z = 2.5$,

$$F(2.5) = \Pr\{Z \leq 2.5\} = .994,$$

from which it follows that

$$\Pr\{Z \geq 2.5\} = 1 - .994 = .006.$$

The probability of more than 15 inches of rain during the forthcoming Spring then is .006.

It should be pointed out that $f(x) > 0$ for *all* values of x from $-\infty$ to $+\infty$. One might reasonably question whether the distribution can be used to represent the distribution of inches of rainfall, which certainly cannot take on negative values, much less values approaching $-\infty$. A similar comment can be made on all of the examples (a) to (d) at the beginning of the section. The answer lies in the fact that although the density function is defined for all values of x, the height of the curve is practically negligible for those values which are far removed from the mean. For example, 99.7 percent of the probability in a normal distribution is contained in an area enclosed by a range of 3 standard deviation units on either side of the mean. It may therefore be reasonable to use this particular distribution, which has an infinite range, to approximate real-world distributions whose true ranges are finite.

Consider the (continuous) joint probability distribution defined by the density function f, where

$$f(x, y) = \frac{1}{2\pi\sigma_1\sigma_2\sqrt{1-\rho^2}} e^{-q/2},$$

and

$$q = \frac{1}{1-\rho^2}\left[\left(\frac{x - \mu_1}{\sigma_1}\right)^2 - 2\rho\left(\frac{x - \mu_1}{\sigma_1}\right)\left(\frac{y - \mu_2}{\sigma_2}\right) + \left(\frac{y - \mu_2}{\sigma_2}\right)^2\right],$$

for $-\infty < x, y < \infty$. The quantities μ_1, μ_2, σ_1, σ_2, and ρ are parameters of the distribution.

One can show the following:

a. For all x, y, $f(x, y) \geq 0$; also

$$\int_{-\infty}^{\infty}\int_{-\infty}^{\infty} f(x, y)\,dx\,dy = 1,$$

i.e., f is in fact a probability density function.

b. If one considers only the random variable X, then its density function g given by

$$g(x) = \int_{-\infty}^{\infty} f(x, y)\,dy$$

is normal with mean μ_1 and variance σ_1^2.

c. If one considers only the random variable Y, then its density function h given by

$$h(y) = \int_{-\infty}^{\infty} f(x, y)\,dx$$

is normal with mean μ_2 and variance σ_2^2.

d. The **correlation** of X and Y is ρ.

This distribution is called the **bivariate normal** distribution, used in Chapter 12. It is sometimes a good model for a situation such as the following. Suppose the target in a bombing mission is located at coordinates (μ_1, μ_2) on the map. Two important random variables associated with the mission are X, the latitude of the bomb impact position, and Y the longitude of the bomb impact position. In many cases it is reasonable to assume both X and Y are normally distributed, with means μ_1 and μ_2, respectively. The correlation ρ is a measure of the relationship between the latitudinal and the longitudinal miss distances. A positive value for ρ would indicate that a "bad shot" in the N-S direction is likely to be bad in the E-W direction as well.

An important theorem in this context is as follows:

Theorem. Suppose X and Y are the latitudinal and longitudinal variables described in the "bombing problem" above and are independent. If (X, Y) is bivariate normal with parameters (μ_1, μ_2), standard deviations (σ_1, σ_2), and X and Y are independent, then the probability that the bomb lands within the ellipse centered at position (μ_1, μ_2) with latitudinal semi-axis length $k\sigma_1$ and longitudinal semi-axis length $k\sigma_2$ is $1 - \exp(-k^2/2)$.

A24   Statistical Sampling

The discussion in the previous section leads naturally to the consideration of the general subject of drawing inferences from limited sample data. A good example of general inferences of this type is to be seen in the early paragraphs of A23 when the notion of the relative frequency diagram was generalized so as to arrive at the smooth probability density curve.

Generalizations such as these are at the very heart of a well-known discipline devoted to the study and analysis of collected sample data. This discipline is referred to under the general heading of **mathematical statistics** or simply **statistics**. In the main body of this text, the part that is most concerned with statistics is Chapter 3 on simulation.

As an example, consider an inspector concerned with quality control of a production process, studying the thicknesses of washers turned out by an automatic machine. Suppose the manufacturer's specifications call for a washer thickness of x_0. The quality control inspector is therefore interested in knowing both the mean washer thickness which is actually being produced by the machine, and the amount of variance about this mean value. To determine these parameters, the inspector might proceed by choosing a sampling of washers at random from the production line and measuring their thickness. It would be sensible to group the sample data into uniform intervals; let x_i be the center of the ith interval. The results could be plotted in the form of a relative frequency diagram and treated as a discrete probability distribution. In this manner, one would then be able to determine the mean value for *this particular sample* by use of (A-9):

$$\bar{x} = \sum_{\text{all } x_i} x_i f(x_i),$$

where $f(x_i)$ is the fraction (relative frequency) of the samples that fall in the ith interval. This quantity is commonly referred to as the **sample mean**. The question which then arises is how confident can one be that the mean thickness of this particular sample is truly representative of the mean thickness of *all* the washers being produced by the machine. The degree of **confidence** one will have in the sample mean will depend, in no small measure, upon the number of measurements included in the sampling. In other words, the hypothesis that the sample mean is truly representative of the so-called **population** mean is subject to certain errors dependent upon both the sample size and the population variance.

To quantify this notion, some notation is introduced. Let X be a random variable which represents a certain characteristic for an entire population. For example, X could be the height of an American male adult, the high temperature in Baltimore on a June day, or the amount of money needed to build a type of aircraft. Let μ be the population mean, i.e., the average value of X over the entire population. It is desired to estimate μ by the sample mean, $\bar{x}$. One expects $\bar{x}$ to be "close" to μ, and calls it an **estimator** for μ. In Chapter 3, formulas are also given for the **sample variance**, the **variance of the sample mean**, and confidence intervals for estimation of the sample mean.

As an example, suppose that the high temperature in Baltimore on June 15 during a five year period has been as given in Figure A.24. It is desired to formulate a 95 percent-confidence interval for the true mean high temperature for June 15 in Baltimore. First, the sample mean is calculated as

$$\bar{x} = (81 + 96 + 78 + 79 + 86)/5 = 84.$$

Next, the sample standard deviation is calculated as

$$s = \sqrt{\frac{1}{5-1}\left[(81-84)^2 + (96-84)^2 + (78-84)^2 + (79-84)^2 + (86-84)^2\right]} = 7.38.$$

Finally, following Chapter 3, the "t-statistic," $t_{(.025,4)}$, is found in tables to be 2.776. A 95 percent confidence interval for μ is

$$\left[84 - 2.776\left(\frac{7.38}{\sqrt{5}}\right), \ 84 + 2.776\left(\frac{7.38}{\sqrt{5}}\right)\right] = [74.8, \ 93.2].$$

Based on the sample data, one can say with 95 percent confidence that the true mean high temperature in Baltimore for the date June 15 is between 74.8° and 93.2°. Note that the analysis depends on the assumption (reasonable in this case) that the high temperatures year by year are in general normally distributed.

FIGURE A.24 HIGH TEMPERATURE IN BALTIMORE

Year	Temperature (°F)
1989	81
1990	96
1991	78
1992	79
1993	86

If the sample size were large, say 30 or more, a confidence interval could be found more easily by observing that by the Central Limit Theorem the distribution of the sample mean is approximately normal; the mean and standard deviation of this distribution are given in Chapter 3.

This example was related solely for the purpose of giving the reader a very brief introduction to the subject of statistics. It can be seen from this that statistics may be viewed as the empirical counterpart to mathematical probability theory.

A25   Other Literature

Olikin [3] is a text book on probability theory and is one of many good introductory texts for this subject. Montgomery and Runger's text [4] is recommended for statistics. A reader seeking a fuller development of the topics addressed in this appendix or to learn about related topics is encouraged to work with textbooks such as these.

[1] Feller, William. *An Introduction to Probability Theory and Its Applications*. Vol I. New York, NY: Wiley, 1957.

[2] Khintchine, A. Y. *Mathematical Methods in the Theory of Queuing*. London, U.K.: Charles Griffin & Co., 1960.

[3] Olikin, Ingram, et al. *Probability Models and Applications. 2nd Edition*. New York, NY: Macmillan, 1994.

[4] Montgomery, Douglas C., and George C. Runger. *Applied Statistics and Probability for Engineers*. New York, NY: John Wiley & Sons, Inc., 1994.

Problems

1. The probability density function may be defined over any domain. Here is a case in which the domain is [0, 2]. Consider the parabola $y = 2x - x^2$. If all the points enclosed between the parabola and the x-axis are equally likely, find the probability density function for the distribution of the distances of random points from the y-axis. First find the density function and then the cumulative distribution function. (Hint: let M and M' denote two straight lines parallel to the y-axis and cutting the x-axis at some points x and $x + dx$. Calculate the probability that a random point will fall between M and M'.).

2. Suppose a search vessel, at 0 in the figure, is moving with constant velocity in the direction indicated by the arrow. The object searched for (life raft, enemy vessel, etc.) is likely to be anywhere on the ocean, and is assumed at rest for simplicity. A simplifying assumption is made (which is not a bad one for some cases) that if the object comes within a radius R of the vessel it will be discovered.

   Relative to the search vessel, the ocean is moving along the parallel paths shown in the figure. The object will also move along one of these relative paths at some distance l from the searching vessel. It is not difficult to see that if the object is placed at random and if it is to be discovered, the value of l will occur at random between the limits $-R$ and R, and the approximate probability that the object, when seen, will be in the interval of length dl about l is given by $dl/(2R)$. This approach will produce a density function in terms of l.

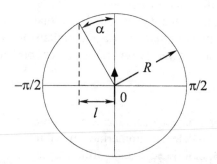

a. What is the probability that the object, if it is discovered, comes into view at a relative bearing α? (You must make a transformation to get the result in terms of α.)

b. Verify that your result satisfies the conditions for a density function.

c. Find the probability that the object will be discovered in the sector 0 to 45 degrees.
d. Show that restricting the lookouts to searching the forward quarter will reduce the probability of sighting by only 30 percent.

3. In Problem 2, find the expected value and the variance of the distribution.

4. In single-ship transits from Pearl to Auckland during World War II, there were 40 sinkings in 1,000 ship-transits.
a. What is the probability that a ship was sunk in one transit?
b. Of 20 ships carrying strategic materials, three were sunk on these individual trips. Does this seem unlikely? What is the probability for this event?
c. Calculate the probability that at most two ships would be sunk in the 20 transits of ships carrying strategic materials.
d. What is the probability that any ship which enters this system will be available for the 11th trip?

5. Consider a box of 200 fuses. It is known that the probability of a particular fuse being defective is .02.

a. What is the probability that at least 6 fuses in the box are defective? (Set up the problem but do not carry out the calculations.)
b. Use the Poisson approximation to obtain an approximation to the probability in a.

6. The probability of detection of a submarine by an ASW ship depends on many variables, among which are speed, depth, water temperature, condition of ASW ship's sonar, and lateral distance. Assume that two ASW ships are part of a screen and that a submarine attempts to penetrate between them somewhat closer to ship A than to ship B. Assume that A's probability of detection is .6 and that of B is .4, and that detection by A and detection by B are independent events. Find the probability that the submarine is detected by at least one of the ships.

7. Six destroyers are conducting an ECM search in a known submarine operating area. Each destroyer is monitoring a specific band of frequencies. There are no overlaps and no gaps in the coverage. Past experience indicates that it is equally likely that the submarine will transmit in any of the six range bands, but not in more than one band simultaneously.
    For problem purposes, assume that an individual destroyer's probability of detecting an emission made in its range band is 1.
    Define the following events:

(1) Event A: destroyers 1, 3, or 5 detect a submarine emission.
(2) Event B: destroyers 2, 4, or 6 detect a submarine emission.
(3) Event C: destroyers 1, 2, 3, or 4 detect a submarine emission.
(4) Event D: destroyers 1, 2, 3, 4, or 5 detect a submarine emission.

a. Are the following independent? (Justify all answers mathematically.)
    i. A and B?

   ii. *A* and *D*?
   iii. *A* and *C*?
   iv. *B* and *C*?
   v.   *B* and *D*?
   vi. *C* and *D*?

b. Answer the questions in (a) for the case where a destroyer's probability of detecting an emission made in its range band is not 1 but is 1/2.

8. Consider a squadron of six submarines, four of which are nuclear and two are nonnuclear. The squadron has been ordered to provide two submarines for off-shore patrols over the Christmas holiday leave period. All of the submarines are fully capable of performing the mission. The decision narrows down to choosing two units to do an unpleasant job. The Squadron Commander decides to choose the two submarines by assigning numbers one through six to the submarines, drawing the numbers out of a hat without replacement, and sending the submarines whose numbers were drawn. Define *A* to be the event that exactly one nonnuclear submarine is sent. Define *B* to be the event that both nonnuclear submarines are sent.

a. Compute $\Pr\{A\}$, $\Pr\{B\}$, and $\Pr\{A \cap B\}$.
b. Are *A* and *B* independent events? Why?
c. Are *A* and *B* mutually exclusive events? Why?

9. Aboard a particular Polaris submarine, statistical records of many trials indicate that the probability of a successful missile launch is 3/5 and that the probability of two successful missile launches in a row is 2/5. Let *A* be the event that one launch is successful and let *B* be the event that two successive launches are successful.

a. Are events *A* and *B* independent?
b. Justify your answer mathematically.

10. Find the probability that on successive rolls with a single die at least two aces will appear in succession by the end of the fifth roll.

11. Solve Problem 5 using the Poisson approximation.

12. Write an expression for the probability of the union of four events, *A*, *B*, *C*, *D*, in terms of $\Pr\{A\}$, $\Pr\{B\}$, $\Pr\{C\}$, $\Pr\{D\}$, and probabilities of the various intersections which may exist. Compare the simplicity of your expression with that of (A-5).

13. Let the random variable *X* denote the number of ones which appear when two dice are thrown. For every possible outcome, list the value of the random variable as in A12.

14. Using the situation in A14, but assuming that ships are as likely to transit the channel at one point as any other, do the following:

a. Derive an expression for the probability density function.
b. Compute the mean value of X.
c. Compute the variance of X and the standard deviation.
d. What commonly used distribution fits this situation?
e. Derive an expression for the cumulative distribution function.
f. Compute the values of $F(250)$, $F(750)$, $F(-250)$, and $F(1250)$.

15. Given E and F are events which are subsets of the same sample space, if $\Pr\{E\} = 1/3$, $\Pr\{E|F\} = 1/2$, and $\Pr\{F|E\} = 1/4$, find

a. $\Pr\{F\}$,
b. $\Pr\{E \cup F\}$.

16. Let E and F be independent events and subsets of the same sample space. If $\Pr\{E\} = 1/4$ and $\Pr\{F\} = 1/3$, find

a. $\Pr\{E \cap F)$,
b. $\Pr\{E \cup F\}$,
c. $\Pr\{E|F\}$,
d. $\Pr\{F|E\}$.

17. Three A-7s, A, B, and C, are sent to bomb a certain target. Each plane is to drop one bomb. The probabilities of a plane's bomb hitting the target are 1/2, 1/3, and 1/4 for planes A, B, and C, respectively. Assuming independence, find the probability that:

a. bombs from all three of the planes hit the target;
b. bombs from exactly two of the planes hit the target;
c. the target is hit at least once;
d. the bomb from plane B hits the target, given that the bomb from plane A hits the target.

18. Two cards are dealt (without replacement) from an ordinary bridge deck. Find the probability that

a. the first card is black;
b. the second card is black given that the first one is black;
c. the second card is black given that the first card is red;
d. the second card is black.

19. A man tosses a coin four times. Assuming that the events associated with each toss are independent, find the probability that

a. the tosses show alternately heads and tails;
b. exactly two of the tosses show heads.

20. An experiment consists of tossing a coin twice. Let X be the random variable whose value, after two tosses, is the number of tails that show on the two tosses. Find

a. $\Pr\{X=0\}$;
b. $\Pr\{X=1\}$;
c. $\Pr\{X=2\}$.

21. Given the following probability function:

$$f(x) = \begin{cases} (x^2 + 7x + 1)/29, & x = 0, 1, 2, \\ 0, & \text{elsewhere.} \end{cases}$$

Find

a. $\Pr\{X=1\}$;
b. $\Pr\{X>0\}$.

22. Given the following density function:

$$f(x) = \begin{cases} 11/8, & 0 \le x \le 8, \\ 0, & \text{elsewhere.} \end{cases}$$

Find

a. $\Pr\{3 \le X \le 5\}$;
b. $\Pr\{4 \le X \le 8\}$;
c. $\Pr\{4 \le X \le 5\}$.

23. Given the following density function:

$$f(x) = \begin{cases} 3x^2/26, & 1 \le x \le 3, \\ 0, & \text{elsewhere.} \end{cases}$$

Find

a. $F(x)$, for all x;
b. $\Pr\{X<2\}$;
c. $\Pr\{X>2\}$.

24. Given that X is a random variable with the following associated possibilities:

$$\Pr\{X=1\} = 1/4,$$
$$\Pr\{X=2\} = 1/2,$$
$$\Pr\{X=3\} = 1/4,$$
$$\Pr\{X \ne 1, 2, 3\} = 0.$$

Find

a. $E[X]$;
b. $E[X^2]$;
c. $E[3X]$;

d. variance of X.

25. Given the following relationships:
$$E[X] = 2 \quad \text{and} \quad E[X^2] = 7.$$
Find

a. variance of X;
b. $E[3X]$;
c. $E[3X+1]$;
d. variance of $3X+1$.

26. Suppose X is a binomial random variable with $n = 4$ and $p = 1/3$. Find

a. $\Pr\{X = 3\}$;
b. $\Pr\{X > 2\}$;
c. $\Pr\{X > 0\}$.

27. An ordinary die is thrown 9 times. If the top face shows 5 or 6 spots, a success occurs. Find the probability of exactly 3 successes.

28. A coin is tossed 5 times. Find the probability that it shows heads

a. twice,
b. at least twice,
c. more than twice.

29. If 3 ordinary dice are thrown simultaneously, the probability that the sum of the spots on the 3 dice is 4 is 1/72. If this experiment is repeated 144 times, find the approximate probability that the sum of the spots on the dice is 4

a. one time;
b. at least one time.

30. An ordinary deck of 52 cards is shuffled, and a card is removed from the deck and placed face down. A guess is made as to what card was removed, the results of the guess checked and the card replaced in the deck. Let this procedure be repeated 104 times. Find the probability of

a. two correct guesses;
b. at least two correct guesses.

31. Given that T is a standardized normal random variable. Find

a. $\Pr\{T < 1.20\}$,

b. $\Pr\{T > 2.70)$,
c. $\Pr\{1.4 < T < 2.4\}$,
d. $\Pr\{T > -1\}$,
e. $\Pr\{-1.2 < T < -1.1\}$,
f. $\Pr\{-.80 < T < .80\}$,
g. $\Pr\{-.80 < T < 1.2\}$.

32. Let T be a standardized normal random variable. Find z so that each of the following probability statements is true:
a. $\Pr\{T < z\} = .964$;
b. $\Pr\{T > z\} = .05$.

33. Given: X is $N(4, 9)$, find

a. $\Pr\{X < 7\}$,
b. $\Pr\{X > 2.5\}$,
c. $\Pr\{-.5 < X < 4.3\}$.

34. Suppose that the lifetime of electronic tubes is a normally distributed random variable. Suppose further that brand A has a lifetime X which is normally distributed with mean 30 hours and standard deviation 6 hours, while brand B has a lifetime Y which is normally distributed with a mean of 34 hours and a standard deviation of 3 hours. Of these two brands, which would you choose for use in an experimental aircraft with

a. 34 hours mission time?
b. 40 hours mission time?

35. A claim is made by suppliers of a medical test for a certain disease:
    If you have that disease, the test will show a positive reaction 95 percent of the time; if you do not have that disease, the test will show a negative reaction 95 percent of the time.
    Assume that .005 of a population as a whole has the disease, and that the claim is correct. Determine how significant the test is; i.e, if a person randomly chosen from the population gets a positive reaction, determine the new probability that he or she has the disease.

Answers to Problems

1. $f(x) = \begin{cases} 3/4\,(2x - x^2), & \text{for } 0 \le x \le 2, \\ 0, & \text{elsewhere.} \end{cases}$ $F(x) = \begin{cases} 1/4\,(3x^2 - x^3), & \text{for } 0 \le x \le 2, \\ 0, & \text{for } x < 0, \\ 1, & \text{for } x > 2. \end{cases}$

2. a. $f(\alpha) = \begin{cases} \dfrac{\cos \alpha}{2}, & -\dfrac{\pi}{2} \le \alpha \le \dfrac{\pi}{2}, \\ 0, & \text{elsewhere,} \end{cases}$ is a probability density function since $\displaystyle\int_{-\pi/2}^{\pi/2} \dfrac{\cos \alpha}{2}\, d\alpha = 1$.

b. (1) $0 \le \dfrac{\cos \alpha}{2} \le 1, \ -\dfrac{\pi}{2} \le \alpha \le \dfrac{\pi}{2}.$

c. $\Pr\{D| \ 0 \le \alpha \le 45°\} = .353.$

d. $\Pr\{D| -45° \le \alpha \le 45°\} = .706$ which is less than a 30 percent reduction in probability.

3. a. $E[\alpha] =$ zero.   b. $\mathrm{Var}[\alpha] = \dfrac{\pi^2}{4} - 2.$

4. a. .04.   b. .0383.   c. .956.   d. .665.

5. $\displaystyle\sum_{x=6}^{200} \binom{200}{x}(.02)^x \,(.98)^{200-x}$.

6. .76.

7. a. (1) no.   (2) no.   (3) yes.   (4) yes.   (5) no.   (6) no.
   b. (1) no.   (2) no.   (3) no.   (4) no.   (5) no.   (6) no.

8. a. 8/15, 1/15, zero.   b. no. c. yes.

9. no.

10. $751/7776 = .0966.$

11. 215.

12. $\Pr\{A\} + \Pr\{B\} + \Pr\{C\} + \Pr\{D\}$
    $- \Pr\{A \cap B\} - \Pr\{A \cap C\} - \Pr\{A \cap D\} - \Pr\{B \cap C\} - \Pr\{B \cap D) - \Pr\{C \cap D\}$
    $+ \Pr\{A \cap B \cap C\} + \Pr\{A \cap B \cap D\} + \Pr\{A \cap C \cap D\} + \Pr\{B \cap C \cap D\}$
    $- \Pr\{A \cap B \cap C \cap D\}$

13. Let zero denote an occurrence other than an ace

outcome	(0, 0)	(0, 1)	(1, 0)	(0, 0)
value of random variable x	zero	one	one	two

14. a. $f(x) = \begin{cases} \dfrac{1}{1000}, & 0 \le x \le 1000, \\ 0, & \text{elsewhere.} \end{cases}$

   b. $E[x] = 500.$ c. $\sigma^2 = 83{,}400, \ \sigma = 295.$ d. rectangular.

e. $F(x) = \begin{cases} \int_0^x \dfrac{1}{1000}\,dx = \dfrac{x}{1000}, & 0 \le x \le 1000, \\ 0, & x < 0, \\ 1, & x > 1000. \end{cases}$

f. $F(250) = .25.$ $F(750) = .75.$ $F(-250) = 0.$ $F(1250) = 1.$

15. a. 1/6.   b. 5/12.

16. a. 1/12.   b. 1/2.   c. 1/4.   d. 1/3.

17. a. 1/24.   b. 1/4.   c. 3/4.   d. 1/3.

18. a. 1/2.   b. 25/51.   c. 26/51.   d. ½.

19. a . 1/16.   b. 3/8.

20. a. 1/4.   b. 1/2.   c. 1/4.

21. a. 9/29.   b. 28/29.

22. a. 1/4.   b. 1/2.   c. 1/8.

23. a. $F(x) = \begin{cases} \dfrac{x^3 - 1}{26}, & 1 \le x \le 3, \\ 0, & x < 1, \\ 1, & x > 3. \end{cases}$

b. 7/26.   c. 19/26.

24. a. two.   b. 9/2.   c. six.   d. ½.

25. a. three.   b. six.   c. seven.   d. 27.

26. a. 8/81.   b. 1/9.   c. 65/81.

27. .273.

28. a. 5/16.   b. 13/16.   c. ½.

29. a. .2706.   b. .8647.

30. a. .2706.   b. .5941.

31. a. .885.   b. .003.   c. .073.   d. .841.   e. .021.   f. .576.   g. .673.

32. a. $z = 1.8$. b. $z = 1.64$.

33. a. .841.   b. .691.   c. .4730.

34. a. *B*.   b. *A*.

35. .087.

APPENDIX B
LINEAR PROGRAMMING FORMULATION
OF MATRIX GAMES

This appendix shows how to solve any matrix game for the optimal mixed strategies for both players by using linear programming. A mixed strategy for the Row Player is a row vector x having the same number of elements as the game matrix has rows. Similarly a mixed strategy for the Column Player is a column vector y having the same number of elements as the game matrix has columns. Recall that the ith element of x, x_i, is the probability that pure strategy i is used by the Row Player and similarly y_j is the probability that pure strategy j is used by the Column Player. Because x and y are vectors of the probabilities the different pure strategies are used by the two players, the sum of the components of each of these vectors must equal 1.

In the course of showing how to formulate the linear programs that will produce optimal mixed strategies, a proof will be given of the minimax theorem for mixed strategies. In this exposition it is presupposed that the reader is familiar with linear programming. Good textbooks covering both matrix games and linear programming are references [1, 2, 3].

B01   Minimax Theorem

Theorem (The Minimax Theorem). Let both the Row Player and the Column Player be permitted to use mixed strategies, with pure strategies as special cases. Let v_* be the highest possible payoff that Row Player can guarantee (no matter what Column Player does). Similarly let v^* be the lowest possible payoff Column Player can guarantee (no matter what Row Player does. Then $v = v_* = v^*$, where v is the value of the game, and hence every matrix game has a value.

To accomplish the above objectives, the following plan will be used. First, the calculation of v_* will be written as a "max min" problem over the set of pairs of mixed strategies for the two players. Then this problem will be reformulated (using some mathematical devices) as a linear program. When the same thing is done for v^*, the minimax theorem will be an easy consequence of the duality theorem of linear programming. It was shown in Chapter 2 that $v_* \le v^*$.

First consider the following lemma.

Lemma. For fixed numbers $a_1, \ldots, a_n$, let the linear function f be given by
$$f(y_1, \ldots, y_n) = a_1 y_1 + \ldots + a_n y_n \quad \text{for all } y_1, \ldots, y_n.$$
Then the minimum of f taken over all nonnegative vectors $y = (y_1, \ldots, y_n) \ge 0$ such that $y_1 + \ldots + y_n = 1$ is $\min\{a_1, \ldots, a_n\}$. Similarly, the maximum of f over the same set is $\max\{a_1, \ldots, a_n\}$.

To see the validity of the lemma, think of the y components as weights and note that the maximum is attained when all of the weight is put into the component with greatest coefficient; similar reasoning with sign reversal applies to the minimum.

Now consider a matrix game, in which the Row Player has pure strategies $i = 1, \ldots, m$, and the Column Player has pure strategies $j = 1, \ldots, n$. Also, let a_{ij} be the payoff from the Column Player to the Row Player if the Row Player chooses i and the Column Player chooses j. If the Row Player uses the mixed strategy $x = (x_1, \cdots, x_m)$ and the Column Player uses the mixed strategy $y = (y_1, \ldots, y_n)$, then the expected playoff from the Column Player to the Row Player is
$$\sum_{i=1}^{m} \sum_{j=1}^{n} a_{ij} x_i y_j.$$

The mathematical statement of the Row Player's max min problem is called problem P1:
$$v_* = \max_{x \in S} \left(\min_{y \in T} \left(\sum_{i=1}^{m} \sum_{j=1}^{n} a_{ij} x_i y_j \right) \right)$$
$$= \max_{x \in S} \left(\min_{y \in T} \left(\sum_{j=1}^{n} \left(\sum_{i=1}^{m} a_{ij} x_i \right) y_j \right) \right)$$
$$= \max_{x \in S} \left(\min_{j=1,\ldots,n} \left(\sum_{i=1}^{m} a_{ij} x_i \right) \right).$$

Here
$$S = \{x : \sum_{i=1}^{m} x_i = 1, \text{ and } x_i \ge 0 \text{ for } i = 1, 2, \ldots, m\},$$
$$T = \{y : \sum_{j=1}^{n} y_j = 1, \text{ and } y_j \ge 0 \text{ for } j = 1, 2, \ldots, n\}.$$

The last equality in problem P1 follows from the Lemma. Now let

$$x_0 = \min_{j=1,\dots,n} \left(\sum_{i=1}^{m} a_{ij} x_i \right).$$

Problem P1 can be rewritten using the above equation and using condition defining S as a constraint, resulting in the following constrained maximization problem, problem P2:

$$v_* = \max x_0,$$

subject to

$$x_0 = \min_{j=1,\dots,n} \left(\sum_{i=1}^{m} a_{ij} x_i \right), \tag{B-1}$$

$$x_1 + \dots + x_m = 1,$$

$$x_i \ge 0 \text{ for } i = 1, \dots, m.$$

To complete the conversion of this constrained maximization problem into a linear program, the constraint (B-1) is replaced by an apparently weaker constraint, but one which is not really weaker because x_0 is being maximized. This new version of the constraint is

$$x_0 \le \sum_{i=1}^{m} a_{ij} x_i \text{ for all } j. \tag{B-2}$$

After moving the expression on the right-hand side of (B-2) to the left of the equality sign and replacing (B-2) with it the transformation is complete. Thus the optimization problem given in P1 has become a standard-looking linear program, which is given next as problem P3:

$$v_* = \max x_0,$$

subject to

$$x_0 - \sum_{i=1}^{m} a_{ij} x_i \le 0 \text{ for } j = 1, \dots, n,$$

$$x_1 + \dots + x_m = 1,$$

$$x_i \ge 0 \text{ for } i = 1, \dots, m.$$

The same procedure is used to obtain a linear program to be solved for the Column Player's optimal mixed strategy y and the value v^* which caps the Column Player's expected loss. The resulting linear program is problem P4 :

$$v^* = \min y_0,$$

subject to

$$y_0 - \sum_{j=1}^{n} a_{ij} y_j \ge 0 \text{ for } i = 1, \dots, m,$$

$$y_1 + \dots + y_n = 1,$$

$$y_j \ge 0 \text{ for } j = 1, \dots, n.$$

Problems P3 and P4 are **dual linear programs**. A pure strategy can be used by either player. Thus for the Row Player this is equivalent to setting x equal to a vector of 0's with a 1 in the component corresponding to the pure strategy chosen. This vector provides a feasible solution for

P3. Similarly a pure strategy for the Column Player provides a feasible solution for P4. Since both members of this pair of dual problems have feasible solutions, the hypothesis of the Dual Theorem of Linear Programming (for example see Theorem 1, p. 129 of [1]) is satisfied and thus both problems have optimal solutions and their objective function values are equal, that is, $v^* = v_*$, so the value of the game $v = v^* = v_*$. This completes the proof of the Minimax Theorem. As this proof shows the Minimax Theorem for two-person zero-sum games and the Dual Theorem of Linear Programming are essentially the same theorem. Historically the Minimax Theorem was discovered and proven first and provided the insights which lead George Dantzig to develop the duality theory of linear programming. The use of simplex algorithm in a constructive proof of the Dual Theorem provides a proof that is much easier to follow than the early proofs of the Minimax Theorem. The duality theory of linear programming tells us that only one player's linear program must be solved for a basic optimal solution and the optimal basis easily provides a basic optimal solution for the other player.

For an example of this approach to finding the optimal mixed strategies for the players of a matrix game consider the game used to illustrate the graphical solution procedure for a $2 \times n$ games in chapter 2. That matrix game has the following payoff matrix:

Red

		R_1	R_2	R_3
Blue	B_1	.6	.3	.4
	B_2	.4	.7	.5

where Blue is the Row Player and Red is the Column Player. So

$$A = \begin{bmatrix} .6 & .3 & .4 \\ .4 & .7 & .5 \end{bmatrix},$$

and for this game P3 specializes to give

$$v_* = \max x_0,$$

subject to

$$x_0 - .6x_1 - .4x_2 \le 0,$$
$$x_0 - .3x_1 - .7x_2 \le 0,$$
$$x_0 - .4x_1 - .5x_2 \le 0,$$
$$x_1 + x_2 = 1,$$
$$x_1 \ge 0, \ x_2 \ge 0.$$

Note that the variable x_0 is unrestricted; it is allowed to take on negative values and will do so when the expected payoff from the Column Player to the Row Player is negative. Taking care in the handling of the lack of nonnegativity requirements on x_0, this problem can be easily solved using the Simplex Method. The optimal solution is $v_* = x_0 = 7/15$, $x_1 = 1/3$, and $x_2 = 2/3$ and the value of the game is 7/15. The Column Player's optimal mixed strategy is the optimal of the linear program which is the dual of the problem just solved. It is easily extracted from the optimal solution just found and is $v^* = y_0 = 7/15$, $y_1 = 1/3$, $y_2 = 0$, and $y_3 = 2/3$.

Formulating the problem of finding the optimal mixed strategies of a matrix game as a linear program is the most practical approach to use for cases where the number of pure strategies available to each player exceeds two. Since both the primal and dual solutions are desired for the resulting linear program the current solution algorithm of choice is the Simplex Method.

B02   Other Literature

[1]   Dantzig, George B. *Linear Programming and Extensions*. Princeton, NJ: Princeton University Press, 1963.

[2]   Hillier, Frederick S., and Gerald J. Lieberman. *Introduction to Operations Research*. 4th Edition. New York, NY: McGraw Hill, 1986.

[3]   Kaplan, E. L. *Mathematical Programming and Games*. New York, NY: Wiley, 1982.

Problems

1. For the following matrix games find the value of the game and the optimal mixed strategies for both players:

a. $A = \begin{bmatrix} 1 & -1 & 2 & 0 \\ -2 & 0 & -3 & 4 \\ -2 & 3 & 1 & 1 \end{bmatrix}$

b. $A = \begin{bmatrix} 2 & 0 & -2 \\ -2 & 2 & 0 \\ -1 & -1 & -1 \end{bmatrix}$

2. Find the value of the game and the optimal mixed strategies for the Colonel Blotto game described in problem 15 of Chapter 2.

Answers to Problems

1. a. $v = 1/7$, $x_1 = 5/7$, $x_2 = 0$, $x_3 = 2/7$, and $y_1 = 4/7$, $y_2 = 3/7$, $y_3 = 0$, and $y_4 = 0$.
    b. $v = -2/3$, $x_1 = 1/3$, $x_2 = 2/3$, $x_3 = 0$, and $y_1 = 1/3$, $y_2 = 0$, $y_3 = 2/3$.

2. Value $= -0.0417$, Let i be the number of battalions assigned to position A and x_i is the probability Blotto's mixed strategy calls for assigning i battalions to A and y_j is the probability Red's mixed strategy calls for assigning j battalions to A. The optimal mixed strategies are:
$x = (.250, .208, 0, .542)$, $y = (.375, .458, .167)$.

APPENDIX C
USE OF DECIBELS

This appendix discusses the **decibel** concept, which is widely used in sonar and radar and is prominent in Chapter 4. In the first section decibels are discussed in abstraction. Decibel usages pertaining to sonar and radar are given in the second and third sections, respectively. Decibels are closely related to logarithms – *all logarithms in this appendix are, as in Chapter* 4, *to the base 10*.

C1   Decibels in Abstraction

If x is an arbitrary positive number then the **decibel value** (abbreviated dB) of x is
$$10 \log x.$$
Thus there is an easily-computed one-to-one correspondence between positive numbers and their decibel values. Since the decibel value of a positive number is proportional to its logarithm (actually for any base of logarithms), the familiar properties of logarithms carry over to decibel values, notably multiplication and division of positive numbers correspond to addition and subtraction of their decibel values, exponentiation corresponds to multiplication by the exponent, and reciprocation corresponds to sign reversal. Generally, the decibel value of x is most useful when x is thought of as a ratio.

For human discourse, the decibel concept has certain advantages: Mental addition and subtraction are easier than mental multiplication and division, and magnitudes of one or two digits or decimal places are generally easier to grasp mentally than magnitudes of several digits or decimal places. As examples consider the correspondences given in Figure C.1 Probably the most widely used of these correspondences is that 3 dB corresponds to a factor of 2. Note that, for example, 1dB + 3dB = 4dB corresponds, in rounded terms, to $(5/4) \times 2 = 5/2$.

FIGURE C.1. DECIBEL VALUES TABLE

dB value of x	-150	-50	-1	0	1	2	3	4
x	10^{-15}	10^{-5}	.79	1	1.26	1.58	1.99	2.51
x rounded	10^{-15}	10^{-5}	4/5	1	5/4	1.6	2	5/2
dB value of x	5	6	7	8	9	10	10^5	10^{15}
x	3.16	3.98	5.01	6.31	7.94	10	50	150
x rounded	3.2	4	5	6.3	8	10	50	150

The term decibel is derived from the term **bel**, named after Alexander Graham Bell: The bel value of $x > 0$ is simply $\log x$. A cognate term, **hemibel**, is used by Morse and Kimball [1] or [2]. Their point is that for an improvement, by OA or other means, to be significant in a complex naval operation with fairly wide uncertainties in estimation of parameters, it should generally be by a factor of three, which is about 5 dB, i.e., half of 10 dB.

C2   Decibel Usages in Sonar

The central importance of decibels in sonar analysis is manifested in the sonar equations (see Chapter 4, Part A); there the sonar terms are given in dB. Thus the independent physical effects that these separate terms represent are combined additively, which is very convenient.

The physical effects themselves are **acoustic intensities** and the corresponding **sound pressure levels**, both referred to specific reference levels. If I_1 and I_r are respectively an acoustic intensity and its reference intensity, and p_1 and p_r are respectively the corresponding sound pressure level and its reference level, then the relation among them is

$$\frac{I_1}{I_r} = \left(\frac{p_1}{p_r} \right)^2,$$

so that the dB value of I_1/I_r is twice the dB value of p_1/p_r; this dB quantity is also denoted SPL. Importantly, L_1 is an intensity level in dB even if expressed in terms of the pressure levels p_1 and p_r.

Direct measurement of pressure is easy, while that for intensity is difficult. Thus intensity levels are usually stated relative to a standard pressure level which is 10^{-6} newtons/sq meter, i.e., 1 micro pascal (1 μpasc). Of interest, an acoustic pressure of 1 μpasc in a plane traveling wave corresponds to approximately 10^{-19} watts/sq meter.

There are two different kinds of levels in the sonar equations. One is an absolute level expressed as the dB value of the ratio of an intensity in watts/sq meter to standard intensity, equivalently as twice the dB value of the ratio of a pressure amplitude to a standard pressure amplitude (1 μpasc). Examples are radiated noise, L_S, and self-noise, L_N.

The second is a relative level expressed as the dB value of the ratio of two intensity values, equivalently as twice the dB value of the ratio of the corresponding two pressure values, measured at different points of the system consisting of sonar, ocean path, and target. Examples are propagation loss, N_W, and target strength, Nts. Propagation loss at range R yards is the decibel value of the ratio of (1) the intensity of sound observed at range R from an acoustical source to (2) the intensity observed at 1 yard from the acoustical center of the source. Target strength is the dB value of the ratio of (1) the plane wave sound intensity that ensonifies a target to (2) the intensity of the sound back-scattered by the target and observed at 1 yard from its acoustical center.

Other relative levels are array gain, A_G, and detection threshold, DT. Array gain is the dB value of the ratio of (1) the sonar's received signal to noise ratio (SNR) measured at a point after array beam processing to (2) the SNR value that an omni-directional hydrophone would observe. Detection threshold is the SNR value required to detect the target with given false alarm and detection probabilities.

See the references in Chapter 4, Part A, for more extensive and complete developments of the brief discussions given above.

C3   Decibel Usages in Radar

The radar range equation is a multiplicative and exponentiated combination of various quantities (primarily measured in power and distance). It would therefore lend itself conveniently to decibel representation. However, that is not usually done for the entire collection of factors in the radar range equation. The equation, in various versions, is ordinarily presented multiplicatively, as is done in Chapter 4, Part B. The use of decibels made in radar analysis is primarily in treatment of widely varying quantities, which are particular factors in the radar range equation.

For this purpose, radar experts have evolved special dB units:

a. The dBW value of a power quantity is its dB value relative to 1 watt, i.e., the dB value of the power quantity expressed in watts.
b. The dBM value of a distance is the dB value of the distance expressed in meters.
c. The dBSM value of an area is the dB value of the area expressed in square meters.

For example, a transmitted power of 30 dBW is 1000 watts, a wave length of 10 dBM is 10 meters, and a radar cross section of -20 dBSM would be .01 square meters (a low observable). As a variant on dBW, the dBm value of a (small) power quantity is its dB value relative to 1 *milli*watt. One must be careful not to confuse dBM and dBm, which pertain to distance and power respectively. Radar echoes tend to be very small signals, perhaps -120 dBm, which would be .000,000,000,001 milliwatts. Expressed in the latter form, this would crowd the display register of most hand-held calculators.

For examples using ordinary dB, see Figure 4.21 of Chapter 4, Part B, which illustrates the effect on radar range from reducing cross section in 12 dB increments. Each increment is a factor of approximately 16 in cross section, so, since by the radar range equation range is proportional to the 4th root of cross section, the range reductions are by a factor of 2 ($16^{1/4} = 2$).

References

[1] Morse, Philip M., and George E. Kimball. *Methods of Operations Research.* Operations Evaluation Group Report 54. Washington, DC: Office of the Chief of Naval Operations, 1946.

[2] Morse, Philip M., and George E. Kimball. *Methods of Operations Research.* Cambridge, MA: MIT Press, 1951.

INDEX

CPSIA information can be obtained
at www.ICGtesting.com
Printed in the USA
BVHW052341240120
570264BV00002B/3